Constancy and Change in
Human Development

Constancy and Change in Human Development

Orville G. Brim, Jr.
Jerome Kagan

Editors

HARVARD UNIVERSITY PRESS
Cambridge, Massachusetts
London, England   1980

This work was commissioned by the Foundation for Child Development, a private organization that makes grants to educational and charitable institutions. Its main interests are in research, social and economic indicators of children's lives, advocacy and public information projects, and service experiments that help translate theoretical knowledge about children into policies and practices that affect their daily lives.

Library of Congress Cataloging in Publication Data

Main entry under title:

Constancy and change in human development.

Includes bibliographical references and index.
1. Developmental psychology.   2.   Constancy.
3.   Change (Psychology)   I.   Brim, Orville Gilbert,
1923-   II.   Kagan, Jerome.   [DNLM: 1.   Human
development.   BF713 C757]
BF713.C66   155   80-13457
ISBN 0-674-16625-6

Contents

Constancy and Change in
Human Development

1 | Constancy and Change: A View of the Issues
Orville G. Brim, Jr., and Jerome Kagan

THE CONCEPTION of human development presented in this volume differs from most Western contemporary thought on the subject. The view that emerges from this work is that humans have a capacity for change across the entire life span. It questions the traditional idea that the experiences of the early years, which have a demonstrated contemporaneous effect, necessarily constrain the characteristics of adolescence and adulthood. As the other thirteen chapters in this volume show, there are important growth changes across the life span from birth to death, many individuals retain a great capacity for change, and the consequences of the events of early childhood are continually transformed by later experiences, making the course of human development more open than many have believed.

Most current research and theory assume that the experiences of infancy and early childhood have a lasting effect on adult behavior and personality. The questions asked, methods selected, and theoretical models used have been colored by the a priori assumption that constancy rather than change characterizes the course of human development. Howard A. Moss and Elizabeth J. Susman (chapter 11) quote E. Lowell Kelly: "Whether one is an extreme hereditarian, an environmentalist, a constitutionalist, or an orthodox psychoanalyst, he is not likely to anticipate major life changes in personality after the first few years of life."

Each discipline has its own reason for insisting that early experience is critical. The behaviorist argues that it is difficult to extinguish behaviors learned during early childhood because of the special quality of the conditions of reinforcement. The psychoanalyst believes that sources of anxiety generated during childhood do not change, that

1

only defenses are altered. One does not resolve intense childhood conflicts but finds new ways to deal with them. Social psychologists call
attention to the developing self-image of the child, noting that the
classification of a child turns into a self-fulfilling prophecy. Children
who are labeled incompetent are treated as such and come to hold this
conception of themselves; as a result, predictions are affirmed. Pedia-
tricians and their colleagues in the biomedical sciences believe that
because nutrition has an important influence on physical growth,
childhood malnutrition may have permanent effects on the integrity
of the brain and, by implication, on intellectual functioning.

To be sure, theories of human development that stress the importance of early experience usually allow for the possibility of later
change and specify the conditions under which change is possible.
John A. Clausen (private communication) points out that "behavior-
ists say that fear can be extinguished by systematic reconditioning;
psychoanalysts believe that through psychoanalysis growth and
change are possible; social psychologists note that in different group
settings and different roles children find new self images." In many
instances, though, the theorists remind us that they think it is very difficult to alter the effects of early experience and that doing so costs
much in time and money invested over the years (for example, ten
years in psychoanalysis).

During the past decade or so, research in the behavioral sciences
has forced scholars to think more carefully about the complementary
themes of constancy and change in human development. Some published studies of the consequences of early family experiences have not
been entirely consistent with the traditional view (Kagan and Moss,
1962; Kagan, 1971; Kagan, Kearsley, and Zelazo, 1978; Clarke and
Clarke, 1976). Also, in the new field of life span development, research on middle-aged and older persons indicates that personality
and behavior are more malleable than most people think (Baltes,
1979).

Constancy and change are inventions of the mind, of course, a
matter of subjective magnitude; the different definitions of the concepts are examined in full in subsequent chapters. Chapters 2 and 3
deal historically with the idea of continuity and change in science, and
the eleven that follow review specific human characteristics, examining the new facts in the light of what is known and noting that ambiguities continue to surround these themes.

An Overview of the Chapters

We intended to cover all the major substantive areas in human
development that had accumulated a large body of empirical data.

The topics first proposed for inclusion in this book were selected at a planning conference of scholars representing neurophysiology, physical growth, psychiatry, psychology, and sociology.

Authors were asked to analyze the data in their fields of specialization with reference to the issue of constancy and change over the life span. Authors had to be selective in the studies they reviewed, for quality of measurement, representativeness of the populations studied, size of the samples, and the number of points in time at which assessments were taken had to be weighed. Although hundreds of investigations purport to deal with the main theme of this volume, many of these sources are not cited. Contributors to this volume were instructed that they were not responsible for citing all the articles whose authors felt they might have been working on the question of constancy versus change but rather for summarizing only the best knowledge that bears on this question. For instance, in the field of crime and delinquency, hundreds of parole prediction studies deal with recidivism, but most have short time spans or small and unrepresentative samples. Similarly, many short-term "longitudinal" investigations on the growth of the child cover only a few years and have unrepresentative samples. The same is true for research on human achievement, for there are thousands of semester or one-year studies of school achievement on undescribed student populations.

Some unique large-scale interdisciplinary studies have not been systematically reviewed in this volume because of their pioneering characteristics; they are not yet part of the cumulative knowledge for specific fields of inquiry. For example, Elder's *Children of the Great Depression* (1974) deals with the differential effects of economic deprivation on adolescents and later adult personality. Inkeles and Smith's *Becoming Modern* (1974) analyzes the role of modernization in several national communities and discusses the way that these changes affect certain personality characteristics of adult workers. Kohn and Schooler's ten-year study (1978) analyzes the interactions in adult personality change between types of work and intellectual functioning. Schaie's work (1979) on the impact of cohort differences in intelligence examines fourteen-year changes in successive cohorts for the entire adult range. References to these unique studies may appear throughout the volume, although these investigations do not fall neatly into any one of the substantive areas.

Some authors had to look at the facts in their field from a new perspective. Hugh F. Cline (chapter 13) had to rearrange the existing data to permit a life span analysis. The facts from key studies in this area had not been organized to permit the analysis of constancy or change because the question had not been asked. A similar situation existed for Barbara Starfield and I. B. Pless (chapter 7), who examined physical health and illness, and for Charles Doering (chapter 6), who studied the data on the endocrine system.

Because of the lack of substantial bodies of fact, the uncertain analytic procedures in many studies, and the vulnerable new hypotheses about life span development, the chapters that follow do not prove that the doctrine of constancy from early childhood onward is invalid. Rather they challenge the traditional Western view of human ontogeny. The burden of proof is being shifted to the larger group, who adhere to the traditional doctrine of constancy, from the minority who suggest that it is a premise requiring evaluation.

Perspectives on Continuity

In chapter 2, the first of two providing perspective on the issue of constancy and change, Jerome Kagan addresses the definitional ambiguity surrounding the terms stability and continuity. He argues that a distinction should be made between the persistence or lack of persistence of a psychological structure and the gradualness or abruptness of change in process. In the central part of the chapter he suggests that Western scholars have been open to the ideas of stability of structure, continuity of process, and derivative change. These ideas can be detected in the Greek notion that immutable entities form the base for the striking diversity in phenomenal nature, and they were articulated during the Enlightenment.

To the premise of continuity Enlightenment scholars added the axioms of genetic and historical necessity and the assumptions of cumulativeness, gradualism, and sacredness of origin. A popular nineteenth-century idea was that civilizations progressed in a linear fashion, with each historical period building on the preceding one. Darwin, as well as other nineteenth-century naturalists, preferred to regard changes in nature as composed of many small steps, because such a view was consistent with the mechanistic outlook of the period. Discontinuities challenged mechanistic explanations because they did not yield easily to propositions that described the smooth sequence of small, connected causes and effects. Gradualism was promoted because it served mechanism.

Kant recognized that the assumption of continuity did not rest on empirical grounds but was one of the mind's necessary constructions; however, his prose in *Critique of Pure Reason* often reads as though he were describing nature, not the mind's invention. Although there has always been a contrapuntal force promoting discontinuity (such as the catastrophe theorists of the nineteenth century and those who believed in spontaneous generation), those who promoted continuity usually dominated the ideological debate. Perhaps one reason for the failure of existentialism to capture the intuitions of more twentieth-century Europeans and Americans was that it required a deeper acceptance of sharp discontinuities in personal experience.

Since classical Chinese society was more skeptical of a philosophy of continuity, it is useful to seek an explanation for this profound cultural difference. Needham has suggested that the Chinese conception of natural phenomena is organic and cyclical, rather than mechanical and linear as it is in the West. The Chinese believe that the structure of the present exerts a profound influence on current phenomena. Since future contexts cannot be predicted easily, the informativeness of the past is limited; hence there is less interest in origins.

Kagan concludes by summarizing some recent published investigations that are not consistent with the traditional supposition of a close connection between early and later development. The inconsistency leads naturally to puzzlement and an attempt to diagnose the emotional needs that are being satisfied by the traditional view.

The Continuous and the Discrete in the History of Science

Everett Mendelsohn (chapter 3) poses the central question in terms of a complementarity between the continuous and the discrete, linking the former to political conservatism and the latter to more radical social change. Mendelsohn's central theme is that there is a link between historical events and continuist or discontinuist epistemologies. Mendelsohn suggests that the immutability assigned to nature by seventeenth-century intellectuals may have been analogous to the timeless authority assumed by the absolute monarchies of the period.

The introduction of disorder into eighteenth- and nineteenth-century European society and the subsequent changes in beliefs and social structures sensitized the citizenry to the possibility of revolution. It may not have been a coincidence that a decade after the French revolution Lamarck offered the incredible suggestion that species could transmute.

Debate over whether species undergo extinction, evolution, or migration can be interpreted as a reflection of attitudes toward the stability of nations and societies. Mendelsohn suggests that "evolution was largely a social theory that came to be transformed into a biological theory." As the twentieth century began, society was experiencing major alterations in its social composition and beliefs, while in the academy Planck's notion of discrete quanta and DeVries's suggestion of discrete genes gave momentum to the discontinuous view, even though in mathematics, the queen of the academy, continuity continued to be a pervading concept. Mendelsohn, like Nisbet and Kant, argues that continuity and discontinuity are inventions of mind, not natural phenomena. A scholar's preference for one mode is affected by the stability of the society to which he looks for principles of nature.

Continuities and Change in Maturational Timing

The enlargement of muscle and the elongation of bone have supplied strong analogies for a continuist view of growth, for the regular increase in body size seems to be imperceptible—a good example of Leibniz's principle of continuity. In addition, boys with more rapid rates of physical growth are likely to have been born to mothers who had relatively early menarche. This last fact implies an inherited mechanism that monitors aspects of development and reminds us that the genetic material can impose a stability on dispositions across generations.

But Stanley M. Garn (chapter 4) also notes that there can be dramatic secular changes in growth and selects menarcheal timing as an example of the way that genetic and secular forces can influence that pubertal phenomenon. Age at menarche has decreased by one full year—from 14 to 13 years—during the last fifty years and by about three years per century in Europe, a relatively large change in a fundamental human characteristic.

Dynamics of Growth, Organization, and Adaptability in the Central Nervous System

One of the most important incentives for entertaining ideas of discontinuity has come from the laboratories of neurobiologists and neurophysiologists. The materialism of nineteenth- and early twentieth-century psychology demanded that a flaw in function must follow major insult to the tissues of the brain. Donald G. Stein and Ronald G. Dawson (chapter 5) summarize recent studies, some of which contradict that supposition.

The authors see the issue of plasticity of brain function as part of a broader controversy dealing with localization versus antilocalization. The latter view, which gives several functions to particular areas of the brain, can explain the recovery of psychological functioning following lesions, a biological analogue to psychological compensation.

The mammalian central nervous system seems to have a greater capacity for regrowth than previously thought. Because some neurons are malleable during the early months of life, there is a period of openness to experiences that can produce divergent growth patterns. Stein and Dawson suggest that animals and humans can show almost complete behavioral recovery following severe trauma to certain areas of the central nervous system—a view in opposition to the classical doctrine of cerebral localization—as long as the injury occurs early in life. This characteristic of young brain tissue is mirrored in the development of psychological competences, for the dispositions of infants are also usually resilient following psychological trauma.

The Endocrine System

Our knowledge of the relation of endocrine function to behavior is not very extensive. This may be one reason that the traditional continuist assumptions are hardier. Charles Doering (chapter 6) summarizes current understanding of the endocrine system and considers some syndromes that show stability over time. For example, androgen levels in the fetus, which influence the morphology of the genitalia, seem also to enhance the energy levels of young girls who experienced excessive androgen prior to birth.

But there is also a discontinuity of puberty when the hypothalamus rather abruptly loses its sensitivity to circulating steroids and triggers the pituitary to begin the pubertal cycle. Boys show rather steep rises in circulating testosterone in the year prior to puberty. And there is a drastic decline in menopause in circulating estradiol which seems to be associated with menopausal symptoms, an illustration of a relatively discontinous process that leads to stable changes.

Physical Health

In chapter 7 the supposition of the "sickly child" is at issue. Barbara Starfield and I. B. Pless address constancy and change by examining three themes: specific diagnoses, use of physicians' services, and general measures of disability.

For some diseases, such as the inherited metabolic and inborn anatomic disorders, there is virtual constancy. An individual with the disorder will always have it even though some of its physical manifestations may be ameliorated with proper therapy. For these and other chronic conditions the major concern is the degree to which psychologic sequalae can be prevented.

There is little evidence, however, regarding the relative balance of constancy and change for most other physical ailments in childhood. Data from the few longitudinal studies in which individual children were followed for many years suggest that the patterns of these illnesses are not randomly distributed in the population. Children who have evidence of illness or disability early in life are a little more likely than other children to have illness later. Conversely, older children who are ill are a little more likely than their peers to have histories of illness earlier in life.

Nevertheless, most children who are sick early in life do not per-

sist in being sick; conversely, many individuals who have manifestations of illness later in life had been healthy earlier. Although information on the effects of social class on patterns of illness over time is
scarce, there is some evidence that poverty increases the likelihood
that ill health and its effects will persist and thus that change in health
status depends in part on having the resources to change one's environment.

The Course of Schizophrenic Psychosis

A basic assumption of twentieth-century psychiatry is that serious
psychopathology has its origins in the early years of life. Psychoanalytic theory rationalized that doctrine by positing unique experiences
surrounding the care of the infant which were necessary precursors of
psychosis. It is still common to hear clinicians announce that the abu-
sive mother had an insecure infancy. Examination of the evidence regarding the development of schizophrenic symptoms is therefore a
relevant topic for this volume. The data do not suggest any strong generalizations. Some investigators fail to find commanding evidence for
deviant signs of future psychosis prior to school entrance. But other
evidence reveals a higher proportion of birth complications and early
parental separation in the lives of adults who later develop schizophrenia. During adolescence, however, the prodromal signs are much
clearer. Adult male schizophrenics tended to be withdrawn from peers
during early adolescence and/or extremely hostile within their family.

Michael J. Goldstein (chapter 8) concludes that no unique developmental path characterizes the child who will become schizophrenic,
noting that male and female schizophrenics show different life courses.
There are hints that the appearance of hallucinations and delusions at
age 20 is the result of a long and gradual process, but no more than
hints. The tension between continuity and discontinuity is also relevant to therapeutic intervention. Some classes of schizophrenia seem
markedly resistant to treatment; the prognosis for those with a good
premorbid history is more optimistic. One schizophrenic course has
the semblance of continuity, and one appears to be more discontinuous, with the latter being more amenable to treatment.

Cognitive Development in Childhood

Psychologists have conceptualized cognitive development as
either the gradual enhancement of a basic talent or as a sequence of
dependent connected stages. In both cases continuity is preserved.
Joachim F. Wohlwill (chapter 9) presents an integrative and critical
review of the literature on cognitive development. Wohlwill distinguishes between the stability of development within an individual
child and the stability of a particular variable measured normatively in

a group of children, across specified age spans. The latter phenomenon describes the extent to which individual differences in a specified group of children are preserved with age.

The review confirms the well-known principle that stability coefficients are low when the predictive assessments occur during infancy and the investigator tries to predict intellectual variables during later childhood and adolescence. But the magnitudes of these coefficients increase steadily with the age of the initial assessment.

Wohlwill documents two major shortcomings in the literature. The first is an overemphasis on the IQ test, with its uncertain conceptual basis and its cultural bias, as the index of intelligence. Another limitation springs from a correlational approach to the assessment of continuity, an approach that abstracts apparent constancy of individual differences from real growth. Wohlwill urges an alternative strategy focusing on the responses of children to particular changes in the environment and often revealing marked susceptibility to change in the intellectual functioning of children.

Cognitive Development in Adulthood

Understandably most of the essays in this volume deal with the formative periods of childhood and young adulthood. Until recently there has been minimal interest in the changes that characterize the years after 40. John L. Horn and Gary Donaldson (chapter 10) provide a broad synthesis of cognitive functioning during this later period.

Unlike Wohlwill, who questions the theoretical utility of the construct of general intellectual ability, Horn and Donaldson promote such a general factor and suggest that it has two parts, *fluid* and *crystallized* intelligence. A fair translation of these terms is that fluid intelligence refers to dynamic competences such as memory, reasoning, and speed of mental work, while crystallized intelligence refers to acquired knowledge, especially information and vocabulary. Horn and Donaldson retain the process-structure distinction endemic to modern psychology. The authors show rather convincingly that performance on fluid intelligence tests decreases with age, especially after age 50, while crystallized intelligence seems to improve even through age 70. To what degree such changes in performance index changes in potential or capacity is a topic for future research (Botwinick, 1977).

The strikingly different growth patterns for these two classes of cognitive ability reveal the difficulty inherent in propositions that refer to intellectual competences as a unity. Indeed, each of the many specific abilities that compose fluid or crystallized intelligence has a different slope of decline or enhancement. The bases for the loss in fluid talent have great theoretical interest. What causes the decline? Can it be reversed or halted (Baltes and Schaie, 1976)? The popular view, still in need of proof, assumes that change in the central nervous system unravels abilities that became organized during the first two years of life and, furthermore, that neurophysiological decline with aging parallels decrement in fluid performance. Whether these changes are gradual or more abrupt is still to be decided. Thus Horn and Donaldson, like the other authors, supply examples of continuity and discontinuity in growth.

Personality Development

The belief that one can preview adult motives, anxieties, and behavior from early childhood qualities is invested with considerable affect because popular belief is committed to the principle that "as one sows, so shall one reap." The average citizen may feel impotent regarding the likelihood of schizophrenia, the onset of puberty, or the loss of memory in senility. But proneness to fear, academic excellence, and aggression are regarded as subject to more personal control. One of the rationales for parental investment in infants and young children is that caretakers will be rewarded for their efforts two decades later.

Howard A. Moss and Elizabeth J. Susman's review of continuity and change in personality development (chapter 11) reflects this premise. The authors assume stability of selected dispositions and try to locate evidence for its presence in the available scientific research. They disagree with Walter Mischel's assumption (1973) of situational control of behaviors and motives and argue for some enduring patterns that generalize across social contexts (see also Block, 1977). Moss and Susman delineate the factors that determine whether individual differences will be discovered (restricted range of scores, time intervals of assessment, variables chosen to analyze), and they summarize findings from the major longitudinal investigations of human development.

The studies of infancy lead the authors to conclude that "behavior remains very plastic during the early years . . . infants are not captives of crystallized behavior patterns." But a review of the studies of older children permits a more positive conclusion: "a pattern of impressive stabilities emerged by middle childhood." The authors note that introversion-extroversion displays a special stability from childhood through early adolescence and merits attention. Other authors have affirmed that theme. A recent review by Costa and McCrae (in press) extends this theme into adulthood.

Values, Attitudes, and Beliefs

Norval D. Glenn (chapter 12) investigates two general hypotheses: that aging leads to a reduced susceptibility to changes in values and attitudes in response to period influences, and that aspects of the aging process lead to changes in certain values and attitudes. The second hypothesis is decomposed into more specific ones.

The first general hypothesis is investigated by examining data from a series of cohort analyses of U.S. national survey data. In general, the cohort data show greater change in the younger adult cohorts than in the older ones during periods of rapid social change, but they nevertheless show substantial change in the older cohorts. Exceptions to this general pattern occur for party identification and attitudes toward a hypothetical black candidate for president. Greater change among the younger cohorts is not explained by ceiling or floor effects, nor is it explained to any appreciable extent by educational differences among the cohorts. However, it could be a cohort rather than an age effect. In any event, it is clear that many attitudes of older adults, including some that reflect "basic values," do not become highly resistant to change.

The specific hypotheses that come under the second general hypothesis relate to possible age effects on values, attitudes, and affective states such as party identification, interest in politics, vocationally related interests, job satisfaction, and happiness. Evidence from cross-sectional, cohort, and panel studies is not conclusive but suggests that several kinds of age effects induce changes; the strongest evidence is that for effects on vocationally related interests between adolescence and middle age. The evidence relating to several kinds of hypothesized age effects (for example, on party identification and personal happiness) was found to be largely negative.

Criminal Behavior over the Life Span

The terms "a life of crime," "the criminal mind," "a born criminal," and "the criminal type" are used frequently. Nevertheless, despite a number of longitudinal studies of criminal behavior, very little is known about constancy of criminal behavior over the life span.

Hugh F. Cline (chapter 13) reviews the major longitudinal studies of delinquency and crime to extract available data on constant and changing criminal behavior through the life span. Data from the Uniform Crime Reports reveal that property crimes are more prevalent among adolescents, crimes of violence are more prevalent among young adults, and white-collar crimes, drunkenness, and crimes against the family are more prevalent in middle age. Whether the same individuals are committing these crimes at different periods in their lives is not known for certain; but what evidence there is implies that different persons are committing these crimes at different ages. Cline describes the need for a research facility to conduct successive longitudinal studies to test theories of criminal behavior and to provide more knowledge for policymaking in criminal justice agencies. Similar statements and suggestions were made some 150 years ago by Quetelet (1835) who was one of the first to study criminality from the perspective of the life span.

Schooling and Occupational Careers

Constancy and change in worldly success—achievements in school, at work, in one's career—is the topic of chapter 14. Is one's success already determined at birth? Can success in life be predicted from one's performance in the early years of elementary school?

David L. Featherman appraises the evidence on the degree to which occupational attainments and earnings over the working life are influenced by scholastic achievements such as grades, class rank, and test scores of school abilities. He examines the work career itself to assess the connections between career beginnings and subsequent jobs and earnings levels. Socioeconomic achievement throughout the life cycle is the fundamental issue in this review of the literature and analysis of newly available data for a national sample of American men.

The life cycle approach is broadened to include continuities that extend across generations as well as within one generation. Thus the commentary about socioeconomic achievement is lodged within a discussion of social mobility patterns in the United States and of recent changes in them for blacks, women, and young white college graduates. Wherever the evidence permits, the analysis of life cycle continuities in achievement is interpreted within a birth cohort perspective. This view suggests that patterns of achievement over the life cycle need not be the same across successive cohorts, for unique historical contexts influence both the organization and pace of the life cycle as well as opportunities for success.

Issues and Questions

New Theory and Research

In his book *On Understanding Science* (1947), James B. Conant argued that no theory is ever displaced by a set of facts that are inconsistent with the theory. A theory, he said, is displaced only when these facts are combined with a new theory that can replace the old one. The traditional view that early experiences strongly influence the entire course of human development is challenged by some of the data summarized in this volume. But since there is not yet any satisfactory alternative theory, the traditional view is likely to remain strong.

There is no theory of life span development; all we have is a perspective and a promise for the future. As Paul B. Baltes (1979) has observed, the life span approach is not a specific theory or collection of specific theories but a general orientation to the study of behavior. The phrase "life span development" describes an emergent intellectual movement, responsive to the possibility of change, trying to formulate its major premises, gather new facts, and conceptualize the developmental span without using chronological age categories. The history of this perspective has recently been described by Baltes (1979) for the field of psychology. During the decade of the sixties the movement began to strengthen and scholarly treatises, both theoretical and methodological in nature, began to appear (Baltes, 1973; Baltes and Schaie, 1973; Huston-Stein and Baltes, 1976; Lerner and Ryff, 1978; Binstock and Shanas, 1976; Birren and Schaie, 1977; Finch and Hayflick, 1977). A similar trend can be seen in sociology (Brim and Wheeler, 1966; Brim, 1976a; Cain, 1964; Riley, 1976; Elder, 1975). Psychoanalytic theory has shown recent increased interest in the work of Carl Jung, who believed in changes in adult personality, and a decline in the influence of Sigmund Freud's theory of human development.

The accumulation of concepts, methods, and new facts about life span development leads to some initial conclusions. First, growth is more individualistic than was thought, and it is difficult to find general patterns. The life span development view is sharply opposed to the notion of adult stages, arguing that stages cast development as unidirectional, hierarchical, sequenced in time, cumulative, and irreversible—ideas not supported by commanding evidence. The facts instead indicate that persons of the same age, particularly beyond adolescence, and the same historical period are undergoing different changes; one person may show an increase in certain attributes while another shows a decline in the same aspects of behavior and personality.

Second, similar changes in people can be caused by different events. Carol Ryff (private communication) observes that the life span researcher is likely to endorse multiple forms of determinism; for example, the causes of male mid-life crisis, for those males for whom it occurs at all, are numerous and vary from male to male. The researcher also describes a more subtle component of this conclusion: similar changes at different ages need not have the same causes. The conditions inducing anxiety in childhood, for instance, can be very different from those inducing anxiety in adulthood.

The life span development view also stimulates imagination about the kinds of biological and environmental events that bring change after childhood. There is an understandable tendency to think most about labeled experiences that change behavior—marriage, divorce, first child, retirement—but the perspective of scholars in life span developmental calls attention to more subtle events that often go unnamed and unrecognized. Many people make fairly effortless passages through the well-known life events because of anticipatory socialization and social supports. Unlabeled events such as "topping out" in the work career, the stress of adolescence, or unanticipated accidents have powerful influences on development (Brim, 1979).

At the present, some new fragile facts challenge theories of development that emphasize the lasting effects of early experience or postulate stages of adult development. Although there is no new systematic theory to deal with these facts, we know what kind of research is needed. We need studies of the same people over long periods of their life span, and these studies must be carried out on successive birth cohorts, that is, in different periods of history, so that the separate effects of individual aging and social change can be seen.

Concentration on Age Periods

Most research on human development is not life span research; it deals instead with specific age periods such as old age, infancy, or adolescence. Our reasons for studying different ages vary. For example, there are a great many studies of children because childhood is believed to be a formative period. Adults are questioned and observed because of their significance in the work force and in the family. Until recently, the aged were studied primarily for humanitarian reasons. Adolescents were studied because in Western society the teenage years are characterized by a great deal of unrest. A typical strategy of investigators has been to focus on a unique characteristic of a particular age period—the attachment of infants, the fears of 4-year-olds, the loss of memory in old age. This tendency is understandable in the formative period of a discipline, but such a strategy has yielded few insights into constancy and change throughout the life span.

Concentrating on age periods makes it difficult to connect facts about human characteristics in one age group with similar facts on an older or younger group, and the study of constancy and change over the life span suffers as a result. For example, research on criminal behavior is highly age-specific. Among the many studies of crime and delinquency, Cline (chapter 13) could find only one that looked at the course of criminal behavior from late childhood into adulthood. For the research on cognitive development, it was necessary to have two chapters, one on childhood and one on adolescence to old age. As for physical health, Starfield and Pless (chapter 7) analyze the data from early childhood to age 20, then note that the field of adult health stands apart, with different bodies of data, assumptions, and social conditions of intervention. Featherman (chapter 14) was readily able to analyze achievement behavior from the first years of childhood through college and graduate education, but he notes that there is a hiatus between studies of academic achievement and studies of occupational achievement and career achievement; different groups of scholars, with different concepts and questions, work the latter areas.

In the years ahead scientists must not focus on just one age period but instead study transformations over the life span. We can visualize a comprehensive grid with chronological age on the side; across the top of the table, in each column, are varied human characteristics (Brim, 1976b). Almost all the themes in this volume could be studied in this manner. Bodily changes, the course of achievement, the nature of social relationships, conformity and independence, or understanding of death could be studied in a way that describes the lifetime passage of each characteristic. Human attributes could be grouped into theoretical classes such as defenses against basic anxieties or political attitudes, and the differential conditions for constancy and change described for each. The challenge is to relate each scholar's work to knowledge of what goes on before and after the age period under study, so that research can contribute to the understanding of constancy and change as well as of a particular age.

Different Cohorts Age in Different Ways

Matilda White Riley (1976; 1978, pp. 39-41) has noted that each new generation as it enters the stream of history "differs from earlier cohorts because of intervening social changes of many sorts: in education, in nutrition, in the occupational and income level at which people begin their careers . . . There is no pure process of aging—the ways in which children enter kindergarten, or adolescents move into adulthood, or older people retire are not preordained. In this view, the life course is not fixed, but widely flexible."

These studies of Riley and of Elder (1974), Schaie (1979), and their colleagues have joined prior scholarship in social history in demonstrating the powerful effects of being a member of a particular birth cohort. The course of history influences the life patterns of different cohorts. The events experienced by today's 50-year-olds are very different from those that occurred when today's 70-year-olds were 50. No cohorts can live exactly the same life course as another. Whether the change is the invention of the printing press, the Crusades, the Civil War, the depression of the thirties, or the war in Vietnam—each of those events caught adolescents and young adults in a special way and had its special influence on them. What makes a birth cohort unique is that it experiences similar events and conditions at similar ages as it moves through its lifetime; this sharing of experiences sets it off both objectively and subjectively from other cohorts (Winsborough, 1978).

Certainly some human characteristics are more subject to secular changes than others, so cohort effects are of different importance for classes of attributes. For instance, changes in diet, smoking, and health practices, as well as the effects of new medical technology, mean that the picture of constancy and change in physical health will be different a decade from now. Conclusions in this volume must be understood as appropriate for this decade, in this society. The story is likely to be different at some other time or in some other place. In fact, Gergen (1977) and Riegel (1976) have argued that because of historical changes, any fact or theory of human development is always in some part undetermined.

The Impact of Changing Social Conditions

The characteristics of given historical periods make individual change more or less likely. Persons may be more interested in and motivated to change, and society may now be more receptive to change—in fact, it may assist in or even demand that persons try to change their behavior or personality. Indeed, the preparation of this volume signifies a reaction to the new interest of scientists in constancy and change.

While Western science and philosophy have struggled with the issue of constancy and change, there has been a simultaneous history of ideas about the possibility of human transformation, a history that exists outside the realm of scholarly thought. Each culture has its own theories of human nature, in the form of myth, legend, and religious belief, theories about the goodness or evil of man, about what is inherited and what is learned, and about whether man is dominant over, subject to, or part of nature. Specifically, all cultures have popular beliefs about the transformation of human personality, about the possibility of change after conception, birth, and early experience.

The possibilities of human metamorphosis are present in Western literature in three great classes of stories about human transformation. Every culture has creation myths and legends about the transformation of man upon death and his existence after death. Between these two are the myths about life span development; until now their functions in various cultures have scarcely been analyzed. The primary source of these tales is the popular literature, ranging from the great myths and legends of the past to the expressions in television, film, magazines, newspapers, and fiction and nonfiction of the present time. A representative group of well-known tales might begin with the pre-Egyptian legends of Osiris, continuing through Ovid's *Metamorphoses* (A.D. 1) and the story of Paul's conversion, and ending with Jan Morris's *Conundrum* (1974) or similar contemporary works.

In these stories two polarities are evident: natural-supernatural and good-evil. One can even hypothesize that man's view of the causes of transformation has changed from supernatural forces (*metamorphosis*, in the precise use of the term) to natural causes such as alterations of environment, deliberate educational programs, psychotherapy, biofeedback, and surgical and chemical operations. Marlowe's *Dr. Faustus* (1588) might be considered a midpoint in this transition. Similarly, one can hypothesize a change from the belief that metamorphosis of mind or body leads to evil consequences to the modern belief that personal change is virtuous. This historical shift can be characterized as one from transmogrification—a grotesque or preposterous metamorphosis—to transfiguration—a change that exalts and transforms one to a higher entity. In many ways, the New Testament story of Paul exemplifies this evolutionary change.

However these hypotheses fare, a matter for intellectual history to decide, such tales about change in personality after childhood center on the two fundamental dramatic conflicts inherent in the process of change. The first is the conflict between the person's wish to change while maintaining a sense of identity. The second is the conflict between the person and society; the person may wish to change, yet society may demand constancy, or the person may wish to remain the same, yet society may demand that the person change.

Individual Conflict over Change

Clausen has observed that the natural state of the person is to be in the process of becoming something different while in many respects remaining the same. Looking deeper into this process reveals that the person wants both to change and to remain the same. There is, on the one hand, a powerful drive to maintain the sense of one's identity, a sense of continuity that allays fears of changing too fast or of being changed against one's will by outside forces. Epstein (1973, p. 405) writes:

> This is well illustrated in the following description by Lauretta Bender of the reactions of a schizophrenic girl on meeting her psychiatrist: Ruth, a five year old, approached the psychiatrist with: "Are you the bogey man? Are you going to fight with my mother? Are you the same mother? Are you the same father? Are you going to be

another mother?'' and finally screaming in
terror, ''I am afraid I am going to be someone else.''

The heroic efforts to maintain one's identity under great stress,
whether as a political prisoner or as a prisoner of war undergoing isolation and torture, are as much as part of the nobility of human character as are the companion heroic efforts of humans to become something they still are not.

On the other hand, each person is, by nature, a purposeful, striving organism with a desire to be more than he or she is now. From
making simple new year's resolutions to undergoing transsexual operations, everyone is trying to become something that he or she is not but
hopes to be. Each person has, as a component of his or her self-theory,
some beliefs about the kind of person he or she might become and
thus, implicitly, a theory of the possibility of personal change.

Unfortunately we know little about how often or how seriously
people want to change their character, and we have no comparative
data over time that would reveal whether the desire to change has increased. Certainly the idea of change, we might say the imagination of
change, seems more widespread today in our society than in other
societies or even in Western society in earlier periods. Although each
generation may believe that it experiences the greatest change, the
thirty-year period from the end of World War II to the present has
challenged the culture's fundamental values as profoundly as any
coherent set of changes since the Enlightenment. The values under
scrutiny include the wisdom and virtue of authority, the sacredness of
autonomy and hard work, and the pleasures inherent in established
status. Many middle-class parents have seen their late adolescent or
young adult offspring reject these values, if even temporarily, leaving
the older generation with at least some doubt about the durability of
their long-cherished standards. Many adults have abrogated their past
by leaving college or resigning from an established and challenging
bureaucratic job to paint scenery in Santa Fe or grow blueberries in
Vermont. These events have made people aware of the possibility of
dramatic change in life-style during adulthood; for many this constitutes a new idea.

The number of people who believe that they could change themselves, if they were to try, is another matter. Certainly the evidence
manifest in group participation indicates that belief in the possibility is
strong enough to motivate many to try. There may also be a developmental component to this belief. One suspects that the child moves
from a fantasy about change to a realistic appraisal of what is pos-

sible; one suspects that, as Carol Ryff has said (private communication), each child travels a path of "ontogenic hopes and disappointments" with respect to change. Our treasured stories about metamorphosis in children—*Alice in Wonderland, Pinnochio, Snow White, Peter Pan*—are especially poignant because they engage children's fascination with transformation of self and at the same time make them realize that there are some inescapable continuities with what they are now. Some 6-year-old boys still believe they can be mothers, and some preadolescents believe they can be black or white when they get older. Only later, due to profound cognitive insights, do they realize that neither sex nor color can be changed. These insights resemble the sense of limitation that comes to a child who falls from a second-story window trying to fly after reading or watching *Peter Pan.*

But times are changing. What was learned must be unlearned, because Jan Morris and Renee Richards changed their sex, as will thousands of persons each month this year. Change and the imagination of change seem to grow in our culture, as does the belief in the possibility of personal change and the expression of desire to do so.

Social Control over Individual Change

Society must transform the raw material of individual biology into persons suitable for the activities and requirements of society. This process of socialization describes how persons acquire the knowledge, skills, and disposition that make them more or less able members of society. Society trains a person in ways that accord with its culture and social organization, and it requires adherence to its beliefs, attitudes, and behavioral habits. Society demands the right behaviors in specified times and places—in specified social roles.

This basic condition of human life generates several kinds of conflict between society and the person. The person may resist socialization, may rebel against societal demands. Then deviant behavior is punished, and individual attempts to change habits, to alter personality, or to break out of the system are restrained by powerful sanctions ranging from ridicule, avoidance, and incarceration to death. But often the person's wish is to conform, not rebel; to become more dependable and predictable in specified roles; to be a better daughter, son, husband, wife, father, mother; to get to work on time, vote in elections, be responsible in community affairs. Society usually supports and facilitates such changes.

Society may demand change after childhood whether the person wishes to change or not. The socialization experiences of childhood cannot prepare one for all the roles that one must fill in later years (Brim, 1966, 1968). As people age they move through a variety of positions in society. Changes in the demands on them arise from their geographic and social mobility and from the customs of society, which may change during their lives. During the rapid social change that characterizes our times, society may have to be more active in adult socialization; it may have to initiate deliberate efforts to change the behavior and beliefs of its members, even against their own wishes, as in affirmative action policies.

Adult socialization occurs at many levels. At the informal and unorganized level are attempts to change the behavior, beliefs, and attitudes of a spouse, a friend, an employee, a neighbor, to adapt to the different culture of one's children, to adopt new attitudes and behaviors toward minority groups, to improve patterns of saving and spending, or to alter religious beliefs and practices.

At a more organized level are the more than six thousand national organizations designed to help individuals change. There is a national organization for almost every conceivable personality change, from Alcoholics Anonymous to Zen, from Transactional Analysis to Transcendental Meditation. The stigma of membership in such groups that was common not too many years ago, when one often kept silent about membership in A.A., for instance, is lessening; these groups are increasingly tolerated by and relied on by the larger society.

At the level of organized government, especially national government, the trend has been to intervene in the lives of citizens in order to change their personalities and behavior. Affirmative action policies are perhaps the most dramatic of these efforts. But there also are adult education programs, job retraining, occupational counseling, drug rehabilitation, and support either directly or indirectly through tax exemption for many of the national voluntary groups just described.

We have touched on some aspects of social conditions relating to constancy and change. These were the belief that change can be carried out under one's own power, without supernatural aid; that change can be good rather than evil; that persons are now more interested in changing themselves and believe it more likely to be possible, and that society is more tolerant and supportive of attempted change than it was in earlier eras.

In summary, the evolution of our views on human transformation parallels a general increase in knowledge and a more intense morality concerned with each individual's rights and dignity. This course constitutes progress in Western civilization. In Western culture the concept of human transformation seems to be a liberating force that joins the ideas of democracy, freedom, rationality, mobility, and humanism. If this conclusion is valid, then the known facts about constancy and change in human development may be different even a decade or two from now, as social conditions facilitating human change increase.

Planned Social Invervention and Social Policies for Children

The chapters in this volume clearly have implications for policies of social investment in human development. The belief that early experiences create lasting characteristics, like the belief in biological and genetic determinism, makes it possible to assume that attempts to improve the course of human development after early childhood are wasted and without consequence. If society believes that it is all over by the third year of life, it can deal harshly with many people in later life because nothing more can be done, and social programs designed to educate, redirect, reverse, or eliminate unwanted human characteristics cannot be justified. Policies of racial, ethnic, and sex discrimination, incarceration rather than rehabilitation of criminals, ignoring urban and rural poverty, and isolation of the elderly have found shelter in the belief in the determinism of the early years of life.

Now this belief has been weakened by new facts, and it will be weakened still further in the years ahead as government and other groups increasingly demand changes in adults and are increasingly successful in changing adult behavior and personality. More family counseling, parent education, adult education for the tens of millions, flu vaccines, on-the-job training, halfway houses, and hundreds of other social investments in adults are being made to prevent losses to society.

It is desirable for those devoted to the children's cause to review their position. In earlier times children were valued and cared for because of their economic contribution to the family and as a future source of support for aging parents. But social change has altered the child's traditional economic value, and in recent times those concerned with child welfare have adopted a ''human capital'' or investment rationale for child care: an argument that investment in child welfare yields a rich return to the larger society.

It is true that facts about human development still support the investment approach to benevolent child care. A prevention strategy aimed at the young, as many of the authors have noted, may be considerably less expensive than a treatment strategy aimed at adults. Although the effects of early experiences are not as powerful as we have thought, and substantial change can be induced in later years, such change is likely to be more costly than improving the young child's environment. One does not abandon a concern with the events of early childhood but seeks to monitor the experiences to which children are exposed, to eliminate those that cause duress, and to maxi-

mize those later experiences that might reverse the deleterious consequences of an unfortunate childhood. Nevertheless, children are not
seen as society's only human capital; the same investment rationale
increasingly will be used to aid the development of humans at all ages.

Those primarily concerned with child welfare may find that the
time has come to strengthen their position by reemphasizing the
child's powerful humanitarian claim on social resources. What the
child can do for us later—or that it is cheaper to be good to children
now—should not be our primary concern. Children should claim our
attention because they engage our humanitarian feelings. A child must
be loved and supported for what the child is now, not just for what the
child can become. The starving child must be fed today, because the
child is hungry today, not just because protein deficiencies might
cause a deficit in intellectual functioning and therefore retard academic progress in grammar school. Children are fellow humans and
claim an equal place with other age groups because they are human
beings, not because they give some future return on investment.

Social policies developed for the aged place the situation of children in perspective. The primary argument for support of federally
financed programs for the aged remains humanitarian. The aged are
viewed as unproductive members of society, needing society's support. True, there are increasing efforts to keep the aging population
useful and productive in society, to make cost-benefit analyses of
capital investment in training older persons and what they return to
society, but the humanitarian concern remains the foundation of
social policy for the aged. Children must share in the same concern
instead of having to petition society for investment in them solely
because of their potential contributions.

These benign public sentiments about children, while well worth
encouraging, do not necessarily bring benefits for the child. Arthur
Koestler wrote in *Darkness at Noon* (1941) that the public conscience
is a diffuse kind of vapor that rarely condenses into workable steam.
There will be occasions when the good feelings of adults toward children should be captured and incorporated in the growing body of
Western law setting forth children's rights (Mnookin, 1978; Vardin
and Brody, 1979; Rosenheim, 1976; *Harvard Educational Review*,
1973, 1974). The transformation of sentiment into law sometimes
occurs naturally when sentiment is strong enough, as in recent legislation on child abuse. More often the transformation requires sustained
moral and intellectual leadership by a few to convince the rest of society. This effort is a companion to the efforts to arouse public sentiment about children, on the one hand, and to enforce existing laws
aiding children, on the other. Older people have shown the way: their

increased numbers enable them to translate humanitarian concerns into laws favoring the elderly. Children cannot claim large numbers, nor do they vote, so their cause is harder. If advocates for children depend only on the public conscience without making it part of the emerging laws concerned with human development, they are likely to lose their battle.

Our new view of human development from a life span perspective must be accompanied by a social policy that endorses continuing investment in the quality of human beings. "As we dispel the myth that there is some optimum time, the nine months *in utero*, for example, or the first year of life, when, if we could intervene, a child could be made perfect forever after, we must at the same time recognize that child development is continuous, and therefore social programs must be developed accordingly" (Zigler and Hunslinger, 1978, p. 13). These programs should derive from both humanitarian values and economic rationale, for young and old, and should assert that where human development is concerned, the assumption that only limited resources are available is unacceptable. The possibility of enhancement of human dignity and happiness is far greater than we can now foresee.

Note

We acknowledge with gratitude the many contributions of Heidi Sigal to chapters 1 and 2.

References

BALTES, P. B. 1973. Prototypical paradigms and questions in life-span research on development and aging. *Gerontologist* 13: 458-467.

———— 1979. Life-span development psychology: some converging observations on history and theory. In P. B. Baltes and O. G. Brim Jr., eds., *Life-span development and behavior*, vol. 2. New York: Academic Press.

BALTES, P. B., and SCHAIE, K. W., eds. 1973. *Life-span developmental psycology: personality and socialization*. New York: Academic Press.

BALTES, P. B., and SCHAIE, K. W. 1976. On the plasticity of intelligence in adulthood and old age: where Horn and Donaldson fail. *American Psychologist* 31: 720-725.

BINSTOCK, R., and SHANAS, E., eds. 1976. *Handbook of aging and the social sciences*. New York: Van Nostrand Reinhold.

BIRREN, J. E., and SCHAIE, K. W., eds. 1977. *Handbook of the psychology of aging*. New York: Van Nostrand Reinhold.

BLOCK, J. 1977. Advancing the science of personality: paradigmatic shift or improving the quality of research? In D. Magnesson and N. S. Endler, eds., *Psychology at the crossroads: current issues in interactional psychology*. Hillsdale, N.J.: Erlbaum Associates (Wiley).

BOTWINICK, J. 1977. Intellectual abilities. In J. E. Birren and K. W. Schaie, eds., *Handbook of the psychology of aging*. New York: Van Nostrand Reinhold.

BRIM, O. G., JR. 1966. Socialization through the life cycle. In O. G. Brim, Jr., and S. Wheeler, eds., *Socialization after childhood: two essays*. New York: John Wiley and Sons.

———— 1968. Adult socialization. In J. A. Clausen, ed., *Socialization and society*. Boston: Little, Brown and Co.

———— 1976a. Theories of the male mid-life crisis. In N. K. Schlossberg and A. D. Entine, eds., *Counseling adults*. California: Brooks/Cole Publishing Co.

———— 1976b. Life-span development of the theory of oneself: implications for child development. In H. W. Reese and L. P. Lipsitt, eds., *Advances in child development and behavior*, vol. 2. New York: Academic Press.

———— 1979. On the properties of life events. Kurt Lewin Memorial Address, American Psychological Association, September 3, New York.

CAIN, L. D., JR. 1964. Life course and social structure. In R. E. L. Faris, ed., *Handbook of modern sociology*. Chicago: McNally.

CLARKE, A. M., and CLARKE, A. D. B. 1976. *Early experience: myth and evidence*. New York: Free Press.

CONANT, J. B. 1947. *On understanding science: an historical approach*. New Haven: Yale University Press.

COSTA, P. T., JR., and McCRAE, R. R. Forthcoming. Still stable after all these years: personality as a key to some issues in aging. In P. B. Baltes and O. G. Brim, Jr., eds., *Life-span development and behavior*, vol. 3. New York: Academic Press.

ELDER, G. H., JR. 1974. *Children of the Great Depression*. Chicago: University of Chicago Press.

———— 1975. Age differentiation in life course perspective. *Annual Review of Sociology* 1: 165-190.

EPSTEIN, S. 1973. The self-concept revisited or a theory of a theory. *American Psychologist* 28: 405-416.

FINCH, C., and HAYFLICK, L., eds. 1977. *Handbook of the biology of aging*. New York: Van Nostrand Reinhold.

GERGEN, K. J. 1977. Stability, change, and chance in understanding human development. In N. Datan and H. W. Reese, eds., *Life-span developmental psychology: dialectical perspectives on experimental research*. New York: Academic

HARVARD EDUCATIONAL REVIEW. 1973. The rights of children, part I, vol. 43.

HARVARD EDUCATIONAL REVIEW. 1974. The rights of children, part II, vol. 44.

HUSTON-STEIN, A., and BALTES, P. B. 1976. Theory and method in life-span developmental psychology: implications for child development. In H. W. Reese and L. P. Lipsitt, eds., *Advances in child development and behavior*, vol. 2. New York: Academic Press.

INKELES, A., and SMITH, D. 1974. *Becoming modern: individual change in six developing countries*. Cambridge, Mass.: Harvard University Press.

KAGAN, J. 1971. *Change and continuity in infancy*. New York: John Wiley and Sons.

KAGAN, J., KEARSLEY, R. B., and ZELAZO, P. R. 1978. *Infancy: its place in human development*. Cambridge, Mass.: Harvard University Press.

KAGAN, J., and MOSS, H. A. 1962. *Birth to maturity*. New York: John Wiley and Sons.

KOHN, M. L., and SCHOOLER, C. 1978. The reciprocal effects of the substantive complexity of work and intellectual functioning: a longitudinal assessment. *American Journal of Sociology* 84: 24-52.

LERNER, R. M., and RYFF, C. D. 1978. Implementation of the life span view of human development: the sample case of attachment. In P. B. Baltes, ed., *Life-span development and behavior*, vol. 1. New York: Academic Press.

MISCHEL, W. 1973. Toward a cognitive social learning: reconceptualization of personality. *Psychological Review* 80: 252-283.

MNOOKIN, R. H. 1978. *Child, family and state: problems and materials on children and the law*. Boston: Little, Brown and Co.

QUETELET, A. 1835. *Sur l'homme et le développement de ses facultés*. Paris.

RIEGEL, K. F. 1976. The dialectics of human development. *American Psychologist* 31: 689-700.

RILEY, M. W. 1976. Age strata in social systems. In R. Binstock and E. Shanas, eds., *Handbook of aging and the social sciences*. New York: Van Nostrand Reinhold.

——— 1978. Aging, social change, and the power of ideas. *Daedalus*, Fall, 39-52.

ROSENHEIM, M. K., ed. 1976. *Pursuing justice for the child*. Chicago: University of Chicago Press.

SCHAIE, K. W. 1979. The primary mental abilities in adulthood: an exploration in the development of psychometric intelligence. In P. B. Baltes and O. G. Brim, Jr., eds., *Life-span development and behavior*, vol. 2. New York: Academic Press.

VARDIN, P. A., and BRODY, I. N., eds. 1979. *Children's rights: contemporary perspectives*. New York: Teachers College Press.

WINSBOROUGH, H. H. 1978. Statistical histories of the life cycle of birth cohorts: the transition from school boy to adult male. In C. Taeuber, J. Sweet, and L. Bumpass, eds., *Social demography*. New York: Academic Press.

ZIGLER, E., and HUNSLINGER, S. 1978. Our neglected children. *Yale Alumni Magazine*, February 2.

2 | Perspectives on Continuity
Jerome Kagan

ONE OF THE BASIC, complementary themes that permeates intellectual inquiry from the earliest period of Greek philosophy to the present is the relation between essence and existence—the invisible and the real. Modern illustrations of these complementary ideas include the relations between competence and performance, between hypothetical construct and operational definition, and between psychology and biology, for many scientists assume that psychological consciousness is the essence for which biological events supply the material, existential base. This theme permeates discussions of continuity and discontinuity in growth. As Robert Nisbet (1969) notes, when the characteristics of plants, animals, children, societies, or civilizations change, there is often an apparent discontinuity at the surface. But the human mind, especially the Western mind, seems inimical to the apparent lawlessness of the emergent form and insists on inventing invisible essences that provide a continuity between the preceding and the succeeding phenomena.

Since change is a salient characteristic of living entities, it is reasonable to ask why social scientists, especially psychologists, invest so much effort searching for threads of continuity in the growth of living forms and inventing a connectivity between past and present.

Many developmental psychologists, partial to a philosophy of continuity, believe that the fears, angers, and loves learned during the first years resist transformation. Some historians, unaware of the fragile empirical basis for this belief, are tempted to relate patterns of societal behavior to early childbearing practices. In trying to account for the brutality, violence, and muting of affect among adults in sixteenth-century England, Lawrence Stone suggests that maternal aloof-

26

ness and the practice of sending infants to wet nurses may have been influential.

> There seem to have been four causes for the development of such a culture. The first was the frequency with which infants at that period were deprived of a single mothering and nurturing figure to whom they could relate during the first 18 months or two years of life. Upper class babies were mostly taken from their real mothers and put out to wet nurses . . . Another psychological consequence of wet nursing was the anxiety experienced by many adults about who they really were. The fairy stories of the time were full of accounts of changelings whose real identity had been concealed by an exchange that had been carried out by the wet nurse . . . Many children of all classes suffered the loss by death of one parent or another at an early age. There is evidence to suggest that throughout the early modern period nearly one in ten of all children under 3 and one in five of all children living at home had experienced this loss . . . Finally, there was the deliberate breaking of the young child's will, first by the harshest physical beating and later by overwhelming psychological pressure which was thought to be the key to successful childrearing in the 16th and 17th centuries. These four factors, the lack of a unique mother figure in the first two years of life, the constant loss of close relatives, siblings, parents, nurses and friends through premature death, the physical imprisonment of the infant in tight swaddling clothes in early months and the deliberate breaking of the child's will all contributed to a psychic numbing which created many adults whose primary responses to others were at best a calculating indifference and at worst a mixture of suspicion and hostility, tyranny and submission, alienation and rage. (Stone, 1977, pp. 99-102)

In a similar vein, John Whiting and Irvin Child (1953) tried to demonstrate that a culture's socialization practices affected the adult personality which, in turn, influenced the beliefs of the society. Analyses of ethnographic data revealed a statistical association between harsh weaning and theories of illness having oral components, such as ingestion of toxic foods or verbal incantations. Whiting and Child's explanation of the relation was that harsh weaning generated anxiety over oral function which, in turn, predisposed the society to invent oral etiologies for illness.

Eastern scholars see more impermanence in nature; because living systems are always changing, much of tomorrow will be independent of today. But the Western mind, frustrated by the irrepressible flux, demands some almost frozen moments—either in the form of hypothetical entities that do not transmute, principles that impose uniform regularity, or, if these cannot be defended, at least periods during which the rate of change slows. We are in a Vermont stream during spring thaw, hoping that the rush of white water will cease for a few moments so that we might determine our location and savor the view.

The Western scholar's assumption of stability of structure and continuous operation of uniform mechanisms has a corollary: Every process or structure in the present contains enough of the past that one should be able to trace the present event to its origin, no matter how far in the past the first critical moment occurred. The exobiologist, for example, assumes that if life ever existed on Mars one should be able to find signs of it today, a supposition that would lead one to suppose that a newly hatched chick should reveal some evidence of the original yolk or that the butterfly should retain signs of the caterpillar. It is also argued that understanding of any event is necessarily enhanced by knowledge of its origin. Some scholars, Isaiah Berlin (1954) being one, contend that explanation is not possible without an insight into origins. Although Nisbet (1969) has written an elegant critique of this view for sociological phenomena, these assumptions have not been questioned seriously by psychologists. Each discipline examines its own house at its own pace when the time is right.

This chapter, which is a continuation of some of the issues raised in chapter 1, provides additional perspective for the rest of the volume by considering three themes.

The first part of the chapter analyzes the terms *stability* and *continuity*. Unfortunately, social scientists, historians, and biologists often have different understandings of these terms. Because it is not possible at the present time to persuade authors to come to a semantic consensus, this initial section may be helpful.

The middle part of the chapter is a historical brief for the proposition that a majority of Western scholars have favored the idea of continuity and have assumed smooth, cumulative transitions for phenomena long before relevant evidence was available. These pages invite the reader to wonder why so many European minds promoted the idea of continuity in nature while their counterparts in China and Japan adopted the opposite attitude.

The final third of the chapter, a review of some recently published evidence regarding the stability of selected psychological dispositions during childhood and adolescence, is not a substitute for the chapters by Moss and Susman and Wohlwill, but an attempt to point out the inconsistency between recent data and older theoretical assumptions.

This chapter is not a brief for discontinuity but an invitation to consider the possibility that for selected domains there may be little connectivity between early and later development.

There are three distinct ways to infer continuity in living systems. One is to hypothesize changeless elements that persist beneath the surface phenomena. The discovery of different classes of neurons in the visual cortex, each responding to different directions of movement or contours of different orientation, is a particularly nice example of this first class.

A second strategy is to discover unchanging mechanisms that operate across epochs of time. In psychological development, it is believed that a nurturant role model who is perceived as commanding power encourages individuals of any age to adopt the model's qualities.

The third basis for positing continuity rests on the assumption that events in a temporal sequence are related either because some structural elements that participated in the earlier event are contained in the later one or because the earlier event established conditions that were necessary for the appearance of the later event. This last argument requires detecting within a sequence of many events those few that cohere in a "causal" chain. The stage theories of Freud and Piaget imply that selected competences or dispositions in the adolescent depend on and are consequences of earlier structures. But these two theories, like all essays on development, whether theoretical or empirical, are essentially histories. They are sets of sentences that attempt to tell a coherent story. In this sense theories of psychological development resemble both *The Origin of Species* and *The Rise and Fall of the Roman Empire.*

Developmental psychology, like history, consists of descriptions of events over a time period and, depending on the author's premises, propositions that attempt to relate the events—the presumed explanation. But the biases of the narrator pose a major problem in both disciplines. Between any two points in time lie many more events than can be seen or recorded. The scholar must select a very small number and ignore many others. Between 1900 and 1978 the automobile, the television, the nuclear weapon, the laser, and the contraceptive pill were invented; the Germans lost World War I, there was an economic depression, Germany was divided following the end of World War II, the People's Republic of China was created, there was a long, bitter struggle in Vietnam, an American president resigned, and the price of oil and postage increased dramatically. Which of these events are part of a coherent sequence and which are not? Only theory can produce an answer to that question. The same problem confronts child psychologists. Between 1 and 15 months of age most infants will smile to a face, show anxiety toward a stranger, sit, stand, walk, and run, solve the object permanence problem, show symbolic play, and begin to speak single words. Which of these phenomena are connected and which not?

The developmental psychologist tries to detect which of these

phenomena are structurally related and to invent reasons. The validity
of the explanation rests, in part, on the accuracy with which the theorist selects from the stream of development the events considered to be
connected. And that selection is guided by suppositions that are not
always articulated, suppositions that also influence the historian's
account of a sequence of events (Collingwood, 1945).

Hayden White (1973) has offered an intriguing analysis of classes
of historical scholarship. He suggests that every historian chooses one
of four modes—romantic, comic, tragic, or satirical—to describe a historical sequence. These stylistic moods reflect the author's evaluation
of human nature as it attempts to reach some desired goal. The scholar
also uses one of four modes of explanation—a detailing of facts, an
organismic, mechanistic, or contextual interpretation. Finally, the
scholar adheres to an ideology that reflects his attitude to change,
from conservative through liberal to radical and anarchic. If one
applies this model to psychology, most developmental psychologists
appear to be romantic, mechanistic, and liberal. They see development as progressing inevitably toward a desired terminal state. They
see the child becoming more competent, stable, logical, and moral; the
adult chooses actions, monitors affects, polishes competences, and
holds beliefs that subdue the impulsiveness, lability, ineptitude, and
rigidity of childhood. The explanatory mode typically chosen by developmental theorists is mechanistic; each event is related to a succeeding event through a long, gradual chain that necessarily links events
and processes that can be detailed. Finally, the developmental theorist
prefers gradual change and is resistant to abrupt discontinuities. The
bases for historical change can provide useful models for psychological development, for in both disciplines new forces induce changes in
an existing structure. Consider seventeenth-century England. Basic
changes in the European family and in attitudes toward children and
toward sensuality occurred between 1600 and 1700 (Stone, 1977). The
family became less patriarchal, parents became more concerned with
the love relation between themselves and their children, and autonomy
and individuality became explicit ego ideals. John Donne diagnosed
the new spirit of egoism.

> For every man alone thinks he hath got
> To be a Phoenix.

Although it is not possible to account completely for these
changes, it is likely that the growth of industry, the rising power of a
middle class emboldened by the spirit of the Protestant Reformation,
and the attraction to intellectual analysis promoted by seventeenth-
century scientific advances cohered to produce an increasingly confi-

dent middle class feeling its economic power, autonomy, and sense of agency. These unpredictable events, introduced into the historical process, induced changes in the society, some of which persist today. Only recently, as a result of increased bureaucratization, have we begun to see some subtle change in these values.

Human development is also influenced by the introduction of new forces. One class of inducer is a new competence resulting from maturation of the central nervous system. For example, when the child's retrieval memory is enhanced at 8 months of age, new psychological competences become possible, including the object concept, imitation, and separation distress. When the capacity for language is inserted into the developmental process the child is able to classify events on symbolic grounds (that is, by membership in a class rather than by physical appearance). When reproductive fertility occurs the adolescent is forced to recognize his new role and correspondingly childishness becomes suppressed.

A less universal source of inducing events is produced within each culture. In our own society, for example, children entering school are placed in a unique social situation. They find themselves with twelve to fifteen other children of the same sex and age in a context in which intellectual talent is being evaluated daily. This situation forces all children to evaluate themselves relative to their same-sex peers and to decide whether they are hopelessly incompetent, of average ability, or superior to their peers. Once that belief is articulated important psychological changes follow, including increased or decreased motivation for academic mastery and movement toward or away from antisocial action.

Definitions of Stability and Continuity

Before trying to understand why the assumption of a necessary relation between an origin and subsequent states is so attractive to Western scholars, we need to define terms such as stability and continuity, especially with respect to psychological development. We shall arbitrarily use *stability* to refer to persistence of psychological structures and behaviors and *continuity* to refer to maintenance of psychological processes or functions, retaining the useful distinction between structure and process.[1]

There are at least four legitimate meanings of stability or continuity, each associated with an empirical strategy of evaluation (see Wohlwill, 1973, and chapter 9 in this volume for slightly different discussions):

1. The persistence of a psychological quality as reflected in minimal rate of change in that quality over time.

2. The persistence of a hierarchical relation between complementary dispositions within an individual (ipsative stability).

3. The preservation of a set of individual ranks on a quality
within a constant cohort (normative stability).

4. The necessary and contingent relation between phenotypically different structures or functions at two points in time due to
the operation of specifiable processes.[2]

A person can be described as possessing certain attributes at two
points in time, each attribute varying in the amount of change displayed across that interval. The four major classes of attributes that
modern psychologists attempt to quantify are overt actions in a context, cognitive structures (beliefs, rules, and concepts), feeling and
motivational states, and cognitive processes (detection, recognition,
interpretation, evaluation, recall, and reasoning). Like energy, each of
these constructs is assumed to exist in two states, either actualized or
capable of being actualized under the proper conditions.

These four classes of constructs are analogous to the colors, cry-
stal shapes, and molecular structures in the chemists' working vocabulary. Although chemists trust that a few grains of salt will retain their
color, chemical structure, and capacity for dissolving into solution as
long as no one disturbs them, biological phenomena are less cooperative. The single-cell amoeba changes its shape continually—especially
when it fissions into two daughter cells—and its internal chemical
composition varies as a function of diet and immediate ecological context. Descriptions of stability in living systems are more tentative than
those applied to inorganic entities. Additionally, statements about
stability are more relativistic.

Consider two two-year intervals in human development, the first
from birth to age 2 and the second from 8 to 10 years of age, and seven
psychological characteristics: (1) number of adjectives in the child's
active vocabulary, (2) frequency of occurrence of the Babinski reflex,
(3) amplitude of the second positive peak (P_2) in the visual evoked
potential, (4) occurrence of guilt following violation of standard, (5)
crying following the mother's departure, (6) length of the string of
numbers recalled immediately after having heard them, and (7) frequency of looking at or approaching the mother when in distress.
Some of these characteristics are relevant only to one of the age periods, and it is therefore meaningless to investigate their stability across
the first ten years of life. The Babinski reflex and crying after the
mother's departure occur in the first two years. Guilt and recall of
digits apply only to the older interval.

The other attributes occur during both periods. The amplitude of the P_2 in the visual evoked potential changes a great deal over the first two years and much less during later childhood. By contrast the number of adjectives in the child's active vocabulary changes less during the first two years than it does during preadolescence. Since we do not know how much change to expect, evaluation of a quality's stability often depends on the stability of another attribute. For example, during the first 4 months the amplitude of the P_2 displays greater change than the Babinski reflex, but from 1 to 2 years of age the reverse is true. That is, if one observed one child or a thousand children each week from birth to 4 months, quantified the P_2 (in millivolts) and the Babinski response (in percentage of occurrence to the proper incentive), and plotted the scores across successive months, the month-to-month differences would be greater for the P_2 than for the Babinski.

An investigator can, for any time period, quantify the occurrence of particular sets of variables, calculate the rate of change in these qualities, and draw conclusions about the relative stability of psychological qualities for a child or for a group. The magnitude of the changes in raw score for each variable will display a growth function. The amount of change across successive time epochs will asymptote earlier for P_2 than for number of adjectives, and one can say that toward the end of the second year the amplitude of P_2 is more stable than the number of adjectives. That statement has empirical meaning.

When biologists declare that the first trimester is a critical period in embryogenesis, they mean that the rate of change in the growth of organs is greatest during the first trimester. Change in the morphology of the central nervous system, for example, is less dramatic from 5 to 8 months than it is during the first 3 months of fetal growth.

When a quality stabilizes (that is, its rate of change slows), we are likely to call that attribute stable. As we shall note later, there are intervals during development when certain behavioral dispositions display such slowing. Rate of change in a measurable quality is perhaps the most meaningful definition of stability in living systems, and when rate of change in one quality is compared with that of others there is a sense of enhanced understanding.

These statements refer to objectively quantified, observable phenomena. Many psychologists, however, are more interested in the stability of hypothetical constructs. They prefer to discuss the stability of intelligence, attachment, or emotional lability rather than the amplitude of the visual evoked potential or the number of adjectives in a child's vocabulary. These scientists have been frustrated by the lack of consensus on the observable phenomena that are supposed to index the constructs. A psychologist interested in the differential stability of intelligence and dependency across the first five years of life is forced to use qualitatively different measures at 1 month and at 5 years, and each measure bears an uncertain and controversial relation to the constructs. As a result, some contend that the statement "Intelligence is more stable than dependency during the first five years" is, at the moment, without empirical meaning.

A closely related definition of stability refers to the relative dominance of one response over a complementary response over a period of time. This idea has been called ipsative stability. Suppose that a child has two mutually exclusive reactions, which are displayed with differential frequency in a specific context. Under these conditions it is meaningful to ask, Is a child's tendency to display response A in preference to response B stable over time? This question differs from the one that asks whether the rate of change in variable A is greater or less than the rate of change in variable B over the same interval.

Consider two responses that a child can make to a maternal request: obedience or disobedience. Suppose that a particular child is always more likely to obey than to disobey across successive sets of 100 parental requests. For each set of 100 requests the child obeys 75 percent of the time and disobeys 25 percent of the time. We could conclude that the dispositional preference to obey rather than to disobey showed stability. But the rate of change for acts of obedience and disobedience across successive six-month periods might be very similar or very different. Thus the persistence within a child of a tendency for one response to dominate another does not have the same meaning as the rates of change of these two responses in the same situation. Both are meaningful but different forms of stability.

When parents remark that their child has always been shy, they may not mean that their child always withdraws from other people or is more timid than most other children. I suspect they mean that their child's initial tendency to avoid contact with strangers has always been slightly more probable than the tendency to initiate encounter. This is an example of ipsative stability. Although ipsative stability has meaning empirically, it is not the meaning typically implied in psychological writing.

Most existing psychological data do not permit either descriptions of rate of change in a quality or conclusions about ipsative stability. Rather, most investigators have been interested in the stability of individual differences in one or more qualities. The evidence used to make these judgments is drawn from a comparison across time periods of the differential magnitudes of a certain variable assigned to a group of subjects.

Consider an obvious example. The statures of 100 children are assessed every six months from 1 to 5 years of age, and correlation coefficients are computed. The correlation from age 1 to 5 is likely to be between 0.4 and 0.5, and it is concluded that height is a stable attribute of children. However, this conclusion is not equivalent to stating that height does not change or that height is more or less stable than another physical attribute. The normative statement that stature is stable means that the *differences* in the heights of the 100 children have remained somewhat constant despite sizable changes in stature over the four-year interval.

In a recently completed longitudinal study, infants were administered the same visual episode at 5, 7, 9, 11, 13, 20, and 29 months while the duration of their attentiveness to the episode was quantified. In one procedure a child watched a hand move an orange rod across an arc of 180 degrees until it touched three light bulbs, which lit upon contact. The lights remained on for several seconds, then the rod was returned to its original position. This procedure was repeated for ten trials. The child then saw a transformation of that event for five trials and then three presentations of the original event. In one analysis we computed the ratio (for pairs of successive ages) of the difference in fixation time between two successive ages divided by the mean fixation time for the pair of ages for trials 2-5 of the original standard. A low ratio indicated minimal change relative to the absolute amount of attentiveness; a ratio of 0 indicated no change. The ratio was lowest for the interval from 9 to 11 months, meaning that absolute attentiveness showed the least change across the two-month period (Kagan, Kearsley, Zelazo, 1978). But the magnitudes of the Pearson product moment correlation coefficients for fixation time across the same successive two-month periods were typically low (less than 0.20) for all pairs of ages, except those between 13 and 20 months, when the coefficient was 0.48. This analysis suggests that the subjects tended to retain their relative rank for fixation time between the ages of 13 and 20 months even though fixation times changed more, in an absolute sense, from 13 to 20 than from 9 to 11 months. Similar results were found for attentiveness to other visual and auditory episodes.

The special character of normatively based propositions about stability of individual difference is seen more clearly when standardized scores are used, as they are for IQ. Absolute scores on the subtests of the Wechsler Intelligence Scale for Children change with age, but because they are standardized within an age cohort, all the real change due to development in psychological competence is removed. Only the relative standings of the children are left. When textbooks say that children's intelligence is stable from 5 to 10 years of age, they do not mean that cognitive ability is stable; it is not. They mean that the differences in test scores among a cohort of children remain stable, despite dramatic changes in the abilities that accompany growth.

Suppose that biologists postulated a concept called health and operationalized it for a particular period by counting the number of colds and fevers, measuring absolute gains in height, weight, and strength of pull, and quantifying time to recover from infections. These six variables display characteristic changes over the first ten years of life. Now suppose that a biologist standardized, within age, each of the six distributions for a thousand children, correlated the transformed scores by successive ages, found an average correlation of 0.5, and concluded that health was a moderately stable attribute across the first ten years of life. That statement may seem misleading; it is analogous to psychological propositions regarding the stability of IQ (McCall, 1977b).

Each species displays invariant sequences of behaviors. Young macaques mouth other monkeys, but this response eventually gives way to rough-and-tumble play. Initially human infants play with one toy at a time, then with two toys simultaneously; finally, they play with toys in a symbolic manner. The existence of replicable, invariant sequences in the ontogeny of all species poses the theoretical problem that many have tried to solve. Which of the responses in these sequences—if any—are part of a continuous process? Further, what is the relation among the structures that are characteristic of each phase? A tangled ball of strings is composed of many separate segments of different lengths. We pick up the end of one and want to know whether it is short or winds its way back to a distant origin in the center of the ball.

How does one know which responses belong to a continuous sequence? More important, how do we determine the nature of the structural connection between successive phases of an ontogenetic sequence, when there is such a connection? (We assume that in some sequences the structural overlap may be minimal.) Let us consider a concrete example from infancy.

Among the many responses that emerge between 5 and 12 months of age are comparative scanning of a new and an old toy (about 6 months of age), crying and inhibition of play in the presence of adult strangers (about 7 months), and reaching for a toy hidden under a cloth (about 8 months). These behaviors are quite different in their surface form, yet it has been conjectured that they are part of an emerging competence involving the ability to retrieve the past and to hold retrieved schemata and current perceptions in active memory (Kagan, 1976). One might speculate further that the ability to remember the location of a hidden object—Piaget's notion of the object concept—builds on the prior competence to recall that an event occurred in the past.

Stated succinctly, this meaning of stability is concerned with the relations between the hidden structures and competences of one stage and those of another, as each competence is embodied in different public actions. The connection is concretized as a process in which the structures or functions of one era are incorporated, completely or partially, into the present. "The ontogenetic formation of the intelligence includes a series of stages . . . each one of which has its origin in a reconstruction, on a new level, of structures built up during the preceding one. And this reconstruction is necessary to the later constructions which will advance beyond the former level. In biological terms, each generation repeats the development of the preceding one, and the new phylogenetic variations as they appear during ontogenesis extend this reconstruction of the past" (Piaget, 1971, p. 147).

Something like this must occur much of the time. The child must know the meaning of number before he can add or subtract. Similar examples abound. But that is not sufficient reason for assuming that all invariant sequences imply connectivity, even though we can always invent a reasonable explanation. The ability to speak a language is always preceded by a period, prior to about 10 months of age, when the infant points at a toy that he wants. But is the pointing a necessary antecedent to speech? Could the prior action have been omitted? Leonard Carmichael's (1926, 1927) anesthetized ambystoma larvae swam without prior practice, even though under normal conditions of growth the swimming movements are always preceded by a stage when much smaller motor movements are observable. But those small movements are not necessary for the mature swimming response. Since not all invariant sequences are epigenetic, we must be skeptical of fast and easy claims of such forms of continuity unless logic, data, and theory provide coherent support.

Theorists, like detectives, enjoy speculating on the relation between different events separated by years and linking pieces of apparently unrelated evidence into a coherent story. Freud believed that excessive resistance to toileting in a 2-year-old and compulsivity in a 12-year-old were part of a continuous sequence. Piaget has contended that the infant's kicking of a mobile and the concrete operational groupings of a 7-year-old belong to a common sequence.

Some believe that the infant's attachment to the caretaker is necessary for a deep love relationship in adulthood or that stimulation of cognitive development during the first three years is necessary for intellectual competence during later childhood. There is, of course, insufficient evidence for any of these speculations. Development represents a grand puzzle, with each scholar guessing at the past's contribution to the present or, on occasion, the present's contribution to the future.

All four classes of stability permit some change. In some cases structures are preserved or enhanced; in others the new quality depends on the existence of earlier ones. But even though many surface changes have close links to the past, it is not necessarily true that every new quality contains remnants of those that came before. Some qualities are replaced; others may vanish. In both cases it is not clear that structural heirs survive.

Let us consider in more detail the four classes of change, two of which are accompanied by stability of structure or continuity of process. We might call them enhancement, derivation, replacement, and disappearance.

In enhancement a particular psychological structure or process becomes better articulated or a process more efficient, but the essential nature of the psychological quality remains unchanged. This idea has its clearest analogy in morphology. Once neurons or muscle spindles form, they grow in size but do not change their fundamental structure. Similarly, many assume that the concept *mammal* becomes cognitively elaborated and better articulated with growth but always retains some key elements over the period of change. In addition, some psychologists contend that recognition memory becomes more efficient and accurate with age but does not undergo qualitative alterations after the first three to five years of life.

Although there is a relation between enhancement and derivation, there is also a subtle distinction. In derivation, which is closely related to the connectivity meaning of continuity, the structure or process that emerges from an earlier one is a transformation of the original and required its prior presence. In embryogenesis the mature genital is a derivative of the genital bud. It is not an enhancement of the original tissue but a transformation of it. Although the haploid gametes produced by meiosis are qualitatively different from their parent cells, they are a material derivative of them.

Many psychological theorists believe that guilt for violating a standard must be preceded by a period when the person fears loss of parental love. Even though the two emotions are different in phenomenology and incentive, the later one is presumed to be a derivative of the former. Or consider a child who, upon seeing a zebra for the first time, infers that it eats and sleeps. That insight is a derivative of existing knowledge, namely, that all animals eat and sleep. Piaget has argued for more profound derivatives; for example, the conservation groupings are assumed to be derivatives of the structures of the earlier sensorimotor and intuitive stages.

Most psychologists regard development as constituted of long chains of derivatives; a process or competence grows out of a prior one, and aspects of the former are incorporated into the later entity.

Replacement is often ignored because on the surface it resembles derivation. In derivation part of the ontogenetically older form continues to exist in the new entity, whether a structure or a process. Fear of loss of love is presumed to remain as an incentive even after guilt emerges as a derivative. In replacement the earlier structure vanishes, although the functions or conditions of occurrence may be similar. More important, however, is that although the parent form constrains the nature of the replacement, it is often the case that more than one replacement could have occurred. The early form did not determine the new one; the new entity was not contingent on the earlier structure or process.

Consider the growth function for initial apprehension to an unfamiliar peer, which emerges between 11 and 20 months of age. Before 11 months there is little behavioral inhibition to an unfamiliar child of the same age. The signs of apprehension to a peer appear soon after the first birthday and are absent by 36 months. Was the inhibition a derivative of earlier fears, such as fear of adult strangers, or was it the result of new cognitive capacities that permitted the child to generate questions that he could not answer? Pairs of children who saw each other monthly from 13 to 27 months showed more apprehension at 20 months of age, after each pair had seen each other seven times, than they did when they were 13 months old. These data suggest that a new cognitive ability, rather than some structural product of past experience, was responsible for the inhibition and its demise. The rough-and-tumble play that follows mouthing in infant macaque monkeys is not obviously contingent on the presence of the latter response even though both responses appear to have similar functions.

Replacement is a common form of change in history. The child-centered attitudes of the late eighteenth century replaced the authoritarian patriarchy of the 1600s, but the latter did not determine the former. Similarly, the use of wet nurses, which ceased in England after the mideighteenth century was replaced by more continuous maternal care. The emergence of new attitudes between 1650 and 1800, which included celebration of sensuality, child centeredness, and personal choice of marital partners, was due to changes in economic and social factors. It is not obvious that the new family was a derivative of the older one; if different economic and social events had occurred, the replacements might have been different. Psychological development may contain many replacements. The fear of strangers shown by 8-month-olds replaces the friendly, smiling posture that 4-month-olds display to unfamiliar adults. The avoidance at 8 months is not a derivative of the earlier amiability but a replacement due to the introduction of new cognitive competences. Reciprocal play between two 30-month-old children replaces a period of timidity that peaked between 15 and 20 months. Timidity need not occur before reciprocal play. New knowledge and the emergence of new cognitive processes permit children to conquer their fears and to initiate reciprocal inter-action with unfamiliar children. There are many examples in psycho-logical development in which maturation of a new competence or in-troduction of an external demand leads to the establishment of a structure that replaces an old one. Replacements imply discontinuity; derivatives imply continuity.

Finally, there are changes in which a structure, stage, or process vanishes and is not followed or replaced by a functionally related one. The trellis cells of the central nervous system vanish after they have accomplished their mission of guiding neurons to their destination, and "in vertebrate animals the main role of the notochord is appar-ently to participate in the formation of the embryonic nervous system. Once the backbone has appeared, the notochord has no further func-tion and largely disintegrates" (Gordon and Jacobson, 1978, p. 112). Indeed, neurobiologists suggest that during development many synapses decay and many neurons die—synapses and cells which par-ticipated in prior experience (Edelman, 1978). In a similar sense, the Moro reflex and the 6-month-old's babbling also vanish without ap-parent replacement. As fear of the dark is conquered by the growing child it is not necessarily replaced by another fear.

Biological evolution, which may provide a fruitful metaphor for psychological development, contains illustrations of all four classes of change. The size of the cerebral cortex has increased in mammalian evolution, the mammalian eye is a derivative of the eye of earlier ver-tebrate forms, the amphibian feet replaced the tail fin of the fish, and reproduction through fission vanished.

Consider some illustrations of the four classes of change for psy-chological qualities, where by psychological quality we mean a com-petence-performance unit. Motor skills typically become enhanced with development; they become more efficient, faster, smoother, and, where appropriate, more forceful. But the basic form of the act often remains unaltered. Language provides a good source of derivatives. When a child first utters the passive sentence "He got hit by his father" instead of the active form "His father hit him," we assume that the passive sentence required prior mastery of the earlier form. When negatives first appear in the child's speech, the child will say "no go"; later the child will say "I no want to go" and "I do not want to go" as apparent derivatives of the simpler phrase. Beliefs, by contrast, are often replaced. The attitude that education is good because it permits pursuit of a skilled vocation replaces a belief in its irrelevance, but the new belief is not a necessary consequent; it is only one of several. The older child might have developed the belief that education is good because it permits understanding or facilitates economic gain. Finally, a belief in ghosts, the babbling of infancy, the 2-year-old's uttering of strings of unrelated numbers, and probably many thousands of representations of vistas and facial expressions which have never been renewed vanish from the psychological repertoire.

These four classes of change are probably not evenly distributed across the life span. Because the newborn is developmentally incomplete, it is likely that maturational processes permit the introduction of new competences. As a result, during the early years we are likely to see replacement and disappearance more often than derivation and enhancement. With growth, structures and processes come to have a longer life and derivatives are likely to become more common.

John Flavell (1972), in an elegant essay on types of developmental sequences, posits five classes of change: addition, substitution, modification, inclusion, and mediation. In Flavell's addition, which is similar to enhancement, two related dispositions develop at different times, but the earlier one remains active or operative even after the later one emerges. In one sense the later one is added to the former. Flavell offers as an example that the 2-year-old, when he becomes capable of a symbolic mode of apprehending objects, does not lose his capacity for an enactive mode. In substitution, which is similar to replacement, the earlier disposition is replaced. "Thus development here consists in the complete substitution of a later acquired form for a functionally similar but formerly different, earlier acquired one, rather than in the mere addition of the former to a cognitive inventory already comprising the latter" (Flavell, 1972, p. 291).

In modification, similar to derivation, the new form is "some sort of improved, perfected, or matured version of X_1; some sort of transformed, derivative, or variant of X_1; in brief, some sort of modification of X_1 in the direction of cognitive maturity" (Flavell, 1972, p. 298). Flavell suggests that differentiation, generalization, and stabilization are three forms of modification.

Flavell's fourth class of change, inclusion, is closely related to the old notion of hierarchic integration. A disposition begins to develop and at some point becomes coordinated with a larger cognitive whole. As I have suggested, inclusion may be one form of a derivative class of change.

In the final form of change, mediation, a disposition facilitates or mediates a new response but does not become a part of the new structure.

Although Flavell is reluctant to acknowledge the possibility that structures may vanish—"it is a fair guess that X_1 is, in fact, seldom if ever irrevocably banished from the repertoire" (p. 292)—he urges investigators to be more receptive to the possibility that developmental sequences that appear to be invariant and cumulative over time might well be cyclical and sequence violating. "We developmentalists would also do well to enrich our vision of cognitive growth by taking seriously the possibility that it has significant asequential aspects" (p. 344).

Although Flavell agrees that it is unlikely that all developmental sequences are composed of connected derivatives, developmental theorists have preferred this interpretation of change. The positing of a closely connected set of stages in the gradual acquisition of a psychological competence—mysteriously they are often six in number—resembles Bonnet's eighteenth-century declaration: "Between the lowest and highest degrees of spiritual and corporal perfection there is an almost infinite number of intermediate degrees. The succession of degrees comprises the universal chain. It unites all beings, ties together all worlds, embraces all the spheres" (cited by Gould, 1977, p. 23).

Since natural phenomena present so many surface discontinuities, Bonnet tried to guess what the intermediate stages might be. He hypothesized that asbestos was intermediate between minerals and fibrous plants, the eel intermediate between reptiles and fish, the ostrich between birds and mammals. The savage, of course, was intermediate between ape and European man.

G. Stanley Hall suggested that some of the fears of childhood were links between the fears of modern man and those of our ancestral adults. Children fear nightfall, Hall believed, because primitive man had to be afraid of predatory animals that roamed at night. And Freud regarded the oral and anal stages of childhood as derivative of animal functioning.

Passages in modern psychological writing have a similar flavor. Some believe that the attachment of 12-month-old infants to their caretakers is an intermediate stage between the skin-to-skin contact of mother and newborn and the adult's capacity for trust and love. The extended pointing of the 7-month-old is considered a preview of spoken requests; the desire to obey one's parents is intermediate between fear of being spanked and the experience of guilt. Even the most recent publications reflect this attraction to a continuity created from a series of derivative structures. "It is theoretically possible to think of moral development as a continuum along which persons or stages can be placed . . . moral development refers to a continuous process formed by gradual qualitative changes in moral reasoning" (Davison, Robbins, and Swanson, 1978, p. 139).

When Maris Rodgon (1976) began her study of early language development during the second year, she assumed a derivative form of continuity from sensory motor structures to holophrases to combinatorial speech. "The literature . . . provides some evidence that the development of holophrases is continuous not only with later linguistic development during the combinatorial period, but also with previous cognitive development on the action level" (p. 23). But she failed to find a strong relation between the child's tendency to use a holophrase (for example, the child said "cookie" but presumably meant "I want a cookie") and the emergence of more complex combinatorial utterances or between the frequency of holophrastic and combinatorial speech. Further, Rodgon found no support for her expectation that certain sensory motor skills would be necessary for holophrastic speech. Although disappointed with these findings, she was still reluctant to question the original assumption of continuity. "It is by no means clear, however, that this implies discontinuity between the two periods" (p. 103). (By the two periods Rodgon meant the phase during which the child uttered single words and the later phase of two- and three-morpheme utterances.)

The stages of the sensorimotor period provide an elegant example of the faith in connectivity. The primary circular reaction, characterized by a repetition of simple acts such as opening and closing the hands, is considered intermediate between the simple automatic reflex of opening or closing the hand to a tactile stimulus and the 1-year-old's self-conscious imitation of an adult opening and closing her hand. The single element of similarity in this sequence is the action of opening and closing the hand. The logic in this argument is identical to the one that Bonnet used in concluding that asbestos and fibrous plants were connected because they shared a rough texture.

Why have social scientists invested so much effort in a search for stability of structure and continuity of process, when the assumptions behind the search are so vulnerable to critical analysis? Listen to James Mark Baldwin: "The genetic treatment of the question is the only fruitful one for a functional psychology or logic. If both the logical and the prelogical are modes or stages of cognition then this transition from one to the other is in its nature but the development of a continuous function" (1975, p. 38). "The canon of continuity: all psychic process is continuous. The fallacy of discontinuity consists in the treating of any psychic event as de novo or as arising in a discontinuous series" (p. 23).

Or consider Piaget on the same theme: "In fact there exist in mental development elements which are variable and others which are invariant, just as the main functions of the living being are identical in all organisms but correspond to organs which are very different in different groups, so also between the child and the adult a continuous creation of varied structures may be observed, although the main functions of thought remain constant" (1952, p. 14).

Finally, Werner and Kaplan have written: "A further issue of equal importance concerns the fate of the genetically earlier modes of functioning when higher functions and forms have emerged. At least with regard to humans it must be maintained that with the attainment of higher levels, lower levels of functioning are not lost" (1963, p. 3).

The general popularity of these views is due, in part, to the fact that the intellectual community believes in stability and continuity in development. The community wants empirical proof of that supposition, and few are overly critical of the quality of the evidence or the logic of the argument. Recently this state of mind has emerged for studies of the inheritance of aspects of psychopathology or personality. When members of a society hold a presupposition with conviction, they tend to be permissive regarding the validity of the supporting facts, and eager for any evidence that maintains the belief. It is time, therefore, to ask why so many Western scholars have favored the notions of stability of structure, continuity of process, and derivative change—a trio that I shall call faith in connectedness.

It may be helpful before presenting the historical background for this belief to consider two issues. First, some scientists see little value in examining the historical bases for current presuppositions. Such speculations are not subject to empirical test, they claim, and are therefore not a proper part of science. Just as many, however, contend that relentless examination of the deepest premises of a discipline is the strongest defense against dogma.

Alfred Wallace, in his 1890 essay "Darwinism," found it useful to review the historical context of Darwin's work.

> In order to appreciate fully the aim and the object of his work and the change which it has effected not only in natural history but in many other sciences, it is necessary to form a clear conception of the meaning of the term *species*, to know what was the general belief regarding them at the time when Mr. Darwin's book first appeared, and to understand what he meant, and what was generally meant, by discovering their origin . . . These opinions of some of the most eminent and influential writers of the pre-Darwinian age seem to us, now, either altogether obsolete or positively absurd; but they nevertheless exhibit the mental condition of even the most advanced section of scientific men on the problem of the nature and origin of species. (pp. 1, 5-6)

The scholar's task is to persuade. His major weapon is the assumption that the audience will be provoked by inconsistency between propositions or between propositions and evidence and will be responsive to coherent argument. Hence by noting premises that do not rest on firm evidence the writer automatically produces dissonance and makes the reader receptive to new views. Facts not relevant to a coherent set of premises are usually insufficient to change minds. For this reason I believe that a historical discussion of continuity is appropriate, for philosophers and natural scientists from Plato to Kant have argued for continuity as a natural law.

The historical consensus provokes a second question: Does the persistent assertion by scholars of continuity in nature reflect a truly connected sequence, or could it be that different sets of conditions over the last twenty-five hundred years have produced similar epistemological assumptions? It is possible that Parmenides' reasons for assuming unchanging essences may have nothing to do with Kant's similar declaration on the permanence of substances.

I argued earlier in this chapter that some historical sequences that seem to be contingently related are not part of a chain of derivatives but rather form a set of noncontingent replacements. Because I have warned against replacements parading as derivatives, I shall try in this historical overview to avoid language that reflects a preference for one or the other position.

Western Belief in Connectedness

The assumption of stability of structures is clearly present in the Greek notion that immutable entities lay behind the diversity and cyclicity in nature's rich display. The first Greek philosophers assumed the existence of a basic material from which real events emerged. For Thales it was water. Anaximenes made air the fundamental entity from which substances were derived by a transformation. Fire resulted from the dilation of air into a rarer form. Wind represented condensation. If that condensation proceeded further, stone was created.

Parmenides turned the essence-existence distinction on its head, denying the possibility of change. The experienced world, he insisted, was the illusion; the reality was the unchanging invisible unity beneath sensory experience. Parmenides' major premise was gratuitous but simple. If an entity exists, then it must be indestructible, eternal, and unchangeable. Parmenides argued that the proposition, Nothing exists, must be self-contradictory; for if something exists it cannot not exist.

Democritus put Parmenides' ideas into a more material form

with two related assumptions which can be detected in the thought of future centuries. "Nothing can come into being from that which is not nor pass away from that which is not . . . atoms are impassive and unalterable." The mind was a material entity constituted of atoms. The difference between the perception of an event (the *nomos*) and the essence of the event (the *physis*) is due to differences in the two motions of the atoms that constitute the mind. But both Thales' water and Democritus' atoms, though dynamic entities, were indestructible. Plato's solution to the problem of surface change was similar. He posited a changing world of events and an unchanging world of *ideai* —objects of thought—maintaining the distinction between existence and essence. Aristotle also assumed that when an object changed into another entity some part of the original endured unchanged, as when clay is worked into a statue of a woman. But Aristotle added an axiom: "He who considers things in their first growth and origin, whether the state or anything else, will obtain the clearest view of them" (Aristotle, *Politics*, Book 1).

The twin ideas of stable, indestructible essences and the explanatory potential of origins are the basic suppositions of modern developmental theory.

The great medieval philosophers—Peter Abelard, Duns Scotus, Thomas Aquinas, William of Ockham—were concerned with questions that turned the mind away from nature. Does God exist? Are there universals? What is the nature of the human soul? These questions were amenable to analysis only through logic and the dialectic, not observation. St. Thomas' defense of God was purely rational and based on the axiom that since every effect had a cause, the original cause was God. (Note the implicit connectedness in this argument.) Reliance on logic led to a separation of thought from the phenomena of life and hence to some measure of indifference to issues concerning the nature of objects and their development. Christianity rejected the Greek view of recurring cycles and substituted the notion of a unique origin and a gradual process of decay from that point. Since God made the world with perfection, change was slanderous (Knowles, 1962).

Some Renaissance scholars believed in the possibility of major changes in human development. Montaigne, for example, declared explicitly that the child's character and dispositions were not an accurate guide to the future. "The evidence of [children's] inclinations is so slight and obscure at that tender age and their promise so uncertain and deceptive that it is hard to arrive at any solid judgment of them . . . Men, falling immediately under the saw of custom, opinion, and law easily change or assume disguises'' (1958, p. 53). As a specific illustration of discontinuity in personality Montaigne mentions the change in character of French youth which he attributes to their college experiences. "There is nothing so charming in France as the young children. But they gradually disappoint the hopes that are conceived of them and when they are grown men we find them to excel in nothing. I have heard men of understanding maintain that it is the colleges to which they are sent—of which there is an abundance—that make them into such brutes'' (1958, p. 71).

The theme of continuity, which became ascendant during the Enlightenment, is captured in its quintessence by Leibniz's insistence on a continuum in nature. "Now this is the axiom which I utilize, namely, that no event can take place by a leap . . . a body in order to go from one place to another must pass through definite intermediate places.''

Leibniz conceived of nature as consisting of distinct monads ranging in hierarchical sequence from God to the lowest grade of life. Although no two monads were alike, each differed from the one just below it and the one above it by the least possible difference. A sentence from a letter captures Leibniz's deep conviction that without such a continuum there would be only disorder. "It is necessary that all the orders of natural beings form but a single chain in which the various classes, like so many rings, are so closely linked one to another that it is impossible for the senses or the imagination to determine precisely the point at which one ends and the next begins'' (quoted in Lovejoy, 1936, p. 145).[3] The implication was that there must be a cause or principle of sufficient reason for each ring; whatever exists must have an origin, and understanding is attained when each of the consequences derived from the origin can be shown to be necessary.

By the late seventeenth and early eighteenth century the notion of cumulativeness was added to the faith in continuity, gradualism, and sacredness of origin. A popular form of this idea is found in Condorcet's optimistic declaration that civilization progresses in a linear fashion, each era building on the era before it: "The history of man from the time when alphabetical writing was known in Greece to the condition of the human race today . . . is linked by an uninterrupted chain of facts and observations (1955, p. 4).

Lovejoy's magnificent summary of the eighteenth-century celebration of the great chain of being suggests that the fusion of Plato's notion of plenitude of forms and Aristotle's notion of continuity led to a conception of the universe as a great chain with an infinite number of links ranging from the meagerest existence through every possible grade up to man. Pope put this idea to poetry.

Vast chain of being! which from God began,
Nature's aethereal, human, angel, man,
Beast, bird, fish, insect, what no eye can see,
No glass can reach; from Infinite to thee
From thee to nothing—On superior pow'rs
Were we to press, inferior might on ours;
Or on the full creation leave a void,
Where, one step broken, the great scale's destroyed;
From Nature's chain whatever link you strike,
Tenth, or ten thousandth, breaks the chain alike.

The gradualism implied by the great chain is one reason for Darwin's insistence on many small steps in evolution and his choice of a tree as a metaphor for evolution. "The limbs divided into great branches, and these into lesser and lesser branches, were themselves once, when the tree was young, budding twigs; and this connection of former and present buds by ramifying branches may well represent the classification of all extinct and living species in groups subordinate to groups."

Darwin recognized that one basis for resistance to discontinuity was the strong desire among seventeenth- and eighteenth-century scholars to designate the mechanisms that mediated change; therefore, they dismissed descriptions in which a great many intermediate, small steps were not obvious. "But the chief cause of our natural unwillingness to admit that one species has given birth to other and distinct species, is that we are always slow in admitting great changes of which we do not see the steps" (Darwin, 1872, p. 180).

Mechanistic explanations, in contrast to those that rely on a coherence of many complex forces, turn the mind to search for a series of little steps. Discontinuities pose serious intellectual challenges to mechanistic explanations because they do not yield easily to descriptions of a series of connected, small causes. Because certainty is the dominant criterion in Western evaluation of knowledge, gradualism was promoted, for it served mechanism. The few eighteenth-century biologists studying reproduction who were not committed to mechanistic explanations, for example, Caspar Wolff, were precisely those who hypothesized major transformations between the undifferentiated cell and the differentiated fetus.[4]

Kant recognized that the assumption of continuity did not rest on empirical grounds but believed it to be one of the mind's necessary constructions. "Neither observation nor insight into the constitution of nature could ever establish it as an objective affirmation [Nevertheless] the method of looking for order in nature according to such a principle and the maxim of admitting such order (though it may be uncertain just where and how far) as existing in nature, certainly constitute a legitimate and excellent regulative principle of reason'' (Kant, 1727, cited by Lovejoy, 1936, p. 241).

Despite this caveat Kant's prose reads as though he were describing nature, not the mind's invention. "All phenomena are therefore continuous quantities . . . as every number must be founded on some unity, every phenomenon, as a unity, is a quantum and, as such, a continuum . . . Of quantities in general we can know one quality only *a priori*, namely, their continuity" (Kant, 1966, pp. 141, 144). Kant restated the Greek notion of stable essences by asserting the principle of the permanence of a substance. "In all changes of phenomena the substance is permanent and its quantum is neither increased nor diminished in nature" (p. 149).

But the section that reflects his views on connectedness most clearly deals with causality.

> Every transition therefore from one state into another takes place in a certain time between two moments, the first of which determines the state from which a thing arises, the second that at which it arrives . . . Every change however has a cause which proves its causality during the whole of the time in which the change takes place. The cause therefore does not produce the change suddenly (in one moment) but during a certain time; so that as the time grows from the initiatory moment a to its completion in b, the quantity of reality also is produced through all the smaller degrees of the first and the last. All change therefore is possible only through a continuous action of causality which, so far as it is uniform, is called a momentum . . . This is the law of continuity in all change, founded on this, that neither time nor a phenomenon in time consists of parts which are the smallest possible and that nevertheless the state of a thing which is being changed passes through all these parts, as elements, to its new state. (1966, pp. 164-165)

Lovejoy notes the sense of harmony that this view generated in the eighteenth and nineteenth centuries.

> The principles of plenitude and continuity . . . usually rested at bottom upon a faith, implicit or explicit of the universe of a rational order, in the sense that there is nothing arbitrary, fortuitous, haphazard, in its constitution . . . For every one of its characteristics, for every kind of being which it contains . . . there must be an ultimate reason, self-explanatory and sufficient. And the second principle follows from the first and was like unto it: there are no sudden leaps in nature; infinitely various as things are, they form an absolutely smooth sequence in which no break appears to baffle the craving of our reason for continuity everywhere. (1936, p. 327)

Lovejoy detects the inconsistencies in the eighteenth-century assumption.

Wherever in any series there appears a new *quale*, a different kind of thing, and not merely a different magnitude and degree of something common to the whole series, there is *eo ipso* a breach of continuity.

And it follows that the principles of plenitude and continuity—though the latter was supposed to be implied by the former—were also at variance with one another. The universe that is full in the sense of exhibiting the maximal diversity of kinds must be chiefly full of leaps. There is at every point an abrupt passage to something different and there is no purely logical principle determining—out of all the infinitely various possible kinds of differentness—which shall come next. (1958, p. 332)

In describing the resistance of nineteenth-century minds to the disruption of the static conception held by the creationists, Barzun comments,

Both should have known that becoming or growing, if it means anything, must mean a change not reducible to the stage before, much less to the original stages of process. Something exists at the end which was not there at the beginning. An oak may come from an acorn, but it is not identical with an acorn, nor even with the acorn plus all that the oak has absorbed of moisture and food in the process of growing upwards. The problem of becoming was the staple of discussion for the whole half century of romantic thought before Darwin and Spencer. To the Germans . . . we owe the establishment of the basic evolutionary notion that being is becoming and that fixity is an abstraction or an illusion. (1958, pp. 51-52)

As Nisbet (1969) notes, the eighteenth century assumed that nature had arranged for a best order of growth for each form. One way to discover this plan was to study the origin before the plan became distorted by life's conditions. The optimal order was believed to be stagelike, progressive, connected, and cumulative. When the relation between two stages was not obvious to the observer, then it was likely that a uniform mechanism or process was at work, veiling the phenotypic variations with sameness and uniformity. Some good examples of uniform causes acting over long periods include natural selection in biological evolution, competition in the growth of the economies of nations, the tension between sociability and egoism, the conflict between libido and the repression of sexuality, the class struggle, and of course assimilation, accommodation, and equilibration. Even if the same process is at work over a long era, however, it does not follow that a set of invariant stages is connected or even cumulative. Wind and sea operate continually at the shoreline, but that does not mean that the form of a New England beach five thousand years ago is present in today's shape, for it ignores the cataclysmic effects of hurricanes. The positing of uniform causes creates the illusion of connected development. What develops is not the shape of the beach but our idea of the shape of the beach. An 8-month-old babbles, an 18-month-old says single words, and a 3-year-old utters ten-word sentences. These are qualitatively different events. By using the word *language* as a categorical descriptor for all three phenomena, we make it easy to conclude that language develops gradually. But we may have created continuity by using the same construct; it is not present in the facts. "There is no historical evidence that macro-changes in time are the cumulative results of small scale linear micro-changes . . . Continuity of change lies in our constructions, not in history (Nisbet, 1969, pp. 288, 284).

The distinguished historian H. A. L. Fisher confesses his disappointment at being unable to find connectedness. "One intellectual excitement has . . . been denied me. Men wiser and more learned than I have discovered in history a plot, a rhythm, a predetermined pattern. These harmonies are concealed from me. I can see only one emergence following upon another as wave follows upon wave, only one great fact with respect to which, since it is unique, there can be no generalizations . . . the play of the contingent and unforeseen" (in Nisbet, 1969, p. 294).

Nisbet provides an example of the role of the unforeseen in the growth of modern English. Had the Norman conquest not occurred and altered Anglo-Saxon into an amalgam of Anglo-Saxon and Norman French, the language we use today would have a much different form.

Several controversies that arose during the nineteenth century implicated the theme of continuity because of their relation to the commitment to mechanism. One dealt with spontaneous generation. The physicalists, who favored spontaneous generation, were on the frontier of science, for they insisted that one did not need to postulate a Creator. Life could have arisen from the inorganic! The more conservative creationists, threatened by that hypothesis, tried to refute any evidence for spontaneous generation. Indeed, most agree that Pasteur's experiments, although adequately designed, were not elegant enough to warrant the acclaim he received. France celebrated Pasteur generously because citizens wanted someone to provide evidence that would refute spontaneous generation. In effect, Pasteur was their "hit man" against the dangerous physicalists.

The hypothesis of spontaneous generation was damaged seriously when progress in genetics revealed that the zygote was produced by the direct fusion of male and female pronuclei. It was clear by the 1870s that there was continuity from cell to cell and therefore from individual to individual. Edmund Wilson wrote, at the end of the nineteenth century, "Life is a continuous stream; the death of the individual involves no breach of continuity in the series of cell divisions by which the life of the race flows onward'' (1896, p. 9).

Those who looked to biology for a model of psychological development favored a position of continuity, for they took Virchow's formula, *Omnis cellula e cellula*—a principle that permitted no break in the chain of events. One can trace each entity through its parent and grandparents to the remote past. If that model were viewed as representative of psychological development, then a position of continuity is intuitively commanding.

When, toward the end of the nineteenth century, the modern view that life might spring from inorganic materials like colloidal gels became a possibility, the stage concept became more clearly articulated, and scientists became more open to a view of psychological development as consisting of a series of stages of increasing complexity that proceed in an invariant order, with each stage containing some of the structures and processes evolved in the preceding stages.[5]

As the twentieth century began, there was an enhancement of the traditional confidence that analysis of an entity into its constituent elements—the mode of natural science—was the most powerful strategy to gain understanding. Clarity was achieved when the experience of a complex event was replaced by a description of the simpler events of which it was composed, complemented by propositions stating the relations among the elements and between the elements and the larger unity.

The complementary view denied any reality to the elemental units since they were only words. Humans were trapped into a world view that was inevitably a product of their language. The twentieth century's skepticism over knowing nature's essence—a mood reminiscent of the doubt that followed the writings of Copernicus and Luther—produced not only an exaggerated concern with the factual bases for belief but, as a second theme, a hint of openness toward discontinuity. The latter, detectable in the writings of Bergson and Whitehead, was celebrated by the existentialists. In Sartre's *Nausea*, the protagonist Roquentin says, ''But as my eyes fell on the pad of white sheets, I was struck by its look and I stayed, pen raised, studying this dazzling paper: so hard and far seeing, so present. The letters I had just inscribed on it were not even dry yet and already they belonged to the past . . . Anyone could have written it. But I . . . wasn't sure I wrote it. The letters glistened no longer, they were dry. That had disappeared too; nothing was left but their ephemeral spark.'' Sartre challenges the notion of continuity of experience by inserting a sliver into the cleft that separates past and present on the stage of consciousness, permitting each self to be free of the constraints of the past and, hence, free to believe anything—an idea that the Greek mind would not understand.

The existentialists became harbingers of a new mood in the social sciences and anticipated the themes in this volume by at least a quarter century. If, as Sartre argues, any person can change his agenda and abrogate the past, the hypothesis of an unbroken trail from childhood to adulthood is flawed. Perhaps one reason why existentialism did not appeal to the majority of Europeans and Americans may be its attitude toward discontinuity in experience.

Several other factors may have promoted contemporary faith in the connectedness of psychological structures from infancy through adulthood. One is our society's egalitarian ethic. Many believe, with John Locke, that the only way to guarantee the attainment of political equality is to assume that all infants are equally skilled or unskilled at birth and to regard experience as unbiased tutor to all. Under these conditions, society could arrange the early environments of all children so that their encounters would be optimal and all would develop equally alert minds. Those who wanted an egalitarian society would be attracted to any psychological theory that insisted that experience was the primary determinant of psychological differences. Since kindergarten children differ so markedly from one another, supporters of this view would conclude that early experience must produce that variation.

A second reason for assuming a relation between early experience and later development comes from the maxim that one must prepare for the future. It is the parents' responsibility to provide the proper early environment—and the earlier, the better. Just as persons in the seventeenth century prepared for salvation through good deeds, parents were urged to prepare their children for psychological health through proper nurturing. The writings of American intellectuals in the eighteenth and nineteenth centuries, influenced strongly by Protestants with an egalitarian ideal, urged mothers to care for their young children, implying that such action was not unlike gathering wood in August to prepare for winter's frigid winds.

A third basis for a belief in stability of dispositions is due to the nature of our language. The adjectives used to describe people rarely refer to the age of actor or the context of action. Like the names of colors, they imply a stability over time and location. We use words like passive, intelligent, or labile to describe infants, children, and adults as if the meanings of these words were not altered by maturation. The use of the same words invites the belief that one is talking about the same process. This tendency is not characteristic of all languages. The Japanese use different terms to describe mental abilities in infants and adults.

The belief in the sustaining power of early experience is also a consequence of entrenched social practices, particularly the tendency to rank children on valued traits. This practice sensitizes every parent to the fact that evaluations of their child's ability at school entrance will influence the quality of the child's education, the probability of gaining entrance into a good college, and, therefore, the child's vocational success, happiness, and wealth. Very few societies practice such a severe grading of children. In most other communities the child is assigned responsibilities when he is ready, not at a particular age. The West's commitment to a meritocratic system forces institutions to select candidates from the best trained. Since training is cumulative, the best colleges will select the best-trained adolescents. Additionally, the well trained affect the less well trained, for the presence of the former persuades the latter that they cannot attain the same level of competence. This belief is established early, perhaps by age 10 and 11; and once articulated, motivations often become fixed. Most parents sense this sequence and therefore want their child to be ahead early in the race, at least by the time they enter school. Since a 6-year-old who is relatively competent, compared with peers, on reading skill or control of aggression is more likely to remain high than to plummet, the child who starts ahead in the development of culturally valued talents or personality attributes is likely to remain ahead. This view, which is partially compatible with the facts, leads parents who want their children to gain positions of status, challenge, dignity, and wealth to assume that psychological differences at school entrance are the result of previous experiences. Hence parents want to guarantee that their children will have the best possible set of early experiences.

Nineteenth-century science contributed to the notion of connectedness between infancy and later development. Psychological science, which is strongly dependent on the natural sciences—especially neurophysiology and neurobiology—is reductionistic. Many believe that it is possible to translate psychological experience into sentences with purely physiological terms. Given the recent claims that experience affects the weight of the brain and that early stimulation can add dendritic spines to cells or alter the sensitivity of the visual cortex to vertical or horizontal lines, one is tempted to regard the central nervous system as similar to John Locke's tablet—a soft surface that accepts material marks, which are difficult to erase, for Locke insisted that no idea could be destroyed. Since most scientists, as well as educated laymen, are receptive to the notion that psychological experience is translated into material changes in the neuron, it is easier to assume that these marks are fixed rather than transient or easily altered. The belief that experience permanently changes the central nervous system, added to the corollary that the brain directs thought and behavior rather than the other way around, leads to the conclusion that early experience must be important, for the first structures, which are permanent, will direct the later ones. The iron filings on the fresh tape, a popular metaphor for mind, will be permanently altered; and if no one erases the message, it will be preserved with fidelity for an indefinite period of time.

There is a fundamental difference between the philosophical assumptions of East and West regarding continuity. The classic Buddhists did not assume a unitary force, God, or monad but favored the hypothesis of multiple forces. Man, wrote the Theravada Buddhists, is made up of matter, feeling, perception, impulse, and consciousness, each impermanent, in perpetual flux, and continually in a state of creation and dissolution. Joseph Needham (1969), who has spent half a career studying science in early Chinese society, notes, "Yet China and Europe differ most profoundly perhaps in the great debate between continuity and discontinuity, for just as Chinese mathematics was always algebraic rather than geometrical so Chinese physics was faithful to a prototypic wave theory and perennially averse to atoms" (p. 17). Needham suggests that the Chinese conception of natural phenomena is organic and cyclical rather than mechanical and linear. Each event is part of an interconnected set of entities and forces. If each unit in the whole reacts in accord with its inherent nature, an orderly alternation of basic cycles is produced. The Chinese never entertained the notion of fixity of species and were receptive to the discontinuity implied by metamorphosis. This difference is evident in the West's eagerness to fix the dates of origins (many seventeenth-century Europeans believed that the world was created on 22 October, 4004 B.C., at 6 P.M.) and the East's relative indifference to beginnings.

An important difference between Chinese and European views of nature is that the Chinese regard the structure of the present as exerting a profound influence on current phenomena. Since future contexts cannot be predicted very well, the informativeness of the past is limited. The Chinese, in extrapolating their ideas about nature to human behavior, regarded each person's position in the social network of the moment as having extraordinary power to control his behavior—a position not unlike that of Walter Mischel and many social psychologists. Further, since social structures change so dramatically with development—from mother-infant, to child-sibling, to child-peer relationships—one would expect to see important changes in behavior that were not necessarily part of a derivative chain.

The treatises on human nature written by scholars in the two cultures may provide some clues to their differential concern with continuity. From Plato through Locke to Whitehead, Western scholars have sanctified the cognitive function of understanding. Two of the most famous essays in Western philosophy are Locke's *Essay on Human Understanding* and Kant's *Critique of Pure Reason*. The initial section of the *Leviathan*, which speculates on the nature of man, begins with a consideration of thought and imagination, not emotion, action, or motivation, each of which is dealt with subsequently. Even Montaigne, who was not friendly to continuity in psychological attributes, celebrated knowledge. "The greatest men make [reflection] their vocation; those for whom to live is to think. It is the occupation of the gods, says Aristotle, the source from which comes their beatitude and ours" (1958, p. 252). In Book 3 of the *Essays*, Montaigne notes, "There is no desire more natural than the desire for knowledge. Truth is so great a thing that we ought not to despise any medium that will conduct us to it" (pp. 343, 344).

Kant, too, assigned reason primacy over motivation or emotion. "If you have recourse to anything else but untrammeled reason . . . you simply render yourself ridiculous" (1966, p. 483). For Kant the central goal was to avoid error, and reason was the greatest weapon in meeting that requirement. Understanding, the function of reason, requires knowledge as a necessary, although not sufficient, condition; and knowledge accumulates. Propositions about the world and material products that derive from knowledge accrue and are phenomenologically stable while emotions are fleeting and cyclical. One mood replaces another; facts remain fixed.

The contemporary neurophysiologist who wishes to understand the neural bases of psychological phenomena selects learning, memory, and consciousness—not feeling or action—as the primary constructs to clarify. Gerald Edelman writes that the efforts of neurobiologists "do not directly address the most challenging problem of neurobiology: the determination of the structural substrates and cellular mechanisms of higher brain functions, particularly those underlying consciousness" (1978, p. 51). A few paragraphs later, while listing the primary phenomena that a theory of brain function must account for, Edelman names only cognitive processes. "It must account for the distributive properties of memory and learning, for associative recall, as well as for the temporal properties and temporal scale of recall" (p. 52). Once one memorizes the Pythagorean theorem, Newton's physics, or Aquinas' philosophy, they remain available indefinitely. Each time these structures are retrieved they seem to have the same form and quality. Knowledge, which is cumulative, lends to each mind a measure of sameness over time.

The Chinese, by contrast, made particular emotional states the central human qualities to attain. *Jen*—best translated as a love of humanity—always takes precedence over understanding. And feeling states, unlike segments of knowledge, are phenomenologically fleeting. An emphasis on affective states leads to a view of human qualities as alterable and evanescent rather than permanent.[6] Moreover, understanding can be attained, at least temporarily. *Jen* is sought! The implication is that one never attains the ideal state but continues to strive for its possession.

Thus one possible basis, although probably not the primary one, for the West's preference and the East's indifference to continuity in human qualities may be that the two cultures created different ideals for humans to achieve. I do not suggest that because the West chose understanding, which is more static than *Jen*, scholars have been friendly to continuity. Rather it is likely that the centrality of rational understanding is one of a coherent set of conditions that led to a preference for continuity as a presupposition (Wing-Sit Chan, 1963).

It is interesting to note what happens when a Western scholar, committed to mechanism and continuity, tries to explain Eastern philosophy. Spiro speculates that the Buddhist notion of karma might be due to certain childhood experiences.

We have seen that in his early years the Burmese lives in a highly uncertain and unpredictable world. Following a period of nurture, the infant for no apparent reason to himself experiences its unpredictable withdrawal. Childhood is an equally uncertain period. At one moment the object of parental attention, in the next the child may be unpredictably shunted aside. For him, fortune and misfortune alike follow each other inexplicably and unpredictably. But since his parents provide him with no clue to their behavior, one would expect him to develop the notion that he must be its cause: he must have done something—though he doesn't know what—to evoke now this, now that, response . . . According to this theory, then, Burmese socialization produces two dimensions of the Burmese cognitive structure—the expectation of uncertainty and the belief in personal responsibility—which, I suggest, form the cognitive bases for their acceptance of the karmic explanation for misfortune and fortune. (1970, p. 137)

As noted earlier, Stone (1977) used the uncertainty of early infancy to explain the violence of sixteenth-century London. Both Spiro and Stone made different adult beliefs and actions at a societal level necessary consequences of the same set of childhood experiences because, I suggest, both shared the Western belief in a connectivity between the experiences of childhood and the beliefs of adulthood.

The Nineteenth and Twentieth Centuries
in Developmental Psychology

Two scientific bases for the developmental psychologist's commitment to stability and continuity are, of course, the theories of Darwin and Freud. Darwin's evolutionary hypothesis assumed gradual change and a connectivity among all forms. Although the gene had not yet been discovered, most supposed that there was a material link between man and animals that bound them in a seamless mural.

Darwin anticipated the demand that gradualism be conserved by insisting that there had been intermediate forms but they had become extinct because proliferation of the new variety, which initially was a transition form, gradually, through competition, led to the extinction of the parent form. The principle of natural selection made it possible for a derivative species to replace its parent, albeit gradually. This idea is present in all major theories of psychological development, including those of Freud and Piaget. A symptom, competence, or affect is the result of the gradual accumulation of many experiences but is always the derivative of earlier structures.

Freud took from Maxwell the notion of a fixed reservoir of energy that was transformed but always conserved, and from Darwin, the central agency of sexuality. For Freud the major puzzle was the existence of psychopathology. Of all the places he might have looked—the patient's current life situation, genetics, social status, or beliefs, Freud selected childhood experience and inborn constitution. Aware of the embryologists' recent discovery that early trauma could result in a malformed fetus, he borrowed the concept of fixation from embryology and applied it to psychological development. Freud's three major premises remain popular in contemporary child psychiatry: (1) The etiology of certain classes of symptomatology lie in the past.(2) The major cause of these symptoms is repression of sexuality. (3) Repression of sexuality has a biological origin in phylogeny, and an experiential source in early family experience. The child's constitution would determine his vulnerability to neurosis; family experience and age of fixation would determine the exact form of the pathology.

Piaget's substages supply particularly nice examples of the connectivity that the Western mind celebrates. "Each stage's general structure results from the preceding one and prepares for the subsequent one; into which it is sooner or later integrated" (Piaget and Inhelder, 1969, p. 153). Piaget, like Darwin, resists the suggestion that new structures or functions might appear without a long period of preparation, despite many biological examples of relatively sudden onset. Reproductive fertility emerges rather quickly between 12 and 14 years of age in most well-fed girls when the hypothalamic sensor for blood-circulating estrogen is raised and the normal inhibition of pituitary secretion of gonadotrophins by the hypothalamus fails. As a result, the consequences of puberty emerge. James Tanner captures the surprise inherent in this sequence. "The oestrogen sensor's responsiveness does not merely lessen; at a certain moment in puberty it seems to be flipped right over" (1978, p. 102). Similarly, the appearance of negatives in the child's speech and the rebellion of privileged, upper-middle-class youth during the late 1960s have an abrupt quality. Nature provides as many examples of relatively sudden onset as of gradual alteration.

During the 1920s and 1930s, when Freudian ideas were gaining popularity and inductive discovery was the prototype for developmental research, several major longitudinal studies were initiated in the United States. The scientists who initiated these unique investigations were looking not for differences between the 12-year-old and the 2-year-old but for the slim thread of sameness. What might those links be? I suspect they were images of dispositions to be fearful, hostile, labile, intelligent, for dispositions were the central descriptors of that period. The implicit metaphor for a person's profile of qualities was a set of piano keys which produced varied melodies firmly connected to unchanging inner structures. It should be possible, theoretically, to infer the inner structure by listening carefully to the music. These investigators ignored the fact that there is no necessary connection between a surface quality and an underlying structure. One cannot, for example, guess the chemical structure of a surface that reflects a particular hue.

The unwritten premise of this first group of investigators was that if one gathered enough information on a growing child, his life course would become clear. In Berkeley, Denver, Boston, and Yellow Springs extensive longitudinal studies of middle- and working-class Caucasian families were initiated. The effort and money would never have been so generously extended if the majority did not believe that the adult could be understood through access to the past. The variables chosen for study reflected conventional dynamic hypotheses—mother's behavior was assumed to influence the child's dependence, aggression, passivity, fearfulness, achievement, dominance, and irritability. It was further believed that pathology in the young was likely to resist change and was, therefore, a harbinger of the future rather than a reflection of a temporary crisis.[7] An early symptom was believed to be the product of an internal conflict—conceived as a structure that grew over time—rather than as an acute reaction, as if a callus on the toe was always due to disease in the underlying layers of the skin rather than to a tight shoe.

A central premise of twentieth-century developmental theory was that anxiety, especially during infancy, was a primary pathogen. Because a second assumption involved continuity, the anxious infant would probably become an anxious child. Psychologists appended to the ancient continuity assumption the modern preoccupation with resolving uncertainty and coping with anxiety and concluded that an infant who was uncertain about the accessibility of his caretakers was likely to be vulnerable to anxiety during the later phases of development.

The existing data, although meager, do not affirm this idea. For example, variation in degree of anxiety over loss of access to attachment figures during the first three years of life (among subjects in the Fels longitudinal sample) predicted no significant behavior in adolescence or adulthood (Kagan and Moss, 1962). Interestingly, one of the behaviorally most secure infants had a serious prepsychotic break at age 18 while her older sister, who showed frequent signs of fearfulness during infancy, became a productive biologist.

In a later longitudinal study (Kagan, 1971) excessive crying and irritability during the first year of life were associated with different derivatives for boys and for girls at 27 months of age. The irritable infant boys became shy 2½-year-olds; the irritable girls became restless and active toddlers. The majority of these children were evaluated again when they were 10 years old. There were no significant differences at age 10 between the irritable infants and those who were placid. Finally, in a recently completed study of day care and home-reared children from 3½ to 29 months of age, no predictive relation emerged between either degree of irritability or intensity of separation distress under 1 year and individual variation on a variety of behaviors at 29 months.

The data on the long-term consequences of differences in early signs of distress are consistent with the published data from several longitudinal studies, all of which imply that variation in many behavioral qualities of infancy are not very predictive of reaction patterns in the distant future. In the Fels Research Institute study (Kagan and Moss, 1962) for example, fearfulness, activity level, irritability, and tantrums during the first three years were not predictive, in the normative sense, of a variety of behaviors during later childhood and adolescence, while differences among 6- to 10-year-olds did predict reasonable variation in adulthood. Similarly, cognitive precocity in infants was not predictive of precocity or level of cognitive development during the school years.

The chapters in this volume, although relying mainly on normative analyses, are in substantial agreement with the Fels study in implying little predictive power from infancy to adolescence and beyond (Moss and Susman, chap. 11; Wohlwill, chap. 9). Even in cases of severe pathology, such as schizophrenia, it has not been possible to find psychological qualities during the first five years that are prolegomena to later psychotic disturbance (Goldstein, chap. 8).[8]

Studies of the consistency of individual differences among school-aged children in the tendency to pause to evaluate the quality of one's cognitive products reveal that the year-to-year correlations are about 0.4 to 0.5, but these correlations decrease in magnitude with time. A nice example of the dynamic changes that typically occur over time is found in longitudinal data collected by Holtzman, Diaz-Guerrero, and Swartz (1975) in a six-year longitudinal study of Mexican and American children from three age groups, 6½, 9½, and 12½ years of age when the study began. For many variables the stability coefficients declined in a linear fashion as the interval between testing increased. There was continuous change in the rank order of the children for particular qualities, but the older the child, the greater the preservation of the rank order. Stability correlations between years 1 and 6 were always lower for the children who were 6-years-old than for those who were 12 years old when the study began.

Similarly, examination of scores on a scale of infant development (similar to the Bayley Scale) administered longitudinally to large numbers of rural Guatemalan children at 6, 15, and 24 months revealed a steady decrease in the magnitude of stability coefficients as the interval between the first and second assessment increased. For example, the relation between scores on the motor scale at 6 and at 15 months was 0.29; the corresponding coefficient for the scores obtained at 6 and 24 months was only 0.14—from 8 to 2 percent of the variance. Some of these children were also administered a battery of cognitive tests at 3, 4, 5, and 6 years of age. Although the language score at 2 years predicted the cognitive score at age 3 ($r = 0.2$), the score at age 2 was uncorrelated with the cognitive assessments at age 6 ($r = 0.16$ for the males, 0.06 for the females). As the interval between assessments increased, the ability to predict the later variation from the earlier scores decreased steadily, implying that the child's qualities were continually subject to change (Klein and Lasky, 1978).

One variable that has shown impressive stability is IQ score, especially its primary component, size of vocabulary. How can we understand the normative stability of individual differences in vocabulary over periods as long as five to ten years? Since all children acquire new words every year, why is the child who knew the meaning of *penny, nickel,* and *fur* at age 5 likely to know the meaning of *secretary* and *establishment* at age 10?

One hypothesis is that children differ in the biological organization of their language abilities. As a result some consistently learn language more easily than others, for the biologically based aptitude acts uniformly over time. One problem with this interpretation is that children with different IQs and vocabulary scores often learn new words equally quickly. (Holtzman, Diaz-Guerrero, and Swartz, 1975; Kagan et al., forthcoming). This fact is inconsistent with the idea that children with large vocabularies and high IQs at ages 5 and 10 naturally acquire new words more quickly.

The stability of the environment, a second explanatory candidate, assumes that children remain similar in their ability to learn new words but that the words to be assessed are heard more often in one environment than in another. Since children usually remain in the same environment, they retain their relative ranks across time. This interpretation has some support. If children are shifted from a family of one social class to that of another, they gain or lose in IQ and vocabulary appropriately. The analogy here is to two plots of land, one rich in minerals and one poor, into which genetically identical seeds are scattered, and the heights of plants are measured across the spring and summer. The seedling growing in the better soil will become the taller plant because of stability in the environment.

Most favor a complex combination of both hypotheses. Some children seem to be more alert to the unusual; they detect discrepant speech forms and seem more motivated to understand them. If these youngsters grow in an environment that supplies more frequent exposure to a variety of language forms, they should remain high in their cohort. This explanation acknowledges the presence of certain inherent qualities of children that remain stable. But if the environment should change, the talent is also likely to change. If a 5-year-old child with a large vocabulary and professional parents should be transferred to a lower-class environment for half a decade, his IQ and vocabulary would change, perhaps dramatically. Corn that is genetically programmed to yield tall seedlings will grow more slowly if it is transferred to poor soil soon after sprouting. Thus stability must be due, in part, to constancies in the environment. For humans this means constancy in the interpretation of experience.

So far I have emphasized the lack of connection between the very early years—typically the first two years—and later development. But stability (in the normative sense) emerges rather clearly after 6 years of age. Almost all investigators find some theoretically reasonable relations between variation in behavior during the years prior to adolescence and variation a decade later. For example, in the Fels Longitudinal Study differences in academic skills and social spontaneity predicted differences in similar qualities in early adulthood. Certain conditions could modify these stabilities, however. For example, differences in aggression—a response inconsistent with the traditional female sex role—were far less stable for females than for males. Individual variation in passivity, which has the opposite sex role profile, was far less stable for males then for females (Kagan and Moss, 1962).

It is reasonable to assume that some dispositions of the preadolescent child might display normative stability. The 7-year-old has generated a belief system about the self which is formed and monitored, in part, by interaction with others. Because most children remain with their family and the same group of peers during the first dozen or so years of life, we would expect these beliefs, and therefore their related behaviors, to be maintained.

Investigations of neural development reveal a lesson that may be applicable to psychological growth. Many classes of neurons are constrained from certain kinds of change while remaining plastic with respect to others. During the period of plasticity it is not possible to predict which of several outcomes will occur because of the indeterminate status of the future environmental constraints that the cell will encounter. For example, there is a period of about a month in the development of adrenergic and cholinergic cells of the autonomic nervous system of the rat—from two weeks prior to birth to approximately two weeks after birth—when a developing neuron is plastic with respect to its final transmitter, whether acetylcholine or norepinephrine. The final outcome is determined, in part, by the action of nearby cells (Patterson, Potter, and Furshpan, 1978). Four weeks is a relatively long time in the life of a rat, considering that this animal reaches reproductive fertility in 3 months, not 156 months, as in the human. Thus it is reasonable to suppose that many psychological dispositions of an infant also remain unusually plastic during the first year or two. How long each of the major psychological systems remains open to change is, of course, unknown.

The available data, though fragile and perhaps not even the most appropriate to generate propositions about stability, imply a few tentative conclusions. There is little firm evidence for the idea that individual differences in psychological qualities displayed during the first two years of life are predictive of similar or theoretically related behaviors a decade hence. I believe that psychological variation during the first two years is often an acute reaction to a transient external provocation, a reflection of differential maturation of cognitive capacities, or the result of a temperamental quality vulnerable to change. A stable belief system about self and others, which is such an important determinant of later behavior, is not articulated by 2 years of age. The reason for the selective appearance of normative stability after 2 years of age may be that the executive functions we call *ego* or *self* do not emerge until later in the second year. Once these functions emerge, the child begins to interpret his experience, and the first expectations begin to be established. Prior to the second birthday, experience does not undergo this critical transduction and, as a result, may be of less consequence.

The moderate stability of individual differences in select variables from preadolescence to later adolescence and adulthood is due, in part, to the consistency of belief systems that happen to find continuous affirmation in the environment. If the beliefs were not affirmed regularly, the stability might be far less obvious. Hence there can be major changes even in early adulthood.

A particularly dramatic demonstration of the difficulties of predicting the later effects of early conflict, trauma, and deviance is found in a Berkeley longitudinal study which followed the lives of 166 men and women from birth through adulthood. When the subjects were seen at age 30, twelve years after their previous interviews, the researchers were shocked by the inaccuracy of their expectations. They were wrong in about two-thirds of the cases, mainly because they had overestimated the damaging effects of early troubles. They had also not foreseen the negative effects of a smooth and successful childhood; a degree of stress and challenge seemed to spur psychological strength and competence. (Skolnick, 1975, p. 710)

In earlier reports (Kagan, 1969, 1971) I introduced the idea of heterotypic continuity to describe the occasions when an investigator invoked the theoretical basis for predictive relation between individual variation on two quite different behaviors at two distant points in time. The relation between fearfulness at age 1 and intellectual precocity at age 5 provides a hypothetical example. The tacit assumption is that the earlier response reflects a disposition within the child that remains dominant and expresses itself later in a different behavioral form. This theorizing is based on the assumptions that I have been criticizing. Since stability is assumed, any theoretically reasonable occurrence of stability is viewed as reflecting an inherent disposition within the child. However, the potential importance of the mediating environment is often ignored.

Consider a real example of this interpretive problem. During the period 13 to 27 months the children in one longitudinal study differed in duration of attentiveness to interesting visual events. At 10 years of age the infants who had been highly attentive at 27 months had higher IQ scores than those who were less attentive. It is easy to argue, after the fact, that infant attentiveness reflects a stable inherent quality, like cognitive alertness. But the social class of the child's family was correlated with both infant attentiveness and preadolescent IQ. When the effects of social class were removed statistically, the relation between early attentiveness and IQ vanished (Kagan, Lapidus, and Moore, 1978). The education and occupation of the child's father is as good a predictor of the child's future vocation as the child's IQ score (McCall, 1977). The first relation leads one to look for continuing influences, the second to a search for inherent dispositions in the child.

In almost all longitudinal studies the investigators have been so eager to find heterotypic continuities that they often failed to consider seriously the possible role of continuing social influences, for their presence would have weakened the conclusion so dearly sought.

I do not suggest that there is little or no stability of structure or continuity of process in development. There is a great deal, and the chapters in this volume document both the qualities that are stable and the relevant eras. Rather my purposes are to point out that the developmental psychologist may have been too quick to assume stability and continuity when the evidence was weak and to suggest why we prefer to look to the past rather than to more recent contexts in interpreting the present.

Popular resistance to the idea that there may not be a strong connection between infancy and later childhood is due partly to the apprehension that some parents will decide that the concern and care they devote to their children are irrelevant to the child's psychological development and hence become indifferent. That is not a reasonable deduction.

The child is influenced by experiences from the moment of birth. There is sound evidence for believing that variation in parental practices during the first two years can produce dramatic variation among children in placidity, irritability, hostility, lability, and cognitive capability. Parents *should* be concerned with the quality of their infants' experience.[9] However, for most children the variation at age 2, although partially the product of family experience, may not be very predictive of behavior a decade hence. The events that fill the years between infancy and adolescence can alter the early dispositions for a great many children.

Thus it is useful to ask why there is currently such intense preoccupation with the opening days and months of life and such a firm conviction that if the biological parents—especially the mother—do not establish a close emotional relationship with the infant, the child's future may be at some risk. Whenever a belief is held strongly without commanding empirical support, it is usually the case that a deep value is being defended. This was as true of Darwin's defense of gradualism in evolution as it was of the more static position of the creationists. [10]

Every theorist starts with a set of tacit axioms. For many developmental theorists concerned with infant development, including Bowlby, Ainsworth, and Sroufe, there seem to be three: (1) An infant is vulnerable to anxiety and must be made to feel secure. (2) Emotional attachment to the parents provides that security. (3) If the infant is secure, it is likely that the older child will also be secure.

Infants are also viewed as vulnerable in many parts of the world, but the sources of weakness have a different quality. Among rural Guatemalan and Javanese families, where morbidity and mortality are typically high among both adults and young children, the infant is regarded as susceptible to dangerous spirits which can bring illness and death. The infant must remain close to the mother for protection. Morbidity and mortality are not high in the United States, but anxiety over trusting adults as well as fear of exploitation by and aggression from others are salient concerns. As in rural, isolated villages mothers are given the primary responsibility for protecting infants from these psychic dangers.

In two modern collectivist societies—Israeli kibbutzim and the People's Republic of China—where anxiety over trusting others may be muted, care of infants is frequently assigned to substitute caretakers. If we presume that adults in these societies are a little less anxious about aggression and exploitation in interpersonal relations, they might be less likely to project these sources of disquiet onto the baby and, perhaps, be less concerned with keeping the infant close to the mother in order to prevent the development of insecurity.

It is possible that the major sources of anxiety among the adults of a community—whatever they may be—are projected onto the infant if a rationale is available. As recognition of the legitimacy of human sensuality reemerged in Europe after 1600, concern with the child's sexual drives increased. Apprehension over masturbatory urges in children during the eighteenth and nineteenth centuries led to an increase in circumcisions in order to mute the motivation. Indeed Freud's ascription of sexuality to the young child was not a novel idea at the close of the nineteenth century but a reflection of the preoccupations of middle-class Europeans at that time.

Modern America is threatened by several ideological crises. One is a distrust of strangers. Since Americans are so mobile, a majority of adults are in daily encounter with others whom they need to trust. But they are not sure of the safety of this posture. Surgeons, we are told, operate excessively; mechanics make unnecessary repairs; moving vans fraudulently add weight to their loads; teachers strike; ministers confess homosexuality; and spouses admit to infidelity. Under such a barrage of deceit it seems wise to worry.

Every society needs at least one transcendental theme to which its members can be loyal. In the past God, the beauty and utility of knowledge, and faithful, romantic love were among the sacred ideas that were beneficial and beautiful. But the facts of modern life have made it difficult for many Americans to be loyal to these ideas.

What is left? The sacredness of the parent-infant bond may be one of the last transcendental themes that remains unsullied. The number of books and articles on infant attachment and the importance of mother-infant contact in the early postnatal days seem to be generated, in part, by strong emotion. The affect that surrounds discussions of who shall care for the baby—parent or surrogate caretaker —suggests that something more than scientific fact is monitoring the discussion. If the infant can be raised by any concerned adult and the biological parents are expendable (note that this has not been proved), then one more sacred column will have fallen. If this analysis has any validity, one would expect resistance to the suggestion that the experiences of the average infant with its biological parents might not have lasting effects.

There may be another reason for the persistence of the idea that variation in adult personality is due largely to early handling. The mind becomes uneasy when there is no explanation for an important phenomenon. Under these conditions the person becomes susceptible to interpretations that may not have been convincing initially. Because an explanation resolves uncertainty, if there are no alternative accounts, the initial dissonance is quickly muted and an initially suspect explanation is accepted. Variation in talent, motivation, and distress among adults is a mysterious fact for most Americans. Early experience and inheritance are the only two popular explanations that receive broad publicity. For the many who resist the hypothesis that variation among adolescents in aggressiveness with peers, timidity with the opposite sex, or difficulty in learning algebra is due to genetic factors, the hypothesis of early experience is the only well-articulated alternative. As a result, faith in this explanation becomes legitimized.

The following experience is illustrative. I was sitting by a small pool in a park watching young children sail their wooden boats. Suddenly I saw a small blue object the size of a fish come to the surface momentarily and then dip below the top of the water for 10 to 20 seconds, simulating the movements of a porpoise. I knew that there could not be a fish in a small artificial pool, but I had no other explanation for what I had seen. The uncertainty provoked me to watch this object more carefully. After several minutes I concluded that the object was a fish because it had all the properties of a fish—proper size, proper color, and proper movements. I was about to leave convinced that I had seen a fish under such unusual circumstances when I spied a man holding a small box that looked like a radio and noted that the man was monitoring the "fish." Minutes later a small boy took a toy submarine from the water. Since the hypothesis of a radio-controlled toy never occurred to me, I had rather quickly accepted an invalid interpretation. Many enigmas in modern psychology provoke much brooding—adult pathology, variation in human intelligence, and the forming of human personality are just a few. Although the idea that significant adult characteristics are shaped by the experiences of infancy may strain some minds when that notion is encountered for the first time, it does reduce uncertainty and is accepted for want of a competing account.

The presupposition of connectedness, which has been and is now held by a great many developmental psychologists, is rarely examined critically. This essay has considered the meanings of the phrases linked to the concept of connectedness and has traced the Western affinity for this idea in order to provoke gentle brooding.

Two ideas are central. First, when change in an observable quality occurs, there is a discontinuity in the external phenomenon. The controversy is not over that fact but rather over our invented ideas about the duration of operation of the hypothetical processes underlying the phenomenon. Of course, no event occurs without some epoch of prior history. But some qualities have a short history, others a long one. Although it is likely that many novel behavioral dispositions have been growing for many years it is not obvious that this axiom applies to all new reactions. That is, although long-term stability of connected forms occurs, its frequency may have been exaggerated. Many instances of developmental change can be characterized by replacement of an old structure or process by a new one, with little or no connectedness between the two hypothetical structures. This suggestion implies that some structures and processes vanish, an assumption that is bothersome to many. Since psychological structures are usually conceived as materialistic in their basic form, intuition is strained by the suggestion that material entities can vanish spontaneously, despite the example of the disappearing trellis cells.

Nontrivial implications flow from what appears to be a purely philosophical debate. Connectedness tempts one to look always for historical explanations and to dismiss the significance of recent or concomitant forces. Although genetic explanations are often the most compelling, some phenomena are not best understood through consideration of early history. Increasing rates of suicide and pregnancy among adolescents in the United States are not likely to be clarified by knowledge of the opening years of life. These phenomena are probably under the influence of more current events, and connectedness diverts attention from contemporary conditions. Retardation in reading skill among school-aged children is many times more frequent in lower-class than in middle-class children. It is likely that this fact can be better explained by examining the values of the child's peer group, the quality of school instruction, and the child's knowledge of letters as he or she entered school than by poring over a complete diary of the first three years of life. Faith in connectedness blunts our motivation to change the present. I am not suggesting that this view is a defense—a way to put off change in current practices—but rather to point out that awarding power to distant origins clouds our vision of local irritants that are difficult to remove. Although the inevitability of spring rains in New England is the result of forces that operated eons ago, today's rain shower was created yesterday.

Notes

I wish to thank Robert McCall for his valuable review and criticism of this chapter. Support for the preparation of this essay came from the Foundation for Child Development and the National Institute of Child Health and Human Development, grant HD 10094.

1. McCall (1977b) uses these terms in a different way. In a thoughtful essay McCall has stability-instability refer to the degree to which individuals in a cohort retain their relative ranks on some variable over time, what I shall call a normative definition of stability. McCall uses continuity-discontinuity to refer to the rate of change in a developmental function for a particular variable. The important distinction is between the continuity or discontinuity of a growth function for an attribute and the degree of stability or instability of individual differences in an attribute.

2. Emmerich (1968) addressed this issue in an earlier essay where he differentiated among a developmental view (epigenesis), differential view (normative analysis), and an ipsative view of continuity and change. Some regard regularity as a form of continuity; it was the core meaning of growth for the ancient Greeks and Chinese. Development contains cycles that repeat themselves—the menstrual cycle is an obvious example. Each part of that cycle contains an orderly set of changes, each part connected to the next. Since the

end of one cycle often acts as an incentive to the next, one assumes a connectivity. But regularity seems a more accurate descriptor for this phenomenon than continuity.

3. Most modern physicists assume that continuity exists beneath the surface discontinuity. If one throws a stone, its traverse follows a parabola. As one increases the force of the throw, the stone goes further but still describes a parabola. But if the force is great enough, it leaves gravity and travels an elliptical course. Physicists assume that despite the discontinuity between parabola and ellipse, theoretically a continuous set of functions bridges the gap between the last parabola and the first ellipse. This idea is of course identical with that behind the great chain of being in biology. One always assumes a smooth series with no discontinuous jumps.

Some of the most sophisticated statistical procedures used to explain complex phenomena, such as path analysis and multivariate analysis of variance, rest on the assumption that causal elements have continuous effects that are linear and additive. For example, social scientists who construct a path analysis model to account for occupational choice as a function of predictors such as IQ, school grades, parental education, and teachers' expectations assume that the predictors combine additively and continuously to influence occupational choice. Since many natural phenomena are the result of coherent forces that do not combine in a linear or cumulative fashion—the relation between temperature and volume of water being one—it is likely that many psychological phenomena also violate the premises demanded by statisticians. But because of faith in the assumption of cumulative and continuous effects, these ideas are not examined with any skepticism.

4. Since most seventeenth-century naturalists were hostile to the notion of dramatic discontinuities in development, they were left with a puzzle when Harvey disproved the popular belief that the fetus developed gradually from a mass of tissue in the uterus. (Harvey simply opened up the womb of an animal soon after rutting and found no tissue.) Because naturalists were unwilling to concede that the differentiated set of organs in the mature fetus could arise from undifferentiated protoplasm, they invented the notion of preformation in an attempt to salvage mechanism and, by implication, gradualism.

5. But close analysis of even the simplest exemplar of psychological development presents the problems inherent in this view. Consider an ontogenetic sequence verified by several psychologists. Prior to 7 weeks the infant presented with a face does not look at the eyes but at the marginal outlines of the figure. After 7 weeks the baby scans the area of the eyes—an obvious discontinuity when compared with the earlier behavior. What produced the change? Is looking at the eyes a complex derivative of scanning the chin or the forehead? Can one claim that looking at the eyes, in contrast to the outline, is a derivative of scanning the frame? It is difficult to imagine the series of small invisible events that will explain the gradual transition from outline to eyes. Two explanations come to mind. One is that maturing competences have permitted the infant to scan inside the frame of the face. Alternatively, it might take about seven weeks for the infant to develop a schema for a human face

with all its elements. When that representation has developed, the presentation of a face engages a schema and leads the child to look at the elements. In both cases an enhancement of a process presumed to be continuous—graded maturation or the graded establishment of a schema for a face—led to a discontinuous change in behavior.

Rather than posit a necessary connection between an early, simpler act and a later, more complex one, it is as reasonable to suggest that scanning the eyes is a novel action made possible by the gradual enhancement of a hidden process having little to do with the bases for the first act in the invariant sequence, namely, scanning the outline of the face. At the level of the facts, we see discrete discontinuity. We invent a hidden gradualism in the mechanism that made the new phenomenon a fact. But although the maturational competence or growth of the face schema may be gradual, there is not a necessary connection between the first response of scanning the outline of the face and the later scanning of the eyes, just because looking is common to both. That is the error Bonnet made in the asbestos example.

6. The influential Chu Hsi, a twelfth-century scholar who integrated disparate intellectual strands into a coherent philosophy with lasting influence, chose a concrete metaphor for nature. He likened nature to a flowing river that is turgid at one moment and clear at another and is always changing its qualities. There is a more compliant, accommodating posture toward change without the need to impose a hidden stability (Wing-Sit Chan, 1963).

The Japanese also make emotion and action more central than cognition. Responsible behavior (*jin*), respect (*gi*), and a combination of trust and trustworthiness (*shin*) are the primary qualities that children and adults should acquire—none is essentially cognitive in nature.

7. It is probably helpful to distinguish among the long-term consequences of different classes of events. Because severe damage to the brainstem can result in permanent motor paralysis, some feel it is permissible to conclude that any anomalous event, such as irregular feeding of the infant, has permanent sequellae. If a structure that participates in a growth phenomenon is damaged, it is likely but not inevitable that certain aspects of functioning will be altered. Temporary starvation produces a loss of weight which is regained if the child is returned to a normal diet, presumably because there was no permanent change in structures. And investigations of the consequences of deprivation of visual stimulation reveal that both vulnerability to modification as well as recovery are enhanced during infancy. Some neurons are more susceptible "to environmental alterations resulting in relatively permanent aberrations," but there is also an "enhanced potential for reversal of deprivation effects if conditions are ameliorated during the critical period. Thus the immediate postnatal period is one of maximum neural plasticity, when functions may be easily modified and reshaped by experience" (Layton, Corrick, and Toga, 1978, p. 361).

Specific child-rearing practices can alter the psychological profile of children. But when these environmental intrusions are removed, the profile may be subject to change. Because we are tempted to view all psychological changes as resting on permanent structural alterations, we are friendly to the notion of infant determinism.

8. Because ipsative analyses were not possible, it remains possible that ipsative stability might be found if such investigations were repeated with that perspective.

However, even if an investigator were to initiate a new longitudinal study using an ipsative strategy, lack of theory would leave the investigator muddled with respect to the variables to select for quantification. Let us say that an investigator studied fifty children during the first two years of life and found that some showed fear rather than initiation of contact to strangers while other children showed the opposite profile. What would the investigator study when these children were 6 years old? Most 6-year-olds do not show fear to unfamiliar adults. Should the investigators assess withdrawal versus active coping with academic tasks; shyness or extraversion with peers? The lack of conviction that surrounds these choices reflects the problem. It is doubtful that such investigations will be initiated until theory becomes more sophisticated.

9. The results of an extensive longitudinal study of children growing up in subsistence farming Guatemalan communities reveals that neither frequency of maternal diarrhea or fever during pregnancy nor frequency of fever, diarrhea, or respiratory illness in the infants during the first six months of life was associated with performance on tests of cognitive development administered when the children were two years old (the r's hovered near zero). But one would not want to recommend on the basis of these results that mothers should not be concerned with their own health or the health of their young infants. Illness is unpleasant and may place a child at slight risk for other physical illnesses (Klein and Lasky, 1978).

10. In contrast to the contemporary assumption that the mother's behavior toward her infant is of critical importance, at least one sixteenth-century philosopher regarded the mother's psychological influence as far less influential. Montaigne viewed women as capricious and therefore incapable of a stable love for their children. "Lacking strength of judgment to choose and embrace those who deserve it they easily allow themselves to be carried away where the promptings of nature are simpler; like animals that only recognize the young while they are pulling at their teats" (1958, p. 153). Montaigne is saddened by the fact that wet nurses give more affection to the infants they are paid to care for than to their own infants. "We see that in most of these women habit soon gives rise to a bastard affection, stronger than the natural, and a greater concern for the wellbeing of others' than of their own" (p. 154). Montaigne's disdain for the role of mother is accompanied not unexpectedly, by the belief that luck, temperament, and an "excellent father" were responsible for his adult character.

References

Baldwin, J. M. 1975. *Thought and things.* New York: Arno Press.

Barzun, J. 1958. *Darwin, Marx, and Wagner.* New York: Doubleday Anchor.

BERLIN, I. 1954. *Historical inevitability.* London: Oxford University Press.

CARMICHAEL, L. 1926. The development of behavior in vertebrates expermentally removed from the influence of external stimulation. *Psychological Review* 33: 51-58.

———— 1927. A further study of the development of behavior in vertebrates experimentally removed from the influence of external stimulation. *Psychological Review* 34: 34-47.

COLLINGWOOD, R. G. 1945. *The idea of nature.* Oxford: Clarendon Press.

CONDORCET. 1955. *Sketch for a historical picture of the progress of the human mind,* tr. June Barraclough. London: Weidenfeld and Nicholson.

DARWIN, C. 1872. *Origin of species,* 6th ed. New York and London: Merrill and Baker.

DAVISON, M. C., ROBBINS, S., and SWANSON, D. B. 1978. Stage structure in objective moral judgments. *Developmental Psychology* 14: 137-146.

EDELMAN, G. M. 1978. Group selection and phasic reentrant signalling: A theory of higher brain function. In G. M. Edelman and V. B. Mountcastle, *The mindful brain.* Cambridge, Mass.: MIT Press.

EMMERICH, W. 1968. Personality development and concepts of structure. *Child Development* 39: 671-690.

FARLEY, J. 1974. *The spontaneous generation controversy from Descartes to Oparin.* Baltimore, Md.: Johns Hopkins University Press.

FLAVELL, J. H. 1972. An analysis of cognitive developmental sequences. *Genetic Psychology Monographs* 86: 279-350.

GORDON, R., and JACOBSON, A. G. 1978. The shaping of tissues in embryos. *Scientific American* 238, no. 6: 106-113.

GOULD, S. J. 1977. *Ontogeny and phylogeny.* Cambridge, Mass.: Harvard University Press.

HOLTZMAN, W. H., DIAZ-GUERRERO, R., and SWARTZ, J. D. 1975. *Personality development in two cultures.* Austin, Tex.: University of Texas Press.

KAGAN, J. 1969. The three faces of continuity in human development. In D. A. Goslin, *Handbook of socialization theory and research.* Chicago: Rand McNally and Company.

———— 1971. *Change and continuity in infancy.* New York: John Wiley.

———— 1976. Emergent themes in human development. *American Scientist* 64: 186-196.

KAGAN, J., KEARSLEY, R. B., and ZELAZO, P. R. 1978. *Infancy: Its place in human development.* Cambridge, Mass.: Harvard University Press.

KAGAN, J., KLEIN, R. E., FINLEY, G., ROGOFF, B., and NOLAN, E. 1979. Cross-cultural study of cognitive development. *Monographs Society Research Child Development* 44 no. 5. Chicago: University of Chicago Press.

KAGAN, J., LAPIDUS, D., and MOORE, M. 1978. Infant antecedents of cognitive functioning. *Child Development* 49: 1005-1023.

KAGAN, J., and MOSS, H. A. 1962. *Birth to maturity.* New York: John Wiley.

KANT, I. 1727. *The seasons.*

———— 1966. *Critique of pure reason.* New York: Anchor Books.

KLEIN, R. E., and LASKY, R. E. The determinants of infant behavioral development in rural Guatemala. INCAP, April 1978.

KNOWLES, D. 1962. *The evolution of medieval thought*. Baltimore, Md.: Helicon Press.

LAYTON, B. S., CORRICK, G. E., and TOGA, A. W. 1978. Sensory restriction and recovery. In S. Finger, ed., *Recovery from brain damage*. New York: Plenum Press.

LOVEJOY, A. O. 1936. *The great chain of being*. Cambridge, Mass.: Harvard University Press.

McCALL, R. B. 1977a. Children's IQ as predictors of adult educational and occupational status. *Science* 197: 485-487.

———— 1977b. Challenges to a science of developmental psychology. *Child Development* 48: 333-344.

MONTAIGNE, M. DE. 1958. *Essays*, tr. by J. N. Cohen. Harmondsworth: Penguin Books.

NEEDHAM, J. 1969. *The grand titration: Science and society in East and West*. London: George Allen and Unwin.

NISBET, R. 1969. *Social change and history*. New York: Oxford University Press.

PATTERSON, P. H., POTTER, D. D., and FURSHPAN, E. J. 1978. The chemical differentiation of nerve cells. *Scientific American* 239, no. 1: 50-59.

PIAGET, J. 1952. *The origins of intelligence in the child*. New York: International Universities Press.

———— 1971. *Biology and knowledge*, tr. Beatrix Walsh. Chicago: University of Chicago Press.

PIAGET, J., and INHELDER, B. 1969. *The psychology of the child*. New York: Basic Books.

RODGON, M. M. 1976. *Single word usage, cognitive development, and the beginnings of combinatorial speech*. Cambridge: Cambridge University Press.

SKOLNICK, A. 1975. The family revisited: themes in recent social science research. *Journal of Interdisciplinary History* 5: 703-719.

SPIRO, M. 1970. *Buddhism and society*. New York: Harper and Row.

STONE, L. 1977. *The family, sex, and marriage: in England 1500-1800*. New York: Harper and Row.

TANNER, J. J. 1978. *Foetus into man: physical growth from conception to maturity*. Cambridge, Mass.: Harvard University Press.

WALLACE, A. R. 1890. *Darwinism: an exposition of the theory of natural selection with some of its applications*. London: MacMillan and Co.

WERNER, H., and KAPLAN, B. 1963. *Symbol formation*. New York: Wiley.

WHITE, H. 1973. *Metahistory: the historical imagination in nineteenth-century Europe*. Baltimore, Md.: Johns Hopkins University Press.

WHITING, J. W. M., and CHILD, I. L. 1953. *Child training and personality*. New Haven, Conn.: Yale University Press.

WILSON, E. B. 1896. *The cell in development and inheritance*. New York.

WING-SIT CHAN. 1963. *A source book on Chinese philosophy*. Princeton, N.J.: Princeton University Press.

WOHLWILL, J. F. 1973. *The study of behavioral development*. New York: Academic Press.

3 | The Continuous and the Discrete in the History of Science
Everett Mendelsohn

As THE NINETEENTH CENTURY drew to a close, the first volume of a remarkable four-volume *History of European Thought in the Nineteenth Century*, by John Theodore Merz, appeared. Toward the end of his final volume Merz gave clear expression to a view that marked the century as a whole and probably gave explicit tone to its theoretical positions. He was discussing the introduction of field concepts in physics (a largely British invention in his view) and the manner in which they were replacing point action. He was proud of the strength of what he called "synoptic views" and the way in which they led to the discovery of new relationships. Nowhere was this shown more forcefully than in the "Darwinian conception of the continuity of organic forms." But, he was forced to add, "The more we study Continuity in nature the more the existence of Discontinuities is forced upon us. The discontinuous may disappear and be smoothed down at one point, but only to reappear again in a more mysterious manner at other points" (Merz, 1914, vol. 4, p. 435).

The urge to believe in continuities is exhibited, that nature does not always fulfill the desire to find continuities is recognized, the position of the nineteenth century as the focal point for the construction of explanatory models displaying continuities is exposed, and the important position of British savants in designing theories embodying continuities is revealed. Indeed, for the historian setting out to examine the position of the discrete and the continuous in the history of science the commanding question rapidly becomes, Are continuity and discontinuity states of matter or primarily states of mind? If the former, what is the evidence; if the latter, what elements beyond the data of nature are involved in the conceptual constructions?

Scanning the issues across time can leave the viewer almost daz-zled by the complexity and changing shape of the arguments and, par-ticularly, the changing uses to which the claims for continuity and dis-continuity are put. One no sooner feels comfortable with the linkages between continuity questions and some specific concepts under exami-nation than the structure of the discourse alters and the focus of con-cern shifts: was the discussion focused on the continuity of life forces being observed, or does it suddenly refer to the discontinuity of a "force vital" and the underlying continuity of matter itself? I think it is fair to say that continuity has always seemed more pleasing to the mind, easier to absorb, and less fraught with challenges than its oppo-site. To pose a discontinuous explanation or solution calls for a break with prior traditions or a departure from conventional wisdom; it pre-supposes a more "activist" solution. It is not surprising, then, that discontinuity is usually linked with social and political challenge or with philosophical radicalism. Similarly, it is not surprising that the ground of the discontinuity discourse shifts with time and circum-stances, and a concept once tied to discrete explanation becomes part of a larger term or other level of continuity.

One thing seems clear. Continuity is a "sprawling concept" (Bochner, 1968, p. 492), with claims being made for it in many fields of human endeavor. Its presence in organized human thought is very old and can be seen in many areas of early philosophy and the sci-ences. Aristotle, in his challenge to the atomism of Leucippus and Democritus, was disturbed by the idea of particles of matter being separated by a vacuity. It was not the reduction to discrete or minimal units of matter that troubled Aristotle but that nothing stood between the parts to mediate their interactions. Not that "nature abhorred a vacuum"; rather Aristotle and the metaphysics that he constructed abhorred a vacuum (Bochner, 1968, p. 495). In the European tradition that developed after the reintroduction of atomic concepts in the late medieval period, atomism was equated with atheism, a fact that adds one more piece of evidence to the tie between the traditional and the continuous in human thought.

But how, then, should we deal with the obvious triumphs of atomistic concepts in the sciences even as continuist theories hold their own? The answer seems to be the abilities of our thought systems to absorb and use dualities and to accommodate to presumed contradic-tions and inconsistencies—indeed, even to elevate dualistic theories to places of special philosophic importance; as occured in the twentieth-century reconciliation between wave and particle characteristics of matter in a theory of "complementarity" (Jammer, 1966, p. 345ff).

The breadth of the concept continuity is further increased as well as some confusions introduced by its relations with a group of other concepts with which it has been identified at various points in its career. It has been tied to constancy, uniformitarianism, seriality, progression, plenitude, and sufficient reason. The first four of these terms refer to relationships of one form to another as, for example, in the belief that species once created remained constant through time, the hereditary mechanism serving only to preserve the continuity of the species. Change—mutability—was disallowed, and a whole ordering of nature depended on the expected continuity and constancy of species form. (When in the nineteenth century species change became acceptable and constancy was deserted, an alternative continuity was asserted, this a continuity not of species form but of the mode of change itself.)

The principle of plenitude, however, provided another kind of base for belief in continuity and gave a strong organizing theme to all observation of nature. A Supreme Being as creator moves according to an understandable model, and for each idea a real object is created and every possibility becomes manifest as reality. Since nothing may be barred from existence, the scheme of created things is full, and what is full does not allow any discontinuity. When brought from its Greek origins and linked to Christian theology, the strong statement is necessary: divine productivity is inexhaustible and creates all possible forms (Formigari, 1968, pp. 325-326; Lovejoy, 1936, p. 152).

It was the seventeenth-century philosopher Leibniz who linked the concept of plenitude with the principle of sufficient reason. "Of everything whatsoever a cause or reason must be assigned alike for its existence or its nonexistence" (Leibniz, *Ethics*, quoted in Lovejoy, 1936, p. 152). Since it was the intellect of God that was in reality the cause of all things, there could be nothing capable of existence that should not exist. Within this explanation is a justification, indeed the necessity, of moral and physical evil. A perfect universe is created in which individual afflictions are included and given their place in the harmonious whole. From the translation of this vision to the idea of a chain of being emerges an "argument in favor of political conservatism . . . If the perfection of the divine plan requires a universe ordered in a hierarchy of beings, each destined to occupy a place in the scale of creatures so that all gradations are filled, then the same law should prevail in the world of men or the moral universe: the norm of behavior should be to live in keeping with one's condition, without subverting any order of society which, like a microcosm, reflects the very order of the universe" (Formigari, 1968, p. 329). (The conservative ideal is not a creation of the Christian West alone; a similar notion of a rightful place for all things is found in the Hindu concept of *Varna*,

also providing for continuity of functions across generations and resulting in the basic conserving of social order.)

A framework for understanding ideas like continuity and discontinuity and their role in the sciences has mixed elements and, consequently, has involved several forms of analysis. One has been direct
philosophical and historical study of the concept itself, its filiation to
other concepts and explanatory models, and the tracing of its metaphysical roots and tacit assumptions. This form of study (of which
Arthur O. Lovejoy's *Great Chain of Being*, 1936, is an exemplar) is
common to the history of ideas and has been the one most fruitfully
adopted to date. Other scholars have touched on the relations of ideas
and evidence from the sciences to the broader concepts of the discrete
and continuous as they turned to analyze specific issues in the sciences
themselves. For example, Stephen Toulmin and June Goodfield in
their very accessible works, *The Architecture of Matter* (1962) and
The Discovery of Time (1965), and John Greene, in *The Death of
Adam: Evolution and Its Impact on Western Thought* (1959), have
generated understanding of some critical episodes in the study of
nature.

One dimension, however, one that seems of particular interest to
us, seems to be missing. Why have concepts been proposed in the
forms used? Why have they been cast at one time in a continuist and at
another in a discontinuist framework? Is nature changeable, at one
period demanding continuity and at another discrete entities? To
understand the reasons for a choice of conceptual mode it seems necessary to look beyond the evidence in nature to that nexus of influences from the religious, the political, and the social spheres that provides the scientist and scholar with the bases for fundamental interpretation. Used in understanding the natural sciences, this form of sociology of knowledge is in its infancy. But already it has exhibited at least
strong suggestive power, if not yet full explanatory power.[1]

If there is a politics and sociology of ideas and concepts, there is
equally a politics and sociology of historical explanation and, indeed,
of epistemology as well. Basic to the epistemologic and historical debates has been the issue whether the development and change of ideas
has been continuous or discontinuous. Have there been epistemologic
breaks, ruptures, and revolution, or has there been a uniform and
continuous unfolding of conceptual novelty? Obviously, no simple
answer to this query can be found, but placing it alongside the issue of
specific scientific changes indicates my belief that there is a link between episodes in history where there have been moves to develop continuist epistemologies and concurrent moves to establish continuist

theories of nature itself. Similarly, discontinuist cognitive structures have often been bracketed in history with revolutionary or discontinuist theories of knowledge for the sciences.

The year 1543 saw the publication of the *De revolutionibus obium caelestium* of Nicolas Copernicus, a treatise of profound importance for human self-perceptions (removal of man from the center of the universe) and great moment for the development of astronomy and physics. It was the same year that Andreas Vesalius, professor of anatomy at Padua, presented his volume on human anatomy, *De humani corporis fabrica*. In this work Vesalius not only broke markedly with previous traditions of anatomical illustration and introduced his famous "living anatomy" but, more important for our discussion, proposed a new mode of gaining knowledge through observation and experience and explicitly severed his science from that of his immediate temporal predecessors, the scholastic anatomists. Furthermore, he consciously cast his new anatomical observations and new methodological procedures in the framework of a discontinuist history. That he also chose to break with the traditional use of late Latin for his text and opted instead to return to the language of Celsus and Cicero seems to fit his self-image as a revolutionary figure. He was using the distant past as a way of breaking with the thought and language of the recent past.

Vesalius fairly bristled as he began the preface to his critique of past practice of anatomy. He denounced those who

> introduced into the schools that detestable procedure by which usually some conduct the dissection of the human body and others present the account of its parts, the latter like jackdaws aloft in their high chair, with egregious arrogance croaking things they have never investigated but merely committed to memory from the bodies of others, or reading what has already been described. The former are so ignorant of languages that they are unable to explain their dissections to the spectators and muddle what ought to be displayed according to the instructions of the physician who, since he has never applied his hand to the dissection of the body, haughtily governs the ship from a manual. (quoted in O'Malley, 1964, pp. 319-320)

The new anatomy was to be created alongside a reborn learning in the tradition of Vesalius's fellow humanists. While willing to celebrate the Golden Age of Greece in contrast with the Dark Ages through which Europe had just passed, he also wanted his fellow physicians to adopt a new method and to "put faith in their own not ineffectual sight and powers of reason rather than in the writings of Galen" (quoted in O'Malley, 1964, p. 320). Original research, observation, and investigation should be the guides to the gaining of knowledge of human anatomy. He claimed that he would not go to the authority of books and indeed intended to read nothing "but the book of the human body that cannot lie" (quoted in Edelstein, 1967, pp. 441-454).

Vesalius cast his own specific new observations in the framework of sharp departures from the texts of the medical authorities. Thus, in the course of his "Letter on Blood-Letting" when he noted a new point, he confided to his readers: "For this opinion of mine on vene-section in pleurisy, conceived by no one previously, I might strive to extract from the statement of Hippocrates in the second book of *The Regimen in Acute Diseases* except it too pointedly contradicts the authority of Galen, which I am afraid of disputing almost no less than if in our very sacred religion I were secretly to doubt the immortality of the soul" (quoted in Edelstein, 1967, p. 449).

These comments by Vesalius not only provide an example of the emergence of novelty in observation and fact in the sciences but also indicate the manner in which a scientist can conceive of his own methodology or epistemology as being discontinuous with the immediate past. He reinterprets history and what happened in it and explicitly chooses a place for himself and his work. For Vesalius this meant the denigration of the scholastic tradition, the celebration of a supposed golden age of Greek learning, and use of the latter as a means of proclaiming epistemologic as well as substantive ruptures with the former.

The new departure in the explanation of the anatomy of the human body was, for Vesalius, cast in a broad and fairly thorough challenge to the concepts, methods, and histories of his predecessors. Its broad context was the emergence of new political and social structures of Renaissance Italy; its immediate context was the institutional framework of Padua University in the Venetian state. The strong new mercantile forces of Venice had given their university a special cast of intellectual freedom. That the next generations would see William Harvey and Galileo Galilei gives some indication of the institutional support and encouragement for conceptual and epistemologic novelty to be gained at Padua (Randall, 1961).

The idea of continuity-discontinuity has a long and involved history. Its own history appears discontinuous and its relations to other concepts and principles changeable. The links it displays with social and political attitudes and realities begs for further examination. It is found both as explanation and description of the natural world and as a structure for the discourse and form of explanation itself. It is the tacit and sometimes explicit guide for history and for epistemology. It often exists in duality challenging the ability of scientists to tolerate ambiguity. Either continuity or discontinuity is often deeply believed in and probably never unequivocably demonstrable.

Continuity and the Sciences

Just what does nature look like to the observer? Aristotle, one of the best and most influential, put it as follows:

Nature proceeds little by little from things lifeless to animal life in such a way that it is impossible to determine the exact line of demarcation, nor on which side thereof an intermediate form should lie. Thus, next after lifeless things in the upward scale comes the plant, and of plants one will differ from another as to its amount of apparent vitality; and, in a word, the whole genus of plants, whilst it is devoid of life as compared with an animal, is endowed with life as compared with other corporeal entities. Indeed, as we just remarked, there is observed in plants a continuous scale of ascent towards the animals . . . And so throughout the entire animal scale there is a graduated differentiation in amount of vitality and in capacity for motion. (Aristotle, *Historia Animalium*, VIII.1, 588b, 4-23)

Continuity was writ large for Aristotle; no void or vacuum separating particles of matter (neither deniable or verifiable by common observation) and no determinable space between the forms of matter organized in ascending scale from inanimate through plants to animals (a proposition visible to the mind's eye but not discernible by any normal form of observation) was permitted. Lovejoy actually credited Aristotle with developing the concept of continuity and providing his successors with a strong definition of the continuum: "Things are said to be continuous whenever there is one and the same limit of both wherein they overlap and which they possess in common (Aristotle, *Metaphysics X*, 1069a, 5, quoted in Lovejoy, 1936, p. 55).

Although it seems clear that Aristotle avoided placing all organization in a single ascending scale, being aware of the diversity of characteristics on which classification might be based, there is an implicit if rough scale of perfection that later became known as the *scala naturae*. Each natural species in the Aristotelian system was fixed and unchanging, and man was given position as the most perfect animal, alone possessing rationality. But the forms adopted and the functions carried out are marked by Aristotle's ideas, final cause and fulfillment. Even the less perfect among the species reaches its proper form (Lloyd, 1968).

The image of what was to be called the great chain of being is already clear in Aristotle and alongside his hierarchy of living beings was a hierarchy of the soul. This scheme of nature implicitly required a search for all the members of the linear continuum, and this became in part a guide for biological exploration and, more important, for biological classification. But it had to be a search. The gaps were most markedly apparent, and only through a system of belief and a willingness to invoke strong inference to supplement evidence could a full chain of being, a real continuum, be proposed. Another nagging problem arose, one that was also recognized by later naturalists: each species itself was discrete, permanently separated from its nearest neighbor above or below in the hierarchy. Continuity was achieved, then, in the face of gaps in the continuum and in spite of the fixed and immutable units making up the elements of the chain.

But the idea of a chain of being was "pleasing to the mind" and provided a means of ordering the multiplicity of living and nonliving forms to be found in nature. The strength of this image and the uses to which it could be put, especially in fixing man's place in nature, were not lost on succeeding generations of scientists and philosophers. Despite the seeming discontinuities of the scientific revolution of the seventeenth century, the image of the chain of being—Aristotelian roots notwithstanding—survived and grew stronger. Leibniz developed the idea with clarity and assured it a firm position in the Enlightenment.

"All the orders of natural beings," Leibniz proclaimed in terms very similar to Aristotle's, "form but a single chain in which the various classes, like so many rings, are so closely linked one to another that it is impossible for the senses or the imagination to determine precisely the point at which one ends and the next begins." But for Leibniz this arrangement of nature was a necessary outcome of what he called "the law of continuity" and he indicated that he would not be surprised if zoophytes—plant-animals—were discovered, for "so great is the force of the principle of continuity." Indeed, he declared, "I am convinced that there must be such creatures, and that natural history will perhaps some day become acquainted with them, when it has further studied that infinity of living things whose small size conceals them from ordinary observation and which are hidden in the bowels of the earth and the depths of the sea" (quoted in Lovejoy, 1936, p. 145). This example of strong theory commitment as a guide to observation is striking coming as it does at the close of the classical period of microscopic research of Antoni von Leeuwenhoek, Robert Hooke, Jan Swammerdam, and others. Indeed, the microscope, a paradigmatic example of the instruments of empirical science, must have been frustrating to many of its users. On the one hand it exposed the existence of a whole world of forms that existed beyond the sight of the eye and encouraged the belief that fuller evidence for the chain of being could be identified. Indeed, Leibniz almost certainly read the evidence optimistically. (When Abraham Trembley in 1739 discovered the hydra, with its regenerative abilities, it was hailed as the missing link between the plant and animal world.) But at the same time it exposed great gaps and striking structural dissimilarities of living forms.

It is fair to say that empirical evidence was never able to resolve the issues of the existence of a chain of being or of a continuum. This dilemma was noticed by more than one contemporary investigator but was stated most elegantly by Pierre Maupertius in his *Essai de Cosmologie* (1750). Of continuity he remarked: "Elle plaît à notre esprit, mais plaît-elle à la Nature?" (It pleases the spirit, but does it please nature?; my translation.)

But the pleasure to the mind in face of the problems of nature was augmented by the very strong position in which humans were placed in this scale of nature. Indeed, man's being given the superior position in a natural chain of being added reality to the Christian belief of man's dominion over nature as proclaimed in *Genesis*. One seventeenth-century author set out the claim in strong form: "In relation therefore to this inferior World of Brutes and Vegetables, the End of Man's Creation was, that he should be the Vice-Roy of the great God of Heaven and Earth in this inferior World . . . And hereby Man was invested with power, authority, right, dominion, trust and care" (Hale, 1677, quoted in Glacken, 1967, p. 481). Humans controlled nature for the sake of the earth itself and for their own sake as well. The hierarchy of life, set out in creation, is kept in order and overseen through man's efforts. "Thus the infinite wisdom of Almighty God chains things together, and fits and accommodates all things suitable to their uses and ends." This special position, based on human intellect and soul, places man in command of nature and justifies the uses to which he puts it—mining, canal building. Indeed, the interference with "brute nature" is fully sanctioned, providing in this way for rational and religious acceptance of the new industries and trades (Hale, 1677). This idea of human dominion was further used to justify European conquest and colonization of the so-called backward areas of the globe such as the Americas, where the native population was seen as degenerate and not sufficiently involved in improving the natural environment (Leiss, 1972, p. 73ff).

The seventeenth century, the period of the scientific revolution, witnessed the introduction or reintroduction of concepts that can be closely linked with the concept of the discrete and the discontinuous. The revival of atomism, with its belief in finite indivisible units of matter which provided the basis of the new physics and the discovery of cells, building blocks of living things, surely suggested that theoretical structures and broad explanatory principles could be discontinuist in form. The very approaches to nature that the new science adopted —analytical, breaking complex structures into component parts that could then be scrutinized—could have been supposed to give fuller understanding of the meaning of discrete units and elements. But as one recent historian put it, "The principle of continuity of all natural processes can be considered the godfather of the new physics which evolved in the seventeenth century" (Hermann, 1971, p. 1). Faced with the problem of matter, which might be conceived of as existing in minute discrete bits, mathematicians developed techniques that could handle them in continuist fashion, the differential and integral calculus. Leibniz, who, along with Isaac Newton, is credited with providing a strong formulation of the calculus (Boyer, 1949, p. 187f), clearly cast the new conceptions within the framework of his *lex continui* (law of continuity). The move to mathematicize nature, especially to quantify matter and motion, has been hailed as a further triumph of the scientific revolution, but its implications for our study are marked. As one historian put it, "In mathematics, continuity is an all-pervading concept (Bochner, 1968, p. 497).

The words, *ex ovo omnia* appear on the frontispiece of the Latin edition of Harvey's book on the generation of animals (Harvey, 1651).[2] To be exact, this motto is inscribed on an egg-shaped box held open in the hands of a likeness of Jove, and from the egg emerges a collection of animals—insects, a bird, a worm, a reptile, a fish, a human infant. Harvey's text is unambiguous and repetitious. One chapter actually carries the title, "An egg is the common origin of all animals" (Harvey, 1651, p. 456). Harvey is staking out a position in embryology—generally Aristotelian in its basis—which clearly demarcates him from the atomists at one point and from the preformationists at another (Mendelsohn, 1968; Needham, 1934, pp. 112-144). He is proposing an underlying continuity of life and form based on his belief that all living things, even those supposedly spontaneously generated, have "in common, that they are engendered from some principle adequate to this effect, and from an efficient cause inherent in the same principle." This primordium from which all life comes is "a certain corporeal something having life in potential" (Harvey, 1651, p. 457). The primordia are the eggs of animals and the seeds of plants. The generalized egg from which all comes is not then the ovum of a fowl or even the germinal vesicle of mammals but the much more general principle that carries life and can impart form. The frontispiece motto and the chapter title were run together, to make an even stronger statement of the implied vital continuum, in the epigram *Omne vivum ex ovo*—every living thing comes out of an egg. The misquotation was widely cited during the eighteenth and nineteenth centuries, appearing in the writings of such scientists as Carl Linnaeus and Lorenz Oken, and even making its way into modern texts and histories. For Harvey there is need not only for material and efficient cause but for final cause as well.

The atomists and corpuscularians, on the other hand, disdained and despised by Harvey, sought another form of continuity through their efforts to establish embryology on the same terms as they would establish physics, from basic laws of matter which they believed underlay the unity of all worldly phenomena (Needham, 1934, p. 135). However, Harvey, undoubtedly the more accomplished observer and experimenter with living phenomena, had no more and no less empirical basis for his stated belief in the continuity of life than did Pierre Gassendi and René Descartes for their claim that particulate matter formed the underlying continuum of all phenomena, animate and inanimate. In each case their specific explanatory models were guided by metaphysical commitment. On Harvey's part it led to a frankly vitalistic position which brought him into direct confrontation with the newly emergent mechanical, atomistic, and reductionist paradigms and became a sustained attempt to outline a principle of the conservation and continuity of life forms.

Although the atomists and mechanists clearly posited an underlying unity in the construction of all things, living and dead, the specific entities formed could be explicitly discontinuous. Thus Descartes, Gassendi, Nathaniel Highmore, and other early seventeenth-century mechanical-atomistic philosophers supported on philosophical grounds the idea of spontaneous generation. This "mistake," as it has been called by historians, grew directly from their theories of matter and its organization. The long-term historical implications of a commitment to this form of generation were discontinuist, and the concept as it was later used challenged vitalist principles and their concomitant assumption of the continuity of life forces.

We can sympathize with the plight of seventeenth-century naturalists. New theories of matter developed largely under the influence of Descartes and other mechanists considered matter itself purely passive. The phenomena of nature was caused by this passive matter in movement, and the laws of motion as they developed were believed to be unchangeable and uniform for all things. While the Cartesian belief in spontaneous generation might be dropped for its inability to explain phenomena, Descartes's clockwork world view became widely shared. Nature was regular, species fixed, generation the same for all living things, chance abhorred. As one contemporary put it, "Nature in all things is one, pure, simple and immutable" (Vallisneri, 1733, quoted in Farley, 1977, p. 11).

I do not want to stretch an interpretive link too far, but I am sympathetic with historian Christopher Hill's view that many seventeenth-century scientific theories, based on strong lawlike statements and exhibiting centralized and timeless authority, were similar in structure to the new absolute monarchies of the age (Hill, 1974). The French image of the sun king seemed almost to caricature the sun-centered universe of the new astronomy. Harvey's image, as set forth in *De motu cordis* (1628), puts all the pieces in their place: "The Heart of creatures is the foundation of life, the Prince of all, the Sun of their Microcosm, on which all vegetation does depend, from whence all vigor and strength does flow. Likewise, the King is the foundation of his Kingdoms, and the Sun of his Microcosm, the *Heart* of his Commonwealth from whence all power and mercy proceeds" (Harvey, 1628, quoted in Hill 1974, p. 160).[3] There seemed to be still another source of support for regularity, uniformity, and continuity.

What is the meaning of this outlook for the understanding of generation? The problem was to bring together the mechanical-physical world view, avoidance of change, the continuity of form and species, and the development of new generations. The answer was a mix of preformationist and preexistence theories. The new conception avoided the Aristotelian epigenetic theory of generation that Harvey had developed and instead relied on a seemingly simple mechanism of generation that required only the expansion of miniature beings that had existed, stored one inside the other, from the time of the first creation. Their unfolding and growth was fully consonant with all principles of matter itself. As this scheme was developed, it came to represent a triumph of rational construction independent of the constraints of empirical verification. Its most direct, and probably fullest, early statement comes from Nicholas Malebranche in 1673.

We may with some sort of certainty affirm that all trees lie in miniature in the cicatride of their seed. Nor does it seem less reasonable to think that there are infinite trees concealed in a single cicatride since it not only contains the future tree whereof it is the seed, but also abundance of other seeds, which may all include in them new trees . . . and thus *in infinitum* . . . We ought to think that all the bodies of men and of beasts which shall be born or produced till the end of the world were possibly created from the beginning of it. I would say that the females of the original creatures were, for aught we know, created together, with all these of the same species which have been, or shall be, begotten or procreated whilst the world stands. (Malebranche, 1673, quoted in Farley, 1977, p. 17)

Aware of the empirical difficulties of theories of this sort, Claude Perrault (1679) attempted to forestall them by claiming that the miniature animals would be too small to be seen by the microscope (Bowler, 1971, p. 241). It was not only the theoretically oriented naturalist who adopted preformationist views; Leeuwenhoek, certainly one of the greatest of the seventeenth-century microscopists, was a cautious advocate of animalculism, one of the several variants of preformationism. But Leeuwenhoek doubted that "we should be able to see or discover the entire shape of a human body" (quoted in Bowler, 1971, p. 233).

The preformation-preexistence theory in its several versions became more popular during the closing decades of the seventeenth century and was the focus for theories of generation through the eighteenth century, recruiting to its support Leibniz, Albrecht von Haller, Charles Bonnet, and numerous other naturalists and philosophers. Indeed, it was primarily a philosophy of generation, and in spite of its empirical difficulties it could survive not only because alternatives were no more successful empirically (embryogenesis proved to be a remarkably intractable problem into the twentieth century) but also because it was the "proper" mode of explanation. Bonnet put the issue directly. Unless there were some directing force or entelechy to rely on for bringing about the organization of the organism, "we must either undertake to explain mechanically the sequential formation of organs . . . or we must admit that the germ contains in miniature all the parts essential to the plant or animal that it represents" (Bonnet, 1762; quoted in Gould, 1977, p. 22). But, we must note, as an explanation this theory was static and preserving.

The Problem of Change: Evolution and Revolution

The scientific vision of the eighteenth century remained ordered and unchanging; the nineteenth century was forced to deal with change. Nothing seemed stable and in place; order was challenged and often disintegrated; authority became tenuous and often changed hands. Traditions of long duration were set aside; the very manner in which humans produced goods and distributed them was altered. Social, political, economic, and religious institutions all underwent significant transformations. Perhaps most important, the day-to-day life of many individuals exhibited marked alterations from the generation of the immediate past. The explainers would gain by constructing theories of change and theories of continuity, but these theories could not avoid the facts of change; they must come to embody them. "The Revolution has razed everything to the ground. Government, morals, habits, everything has to be rebuilt. What a magnificent site for the architects! What a grand opportunity of making use of all the fine and excellent ideas that had remained speculative, of employing so many materials that could not be used before, of rejecting so many others that had been obstructions for centuries and which one had been forced to use" (*Décade Philosophique*, I, 1794, quoted in Hayek, 1952, p. 109).

The French Revolution set the pattern for one model of societal change and gave a new meaning to the term *revolution*.[4] Sharp, violent change on a broad scale became the definition associated with the 1790s in France. The repeated attempts during the next half-century to overthrow political regimes and social order give a special background to all intellectual developments that took place. The years 1815, 1830, and 1848 evoke images of martial events and the acting out of deep-seated conflicts. "A specter is haunting Europe," Karl Marx and Friedrich Engels declared as they opened their *Manifesto of the Communist Party* in 1848, and with it they provided their vision of the past: "The history of all hitherto existing society is the history of class struggles." The images to which they could turn were those of deep divisions and actual insurrections.

> When our reign arrives
> When your reign shall end
> Then we shall weave the shroud
>   of the old world
> For hear! revolt is rumbling. (quoted in Struik, 1971, p. 23)

These words of challenge addressed by the silk weavers of Lyons to their employers in the 1830s had many sympathetic hearers. A similar revolt in Germany by the Silesian weavers in 1844 was poetically celebrated by Heinrich Heine.

> Without a tear in their grim eyes,
> They sit at the loom, the rage of despair
>   on their faces:
> We have suffered and hunger'd long
>   enough
> Old Germany, we are weaving a
>   shroud for thee
> And weaving it with a triple cause.
> We are weaving, weaving. (quoted in Struik, 1971, p. 24)

Even England, which in the nineteenth century avoided large-scale direct confrontations, felt the force of the other revolution of the age, the industrial revolution, which created its own dislocations, deep class antagonisms and actual, if limited, struggles. Following an attack by the militia on a meeting of sixty thousand workers in Manchester in 1819, Shelly wrote in his "Mask of Anarchy":

> Rise, like lions after slumber,
> In unvanquishable number,
> Shake your chains to earth like dew
> Which in sleep has fallen on you.
> Ye are many, they are few! (quoted in Struik, 1971, p. 21)

The twin revolutions in France and England that greeted the nine-teenth century provided overlapping but contrasting images of the processes of change. The magnitude of change might be equally great, but the industrial revolution which got underway in England about 1770 was pervasive, manifold in its acts and events, and understood only as the sum of the numerous small acts. The French Revolution by contrast was cataclysmic in form, reflecting sharp breaks and single-stroke major changes.

By 1799 J. B. Lamarck, a professor at the Muséum d'Histoire Naturelle and a sympathizer with the revolution, had developed a theory of the transmutation of species (Burkhardt, 1977). Although some eighteenth-century naturalists had advanced limited theories of organic change through hybridization or degeneration, Lamarck offered the first full-scale theory of organic mutability. Gone was the concept of fixed species; in its place he developed a system that called for malleable forms capable of influence by the environment and change toward greater complexity. In addition, Lamarck adopted the belief that lower, simple organisms could be spontaneously generated —"nature's productions"—and that these in turn could undergo change. He provided a dynamic explanation for the diversity of forms in nature. He believed in a scale of organic complexity, but his trans-formation theory indicated that it must be interpreted phylogenetically (Burkhardt, 1977, p. 140). By the time he published his last account in 1815, he felt he had set forth a "truly general theory." He had dealt with nature's creation of the simplest life forms, the increasing com-plexity of organization of animals, the emergence of higher animal faculties, and the influence of particular circumstances (environmen-tal) in developing special structural and behavioral attitudes (Burk-hardt, 1977, p. 143).

In the politics of the science of the times, Lamarck's theories rep-resented a sharp discontinuity. Although a number of other natural-ists in the early decades of the nineteenth century were exploring the mutability of species, none developed anything resembling a full theory of organic change. Lamarck himself was aware of the degree to which he was an "outsider" within the gathering of Parisian scientists and the degree to which his theory was at odds with the current beliefs of the naturalists. "I am well aware that the novelty of the considera-tions exposed in this work and especially their extreme dissimilarity with what is commonly thought in these matters calls for a more ex-tensive treatment" (quoted in Burkhardt, 1970, p. 287).

Our response to the structure of Lamarck's theory, however, is more problematic. Change was recognized and, indeed, diversity had been accomplished through the mutation of the species. Constancy of

species was abandoned. But the nature of the change itself was orderly, a "marche de la nature," with the simplest living beings giving
rise to, and in succession with, all others. The environment or particular circumstances could intervene, but not to affect the major thrust in
an almost linear series. Rather, it had effect only at the margins, the
lateral branches.

Fossils were the problem. They had been the focus of much of
Lamarck's empirical work, and they seemed to hold the key to the
nagging question, Had some species become extinct in the course of
the earth's history? The answer was given by another naturalist from
the Muséum, Georges Cuvier, on January 21, 1796 (Rudwick, 1972).
Living things that then existed, he claimed, were replacing others that
catastrophes had destroyed. To bolster his claim, he presented a study
of the comparative anatomy of elephants. From this emerged his questions. "But what, then, was this primitive earth where all the beings
differed from those that have succeeded them? What nature was this
that was not subject to man's dominion? And what revolution was
capable of destroying it to the point of leaving as trace of it only some
half-decomposed bones?" (Cuvier, 1796, quoted in Burkhardt, 1977,
p. 129). In 1796 in Paris the work *revolution* was not used with inno-
cence. It carried the political overtones of violence, and certainly this
was the sense in which Cuvier used it. The whole of the earth's history
was punctuated by revolutions. If the institutions and structures of the
ancien regime had been swept away to be succeeded by new ones, the
fossils that Cuvier examined seemed "to prove the existence of a
world anterior to ours, destroyed by some kind of catastrophe"
(quoted in Rudwick, 1972, p. 109). No slow environmental change
could account for extinction; therefore, one of the earth's revolutions
must be responsible. Indeed, continental geologists had gathered a
good deal of evidence, some of it as recent as a few thousand years
before, that catastrophes such as flood had caused major discontinuities in the earth's history.

The evidence that Cuvier proceeded to gather confirmed that animals which had inhabited the earth in the relatively recent past were
no longer known to exist. The new question that he posed to himself
was whether the species that no longer existed had been destroyed, or
merely modified in their form, or transported from one climate to another (Rudwick, 1972, p. 115). There are three clear alternatives: extinction, evolution, or migration. The last, while possible for some
marine forms, had to be ruled out for the mammoths. Lamarck had
opted for "modification" evolution; Cuvier chose extinction.

Here, of course, lay irony and paradox. Two scientists of the
French Revolution responded. One developed a novel theory of

change and mutability for the species in which the change was slow and orderly. Another recognized in nature's history significant violent changes called revolutions but considered the species fixed and unmodifiable. The first postulated a graded continuous scale of nature through which the modifications traveled. The other firmly denied the existence of a single scale of beings and believed instead that the history of life is not only punctuated by occasional discontinuities but is also in some sense progressive (Rudwick, 1972, p. 142).

The young Engels traveled to Manchester, England, in the early 1840s to study the effects of the industrial revolution. On returning to Germany in 1844 he set down his report, *The Condition of the Working Class in England*. The nascent revolutionary was sharp in his criticism. He confided to his new associate, Marx: "I shall present the English with a fine bill of indictment. At the bar of world opinion I charge the English middle classes with mass murder, wholesale robbery, and all the other crimes in the calendar" (Engels, 1844, p. xxil). Engels confidently expected a violent revolution, but it never came. In one important sense Charles Darwin may have been a better observer of industrial England than his German contemporary. As Marx wrote to Engels in 1862, shortly after reading the *Origin of Species*: "It is remarkable how Darwin recognizes among beasts and plants his English society with its division of labor, competition, opening up of new markets, 'invention', and the Malthusian 'struggle for existence' " (quoted in Gould, 1977b, p. 12). Darwin saw in struggle the motor for change, but he eschewed revolutions, violence, and catastrophe and reduced the elements of conflict to part of a system of long, slow, orderly transformation. Nature, he seemed to be saying along with his British naturalist colleagues, was generous of time and parsimonious of violence (Wilkie, 1959).

Much of the science that Darwin needed was available to him. A new, primarily British, theory of uniformitarianism in geology claimed that, contrary to the theory that the history of the earth was punctuated by "revolutions," the forces of nature had been slow, uniform, and roughly equal in magnitude through time. The fossil evidence, both continental and British, seemed to show progression of species forms (although a group of British naturalists gave a theological interpretation calling for a progressive series of special creations following each catastrophe, Bowler, 1976). Darwin had been exposed to the great diversity of natural forms and the problems of geographic distribution during the five years (1831-1836) that he spent aboard the British exploring vessel the *Beagle*, as it circumnavigated the globe. (Indeed, he was able to learn at first hand that in the midnineteenth century "the sun never set on Great Britain.") Even as Darwin set about his own investigations of transmutation of species, another British author wrote a popular and full account of a theory of evolution: Robert Chambers's anonymously published *Vestiges of the Natural History of Creation* (1844).

Aware of the negative criticism that had greeted Lamarck's theories and watching the response to Chambers's efforts, Darwin was seeking a mechanism for change in nature that did not rely on the seeming innate urge to complexity of Lamarck or include the violence that was implied from the catastrophists. While he ransacked the biological literature for evidence of species mutations, he also turned to the social literature; there he ultimately found in the political-economic treatise of Thomas Malthus a model that he could adapt to biology. In 1838 Darwin was led to Auguste Comte by reading David Brewster's review. In the works of the French social philosopher he found the concept of artificial selection. Then he went on to the Belgian statistician Adolph Quetelet from whom he was led back to Malthus. He was becoming acquainted with proposed statistical laws for social phenomena as well as the forces governing human reproduction. Malthus had spelled out a clear, if controversial, quantitative and deterministic rule of superfecundity. It was this rule that became the force behind natural selection, the mechanism that Darwin invented to account for organic change. His notebooks show that he was reading the Scottish political economists as well—Adam Smith, Dugald Stewart, and James McIntosh. He examined the reformist tracts of Henry Lord Brougham which lay behind the 1830s reform measures in England. He explored the philosophical treatises of William Whewell and John Herschel, where he found Francis Bacon's rules of inductive method—the accumulation of numerous bits of evidence out of which laws of nature were constructed—revived and set forth as the appropriate philosophy for science (Young, 1969; Schweber, 1977; Manier, 1977). A number of underlying themes can be recognized; there is a sense of stability, including societal stability and the concept of the "average man"; there are underlying continuous laws of nature (struggle) and of society and the economy (competition yielding regular and predictable patterns).

Darwin read still another English social philosopher, Herbert Spencer, who had constructed for society a comparable theory to account for change: It relied on continuous competition, a "struggle for existence" among humans and led to the "survival of the fittest." The evolutionary system that Spencer developed, just prior to Darwin's publication of the *Origin*, was strongly Lamarckian in character. Social evolution occurred through human adaptations to the environment; these adaptations were themselves heritable. "In common with every other creature, Man is modifiable—since his modifications, like those of every other creature, are ultimately determined by surrounding conditions; and it is continually thrust on men's attention . . . [that] faculties and powers of all orders, while they grow by exercise, dwindle when not used; and that alterations of nature descend to posterity" (Spencer, 1874, quoted in Peel, 1971, pp. 147-148). The social implications of Spencerian social evolution were understood by Spencer and, most important, were widely adopted by those in British society who used them to provide scientific justification for laissez faire economics and opposition to all elements of the welfare state.

The political doctrine that emerged from these biological and sociological works became known as social Darwinism, although its outlines were fully developed before the publication of Darwin's evolutionary theories. Built on the works of Spencer, these theories immediately adopted natural selection and its theory of the struggle of nature. The core of this thought was fundamentally continuist. Humans with their present characteristics came into being through a process of continuing evolution in which those who survived were the strong and able. The whole character of society depended on the aggregate of the units; therefore any attempt to interfere with the process of adaptation and to ameliorate the condition of the ill adapted would be detrimental to continued human development. Social welfare legislation would prevent evolution by reducing incentives to adapt to the social state. "From the biological laws we have been contemplating, it is, on the one hand, an inevitable corollary that if these conditions are maintained, human nature will slowly adapt itself to them: while, on the other hand, it is an inevitable corollary that by no other discipline than subjection to these conditions, can fitness to the social state be produced" (Spencer, 1874, quoted in Peel, 1971, p. 148).

There was also seen to be a natural rhythm to change. It was biological in its basis. Human interference could only be detrimental. The present state of society with its strong and weak, rich and poor, was the natural condition of things. The continuity of nature and of nature's laws was to be preserved. (In fact, toward the end of his life, Alfred Russell Wallace drew back from his beliefs in natural selection, of which he was codiscoverer, in relation to human physical, social, and mental development because he saw it leading to fatalism and standing in the way of the socialism he favored.)

Recent scholarship shows Darwin to have been a believer in social evolution from early in his career. The views that he put forth in *The Descent of Man* (consciously held back from the *Origin*) show that he was deeply influenced by the type of thought later called social Darwinism and that, in turn, the general arguments advanced in the *Ori-*

gin gave strong support to this point of view (Greene, 1977). On numerous occasions he stressed the theme of not wanting to interfere with the course of human natural evolution which had advanced man to his high state. "Hence our natural rate of increase, though leading to many and obvious evils, must not be greatly diminished by any means. There should be open competition for all men; and the most able should not be prevented by laws or customs from succeeding best and rearing the largest number of offspring" (Darwin, 1871, quoted in Greene, 1977, p. 3). Not only were there marked and often used social implications of evolution as it developed in the nineteenth century, but I contend that evolution was largely a social theory that was transformed into a biological theory only to turn once again to social explanation and justification. It provided scientific sanction for interpreting social ills. It suggested social remedies such as social Darwinism and, later in the century, eugenics or controlled procreation. Recent studies suggest that Darwin and evolutionary theory were more widely known and more popular in their social form than in the narrower biological form. The whole pattern of the reception of Darwinism gives strong credence to this view, especially in the manner in which Darwinism was accepted outside Europe (Glick, 1972).

During the course of the nineteenth century the term *evolution* came to be contrasted directly with *revolution*. It carried with it, by analogy to the natural science usage, implications of slow modification by one of the several means advocated by biologists. Old institutions, having become nonadaptive, would give way to newer, higher forms. In contrast to revolutionary change, evolution was suggested to be "the unrolling of something already implicitly formed (like a *national way of life*), or the *development* of something according to its inherent tendencies (like an existing constitution or economic system)" (Williams, 1976, p. 105). Revolutionary or radical changes by contrast were connected with violence rather than continuous growth and, in rejecting existing institutions or structures, were considered unnatural.

During the nineteenth century biologists tended not to use the word *evolution* very widely. Darwin does not mention it even once in the *Origin* and uses the term *evolve* just once—the very last word of the book! (Bowler, 1975). The biological theory was generally referred to as transmutation or transformation theory, with Darwin, until late in his life, speaking of "descent with modification" (Gould, 1977, pp. 28-32). It was Spencer who first used evolution to mean "a change from an indefinite, incoherent homogeneity to a definite, coherent heterogeneity; through continuous differentiations and integrations" (Spencer, 1865, quoted in Gould, 1977, p. 31).[5] The term was thus not limited to organic change but was linked to progressive alteration toward greater complexity. William James, who on first reading Spencer had become a convert, fairly rapidly deserted the ranks and became a sharp critic of his views. When reading Spencer's concept of evolution in the *First Principles*, he marked up the margins with critical and uncomplimentary remarks that parodied Spencer's concept. "Evolution is a change from a nohowish untalkaboutable all-alikeness to a somehowish and in general talkaboutable not-all-alikeness by continuous sticktogetherations and somethingelseifications" (Hofstadter, 1955, p. 129). James was objecting to the determinism of Spencer's view because it left no room for human efforts to improve the quality of life.

The sciences of the nineteenth century, reflecting in part the same broad influences that shaped the theory of evolution, gave an overall sense that nature was a series of processes, structures, and forms, all exhibiting continuity. The theory of the conservation of energy, although born of reductionist intentions, showed that all forces in nature were convertible into each other and that energy could be neither produced nor destroyed but only transformed. Instead of relying on a model of billiard ball atoms depending for action on direct contact, the concept of field which could fill all space gave to the concept of matter a unity and continuity. Cells, conceived of as the ultimate units of life and, in the theory of Theodor Schwann (1839), seen as arising de novo from inanimate matter, were brought into a scheme of a "new vitalism" by Rudolf Virchow with his proclamation *omni cellula e cellua* (all cells from cells). Life itself, thought by Lamarck and others to be capable of spontaneous generation, was shown by Louis Pasteur always to be dependent on previously existing life in the form of airborne germs or spores. Indeed, each of these episodes seemed to demonstrate that continuity was the underlying principle of all nature —the living and the inanimate. But as Merz warned, discontinuities always seemed to reappear or make themselves known at some unexpected point.

The Collapse of Confidence in Continuity

On December 14, 1900, Max Planck presented his paper on the law of black-body radiation to the Physikalische Gesellschaft in Berlin. In this paper he overthrew "the principle of continuity of physical processes by his introduction of the discrete energy levels of a linear oscillator" and consequently set the basis for quantum theory (Hermann, 1971, p. 1). In the same year three biologists, Hugo DeVries, Carl Correns, and Erich von Tschermak, simultaneously rediscovered an 1865 paper by Gregor Mendel in which he advanced a theory attributing the carrying of hereditary information to discrete units. Even while announcing the rediscovery of Mendel, DeVries was completing the first volume of this *Mutationstheorie* (published in 1901). In this work he proposed, on the basis of experimental research, that complexes of new characters arose in a single step, a mutation, which he felt was probably *the* mode by which new species arose (Dunn, 1965). The era of genetics had been opened on the note of unit characters and discontinuous jumps in the evolution of species.

In two widely separated fields of science the belief in continuity was shaken by discoveries of discontinuity in the very same years. This coincidence caught the attention of several commentators and provoked speculation. In the very years when the new theories were being debated, Merz sensed the implications and challenge. "It seems, indeed, impossible for an ultimate explanation to conceive of a plenum or continuum in space without assuming at the same time that such a plenum contains discontinuities which admit of portions of this plenum contains discontinuities which admit of portions of this plenum being defined, and preserving their identity: this introduces again the atomic view, the conception of discrete particles" (Merz, 1914, vol. 3, p. 574). Almost half a century later the physicist Erwin Schrödinger wrestled with the same issues and was forced to conclude that discontinuity may now "come to dominate our entire conception of nature" (1956, p. 242). The significance of this for him was that discrete things could be counted or handled directly with mathematical equipment. He concluded that "the universality of discreteness, as now recognized, appears to show that the method of enumeration, the method of the integer, is really the royal road, the only road by which we may hope to achieve real insight" (1956, p. 243). The underlying implication is that nature may consist of discrete units and that in the integer, which he described as the one fully understood mathematical concept, is the clue to the successful and proper methods of the study of nature. (He cites in a footnote the remark of Leopold Kronecker: "Integers were made by God, everything else is the work of man.") But even Schrödinger, who in his early essays, particularly those written in the mid and late 1940s, seemed to celebrate discontinuity as found in the scientific study of nature and to link it to basic human thought processes, drew back in his papers of the 1950s. In these he became critical of some of the discontinuous phenomena he had previously discussed and threw doubt on some of their meanings. He was responding to the shift in opinions among geneticists, which led them back from the belief that natural selection was based on "quantum jumps" (Schrödinger, 1956, p. iii). Perhaps it was the shock of the Second World War that motivated Schrödinger's explorations of and deep interest in the discrete and the discontinuous in life and matter while an intervening decade of European reconstruction led to his partial retreat from these concepts.

What led Planck to his development of quantum theory is not clear. Certainly experimental evidence, the product of new techniques and technologies, lent urgency to new explanations. As Schrödinger put it, "The great revelation of quantum theory was that features of discreteness were discovered in the Book of Nature, in a context in which anything other than continuity seemed to be absurd according to the views held until then" (1956, p. 49). It seemed to the observer in 1900 not only that matter behaved as though it were made up of discrete bundles but that energy or force also behaved as though it existed only in discrete amounts. Working theoretically, Planck discovered discontinuity where it was least expected, in the energy exchange between an atom or molecule and the radiation of heat and light. Each atom could hold only precisely defined units of energy; normally at one of these energy levels the atom would change abruptly to another energy level. In change an atom radiated or absorbed energy in unit amounts from the environment, hence the term light quanta or photons introduced by Einstein in 1905 (Schrödinger, 1956, p. 136).

It would be misleading to say that Planck immediately understood the full impact of his discovery and realized that he had overthrown the continuity principle. That understanding was to come in just over a decade when Niels Bohr in 1913 extended the Planck assumptions in two directions, providing a solution to the problem of the structure of the atom (Hermann, 1971).

But Planck was a "reluctant revolutionary" (Hermann, 1971, p. 1, 22; Schrödinger, p. 136). First, he was slow to move from being an opponent to being a proponent of the atomic theory; even then, he continued to have reservations about definite models of the atom. Second, he was hesitant to adopt the view that radiation was divided into units, or quanta. Reflecting on his moves several years later in a letter, he relates:

> What I did can be described as simply an act of desperation. By nature I am peacefully inclined and reject all doubtful adventures. But by then I had been wrestling unsuccessfully for six years (since 1894) with the problem of equilibrium between radiation and matter and I know that this problem was of fundamental importance to physics; I also know the formula that express the energy distribution in normal spectra. A theoretical interpretation therefore *had* to be found at any cost, no matter how high . . . I was ready to sacrifice every one of my previous convictions about physical laws. (Hermann, 1971, p. 23)

The reluctance to give up continuity interpretations of natural phenomena was not Planck's alone. Even Bohr who found himself in the midst of the effort persistently refused to accept the idea of light quanta even after Einstein's paper of 1905. His commitment to the validity of the wave concept emerges from an incident related by a colleague. Upon receiving a letter from Einstein criticizing Bohr's opposition to light quanta, Bohr is said to have remarked that even if Einstein had sent a telegram indicating that there was now irrefutable proof of the physical existence of light quanta, "the telegram could only reach me by radio on account of the waves which are there" (Jammer, 1966, p. 187).

The sharpness of the division between the old physics and the new is reflected by the slowness with which the Planck quantum hypothesis was adopted. Neither the older nor the younger generation of physicists fully recognized the broad implications of the work. However, the young theoretical physicist Albert Einstein first comprehended the full philosophical implications of Planck's work and, indeed, added to it his proposal for a quantum of light—the photon. This idea also was initially rejected (McCormach, 1971, pp. xvii-xxiv). Einstein shared with Planck a dissatisfaction with the then current world views within physics and did not hesitate to stake out new ground. A provocative study by Lewis Feuer has linked the young Einstein's willingness to adopt a heterodox view in the case of his special theory of relativity to his involvement in the circle of radical philosophers and political activists with whom he was closely associated during his early years in Zurich (Feuer, 1974a).

On the other side, the reluctance on the part of the other physicists to accept the implications of discontinuity in Planck's theory seemed also to reflect their views and beliefs outside the narrower limits of physical theory and data. As late as 1911, when the first Solvay Congress gathered, there was only a handful of advocates of the quantum theory—even though Einstein was joined by another young physicist, Paul Ehrenfest, in providing strong theoretical support for the theory. The quantum was not accepted until several of the senior figures in physics, Henri Poincaré and James Jeans, became convinced in 1913 of its validity. Jeans had tried to reconcile the new laws of radiation with classical mechanics and failed, so that he was finally forced to acknowledge the evidence that was piling up. His hesitations were clear even in his announcement of support in his "Report on Radiation and the Quantum Theory" in 1914. "The keynote of the old mechanics" he wrote, "was continuity, *natura non facit saltus*," while that of quantum theory is discontinuity. Jeans cited Poincaré's words. "A physical system is only susceptible of a finite number of distinct states; it jumps from one of these states to another without passing through a continuous series of intermediate states" (Feuer, 1974b, p. 278).

The reasons advanced by historians and others for the break with continuity that occurred in physics around 1900 seem to me less than satisfactory. Russell McCormmach advances the explanation that physicists were concerned with the world view in their science. They were facing the dissolution of a long-held mechanical world view during the closing years of the nineteenth century, and this view conflicted with their need for coherence in the sciences, which was matched by the need for coherence in German scholarship in general (McCormmach, 1971). Feuer takes up the model of generational conflicts and collaborations and sees elements of both involved in the complex Planck-Einstein-Poincaré network (Feuer, 1974b). Armin Hermann and Max Jammer, interested primarily in the development of the technical concepts of physics itself, treat the introduction of quantum theory largely as a steady emergence of new explanations in the face of the inadequacy of the old theories to handle anomalous data.

Despite the lack of a cogent historical explanation and a reluctance to accept the deep implications of discontinuist theories, continuity as a guiding principle in physics was lost, never to be fully regained. There was the conscious attempt by Bohr to reconcile wave and particle concepts and to write into physical theory a principled tolerance for ambiguity, but nothing like the nineteenth-century view of a world governed by great laws of continuity has been recovered.

William Bateson, the British biologist, foreshadowed the events of 1900 in genetics when some six years earlier, in 1894, he published his substantial work *Materials for the Study of Variation*. The subtitle of the book proclaims its thesis: "Treated with Especial Regard to DISCONTINUITY in the Origin of Species" (the capital letters are Bateson's) (Dunn, 1965, p. 58). By the close of the nineteenth century the Darwinian model of evolution had come under attack from a number of sides. While it would be fair to say that evolution itself was widely accepted in biology, the model of natural selection working on continuous variations was far from being universally adopted. The discontinuity of species in nature was still apparent, and from several sides discontinuous variation was being proposed as an alternative explanation for variety in nature.

In England, however, Bateson found that despite criticisms of Darwinism, discontinuity was not easily accepted. How discontinuity might work in nature was not easy to envisage. In a letter defending his 1894 book he wrote, "Part of the difficulty, that will I fear stand in the way of any general acceptance of the suggestion of Discontinuity, lies in the impossibility of at once giving it a definite expression" (quoted in Bateson, 1928, p. 57). Bateson was unwilling to put forward "a definite expression" because far too little evidence existed on which to build it. He commented in the closing pages of his 1894 report: "The only way in which we may hope to get at the truth is by the organisation of systematic experiments in breeding, a class of research that calls perhaps for more patience and more resources than any form of biological inquiry" (quoted in Bateson, 1928, p. 57). But notice what Bateson was doing. In spite of scant evidence and little support, he proposed an explanation of evolution that ran counter to prevailing opinion in the community of scientists. He expressed a belief with an implied metaphysics behind it.

Thirty years earlier Mendel had similarly proposed an explanation for heredity that also ran counter to current scientific beliefs and, more important, interests. It was thus largely ignored by the biologists who could have understood it. Mendel, an Augustinian monk, was operating at the margins of organized science and, although published, was not widely read. Bateson was at Cambridge University but had a minor position, was young, and was largely marginal to established biology. The recognized heirs of Darwin were Karl Pearson and the biometricians. For them the small variations that Darwinian natural selection required were the basis of a well-constructed new statistical approach to nature and evolution. These were the scientific foes whom Bateson battled; prior to 1900 the contest was strikingly unequal.

Little wonder then that the rediscovery of Mendel's papers in 1900 with their discussion of particulate inheritance relying on units or "factors" was "hailed with a kind of triumphant gladness by Will" (as Bateson's wife, Beatrice, reports her husband's response). To Bateson the implication was clear: "Those who accepted Mendelism could not reject Discontinuity" (Bateson, 1928, p. 70). This support was quite welcome in that it confirmed the views he had been developing and seemed to set the lines of conflict more sharply than ever. On the eve of the Mendelian rediscovery, at a time when he was finding it difficult to have his papers published (Feuer, 1974b, p. 279), Bateson pushed his points hard at a meeting of the Royal Horticultural Society. Discontinuity, he claimed, would account for evolution. He challenged his listeners.

> We are taught that Evolution is a very slow process, going forward by infinitesimal steps. To the horticulturist it is rarely anything of the kind. In the lifetime of the older men here present it is not Evolution but Revolution that has come about in very many of the best-known Orders of horticultural plants. Even the younger of us have seen vast changes. It may have seemed a slow process to individual men in the case of their own specialty. It may have taken all their lives to obtain and fix a strain; but in Evolution that is nothing. It is going at a gallop! (quoted in Bateson, 1928, p. 165)

While Bateson hammered away at evidence of discontinuous variation, the Dutch plant breeder DeVries, one of the three rediscoverers of Mendel, put discontinuity into the framework of a full-fledged theory of experimental evolution. As L.C. Dunn noted, the mutation theory "gave for the first time the hope of directly observing and possibly controlling evolutionary processes" (1965, p. 59). Mutation theory as proposed depended on Mendelian genetics but went beyond it to deal with the mechanism of evolution. DeVries claimed in the *Mutationstheorie* (1901-1903) that he had discovered the mode by which new species originated. His theory was both controversial and fruitful, challenging the role of selection and demonstrating that the problem of the origin of species could be studied experimentally.

The reception of mutation theory gives some clues to scientists' reasons for deserting their long-held commitment to continuity in favor of discontinuous jumps in evolution. First, it had the promise of yielding to experimentation, thus differentiating it from evolution which depended almost totally on comparative study. It could be observed directly and could be linked to basic physiological processes. It was in fact the physiologists and embryologists, such as Jacques Loeb and Thomas Hunt Morgan, who most enthusiastically received mutation theory. This theory further separated scientists by discipline, the field biologists largely staying with natural selection while the experimentalists, the laboratory scientists, opted for mutation theory. It also reflected generational choice, with more younger than older biologists supporting Mendelian genetics. Nationalities also split in their responses, with Americans greeting it very favorably. Indeed DeVries was invited quite early to present his ideas at the opening of the newly established experimental genetic facilities at Cold Spring Harbor, New York.

But another important element suggests an added dimension in the positive reception of mutation theory. Despite DeVries's assumption that he was working within the Darwinian framework, other biologists interpreted his discoveries as embodying a fundamental attack on the underlying philosophy of Darwinism (Bowler, 1978; Allen, 1975). Thomas Case, reviewing the mutation theory in the American journal *Science* (1905), showed one reason for popular reception. "If we conceive that man originated abruptly by some unaccountable molecular change . . . then there can be no doubt of the time when man became immortal, whereas there would be necessarily much, much uncertainty as to the time when this occurred among the successive infinitesimal increments of brain development necessitated by Darwinian theory" (quoted in Eiseley, 1958, p. 250). The theologian could take comfort in this sort of interpretation. Further, the American experimental embryologist Morgan gives an additional clue about what was being rejected and what was being accepted. Mutation theory seemed to provide an escape from the strong social Darwinian image carried by natural selection or, as Morgan put it, the "dreadful calamity of nature, pictured as the battle for existence" (1903, p. 116). Morgan and others disliked the vision of nature's proceeding on the basis of suffering and struggle. Eiseley expressed this: "The more repugnant aspects of Darwinian thought—its constant emphasis upon struggle, its mechanistic, utilitarian philosophy which to many, seemed as dingy as a Victorian factory" (1958, p. 250). Morgan never fully explored the social implications of his "biological" views but they were important and were not dropped even after he had modified his views on large mutations and adopted instead a belief in smaller mutations on which natural selection might operate. He stressed that although favorable mutations might spread through a population, this would not mean that the unchanged would suffer. The new view, as he put it forward, "gives a somewhat different picture of the process of evolution from the old idea of a ferocious struggle between individuals of a species with the survival of the fittest and the annihilation of the less fit" (1913, pp. 87-88). Morgan was pleased to be able to claim that in the synthesis he was creating, "evolution assumes a more peaceful aspect" (1913, pp. 87-88).

A mix of motives led biologists to adopt a discontinuist view of evolution. For all of them an explicit desire to explain change in nature and how it might occur was strong. Some were dissatisfied with the methodology of traditional Darwinism and wished to introduce a more experimental mode. Others were attracted to the alternative view of evolution without struggle and competition.

DeVries's mutation theory, relying on large jumps in nature, was influential for a little more than a decade, during which Mendelian explanations of heredity gained wide currency and the idea of mutation became accepted and modified. Ultimately, however, the steps in nature were reduced in size and accommodated to a new theory of evolution that united Mendelian genetics (including micro mutations) and Darwinian natural selection (now modified to act on variations produced by mutations). Created was a theory of continuity in evolution, based on discontinuous steps in nature. In structure, then, the new genetics—evolution—resembled the compromise achieved in physics, where the new quantum mechanics included both particles and waves.

Scientific Revolutions

Even the discussion of how to gain knowledge of nature, indeed the problem of knowledge in general, has been a site of controversy over continuous versus discontinuous processes. Philosophers, sociologists, and historians of science are even now engaged in deep combat over epistemological issues, arguing whether knowledge is achieved by revolutionary jumps or by evolutionary adjustments. Does epistemology exhibit ruptures and breaks? Or does it demonstrate slow, cumulative growth? Karl Popper titles his most recent collection of essays *Objective Knowledge: An Evolutionary Approach* (1972), and Stephen Toulmin chooses *Human Understanding. Part I: The Collective Use and Evolution of Concepts* (1972). Thomas Kuhn, on the other hand, provided a sharp focus for the most recent epistemological controversy with his volume *The Structure of Scientific Revolutions* (1962, 2d. ed. 1970).

Although these authors seem to suggest that the controversy is a new one, one historian has recently examined the older and almost commonplace phrase the "scientific revolution." I. Bernard Cohen, in tracing the words and the concept, has found that the earliest uses are based on analogy to the English "glorious revolution" of 1688. Most striking to my mind is that although the term *revolution* has its origins in the sciences (astronomy, to be exact), its use in referring to the sciences was almost always drawn by analogy from the newer political usage (Cohen, 1976). During the eighteenth century, as the term gained currency, the language used in retrospect to describe the actions of the scientists was clearly that of political revolutionary movements. Jean d'Alembert in his *Preliminary Discourse* to the great *Encyclopédie* talks of Descartes and refers to his great "révolte" and the manner in which he had shown "intelligent minds how to throw off the yoke of scholasticism, of opinion, of authority." Descartes is portrayed "as a leader of conspirators who, before anyone else, had the courage to rise against a despotic and arbitrary power and who, in preparing a resounding revolution, laid the foundations of a more just and happier government, which he himself was not able to see established (quoted in Cohen, 1976, p. 270). While d'Alembert and his fellow encyclopedist Denis Diderot explored the facets of that midseventeenth-century series of events that came to be called the scientific revolution, they implied most often that the changes they were referring to were sharp breaks. But sometimes the notions of revolution, even as they used it, also had overtones of the earlier meaning of a cyclical process of change.

During the decade of the French Revolution, however, the term *revolution* in general and *scientific revolution* in particular were fixed in their meaning of a discontinuous break with the past, political or conceptual, and the institution of a new order of society or of scientific theory and method. As Cohen aptly notes, those sympathetic with the political changes of the day, Condorcet, Antoine Lavoisier, and the English advocate Joseph Priestley, found it easy to transfer the concepts of revolution from the political to the scientific scene. (All three could talk easily about the chemical revolution occurring at the time in which the latter two were active participants). Those unsympathetic or cautious in their judgments were more restrained. Samuel Miller, an American cleric with an anti-French bias, noted in his 1803 *Brief Retrospect of the Eighteenth Century* that people more than ever before had learned to "throw off the authority of distinguished names . . . to discard all opinions, to overturn systems which were supposed to rest on everlasting foundations . . . [to create] revolutions of the human mind" (quoted in Cohen, 1976, p. 286). As Cohen put it, "the image thus conjured is one of intellectual *sans-culottes* running rampant" (1976, p. 286).

A picture, then, of conceptual revolutions, involving a rupture with past traditions, relying on the work of an individual or a group whose activities could be located in time and place, is most often seen in periods of political and social upheaval and is most easily proposed by those sympathetic to radical challenge or radical proposals for social reorganization (Mendelsohn, 1977).

The current debates in the epistemology of science show these same characteristics, although with the discussion still under way it is too early to delineate all the contours. The issue in science arose from the challenge to the authority of positivist ideals of scientific knowledge which date back to the nineteenth century and which envisage science broadly as the progressive cumulation of many bits of new knowledge. While others had raised these issues before him, Kuhn put the challenge and an alternative theory of knowledge in the context of an explicitly revolutionary model. The process that he describes is one of "normal science" periodically interrupted by a period of "revolutionary science" from which a new guiding "paradigm" or conceptual scheme emerges, in turn shaping the work of a new epoch of normal science. "Scientific revolutions are here taken to be those non-cumulative developmental episodes in which an older paradigm is replaced in whole or in part by an incompatible new one" (Kuhn, 1970, p. 92). The analogy with the political sphere is explicitly drawn and defended, even while some differences are noted. "Political revolutions are inaugurated by a growing sense, often restricted to a segment of the political community, that existing institutions have ceased adequately to meet the problems posed by an environment that they have in part created. In much the same way, scientific revolutions are inaugurated by a growing sense, again often restricted to a narrow sub-division of the scientific community, that an existing paradigm has ceased to function adequately in the explorations of an aspect of nature"

(Kuhn, 1970, p. 92). The elements of extralegality, crisis, institutional collapse, and polarization are all explored. Indeed, Kuhn actually means "revolution" in the sciences. His model, even after the give-and-take of the several years of debates, remains fundamentally discontinuist in its theory of knowledge, and it is exactly this aspect that has most troubled his critics.[6]

The most sustained criticisms have come from those who reject revolutionary changes if they mean epistemological discontinuity. Thus Toulmin takes direct aim at the Kuhnian position. "Any suggestion that a complete paradigm-switch involves conceptual changes of a totally different kind from those that take place within the limits of a single overall paradigm—that they represent some sort of a 'rational discontinuity', and lead to inescapable incomprehension—is quite misleading" (1972, p. 118). Toulmin sees the two types of conceptual changes as differing in degree only. He wants to replace Kuhn's revolutionary model of conceptual change with an evolutionary model. Changes of lesser or greater degree might occur, but by analogy with uniformitarian geology the changes are just alternative outcomes of the very same factors working together in differing ways (Toulmin, 1972, p. 122). If the Darwinian or evolutionary idea of "conceptual populations" is adopted, then according to Toulmin, "the occurrence of a 'scientific revolution' no longer amounts to a dramatic interruption in the 'normal' continuous consolidation of science: instead, it becomes a mere 'unit of variation' within the very process of scientific change" (Toulmin, 1970, p. 45).

Without doubt Toulmin presents the fullest and most challenging evolutionary model of conceptual change and growth. It parallels modern evolutionary thought in biology and takes full advantage of the many subtleties introduced into that theory. But like evolution from the nineteenth century to the present, it has the urgent, if often tacit, assumption that change must be harnessed—it must not be wild, anarchistic, catastrophic, or revolutionary. Other critics have amplified this point. Indeed, the reluctance to include these disruptive elements and images and a desire to avoid the very ideas of "crisis" that Kuhn put forward to explain change are what lie behind the sharp criticisms of Imre Lakatos. In addition Lakatos wishes to avoid an implicit relativism that he sees in the discontinuist approach. At one point in his exposition these elements burst out. "Each paradigm contains its own standards. The crisis sweeps away not only the old theories and rules but also the standards which made us respect them. The new paradigm brings a totally new rationality. There are no super-paradigmatic standards. The change is a bandwagon effect. Thus *in Kuhn's view scientific revolution is irrational, a matter for mob psy-*

chology" (Lakatos, 1970, p. 178; my ital.). Science in Lakatos's view operates in modes strikingly different from those envisaged by Kuhn. Lakatos has a very specific alternative demand. "This *requirement of continuous growth* is my rational reconstruction of the widely acknowledged requirement of 'unity' or 'beauty' of science" (1970, p. 175; my ital.).

The background claim of evolutionary continuity of scientific concepts comes from Popper, who explicitly put forward the idea just a year before Kuhn proposed his revolutionary alternative. "The growth of our knowledge," Popper wrote in his Herbert Spencer Lecture, 1961, "is the result of a process closely resembling what Darwin called 'natural selection'; that is, *the natural selection of hypotheses*" (Popper, 1972, p. 261; my ital.). The knowledge we possess at any given time represents the hypotheses that have survived in a struggle for existence by demonstrating their greater fitness. They have overcome and eliminated the hypotheses that were unfit. Popper makes the element of evolutionary continuity clear. "This interpretation may be applied to animal knowledge, pre-scientific knowledge, and to scientific knowledge . . . From the amoeba to Einstein, the growth of knowledge is always the same; we try to solve our problems, and to obtain, by a process of elimination, something approaching adequacy in our tentative solutions" (Popper, 1972, p. 261).

That the 1960s were the period during which a strong assault was made on the idea of smooth continuity and ordered growth should not be surprising. Nor is it surprising that others made concerted efforts to save the phenomenon of the theory of progressive growth of scientific knowledge. The analogous battle was being fought on the political and the social scenes. The advances of science and its technologies were being heralded and the race to the moon was being run. At the same time the profoundest challenges to scientific knowledge and its uses were being launched. The missile era and all that it symbolized about the measure of rationality had brought the several criticisms that science had confronted in more than a century. But, more broadly, the challenges to science and to the specialness of its epistemology, were part of a broader series of objections to the very structure of social order and the patterns of political authority. Whether reflected in the civil rights campaign or antiwar movements in the United States or the days of May 1968 in France and on the continent, the whole Western world was experiencing a breakdown of national consensus and social cohesion; new groups, new parties, new generations were questioning and attempting to overturn the order of things. The polite dialogues within the philosophy of science were matched by more explicitly politically and radically oriented objections from outside. Theodore Roszak in his provocative *Making of a Counter Culture* (1969) questioned the very existence of objective knowledge, and Herbert Marcuse in his neo-Marxist text in the sociology of knowledge, *One Dimensional Man* (1964), raised the specter that science and technology were constructed on an epistemology of domination. To the students and young scholars of the 1960s rupture with the past and challenge to authority became a mode of thought and action. They were the receptive readers and the supporters of ideas of conceptual revolution and cognitive discontinuities. Indeed, they often seemed consciously to aim at creating discomfort of the mind. Claims of continuity, in this context, evoked images of support for the rejected past.

Continuity and discontinuity, I would argue, are not constructs of nature but constructs of the human mind used to interpret nature. It is the observer and the interpreter of the physical world who posit continuities and discontinuities in the materials before them. Indeed here we seem to have excellent examples of theory-laden and metaphysics-laden observation. The whole range of cases that we have been examining indicate the very strong role that prior commitment to types or forms of explanations and theories play, not only in empirical investigations but in concept and theory construction itself. The influence of an immediate historical and social context has become visible on a number of occasions and strongly suggests that for broad organizing themes like continuity and discontinuity structures of discourse and thought can pervade segments of a society or historical epoch and mark the structure of theories across the traditional boundaries of discipline and field.

Continuist and discontinuist explanations allow themselves to be used for different ends and permit different tones to be given to means and methods as well. Continuist themes place the influence of the past and its ways on the present and the future. Novelty and change are viewed as rooted in anterior experience and precedent; deterministic explanation becomes the normal mode. Discontinuist approaches can seem more disconcerting; they are often more pluralistic and make external influences more acceptable. Innovation and variety can be viewed as reflecting new circumstances and new opportunities. In political and social discourse continuity is conserving of past and present forms, procedures and traditions, while discontinuity invites rupture with the past and creates the sense of necessity for invention. Those comfortable with the present welcome continuity; those unsatisfied with it seek a rupture.

What are the consequences of the use of these two modes of thought? The strong continuist theories developed during the nineteenth century show the ability to incorporate many bits of disparate evidence within broad explanatory frameworks. They served as guides to research, exploration, and experiment and reserved a place for the data being sought. But too deep a commitment to continuist views can so direct what is sought that it can determine what can be found. Was the search for continuity, for example, responsible at least in part for the failure to understand and utilize Mendel's genetic discoveries? It seems that the unexpected and the anomalous can be more readily utilized and understood if analyzed within a discontinuist structure. Novelty and radical innovation are probably more readily accepted where continuities are not too strongly postulated.

But one other overriding truth seems to come from historical reflections: continuous and discontinuous organizing modes have seldom held monopolies over explanation for very long. Rather they have seemed to live in tension with each other, thus allowing historical perspective and the organization of tradition to coexist, probably healthily, with the challenge of change and the thrust toward revolt.

Notes

1. The recent works of authors such as Barry Barnes, David Bloor, Paul Forman, Jerome Ravetz, and David Edge provided some guidelines and examples. My own attempt to locate the choice made by German physiologists of the 1840s for a strong physical-reductionist explanatory system in the social revolutions of the period added to my understanding of the manner in which concepts and techniques in the sciences can become thoroughly interactive with the contemporary political and social scene. Everett Mendelsohn, "Revolution and Reduction: The Sociology of Methodological and Philosophical Concerns in Nineteenth-Century Biology," in Y. Elkana, ed., *The Interaction between Science and Philosophy*, Atlantic Highlands, N.Y.: Humanities, 1974, pp. 407-426.

2. An interesting discussion of the inconography of the illustration is I. Bernard Cohen's "A Note on Harvey's 'Egg' as Pandora's 'Box,' " in Mikulas Teich and Robert Young, eds., *Changing Perspectives in the History of Science: Essays in Honour of Joseph Needham* (London: Hutchinson, 1973), pp. 233-249.

3. From Harvey's dedication which was addressed to Charles I, whom he served as personal physician. There is a lively debate about Harvey's meaning and intent to be found on subsequent pages of Webster, 1974.

4. The special modern sense of violent overthrow and establishment of a new social order belongs to the 1790s. See the interesting discussion in Williams, 1976.

5. Spencer used *evolution* as early as 1852 in his essay *The Development Hypothesis*.

6. Ironically, Kuhn is also attacked from the materialist left by Dominique Lecourt, a French communist historian-philosopher of science, in his

book *Marxism and Epistemology: Bachelard, Canguilhem and Foucault,* (trans. Ben Brewster, London: New Left Books, 1975). While Lecourt applauds the noncontinuism exhibited by Kuhn's concept of revolutionary paradigm shifts and compares it with the earlier concepts of Gaston Bachelard, who introduced the notion of epistemological ruptures, Lecourt finally dismisses Kuhn's efforts as being ultimately in the idealist mode (pp. 17-19).

References

ALLEN, GARLAND A. 1975. *Life science in the twentieth century.* New York: Wiley.

ARISTOTLE. *Historia animalium.* Trans. D'Arcy Wentworth Thompson. Oxford: Oxford University Press, 1910.

—— *Metaphysics.* In Lovejoy, 1936, p. 55.

BATESON, BEATRICE. 1928. *William Bateson, F.R.S. naturalist.* Cambridge: Cambridge University Press.

BOCHNER, SALOMON. 1968. Continuity and discontinuity. In *Dictionary of the History of Ideas.* New York: C. Scribner's Sons. 1:492-505.

BONNET, CHARLES. 1762. *Considérations sur les corps organisés.* In Gould, 1977a, p. 22.

BOWLER, PETER. 1971. Preformation and pre-existence in the seventeenth century: a brief analysis. *Journal of the History of Biology* 4:221-244.

—— 1975. The changing meaning of "evolution." *Journal of the History of Ideas* 36: 95-114.

—— 1976. *Fossils and progress: paleontology and the idea of progressive evolution in the nineteenth century.* New York: Science History Publications.

—— 1978. Hugo DeVries and Thomas Hunt Morgan: the mutation theory and the spirit of Darwinism. *Annals of Science* 35: 55-73.

BOYER, CARL. 1949. *The history of the calculus and its conceptual development.* New York: Dover.

BURKHARDT, RICHARD W., JR. 1970. Lamarck, evolution and the politics of science. *Journal of the History of Biology* 3:275-298.

—— 1977. *The spirit of system: Lamarck and evolutionary biology.* Cambridge, Mass.: Harvard University Press.

COHEN, I. BERNARD. 1976. The eighteenth-century origins of the concept of scientific revolution. *Journal of the History of Ideas* 37:257-288.

CUVIER, GEORGES. 1796. Mémoire sur les espèces d'elephans vivantes et fossiles. In Burkhardt, 1977, p. 129.

DARWIN, CHARLES. 1871. *The descent of man.* In Greene, 1977, p. 26.

DUNN, LESLIE C. 1965. *A short history of genetics: the development of the main lines of thought, 1864-1939.* New York: McGraw-Hill.

EDELSTEIN, LUDWIG. 1967. Andreas Vesalius, the humanist. In *Ancient medicine: selected papers of Ludwig Edelstein,* ed. O. Temkin and C. Temkin. Baltimore, Md.: Johns Hopkins Press.

EISELEY, LOREN. 1958. *Darwin's century.* New York: Doubleday.

ENGELS, FRIEDRICH. 1844. Engels to Marx, 19 November 1844. In editors' introduction. *The condition of the working class in England,* ed. W. O.

Henderson and W. H. Chalomer. Stanford, Calif.: Stanford University Press, 1958.

FARLEY, JOHN. 1977. *The spontaneous generation controversy*. Baltimore, Md.: Johns Hopkins Press.

FEUER, LEWIS S. 1974a. The social roots of Einstein's theory of relativity. In *Einstein and the generations of science*, ed. L. Feuer. New York: Basic Books.

—— 1974b. Generational movements and scientific revolution. In *Einstein and the generations of science*, ed. L. Feuer. New York: Basic Books.

FORMIGARI, LIA. 1968. Chain of being. *Dictionary of the History of Ideas*. New York: Charles Scribner's Sons. 1:325-335.

GLACKEN, CLARENCE J. 1967. *Traces on the Rhodian shore*. Berkeley and Los Angeles: University of California Press.

GLICK, THOMAS F. 1972. *The comparative reception of Darwin*. Austin, Tex.: University of Texas Press.

GREENE, JOHN C. 1977. Darwin as a social evolutionist. *Journal of the History of Biology* 10:1-27.

GOULD, STEPHEN JAY. 1977a. *Ontogeny and phylogeny*. Cambridge, Mass.: Harvard University Press.

—— 1977b. Evolution's erratic pace. *Natural History* (May).

HALE, SIR MATTHEW. 1677. The primitive organization of the mind. In Glacken, 1967, p. 481-482.

HARVEY, WILLIAM. 1628. *De motu cordis et sanguinis*. In Hill, 1974, p. 160.

—— 1651. *On the generation of animals*. As, Exercise the Sixty Second. In *The works of William Harvey, M.D.,* trans. Robert Willis London: Sydenham Society, 1847.

HAYEK, F. A. 1952. *The counter revolution of science: studies on the abuse of reason*. Glencoe, Ill.: Free Press.

HERMANN, ARMIN. 1971. *The genesis of quantum theory (1899-1913)*. Cambridge, Mass.: MIT Press.

HILL, CHRISTOPHER. 1974. William Harvey and the idea of monarchy. In Webster, 1974.

HOFSTADTER, RICHARD. 1955. *Social Darwinism in American thought*. Boston: Beacon Press.

JAMMER, MAX. 1966. *The conceptual development of quantum mechanics*. New York: McGraw-Hill.

KUHN, THOMAS S. 1970. *The structure of scientific revolutions*. Chicago: University of Chicago Press.

LAKATOS, IMRE. 1970. Falsification and the methodology of scientific research programs. In *Criticism and the growth of knowledge*, ed. 1. Lakatos and A. Musgrave. Cambridge: Cambridge University Press.

LEIBNIZ, GOTTFRIED WILHELM. *Ethics*. In Lovejoy 1936, p. 145.

LEISS, WILLIAM. 1972. *The domination of nature*. New York: G. Braziller.

LLOYD, G. E. R. 1968. *Aristotle: the growth and structure of his thought*. Cambridge: Cambridge University Press.

LOVEJOY, ARTHUR O. 1936. *The great chain of being*. Cambridge, Mass.: Harvard University Press.

MALEBRANCHE, NICHOLAS. 1673. De la recherche vérité. In Farley, 1977, p. 17.

MANIER, EDWARD. 1977. *The young Darwin and his cultural circle.* Dordrecht: D. Reidel Publishing Co.

MAUPERTVIS, PIERRE LOUIS MOREAU DE. 1750. Essai de cosmologie. *Oeuvres I.* In Formigari, 1968.

MCCORMMACH, RUSSELL. 1971. Editorial preface. *Historical Studies in the Physical Sciences* 3.

MENDELSOHN, E. 1968. Philosophical biology vs. experimental biology: spontaneous generation in the seventeenth century. *Actes Congrès International d'Histoire des Sciences.* IB:201-226.

———— 1977. The social construction of scientific knowledge. In *The social production of scientific knowledge,* ed. E. Mendelsohn, P. Weingart, and R. Whitley. Dordrecht: D. Reidel Publishing Co.

MERZ, JOHN THEODORE. 1914. *A history of European thought in the nineteenth century,* 4 vols. Edinburgh: W. Blackwood and Sons.

MORGAN, T. H. 1903. *Evolution and adaptation.* In Bowler, 1978.

———— 1913. *A critique of the theory of evolution.* In Bowler, 1978.

NEEDHAM, JOSEPH. 1934. *A History of embryology.* Cambridge: Cambridge University Press.

O'MALLEY, CHARLES D. 1964. *Andreas Vesalius of Brussels, 1514-1564.* Berkeley and Los Angeles: University of California Press.

PEEL, J. D. Y. 1971. *Herbert Spencer: the evolution of a sociologist.* New York: Basic Books.

POPPER, KARL. 1972. Evolution and the tree of knowledge. In *Objective knowledge: an evolutionary approach.* Oxford: Clarendon Press.

RANDALL, JOHN HERMANN, JR. 1961. *The school of Padua and the emergence of modern science.* Padua: Antenore.

RUDWICK, MARTIN J. S. 1972. *The meaning of fossils.* New York: American Elsevier.

SCHRÖDINGER, ERWIN. 1956. *What is life and other scientific essays.* New York: Macmillan.

SCHWEBER, SYLVAN. 1977. The origin of the *Origin* revisted. *Journal of the History of Biology* 10:229-316.

SPENCER, HERBERT. 1865. *First principles of a new system of philosophy.* In Gould, 1977, p. 31.

———— 1874. The study of sociology. In Peel, 1971, pp. 147-148.

STRUIK, DIRK J. 1971. *Birth of the Communist Manifesto.* New York: International Publishing Co.

TOULMIN, STEPHEN. 1970. Does the distinction between normal and revolutionary science hold water? In *Criticism and the Growth of Knowledge,* ed. I. Lakatos and A. Musgrave. Cambridge: Cambridge University Press.

———— 1972. *Human understanding. Part I: The collective use and evolution of concepts.* Princeton, N.J.: Princeton University Press.

VALLISNERI, ANTONIO. 1733. *Opere fisciso mediche.* In Farley, 1977, p. 11.

WEBSTER, CHARLES, ed. 1974. *The intellectual revolution of the seventeenth century.* London: Routledge, Kegan, Paul.

WILKIE, J. S. 1959. Buffon, Lamarck and Darwin: The originality of Darwin's theory of evolution. In *Darwin's biological work: some aspects recon-sidered*, ed. P. R. Bell. Cambridge: Cambridge University Press.

WILLIAMS, RAYMOND. 1976. *Keywords, a vocabulary of culture and society*. New York: Oxford University Press.

YOUNG, ROBERT M. 1969. Malthus and the evolutionists: the common context of biological and social theory. *Past and Present* 43: 109-141.

4 | Continuities and Change in Maturational Timing

Stanley M. Garn

STUDENTS OF PHYSICAL (or biological) growth and development have long been concerned with continuity and change. In fact, both continuity and change were the concerns of the very first longitudinal growth study (Scammon, 1927) which took place over two hundred years ago. Many questions related to continuity may be explored; they concern, for the larger part, dimensional growth and problems of growth assessment, growth prediction, and growth evaluation. Whether small babies remain small as children, whether small children are still small as adolescents, and whether differences in the duration of growth (or the magnitude of the adolescent spurt) may bring dimensionally small school-age boys and girls to average or above-average size as adults are all very practical concerns.

Very early, therefore, students of physical growth and development directed attention to sources of continuity and to regularities in the directions of change. By investigating siblings rather than isolated children, and then siblings in family-line context, they were able to clarify the familial nature of continuities as well as the family-line similarities in change. Of course, tall parents tend to have tall children and short parents tend to have short children, but family-line similarities in growth path also become apparent. Some women have large babies who become small adults. Some families tend to have developmentally advanced infants who are nevertheless retarded in maturational timing. With two-generational longitudinal growth data available for study, it was even possible to show parent-child continuities in ossification timing and in the sequence or order of such maturational events. Comparing relative growth rates of major long bones made it possible to demonstrate developmental continuities in relative size or

113

proportions, as well as familial changes in both size and proportions, and family-line continuities in the rates of change.

Familial and Situational Sources of Continuity and Change

Yet it scarcely escaped notice that growth continuities and change were unequally distributed with reference to socioeconomic class and to race, ethnicity, and national origins. In prewar Czarist Russia, growth investigations observed that children's sizes could be grouped according to paternal education, the single exception being the children of blacksmiths (who were taller and heavier than paternal education would predict). American growth investigations, following the children of immigrants, discovered major dimensional differences and changes according to the country of origin.

Such studies, which are being conducted in the present day with increasing attention to nutritional status, are directed to the sources of continuities and the factors that direct developmental change. We now realize the extent to which caloric deprivation can slow growth, delay development, and delay the end of "adolescence." Families, we find, may have small children for reasons that involve nutritional knowledge, food utilization, and attitudes toward both eating and exercise. Other families, even of comparable incomes and education, may speed dimensional growth and developmental timing by pushing calories, by using food as a reward, and by encouraging energy conservation rather than active energy expenditure.

Thus, continuities in growth and development (including continuities in fatness) may be familial yet not necessarily genetic. Some changes in size and proportions may be both familial and genetic, while still other aspects of change may demonstrate continuities that transcend time and space.

Continuities and Change within Individuals

To some extent, large or long newborn babies tend to remain large or long as they move into childhood. This simple phenomenon, continuity in the sense of the present volume, is termed *channelization* by most American investigators in physical growth and *canalization* by the English and some others.

Continuity (or channelization or canalization) in size or weight is of both practical as well as theoretical importance. It is of practical importance in growth appraisal, by the Boston, Iowa, or National Center for Health Statistics (NCHS) growth charts. Indeed, all growth charts assume some degree of channelization; otherwise the percentiles have no operational value in following growth. Systems of bone age appraisal (skeletal age appraisal) also assume some degree of continuity, in biological as apart from chronological timing. Stature prediction, a specialized but important application of growth research, also assumes some degree of continuity—otherwise the predictions are not predictions at all.

Now canalization (or continuity) does occur within set temporal limits. Size at birth (for normal term infants) is a fairly good predictor of size during the first seven years of life, as exemplified by the black females of figure 4.1. Children in the lower weight percentiles gener-

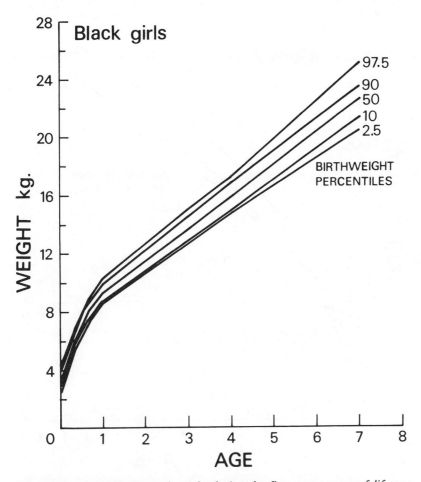

Figure 4.1. *Channelization of weight during the first seven years of life as shown in over four thousand black female participants in the NINCDS collaborative study. With sufficiently large samples, boys and girls of different birthweight percentiles tend to different weights and lengths through the school years.*

Stanley M. Garn

ally remain in the lower weight percentiles and infants of the higher weight percentiles tend to remain in the higher weight percentiles through the early school years. Moreover, since dimensions and weights are all highly correlated during the growing years, the starting percentile in one dimension tends to be characterized by continuity in a second dimension as shown in figure 4.2. (Figures 4.1 and 4.2 are each based on over four thousand children followed in truly longitudinal fashion.)

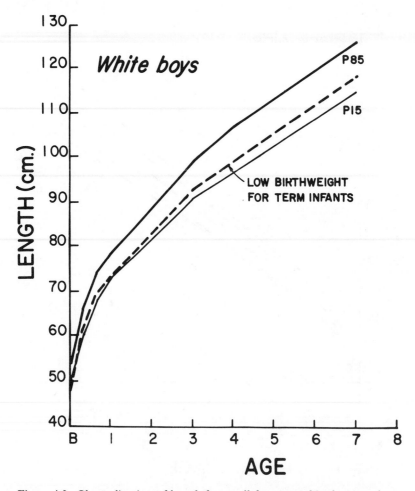

Figure 4.2. *Channelization of length for small-for-term white boys as shown in over four thousand white male participants in the NINCDS collaborative study. Though small-for-term infants may not remain comparably small throughout the growth period and eventually approximate the fiftieth percentile, the small do remain small during the first seven years of life.*

Such continuity as demonstrated in these two figures, from the largest longitudinal study (the NINCDS collaborative study), introduces a further modification to all traditional growth charts. Since birth size is a major determinant of size through 7 years, it follows that the accuracy of the growth charts' predictions may be increased considerably if they include different lines or different "channels" according to size at birth (Garn, Shaw, and McCabe, 1977). Having demonstrated continuity, we may use continuity to improve growth assessment, at least for term infants apart from those prematurely or postmaturely born!

At the same time, few intraindividual dimensional and developmental continuities actually persist from birth right through maturity. Except at the extremes of size, the big (or small) full-term infant rarely achieves equally big (or small) adult dimensions. Many a bouncing heavyweight of a baby ends as a size-diminished adult. Many a truly small neonate attains above-average adult stature. (Remember the over-sized bully of our grade-school days. How big is that bully now? Remember also, Mickey Rooney once was Andy Hardy.)

The lack of complete dimensional continuity from birth through maturity, however, may not be just regression toward the mean. Rather, as we now understand growth, it can represent a different kind of continuity related to growth duration. A developmentally advanced subteen may be larger earlier (by virtue of physiologic advancement) yet smaller later because of premature growth cessation. (Remember Andy Hardy?) Conversely, a short or small child who is developmentally retarded may well attain average or even above-average size if growth is long maintained. These possibilities will be explored in greater detail in later sections, especially when we consider menarcheal timing.

Several other factors may explain the lack of complete dimensional continuity. A baby may be large because that baby had the advantage of a large placenta or even a large uterus. These advantages may not long persist in postnatal time. Another baby may well be size-reduced because of placental insufficiency or intrauterine competition. Although there are long-term effects of placental size, uterine size, or a shared uterus, as with twins and other multiple births, the postnatal environment and the genetic endowment introduce new continuities of their own.

Of course there are some continuities in size, clearly demonstrated in long-term perspective. Over any five-year interval between birth and early adolescence, both dimensional and developmental continuities are sufficiently real to justify the percentile lines on the growth charts and to warrant stature prediction. Over a longer time period, however, differences in maturity status inevitably intervene, so that the large may become the small (given earlier maturity) and the small may end up large (given later maturity). Dr. Alex Roche, whose stature predictions are the most complete of them all, does not presume to predict adult stature from size at birth.

Dimensional Continuities between Generations

It is no secret that tall parents have tall children and that short parents have short children. This is an example of intergenerational dimensional continuity, not altered by intergenerational secular changes. While there are complications at both ends of the size continuum, parent-child correlations and two-parent or mid-parent-child correlations are of the approximate order that might be expected for polygenic inheritance (Garn and Bailey, 1978; Garn, Robinow, and Bailey, 1979).

From longitudinal growth studies, the Fels study in particular, it is also possible to document parent-child continuities in ossification timing given a parent and a child at the same age (using stored longitudinal data). Early parental advancement in ossification is associated with early advancement of the children, and vice versa (Garn and Shamir, 1958). Parent-child similarities and continuities in menarcheal timing are another example.

The parent-child correlation in height has obvious implications for growth assessment and growth evaluation. There is need for parent-specific growth tables so that we do not evaluate the dimensional growth of a child in a dimensional near-vacuum. Conventional growth tables and growth charts (Stuart-Stevenson, Meredith, or even NCHS) quite ignore parental size. In application, they may do a disservice to the progeny of both tall and short parents through facilitating inaccurate predictions.

Parent-specific growth charts and growth tables not only illustrate dimensional continuities between generations but also place them in a useful perspective. With such charts or tables we can better estimate the growth progress of the children of the tall as against the progeny of the short. Table 4.1 reprints in detail the growth progress of children of different parental size combinations (Garn and Rohmann, 1966). Similar tables and charts have been developed for English and continental families by J. M. Tanner, H. Goldstein, and R. H. Whitehouse (1970) and for San Francisco area families by J. Wingerd, I. K. Solomon, and E. J. Schoen (1973).

Such parent-specific growth charts and tables are most useful in the growth appraisal and growth evaluation of the children of homogamous (similar) matings. Tall parents (tall X tall) tend to produce tall

Table 4.1. Parent-specific height standards for boys using parental midpoint stature $\left[\dfrac{\text{father} + \text{mother}}{2}\right]$.[a]

	Parental midpoint (cm)								
Age	163	165	167	169	171	173	175	177	178
Birth	47.1	49.7	50.3	50.0	48.3	50.7	50.0	51.5	51.4
0-1	52.7	54.6	54.7	57.6	53.2	53.6	52.2	55.6	55.9
0-3	58.9	60.8	60.0	62.2	57.4	60.8	61.2	61.4	62.6
0-6	65.1	66.2	66.8	67.4	65.8	70.2	69.0	70.2	70.3
0-9	70.7	72.9	73.8	73.2	71.0	74.8	75.2	77.1	75.7
1-0	73.1	75.6	75.7	75.1	73.4	76.6	77.1	79.6	77.8
1-6	79.9	82.4	81.7	82.0	81.2	82.6	83.4	86.8	85.2
2-0	85.4	87.2	87.0	87.4	87.8	88.0	88.9	92.0	91.3
2-6	88.8	91.3	92.0	92.1	93.2	93.5	94.0	96.7	96.0
3-0	93.2	94.9	96.1	96.0	97.2	98.1	98.3	100.7	99.9
3-6	96.3	98.4	100.0	99.5	101.0	102.3	102.6	104.5	103.5
4-0	99.5	102.2	103.5	103.1	104.6	106.0	106.3	108.0	107.0
4-6	102.7	105.4	107.1	106.6	108.0	109.6	109.6	111.4	110.4
5-0	105.6	108.5	110.6	110.0	111.5	113.2	112.7	114.6	113.8
5-6	108.3	111.3	113.4	112.7	114.5	116.3	115.8	117.4	116.8
6-0	110.9	114.1	116.4	115.4	117.4	119.4	118.7	120.4	119.8
6-6	113.6	116.9	119.3	118.4	120.3	122.4	121.7	123.4	122.8
7-0	116.2	119.7	122.3	121.3	123.2	125.6	124.6	126.4	125.6
7-6	118.9	122.5	125.1	124.3	126.1	128.8	127.6	129.5	128.4
8-0	121.6	125.0	127.8	126.8	128.8	131.6	130.4	132.8	131.6
8-6	124.2	127.6	130.7	129.3	131.5	134.9	133.2	135.9	134.6
9-0	126.9	130.4	133.3	131.9	134.1	138.0	136.0	138.8	137.5
9-6	129.9	132.9	136.1	134.6	136.9	141.0	138.8	142.0	140.5
10-0	132.5	135.8	138.8	137.4	139.8	143.8	141.5	145.3	143.2
10-6	135.6	138.8	141.5	140.3	142.6	146.8	144.3	148.6	146.0
11-0	138.5	141.8	144.1	143.0	145.4	149.9	146.8	151.9	148.9
11-6	141.6	144.9	146.9	145.6	148.3	152.8	149.6	155.4	151.6
12-0	144.7	148.0	149.7	148.4	151.4	155.7	152.4	158.8	154.5
12-6	147.7	151.1	152.6	151.6	154.6	158.3	155.8	162.6	157.5
13-0	151.0	154.2	155.7	154.9	158.0	161.7	159.6	166.3	160.5
13-6	154.5	157.7	158.9	158.1	161.6	164.6	163.6	170.1	163.8
14-0	158.8	161.7	162.3	161.6	165.7	167.6	167.8	173.4	166.9
14-6	162.6	164.9	165.9	164.8	169.6	170.3	172.0	175.2	171.3
15-0	165.8	168.1	169.1	167.9	172.9	173.0	174.7	176.4	175.2
15-6	168.0	171.3	172.0	170.6	174.5	175.6	175.8	177.0	178.6
16-0	169.4	173.3	174.3	172.8	177.3	177.5	176.6	177.4	181.2
16-6	170.3	174.2	175.8	174.4	178.4	178.7	177.3	177.4	182.8

(continued)

Table 4.1 continued

Age	Parental midpoint (cm)								
	163	*165*	*167*	*169*	*171*	*173*	*175*	*177*	*178*
17-0	170.9	174.7	176.8	175.4	179.2	179.4	177.8	177.5	184.3
17-6	171.2	174.9	174.4	176.0	180.0	179.9	178.2	177.6	185.4
18-0	171.5	175.0	177.9	176.2	180.5	180.2	178.6	177.6	186.3

Source: Garn and Rohmann (1966).
a. For other parent-specific growth charts see text.

children, for whom conventional growth charts are hardly suitable. Short parents (short X short) generally produce short children, for whom the Stuart-Stevenson, Meredith, or NCHS charts are scarcely applicable. Intergenerational continuities are thus confirmed. But if the parents are of opposite dimensional extremes (tall X short, short X tall), dimensional variability of the children is then increased, and these "new" parent-specific charts are no better than the old.

Such parent-specific height and weight tables that account for the parents' sizes are of practical and theoretical use within the limits stated. Practically, they make better use of continuities. Theoretically (following theory), they confirm continuities. They might also lead us to assume that dimensions are primarily under genetic control, since the tall beget the tall and the short beget the short. Yet parents and their children share more than genes in common, and there may be more to parent-child resemblances and continuities than the genetic hypothesis alone allows. (For discussion see Garn and Bailey, 1978; Garn, Robinow, and Bailey, 1979).

Strategies in Explaining Intragenerational and Intergenerational Continuities

Intraindividual and intergenerational continuities in growth rates and developmental timing are attributed to genetic control mechanisms operating at the target-organ level (such as bones and muscles), at the endocrine level, or at both levels. The fact that sibling resemblances in size exceed parent-child resemblances in size is in accordance with the proportion of genes held in common, as is the often-repeated demonstration that monozygotic twins are more alike than dizygotic twins, who are in effect simultaneous siblings. Such intragenerational and intergenerational continuities can also be demonstrated for individual bones or contiguous bones, accounting for similarities in segmental lengths and differences in proportions. As shown over fifty years ago, some "racial" differences in relative limb lengths may be demonstrated rather early in fetal development. And in some malformation syndromes, marked differences in limb proportions can be documented very early in prenatal time, with patterned continuities continuing well into adult life (cf. Poznanski et al., 1977).

But it is obvious that some intragenerational continuities in growth rates and some intergenerational continuities in size must also stem from the shared environment, with the caloric balance of major importance. A reduced caloric intake or an increased caloric expenditure can restrict growth rates and limit ultimate size and, if shared by siblings, can account for some proportion of dimensional continuities and some proportion of resemblance in growth rates. To the extent that parents and children share nutritional deprivation, or even parsimonious attitudes toward food and eating, dimensional and developmental continuities may then be familial but not necessarily genetic (Garn and Bailey, 1978; Garn, Robinow, and Bailey, 1979; Garn, Cole, and Bailey, 1977).

As a practical strategy, the question of genetic versus nongenetic sources of family-line continuities in size, growth rates, and developmental timing may be resolved by comparison of genetically unrelated individuals living together. (This strategy's complement would involve comparison of genetically related individuals living apart.) Genetically unrelated individuals living together include (a) "parents" not genetically related to children and (b) genetically unrelated "sibling" pairs.

When these situations occur through adoption, the strategy obviously involves a simple comparison between parent and unrelated (adopted) child, or between unrelated (adopted) siblings. However, both situations (a) and (b) may result from remarriage as well as adoption. Homes in which a child is genetically related to one parent and genetically unrelated to the other are common; therefore, with but two parents and one child it is possible to make a simultaneous comparison of a biological parent-child pair and an unrelated parent-child pair. If both parents have a biological child from a previous marriage, the comparison of four such parent-child pairs as well as of a pair of genetically unrelated siblings is possible (figure 4.3). Further strategic variables then include (1) the age at adoption (or entrance into the nonrelated family situation), (2) the duration of living together, and (3) the age at separation, if this occurs.

Using the "parent" versus adopted child comparison (in contrast to comparisons of biologically verified parent-child pairs) provides evidence that adopted children may come to resemble their adopted parents in a great many dimensional variables. In similar fashion,

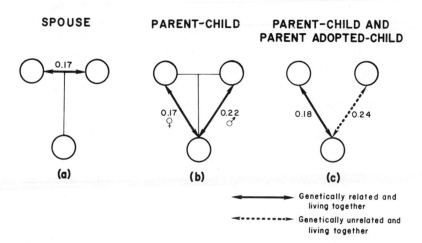

Figure 4.3. *Strategies for ascertaining the environmental component of intergenerational continuities through the study of genetically related and genetically unrelated individuals living together. As shown here for the triceps fatfolds, spouse fatfold correlations (a) are the same order of magnitude as parent-child correlations (b). Similarly, correlations between parents and their biological children are not notably different from fatfold correlations between parents and adopted children (c). Such findings, which pertain to many conventional measures of size and body mass, are indicative of the influence of the shared environment on dimensional and developmental continuities. (Garn and Bailey, 1978.)*

adoptive (genetically unrelated) siblings sharing a common environment may evidence greater similarity than the genetic explanation alone would allow (see Garn and Bailey, 1978, for references; Garn, Bailey, and Cole, 1976; Garn, Bailey, Cole, and Higgins, 1978).

Thus family-line intragenerational and intergenerational continuities in growth rates, size, and developmental timing may not be exclusively genetic. To a greater or lesser degree, there are nongenetic sources of continuity (just as there are nongenetic sources of change). The study of genetically unrelated individuals living together, which includes most husbands and wives, constitutes an important strategy in ascertaining the sources of family-line intragenerational and intergenerational continuities in size and development.

The Secular Trend: An Example of Change

Simply by collecting and comparing dimensional data, decade after decade, the *secular* (or generational) trend was discovered. As was especially well-documented in the United States over a century ago and has since been reported in detail for hundreds of different groups worldwide (table 4.2), secular change is of major importance

Table 4.2. Secular changes in bodily dimensions and menarcheal timing.

Author	*Comment*
	The secular trend
Boas (1912a, b)	Combined secular change and migration effect on 18,000 children of immigrants.
Bowles (1932)	Changes, largely in old Americans, since the Revolutionary War, changes in Eastern college undergraduates since 1880.
Boas (1940)	The secular change in anthropometric measurements.
Meredith and Meredith (1942)	The secular change in Toronto school children since Boas's report of 1898.
Trotter and Gleser (1951)	Secular change in blacks and whites, 1840-1950.
Howe and Schiller (1952)	Wartime interruptions in the secular trend in Germany and other countries.
Meredith (1963)	The secular change in stature and weight in the United States, 1880-1960.
Bakwin and McLaughlin (1964), Garn and French (1967)	The end of the secular trend in favored groups.
Damon (1965)	Maximum secular change in Neapolitans in the Boston area.
	Menarcheal timing
Popenoe (1928), Gould and Gould (1932)	Mother-daughter and sister-sister resemblances in menarcheal age.
Garn and Haskell (1959, 1960)	Effect of fatness on maturational timing of children of both sexes.
Tanner (1962), Eveleth and Tanner (1978, pp. 212-220)	Reviews and references on the secular trend in menarche.
Damon et al. (1969)	Accuracy of recall in two-generational mother-daughter comparison.
Frisch and Revelle (1971)	Early exposition of the "critical weight" hypothesis, since repeatedly modified.
Garn, Cole, and Wainwright (1978)	Evidence that family-line resemblances in menarcheal timing are not due to socioeconomic status or fatness in common.

in every developed country. The secular trend is also of importance in emerging countries and to previously marginal groups. Even the South African Bushmen (beloved of anthropologists and *National Geographic* readers) have undergone a secular trend in stature since 1915.

Briefly stated, the secular change involves increasing body size. Children are taller, adolescents are taller, and adults are taller, at a rate approximating 1 centimeter per decade, or 1 inch every twenty-five years. As a result of this secular change, we now stand some 10 centimeters taller than our Civil War ancestors, and we are also far heavier. For all Westernized countries, this secular change has involved size (stature), weight, and bodily proportions. Japanese born since 1946 have evidenced an especially large secular increase in size and weight and proportions.

There are very real and important questions concerning the sources of these secular dimensional changes. We do know that bigger mothers produce bigger babies. A changed infant diet, with emphasis on cow's milk, may well also be a factor. Changes in both energy intake and in energy expenditure play a role as well. The school bus, improved home heating, the availability of snacks, and even the shift to spectator sports may all contribute to this trend.

Economic implications of the secular trend in body size may be given in terms of food, fiber, and fuel. Bigger people need more food to fuel them, and this has further implications for the world food supply. Being bigger, they also require more fiber to cover them; this has important implications for wool growers, cotton planters, and producers of synthetic yarns. Also, larger people require larger work space, larger home space, and more space in travel—all of which demand additional fuel.

The point is that there has been a very major change in size and proportions (and developmental rates). Because stature and weight are given as hard numbers, and because radiographic measures of developmental status can be expressed in absolute terms, we can document change and rates of change. We can also express worldwide continuities in the rates of dimensional and developmental change over the past century and more.

Effects of the Secular Change in Menarcheal Timing

Nearly coincident with the discovery of the secular change in body size was the discovery of the secular trend in the age at menarche, that is, the timing of the first menstruation. As stature and body weight increased, over time, the age at menarche decreased from 16 or more a bit over a century ago to 13 and less over the last decade or so, in approximately linear fashion (see table 4.2 for references concerning these discoveries).

This decrease in the age at menarche has influenced aspects of many American conventions. Educational policy has been undergoing changes, as some school authorities have considered a need to return to a four-year high school program in order to become more "socially appropriate." The decrease in the age at menarche has had its effect on clothing design and clothing tariffs, on the cosmetic industry, and on the reading habits and entertainment interests of the "adolescent" population.

Such a decrease in menarcheal timing, which has characterized all developed nations, is no less important to the world economy than is the secular increase in body size. But of far greater worldwide importance than the immediate effects in body size on the world economy are the future implications of the decrease in menarcheal timing.

The earlier age at menarche has led to an earlier attainment of fertility and to a prolongation of the fertile period. Since the age at menopause has not decreased (and may have increased somewhat), the capacity for reproduction now begins earlier and stretches over a longer span of years. As a result, the potential for population expansion is now greater than ever before. Even where contraception is widely practiced, the increase in the number of teenage pregnancies may be attributed in part to the secular decrease in the age at sexual maturation. Despite the transient period of adolescent infertility (which extends approximately one year beyond menarche), there are now many 12-year-olds and even 11-year-olds who are capable of maintaining a conceptus. As a result of the secular decrease in the age at menarche, there is an increasing number of mothers who are ill prepared for the task of mothering, thus creating both biological and psychological hazards to themselves and their progeny.

Problems of Continuity and Change in Menarcheal Timing

While the secular (or generational) change in the age at menarche thus emerges as a special example of change in physical (or biological) growth and development, there are necessarily many investigative problems of continuity and change in menarcheal timing remaining to be explored.

One problem is both descriptive and comparative—that of obtaining long-term data on the secular change in menarche in the United States. Recent menarcheal data from the United States are meager compared with data from Europe, especially for groups other than those of European descent, "whites" in census terminology. It is one purpose of this chapter to provide new recent data on the secular change in the age at menarche from a number of large-scale population surveys.

A second problem, that of continuity in change, has to do with the effect of socioeconomic status (SES) on the secular decrease in menarcheal timing. Menarche is earlier in more affluent girls and later in those who are poorer. Another purpose of this chapter, then, is to provide new information on the effect of socioeconomic status—as variously measured—on menarcheal timing and the secular decrease in the age at menarche.

A third problem scarcely explored so far is the long-term consequences of differences in menarcheal timing. This is a problem of continuity despite change, for it can be shown that early-maturing females and late-maturing females differ in many respects, even sixty years after the event of menarche! New data will be offered on a long-term retrospective basis.

A fourth problem, still related to menarcheal timing, is continuity across the generations and continuity across the sexes. Are there differences in growth and development between the children of early-maturing mothers and the children of late-maturing mothers? For that matter, do the children of early-maturing mothers mature earlier than the children of late-maturing mothers?

A fifth problem is again continuity in menarcheal timing, as seen in mothers and daughters and in sisters alike. Mother-daughter and sister-sister similarities in menarcheal timing have been reported, but the question is, Do these result from genes held in common or simply from similarities in the way of life?

A sixth problem, involving both change and continuity, concerns the interactions between fatness and menarcheal timing. The question to pose is whether nutritional level (and stored fat) is merely causally related to menarcheal timing or whether, in exactly converse fashion, menarcheal timing has both retrospective and prospective relationships to fatness and to obesity.

These questions are questions that will be resolved in this chapter on continuity and change. They bear on menarcheal timing, specifically, but they also bear on continuity and change in physical or biological growth and development in general. They bear on boys as well as on girls, with respect to both size and maturational timing. They show how continuities and changes may be related, that there are continuities in change (in biological growth and development), and changes in continuities. Finally, they relate to basic problems of maturational timing, to the long-term secular change, and to mechanisms that yield continuities and processes that yield change, over time, in human growth and development.

New Data for the Study of Continuity and Change in Menarcheal Timing

This investigative report is based on menarcheal age records, anthropometric and developmental data, and measurements of outer fatness on 85,207 individuals from three major studies of broad scope and design. (A numerical breakdown of the samples in these studies is given in table 4.3.) The first of these, the Tecumseh Community Health Survey of the University of Michigan, provides menarcheal data for 3,524 females over 15 years of age, while the mother-child comparisons include 1,488 mothers and 3,543 children (all serologically verified). A unique feature of this study is that older children were available for the investigation of maternal menarcheal timing as it relates to the size and fatness of the offspring.

The second of these is the Ten-State Nutrition Survey of 1968-1970, which involves data from ten states and New York City. Menarcheal data are given for 10,194 females aged 15 and over, though certain early ages are also included in parts of the data analysis. Mother-children comparisons include 1,702 mothers and 3,454 children. These latter samples are restricted to individuals providing full anthropometric and developmental data, particularly for ossification timing (derived from radiographs). The third study involves the Collaborative Perinatal Project of the National Institutes of Neurological and Communicative Disorders and Stroke (NINCDS). Prime data are derived from 18,866 records of menarcheal timing and for 18,866 paired mother-child records (with serial anthropometric measurements on normal-term singling children through age 7).

Table 4.3. Sample sizes in the menarcheal study.

Data base	Number of menarcheal records	Number of mothers	Number of children
Tecumseh (Michigan) Community Health Survey	3,524	1,488	3,543
Ten-State Nutrition Survey[a]	14,898	1,702	3,454
Collaborative Perinatal Project NINCDS[a]	18,866[b]	18,866[b]	18,866[b]
Total	37,288	22,056	25,863

a. Blacks, whites, Mexican-Americans, and Puerto Ricans analyzed separately.

b. Mothers of normal-term singlings only.

The Tecumseh (Michigan) data were for individuals of Northwest European ancestry living in that community. For the Ten-State data base, data on blacks, whites, Puerto Ricans, and Mexican-Americans were separately tabulated and analyzed, though data on blacks and whites are of primary interest here. NINCDS data included blacks, whites, "Orientals," and Puerto Ricans, though blacks and whites are the primary concern because of sample size.

In all three data bases we have given attention to socioeconomic status (SES) as variously measured by such indexes as income, per capita income, education, and occupation. Such division was necessary because the poor are later-maturing: far too few research studies take SES into account.

Anthropometric measurements include stature (or recumbent length in the earlier years) and weight, as well as several fatfolds for the Ten-State and the Tecumseh studies. Fatfolds, sometimes called "skinfolds," are objective, independent measures of outer fatness.

The independent measure of maturational timing, appropriate for both sexes, was the presence or absence of the adductor sesamoid as seen on postero-anterior hand radiographs. This highly objective measure was employed only for the Ten-State Nutrition Survey, with separate analyses for blacks and whites because ossification timing differs between populations even after correction for income, education, and occupation.

More detailed references are given for specific methodologies; three references apply to the major studies. For the Ten-State Nutrition Survey the key reference is the four-volume Department of Health, Education and Welfare report *The Ten-State Nutrition Survey* (1972). For the NINCDS Collaborative Perinatal Study, the appropriate reference is H. R. Niswander and M. Gordon (1972). The official description of the Tecumseh (Michigan) Community Health Study is that of J. A. Napier, B. C. Johnson, and F. H. Epstein (1971).

A Note on the Validity of Menarcheal Recall Data

Except in truly longitudinal studies of growing children, where menarcheal ages can be ascertained in prospective fashion (and within narrow age limits), age at menarche is ordinarily obtained in purely retrospective fashion (by recollection). This method of obtaining data introduces the problem of class intervals, since the data are customarily reported as of the previous birthday. Nonetheless, with sufficiently large samples, the data can be corrected by adding half the class interval either prior to the data reduction or in the final graphic and tabular representations. Consequently, the one-year class interval need not pose any particular statistical problem as compared with exact age information on menarcheal timing.

Some authors have argued that menarcheal-age studies and studies relating to the secular trend are invalid because of random errors in recollection. This criticism can be answered in several ways. First, it is possible to compare "recollected" ages, obtained on different occasions. Second, it is possible to compare prospective and retrospective ages at menarche, obtained at different times from the same sample. A. Damon et al. (1969) have addressed many of these problems.

A third set of tests which aids in defending the accuracy of the data involves comparison of different data sets with attention to internal consistencies. If, in numerous studies conducted in different countries and in different decades, secular changes in menarcheal timing are comparable, then it is unlikely that random errors in recollection are at work. If, in numerous studies, the effects of income, or education, or occupation are very much the same, it is again unlikely that systematic errors in recollecting the age at menarche are at fault.

In this study of continuity and change in menarcheal timing, we find that fatness (even as late as age 70) relates to reported menarcheal timing, in blacks, in whites, and in other groups. Mothers who report early menarcheal ages have sons who are systematically early in ossification timing. Such internal consistencies, tested very early in our data analysis, are unlikely to be the product of either random or systematic errors in recollection. Since it is difficult to imagine a bias in maternal recollection of menarcheal age that would systematically relate to a covert phenomenon visible on radiographs of their sons and daughters, internal consistency provides an operational test of validity in these two-generational data.

The Secular Change in Menarcheal Timing in the United States

Having reviewed worldwide (or generational) decrease in the age at menarche, and noting the average decrease of three years over the last century in Europe claimed in some summarizations, the first task was to provide new, updated information for the United States. There was need for a new, comparable estimate of the amount and rate of change and for separate estimates for different population samples and different socioeconomic groupings. There was no reason to believe that the age at menarche would decrease at the same rate for the poor and the affluent or that data on whites, blacks, Mexican-Americans, and other groups would prove identical.

We have examined our data, therefore, and made necessary exclusions. The Collaborative Perinatal Program (NINCDS) covered too few birth decades to meter indications of long-term trends. Data from the Ten-State Nutrition Survey were sufficient for blacks, whites, and Mexican-Americans but not for Puerto Ricans. For the most part data were sufficient for the six birth decades from 1900 through 1950. Use of the 1960 birth decade was inadvisable for both the Ten-State Survey of 1968-1970 and the Tecumseh Community Health Survey, at least for Examination Round 1. In all, our sample amounted to slightly under fourteen thousand for this stage of the study, with decade-specific means uniformly calculated and uniformly adjusted by +0.5 years.

The results, given in table 4.4, are divided into two major survey groupings (Ten-State and Tecumseh), and the former are divided into whites, blacks, and Mexican-Americans. The degree of agreement is surprisingly high. The results show a decade-specific mean of about 13.9 years for birth decade 1900. They also show a systematic decrease after birth decade 1900 and a mean age at menarche close to 13.0 years for the 1950 birth decade. Using other computational methods (medians rather than means, probability estimates) the results are very much the same, after correction.

It seems safe, therefore, to say that the age at menarche has decreased from approximately 14.0 years (in 1913-14) for the 1900 birth decade to 13.0 years (in 1962-63) for the 1950 birth decade. This decrease, amounting to 1.0 year in half a century, extrapolated to 2.0 years per century, is surprisingly similar for whites, blacks, and Mexi-

Table 4.4. The secular trend in the age at menarche (M) in four recent U.S. samples.[a]

| | Ten-State | | | | | | Tecumseh | |
| | White | | Black | | Mexican-American | | White | |
Birth decade	N	M	N	M	N	M	N	M
1890	—	—	—	—	—	—	162	13.6
1900	688	13.6	274	13.5	33	13.4	246	13.3
1910	782	13.3	434	13.4	44	13.2	371	13.1
1920	925	13.1	588	13.2	119	13.5	597	13.0
1930	972	12.9	676	13.2	207	13.2	690	12.8
1940	1289	12.5	785	12.9	226	12.9	487	12.6
1950[b]	1470	12.6	1302	12.7	366	12.5	—	—

a. For corrected or adjusted ages add 0.5 years. Totel $N = 13,746$.
b. Not applicable to Tecumseh Community Health Survey Record.

can-Americans, and for both the Tecumseh and the Ten-State Survey data. Given the sample sizes ($N = 995$-$6,135$) and the uniform method of calculation, this estimate of the secular trend in the age at menarche seems valid.

Figure 4.4 pictures the secular decrease in the age at menarche for 2,553 females in the Tecumseh community and for birth decades 1890 through 1940. Raw (uncorrected) menarcheal ages are given on the left and adjusted (corrected) menarcheal ages on the right. This sample is selected for graphic illustration simply because it is a single community, with genetic continuity, and with the older women the mothers (and grandmothers) of the younger women. In fact, figure 4.4 is unique in being the only representation of the secular change in menarcheal timing within a single U.S. community that I know of.

Socioeconomic Effects

The data given in table 4.4 (for whites, blacks, and Mexican-Americans) and the tidy trend line in figure 4.4 provide a convincing estimate of the magnitude of the secular decrease in menarcheal timing over the past half century. In fact, they also hint at the "plateau" effect; that is, the slowing up of the secular decrease in the last few decades. But the table and the trend line deliberately ignore socioeco-

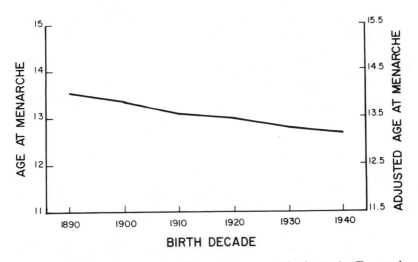

Figure 4.4. *Secular (generational) trend in menarcheal age in Tecumseh (Michigan) women arranged by birth decade. In this series of more than twenty-five hundred white women, the fifty-year decrease in the age at menarche approximates 1.0 years, equivalent to 2.0 years per century.*

nomic status and its bearing on the age at menarche and the secular change in the age at menarche.

Fortunately, all three survey studies contain socioeconomic information. The Ten-State Survey included income and family size and therefore per capita income. The Tecumseh Community Health Survey included a variety of educational measures as well. The Collaborative Perinatal Project (NINCDS) further included education, occupation, and income and all the makings of the Bureau of Census Socioeconomic Index. With such a wealth of socioeconomic data available, only a sampling can be included here (table 4.5).

The first sampling is given for over 5,000 black and white women in the Ten-State Survey and for two per capita income groupings— poverty level and below, and median income and above. This comparison, which intentionally leaves out the grouping between the poverty level and the median, has the great advantage of comparing blacks and whites at comparable income levels. And the results of this comparison are simple enough. First, the income-restricted comparisons show the same kind of secular trend in menarcheal age illustrated in table 4.4 and figure 4.4. Second, these income-restricted comparisons provide an indication of the socioeconomic effect—which may be of the order of 0.4-0.5 years in whites.

We can express the results in purely graphic form, as in figure 4.5.

Table 4.5. Menarcheal ages (M) for 5,040 poverty-level and median-income black and white women arranged by birth decade.[a]

	Whites				Blacks			
	Poverty level[b]		Median income[c]		Poverty level[b]		Median income[c]	
Birth decade	N	M	N	M	N	M	N	M
1900	123	14.0	153	13.5	134	13.5	18	13.7
1910	128	13.6	289	13.4	182	13.6	39	12.7
1920	127	13.7	375	12.9	246	13.4	65	12.9
1930	203	13.1	225	12.7	383	13.3	46	13.3
1940	220	12.7	299	12.5	406	12.9	50	12.7
1950	270	12.7	259	12.4	754	12.6	46	12.9

a. All data are from the Ten-State Nutrition Survey of 1968-1970 (1972).
b. Poverty level and below, $799 per capita.
c. $2,400 per capita and above.

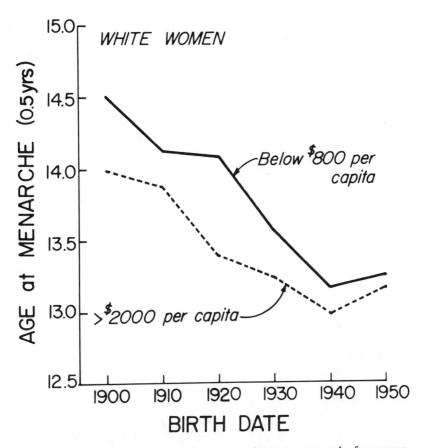

Figure 4.5. *Effect of socioeconomic status on the age at menarche for women in the Ten-State Nutrition Survey. As shown here for white women, those of higher per capita income (dashed line) report a systematically lower age at menarche than those below the poverty line (solid line). Education, occupation, and income show comparable relationships to menarcheal age.*

Three generalizations are clear. First, the secular trend in menarche is much the same for median-income women and for poverty-level women. Second, at all birth decades represented, median-income women report an earlier age at menarche. Third, in the Ten-State data, there seems to be a leveling off of the secular trend, as for birth decade 1940.

Attention to the Collaborative Perinatal Project (NINCDS) gives surprisingly similar information with respect to the effect of income (more specifically present income) on menarcheal age. The Tecumseh (Michigan) survey data confirm the existence of two secular trends, one for the poor and one for the more affluent. In the total-population context of the Tecumseh community with its notable intergenerational continuity, both educational level and economic level are related to the age at menarche. The menarcheal trend lines are parallel from birth dates 1890 to 1940. They evidence a downward trend, but they remain apart.

As we see it now, the poor and the more affluent have both decreased in the age at menarche, over the past half century. Over this same time period menarcheal age has remained systematically later for the poor or poverty-level girl and somewhat earlier for the girl having the advantage of a median per capita income or a high school education. We have insufficient data on the menarcheal ages of high-income women, from any of the survey populations, or on those having professional-level educations.

Continuities in Dimensional Differences between Early-Maturing and Late-Maturing Women

To summarize from a number of studies, early-maturing girls tend to be taller earlier in life but ultimately shorter, consistent with an earlier cessation of growth. Early-maturing girls tend to be heavier and fatter and apparently both heavier and fatter into the adult years. These observations open the opportunity to seek for continuities in all the data we have.

Turning first to the Tecumseh Community Health Survey, which contains data on a number of fatfolds, menarcheal age is clearly related to the level of fatness and vice versa. Taking data on over twenty-five hundred Tecumseh women, born between 1890 and 1940 reveals clear trends (table 4.6). When lean, medium, and obese Tecumseh women are compared with respect to the mean age at menarche (after grouping for birth decades), the lean women report the latest menarcheal ages and the obese women report the earliest menarcheal ages.

Studied in retrospective fashion, with fatfold measurements employed to separate the lean from the obese, the degree of continuity is remarkable. Even at age 70, and nearly fifty-five years after the attainment of menarche, obese Tecumseh women still report lower menarcheal ages than the lean—by 0.5 years or so.

If we turn to the Ten-State Survey (and to figure 4.6), the same trends are abundantly clear. Lean black women aged 15 and over are associated with later menarcheal ages, even into the seventh decade. Since the basis of comparison is the same, birth decade by birth decade, and since the definitions of "lean" and "obese" are similar in both illustrations, the comparisons between figure 4.6 and table 4.4 are striking. One survey of suitably large size confirms a second survey

Table 4.6. Menarcheal ages (M) of 2,590 women defined as lean, medium, or obese at the time of examination.[a]

Birth decade	Mean age at menarche					
	Lean[b]		Medium		Obese[b]	
	N	M	N	M	N	M
1890	18	12.8	127	13.6	16	13.9
1900	39	13.5	167	13.4	39	12.9
1910	51	13.1	267	13.1	52	12.9
1920	95	13.1	396	13.1	103	12.5
1930	113	13.1	468	12.7	108	12.6
1940	62	12.9	349	12.7	76	12.3

a. All data are for Tecumseh Community Survey, Round 1.

b. Lean and obese defined with respect to the fifteenth and eighty-fifth percentiles for triceps fatfolds for the birth decade given.

of ample size, even crossing race, socioeconomic status, and geographical location. In fact, figure 4.6 is indicative of the long-term differences in fatness between early-maturing and late-maturing women.

Figures 4.7 and 4.8, relating to stature and weight, may be taken together. Here turning to the Ten-State data, it is clear that early-maturing white women are shorter from age 20 through age 70. As shown in figure 4.8 for black women, early-maturing women (though shorter) are still heavier at all ages considered. These examples are selected—to save space—but the results are hardly equivocal. Black or white, early-maturing women are shorter and late-maturing women are taller, through the seventh decade at least. Black or white (and with similar trends for other groups) early-maturing women are heavier, at least through the seventh decade, in the Ten-State Survey data.

Exactly the same trends hold for the women in the massive Collaborative Perinatal Project (NINCDS). Though the range of birth decades is compressed, effectively 1930-1950, the trends are the same. Early-maturing women in the NINCDS survey prove to be heavier and at the same time shorter, having a markedly different height-to-weight ratio, or "ponderal index." The Tecumseh study also confirms these results, as illustrated in figure 4.9.

These data, drawn from three different population surveys, are utterly consistent. Studied in retrospective fashion, early-maturing

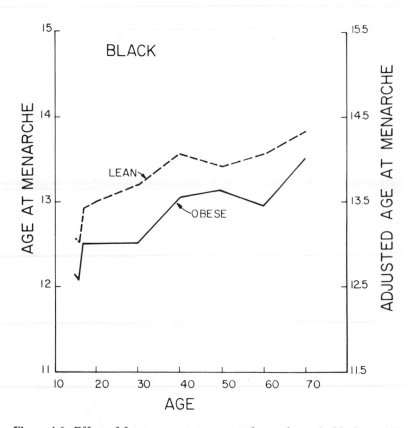

Figure 4.6. *Effect of fatness on age at menarche as shown in black participants in the Ten-State Nutrition Survey. From age 20 through the seventh decade, lean women (below the fifteenth percentile for fatness) report systematically later ages at menarche than do obese women (above the eighty-fifth percentile for fatness).*

woman are shorter but heavier and fatter. Retrospectively studied, late-maturing women prove to be taller in stature but lighter in weight and less fat as measured by triceps and subscapular fatfolds.

We are presented here with an unusual example of continuity, covering a full six birth decades, from 1900 on, and a range of ages through age 70. The continuity includes whites (from three survey studies), blacks from two survey studies, and Puerto Ricans, and Mexican-Americans, too. Without question, given the total sample size and the number of different subsamples, there is continuity in the dimensional differences between early-maturing and late-maturing women. However analyzed, menarcheal timing has long-term effects on size (stature), weight, and fatness, the last confirmed by fatfold measurements on the arms and the backs of thousands of women.

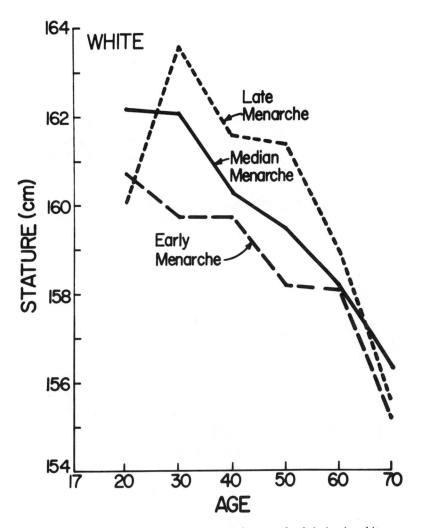

Figure 4.7. *Relationship between stature and menarcheal timing in white participants in the Ten-State Nutrition Survey. From the second decade through the sixth decade, late-maturing white women are approximately 2 centimeters taller than early-maturing women.*

Maternal Menarcheal Timing and the Growth Rate of the Children

Given the consistent dimensional differences between early-maturing and late-maturing women, including stature, weight, and fatfolds, one might anticipate dimensional differences in the children during either the growing years or adulthood, or both. Given the fact that early-maturing girls themselves are larger, at least until maturity,

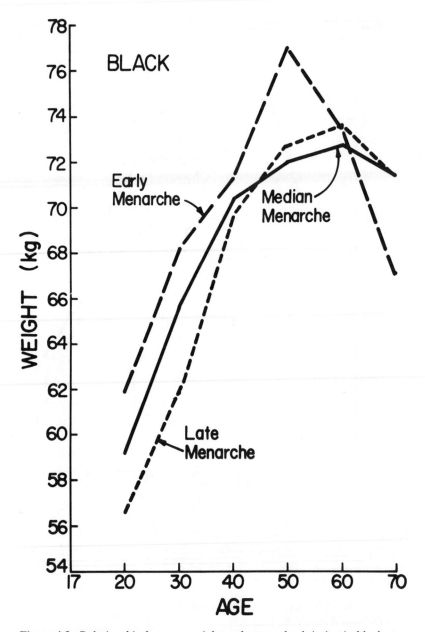

Figure 4.8. *Relationship between weight and menarcheal timing in black participants in the Ten-State Nutrition Survey. In this survey, as in the Tecumseh Community Health Survey and the Collaborative Perinatal Project (NINCDS), early-maturing women consistently weigh more than their late-maturing age-peers.*

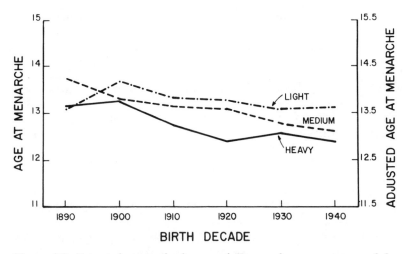

Figure 4.9. *Reported menarcheal ages of Tecumseh women arranged by weight groupings for birth decades 1890-1940. Heavy women (above the eighty-fifth percentile for weight) systematically report earlier menarcheal ages than do women of lower weight at the time of examination.*

while later-maturing girls are smaller (until maturity), one might expect differences in the relative growth rates of children thus arranged by maternal menarcheal timing.

Starting first with the boys and girls included in the National Collaborative Perinatal Project (NINCDS), it is indeed clear that the children of early-maturing women have dimensional advantages over the sons and daughters of late-maturing women, increasingly so with time. This statement holds true both for length and for weight, both for boys and for girls, and both for blacks and for whites. To save space in this chapter, documentation is given only for 3,048 normal, white, full-term singlings followed in fully longitudinal survey fashion from birth through 7.0 years. Comparing the sons and daughters of early-maturing mothers (the earliest 15%) and the sons and daughters of the latest-maturing women (the latest 15%) the trends are clear-cut, indeed, as shown in table 4.7.

For children in the Collaborative Perinatal Project, similar trends can be shown for stature as well as for weight and for the total sample (including those originally excluded on the basis of minor defects observable at birth). Very similar results occur when "fixed-age" cuts for maternal maturational timing are employed, generally defining "early" maturation as twelve years and less and "late" as age fourteen and beyond. Moreover, when the seven-year weight gains of the progeny of early-maturing and late-maturing mothers are compared,

Table 4.7. Comparative weight growth of children of early-maturing and late-maturing white mothers.[a]

| | Boys | | Girls | |
Age	Earliest 15%	Latest 15%	Earliest 15%	Latest 15%
Birth	3.43	3.43	3.28	3.26
0.33	6.77	6.77	6.21	6.14
0.66	9.04	9.03	8.42	8.26
1.00	10.25	10.29	9.71	9.49
3.00	14.88	14.66	14.31	13.83
4.00	16.91	16.82	16.56	15.96
7.00	24.15	23.45	24.01	22.61

a. Sample consists of 3,048 normal-term singlings drawn from the Collaborative Perinatal Project (NINCDS). All weights in kg.

even after attention to maternal birth decade, it is clear that the long-term weight gain of children of early-maturing mothers exceeds the seven-year weight gain of the children of late-maturing mothers by nearly 5%.

Very similar results hold for the data from the Ten-State Nutrition Survey and for the Tecumseh Community Health Survey. In both studies, from infancy through adulthood, for boys and girls, and for whites and blacks, children of early-maturing mothers are taller and heavier than the children of late-maturing mothers (figure 4.10).

The problem of summarizing so much data, involving individual age groups for two sexes, can be simplified by the use of Z-scores (or standard scores) for height, weight, and fatfolds. When this is done, and with the use of broad age groupings (as in figure 4.11), the effects of maternal menarcheal timing on the size and growth of their offspring are dramatic indeed. Clearly, the stature of children of early-maturing women tends to exceed the stature of late-maturing women by about 0.4 Z-scores (0.4 standard deviations) until maturity. In similar fashion, and as shown in figure 4.12, the fatfolds of the children of early-maturing women tend to exceed the fatfolds of the children of late-maturing women by approximately 0.4 Z-scores. These examples, taken from the Tecumseh Community Health Survey, Examination Round 1, clearly picture the dimensional differences between the children of early-maturing and late-maturing mothers.

Since menarcheal timing is affected by a variety of socioeconomic variables, including education, income, and occupation, it is useful to look at the findings after restricting the socioeconomic range. This is

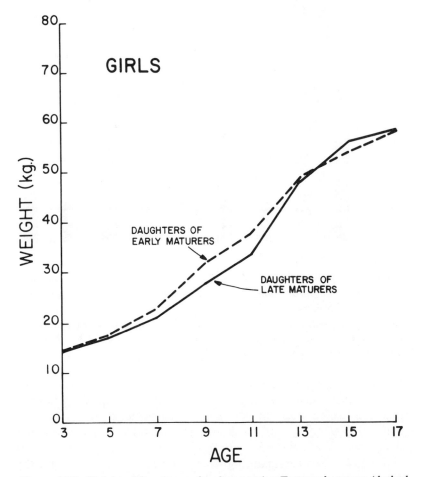

Figure 4.10. *Weight of daughters of early-maturing Tecumseh women (dashed line) and late-maturing Tecumseh women (solid line). From infancy through adolescence and in all three surveys analyzed, both the sons and the daughters of early-maturing women tend to higher weight than the children of late-maturing women.*

most easily accomplished for maternal education, which is not affected by marriage and family size or by upward or downward social mobility. So we have examined the size of children of early- and late-maturing mothers after restricting the sample range to women whose education extends to high school and no further. As shown in figure 4.13, when the age-specific Z-scores from birth through maturity are pooled and the educational range is restricted, the children of early maturers (open bars) are above average for weight and the children of

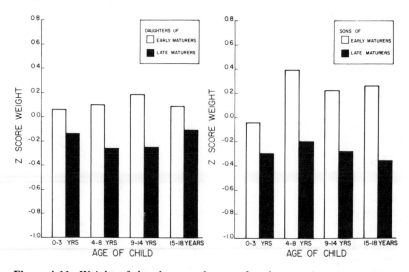

Figure 4.11. *Weight of daughters and sons of early-maturing women (open bars) and late-maturing women (solid bars) enrolled in the Tecumseh Community Health Survey. The greater weight of children of early-maturing women is apparent at all ages. The weight difference between the children of early-maturing women (open bars) and late-maturing women (solid bars) approximates 0.5 standard deviation units.*

late-maturing women (solid bars) are below average for weight. The differences associated with maternal menarcheal timing are present to a greater degree when the data analysis is further extended to adult children (beyond age 18). As shown in figure 4.13, the adult sons and daughters of early-maturing women are far heavier and the adult sons and daughters of late-maturing women are far lighter in weight, (by almost 1 standard deviation).

So there is continuity in the differential growth and development of the children of early-maturing and late-maturing women. Maternal menarcheal timing affects stature, weight, and fatfold thickness of both the sons and the daughters, thus the effect is not sex linked. Continuities in developmental rate persist well into adulthood, at least through the fourth decade. The children of early-maturing women are faster growing, but, reaching maturity earlier, they are ultimately shorter. The slower-growing children of late-maturing mothers grow at a lesser rate but for a longer time period, they are lighter at all ages from infancy through adulthood, and they are consistently leaner at all ages. Thus maternal menarcheal timing is evidenced in the next generation not only by continuities but also by consistencies in change.

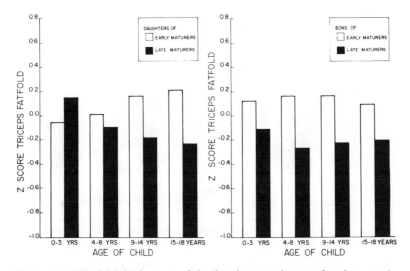

Figure 4.12. *Fatfold thicknesses of the daughters and sons of early-maturing women and late-maturing women in the Tecumseh Community Health Survey. Throughout the age range considered and for sons and daughters alike fatfold thickness tends to be greater in the children of early-maturing women. This generalization holds for both the triceps fatfold and the subscapular fatfold and for the two-generational data in the Ten-State Nutrition Survey as well.*

Menarcheal Timing as a Factor in Fatness

The retrospectively collected menarcheal data used in this study show that menarcheal timing relates to fatness at every age considered. Not only are fatter girls earlier to mature, as we demonstrated years ago (Garn and Haskell, 1959), but women who report earlier menarcheal ages are fatter, even into the seventh decade (table 4.8). Conversely, analysis of the NINCDS data show that super-obese women (S-OBS) report still earlier menarcheal ages than the obese (OBS) and that the super-lean (S-LEN) are characterized by still later menarcheal ages than the lean (LEN).

Studied in prospective fashion, the data show that early-maturing mothers have both sons and daughters who are fatter than average, as shown in the Ten-State Survey (table 4.9). Next, using the two-generational parent-child fatfold comparisons from the Tecumseh Health Survey, it is remarkable that as late as age 40 the children of early-maturing mothers are still fatter than those of late-maturing mothers. So maternal menarcheal timing introduces continuity for fatness,

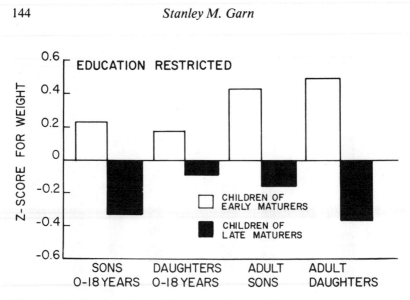

Figure 4.13. *Comparative weight values for the children of early and late-maturing mothers through the growing years and into adulthood. With all available two-generational data from the Tecumseh Health Survey pooled, it is clear that the children of early-maturing women tend to be heavier than the children of late-maturing women even after removing the educational effect by using an education-restricted group throughout. Through adulthood, children of early and late-maturing women differ by approximately 1 standard deviation in weight.*

whether in retrospective analysis of the mothers themselves, as in table 4.8 and figure 4.9, or in prospective analysis of their children of both sexes, as in table 4.9 and figure 4.12.

Were we limited to the purely retrospective fatfold data, we might view the findings as simply confirming continuity in fatness. This interpretation would be a useful one, suggesting that fatness levels attained by age 12-15 are long maintained—as late as the seventh and eighth decades, in fact. This suggestion alone would be valuable because of the current interest in fatness and the age at which adult fatness levels are apparently established.

But the prospective two-generational parent-child comparisons here offer an alternative explanation. Since early-maturing women tend to have fatter children and late-maturing women tend to have leaner children, it is possible that maternal menarcheal timing is itself a factor in fatness, possibly the first truly biological factor to be identified. A third explanation, of course, is that maternal fatness is attained early and then socially transmitted to the children. A two-way analysis of variance does not fully resolve the problem, and the latter explanation therefore remains viable.

Table 4.8. Comparative fatness (mm) of early-maturing and late-maturing women by birth decade.[a]

Birth decade	Early-maturing women[b]		Late-maturing women[b]	
	N	Mean	N	Mean
1900	32	25.8	104	23.2
1910	54	25.4	126	22.5
1920	102	23.6	192	17.7
1930	130	18.8	175	14.9
1940	102	17.1	111	14.6

a. Subscapular fatfolds (mm) of women from the Tecumseh Community Health Project.

b. Earliest 15% and latest 15% maturing women.

However explained, maternal menarcheal timing and fatness are clearly related, in both retrospective and prospective fashion. Without question, maternal menarcheal timing is a factor in fatness.

Family-Line Continuities in Menarcheal Timing

Reported mother-daughter correlations for the age at menarche are of the order of 0.2-0.3, suggesting an effect that transcends gener-

Table 4.9. Comparative fatness (mm) of the sons of early-maturing and late-maturing white women.[a]

Age	Early-maturing mothers[b]		Late-maturing women[b]	
	N	Mean	N	Mean
1	37	7.2	37	6.9
3	52	6.3	52	6.2
5	56	6.1	65	5.6
7	72	5.4	82	5.3
9	71	7.2	64	6.7
11	92	8.6	74	8.3
13	64	10.2	68	8.1
15	41	11.5	52	10.7
17	39	11.0	33	9.7

a. Subscapular fatfolds (mm).

b. Earliest 15% and latest 15% maturing women respectively in the Ten-State Nutrition Survey (1972).

ations. While not large, as most correlations go, these values of *r* are of a magnitude that would be expected for genetically determined traits—as calculated by R. A. Fisher (1950), D. S. Falconer (1960), and numerous others. Such values, moreover, are in accordance with values of *r* for various anthropometric measurements (Garn and Bailey, 1978). This agreement increases the probability that the intergenerational continuity for the age at menarche actually has a genetic basis.

At the same time, mother-daughter similarities in maturational timing must be viewed with some skepticism. A single value of *r*, no matter how reasonable, does not confirm a genetic model, just as a single swallow does not make a summer. With small samples (less than 100) obtained values of *r* may be both lower than and higher than the true value, as can be demonstrated by appropriate computer programs as well as in theory. Furthermore, family-line similarities may be exaggerated by a variety of shared environmental factors. Since menarcheal timing is influenced by the level of fatness (Garn and Haskell, 1959, 1960) and since there are notable mother-daughter similarities in measured fatness, mother-daughter resemblances in menarcheal timing could be the result of fatness levels shared in families. Since menarcheal timing is also a function of socioeconomic status (as demonstrated earlier in this chapter), and since socioeconomic status runs in families, apparent continuity in maturational timing might also result from "social" inheritance rather than from common genes.

To clarify this complex problem we have made use of 552 mother-daughter pairings and 337 sister-sister pairings, using new data from Examination Round I of the Tecumseh Community Health Survey. The problem of secular trend was resolved by computing decade-specific correlations and then pooling the results. In all, the nearly nine hundred menarcheal-age pairings provide a useful estimate of the degree of similarity in menarcheal timing with a standard error of .03. The spectrum of mother-daughter correlations is detailed in table 4.10.

The problem of fatness, or the influence of fatness, was then corrected by calculating partial (fatness-corrected) correlations—$r_{12.3}$—for nearly all the 552 mother-daughter and 337 sister-sister pairings. In similar fashion, both fatness *and* socioeconomic status were also partialed out, using maternal education as the single most useful socioeconomic indicator throughout (table 4.10).

As shown in table 4.10, mother-daughter correlations for menarcheal age approximate 0.23, quite in accordance with the genetic hypothesis. Sister-sister correlations are very similar (0.21). These raw-order (uncorrected) mother-daughter and sister-sister correlations

Table 4.10. Raw-order (r_0) and corrected family-line correlations for menarcheal age.[a]

| Birth decade[b] | Raw order | | Corrected for | | | |
| | | | Fatness | | Fatness and education | |
	N	r	N	r	N	r
	Mother-daughter correlations[c]					
1910	37	0.15	36	0.09	33	0.11
1920	84	0.27	83	0.24	82	0.27
1930	137	0.18	135	0.17	130	0.18
1940	289	0.27	288	0.26	281	0.27
Total	552	0.23	548	0.22	530	0.24
	Sister-sister correlations[c]					
1900	23	0.19	23	0.21	22	0.20
1910	27	0.03	27	−0.12	26	−0.05
1920	61	0.02	60	0.05	58	0.02
1930	98	0.23	98	0.17	93	0.18
1940	122	0.31	122	0.33	116	0.31
Total	337	0.21	336	0.19	319	0.18

a. All data from Tecumseh Michigan, Examination Round 1.

b. Daughters' birth decade or younger sisters' birth decade.

c. Calculated by the pairwise estimator method (Rosner, Donner, and Henneken, 1977).

for the age at menarche in the Tecumseh data base are not appreciably diminished when fatness or both fatness and education are taken into account. The results are given in the second and third columns of table 4.10, along with substantiating values of *r* and the sample sizes (*N*).

Under these circumstances, using a single data base (Tecumseh) with correction for secular trend, fatness shared in common, and the educational variable, it is possible to confirm the genetic hypothesis. Examination of resemblances between adoptive mother and adopted daughters further supports this hypothesis.

Continuity, albeit small, between mothers and their daughters and between older sisters and younger sisters in the age at menarche, is indeed consistent with the genetic hypothesis, but it does not contradict the massive evidence supporting secular change. As with stature (where taller mothers have taller daughters and shorter mothers tend to generate shorter daughters), the intergenerational change in menarche does not contradict continuity, and the continuity does not preclude secular change in menarcheal timing.

We have been able to demonstrate continuity in menarcheal timing, beyond that shown by F. Boas, (1940) and by H. N. Gould and M. R. Gould (1932), both for mothers and daughters and for sisters as well. Moreover, having considered both fatness (which relates to menarcheal timing) and educational level (among other socioeconomic variables examined), we are now convinced that the bulk of family-line similarities in menarcheal timing does indeed have a genetic basis. Though subject to the generational change and to socioeconomic effects, menarcheal timing still exhibits continuity, and that continuity resides largely in the genes.

Continuities in Maturational Timing in Progeny of Both Sexes

Given the mother-daughter continuities in menarcheal timing, it is appropriate to look for confirmatory data on mothers and their sons. Such confirmation might provide indications as to the mode of inheritance of maturational timing—autosomal or sex linked. But males do not menstruate, and therefore the critical mother-son continuities in maturational timing might at first appear impossible to demonstrate.

However, there is a useful, objective measure of maturational timing that is appropriate to both sexes. The measure in question is radiographically demonstrable as the ossification of the adductor sesamoid bone of the thumb (figure 4.14). Ossification of the adductor sesamoid bone is highly correlated with menarche (Frisancho, Garn, and Rohmann, 1969) and in delayed sexual development this little bone is also delayed (Garn and Rohmann, 1962). Theoretically, at least, ossification of the adductor sesamoid in boys with a suitable age range would make it possible to test for two-generational mother-son continuities in maturational timing.

Information on both menarcheal timing of the mothers and suitable postero-anterior hand radiographs of their offspring makes it possible to explore two types of developmental continuities. The first, accomplished in *prospective* fashion, would compare the progeny of early-maturing and late-maturing mothers. (At any given age, a greater proportion of the offspring of early-maturing mothers should have attained ossification of the adductor sesamoid.) The second test of maturational continuity, the *retrospective* test, compares the reported menarcheal timing of the mothers of early-to-ossify and late-to-ossify children. Both the prospective (forward-looking) and retrospective (backward-looking) tests for continuity can be made for

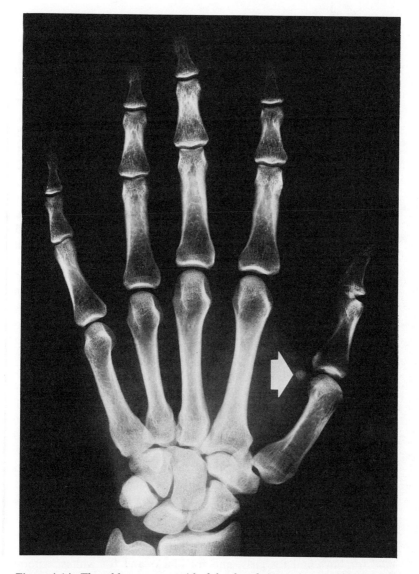

Figure 4.14. *The adductor sesamoid of the thumb (arrow) as seen in a postero-anterior hand-wrist radiograph. The time of appearance of this seedlike bone is highly correlated with the age at menarche. The measure is highly objective and equally useful in both sexes (Garn and Rohmann, 1962; Frisancho, Garn, and Rohmann, 1969).*

mother-child pairs if hand-wrist radiographs are available for children in the 10-15 year age range, and if there are menarcheal age data on the mothers.

Fortunately, we have just such complete menarcheal and radiographic data from the Ten-State Nutrition Survey of 1968-1970, which was providentially set up on a family-line basis at our original suggestion. Paired maternal history and radiographic evaluations were available for over four thousand mother-child pairs, allowing both the prospective and the retrospective tests for continuity. In the tests data on blacks and whites were necessarily separated (for ossification tends to be earlier or advanced in black infants, children, and adolescents, as we have demonstrated in detail). Data on both sons and daughters were separately analyzed.

With the prospective test, confirming continuity in boys and girls and blacks and whites is simple. For all four sex-race groups, the children of early-maturing mothers are advanced in adductor-sesamoid ossification and the progeny of late-maturing mothers are behind or retarded in ossification of this small bone of the hand. This is shown graphically in figure 4.15 for black boys. Overall, taking white boys, white girls, black boys, and black girls all into account, progeny of early-maturing mothers are advanced in adductor-sesamoid ossification by approximately 0.75 years. Clearly, maternal menarcheal timing is reflected in adductor-sesamoid ossification of their progeny. This confirms continuity in maturational development and the intergenerational effect. Both blacks and whites are affected, and equally so. This demonstrates a cross-population effect. So ossification timing of boys and girls of both races is affected by maternal menarcheal timing, with implications for the mode of inheritance.

Taken in reverse order for the retrospective analyses, the two-generational radiographic and menarcheal data yield similar results. For both races the mothers of children early in adductor-sesamoid ossification proved to be early-maturing mothers. Conversely, the mothers of children late in adductor-sesamoid ossification were late-maturing mothers. These generalizations, summarized in figure 4.16, hold for boys and for girls, and for blacks and for whites, without exception. Developmentally advanced boys and girls are associated with earlier maternal menarcheal timing.

In fact, the continuities here revealed suggest a greater relationship between sesamoid timing and maternal menarcheal timing in boys as compared with girls, and this in turn suggests some effect of the X chromosome (since boys derive their single X chromosome from their mothers whereas girls derive one X chromosome from each parent).

Now there is considerable clinical evidence suggesting that early-maturing women do have early-maturing progeny, and we have fol-

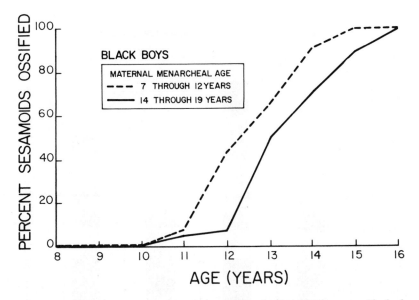

Figure 4.15. *Sesamoid ossification in sons of early-maturing women (dashed line) and late-maturing women (solid line). As shown here for black boys in the Ten-State Nutrition Survey, early maternal maturational attainment is reflected in advanced ossification time of their children. Similar results hold for black girls and for white children of both sexes.*

lowed the sexual development of the sons of some clinical examples of maternal sexual precocity. But the data here presented allow more useful generalization than such clinical extremes. Not only is there continuity in menarcheal timing (as previously shown by mother-daughter pairs), but this continuity extends to the sons as well (here using adductor-sesamoid timing as the maturational measure).

Analyzed both prospectively (looking toward the children) and retrospectively (looking backward at the mothers), the data confirm major maturational continuity. Such maturational continuity characterizes both sexes and not just the daughters. There is maturational continuity for both blacks and whites (as pictured here), and for other groups as well. If anything, the sons depict maturational continuity even more than do the daughters. Given the two-generational sample size used in this study, these important generalizations about continuity in maturational timing are likely to stand.

Body Size Menarcheal Timing and the "Critical Weight" Hypothesis

Although this chapter is concerned primarily with continuities and change in menarcheal timing, it is not quite possible to conclude it

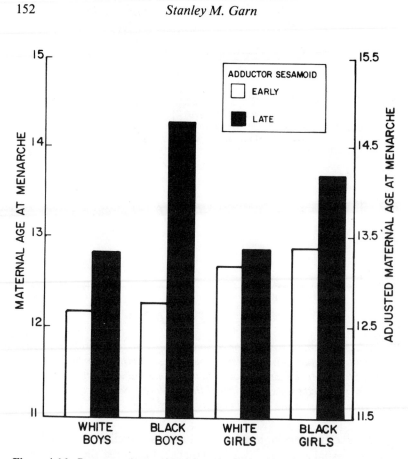

Figure 4.16. *Retrospective analysis showing maternal menarcheal ages of children early in ossification timing (open bars) and late in ossification timing (solid bars). As shown for both sexes and for blacks and whites alike, advanced sesamoid ossification is associated with earlier maternal menarcheal ages, and delayed ossification (as seen in the children) is associated with later maternal menarcheal ages.*

without some mention of the critical weight hypothesis. Besides, we have dimensional data on girls who have and have not attained menarche at each age from 10 through 17, numbering 3,188 for Ten-State whites and blacks alone, and on the reproductive histories of many hundreds of women below the so-called critical weight.

There is no doubt that heavier or fatter or better-nourished girls attain menarche earlier than lower-weight, leaner, or poorly nourished girls; years ago we showed that fatness predisposes to maturational advancement in both sexes (Garn and Haskell, 1960). And of course there is an average weight or an average fatness associated with the time of menarche or the time of second molar tooth emergence or of axillary hair development, though one does not necessarily trigger the other.

There are population arguments against a critical weight hypothesis, since average weight at menarche differs markedly between populations. Inasmuch as menarcheal age also differs between socioeconomic groups, a socioeconomic correction would be appropriate. Moreover, since there are changes in menarcheal age over time, a chronological correction might be suggested for a critical weight.

Yet the most cogent data are the data comparing menarcheal attainments of various groups as a whole and those individuals below some critical value. If we take 47.3 kg (104 lbs), often given as a critical weight (and which also corresponds to the fifth percentile for adult women), then the following generalizations can be made from newly analyzed data of considerable size.

1. For both whites and blacks in the Ten-State Nutrition Survey of 1968-1970, low-weight girls (47.3 kg) are slightly delayed in menarcheal attainment; nevertheless, some do attain menarche at every age. All such low-weight girls attain menarche, sooner or later, as shown in figure 4.17. Whether we use the 47.3 kg cutoff (104 lbs) or an even lower value, there is no critical weight, in any proper sense of the term.

2. For 599 Mexican-American girls in the Ten-State Survey (with menarcheal data completely given in table 4.11), there is a slight developmental advantage for the total series over those with weights of 47.3 kg and below. For these girls—as for Puerto Rican girls—body weights during adolescence are rather less than for blacks or whites, but there is no critical weight below which menarche does not ultimately take place.

A substantial number of mothers in the Collaborative Perinatal Project (NINCDS) have become pregnant at 47.3 kg or less, and some were as old as age 40. Thus there is not even a critical weight below which pregnancy does not take place. Further examination of pregnant women and mothers enrolled in the Ten-State Survey reveals a substantial number who are (a) pregnant or (b) mothers of one or more children, yet below 47 kg in measured body weight. So it is possible to become pregnant or even to attain advanced parity at or below 47 kg, or virtually any weight that may be set. The same generalizations also apply to fatness.

From these new studies it is possible to agree that greater weight or fatness or body mass is associated with menarcheal advancement, consistent with other evidence we have adduced so far. But there is no

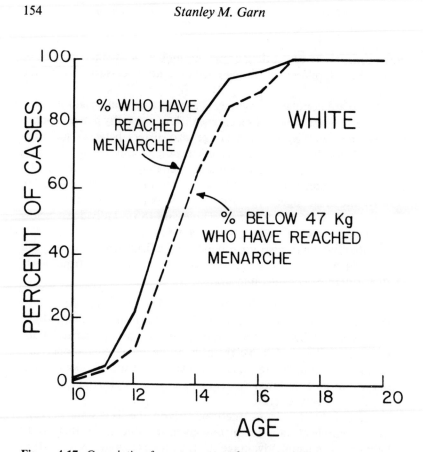

Figure 4.17. *Cumulative frequency curve for menarcheal attainment in the total sample of white girls (solid lines) and in girls below 47 kg (dashed line). While menarcheal attainment is later in low-weight black and white girls (by approximately 0.40 years overall), body weight is by no means "critical" for menarcheal attainment; by age 17 or so all the low-weight girls have attained menarche. For Puerto Rican and Mexican-American girls (who generally have lower body weight) the average weight at menarche is lower still (see table 4.11).*

"critical" weight, below which menarche fails to take place—or even conception, for that matter, or parturition, or repeated pregnancies. While agreeing that the bigger or heavier or fatter girl is apt to be maturationally advanced, we may question whether there is a critical weight or a critical fatness, in any precise use of the term.

With menarcheal data for over 4,000 girls aged 10 through 17, we can be truly critical of the critical weight hypothesis.

Discussion and Comments

From these new findings, based on nearly fifty thousand menarcheal records from three different population surveys, it should be

Table 4.11. Menarcheal attainment in 599 Mexican-American girls, including those of low weight (less than 47 kg).[a]

Age midpoint	N	Percentage reaching menarche	
		Total[b]	—47 kg
10	76	3.9	0
11	88	13.6	12.3
12	83	37.3	35.5
13	93	67.7	60.3
14	82	74.6	84.2
15	77	89.6	88.5
16	54	94.4	94.4
17	46	97.8	100.0

a. These data are from the Ten-State Nutrition Survey of 1968-1970 (1972).
b. Total sample with Ns as shown.

clear that menarcheal timing reflects both constancy and change. In fact, the two-generational data employed here and the family-line analyses attest to both continuity between generations and changes, even within a generation.

Change, of course, is extremely well documented for menarcheal timing. The rate of change for many European countries has approximated 0.3 years per decade, or 3.0 years in a century. Over the last fifty years in the United States the rate of change appears to be somewhat less, approximately 0.2 years per decade extrapolated to 2.0 years in a century.

Nevertheless, the decrease in menarcheal age has been dramatic—from age 15 or 16 down to 13 or even less, depending on the population sampled, the country, and the reporting dates. When making such statements, of course, it is necessary to assure continuity in the population segments sampled, for socioeconomic status affects menarcheal timing in all groups considered in this chapter.

Still, the decrease in the age at menarche characterizes both poverty-level women and those at median income, although average menarcheal age may vary between groups. Blacks, whites, Puerto Ricans, and Mexican-Americans all share in this secular decrease, though the decade-specific curves differ. Even in the massive Collaborative Perinatal Project (NINCDS) data there is evidence of a secular decrease, statistically significant because of the huge sample number.

Now-obese women and women currently lean show equal evidence of a secular decrease in the age at menarche, documenting constancy in this particular change. Yet it is equally clear that the reported

age at menarche is lower for women currently obese and higher for
women currently more affluent. These two observations, derived from
thousands of examinations and case records, do much to explain the
mechanisms behind the secular change in menarcheal age. Improvement in the caloric reserve surely underlies the decrease in menarcheal
age, though there are still other and more direct correlates of fatness.

Still, the decrease in the age at menarche (like the secular increase
in stature) seems to be at an end in the United States, and in many
Western European countries. For the data we have amassed, the secular decrease seems to have "plateaued" out for those in the 1940 birth
decade on. There is little evidence of a continuing decrease in the age
at menarche in most samples of median income and above, though
there is evidence that it is still decreasing in the poor and in recent immigrant groups from Central America and the Caribbean. With these
exceptions, duly noted, menarcheal-age change seems to be nearly at
an end.

Yet despite change in menarcheal age over the past century, and
more, with major implications to population expansion, there are also
constancies in age at menarche. Mothers and daughters show the degree of similarity in menarcheal timing that would be expected for a
genetically determined trait ($r = 0.25$) and when comparing menarcheal ages of the daughters of maturational extremes. Corrected for
the secular trends, by the method of calculation, further corrected for
socioeconomic status in various ways, and even corrected for fatness,
the mother-daughter correlations in age at menarche are much the
same as the raw-order (r_0) correlations. The two-generational menarcheal constancies, therefore, may be presumed to have a genetic basis.
In much the same fashion, sister-sister correlations in age at menarche
hold constant after correction for (1) birth decade, (2) for socioeconomic status, and (3) for fatness. With these shared familial similarities excluded from the correlations, the genetic explanation becomes
more tenable.

Maternal menarcheal timing, moreover, relates to the size,
growth, and maturational timing of the offspring of both sexes, and in
blacks and whites and Puerto Ricans. In all groups studied, early-
maturing mothers have children who are taller from infancy through
adolescence. Also, early-maturing mothers have sons and daughters
who are heavier from infancy through adulthood. These statements,
based on thousands of longitudinal and semilongitudinal examinations, indicate that maternal maturational timing has effects that truly
transcend sex and that fully transcend generations.

Early-maturing mothers (defined by the age at menarche) have
early-maturing sons and daughters, as indicated by adductor-sesamoid

ossification. Late-maturing mothers, (defined by the age at menarche), have late-maturing sons and daughters as shown on posteroanterior hand radiographs. Maternal menarcheal timing therefore transcends sex; it transcends generations, and it even transcends target-organ or tissue. So this maturational variable is neither sex limited; nor just a measure of uterine response to cyclic estrogen withdrawal, but it is a basic developmental variable. Growth rates, size, proportions, and maturational timing are all involved. Early maturers and their progeny are taller during the growing period but ultimately shorter, heavier at all ages (through the fifth decade at least), and early-maturing in numerous developmental parameters. So there is true constancy, despite secular change.

Menarcheal timing relates to fatness in both predictable and unexpected ways. Not surprisingly, fatter girls mature earlier as we first showed 20 years ago. Fatter girls (like better-fed domestic animals) mature earlier and leaner girls (like ration-restricted farm animals) mature far later. The extremes of fatness are associated with extremes of menarche from about 8 years—in the Pickwickian extreme —to 15-16 years and more in the very lean. Even later menarcheal ages occur in malabsorption syndromes, in cases of childhood deprivation, and during famine conditions. That menarche has a nutritional determinant, easily measured as stored fat, is not remarkable. It helps to explain why Westernized girls reach menarche earlier; it helps to explain why menarche has become earlier as the nutritional status has improved and why the earliest-maturing populations are—in general —the fattest. Clearly maturational timing can be manipulated by altering the caloric reserve, in *Homo* as in other species.

To some extent our massive *retrospective* data relating fatness later in life to earlier menarcheal timing might appear to be a simple extension of nutritional facts. Women who are obese at 40, 50, 60, and 70 report earlier menarcheal ages than those who are lean at each of these decades. This seems to be a case of simple continuity. If fatness speeds menarche, as we have shown, and if the obese remain obese and the lean remain lean, then it is no wonder the obese septuagenerians were earlier to mature than their now-lean decade-mates. This might also seem to be simple continuity in fatness, an interesting fact in itself.

But the *prospective* two-generational data offer an alternative, exciting possibility. For the children of early-maturing women are both heavier and fatter than the children of late-maturing women, not just as infants and adolescents, but as adults, too. Early-maturing mothers have fat 40-year-old sons and daughters. Late-maturing mothers have lean infants, children, adolescents, and even adult sons and daughters. Either the early-maturing women, who are fatter, re-plicate their fatness through precept and instruction (which alone would be important to the study of obesity), or there is something even more fundamental in this continuity. By various analytical de-signs it is possible to show that maternal maturational timing is still linked to the fatness level of their offspring after exclusion of mater-nal fatness per se and after exclusion of various socioeconomic vari-ables. There does seem to be a fundamental relationship between ma-ternal maturational timing and fatness level over the generations and in both sexes, a relationship that is not entirely explained by the living-together effect (cohabitation).

With these examples of continuity and change in menarcheal tim-ing, and the two-generational cross-sex relationship to measured fat-ness, there remain two considerations to explore. The first of these is the allegation, made from time to time, that reported menarcheal tim-ing is too imprecise and too subject to error to serve as useful scientific data. Indeed, the custom of reporting age at menarche to the nearest whole year, or more commonly the past year, does constitute a report-ing error of considerable magnitude. If age 12 is reported as the age at menarche, with a midpoint age of 12.5, the resulting error is .5 years, or nearly half of a standard deviation (= 1.1 years). Even greater indi-vidual errors may then occur if the nearest age rather than the past age was reported instead.

Yet the continuities within the data given here are indeed impres-sive. Even at age 70 women reporting early ages at menarche (decade corrected) are shorter but fatter than women reporting late menar-cheal ages. The progeny of the women reporting an early menarcheal age are both shorter and fatter than those of the septuagenarians re-porting late menarcheal ages. At age 40 the children of black and white and poor and rich early-maturing women differ dimensionally from the children of those women who report late menarcheal ages. Birth records in the Collaborative Perinatal Project similarly distin-guish the neonates of early-maturing and late-maturing women. Anthropometric data confirm the size differences in the offspring of early-maturing and late-maturing Tecumseh mothers. Fatfolds mea-sured on the children in ten states agree with maternal menarcheal records in the Ten-State Survey. Even serum and urinary measures confirm the difference. It is doubtful whether random errors or sys-tematic errors in recalling the age at menarche could possibly result in such systematic cross-generational cross-survey results.

Finally we come to the often-asked question of a "critical weight" for menarche and the critical weight hypothesis in general. But the results are far from supporting this simplistic generalization. While there is an average weight at the time of menarche, this differs from group to group (lower in Puerto Ricans and Mexican-Americans). It differs, moreover, in the poor and the more affluent. Nor is it a "critical" weight, in the proper sense of the word. In every group studied some girls reach menarche far below the critical weight, and some do not attain it until a far greater weight. In blacks and whites and Puerto Ricans some became pregnant below the 47.3 kg "critical weight," and some are multiparas well below that weight. By age 17 or 18, in fact, virtually all girls attain menarche, regardless of weight (or fatness). The critical weight is scarcely "critical" in any proper use of the term.

Coda

Apart from the critical weight hypothesis, which falls because of insufficient supportive findings, there are four things we would like to say about menarcheal timing. First, it is susceptible to marked change according to the degree of nutritional insufficiency or caloric excess. In this sense menarcheal timing exemplifies change. Second, menarcheal timing shows itself to be familial and hereditary (though susceptible to change) and reflected in the developmental timing of the next generation regardless of sex. In this respect menarcheal timing, carefully explored, exemplifies continuity.

Third (not assignable to either continuity or change), is the association between menarcheal timing and size and growth. Without doubt, children of early-maturing women are taller earlier in life though not in the long run. They are heavier earlier and through adulthood as well. So maturational timing is not independent of size and growth; as a variable it is associated with demonstrable differences from womb to tomb.

Fourth, and last, menarcheal timing has a remarkable relationship to fatness and provides a biological basis for fatness. It is not surprising that fatter girls reach menarche earlier nor totally amazing that early and late maturational timing are reflected by fatness differences as late as the seventieth year. But early-maturing women have fatter infants, fatter children, fatter adolescents—and even fatter adult children. Thus menarcheal timing emerges as an example of continuity and of change, of relevance to size and growth throughout the life cycle and to fatness and obesity as well.

Notes

Work described in this paper was supported by a grant from Weight Watchers Foundation (Fatness and Lipid Levels), Grant HD 09538 (Socioeconomic and Genetic Determinants of Obesity) from the National Institutes of

Health and Contract NOT-NS-5-2308 with the National Institute of Neurological and Communicative Disorders and Stroke (NINCDS).

Data analysis was originally conducted with Patricia E. Cole, coauthor of an earlier paper in this area, and completed with the assistance of Karen Rosenberg. The manuscript was completed with the assistance of Patricia S. Bridges and Jody I. Rein.

References

BAKWIN, H., and McLAUGHLIN, J. D. 1964. Secular increase in height: is the end in sight? *Lancet* 2: 1195-96.

BOAS, F. 1912a. *Changes in bodily form of the descendants of immigrants.* New York: Columbia University Press.

—— 1912b. Changes in bodily form of descendants of immigrants. *American Anthropologist* 19: 530-562.

—— 1940. Age changes and secular changes in anthropometric measurements. *American Journal of Physical Anthropology* 26: 63-68.

BOWLES, G. T. 1932. *New types of old Americans at Harvard and eastern women's colleges.* Cambridge, Mass.: Harvard University Press.

DAMON, A. 1965. Stature increase among Italian-Americans: environmental, genetic or both? *American Journal of Physical Anthropology* 23: 401-408.

DAMON, A., DAMON, S. T., REED, R. B., and VALADIAN, I. 1969. Age at menarche of mothers and daughters with a note on accuracy of recall. *Human Biology* 41: 161-175.

EVELETH, P. B., and TANNER, J. M. 1976. *Worldwide variation in human growth.* New York: Cambridge University Press.

FALCONER, D. S. 1960. *Introduction to quantitative genetics.* New York: Ronald Press.

FISHER, R. A. 1950. *Statistical methods for research workers.* London: Oliver and Boyd.

FRISANCHO, A. R., GARN, S. M., and ROHMANN, C. G. 1969. Age at menarche: a new method of prediction and retrospective assessment based on X-rays. *Human Biology* 41: 42-50.

FRISCH, R. E., and REVELLE, R. 1971. Height and weight at menarche and a hypothesis of menarche. *Archives of Diseases in Childhood* 46: 695-701.

GARN, S. M., and BAILEY, S. M. 1978. Genetics of maturational processes. In F. Faulkner and J. M. Tanner, eds., *Human growth.* New York: Plenum Press.

GARN, S. M., BAILEY, S. M., and COLE, P. E. 1976. Similarities between parents and their adopted children. *American Journal of Physical Anthropology*, 45: 539-543.

GARN, S. M., BAILEY, S. M., COLE, P. E., and HIGGINS, I. T. T. 1978. Evidence for the social inheritance of obesity in childhood and adolescence. In L. Gedda and P. Parisi, eds., *Auxology: human growth in health and disorder*, Proceedings of the Serono Symposia 13: 217-223. London: Academic Press.

GARN, S. M., COLE, P. E., and BAILEY, S. M. 1977. Effect of parental fatness levels on the fatness of biological and adoptive children. *Ecology of Food and Nutrition* 6th (no. 2): 91-93.

GARN, W. M., COLE, P. E., and WAINRIGHT, R. L. 1978. Effect of maternal menarcheal age on the somatic and sexual development of the offspring. *American Journal of Physical Anthropology* 48: 397.

GARN, S. M., and FRENCH, Y. 1967. *Magnitude of secular trend in the Fels population: stature and weight.* Privately printed.

GARN, S. M., and HASKELL, J. A. 1959. Fat and growth during childhood. *Science* 130:1711-12.

——— 1960. Fat thickness and developmental status in childhood and adolescence. *Journal of Diseases of Children* 99: 746-751.

GARN, S. M., ROBINOW, M., and BAILEY, S. M. 1979. Genetical and nutritional interactions in growth and development. In D. Jelliffe and P. Jellife, eds., *Nutrition and growth*, New York: Plenum Press.

GARN, S. M., and ROHMANN, C. G. 1962. The adductor sesamoid of the thumb. *American Journal of Physical Anthropology* 20: 297-302.

——— 1966. Interaction of nutrition and genetics in the timing of growth and development. *Pediatric Clinics of North America* 13: 353-379.

GARN, S. M., and SHAMIR, Z. 1958. *Methods for research in human growth.* Springfield, Ill.: C. C. Thomas.

GARN, S. M., SHAW, H. A., and McCABE, K. 1977. Birth size and growth appraisal. *Journal of Pediatrics* 90th (no. 6): 1049-51.

GOULD, H. N., and GOULD, M. R. 1932. Age of first menstruation in mothers and daughters. *Journal of the American Medical Association* 98: 1349-52.

HOWE, P. E., and SCHILLER, M. 1952. Growth responses of the school child to changes in diet and environmental factors. *Journal of Applied Physiology* 5: 51-61.

MEREDITH, H. V. 1963. Changes in the stature and body weight of North American boys during the last 80 years. In L. D. Lipsett and C. C. Spiker, eds., *Advances in child development and behavior*, vol. 1. New York: Academic Press.

MEREDITH, H. V., and MEREDITH, E. M. 1942. The stature of Toronto children half a century ago and today. *Human Biology* 16: 126-131.

NAPIER, J. A., JOHNSON, B. C., and EPSTEIN, F. H. 1971. The Tecumseh Community Health Study. In I. I. Tessler and M. L. Lesen, eds., *Case book of community study*. Baltimore, Md.: Johns Hopkins Press.

NISWANDER, H. R., and GORDON, M. 1972. *The women and their pregnancies* (DHEW Publication No. NIH 73-379). Washington, D.C.: Department of Health, Education, and Welfare.

POPENOE, P. 1928. Inheritance of age of onset of menstruation. *Eugenics News* 13: 101.

POZNANSKI, A. K., GARN, S. M., KUHNS, L. R., and SHAW, H. A. 1977. Disharmonic skeletal maturation in the congenital malformation syndromes. *Birth Defects: Original Article Series* 13 (3C): 45-65.

ROSNER, B., DONNER, A., and HENNEKENS, C. H. 1977. Estimation of interclass correlation from familial data. *Applied Statistics* 25: 179-187.

SCAMMON, R. E. 1927. The first seriatim study of human growth. *American Journal of Physical Anthropology* 10: 329-336.

TANNER, J. M. 1962. *Growth at adolescence.* Oxford: Blackwell Scientific Publications.

TANNER, J. M., GOLDSTEIN, H., and WHITEHOUSE, R. H. 1970. Standards for children's height at ages 2-9 years allowing for height of parents. *Archives of Disease in Childhood* 45 (no. 244).

TEN-STATE NUTRITION SURVEY 1972. (DHEW Publication No. HSM 72-8130). Atlanta, Ga.: Department of Health, Education, and Welfare.

TROTTER, M., and GLESER, G. C. 1951. Trends in stature of American whites and negroes born between 1840 and 1924. *American Journal of Physical Anthropology* 9: 427-440.

WINGERD, J., SOLOMON, I. L., and SCHOEN, E. J. 1973. Parent-specific height standards for preadolescent children of three racial groups, with method for rapid determination. *Pediatrics* 52: 556.

5 | The Dynamics of Growth, Organization, and Adaptability in the Central Nervous System
Donald G. Stein and
Ronald G. Dawson

THE NATURE AND SIGNIFICANCE of neuronal plasticity have long been focal points for argument in the neurosciences. the nature-nurture controversy and the localizationist-antilocalizationist arguments are two outstanding cases of the polarization of opinion concerning the factors that shape the development of the nervous system or best describe the relationships between structure and function. Wide differences of opinion about neuronal plasticity can be found within these two controversies. The issue in the nature-nurture conflict is the degree to which the nature of an organism (its genetic material) constrains its ability to interact with the environment and the degree to which these constraints are set by the environment in which the organism develops. To give the two extreme examples, neurogenesis (the development of the nervous system) can be viewed as the unfolding of a preprogrammed genetic plan, unaffected by the environment and not modifiable. Alternatively, neurogenesis might be conceived of as the proliferation of neural elements that make random connections among one another, with the environment supplying the information about which of the connections are adaptively significant. The capacity for sustaining adaptively significant connections would give such a nervous system great flexibility.

A different conception of neuronal plasticity arises from the localizationist-antilocalizationist controversies. At issue here is whether the functions of the nervous system can be localized in discrete regions of neural tissue. In other words, do particular regions of the nervous system perform particular functions and only those functions? Or might the functions performed by one part of the nervous system be changed, for example, as a result of injury or a change in the organism's environment?

Only within the last few decades have neuroscientists attempted to measure central neuronal events directly in the hope of clarifying these questions, which had been raised almost exclusively on the basis of behavioral observations. For example, mammals were viewed as having more plastic nervous systems than reptiles and amphibians because they had adapted successfully to a wider range of environments than the last two groups and had showed a greater capacity for learning in controlled experiments. Some issues have been reformulated to incorporate the data obtained at the neuronal level (Gottlieb, 1976; Sperry, 1968), but there are still wide gaps between the hypothetically inferred and the directly measured phenomena. We now know that the mammalian nervous system possesses a much greater capacity for regrowth following injury than was previously thought, yet the relationship between such regrowth and the recovery of function is still far from clear. Many of the constructs that have their origins in behavioral research still have no explanation at the neuronal level; similarly there is much uncertainty about the behavioral significance of some of the neuronal mechanisms under investigation. Our task is to bring these two levels of research closer together, by reviewing the use of different notions of neuronal plasticity and examining the most reasonable of them in the light of more recent research.

In the early part of the twentieth century the prospect of central neuronal reorganization dominated thought and practice in clinical neurology. It was believed that adaptive behavior could be restored in patients with nerve damage or muscle atrophy by reconnecting foreign nerves to sound muscles or by transplanting normally innervated muscles into foreign locations.

The belief that the mammalian nervous system could adapt to these abnormalities of connectivity by some form of central reorganization was based on studies of behavioral conditioning. Some researchers believed that almost any stimulus might be made to elicit any response in an animal's repertoire, if that stimulus was given adaptive significance. That is, the conditioning procedures could override any natural preferences of the animals to respond to a stimulus in a particular manner. Furthermore, there were numerous reports that animals could transfer what they had learned in one conditioning situation to another requiring a different set of adaptive responses. In one widely cited experiment Liddell (1942) trained a sheep to avoid a footshock by flexing its leg at the onset of a signal. The animal was then placed on its back with its head near the shock plate. At the onset of the signal the animal stiffened its legs and attempted to lift its head instead of flexing its foreleg.

Following this and other demonstrations of transfer of learning (Lashley and McCarthy, 1926; Tolman, 1948) the nervous system was thought to be able not only to develop connectivity between stimuli and responses as a result of learning but also to reorganize the connectivity utilizing other response systems when it was adaptive to do so. The feeling was that in the clinical cases central neuronal reorganization might in some analogous fashion produce normal movement as long as some form of nerve-to-nerve or nerve-to-muscle connectivity could be reestablished surgically.

There was a second, purely practical reason to intervene surgically in these cases. Studies of residual growth in the mammalian nervous system following injury indicated that central neural regeneration was at best short-lived (Cajal, 1928), and in the peripheral nervous system several factors combined to prevent the reestablishment of the normal pattern of reinnervation following peripheral nerve damage (Langley, 1918; Cajal, 1928). Many experiments on nerve crossing and regeneration in humans and lower animals followed, and the results were generally claimed to be successful. The feeling at the time, therefore, was that the mammalian central nervous system was not plastic in the sense that it had no residual growth potential that might restore normal function after injury but plastic in the sense that the functions of residual neurons could be respecified, as was indicated generally in the learning literature and specifically in the nerve-crossing experiments.

At approximately the same time the search for the neural substrates of conditioning and learning had also begun (see Lashley's collected works in Beach et al., 1960). However, the hypothetical processes of central neural reorganization appeared to be so ubiquitous as to deny any successful search for the mechanisms of learning on which they depended. In one example illustrating this point Lashley (in Beach et al., 1960) attempted to isolate the locus in the brain where the connections that support motor learning occur. He destroyed the precentral gyrus of a monkey unilaterally, thus interrupting much of the brain's control over the contralateral arm and leg, which were paralyzed as a result. He then trained the monkey to perform a series of latch-box tasks with the sound hand. The tasks demanded a great deal of dexterity since a series of latches had to be opened in a precise order in order to solve each task. The remaining side of the precentral gyrus was then destroyed, paralyzing the arm and the hand that had been used to solve the tasks. When the animal recovered from the immediate effects of surgery, the limbs on the side that was first paralyzed showed signs of recovery, and the monkey quickly solved the latch-box tasks using the previously untrained hand. This experiment was taken to indicate not only that motor memory for the task did not reside in the precentral gyrus but also that the connections made during learning were not the same as those used during relearning, since different hands were used for each.

Numerous other studies showed that animals were able to relearn both motor and sensory tasks after recovering from the initial effects of injury to cortical sensory and motor projection areas. These areas were, incidentally, thought to be the ones most likely to participate in the formation of connections between stimuli and responses. Therefore, while no learning mechanisms were isolated, the experimental findings in these studies confirmed the general belief that the functions of central nervous system neurons could be specified and respecified because animals were able to readapt. For example, Lashley (1920) demonstrated that preoperatively learned visual discrimination in rats was lost after striate cortex lesions, but the animals were able to relearn the task within the same time that it had taken them to learn the task before brain surgery.

Ideas concerning the factors that shaped the development of the nervous system were also influenced by these beliefs. Neurogenesis was viewed primarily as a set of haphazard processes of cell division, migration, and connection formation between the various neuronal elements, themselves endowed with an extreme form of plasticity. Experience subsequently played the major role in determining which of these connections would be functionally adaptive (Holt, 1937). Lashley (1937) even suggested that the particulars of structure may be irrelevant to understanding how the nervous system supports adaptive behavior. Lashley meant that it may be inappropriate to conclude that two regions of an animal's cortex do different things because they are anatomically dissimilar, since the plasticity of their functional connectivity may be sufficient for experience to dictate that they do the same thing.

It was not until Sperry's (1945) monograph that these views were questioned seriously. On the basis of intensive studies of the original research reports and the results of his own research, Sperry concluded that central neuronal reorganization following nerve crossing or muscle transposition did not occur. Successful adaptation, when observed, could be attributed in all cases to the functioning of residual intact connections. There appeared to be two major reasons for the earlier research workers' belief that central neural reorganization had occurred in their experiments. First, they often chose to disconnect and cross minor nerves which innervated small regions of muscle. Second, after performing a minor nerve-cross operation they studied gross responses, such as an animal's ability to use a limb to walk or a wing to fly, rather than looking at the specific nerve-muscle relationships that had been changed (Sperry, 1945). Close examination of the nerve-muscle relationships shows that when normal functioning is restored it is often because nerves regenerate to their original muscles even after the nerves have been crossed.

Sperry (1943) showed that in cases where neural regeneration could be studied uncomplicated by the many factors hindering mammalian nerve regrowth (for example, the visual systems of amphibia), persistent and maladaptive behavior could be readily demonstrated. These demonstrations were puzzling in the light of the prevailing view, since it was presumed that the connections formed when neurons regenerated would be made adaptive by the joint effects of experience and the capacity of central neuronal reorganization.

In the newt the connections between the eye and the brain are made by retinal ganglion cells which send their axons in the optic nerve to the optic tectum, the rough equivalent of the visual cortex in mammals. If these connections are cut, by sectioning the optic nerve, the axons will regenerate into the tectum. Sperry (1943) showed that if the eyeball was rotated 180° in the orbit following optic nerve section, the regenerating axons restored vision, but it was upside down and laterally switched, as it would be if the optic nerve had not been sectioned and the eye had merely been rotated. Also, if one eye was transplanted from one orbit to the other such that only the vertical visual axis was switched around, vision about this axis was inverted while vision about the horizontal axis was normal (if the left eye was transplanted into the right orbit, its nasal side would be temporal and its temporal side would be nasal). The inescapable conclusion was that the optic nerve axons had regenerated into their original locations in the tectum, relaying precise, though completely misleading, information about what parts of the visual field they represented. A somewhat similar experiment by Stone (1944) cast more doubt on the idea that experience was the major factor in the formation of adaptive neural connections. He showed that if the eyes of young salamanders were rotated very early in life, vision was laterally switched and inverted in adulthood. This experiment indicated that the precise ordering demonstrated in the optic nerve regeneration studies appeared to be present before the optic nerve axons made their first connections with the tectum during development.

Since maladaptive connections could also be made to form during development, neurogenesis in this instance was clearly not a haphazard set of processes subsequently made adaptive by learning. On the contrary, later research has revealed other examples of the precise order present in the developing nervous systems of mammals as well as amphibians, and there is no longer any doubt that this order often appears long before an organism has any opportunity to test the appropriateness of such order by its own individual experiences (Sperry, 1965).

However, Schneirla (1956) and others argued that the appearance of orderly growth and specificity of neuronal activity, without prior learning about the environment, is not conclusive evidence that there is no plasticity during the development of such ordered systems. Schneirla's arguments were directed primarily to ethologists, who thought that instinctive behavior was genetically predetermined because many instinctive acts appeared to be stereotyped (ordered) and invariant across individual members of a species, but they apply equally well here. The crux of Schneirla's argument was that behaviors may emerge without the organism's having had an opportunity to learn them but where experience, in a sense broader than mere associative learning, could be shown to have played a role.

All that is needed to sustain this argument are cases for which the emergence of a particular pattern of behavior has changed as a result of a prior change in a developing organism's environment. In one such case Gottlieb (1976) examined the development of the Peking duck's response to the natural "assembly" call of the species. The development of this selective response depends on the exposure of the duck embryo to its own vocalizations, or to those of its siblings, for a period of days prior to hatching. Ducklings deprived of hearing either source of vocalizations while still in the egg developed only an immature response to the call (overt activity was inhibited), while ducklings exposed to sibling calls one day earlier than normal passed through the immature stage and showed the more mature excitatory reactions, typical of a later stage of the development of the response, one day earlier than usual. There are also cases for which the type of behavior depends on prior environmental effects. For example, Wiens (1970) showed that frogs selectively acquired a preference for a striped pattern rather than a squared pattern if they were reared on a striped substrate in the tadpole stage. In this case it seems clear that the type of prior experience was critical in determining the adult preference. In both these experiments the environmental effects were outside the realm of what is typically called learning. The ducklings' selective response to the maternal call developed as a result of exposure to their own vocalizations and not to the maternal call. The tadpoles were never taught a preference. They were merely raised on one substrate or the other. In neither case did the animals test the appropriateness of the developing responses, yet experience affected what developed. It therefore becomes a matter of contention whether the precise order of the development of neural connections is a result of genetic influences alone.

In their search for neuronal specificity, that is, the determination of each and every action (and reaction) in a neuron, some researchers tend to forget that what is predetermined or inherited is not a specific phenotypic trait or character (whether at the organismic or neuronal level) but rather a genotypic potential for the organism's response to its environment. In discussing this issue, Dobzhansky pointed out that "a genetic potentiality for an organism's developmental response to its environment, given a certain genotype and a certain sequence of environmental situations, the development follows a certain path. The carriers of other genetic endowments in the same environmental sequence might well develop differently, but, also, a given genotype might well develop phenotypically along different paths in different environments" (1969, p. 77).

Recent interest in the possibility that visual information could be incorporated into the developing nervous system has come from studies of the development of neuronal activity patterns in the visual system. This system is amenable to the analysis of such questions, since the opening of an animal's eyes provides a precise point at which visual experience may begin to influence developmental directions, though, of course, visual stimulation through the closed eyelids of an animal may have a role in development. Moreover, it is relatively easy to prevent or restrict an animal's visual input. Such experience serves merely to sustain or facilitate central nervous system development, which presumably gets its direction from the genes. Some recent experiments on visual development which may be taken to suggest that an animal's early visual environment may exert a selective effect on what develops.

Sperry's research directed attention back toward the study of the residual growth potential of the mammalian nervous system. Since surgical attempts to restore function by producing abnormal connectivity had failed, it became more important to determine whether the mammalian nervous system has the capacity to restore function, in similar fashion to the amphibians, by regrowing its connections after injury. The first positive report occurred in 1958, when Lui and Chambers (1958) discovered axonal regrowth in the spinal cord. Since that time, the study of residual growth processes in the spinal cord and brain has blossomed.

The significance of recovery of function following central nervous system lesions as evidence of neuronal plasticity has been difficult to evaluate within the context of the previous experimental results. In the past, neuronal regrowth was never seriously entertained as an explanation, though many more researchers now consider this possibility. For this reason most of the explanations of behavioral recovery have embodied the notion that the functions of damaged structures are "taken over" by undamaged structures. However, since the early studies made no serious attempt to describe what was damaged as the result of a lesion, save circumscribing the focal area of tissue loss, and since the lesion was in turn used to assess the functions of the damaged areas, the likelihood that recovery was mediated by way of intact residual connections could never be ruled out.

Experience and Development of Neuronal Activity in the Visual System

One of the most productive areas of neurophysiological research in the last twenty years has been concerned with delineating the response characteristics of individual sensory neurons, in particular, neurons in the visual system. The first indication that such studies might increase our understanding of how we see the world came from research by Lettvin et al. (1959), who showed that neurons in the tectum of the frog responded to particular features of the visual environment (shapes, angles, moving spots). Moreover, the types of features represented were seen to be consistent with the frog's responses to the visual environment. For example, certain cells responded best to small patches or spots moved in the visual field (bug detectors?).

Subsequent work by Hubel and Wiesel (1959, 1962, 1963a) showed that neurons in the primary visual cortex of the cat were excited when particular features were moved in a specific area of the visual field (the receptive field of the cell). These cortical cellular responses in the cat were more complex than those found in the frog tectum, and four parameters of stimulation were found to affect the firing rates of the cells: the size of the (typically rectangular) stimulus, the presence of a constrasting border, the speed and direction of motion of a feature, and the orientation of a bar of light or shadow. The response of a cell might be modified by any one, or a number, of these parameters, and the specific combination that produced the maximal response was the same for both eyes. Generally, this so-called optimal stimulus was equally effective in producing a response from either eye, though there might be ocular dominance. Finally, when the cell was stimulated binocularly, the response could be modified by displacing either of the two stimuli laterally in the visual field. This was termed disparity sensitivity, and the stimulus positions producing the maximum cell firing were termed corresponding points.

A good argument could be advanced that the response characteristics of the neurons in the frog tectum were genetically determined, since the responses were simple and the frog had adapted to a highly restricted environment. It was less clear that the complex cell response characteristics of the cortical neurons of the cat were programmed in the genes. Furthermore, it made sense for a mammal to have its feature detectors specified by the environment rather than by the genome, since this would allow the animal to adapt to radically different visual environments. This amounts to a restatement of the old nature-nurture problem at the level of the individual cell. Are the response characteristics of individual cells in the visual system specified by heredity, or are they undetermined (plastic) and specified by the environment?

Hubel and Wiesel set out to answer this question in a now-classic series of experiments on young kittens (Hubel and Wiesel, 1963b, 1965; Wiesel and Hubel, 1963, 1965). They showed that the appearance of the normal pattern of binocular cellular response characteristics could be prevented by any one of several procedures that altered the kittens' visual environment if such procedures were carried out during the first three months of life. Thus, if one eye of a visually naive kitten was sutured closed or occluded with a translucent disk placed over that eye for a period of two to three months, very few responses could be recorded from opposite cortical cells when the eye was stimulated. In contrast, responses from the open eye appeared to be normal. Furthermore, if both eyes were allowed to see a normal patterned environment, but concurrent binocular vision was prevented by switching the occluder from one eye to the other daily, or by eliminating the normal overlap between the visual fields by cutting an external ocular muscle, two separate monocular populations of cells resulted. The normal pattern of binocular activation, therefore, seemed to depend on the preservation of concurrent inputs to the two eyes from the same areas in visual space during a critical period of early visual development.

The results of two other sets of experiments forced Hubel and Wiesel to come to a completely opposite conclusion. First, they showed that cortical cells of visually naive kittens could be excited by stimuli delivered to either eye. Moreover, the cells had similar orientation and movement preference to stimulus features delivered to either eye. They then showed that suturing both eyes closed for a two- to three-month period did not lead to any deterioration in the pattern of response specificity which they had demonstrated in the visually naive kittens. They were therefore forced to conclude that much of the complexity of firing of kitten visual cortical cells developed in the absence of either patterned stimulation or binocular vision. The crucial factor in the disruption of the normal binocular responses in the earlier experiments was assumed to be something other than the prevention of binocular vision, since binocular suturing clearly achieved that end but did not seem to affect binocular cortical cellular responses.

Had Hubel and Wiesel's (quite tentative) conclusions been correct, the effect would have been to remove much of the promise from the study of individual cortical cellular firing patterns. Since neuronal activity is considered to be such a unit of perception, one might expect that activity might conform more closely to the behavioral changes that follow visual deprivation. For example, cats tested during the initial postdeprivation period often seem completely blind; they bump into objects, show abnormal gait, and tend to "freeze" or show extreme hyperactivity when presented with novel stimuli. The implication was that one would be forced to look elsewhere in the nervous system for an explanation for these behavioral effects. Fortunately, subsequent studies have been more encouraging.

Pettigrew (1974) has reexamined the activity of cortical cells in the visually naive and visually deprived kitten. He found, as did Hubel and Wiesel, that cortical cells could be excited by stimuli delivered to either eye, although the cells were not sensitive to retinal disparity and therefore could not support depth discriminations which are a feature of binocular vision in adults. Furthermore, although many of the cells responded to the direction of motion of objects in the visual field, they did not show any sensitivity to orientation. More important, Pettigrew showed that binocularity and orientation sensitivity were in a similar undeveloped state in kittens who had both eyes sutured closed for six weeks after they would normally open. In cats not so deprived these response specificities developed normally. Visual deprivation, then, appears to delay development of response specificity. The implication is that the formation of these two types of response patterns—orientation and binocularity—may be determined by visual experience. There has been much controversy in recent years concerning the evidence that can be accepted as confirmation that this is the case.

In the normal adult cat orientation specificity and disparity sensitivity can be found in the same cell (the cell is best stimulated by the same stimulus orientation in either eye, and when both eyes are stimulated, the cell responds best when the two stimuli are a particular distance apart laterally). Also, the cat's orientation-specific cells are not all sensitive to the same orientations. Many respond to any one of the remaining diagonal positions.

Hirsch and Spinelli (1970) were the first to argue that orientation-sensitive cells could be induced to respond to the particular orientations (horizontal or vertical stripes) of stimulus patterns, if these patterns constituted their only visual experience. These authors raised kittens in total darkness for the first 3 months of life except for periods of 8 hours a day during which one eye was exposed to black and white vertical lines and the other eye was exposed to black and white horizontal lines. They found that after this selective visual experience, cells "driven" from the eye previously exposed to vertical lines were successfully excited only by vertically oriented line stimuli, and cells "driven" from the eye previously exposed to horizontal lines were successfully excited only by horizontally oriented line stimuli. Similar results have also been reported by Stryker and Sherk (1975).

Blakemore and Cooper (1970) reported that cellular orientation "preferences" could also be changed if kittens were allowed to view either horizontal or vertical line patterns binocularly. However, this result has been disputed (Stryker and Sherk, 1975; Shinkman and Bruce, 1977). These kinds of observations have been taken to indicate that the orientation-sensitive cells somehow "mirror" the environment. That is, the orientation-sensitive cells are presumed to develop their maximal response to the particular orientation to which the animals were exposed, and this response characteristic is in some sense a memory of that experience. If this were the case, it would serve as a clear example of neuronal adaptibility since, it is argued, an orientation detector detects the orientation it does because it has been exposed to that particular orientation during development.

Recent findings make it unlikely that previous results have so straightforward an interpretation. Leventhal and Hirsch (1975) have shown that similar distributions of cells with either horizontal or vertical preference response characteristics can be produced by limiting cats' early visual experience to the viewing of different diagonal patterns by each eye. Following this procedure, they found cells that responded best to horizontal, vertical, or diagonal orientations. If the cats were allowed to view horizontal and vertical patterns (one by each eye), no cells responsive to diagonal orientations could be found. These authors therefore concluded that precise information about diagonal orientations might be a prerequisite for the development of cells sensitive to those orientations but that horizontal and vertical preferences developed even though the cats were never allowed to view horizontal or vertical lines. Cynader, Berman, and Hein (1975) found that animals raised in an environment of irregularly shaped patterns moving constantly to the left had a predominance of cortical cells whose maximal response was to vertical orientations. This result has no ready explanation, but it illustrates that the appearance of particular orientation preferences by cortical cells need not reflect a specific memory for the environment.

There is a second objection to the idea that orientation-detecting cells can become "tuned" to particular orientations in the environment and as a result are a memory of those orientations. When animals are tested behaviorally after these selective exposure procedures, they react no better to the features to which they were exposed than do normal animals, even though the presumed effect is to make the cells maximally responsive to those features. Muir and Mitchell (1973) found that cats raised in either horizontal or vertical striped environments were no better than normals in discriminating between stimulus orientations close to the ones in which they had been reared. Blakemore and Cooper (1970) found only detrimental effects of selective rearing; they found that such cats were worse than normals in reaching for stimuli in planes orthogonal to the ones to which they were exposed.

There is insufficient evidence, at present, to evaluate the significance of these reports since cell loss, specific induction (diagonal lines induce diagonal preferences), and nonspecific induction (moving shapes induce vertical preferences) could all be involved. Each of these possibilities has different implications for any discussion of cellular plasticity. What can be said at present is that under some circumstances the orientation-sensitive activity patterns of cortical cells appear to have been modified as a result of the animal's early experience. The more specific claim that information about the orientations present in the environment has become incorporated into the cells as some form of memory of the early environment does not appear to be substantiated.

Binocular Interactions and Early Experience

A much clearer statement can be made concerning the effects of experience on the binocular activity patterns of individual cortical cells. The specificity exhibited by many cortical cells is precisely mirrored in each eye. That is, the cell responds to corresponding points in the two visual fields. When the visual fields are misaligned early in life, there is evidence that the cellular response specificities in the two eyes shift in a direction that appears to compensate for these misalignments. Shlaer (1971) had kittens wear prisms that induced a relative vertical disparity of 4° between the two eyes. The cells that he monitored did not respond to corresponding points after the prisms were removed but to points misaligned vertically by approximately the same amount that the visual fields had been misaligned. Shinkman and Bruce (1977) have reported similar compensatory adjustments in orientation sensitivity following early experience during which prisms were used to rotate the visual axis of the two eyes with respect to each other. They showed that if inputs to the two eyes of young, visually naive cats were rotated relative to each other by 16° (the prisms produced the same result that would have been achieved by rotating one eye clockwise by 8° and the other eye counterclockwise by 8°) the kittens appeared to develop quite normally when their sole visual experience was gained during the first 12 weeks of life during a series of 1- to 2-hour sessions in a "playroom." Visual orientation and depth discrimination in particular appeared to develop normally. Subsequent recording of the binocular orientation preferences of cortical cells indicated that the most effective (optimal) stimuli for each were not in the same plane as they are in normally reared animals but in planes rotated relative to each other by approximately the same amount as the prisms rotated the visual fields. Here, there is clear evidence that visual experience changes orientation sensitivity in the two eyes and by doing so preserves binocular vision—a clear case of adaptive plasticity, as the term is currently used.

Apart from these experiments, there is little evidence that abnormal rearing conditions give the animals an adaptive advantage by allowing them to discriminate the patterns to which they were exposed better than the normally reared animal could. Rather the animals are deficient in the ability to discriminate patterns to which they were not exposed. The final question is whether the deficits produced are permanent and, if not, what additional evidence of visual system plasticity is revealed in the type of recovery observed.

A number of findings suggest that recovery of visual function after severe deprivation may occur following postoperative training. Riesen (1947) raised chimpanzees for 16 months in total darkness. When they emerged from this situation, the animals appeared to be blind; however, with intensive postdeprivation training, many of the deficits initially observed disappeared even though prolonged rearing in the dark produced clouding of the optic disk and degeneration of retinal ganglion cells. Ganz and Fitch (1968) raised kittens from birth for 1-6 months with one pair of eyelids sutured closed. When the suture was removed, the acuity of the deprived eye was significantly less than that of the experienced eye. The experienced eye was then sutured closed and the cats were forced to use the peviously deprived eye. As a result of this training, visual acuity using the previously deprived eye improved to the same level as that demonstrated using the experienced eye.

Two similar demonstrations suggest differing explanations of the mechanism of recovery. Chow and Stewart's (1972) study of monocular pattern discrimination indicated that intensive training with the deprived eye open causes initially abnormal striate neurons to respond to visual inputs. Rizzolatti and Tradardi (1971) suggest that their animals used a different strategy when solving pattern discriminations with the previously deprived eye. These authors noted that the animals made large sweeping head movements as if they were scanning the visual targets presented to them. Rizzolatti and Tradardi hypothesized that the cortical disorganization produced by the early sensory restriction forced the animals to use subcortical centers that are normally insensitive to shape and orientation of stimuli but can respond to the displacement of targets. This implied shift in mediation of visual function from one area of the central nervous system to another can also be taken as an example of the adaptive plasticity of brain functions. Such shifts in function have also been proposed to account for the ability of animals under certain conditions to learn to solve complex pattern discriminations after total, bilateral removals of visual cortex (Spear and Braun, 1969; Spear and Barbas, 1975).

Whether extensive training or retraining is necessary for adaptive response to visual deprivation during development has not been completely resolved. In a recent experiment Kratz, Spear, and Smith (1976) sutured one eye of kittens closed until the animals were 4-8 months of age. The kittens under these conditions had hardly any cells in their striate (visual) cortex that could be driven by visual stimulation of the depressed eye. Such data could be taken to suggest that the lid suturing during a "critical" stage of development permanently eliminates visual-cortical function in these animals. However, Kratz, Spear, and Smith raised another group of kittens to 4-5 months of age with lid sutured and, just prior to the opening of the eye, enucleated the animals' normal (previously used) eye. Recording on the day of enucleation from the side of the visual cortex receiving projections from the deprived eye showed that 29%-39% of the cells respond to visual stimulation although, as might be expected, their response was not normal. That is, receptive fields were nonspecific and only 39% were direction sensitive.

Kratz, Spear, and Smith suggest that the immediate response of cells from the deprived eye is due to release from tonic inhibition imposed by the development of activity in the normal eye. The cells were not eliminated by the prolonged deprivation, but their functional activity was altered, demonstrating that experience plays a critical role in determining the brain's response to environmental stimulation.

However, visual deprivation has profound peripheral effects, and the initial deficits may reflect those peripheral abnormalities. Wiesel and Raviola (1976) have shown that an eye of a rhesus monkey grew significantly larger over the eighteen-month period during which its lids were sutured than the open eye. The animal was myopic in the sutured eye as a direct consequence of the growth. Thus one may not safely ascribe all the deficits following visual deprivation to the changes produced in the central nervous system, since they could have a peripheral origin. That is not to say that a peripheral change may not subsequently cause a change more centrally. For example, Mitchell and his co-workers have shown that the acuity deficits in astigmats, who have one visual axis out of focus because of a lens defect, cannot be corrected optically by making all planes equally well in focus on the back of the eye. The source of the deficit is more central in the visual system. Apparently the consequences of childhood experience with blurred vision in one axis had influenced the development of visual neural elements.

Similar long-term acuity deficits can also be produced after short periods of restricted visual input. Muir and Mitchell (1973) showed that cats kept in either horizontal or vertical restricted environments for the first 4 months of life performed as well as normals when the gratings were oriented in the same plane as the stripes they saw as kittens, while their performance on gratings that were orthogonal to those on which they were raised was impaired. The deficits in acuity discrimination were observed for as long as 30 months following normal visual stimulation. It is probably the case, however, that numerous other aspects of human vision can be modified in later stages of life. There is an interesting parallel between the animal analogues, where prism rotations affect cortical cellular activity in predictable ways, and human research, where it has been shown that humans can adapt to prisms that invert normal vision.

In summary, studies of the development of individual, cortical, cellular response patterns in the cat can be taken to indicate that these patterns are highly malleable during the first few months of life after the eyes open. The formation of the normal binocular response patterns appears to depend on the fact that the two visual fields are normally fairly well aligned since the cortical cell firing patterns demonstrate that the visual system compensates for misalignments. A rudimentary form of binocular activation of cortical cells appears to be present before eye opening, but this can be interfered with by altering the early visual environment. The results obtained after suturing one or both eyes closed are taken to indicate that visual experience is necessary for the subsequent elaboration of initial response patterns, but subsequent studies of behavior following such procedures suggest that training can overcome at least some of the deficits produced. These observations lead to the suggestion that early visual experience may not be critical for the elaboration of some aspects of vision, and the visual system seems to retain the plasticity necessary for adaptive modification at later stages of development.

Growth and Regeneration in the Central Nervous System

The subject of neural growth and regeneration, with the possibility that such regeneration might serve as the basis for function restitution after damage to the central nervous system, has recently become one of the most active areas of research in neurobiology. Since the early work of Cajal (1928), it has been known that there is some regeneration of axons after spinal cord injury, but under Cajal's experimental conditions regeneration was limited and therefore not considered to be of any functional significance. As a result of early failures, that regeneration in the CNS of higher mammals did not exist became a fundamental concept. If, however, it could be shown that under certain conditions the damaged central nervous system did respond with changes in structure based on regeneration of anomalous, or collateral, fibers to replace those that were lost, it might then be possible to relate these changes to functional restitution sometimes observed in the clinic or the behavioral laboratory. Modification of the nervous system in this sense represents a positive aspect of plasticity through renewal of synaptic contacts rather than a negative process (such as producing deficits in binocularity by altering neuronal functions).

Although in its broadest sense regeneration of any kind could be considered a second example of adaptability to injury, we would like to argue for a more restricted use of the term. If one is concerned only with the question whether any type of regeneration occurs, this could be seen as a simple definition of plasticity since such growth or hypertrophy would represent morphological change in an existing anatomical structure. However, one need not be concerned with whether such regrowth was orderly or whether it had any functional significance for the brain-damaged organism. An example is reported in a recent paper by Geschwind (1974), in which he describes a disorder known as palatal myoclonus. As a result of a lesion in the dentate nucleus (a part of the cerebellum), the patient develops a rapid striking movement of the soft palate, pharynx, and larynx. The symptoms take about a year after the lesion to develop. If the patient dies, postmortem autopsy would reveal extensive hypertrophy of the olive (another cerebellar nucleus) on the side opposite the lesion. "Microscopically, the neurons in the olive are grossly enlarged with tremendous thickening and tortuousity of the dendrites" (p. 476). In this instance, anomalous growth is of very limited value to the organism. A much more important question for those interested in nervous system function should be, What do the new fibers or terminals do? For example, do new fibers return to the same regions they previously innervated? What happens to regenerating fibers when the regions they previously innervated are removed? What are the consequences of anomalous innervation by newly regenerated fibers? Are parallel pathways capable of carrying the same "information" as those that have been destroyed by lesion or traumatic injury? Are the processes involved in morphological reorganization after injury closely related to growth processes that occur in the normal organism? These are but a few of the areas under study by investigators seeking to determine the bases of functional recovery.

Some of the earliest work on neural specificity and regeneration was initiated by Sperry (1943, 1944). Much of this work has used the eye and the brain of the goldfish because it is a relatively simple system in which fibers from the retina project directly and in topographical fashion to the optic lobe of the opposite hemisphere (Meyer and Sperry, 1974). By cutting the nerve fibers and studying the pattern of regeneration, Sperry showed that the regenerating fibers grow along specific pathways to reach very specific target points in the tectum. Even when the fibers are divided or scrambled, "they somehow unsort themselves and regrow the appropriate topographic projections required for optokinetic, orienting and visual discrimination behavior" (p. 47). In some cases Sperry (1943, 1944) rotated the eyeball of the fish so that the animals were obliged to view the world upside down. This state resulted from the fact that the nerve fibers grew back into their original location. No amount of training or environmental experience could overcome the behavioral abnormalities produced by these experimental procedures. That the regeneration and remapping were so precise and orderly suggested to Sperry that target cells in the optic tectum must give off a sort of chemical marker that leads the regenerating retinal axon to its precise terminus even though such regeneration may result in functionally maladaptive consequences for the organism.

Recently, Yoon (1975) was able to demonstrate essentially the same degree of precision of retinotectal projections in the adult goldfish. (Many of the earlier studies had used apparently immature specimens, and it was believed that there might have been a restricted "critical period" for regeneration.) Yoon removed pieces of tectum and rotated the slabs around the dorsoventral axis or placed the tissue upside down with respect to its laminar structure. After a period of recovery, recordings were made from single neurons in the transplanted areas and compared with tectal responses in normal animals. The reimplanted slabs in the adult fish became innervated by the regenerating optic fibers. Yoon found that the reimplanted slabs "retained their original topographic polarity *regardless* of the orientation of reimplantation" (p. 152). One surprising (and inexplicable) finding was that although the topographic arrangements of regenerating optic fibers were the same as in the intact goldfish, the reimplanted tectum showed "a severe (morphological) disarrangement in its laminar structures." Thus the specificity of the regeneration may not have been due to the integrity of the target issue, as Sperry (1944) had suggested; the regenerating fibers "knew" where to go in spite of the marked disarrangement of the receptor areas to which they were directed.

Although these studies were experimental demonstrations of a type of anomalous growth in the nervous system, any extrapolation to clinical phenomena is limited by the fact that the nervous systems of the fish, the newt, and the frog are thought to be less complex than that of the mammal. Thus, while we can accept the possibility of extensive regeneration in poikilothermic teleosts, some workers have felt more hesitation in applying the same principles of neural organization to the brain of adult mammals. Cajal (1928) stated: "Once development was ended, the founts of growth and regeneration of the axons and dendrites dried up irrevocably. In adult centers, the nerve paths are something fixed, and immutable; everything may die, nothing may be regenerated" (p. 750). Only within the last six to ten years has regenerative capacity been demonstrated in the adult, mammalian nervous system. However, there are only hints, not yet conclusive evidence, that regenerated terminals serve as the substrate for behavioral restitution after brain damage.

At the present at least two types of growth have been observed in the central nervous systems of developing and adult mammals. The first type has been called *regenerative sprouting* and represents the type of neuronal change in response to injury that we have already discussed. (Indeed, some workers have suggested that regenerative sprouting represents an aspect of the growth process that can be seen in normal organisms; Sotelo and Palay, 1971.) In this situation the axons of cells are cut and the distal portion begins to degenerate. The remaining stump (including the cell body) begins to form growth cones and regenerate new terminals (Moore, 1974). The second type of growth in response to nerve injury has been called *collateral sprouting*. In this case a certain number of cells innervating a given structure are destroyed and their terminals degenerate. However, remaining, intact cells begin to grow additional new terminals (sprouting) that innervate the target area evacuated by the damaged neurons; thus the degenerated inputs were replaced by terminals arriving from intact neurons.

Studies on regeneration (as opposed to collateral sprouting or anomalous sprouting) have been concerned primarily with investigation of central adrenergic neurons.[1] Within a very short time after an adrenergic axon transection there is an accumulation of amine in the stump (Björklund and Stenevi, 1971) which continues to increase over the next few days. After about two or three weeks, there is a significant increase in the number of fluorescent fibers along the lesion border that remain "as a permanent feature of the reorganized nervous system."[2] Often the sprouting fibers grow into blood vessels or into the area of the lesion, but such nerve terminals would be unlikely to result in significant functional contacts that might be implicated in behavioral recovery (Stenevi, Björklund, and Moore, 1973). In addition, to demonstrate functional significance, the pattern of regeneration should be similar to the original pattern of innervation, as shown by the work of Meyer and Sperry (1974) or Yoon (1975).

To test the hypothesis that regenerated adrenergic sprouts could make functional and organized synaptic contacts, Björklund and his colleagues at Lund, Sweden, performed a series of elegant experiments. They removed pieces of the iris (which is adrenergically innervated) from rats and transplanted the tissue into the animal's medial forebrain bundle which contains both the ascending and descending pathways of the adrenergic neuronal system (Björklund and Stenevi, 1971). Obviously, when removed from the eye, the iris loses all its "normal" innervation, but it can serve as a target organ for regenerating adrenergic neurons. The animals with transplants were then killed at various stages after the surgery and their brains examined for evidence of regeneration. At first (3-5 days after transplantation) there was the typical pattern of accumulation of amines in the proximal stumps of the cut axons but no growth of fibers into the transplanted iris. About 1 week after the operation very "delicate, varicose fibers" could be seen near or on the surface of the iris, but they did not penetrate it. About 2 weeks after the transplant the regenerating fibers entered into the iris in bundles of axons with specific orientations. At longer survival periods numerous adrenergic fibers were present "and at this stage, the arrangement of fibers is in places very similar to the innervation pattern of the intact iris innervated by peripheral sympathetic neurons" (Stenevi, Björklund, and Moore, 1973). Histochemical studies of the reinnervated transplant revealed that most of the regenerated fibers were adrenergic, and tissue examined 6 months after the transplant showed a picture identical to that of 40 days.

To test further the idea of the specificity of the reinnervation and the possibility that the terminals may be physiologically active, Svengaard, Björklund, and Stenevi (1975) introduced other types of tissue (mitral valve from the heart, which is adrenergic; pieces of diaphragm or uterus, which are not) into the region of the medial forebrain bundle. The tissues that are adrenergically innervated had patterns of reinnervation that closely resembled their normal state. With the other pieces of tissue the regenerating sprouts did not enter the transplant, grew in somewhat haphazard order around the material, and did not establish functional contacts. These studies support the work of Sperry, since they demonstrated that the target area is important in directing the growth and affinity patterns of the regenerating neurons. In the face of such results one might justifiably ask why there is not a greater degree of functional restitution than is usually observed in clinical cases. The answers are, unfortunately, quite complex. First, after traumatic injury severe displacement of tissue may prevent the growing neurons from following preestablished pathways to their appropriate target organs. Second, in uncontrolled (and even in experimental) traumatic injury there is often a dramatic decrease or change in the vascular and metabolic patterns of the damaged tissue which could prevent or reduce reinnervation. Third, there is almost always a marked glial and connective tissue reaction which could serve as a physical barrier to the regenerating cells. Age and the general condition of the organism at the time of injury could play important roles, but these variables are only just now being given serious experimental consideration.

Although little is known about the conditions that can promote neural regeneration in the CNS, some important and exciting findings have recently been reported. Björklund and his colleagues have been working with a complex protein called *nerve growth factor* (NGF) that was isolated in mammals by Levi-Montalcini (Levi-Montalcini and Angeletti, 1968). In the mammalian brain NGF administered intracerebrally or intraventricularly enhances the rate of regeneration of adrenergic fibers (Björklund and Stenevi, 1972; Björklund, Bjerre, and Stenevi, 1974). In one experiment, Björklund and his colleagues used 4 to 5-week-old mice that had first been treated with 6 hydroxydopamine (6-OH-DA), a neurotoxin that causes degeneration of adrenergic terminals in the sympathetic system. The authors report that there is complete degeneration of terminals as soon as twenty-four hours after a single injection of the drug. Some of the mice were given 6-OH-DA and were then treated with NGF for six days. In most of the tissues they studied (iris, salivary glands, intestine, pancreas) NGF-treated mice showed a much greater fluorescence intensity, indicating preservation of nonadrenergic terminals, compared with those that were given 6-OH-DA alone. In addition, there was an increase in the rate of recovery of the endogenous NGF taken from the salivary glands.

In another series of experiments, the Swedish group transplanted pieces of iris in the medial forebrain bundle (MFB) and then immediately gave an intracerebral injection of NGF. These workers noted a significant increase in the rate and number of adrenergic regenerating fibers that penetrated the transplant within the first 7 days. The maximum effects of the NGF treatment were seen if the protein was given at the time of transplantation; even if the injections were delayed by a few hours, there was less effect, which in any case is not seen until 7 days after NGF treatment.

The pharmacological and biochemical mechanisms of NGF on regeneration are not yet completely understood, although there seems to be some evidence that the compound is taken up by retrograde axonal transport in adrenergic neurons (Stöeckel and Thöenen, 1975) where it is said to increase glucose utilization and lipid and protein synthesis (Levi-Montalcini and Angeletti, 1968). In a recent report Varon (1975) cites evidence to suggest that NGF affects intracellular dopamine beta-hydroxylase and tyrosine hydrosylase activity and may play a role in regulating RNA synthesis and in regulating glucose metabolism. Varon also mentions the possibility that NGF may alter membrane permeability and enhance the ability of neurons to adhere to other nonneural structures such as glial cells, which have been shown to play an important role in guiding neurons to their appropriate target organs during development (Rakic, 1975).

Despite the potential importance of NGF for regeneration of damaged neural tissue, almost nothing has been done to explore the behavioral consequences of administering the compound to brain-damaged subjects. Berger, Wise, and Stein (1973) demonstrated that adult rats made adipsic and aphagic by bilateral hypothalamic damage were able to recover and eat normally if high doses of NGF were administered after surgery. In recovered hypothalamic rats administration of the NGF blocked reappearance of symptoms caused by administration of 6-OH-DA (6-hydroxy-dopamine), the neurotoxin that destroys adrenergic cells.

In our laboratory at Clark University we have been concerned with whether NGF administration can repair the damage and subsequent behavioral deficits produced by bilateral lesions of the caudate nucleus. This structure has been implicated in the control of motor behavior, and severe impairments on tasks involving motor coordination often result when this tissue is damaged (Schultze and Stein, 1975). In one experiment (Hart et al., 1978) we made bilateral lesions of the caudate-putamen complex in adult male rats and then immediately injected (bilaterally) the animals with either 125 biological units of NGF per side, in buffer solution, or gave control animals just an injection of buffer solution in the same volume. Both NGF and buffer solution injections were given intracerebrally in an attempt to place the solutions in the adrenergic area of terminals coming to the cau-date-putamen complex from the medial forebrain bundle and sub-stantia nigra. The performance of the two brain-damaged groups was compared to intact rats. Analysis of our behavioral results revealed that the NGF-treated rats perseverated significantly less than buffer-treated animals (perseveration is a classic symptom of caudate lesions in rats) and were less emotional. However, NGF-treated subjects made no more avoidance to electric shock than did brain-damaged rats without the NGF. In sum, there were no statistically significant differences between NGF-treated, brain-damaged rats and intact, unoperated controls on some of the learning measures employed. To our knowledge this is the first attempt to demonstrate that NGF may have important functional consequences for congitive and emotional behavior in brain-damaged subjects. However, until all the evidence is in, one should be careful in attributing this recovery to specific regen-erative or growth properties of the NGF. Our analysis of brain sec-tions revealed no differences in the number of healthy neurons re-maining in the caudate nucleus of brain-damaged NGF-treated or brain-damaged control rats, although there were differences in glia-to-neuron ratios, with the NGF-treated rats having fewer glial cells. One could also argue that NGF serves merely as a neural stimulant to in-crease vigilance or arousal, perhaps by modifying tyrosine hydroxylase or other transmitter activity. Recovery of behavioral function after brain damage has been induced by amphetamine injections that might have nothing to do with regeneration per se (Glick, 1974); rather, the drug increases the overall level of arousal in the CNS. Lewis (1977) tested the hypothesis that NGF could have ameliorating effects on brain damage by injecting the substance into the region of the sub-stantia nigra in rats given bilateral 6-hydroxydopamine-induced le-sions of the nucleus accumbens (a subcortical structure that may play a role in motor activity). Lewis hypothesized that the NGF treatment would cause remaining intact, catacholaminergic terminals from sub-stantia nigra (a brain stem nucleus implicated in sleep and arousal) to sprout into the denervated region created by the lesion and thus facili-tate the recovery of normal amphetamine-induced motor activity that is diminished or eliminated following damage to the n. accumbens. Lewis further speculated that if recovery of function was observed, it would be due to nearly normal steady-state levels of NA or DA re-leased by the ascending nigrostriatal system and that these enhanced levels of the catecholomines would reflect NGF-induced neural activ-ity.

As with the previous study, administration of NGF facilitated behavioral recovery of normal activity levels in rats with lesions of nucleus accumbens, but the biochemical analysis did not reveal any significant change in steady-state levels of either NA or DA, which suggests that catecholaminergic neural growth may not have mediated behavioral recovery. Subsequent experiments to determine whether turnover of these catecholamines was affected were also somewhat inconclusive but suggested that altered rates of neurotransmitter synthesis may be important in initiating trophic responses of regenerating neurons to their appropriate target areas. Despite the difficulty in assessing the biochemical substrates of recovery of function induced by NGF, there is now reason to believe that the substance may play an important role in reorganization of function following CNS injury. However, we remain cautious in interpreting these findings until more data can be obtained and evaluated. Further research in this area promises to be both exciting and worthwhile with respect to its clinical possibilities.

Functional Recovery in Developing Animals

Collateral sprouting, defined as the replacement of degenerated terminals by growth of neighboring, intact axonal sprouts, is another type of neuronal adaptability that may be involved in functional restitution after brain damage. The most obvious examples of alterations in growth patterns of neural pathways have come from research on neonatal subjects, where there appears to be a greater degree of behavioral recovery after brain damage (Kennard, 1938; Stewart and Reisen, 1972). If plasticity is limited to neonatal preparations, it would be important to demonstrate whether there is a critical period during which anomalous projections can be formed. If there is a critical period of neuronal regrowth in response to injury, one expects that no regeneration or anomalous sprouting would be possible once the stage has passed. However, there appears to be evidence both for and against the notion that regeneration is limited to a specific period in early development.

Lund, Cunningham, and Lund (1973) compared the responses of infant and adult nervous systems to injury. Lund and colleagues removed an eye in newborn or mature rats and then studied the distribution of optic terminals from the remaining eye to either the superior colliculus or the dorsal lateral geniculate body (both structures are parts of the thalamus that receive projections from the optic nerve). The albino rat is a good preparation for this type of experiment because each retina projects very heavily on the contralateral superior colliculus, with only a very few fibers going to the ipsilateral colliculus at the level of the stratum opticum. Lund showed that if one eye is removed at birth, the projections from the remaining eye will grow to cover the entire area of the colliculus. In contrast, if the eye is removed 10 days after birth, this increased growth does not occur. This result suggests that the critical period for this neuroplasticity is limited to the first 10 days of postnatal life.

To test this hypothesis, Lund, Cunningham, and Lund (1973) studied the effects of eye removal in rats from 1 day to 100 days of age. At varying points in time (3-22 months after the first operation), the second eye was removed in order to study the distribution of fibers by degeneration techniques.[3] The authors were able to show that when the eye is removed during the first 2 weeks after birth, there is substantial reorganization in growth patterns but very little after the first 2 postnatal weeks. They found considerable transneuronal degeneration; cells in the superior colliculus were reduced by as much as 54% of their normal number. There was an increase in the number of ipsilateral fibers replacing the crossed fibers that had been destroyed by removal of one eye. After 10 days of age the pattern of degeneration following removal of the second eye revealed no increase in distribution of ipsilateral fibers, indicating that the capacity to reorganize after damage to the central nervous system apparently becomes severely restricted.

Lund and his colleagues suggested that the enlarged ipsilateral pathway results from a rerouting of immature fibers, caused by the eye removal, that are still in the process of growth and would normally cross at the optic chiasm to innervate the contralateral colliculus. They proposed that once the optic fibers crossed the chiasm (the growth taking 5-10 days), plasticity is reduced, and this fact would account for the lack of effects seen after eye removal in older animals. Lund and his co-workers distinguish between actual growth of new neurons into an area (rerouting) and collateral sprouting in which mature neurons sprout additional terminals to replace those that have been destroyed by injury.

More recently, So and Schneider (1978) also demonstrated that collateral sprouting may be age dependent and limited to the first 14 days of postnatal life. In newborn hamsters removal of the superficial layers of the right superior colliculus (SC) causes fibers coming from the right eye to cross the animal's midline (a phenomenon not seen in intact animals) and terminate in the left SC. If, at birth, the hamster's right eye is also removed, the anomalous fibers coming from the left eye spread across the entire right SC, but if eye removal is delayed 7-14 days, this spread is markedly reduced or does not occur at all. Clearly, then, the growth of anomalous projections seems to occur for only a short period of time after birth, at least for the visual system. However, similar growth processes in response to injury are believed to occur in adult subjects.

Anomalous fiber projections resulting from CNS injury in young animals are not limited to the visual system. In an elegant study Hicks and d'Amato (1975) created lesions in the motor-sensory cortices of adult or developing rats and found that both young and adult subjects were impaired when required to run on difficult terrain (an elevated, narrow runway). In rats given lesions as infants Hicks and D'Amato noted small, aberrant circuits in the corticospinal tract that projected into the reticular formation, trigeminal region, and spinal cord in a manner similar to the normal animal. If lesions were made after 9 days of age, the aberrant fiber bundles did not develop—a pattern of growth similar to that observed by Lund and his colleagues for the visual system.

The most extensive series of experiments on the anatomical bases of functional restitution after brain damage have been carried out by Schneider (1973) and Schneider and Jhavari (1974). Schneider chose the hamster as an experimental subject because this animal is born, after a very short gestation period (16 days), with an immature CNS that grows rapidly to maturity within 3 months. In addition, the superior colliculus and visual cortex are easy to manipulate surgically (the colliculus is completely exposed; there is no cortex overlying it). If the superficial layers of the superior colliculus are ablated at birth, what happens to the fibers arriving from the optic tract? Schneider observed a new projection going to the lateral posterior nucleus of the thalamus and an increase in the number of projections in the ventral nucleus of the lateral geniculate body. "The abnormalities in the diencephalon occur in just those areas normally receiving projections from the superficial layers of the superior colliculus" (p. 73). Schneider also demonstrated that the extent of the retinotectal connection is directly correlated with the sparing (or recovery) of turning behavior toward a visual stimulus (sunflower seed). If the lesions in the tectum were large and prevented retinofugal fibers from reaching the dorsal midbrain, there was little or no sparing of the visually guided turning behavior— the greater the extent of the abnormal midbrain projection, the greater the degree of visual sparing observed. However, Schneider and Jhavari (1974) pointed out that not all anomalous projections were beneficial. Thus, in some cases, early unilateral tectal lesions resulted in abnormal retinal projections to the wrong side of the midbrain; the fibers crossed the midline and innervated the intact colliculus. In this situation the hamsters would turn away from the visual stimulus instead of toward it.

More recently, Devor (1975) described how axonal rearrangement can have either adaptive or pathological consequences, depending on the type and nature of the new connections formed. Devor studied mating behavior in male hamsters because this behavior is almost completely dependent on the sense of smell. Cutting the lateral olfactory tract (LOT) eliminates this input and the mating behavior that depends on its integrity. Cutting the LOT in neonatal or adult subjects would then provide information about the extent and nature of neural growth in these animals as well as the capacity for functional restitution of this relatively straightforward and easily observed behavior. Devor showed that complete transection of the LOT in the adult hamster eliminates mating behavior with no subsequent recovery. After complete LOT transection in the neonatal hamster, mating capacity is spared when the animals are tested as adults. If the LOT is only partially damaged in the neonate, mating capacity in later life is impaired; partial LOT transection in adults has much less severe consequences, with normal mating often observed.

Devor's anatomical data revealed that complete LOT section at 6 weeks of age or later was followed by total degeneration of nerve fibers and no subsequent mating (apparently intact fibers from the olfactory tubercle are not themselves sufficient to maintain mating). Following complete transection at 3 days of age, there was partial reinnervation of the rhinal cortex by fibers from the olfactory bulb or tubercle. LOT axons also sprouted new terminals into the limbic and neocortex of the rhinal sulcus. When the cuts were made at 7-10 days of age, the sprouting was much more restricted and there was no functional recovery. Apparently, the early lesions (3 days of age) permit the transected axons to sprout new terminals that reinnervate the deafferented cortex. The partial transections in the young animals permit some sprouting, but the intact fibers are also rearranged. The latter also grow into the denervated region but seem to cause a stunted growth of the transected axons which cannot keep pace with the rapidly growing cortex (Schneider and Jhavari, 1974) and thus result in less functional recovery.

It appears from these data that both collateral and regenerative sprouting occur more easily in young than in adult animals. Nonetheless, recent experiments have demonstrated that collateral sprouting in mature subjects is possible and that the new, additional terminals may be responsible for functional recovery from brain injury.

Anomalous Growth in Mature Subjects

Perhaps the best-known example of neural plasticity in mature subjects comes from the work of Raisman (1969). Raisman showed that two afferent fiber systems converge on the medial nucleus of the septum. One set of afferents arrive from the hippocampus via the fimbria and terminates on only the dendrites of the cell bodies in the septal nucleus. Fibers originating in the hypothalamus also terminate in the same septal nucleus but primarily on the soma of the cells as well as on some of the dendrites. If lesions were made in one of the fiber systems and a long survival period permitted, and a second lesion made (with short survival period) in the remaining system, a dramatic reorganization of the terminal projections took place in the latter. Thus if the lesion was placed in the fimbrial fiber system, there was, as might be expected, considerable degeneration of the synaptic terminals making contact with dendrites of the septal cells. In response to this degeneration fibers arriving from the hypothalamus sprouted new terminals, which had their contacts primarily on the regions evacuated by the degenerated fimbrial elements. Conversely, if hypothalamic fibers were transected, the fimbrial axons sprouted terminals that occupied sites along the soma of the septal cells. These findings were confirmed more recently by Raisman and Field (1973). The type of collateral sprouting described by Raisman and colleagues represents a generalized type of growth, since fibers from one system (fimbria) are replaced by terminal growths coming from another system (medial forebrain bundle). Moore, Björklund, and Stenevi (1971) have shown that the fibers coming from the MFB are primarily nonadrenergic, and when these sprout into synaptic areas evacuated by destruction of hippocampal inputs to septum, they are replacing terminals that are quite likely to be cholinergic or at least nonadrenergic.

One question that arises, then, is whether the nonspecific collateral sprouting of the type described by Moore, Björklund, and Stenevi (1971) and by Stenevi, Björklund, and Moore (1973) occurs more generally in the CNS. Such sprouting, if it occurs, would be a dramatic example of morphological plasticity in which one set of neurons, with one neurotransmitter action, could replace another set with a totally different transmitter action. Unfortunately, these studies were not concerned with the question of functional restitution, so whether behavioral recovery was mediated by the collaterals was never resolved.

The kind of nonspecificity of collateral sprouts described by Stenevi, Björklund, and Moore (1973) has been questioned by Goodman, Bogdesarian and Horel (1973). These investigators were concerned with axonal sprouting of retinal projections in adult rats after removal of one eye. They demonstrated, using degeneration stain techniques, that sprouting of uncrossed retinal projections occurs in regions where the uncrossed (retinal) projections normally terminate. However, Goodman and co-workers did not observe collateral sprouts coming into the denervated area from other associated neural systems, that is, anomalous projections. Thus the observed sprouting was limited to fibers from the uncrossed portion of the visual system itself. The authors suggest that this "priority" of "within-system" sprouting "should be most effective in establishing system repair and maintenance or recovery of function where *small numbers of neurons* of a system are destroyed in the adult brain" (p. 41). They stressed that at least for the adult brain, if sprouting is to occur, the system must be no more than partially destroyed so that the remaining intact neurons can grow into the terminal areas normally innervated by that particular system. These authors do not rule out the possibility that the sprouting they observed may be representative of normal growth and reparative processes observed by Sotelo and Palay (1971). The latter suggest that there is a continuous remodeling of axonal connections in the normal brain and that throughout life there are always some nerve endings that degenerate, with adjacent axons sprouting to establish new contacts. It may also be that dendritic fields enlarge or contract to accommodate changes in the axonal remodeling, although much less is known about this aspect of neuromorphological growth.

Functional and morphological changes in cerebral dendritic fields as a response to injury have recently received careful attention by Lynch and his co-workers. Using mature rats as subjects, they studied the morphological, chemical, and physiological responses of the dendate gyrus of the hippocampus to interruption of some of its primary afferent pathways. According to Lynch and Cotman (1975), the hippocampus is an ideal system for the study of synaptic modeling because its afferent and efferent pathways are highly specific. Also the dentate gyrus of the hippocampus is a layered structure, with well-defined afferents arising in the septum and entorhinal cortex. These afferents project in rigidly ordered fashion to the different layers of dentate, and this makes it possible to determine the morphological changes that occur after one or the other of the afferent systems is damaged or eliminated.

In one of their first experiments (Lynch et al., 1972) unilateral lesions were created in entorhinal cortex, and the hippocampus was examined for levels of acetylcholinesterase (ACHe). Lynch and his co-workers hypothesized that loss of entorhinal inputs into the dentate would trigger a massive growth of ACHe-containing fibers coming from the intact septal region. In the normal animal the outer molecular layer of the dentate shows very little ACHe response, that is, when entorhinal afferent projections are present. After the lesion, however, they found dense cholinesterase staining where it normally should not be. Did the ACHe-containing fibers, in fact, arise from anomalous septal projections replacing those that had been lost through damage? To answer this question, these workers created electrolytic lesions in the medial septal nuclei 30 days after an initial entorhinal lesion. Five days later the rats were killed and the molecular layer of the dentate evaluated for the presence of ACHe. As expected, the septal lesion completely eliminated all ACHe bands seen in animals with entorhinal lesions only. These data provide strong evidence for synaptic remodeling resulting from brain damage. It seems apparent that the adult CNS has the capacity for relocalization of terminals from one area or region to another and that the process of collateral reinnervation may occur as efficiently in the mature nervous system as in the developing brain.

Although the results of this experiment coincide nicely with other anatomical findings of sprouting in the adult mammalian brain, there is still the problem whether such new terminals are physiologically and/or behaviorally functional. One way of determining whether new sprouts are functional is to use electrophysiological recording in the reinnervated area. Using this approach, Steward, Cotman, and Lynch (1974) ablated entorhinal cortex in mature rats in order to eliminate synaptic input to the granular cells of the ipsilateral dentate gyrus. They then traced fiber projections from the intact, contralateral entorhinal cortex and found that 60 days after the initial lesion new fibers from the intact side of the brain grew into the denervated region and terminated on cells that normally received ipsilateral entorhinal input. To determine whether the new contacts were functional, Steward, Cotman, and Lynch (1973) stimulated entorhinal cortex contralateral to the damaged side and found that there was a short latency activation of the previously denervated region. In normal animals contralateral stimulation does not produce such activation. The response to stimulation does not appear immediately but rather takes about 9-15 days to mature functionally and then remains stable for as long as 200 days. The authors conclude that "the new synapses are formed rapidly in response to a deafferenting lesion and remain permanently capable of activating the dentate granule cells which had been deprived of ipsilateral entorhinal input" (p. 45). These results can be taken to demonstrate that adult CNS neurons are capable of considerable regenerative capacity; lesions somehow entrain a highly specific and rapid pattern of reconnection that appears to be electrophysiologically functional.

The important question, of course, is whether the new terminals are behaviorally functional. On this point there is no direct evidence. However, Loesche and Steward (1977) recently carried out a series of experiments in which they attempted to correlate behavioral recovery with the time course required for proliferation of new synaptic connections in adult rats. They created both bilateral and unilateral lesions of the entorhinal cortex (EC) and examined alternation performance of the brain-damaged animals in comparison with sham controls. Rats with bilateral lesions showed profound deficits on the spatial task and did not recover within the time period studied. In contrast, the rats with unilateral EC lesions permitted a 10-day postoperative recovery period performed as well as normals, although another group that began testing 3 days after surgery showed an initial deficit which recovered at control levels of performance by 10 days postoperatively.

Loesche and Steward next damaged the contralateral EC and found that this second operation in the unilaterally operated rats resulted in profound and long-lasting disruption of the alternation performance that had recovered following the primary, unilateral EC lesion (1977). Loesche and Steward concluded that the observed recovery depends on the integrity of the EC and is a time-dependent process as well. They note a strong coincidence between the time period for recovery of alternation performance and the time required for reinnervation of the dentate gyrus by the contralateral, intact EC (West et al., 1975) and reappearance of dendritic field potentials in rats with unilateral EC lesions. The authors feel that their position is supported by their finding that bilateral EC lesions result in profound impairments, even if there is a large interval between operations. Their data can be interpreted as strong evidence for the role of sprouting as a mechanism underlying functional recovery, and their position receives support from other investigators as well (Goldberger, 1974; Murray and Goldberger, 1974; Patrissi and Stein, 1975).

Still at issue is whether sprouting underlies all aspects of recovery. Indeed some argue that collateral or anomalous reinnervation may be maladaptive in some cases (Raisman, 1969; Schneider and Jhavari, 1974). However, as the data continue to develop, it seems clear that dynamic reinnervation must be given serious consideration as a possible mechanism for behavioral recovery in adult organisms even though under some conditions such reinnervation could have maladaptive consequences or no effects at all for the particular behavior under study.

Another recent and highly provocative finding may have direct bearing on the question of synaptic remodeling and its implications for plasticity. Descarries, Beaudet, and Watkins (1975) performed an exhaustive electron microscopic examination of the distribution and morphology of serotonin nerve terminals in the adult rat neocortex that had been labeled with tritiated serotonin (^{3}H/5-HT). They found that most of the terminals were located in the first three layers of the frontal-parietal cortex and that the terminal boutons observed had morphological characteristics comparable to those found in other regions of the CNS. The striking finding obtained by Descarries, Beaudet, and Watkins was that only 5% of the terminals seen after extensive sampling had genuine synaptic relationships: "Indeed, the low incidence of junctional complexes between 5-HT varicosities and adjacent dendrites is in striking contrast with the high proportion found in a random population of unlabelled axonal boutons from the surrounding neuropil" (p. 585). According to their observations, these "free" terminals possess the same morphological qualities as those making typical synaptic connections and can store and liberate serotonin (5-HT). The authors conclude that "the morphological characteristics of cortical 5-HT fibers are hardly compatible with the *preconceived notion* (italics ours) that these are part of a fixed pattern of neuronal circuitry. All functional constituents present in varicosities are known to possess intra-axonal mobility. It is conceivable that the minute varicosities, distributed along tenuous processes lying free in the neuropil, are themselves submitted to incessant translocation and/or reshaping. Such intrinsic dynamic properties could be determinant in the mode of action and function of 5-HT fibers, contribute to their plasticity and promote their capacity for regrowth" (p. 585). If such synaptic remodeling is the rule rather than the exception, then attempts to define fixed circuitry and structure-function relationships based on postmortem examination of preserved tissue would result in inappropriate conceptions about the organization of the brain in the mature organism.

All these studies point to the intriguing possibility that different types of neuronal regeneration may be an important factor in mediating functional recovery after brain injury; certainly, at least, the pessimistic statement issued earlier in the century by Cajal has not been supported by the facts.

While there is now considerable evidence to indicate regenerative and collateral sprouting in young and adult organisms, it would be incautious to suppose that all regeneration may serve as the basis for functional restitution. Indeed, some forms of morphological plasticity may actually result in maladaptive behavioral consequences. Schneider and Jhavari (1974) and Devor and Schneider (1975), among others, have pointed out that there is a limited amount of synaptic space available in the CNS. If damage to one part of the brain serves as a stimulus for collateral sprouts into an intact region, the newly arriving terminals would compete for synaptic areas with fibers that normally grow into the area. The anomalous projections, by providing inappropriate sensory input, or "crowding," could introduce a degree of noise into the intact system that might produce greater disruption of behavior than partial destruction. Noisy inputs into healthy remaining tissue might also inhibit functional reorganization. In the study by Raisman and Field (1973) there would be no a priori reason to assume that medial forebrain inputs to septum provide the same information as hippocampal fibers. If one system replaces the other, the normal pattern of afferent input is destroyed and this might result in the neurological equivalent of "jamming" the system and causing greater functional disruption.

In the clinic one must be even more careful about jumping to unwarranted conclusions concerning mechanisms. Damage to the CNS is often not well localized, and it is more often the case that significant changes resulting from traumatic injury are produced throughout the brain, especially widespread axonal and terminal degeneration caused by the damage. In addition, one might expect destruction of fibers of passage as well as loss of cell bodies. In this situation anomalous or collateral growth could occur but might be maldirected by glial scars, for example, as fibers begin to sprout into regions that do not ordinarily receive projections. Other factors that could influence regeneration in the CNS, under the assumption that sprouting can lead to functional restitution, would be the age of the subject, the general condition or well-being of the organism at the time of injury, and its genetic constitution. All the variables require further research before any definitive answers can be given.

Latent Synapses

Recently an alternative to collateral sprouting has been proposed as a mechanism underlying plasticity in the CNS. Anomalous sprouting can, under some conditions, introduce a certain amount of noise if projections to a deinnervated area are not correctly wired in. If there is only a limited amount of sprouting, recovery may be partial or it may not occur at all. As one alternative to explanations of recovery based on collateral sprouting, Wall (1975) and his associates have recently proposed that functional reorganization may be mediated by existing but "relatively ineffective" pathways that are disinhibited when the primary sensory afferentation that suppresses their activity is removed.

In one experiment Wall and Egger (1971) destroyed the nucleus gracilis (a sensory relay nucleus located in the medulla of the brain stem) in rats and thereby eliminated hindlimb sensory representation to the nucleus ventralis lateralis of the thalamus. After removal of the gracilis, the medial part of this thalamic nucleus does not respond to skin stimulation of the hindlimb but does respond to skin stimulation of the forelimbs. When the rats were allowed to survive, it appeared that the area responding to forelimb stimulation expanded "in an orderly fashion into the area which had previously responded to the hindlimb." Although these findings could be interpreted in terms of sprouting of forelimb afferents into the denervated hindlimb area, Wall proposed that there might have been "silent cells already connected to the area which do not function in the intact animal," but which can become active when primary afferents are removed.

To test this hypothesis, Merrill and Wall (1972) studied the receptive field properties of afferents into lamina 4 of the cat spinal cord. Neurons in this area have very restricted receptive fields which do not vary and have a very definite edge. By sectioning the dorsal roots or blocking them, Merrill and Wall were able to show that all the afferents into the lamina are limited to a very small micro bundle consisting of a few fibers. When the fibers were blocked, the receptive field disappeared. Merrill and Wall then stimulated neighboring dorsal roots electrically (instead of with tactile stimulation, which was ineffective) and the same cell again responded. The authors claim that the electrical stimulation was able to trigger a volley in masked, ineffective terminals that fed into the same cell from neighboring afferents. Natural stimulation failed to produce effective excitation of the cell. Wall suggests that the response of these "relatively ineffective afferents" occurs almost immediately after deafferentation of the primary roots and that the reappearance of the unit response is therefore not likely to be due to the replacement with anomalous sprouts of the normal afferents that were damaged in the adult animals.

To support further his position, Wall (1975) provides evidence derived from experiments using acute and reversible techniques of deafferentation. Wall mapped the receptive field properties of the dorsal column nuclei and then selected cells that responded to the stimulation of the foot. He then blocked the activity of the spinal cord in the L4 segment with ice technique. Wall found that most of the cells lost their response to peripheral stimulations but were capable of ongoing activity. Some of the cells, however, lost their receptive fields on the foot and gained one on the abdomen. When the cold block was removed, the receptive fields reverted to the foot. Wall interpreted his data to indicate that at least some of the cells in the spinal cord have alternative inputs which can become effective (unmasked) as soon as normal input is removed. Similar findings and interpretations have recently been made by Eidelberg and his colleagues (Eidelberg, Kreinick, and Langeschied, 1975) and are similar to the interpretation provided by Kratz, Spear, and Smith (1976) in their explanation of how neurons in the cortex of monocularly, visually deprived cats begin to respond immediately when the inputs from the normal eye are removed.

In essence, Wall and others have provided physiological evidence for a type of redundant mechanism capable of mediating functional activity in the CNS, but more research needs to be done to determine whether the presence of relatively ineffective synapses can mediate functional restitution after brain damage. That neurons in the thalamus previously responding to hindlimb stimulation can, after deafferentation of hindlimb, respond to more intense forelimb stimulation indicates only that the subject may perceive that he suddenly has three hands and one foot—hardly an adaptive mechanism for functional recovery! Wall's data and interpretation demand further thought and examination, however, especially in the light of evidence beginning to appear from other laboratories. If the existence of parallel pathways can be understood in terms of the role they may play in reorganizing the activity of the CNS after damage, Wall's findings may have very important practical and theoretical consequences. (See also Bach-y-Rita, 1972, for other approaches to sensory substitution research and theory.)

Behavioral Recovery

Although progress is certainly being made toward understanding CNS functions, one of the most interesting and least understood phenomena in the neurosciences is that under certain conditions animals and humans are capable of almost complete behavioral recovery following severe traumatic injury to the CNS. Such recovery from brain damage has been known for a very long time (see Rosner, 1974, for a historical review, or Prince, 1910, for an early discussion of the problem), especially in the clinic. Until very recently, however, laboratory investigators have tended to ignore or attack the principle of behavioral recovery as described in the classical work of Kennard (1938) or Luria (1963). There are reasons for rejecting the notion of restitution of function, some based on unspoken (and sometimes emotional) assumptions about how the nervous system is organized rather than empirically gathered facts or clinical observations. The classical doctrine of cerebral localization insists that specific anatomical regions, systems, centers, or areas, are both necessary and critical for the elicitation and/or control of specific behaviors. Thus the hypothalamus is seen as the center for appetitive behavior while the hippocampus is seen as critical for processing or storing short-term memory. These conclusions are based on the fact that severe deficits are often produced when bilateral damage or removal of specific brain areas is carried out, especially in adults. The observation of specific deficits (loss of speech, vision) following brain damage serves as the basis for the inference that the damaged structure must have mediated the impaired function, especially if other lesions do not produce the same symptoms.

Early Lesions

Many investigators concerned with defining structure-function relationships in the brain are willing to admit that early lesions result in considerably more sparing than when the same damage is inflicted in adult subjects although even this assumption recently has been vigorously (and, in some aspects, justifiably) attacked (Isaacson, 1975). In general, it has been suggested that the immature nervous system is more capable of reorganization (is more "plastic") after injury; indeed, anomalous sprouting is more likely to occur in young than in adult subjects (Goodman, Bogdasarian, and Horel, 1973; So and Schneider, 1978).

As the organism approaches maturity, brain damage is believed to result in severe and permanent deficits although even this long-held assumption is beginning to be questioned. For example, in one study, Benjamin and Thompson (1959) created bilateral lesions of the somatosensory cortex in neonatal and adult cats and then tested the animals on a battery of tactile discrimination tasks. The cats with lesions suffered in the first week of life were able to solve all the tasks as adults, but those with lesions placed as adults were unable to learn even the simplest of the tests presented to them. Similarly, Tucker and Kling (1967) removed the frontal cortex in neonatal monkeys and found that the animals could solve a delayed response task that animals operated later in life were unable to do. Similar findings have been reported by Harlow and his colleagues (1968).

Some of the earliest systematic investigations of recovery of function in young animals were performed by Kennard (1938). She ablated areas 4 and 6 of the motor cortex in infant and mature rhesus monkeys and found that the animal's ability to recover the use of its limbs was directly related to its age at the time of surgery—the earlier the lesion, the better the functional recovery measured later in life. Although recent evidence suggests that the question of early versus late lesions is not as simple as it once seemed, studies such as Kennard's led to the conclusion that damage to the adult nervous system results in more marked and less reversible effects than similar brain damage inflicted during development. Acceptance of this doctrine has led in turn to the assumption that little reorganization of function can occur after injury to the mature mammalian nervous system and that most structure-function relationships are fixed in early life.

Although sparing of function after some types of brain damage has been repeatedly demonstrated, it should not be assumed that such adaptability is a general characteristic of the CNS or that all behaviors are equally spared after early rather than late lesions. In fact, there now seems to be some clinical evidence that a price must be paid for functional recovery after infant lesions in human subjects. Milner (1974) observed that patients who suffered early damage to either the right or left hemispheres in infancy may have considerable sparing of language functions, but they often have low verbal and nonverbal IQ scores. She argues that their generally lowered intellectual capacity results because the early lesions force the remaining intact tissue to mediate the functions normally controlled by the language area in the dominant hemisphere. This crowding of functions into remaining tissue then results in overall reduction in intellectual capacity that may not be seen without careful testing procedures. Milner interpreted her results to indicate that recovery of language and other intellectual capacities after lesions may depend on whether the dominant hemisphere is damaged. Thus in one study she found that there was frequently recovery of function after right dorsolateral frontal lobectomy but not if the left side was damaged.

Milner further hypothesizes that in very young children, both the right and left hemispheres participate in the development of language, although probably not to an equal extent. She suggests that as the left hemisphere matures and develops greater linguistic capacity, it suppresses or inhibits the right-hemisphere language function. Recovery of language after lesions in childhood represents, for Milner, a release from inhibitory influences of the left hemisphere, permitting the right side to manifest its otherwise suppressed functions, which it may perform but in a relatively inefficient manner (Wall, pp. 30-32).

Although intellectual capacity appears to be diminished when lesions and damage to the CNS occur early in life, it still appears that, in general, the younger the subject at the time of injury, the more likely is sparing of functions. According to Teuber (1975) even a few years seem to make a difference. Teuber and his students studied children from ages 8 to 18 who suffered prenatal or early postnatal brain damage to the left or right cerebral hemispheres and compared their verbal performance to that of normal siblings. Analysis of their data showed that early lesions of the left hemisphere resulted in deficits on both verbal and nonverbal tasks, but no aphasia. Early right-hemisphere lesions spared verbal performance but affected spatial tasks. Here is an asymmetry in the effects of early lesions that may be due to different rates of maturation of the two hemispheres—a hypothesis subsequently verified by Goldman (1974, 1975).

Although traumatic head injuries in later life are more disruptive, Teuber (1975) has shown that improvement is considerably greater when damage occurs at a younger age. Teuber and his colleagues examined 167 cases of brain damage in Korean war veterans who were first tested within one week after injury and received a follow-up examination twenty years later. With respect to motor deficits, somatosensory deficits, visual field deficits, and initial dysphasia, patients who were injured between 17 and 20 years of age showed a greater percentage of improvements than subjects in the 21-25 or 26+ age groups. Thus even in young adulthood there seem to be significant differences in functional capacities of the brain in response to injury; however, the specific mechanisms underlying this important finding remain elusive.

The hypothesis that the role of different CNS structures (left hemisphere maturing into the region responsible for language mediation) changes as a function of age has been confirmed recently in a series of experiments by Goldman (1974, 1975). She showed that removal of the dorsolateral cortex in infant rhesus monkeys had no effect on performance of spatial delayed-response tasks when the animals were tested as juveniles; this type of lesion produces dramatic impairments in mature subjects. In contrast, removal of the orbital prefrontal region in infancy produced massive impairment of spatial performance when the animals were tested at 12 months of age, suggesting that the functions of some structures, such as orbitofrontal cortex, are "fixed" early in life, while others (dorsolateral cortex, for example) undergo a longer period of development during which functional specification has not yet occurred. Thus removing the tissue before it has matured would have less effect than a lesion in an area programmed for a specific function or behavior. Goldman examined the behavior of the monkeys at 24 months of age and again at 34 months. She found that the animals with dorsolateral lesions that initially showed no signs of impairment on spatial tasks began to show a deficit that grew progressively worse with age because this structure became necessary for normal spatial performance but was previously ablated. In contrast, the monkeys with orbital frontal lesions, who were initially very disturbed, eventually outgrew their deficits. Goldman suggests that this was because the dorsolateral cortex "grew into" its role of mediating spatial behaviors and could thus compensate for damage to the orbital region while the reverse was not true for the orbital region. That is, an intact, mature orbital cortex could not compensate for removal of dorsolateral cortex. Goldman (1974) interpreted these findings to indicate that the dorsolateral cortex does not become fully functional until about 2 years of age (the time at which deficits following infant lesions first begin to be observed).

Goldman's (and Teuber's) findings can be taken to indicate that the maturational status of the nervous system at the time of injury has to be considered in any explanation of recovery or sparing of function after early brain damage. If subjects are tested at a time when the "substrate" for a particular function has not yet developed, they will appear to have been spared the effects of the lesions. "Indeed, functions will appear to have been compensated when, in fact, they had not been lost" (p. 168). While Goldman argues that there is at least a limited degree of plasticity in the developing central nervous system of mammals, others consider the very concept of recovery after early brain damage a myth. Isaacson (1975) suggests that early brain damage "must be considered to be more disastrous than later brain damage" (p. 5) and cites the fact that early lesions often result in the formation of anomalous pathways and overall shrinking of brain size. He also argues that most tests used to assess the residual effects of brain damage are insensitive to the "real" impairments that remain long after temporary effects of the injury have dissipated. While no one can overlook the tragic cases of mental retardation resulting from systemic, biochemical, or morphological abnormalities in embryonic development, it is too strong to argue that relatively localized injury cannot be compensated for by remaining nondamaged portions of the brain. Cases in which complete sparing of functions is observed after early lesions cannot be explained as mere exceptions. Such an approach would be equivalent to ignoring an apple falling upward in a normal gravitational field because it, too, is only an exception to the law of gravity. Bjursten, Norsell, and Norsell (1976) removed all the cortex bilaterally in neonatal cats and then tested the animals repeatedly as they matured to adulthood. They found that the subjects were able to perform most normal behaviors adequately and were even able to solve a visual discrimination problem in a T-maze. In the human clinical literature Smith and Sugar (1975) recently reported a case of above-normal language and intelligence in an adult male 21 years after total removal of his left hemisphere. The patient received a battery of 29 tests and performed at the normal or above-normal range on almost all of them. Such cases cannot be dismissed as minor exceptions to functional specificity. It is difficult to infer from these data that early brain damage must be more disastrous than that occuring later in life. The real explanation of functional recovery after infant lesions probably lies somewhere between the claim that any recovery is a myth and the claim that there is a total lack of specificity and therefore complete plasticity in the developing brain. Recent experiments have shown that early lesions sometimes have less deleterious effects than later lesions, but one must always be concerned with the specific type of behaviors being studied, the general health of the subjects at the time of injury, and the task or test demands required of the subjects.

Recovery in Adults

That lesions of the spinal cord or central nervous system in adults do not always result in permanent deficits has been known for a long time, but the mechanisms that underlie sparing or recovery of function are still unknown despite a recent upsurge of interest in research on this problem. In the mature subject suffering from CNS injury any behavioral sparing that is observed is often thought to reflect residual functions of remaining intact tissue, while observed deficits have been taken to reflect the loss of specific function controlled or mediated by a specific area. The adult nervous system is considered too stable and too programmed in terms of specificity of its anatomical and morphological characteristics to be capable of reorganization or recovery (Dawson, 1973; LeVere, 1975). According to this definition, any sparing after traumatic injury can be dismissed because the damaged area was not involved in the behavior under study or because the tests used to measure behavior were too insensitive or inappropriate to reveal the true deficits. These assumptions presuppose a strict relationship between structure and function in the brain and serve as the basis for the principle of localization of function in the CNS. If there are conditions under which lesions that normally result in severe deficits have little effect on behavior, then it would be more difficult to argue that structure-function relationships in the adult CNS are fixed or that mature subjects are less capable of recovery than young ones.

Some approaches to the study of recovery from brain damage in adults are concerned with testing the principle of functional localization. One such paradigm entails the use of serial lesion techniques. Bilateral brain damage is inflicted in two or more operations with a fixed period of time between each stage of surgery, usually several weeks or more. Subjects so treated are always compared with their age-matched counterparts receiving the same operation in a single stage and are given the same total amount of postoperative recovery time. Both surgical groups are compared with intact controls to determine whether the lesions result in the same symptomatology.

Under these conditions recovery (or sparing) of function is said to occur if the animals with serial lesions perform significantly better than subjects inflicted with the same locus and extent of damage in a single operation. The behavioral tests administered to the subjects are chosen because they are known to detect the effects of bilateral damage inflicted in a single stage. Thus, if animals with serial lesions perform as well as intact controls, it becomes difficult to infer that a given structure is required for the mediation of a given behavior (doctrine of localization), when no differences are observed between normal, intact animals and those without the "critical" part. Although the question of cerebral localization is interesting from a philosophical point of view (Laurence and Stein, 1978), we shall limit this discussion to some of the conditions under which adults are capable of showing recovery from brain damage and what the limits of such recovery are.

There are certain differences between recovery of function and sparing of function (Teuber, 1974). In the first case subjects are trained prior to receiving lesions and are tested after surgery to determine the conditions under which performance can, or cannot, return to preoperative levels. In this situation recovery may be due to the subject's use of different cues in the same test or to considerable preoperative experience, which would render the task less difficult. In the second case training or testing does not begin until after all surgery has been completed; there is no opportunity for the subjects to gain pre- or interoperative experience with the test conditions. The subject is expected to perform as well as an intact control without the area generally thought responsible for the mediation of the behaviors under study, indicating that the function in question has been spared from the effects of sequential surgery. There are several recent detailed and critical reviews of serial lesion phenomena (Finger, Walbran, and Stein, 1973; Finger, 1978), so we can limit our presentation to a few relevant examples.

In a series of experiments (Stein et al., 1969) we examined the effects of one- or two-stage bilateral removals of the anterior (frontal) cortex, hippocampus, amygdala (McIntyre and Stein, 1973), and caudate nucleus (Schultze and Stein, 1975) in adult rats. We chose these areas because a large number of studies have demonstrated that bilateral single-stage lesions almost always result in severe and irreversible deficits of learning and retention capacity. We tested subjects on a battery of tasks, including successive discrimination learning and reversal, passive avoidance, pattern discrimination learning and reversal, delayed spatial alternation, and various tests of activity and emotionality, although no one group received all these tests.

In each case we found that rats with serial lesions spaced 25-30 days apart (removal of structure in one hemisphere, removal of the contralateral structure 30 days later) performed significantly better than animals with the same extent and locus of damage inflicted in a single operation. In fact, the animals with two-stage lesions performed as well as intact controls. One surprising finding in this group of experiments was that rats with two-stage caudate lesions (Schultze and Stein, 1975) performed a passive avoidance task better than intact rats while their one-stage counterparts were not significantly different from the normal animals. This suggested that while successive damage to the CNS clearly does not result in the same deficits as injury inflicted in a single bilateral operation, the recovered animal is not necessarily neurologically or behaviorally the same as an intact control. We have proposed elsewhere (Schultze and Stein, 1975) that the sequential lesions may result in total reorganization of the damaged brain in such a way that remaining individual structures may change their functions (or activity).

We tested this hypothesis by studying recovery of a behavior that is less dependent on complex cognitive processes but at the same time is sensitive to bilateral lesions. For this purpose we chose to examine the effects of damage to the lateral hypothalamic area (LHA) on food intake and weight regulation in adult male rats (Fass et al., 1975). Damage to the LHA produces severe aphagia and adipsia, and animals often die if not force-fed for a long period of time. Consistent with previous reports, animals with one-stage LHA damage showed a significant and dramatic drop in body weight. In the two-stage group there was an initial decline in body weight after the first operation, but the rats gradually recovered to levels approaching that of normal controls. The two-stage rats did not regain the level of weight of their nonoperated counterparts by the time of their second lesion in the contralateral LHA, but this second operation had no effect on subsequent weight regulation. The two-stage rats continued to gain weight and eventually approximated that of the sham-operated group.

These data suggest that the LHA probably plays a critical role in normally mediating weight regulation, for a significant deficit is observed after a unilateral lesion. However, the unilateral lesion apparently triggers a change in CNS activity such that the intact, contralateral LHA either alters its function or becomes less important since its removal has no subsequent effects on weight regulation. Extensive morphological and physiological alterations take place after CNS damage, so it should not come as a surprise that some types of functional reorganization after injury should be possible even though evidence for a correlation between structural and behavioral changes underlying recovery is still difficult to produce.

Regardless of the explanations proposed, dramatic recovery of function following serial lesions has been seen in different laboratories examining different CNS regions in rodents, cats, and monkeys (see Finger, Walbran, and Stein, 1973; and Finger, 1978), including somatosensory cortex, visual system, and limbic areas. But there have also been persistent reports of failure to find recovery after serial lesions, especially those involving the limbic system (Butters et al., 1973; LeVere and Weiss, 1973; Loesche and Steward, 1977). Such failures to find recovery after serial surgery may be due in part to the possibility that different structures require different periods of time for reorganization. Thus three weeks between operations may be sufficient to permit functional recovery from LHA lesions, but it may be too short to permit recovery from hippocampal damage. Recently Patrissi and Stein (1975) created serial lesions in frontal areas of rats with either 10-, 20-, or 30-day intervals between first and second removals. The groups with serial lesions were compared with rats having one-stage lesions and with nonoperated controls. These authors found that animals with only a 10-day interoperative interval were very impaired on tests of spatial behavior, but even they performed better than rats with simultaneous removals of the frontal area. The rats with 20- and 30-day interoperative intervals performed as well as the intact controls. Thus there appears to be a minimum time required for processes underlying functional recovery to be effective, and it is quite likely that this time may vary as a function of age at surgery, general health of the organism, morphological complexity (number of different cell groups, number of final common paths terminating or originating in the damaged region, and so on), and demands of the pre- or postoperative environment on the organism. None of these variables has yet been sufficiently explored to warrant conclusions regarding the reasons for failing to find recovery in certain cases and not others (see Isaacson, 1975, for a more detailed discussion of this problem).

Recovery in Senescent Subjects

The experiments showing recovery or sparing of function in adult organisms demonstrate that adaptability of the nervous system to injury is not limited to immature organisms, even though we are not quite sure what mechanisms subserve recovery. One important question is whether the CNS shows a gradually diminishing capacity for recovery with advancing age. Goldman's work (1974, 1975) suggests that the functions of certain areas of the brain develop more slowly than others or change as the subject approaches maturity. In our laboratory we were concerned with whether CNS "development" continues past maturity. More specifically, we asked whether the functions of the adult brain also change with time. We have just begun to attack the problem of brain function and aging, but we can report on the results of a recent study by Stein and Firl (1976). Using the serial lesion paradigm, Stein and Firl removed the frontal area of 675- to 700-day-old rats in either one or two stages and compared the performance of the brain-damaged animals on delayed spatial alternation and active avoidance of foot shock with the performance of unoperated animals of the same age. All the aged animals were then compared with young but mature counterparts with one- or two-stage lesions of the same area.

This study produced no evidence of recovery or sparing of function in the old rats; those with two-stage lesions were not significantly better than those with one-stage operations. (Walbran, 1976, obtained similar results using tactile discrimination tasks.) In fact, the aged rats with brain damage performed the spatial task as well as their aged, nonoperated counterparts. This was surprising because bilateral removals of the same tissue in young but mature rats produce severe deficits on the spatial tasks. Although the old rats performed similarly whether they had a lesion or not, they performed more poorly than the young animals with serial lesions and more poorly than young, intact controls. Stein and Firl (1976) reported that frontal lesions at maturity produce severe deficits, but the same damage inflicted toward the end of life has little effect on spatial behavior. On the shock avoidance task the old animals showed an effect of lesions; the brain-damaged groups performed much worse than their age-matched, unoperated controls.

At the end of testing the rats were killed and their brains prepared for histological examination. The frontal lesions were just as large as those produced in younger rats, so the failure to find deficits in the aged animals was not due to their having smaller lesions. The number of cells in the dorsomedial nucleus of the thalamus (whose cells project to frontal cortex) were counted in aged and younger animals with both one- and two-stage lesions, and these results were compared with cell counts taken from young and aged unoperated standards. In the frontal cortex of the old, unoperated rats there was a marked reduction in the number of normal cells. In the dorsomedial nucleus of the thalamus young unoperated controls had almost six times the number of cells as the aged animals. In fact, there were no differences in the number of neurons between old operated and old intact rats. We interpret this to indicate that the reason for the lack of deficit on spatial performance after lesions in aged rats was that ablated tissue had been functionally dead before the surgery. Also reflecting this possibility was the fact that intact aged rats performed the task worse than younger controls or young rats that had recovered their spatial abilities.

Recently we completed another experiment that followed the paradigm used by Goldman (1974). We made small (limited to frontal pole with minimal medial and cingulate damage) one- or two-stage lesions of the frontal cortex in young but mature rats (approximately 6 months of age at the beginning of the experiment) and tested all the animals on delayed spatial alternation at different times after surgery, beginning 2-6 weeks after all damage had been inflicted. At first the lesions did not impair learning; both one- and two-stage rats performed at the same levels as unoperated controls. Six months after all Ss completed training, they were again retested on the DA task. At about 1 year of age deficits in the brain-damaged rats clearly emerged and there was no evident sparing resulting from the serial lesions as had been observed in previous experiments, at least for the testing periods we have now completed. Thus, like Goldman, we found that after frontal damage rats may grow into their deficits as they age (and even grow out of them again). This finding supports the notion of continuous "shifting" or reorganization of functions as the organism changes from one end of the developmental continuum to the other. It is now clear that to assess the effects of brain damage, one must consider the developmental status of the victim in order to study the relationship between structures and their alleged functions.

In summary, it now appears that the organization of the brain and its response to injury may change with advancing age although more research is needed to know whether this is a general characteristic of the CNS or whether it is limited to the cortical areas studied thus far. In any case, if such reorganization does occur, then the question of localization of functions even in the mature central nervous system must be examined more closely in order to determine not only where a given function is mediated but when.

We can give another example of the difficulty involved in trying to specify structure-function relationships on the basis of anatomical or physiological variables per se. One criticism of recovery-of-function experiments is that when restitution is observed, what one sees is not recovery per se but the residual functions that were not affected by the lesions. Further, it is sometimes suggested (Dawson, 1973; Isaacson, 1975) that tests are too insensitive to reveal the permanent deficits produced by the lesion. Here one must ask what constitutes a permanent deficit. Is the "function" removed by a particular lesion? These questions have been approached in a series of intriguing experiments by Meyer (1972) and his colleagues. These workers made complete bilateral removals of the occipital cortex in cats which included the lateral and posterior lateral gyri, mid- and posterior suprasylvian gyri, the entire Clare-Bishop area, and the medial visual gyrus. Under these conditions the animals show a dramatic impairment in visually guided placing responses (extending the forepaws to land on a platform, striking at objects). However, after testing the initial impairment, the investigators gave the cats an injection of d-amphetamine. Under the influence of the drug the normal placing response returned, and waned as the effects of the drug wore off. Meyer interpreted his results to indicate that the lesions do not remove a critical area for behavioral function but block access to retrieval of the engrams (the coded pattern of organization required to make a given response) necessary to organize complex behavior. Apparently, under certain conditions of high arousal (here produced by the amphetamine), access to the engrams occurs and permits apparently normal behavior until arousal dissipates. Regardless of the explanation, the behavior is not obliterated following extensive lesions, nor is extensive training or handling required for its reappearance.

Diaschisis

Although behavioral recovery from brain damage may be considered one of the more dramatic examples of CNS plasticity, the neural bases for this phenomenon are hardly understood and are just beginning to be explored seriously (Finger, Walbran, and Stein, 1973; Eidelberg and Stein, 1974; Rosner, 1970). Clinical examples of recovery from brain damage found in the early neurological literature fueled the often acrimonious disagreements between supporters and opponents of the doctrine of cerebral localization of function. Since several recent reviews have discussed theories of recovery from brain damage, only a few examples are evaluated here. For more detailed presentation see Isaacson (1975), Rosner (1970), Schoenfeld and Hamilton (1977), and Laurence and Stein (1978).

One of the early attempts to explain recovery from brain damage was proposed by Von Monakow in 1914. He attributed symptoms following lesions to the destruction of specific portions of the brain followed by the trauma-induced suppression of activity in healthy areas of brain adjacent, or connected to, the damaged area. Von Monakow termed the shock-induced inhibition of neural activity *diaschisis*, and this term is often used as an "explanation" of both deficits and recovery that follow brain injuries. Von Monakow suggested that the diaschisis gradually disappears, and as it recedes, suppressed functions mediated by intact tissue gradually begin to reemerge so that behavioral recovery is a function of the extent to which the surgical shock (diaschisis) can dissipate.

Although the term itself is often applied to clinical cases of recovery, the concept of diaschisis has not received much experimental verification. In a sense the observed recovery is "explained" by giving the observation of behavioral sparing a different name: dissipation of diaschisis. Within the last few years, however, several investigators have attempted to directly manipulate surgically induced cerebral shock and its disappearance. In one experiment with adult cats, Glassman (1971) made small and well-localized lesions of motor cortex after having recorded evoked potentials induced by the animals reaching into a narrow tube to obtain a bit of food. When punctate lesions were created by passing direct current through the recording electrodes, Glassman observed a severe but transient deficit in reaching. Concomitantly with the behavioral impairment, there was a flattening and disappearance of the evoked potentials in the damaged and adjacent intact regions of the motor cortex. As the cats began to recover their ability to reach into the tube, there was a gradual reinstatement of the evoked potentials from the undamaged adjacent cortex. By the time the cortical potentials returned to preoperative levels, the animals demonstrated a complete recovery of the reaching response. Glassman's findings can be taken to indicate that surgically induced shock in cortex adjacent to the lesion may have been reduced, thus permitting the nondamaged (equipotential?) regions of the motor area to mediate the animal's reaching behavior.

West and his colleagues (1976) proposed to test the concept of diaschisis directly in an electrophysiological experiment. These workers recorded extracellular, hippocampal dendritic field potentials in rats before and at various times after entorhinal cortex lesions placed to eliminate contralateral inputs to the dentate gyrus. Their hypothesis was that if diaschisis was produced by the lesion (suppression or inhibition of neuronal activity), removal of contralateral afferents to the dentate would make the granule cells of the structure less responsive to its remaining afferents. In the few animals studied, monosynaptic stimulation of the CA3 field (a region of the hippocampus whose cells receive inputs from the entorhinal cortex) of the dentate gyrus produced the same frequency, wave form, latency, and amplitude of dendritic potentials seen in normal rats; the entorhinal lesions had no effect on electrophysiological activity at any of the time periods studied. West and colleagues concluded that while their findings may not generalize to all brain structures, they suggest that "shock" effects are not to be found at the projection sites of a "lesioned" structure. This of course does not preclude their occurrence at areas surrounding or encroached upon by the lesion (Glassman, 1971).

Despite the negative findings, the issue whether diaschisis is a valid explanation of behavioral recovery from brain damage is unresolved. In fact, several researchers have argued that diaschisis is an a posteriori attempt at explanation that does nothing more than give a different label to the observed sparing or amelioration of symptoms following CNS injury. Yet, despite the lack of experimental confirmation of Von Monakow's hypothesis at the neuronal level, diaschisis remains an enticing concept in clinical neuropsychology because certain aspects of recovery seem to fit the notion of a release from neural inhibition with time. Teuber (1974) cites the case of a young sailor in WW II whose speech was reduced to "a few grunts after massive temporo-parietal lesion. Retrained daily for 30 days by a young lady from Connecticut, he began to speak again, at which point the trainer wanted to resign her post because, she asserted, he had evidently simulated his condition. Though retrained by a person speaking in Yankee accents, the patient spoke his first words a month after the injury, in his original hillbilly dialect" (p. 205).

That lesion-induced behavioral deficits and symptoms may be the result of suppression or inhibition of CNS activity cannot be dismissed in spite of the negative electrophysiological evidence produced by West et al. (1976). We must again consider the evidence of Meyer and his students, who reported that neodecorticated cats were able to make normal placing responses while under the effects of the stimulant d-amphetamine but were completely impaired when the temporary effects of the drug wore off. In reviewing his experiments, Meyer (1972) suggested that the amphetamine activates access to the neural programs (engrams) mediating visually guided behavior, and as the drug diminishes, the inhibition of access to the engram can be said to return.

In a corollary experiment with monkeys, Faugier-Grimaud, Frenois, and Stein (1978) found that lesions of areas 5 and 7 of the parietal cortex in the Java monkey produce temporary deficits in visually guided reaching for food. These deficits are manifested by an abnormal posturing of the hands, misreaching for the target (apraxia), and abnormal grasp once the reward object is obtained—a behavior similar to the Ballint syndrome seen after parietal damage in man (Hecaèn and DeAjuriaguerra, 1954). These deficits usually disappear within 10-14 days after surgery. In the affected animals testing continued long after surgery was completed, and video and cinematographic analyses of the monkeys' movements revealed perfectly normal visually guided reaching movements toward the small morsels of food. After this long postoperative recovery period each of the monkeys (some with unilateral, some with bilateral lesions) were given a single injection of short-acting anesthetic (ketamine) at 2.5% of the dose required for anesthesia and were then retested within a few minutes to 180 minutes after the injection. The response to the ketamine was dramatic; each animal demonstrated a complete reappearance of all the symptoms produced by the lesions—the effects lasting until the effects of the drug wore off. Here, it would seem that a decrease in CNS activity resulted in a reappearance of symptomatology exactly mimicking that produced by the lesion. As the effects of the drug diminished, the reemergent deficits disappeared as completely as they previously had but could be reinstated at any time with a subsequent injection of the ketamine. In one case a single injection six months after surgery produced the same symptoms and patterns of recovery as observed immediately after the operation. This experiment may have implications for all theories of recovery, but for the present the results can be interpreted to suggest that recovery of behavioral functions depends on a reorganization of CNS activity that must be maintained at some minimal level of efficiency, for want of a better term. The data of Faugier-Grimaud, Frenois, and Stein certainly support the notion that lesion-induced inhibition (diaschisis) plays a role in behavioral recovery. But, again, the specific hypothesis of neuronal diaschisis has not been tested directly. Taken together with Meyer's findings and Teuber's anecdotal report (1974), these results make it difficult to reject Von Monakow's concept as totally inappropriate, at least at the behavioral level of analysis.

Denervation Supersensitivity

Although the concept of diaschisis may have certain heuristic value, the relatively gradual diminution of surgically induced inhibition has not been experimentally verified (West et al., 1976). What is observed is a gradual restoration of behavioral function, and one should not overlook that the "inhibition" refers to an organism's (temporary?) lack of ability to initiate a desired response rather than some specific neuronal process.

One attempt to provide a neurophysiological and biochemical explanation for the post-traumatic restoration of function that occurs over time is derived from a phenomenon seen more often in the peripheral than in the central nervous system, more specifically, in the response of muscle fibers to denervation. When a muscle fiber is denervated, its sensitivity to acetylcholine (ACh) delivered to the motor endplate, increases enormously over a period of 1-2 weeks. The enhanced response has been called *denervation supersensitivity*. This reaction is apparently due, not to greater release of ACh from those presynaptic terminals that are still intact, but to an increase in the number and sensitivity of postjunctional receptor sites on the muscle fibers. As the muscle fibers become reinnervated by regenerating nerves, the receptor sites disappear and the activity of the fibers once again becomes controlled by the release and reuptake of ACh in the terminal nerve endfeet. The denervation supersensitivity seen in the muscle fibers has been taken as a model for recovery of function after damage to the CNS. In fact, it has been suggested that such supersensitivity may be a necessary chemical stimulus to attract collateral sprouts to the denervated areas (Glick, 1974; Goldberger, 1974).

Denervation supersensitivity has not been directly demonstrated in the brain. Rather, the response of a brain-damaged subject to neurotransmitter agonists (stimulants) or antagonists (inhibitors) has been taken as evidence to support the model. Areas of the brain that are partially denervated by lesions are assumed to become supersensitive to remaining inputs, and return of function over time is taken as support of this hypothesis. One example of possible recovery of function mediated by denervation supersensitivity has been described by Glick (1974). If the model is correct, rendering an area of the brain supersensitive by administration of a drug that reduces the release of neurotransmitters to an area, or by a lesion in another part of the brain that partially eliminates inputs to the CNS area under study, should facilitate the recovery of function. To test the model, Glick and Greenstein (1972) first created frontal lesions in rats to eliminate some of the catecholaminergic inputs into the lateral hypothalamic area and thus render the neurons of the LHA supersensitive. Thirty days later Glick and Greenstein damaged the LH and reasoned that the neurons remaining and functioning in the LH would have been, by virtue of their supersensitivity, more capable of mediating weight regulation. The results were consistent with their hypothesis. However, in rats that had received frontal lesions at the same time as LHA lesions, no recovery was observed because, supposedly, there was no time for supersensitivity to develop.

Another way to test the model was to administer a drug that blocks the synthesis of the neurotransmitters thought to be involved in mediation of feeding and drinking behaviors. One such drug is alpha-methyl-paratyrosine (a-MPT) which inhibits dopamine and norephenephrine by blocking an enzyme necessary for their synthesis. Rats were given a-MPT for 3 days prior to lesions of the lateral hypothalamus to make the neurons subserving recovery more supersensitive and capable of mediating weight regulation. The rats given a-MPT prior to LH lesions quickly regained postoperative weight regulation, while those given a-MPT immediately after surgery (further depleting transmitter levels) lost weight and died. While these experimental findings and others (see Glick, 1974, for details) are interesting and can be taken as support of the supersensitivity model, the data so far are limited to relatively discrete catecholamine systems involved in simple behavioral responses (activity and eating). In addition, certain problems limit the extent to which the concept of denervation supersensitivity may explain brain adaptability to injury. It would be presumptuous to assume that drugs such as a-MPT act only on areas that are specifically denervated, especially since catecholamine-containing neurons are found almost throughout the brain. Thus supersensitivity, or any other response to the drug, may be occurring in sites far removed from the damaged area, and recovery may be mediated by "distant" structures whose patterns of response may be changed by the drug administration or by the brain's "systemic" reaction to a lesion. Thus as Schoenfeld and Hamilton (1977) point out, a lesion may produce widespread alterations in the activity and concentration of neurochemicals throughout the brain, and indeed, throughout the entire organism, especially if metabolism is altered by the lesion(s). "Localized lesions rarely produce damage to only a neuronal system of main neurochemical identity, even if that is the target. The observed neurochemical depletion, therefore, may not be the only secondary effect of significance to the overall lesion effect. Hence, the utility of assessing neurochemical depletion, or a secondary effect of lesions may be restricted to a small percentage of systems in the brain and to a small proportion of the organism's total behavioral repertoire as influenced by such systems" (Schoenfeld and Hamilton, 1977, p. 959). Laurence and Stein (1978) have pointed out that the model cannot apply in cases where both afferents to an area and the area itself are damaged or destroyed. This must be the case, for example, when the visual cortex is removed (Spear and Barbas, 1975; Spear, 1978) and animals are still capable of pattern discrimination and when normal patterns of movement are seen following bilateral, total extirpation of motor cortex (Gentile et al., 1978). The problem is not that denervation supersensitivity might not occur following extensive brain damage but that such supersensitivity is considered to be limited to a specific neuronal system (Glick, 1974). Extensive cortical damage, in which fibers of passage are often cut, leads to widespread degeneration throughout the brain (Gentile et al., 1978) so if supersensitivity is involved in the initiation or mediation of adaptive response to injury, it must be a general response of the brain rather than a limited effect.

Finally, if denervation supersensitivity mediates recovery, does it do it in the same way as if the organism were intact? Are food preferences the same? Are the same amounts ingested? Is the animal's behavior really identical to the intact control?

The supersensitivity model is taken from observations of neuromuscular activity, and here, as supersensitivity develops, random muscle twitches resulting in muscle fibrillation are seen. The motor response is, therefore, quite abnormal and is not considered to be recovered until nerve regeneration into the muscle is completed. No such constraints have yet been placed on the model as it is applied to recovery from central nervous system damage.

Vicarious Function and Multiple Control

Whether it is called diaschisis or not, release from inhibition as a mechanism for recovery of function (diaschisis) depends on a corollary notion that remaining intact tissue can mediate the same function(s) of the regions destroyed by a lesion. This capacity has been called *vicarious function* by some workers (Jacobsen, 1936; Rosner, 1970) but strong experimental evidence in direct support of the concept (Laurence and Stein, 1978) is difficult to obtain. However, much of the work on collateral or anomalous sprouting (discussed earlier in this chapter) can be taken as an example of vicarious functioning after CNS damage. Thus if intact neurons give off new terminals to areas previously denervated by a lesion and this sprouting can be correlated with restitution of behavior, one can argue that the new region mediates the functions of the previously deafferented structures (Loesche and Steward, 1977; Steward, Loesche, and Horton, 1977). As is often the case, direct manipulation of vicarious function has eluded most workers in the field. In one study Cytawa and Teitelbaum (1967) created lesions of the lateral hypothalamus in rats and observed the symptoms of adipsia and aphagia. In time the animals went through stages of recovery and eventually approximated normal animals in their patterns of food intake. Once the rats had recovered, Cytawa and Tietelbaum placed potassium chloride on the frontal cortex to cause spreading depression (a reversible suppression of cortical-electrical activity); as a result, the lateral hypothalamic syndrome returned, even though frontal cortical lesions alone did not produce the syndrome. One might argue that the frontal cortex vicariously served the functions of the damaged hypothalamic region, but many factors change after bilateral ablations or chemical alteration of the CNS; it is highly unlikely that the changes are limited only to the structures under study, a point forcefully argued by Isaacson (1975) and by Schoenfeld and Hamilton (1977) in their recent reviews. Perhaps vicarious function might better be evaluated in more specifically organized neuronal systems, such as the descending motor pathways. In one experiment Lawrence and Kuypers (1968) cut the pyramidal tracts of adult monkeys at the level of the medulla and found that the animals could walk, climb, and gather food with difficulty. Nonetheless, the monkeys were able to navigate by executing a novel series of movements that were not used prior to surgery. Kuypers (1974) argued that whatever motor control was recovered after bilateral pyridotomy depends on descending brain stem paths that have terminals in common with the pyramidal fibers. To test this hypothesis, Lawrence and Kuypers (1968) cut the lateral and medial brain stem paths in monkeys that had already recovered from the pyramid lesions. These workers then observed persistent deficits in independent movements in walking, righting, and turning and suggested that the previous recovery was mediated by the "shared" motor system now destroyed. The concept of vicarious function and/or multiple control, however, can lead to an infinite regress (Laurence and Stein, 1978); each time recovery of function is observed, one can claim a posteriori that another structure takes over the functions of the damaged tissue. Of course, this claim implies redundancy in the system itself, which would argue against the hypothesis of discrete, cerebral localization. In any case it is unlikely that neural systems not normally implicated in a given behavior can vicariously mediate that behavior after the critical areas have been removed. Vicariation, if it occurs at all, would probably be limited to intact areas within the same system, as Lund, Cunningham, and Lund have suggested (1973).

Perhaps the most dramatic example of functional recovery, based on compensation by other related areas of the brain, comes from studies in which the visual cortex is damaged in neonatal or adult preparations. Spear (1978) recently described an elegant series of experiments. In cats, bilateral removals of the visual cortex cause a severe impairment of pattern and form discrimination, but the animals are capable of relearning. Spear suggests that the suprasylvian gyrus (an area of cortex adjacent to the visual cortex) assumes a new importance in mediating pattern vision when the visual cortex is damaged. To test this hypothesis, Wood, Spear, and Braun (1974) damaged the suprasylvian gyrus in cats but left the visual cortex intact. This lesion resulted in little or no loss of ability to discriminate horizontal from vertical stripes. Spear and his colleagues then subjected cats to removals of visual cortex (areas 17, 18, 19) after they had been trained on a pattern discrimination task. As expected, the animals were impaired but were able to relearn. Subsequent removals of suprasylvian gyrus abolished the relearned discrimination. Spear and Baumann (in preparation) using microelectrode technique, showed that after visual cortex damage individual neurons in the lateral suprasylvian gyrus change their response characteristics to visual stimulation (about 86% of neurons recorded became activated exclusively by the contralateral eye compared with only 33% in normal cats). Spear (1978) argues that this change in neuronal activity permits restoration of visual form discrimination even though it may not be as precise or as efficient as in the intact animal.

More important, if the same damage to visual cortex is inflicted on neonatal cats, the receptive fields in the lateral suprasylvian gyrus (LS) appear normal—in spite of the absence of visual cortex (cells retain their directional sensitivity and the percentage of binocularly driven cells is the same as in intact animals). Apparently the "normal" function is mediated by anomalous projections to the LS cortex that arise in the lateral geniculate body of the thalamus, after it, in turn, receives anomalous fibers from the retina that were caused to sprout by the visual cortex lesion.

Spear's (1978) findings can be interpreted to suggest that there may be vicarious function within related systems of the brain. The pattern of dynamic regrowth in the neonatal preparation that led to normal pattern discrimination is consistent with the argument of within-system vicariation proposed by Lund, Cunningham, and Lund (1973) and is particularly dramatic since it is still a common belief that removal of the visual system can only result in total blindness.

In general, static theories of recovery based on the concept of vicarious function or multiple control cannot predict or account for the differential effects produced by serial lesions. This is one of the major weaknesses of the concept. Thus when damage to a given area of the brain is inflicted slowly (Finger, 1978), the deficits or perturbations observed are often much less severe than when the same damage is created in a single operation. Not only is there often total sparing of function after seriatum lesions, but also the experimental subjects show behaviors quite different from those of their conspecifics receiving the same damage in a single sitting (Schultze and Stein, 1975).

More recently, it has been demonstrated that serial lesions per se may not be the only factor promoting sparing or recovery; the order of surgery may also be an important variable, and such findings would not be predicted on the bases of vicarious function or multiple control models. Treichler (1975) recently demonstrated that recovery of spatial learning after removal of the principal sulcus in the monkey depends on the order in which the banks of the sulci are damaged; removing upper banks first caused severe deficits on tests of alternation and spatial reversal while removal of lower banks first spared spatial performance. Similarly, Stein, Rosen, and Butters (1977), showed that four-stage removals of principalis resulted in greater sparing of spatial behaviors than either one- or two-stage damage even though the former were significantly larger lesions than the latter.

In the rat, Isseroff et al. (1976) showed that bilateral serial lesions of the hippocampus had different consequences, depending on the order of surgery. If the dorsal and ventral hippocampus was unilaterally destroyed and similar contralateral damage followed 30 days later, there was no recovery or learning a spatial task; the rats were just as impaired as one-stage, bilateral operates. If, however, bilateral dorsal hippocampal lesions were followed 30 days later by bilateral ventral damage, the rats were less impaired on behavioral tests of learning and emotionality, even though the overall extent of damage was equivalent for all brain-damaged groups. The sequence of surgery as a variable influencing behavioral outcomes has received little experimental attention but obviously has important implications for theories of brain-behavior relationships. Order of surgery may affect the secondary changes that follow brain injury (Schoenfeld and Hamilton, 1977), which in turn, affect the capacity of the subject to adapt appropriately and efficiently to its postinjury condition. One such variable that has received little attention is the change in vascularity after lesions; the rate and order of decreased blood supply to cortical or subcortical structures may be very important, but there is hardly any literature on this subject.

Response Substitution

Because of the inconsistencies inherent in the concepts of multiple control and vicarious function, some workers have proposed that there is no real recovery of function, if one takes the term to imply a complete restitution of premorbid response patterns. It can be argued that when "recovery" is observed, it results either because tests used to evaluate the behavior are insensitive (Dawson, 1973) to the subtle nature of the residual deficits or because the subject learns to substitute one pattern of responses for those lost as a result of the traumatic injury. In considering this approach to the problem of recovery from brain damage, others have stressed the need for a means-end analysis (Laurence and Stein, 1978) to determine how a subject solves a problem (attains a goal) even though it has lost a part of its nervous system thought to be critical for the mediation of specific behavior patterns. Those supporting substitution theories of recovery argue that the brain-damaged subject develops, through experience, a new set of behavioral strategies that allow it to cope with the environment. Perhaps the simplest example is an animal who, deprived of its eyesight, uses olfactory cues to run a labyrinth and obtain food reward, even though this may be a far less efficient way to solve the problem.

The most forceful argument for response substitution as a mechanism for recovery comes from the work of Sperry (1945) and Goldberger (1972, 1974). The latter trained young adult monkeys to grasp and release a lever in order to obtain food reward and then subjected the animals to bilateral cortical lesions of arcuate sulcus (area 6 of Brodmann). This made it impossible for the animals to release the lever once grasped or to avoid grasping a tactile stimulus. Such a postoperative response would be quite maladaptive because the monkeys, given the experimental paradigm, would not be able to obtain the food reward offered them. The monkeys compensated for this impairment by developing the response of tactile evasion; since they could not release an object once grasped, they refused to grasp at all. They obtained the food reward by using a different behavioral maneuver, what Sperry (1944) and Goldberger would call a trick, to resolve the problem and attain the appropriate goal.

In the response substitution model it is not necessary to hypothesize that other structures take over the functions of the lost areas, nor is anomalous, or collateral, sprouting required for restitution. The subject learns to use whatever remaining capacity it has to attain a particular goal. The effectiveness of the response would, of course, depend on the severity of the initial deficits, the integrity of the remaining systems, and perhaps the past experience and training history of the organism under examination. Thus the extent of recovery would be determined only by the responses and cues that remain available to the subject (Goldberger, 1974) and the opportunities for eliciting such responses in the brain-damaged organism. As Goldberger suggests (1974), "the possibility of utilizing this notion in experimental animals or even neurological patients in order to discover and enhance *surviving functions* following CNS lesions rather than 'reeducating' the nervous system to take over the functions is intriguing" (p. 93).

The substitution model can, however, incorporate the idea that collateral or anomalous sprouting of undamaged neurons in response to injury plays a role in recovery of function. Although in some cases anomalous projections result in maladaptive behavior, it is also possible that new connections can provide the subject with response patterns not previously available. Again a means-end analysis of behavior would be required to determine whether the appearance of new patterns of response to compensate fully or partially for those lost would be adaptive (Murray and Goldberger, 1974; Goldberger, 1977).

The work of Goldberger can be taken to suggest that collateral sprouting may play a role in mediating functional recovery. He points out that the recovered behavior is never as precise as in the behavior of the intact animal and that a different motor strategy appears to replace movement patterns lost after the injury.

The issue, however, is rendered more complex by a recent study by Gentile and her colleagues (1978). Single-stage or two-stage lesions of motor-parietal cortex in rats were performed to determine whether the animals could recover their ability to run on a narrow, elevated runway for water reward. To assess the extent of recovery or lack of impairments, Gentile and her co-workers filmed the rats with a high-speed camera (64 frames/sec) and analyzed the data quantitatively with a Vanguard Motion Analyzer. This device permitted a frame-by-frame evaluation of the movement patterns on the runway and a precise examination of the ballistic and temporal movements of front and hind paws. The intent of the study was to determine whether there was substitution or restitution of function after serial lesions of the motor cortex. If the latter, the recovered animals would evidence their pre-operative motor patterns. If the former, the postoperative motor sequence would be markedly different. These investigators found that both restitution and substitution occurred, depending on the surgical conditions. Rats suffering one-stage lesions were more impaired on the runway than two-stage counterparts, but they eventually recovered; however, their postoperative response pattern was significantly different from that used in their premorbid condition. Here is an example of response substitution serving as a basis for functional recovery. In contrast, a number of the rats with serial lesions used essentially the same movement pattern as that used preoperatively; they evidenced a restitution of function, which was rendered more dramatic by their greater impairment when testing on the elevated runway began.

Subsequent evaluation of histological sections revealed that both one- and two-stage lesions caused the same extent of damage at the cortical level. In addition, retrograde degeneration in the thalamic projection areas to the motor cortex was the same for both groups. Such data can be taken to indicate that the serial lesions spared the behavior but not neurons. It is likely that the secondary consequences of two-stage surgery are different from those following a single operation even though the histological techniques available to Gentile and her colleagues did not reveal them.

Scheff, Bernardo, and Cotman (1977) recently reported that serial lesions of the entorhinal cortex result in more rapid and dense collateral sprouting than single-stage damage. These workers suggest that the seriatum technique may prime the areas likely to sprout; that is, it may provide the stimulus necessary to initiate the collateral, axonal growth into the deinnervated areas. Only more research can determine whether this is so and whether the sprouts in the CNS are functionally adaptive.

There are many hypotheses concerning the underlying nature or mechanisms of behavioral recovery (see Goldberger, 1974; Eidelberg and Stein, 1974; Finger, 1978, for examples), but no approach seems capable of explaining the complexity of the phenomenon. As Stein and Lewis (1975) and Schoenfeld and Hamilton (1977) have pointed out, so many variables can affect the outcome of brain damage that it is not surprising that there are so many different ideas about what constitutes recovery from CNS damage and even more controversy about what mediates it. As the English neurologist John Hughlings Jackson said in 1888, "what all of us dislike is the complex. We may easily err in taking the subjective confusion produced in us to be in the objective thing contemplated, which is really only very complex."

Notes

This paper was written with the support of a research career development award (Type 2) from the National Institute of Mental Health and a grant from the National Institute on Aging (1 RO1 AG00295-01). Mrs. Alfhild Bassett deserves special thanks for her unswerving patience and good humor in typing the various versions of this manuscript.

1. Recently, Björklund et al. (1975) placed sections of portal vein in caudal diencephalon of rats. Thirty days later the animals were killed and examined with the histofluorescence method for AChE. These authors showed AChE axons coming from the septo-hippocampal pathways which are known to be cholinergic.

2. Fibers containing serotonin or noradrenalin can be made to fluoresce and are seen to glow green and yellow under the microscope when chemically treated to produce this reaction. The intensity of this reaction is taken as an indication of regrowth into a previously denervated region—the brighter the fluorescence, the more regrowth.

3. Silver strain degeneration techniques employ a method developed by Nauta and later modified by Fink and Heimer (1967). Staining of normal fibers is suppressed but degenerated axons and terminals can be seen because they have a dramatic argyrophyllic reaction characterized by black, swollen, and irregular pieces of axonal material and by a "dust" of terminals resembling grains of ground black pepper of irregular size.

References

BACH-Y-RITA, P. 1972. *Brain mechanisms in sensory substitution*. New York: Academic Press.

BEACH, F. A., HEBB, D. O., MORGAN, C. T., and NISSON, H. W., eds. 1960. *The neuropsychology of Lashley*. New York: McGraw-Hill.

BENJAMIN, R. M., and THOMPSON, R. F. 1959. Differential effects of cortical lesions in infants and adult cats on roughness discrimination. *Experimental Neurology* 1: 305-321.

BERGER, B. D., WISE, B. C., and STEIN, L. 1973. Nerve growth factor: enhanced recovery of feeding after hypothalamic damage. *Science*, 180: 506-508.

BJÖRKLUND, A., and STENEVI, U. 1971. Growth of central catecholamine neurones into smooth grafts in the rat mesencephalon. *Brain Research* 31: 1-20.

——— 1972. Nerve growth factor: stimulation of regenerative growth of central noradrenergic neurons. *Science*, 175: 1251-53.

BJÖRKLUND, A., BJERRE, B., and STENEVI, U. 1974. Has nerve growth factor a role in the regeneration of central and peripheral catecholamine neurons? In K. Fuxe, L. Olson, and U. Zotterman, eds., *Dynamics of degeneration and growth in neurons*. New York: Pergamon Press.

BJÖRKLUND, A., JOHANSSON, B., STENEVI, U., and SVENGAARD, N. 1975. Reestablishment of functional connections by regenerating central adrenergic and cholinergic axons. *Nature* 253: 446-448.

BJURSTEN, L. M., NORRSELL, K., and NORRSELL, U. 1976. Behavioural repertory of cats without cerebral cortex from infancy. *Experimental Brain Research* 25: 115-130.

BLAKEMORE, C., and COOPER, G. F. 1970. Development of the brain depends on the visual environment. *Nature* 228: 477-478.

BUTTERS, N., BUTTERS, C., ROSEN, J., and STEIN, D. G. 1973. Behavioral effects of sequential and one-stage ablations of orbital prefrontal cortex in the monkey. *Experimental Neurology* 39: 204-214.

CAJAL, RAMON Y, S. 1928. *Degeneration and regeneration of the nervous system*. Translated by R. M. May. London: Oxford University Press.

CHOW, K. L., and STEWART, D. L. 1972. Reversal of structural and functional effects of long-term visual deprivation in cats. *Experimental Neurology* 34: 409-433.

CYNADER, M., BERMAN, N., and HEIN, A. 1975. Cats raised in a one-directional world: effects on receptive fields in visual cortex and superior colliculus. *Experimental Brain Research* 22: 267-280.

CYTAWA, J., and TEITELBAUM, P. 1967. Spreading depression and recovery of subcortical functions. *Acta Biologica Experimentalis* 27: 345-353.

DAWSON, R. G. 1973. Recovery of function: implications for theories of brain function. *Behavioral Biology* 8: 439-460.

DESCARRIES, L., BEAUDET, A., and WATKINS, K. C. 1975. Serotonin nerve terminals in adult rat neocortex. *Brain Research* 100: 563-588.

DEVOR, M. 1975. Neuroplasticity in the sparing or deterioration of function after early olfactory tract lesions. *Science* 190: 998-1000.

DEVOR, M., and SCHNEIDER, G. E. 1975. Neuroanatomical plasticity: the principle of conservation of total axonal arborization. In F. Vital Durand and M. Jeannerod, eds., *Aspects of neural plasticity*. Lyons: Colloque INSERM 43: 191-202.

DOBZHANSKY, T. 1969. Introduction. In M. Mead, T. Dobzhansky, E. Tobach, and R. E. Light, eds., *Science and the concept of rate*, New York: Columbia University Press.

EIDELBERG, E., KREINICK, C. J., and LANGESCHIED, C. 1975. On the possible functional role of afferent pathways in skin sensation. *Experimental Neurology* 47: 419-432.

EIDELBERG, E., and STEIN, D. G. 1974. Functional recovery after lesions of the nervous system. *Neurosciences Research Program Bulletin* 12, No. 2.

FASS, B., JORDAN, H., RUBMAN, A., SEIBEL, S., and STEIN, D. G. 1975. Recovery of function after serial or one-stage lesions of the lateral hypothalamic area in rats. *Behavioral Biology* 14: 283-294.

FAUGIER-GRIMAUD, S., FRENOIS, C., and STEIN, D. G. 1978. Effects of posterior parietal lesions on visually guided behavior in monkeys. *Neuropsychologia* (in press).

FINGER, S. 1978. Lesion momentum and behavior. In S. Finger, ed., *Brain damage, behavior, and the concept of recovery*. New York: Plenum Press.

FINGER, S., WALBRAN B., and STEIN, D. G. 1973. Brain damage and behavioral recovery: serial lesion phenomena. *Brain Research* 63: 1-18.

FINK, R. P., and HEIMER, L. 1967. Two methods for selective silver impregnation of degenerating axons and their synaptic endings in the central nervous system. *Brain Research* 4: 369-374.

GANZ, L. 1975. Orientation in visual space by neonates and its modification by visual deprivation. In A. H. Riesen, ed., *The developmental neuropsychology of sensory deprivation*. New York: Academic Press.

GANZ, L., and FITCH, M. 1968. The effect of visual deprivation on perceptual behavior. *Experimental Neurology* 22: 638-660.

GENTILE, A. M., GREEN, S., NIEBURGS, A., SCHMELTZER, W., and STEIN, D. G. 1978. Disruption and recovery of locomotor and manipulatory behavior following cortical lesions in rats. *Behavioral Biology* 22: 417-455.

GESCHWIND, N. 1974. Late changes in the nervous system: an overview. In D. G. Stein, J. Rosen, and N. Butters, eds., *Plasticity and recovery of function in the central nervous system*. New York: Academic Press.

GLASSMAN, R. B. 1971. Recovery following sensorimotor cortical damage: evoked potentials, brain stimulation, and motor control. *Experimental Neurology* 33: 16-29.

GLICK, S. D. 1974. Changes in drug sensitivity and mechanisms of functional recovery following brain damage. In D. G. Stein, J. J. Rosen, and N. Butters, eds., *Plasticity and recovery of function in the central nervous system*. New York: Academic Press.

GLICK, S. D., and GREENSTEIN, S. 1972. Facilitation of recovery after lateral hypothalamic damage by prior ablation of frontal cortex. *Nature New Biology* 239: 187-188.

GOLDBERGER, M. 1972. Restitution of function in the CNS: the pathologic grasp reflex. *Experimental Brain Research* 15: 79-96.

—— 1974. Recovery of movement after CNS lesions in monkeys. In D. G. Stein, J. J. Rosen, and N. Butters, eds., *Plasticity and recovery of function in the central nervous system*. New York: Academic Press.

—— 1977. Locomotor recovery after unilateral hindlimb deafferentation in cats. *Brain Research* 123: 59-74.

GOLDMAN, P. 1974. An alternative to developmental plasticity: heterology of CNS structures in infants and adults. In D. G. Stein, J. J. Rosen, and N. Butters, eds., *Plasticity and recovery of function in the central nervous system*. New York: Academic Press.

—— 1975. Age, sex, and experience as related to the neural basis of cognitive development. In N. A. Buchwald and M. A. B. Brazier, eds., *Brain mechanisms in mental retardation*. New York: Academic Press.

GOLDSTEIN, K. 1939. *The organism*. New York: American Book Company.

GOODMAN, D. C., BOGDASARIAN, R. S., and HOREL, J. A. 1973. Axonal sprouting of ipsilateral optic tract following opposite eye removal. *Brain, Behavior, and Evolution* 8: 27-50.

GOTTLIEB, G. 1976. The roles of experience in the development of behavior and the nervous system. In G. Gottlieb, ed., *Neural and behavioral specificity*. New York: Academic Press.

HARLOW, H. F., BLOOMQUIST, A. J., THOMPSON, C. I., SCHLITZ, K. A., and HARLOW, M. K. 1968. Effects of induction age and size of frontal lobe lesions on learning in rhesus monkeys. In R. L. Isaacson, ed., *The neuropsychology of development*. New York: John Wiley and Sons.

HART, T., CHAIMAS, N., MOORE, R. Y., and STEIN, D. G. 1978. Effects of nerve growth factor on behavioral recovery following caudate nucleus lesions in rats. *Brain Research Bulletin*, in press.

HECAÈN, H., and DEAJURIAGUERRA, J. 1954. Balint's syndrome (psychic paralysis of visual fixation) and its minor forms. *Brain* 77: 373-400.

HICKS, S. P., and D'AMATO, C. J. 1975. Motor sensory cortex-corticospinal system and developing locomotion and placing in rats. *American Journal of Anatomy* 143: 1-42.

HIRSCH, H. V. B., and SPINELLI, D. 1970. Visual experience modifies distribution of horizontally and vertically oriented receptive fields in cats. *Science* 168: 869-871.

HOLT, E. B. 1937. *Animal drive and the learning process*. London: Williams and Noorgate.

HUBEL, D. N., and WIESEL, T. N. 1959. Receptive fields of single neurones in the cat's striate cortex. *Journal of Physiology* (London) 148: 574-591.

———— 1962. Receptive fields, binocular interaction, and functional architecture in the cat's visual cortex. *Journal of Physiology (London)* 160: 106-154.

———— 1963a. Shape and arrangement of columns in the cat's striate cortex. *Journal of Physiology* (London) 165: 559-568.

———— 1963b. Receptive fields of cells in striate cortex of very young visually inexperienced kittens. *Journal of Neurophysiology* 26: 994-1002.

———— 1965. Binocular interaction in striate cortex of kittens reared with artificial squint. *Journal of Neurophysiology* 28: 1041-59.

ISAACSON, R. L. 1975. The myth of recovery from early brain damage. In N. R. Ellis, ed., *Aberrant development in infancy*. Potomac, Md.: Lawrence Erlbaum Associates.

ISSEROFF, A., LEVETON, L., FREEMAN, G., LEWIS, M. E., and STEIN, D. G. 1976. Differences in the behavioral effects of single-stage and serial lesions of the hippocampus. *Experimental Neurology* 53: 339-354.

JACOBSEN, C. F. 1936. Studies of cerebral function in primates. *Comparative Psychology Monograph* 13: 1-68.

JACKSON, J. H. 1888. Remarks on the diagnosis and treatment of diseases of the brain. *British Medical Journal* 2: 59-63.

KENNARD, M. A. 1938. Reorganization of motor function in the cerebral cortex of monkeys deprived of motor and premotor areas in infancy. *Journal of Neurophysiology* 1: 477-496.

KRATZ, K. E., SPEAR, P. D., and SMITH, D. C. 1976. Postcritical-period reversal of effects of monocular deprivation on striate cortex cells in the cat. *Journal of Neurophysiology* 39: 501-511.

KUYPERS, H. G. J. M. 1974. Recovery of motor function in monkeys. *Neurosciences Research Program Bulletin* 12: 240-244.

LANGLEY, J. N. 1918. On the separate suture of nerves in nerve trunks. *British Medical Journal* 1: 45-47.

LASHLEY, K. S. 1920. Studies of cerebral functioning in learning. *Psychobiology* 2: 55-135.

——— 1937. Functional determinants of cerebral localization. *Archives of Neurological Psychiatry* 38: 371-387.

——— 1960. Studies of cerebral function in learning. V: The retention of motor habits after destruction of the so-called motor areas in primates. In F. A. Beach, D. O. Hebb, C. T. Morgan, and H. W. Nissen, eds., *The neuropsychology of Lashley*. New York: McGraw-Hill.

LASHLEY, K. S., and MCCARTHY, D. A. 1926. The survival of the maze habit after cerebellar injuries. *Journal of Comparative Psychology* 6: 423-433.

LAURENCE, S., and STEIN, D. G. 1978. Recovery of function after brain damage and the concept of localization. In S. Finger, ed., *Brain damage, behavior, and the concept of recovery*. New York: Plenum Press (forthcoming).

LAWRENCE, D. G., and KUYPERS, H. G. J. M. 1968. The functional organization of the motor system of the monkey. II: The effects of lesions of the descending brain-stem pathway. *Brain* 91: 15-36.

LETTVIN, J. Y., MATURANA, H. R., MCCULLOCH, W. S., and PITTS, W. H. 1959. What the frog's eye tells the frog's brain. *Proceedings of the Institute of Radio Engineers* 47: 1940-59.

LEVENTHAL, A. G., and HIRSCH, H. V. B. 1975. Cortical effect of early selective exposure to diagonal lines. *Science* 190: 902-904.

LEVERE, T. E., and WEISS, J. 1973. Failure of seriatum dorsal hippocampal lesions to spare spatial reversal behavior in rats. *Journal of Comparative Physiology and Psychology* 82: 205-210.

LEVERE, T. S. 1975. Neural stability, sparing and behavioral recovery following brain damage. *Psychological Reviews* 82: 344-368.

LEVI-MONTALCINI, R., and ANGELETTI, P. U. 1968. Nerve growth factor. *Physiological Reviews* 48: 534-569.

LEWIS, M. 1977. The influence of early experience on the effects of one- and two-stage hippocampal lesions in male rats. Doctoral dissertation, Clark University.

LIDDELL, H. S. 1942. The conditioned reflex. In F. A. Moss, ed., *Comparative psychology*. Englewood Cliffs, N.J.: Prentice-Hall.

LOESCHE, J., and STEWARD, O. 1977. Behavioral correlates of denervation and reinnervation of the hippocampal formation of the rat: recovery of alternation performance following unilateral entorhinal cortex lesions. *Brain Research Bulletin* 2: 31-39.

LUI, C. N., and CHAMBERS, R. W. 1958. Intraspinal sprouting of dorsal root axons. *Archives of Neurology* (Chicago) 79: 46-61.

LUND, R. D., CUNNINGHAM, T. J., and LUND, J. S. 1973. Modified optic projections after unilateral eye removal in young rats. *Brain, Behavior, and Evolution* 8: 51-72.

LURIA, A. 1963. *Restoration of function after brain injury*. Oxford: Pergamon Press.

LYNCH. G., and COTMAN, C. 1975. The hippocampus as a model for studying anatomical plasticity in the adult brain. In R. L. Isaacson and K. Pribram, eds., *The hippocampus*. New York: Plenum Press.

LYNCH, G., MATTHEWS, D. A., MOSKO, S., PARKS, T., and COTMAN, C. 1972.

Induced acetylcholinesterase-rich layer in rat dentate gyrus following entorhinal lesions. *Brain Research* 42: 311-318.

McINTYRE, M., and STEIN, D. G. 1973. Differential effects of one- vs. two-stage amygdaloid lesions on activity, exploratory, and avoidance behavior in the albino rat. *Behavioral Biology* 9: 454-466.

MERRILL, E. G., and WALL, P. D. 1972. Factors forming the edge of a receptive field: the presence of relatively ineffective afferent terminals. *Journal of Physiology (London)* 226.

MEYER, D. R. 1972. Access to engrams. *American Psychologist* 27: 124-133.

MEYER, P. E. 1974. Recovery of function following lesions of the subcortex and neocortex. In D. G. Stein, J. J. Rosen, and N. Butters, eds., *Plasticity and recovery of function in the central nervous system*. New York: Academic Press.

MEYER, R. L., and SPERRY, R. W. 1974. Explanatory models for neuroplasticity in retinotectal connections. In D. G. Stein, J. J. Rosen, and N. Butters, eds., *Plasticity and recovery of function in the central nervous system*. New York: Academic Press.

MILNER, B. 1974. Sparing of language functions after early unilateral brain damage. In E. Eidelberg and D. G. Stein, eds., *Functional recovery after lesions of the nervous system*. Neurosciences Research Program Bulletin No. 12, pp. 213-216.

MOORE, R. Y. 1974. Central regeneration and recovery of function: the problem of collateral reinnervation. In D. G. Stein, J. J. Rosen, and N. Butters, eds., *Plasticity and recovery of function in the central nervous system*. New York: Academic Press.

MOORE, R. Y., BJÖRKLUND, A., and STENEVI, U. 1971. Plastic changes in the adrenergic innervation of the rat septal area in response to denervation. *Brain Research* 33: 13-35.

MUIR, D. W., and MITCHELL, D. E. 1973. Visual resolution and experience: acuity deficits in cats following early selective visual deprivation. *Science* 180: 420-422.

MURRAY, M., and GOLDBERGER, M. 1974. Restitution of function and collateral sprouting in the cat spinal cord: the deafferented animal. *Journal of Comparative Neurology* 158: 37-54.

PATRISSI, G., and STEIN, D. G. 1975. Temporal factors in recovery of function after brain damage. *Experimental Neurology* 47: 470-480.

PETTIGREW, J. D. 1974. The effect of visual experience on the development of stimulus specificity by kitten cortical neurons. *Journal of Physiology (London)* 237: 49-74.

PRINCE, M. 1910. Cerebral localization from the point of view of function and symptoms. *Journal of Nervous and Mental Diseases* 37: 337-354.

RAISMAN, G. 1969. Neuronal plasticity in the septal nuclei of the adult brain. *Brain Research* 14: 25-48.

RAISMAN, G., and FIELD, P. M. 1973. A quantitative investigation of the development of collateral reinnervation after partial deafferentation of the septal nuclei. *Brain Research* 50: 241-264.

RAKIC, P. 1975. Timing of major ontogenetic events in the visual cortex of the rhesus monkey. In N. A. Buchwald and M. A. B. Brazier, eds., *Brain mechanisms in mental retardation*. New York: Academic Press.

RIESEN, A. H. 1947. The development of visual perception in man and chimpanzee. *Science* 106: 197-208.

――― 1971. Problems in correlating behavioral and physiological development. In M. B. Sterman, D. J. McGinty, and A. M. Adinolfi, eds., *Brain development and behavior*. New York: Academic Press.

RIZZOLATTI, G., and TRADARDI, V. 1971. Pattern discrimination in monocularly reared cats. *Experimental Neurology* 33: 181-194.

ROSNER, B. 1970. Brain functions. *Annual Review of Psychology* 21: 555-594.

――― 1974. Recovery of function and localization of function in historical perspective. In D. G. Stein, J. J. Rosen, and N. Butters, eds., *Plasticity and recovery of function in the central nervous system*. New York: Academic Press.

SCHEFF, S., BERNARDO L., and COTMAN, C. 1977. Progressive brain damage accelerates axon sprouting in the adult rat. *Science* 197: 795-797.

SCHNEIDER, G. E. 1973. Early lesions of superior colliculus: factors affecting the formation of abnormal retinal projections. *Brain, Behavior, and Evolution* 8: 73-109.

SCHNEIDER, G. E., and JHAVARI, S. R. 1974. Neuroanatomical correlates of spared or altered function after brain lesions in the newborn hamster. In D. G. Stein, J. J. Rosen, and N. Butters, eds., *Plasticity and recovery of function in the central nervous system*. New York: Academic Press.

SCHNEIRLA, T. C. 1956. Interrelationships of the "innate" and the "acquired" in instinctive behavior. In P. P. Grasse, ed., *L'Instinct dans le comportement des animaux et l'homme*. Paris: Masson.

SCHOENFELD, T. A., and HAMILTON, L. W. 1977. Secondary brain changes following lesions: a new paradigm for lesion experimentation. *Physiology and behavior* 18: 951-1067.

SCHULTZE, M., and STEIN, D. G. 1975. Recovery of function in the albino rat following either simultaneous or seriatum lesions of the coudate nucleus. *Experimental Neurology* 46: 291-301.

SHINKMAN, P. G., and BRUCE, C. J. 1977. Binocular differences in cortical receptive fields of kittens after rotationally disparate binocular experience. *Science* 197: 285-286.

SHLAER, R. 1971. Shift in binocular disparity causes compensating change in the cortical structure of kittens. *Science* 173: 638-641.

SMITH, A., and SUGAR, O. 1975. Development of above normal language and intelligence 21 years after left hemispherectomy. *Neurology* 25: 813-818.

SO, K., and SCHNEIDER, G. E. 1978. Abnormal recrossing retinotectal projections after early lesions in Syrian hamsters: age related effects. *Brain Research* 147: 277-295.

SOTELO, C., and PALAY, S. L. 1971. Altered axons and axon terminals in the lateral vestibular nucleus of the rat: possible example of neuronal remodeling. *Laboratory Investigation* 25: 633-672.

SPEAR, P. D. 1978. Behavioral and neurophysiological consequences of visual cortex damage: mechanisms of recovery. In J. M. Sprague, and A. N. Epstein, eds., *Progress in psychobiology and physiological psychology*, vol. 7. New York: Academic Press.

SPEAR, P. D., and BARBAS, H. 1975. Recovery of pattern discrimination ability in rats receiving serial or one-stage visual cortex lesions. *Brain Research* 94: 337-346.

SPEAR, P. D., and BAUMANN, T. P. Response properties of cells in the cat's lateral suprasylvian visual area following behavioral recovery from visual cortex damage (in preparation).

SPEAR, P. D., and BRAUN, J. J. 1969. Pattern discrimination following removal of visual neocortex in the cat. *Experimental Neurology* 25: 331-348.

SPERRY, R. W. 1943. Visuomotor coordination in the newt (triturus viridescens) after regeneration of the optic nerve. *Journal of Comparative Neurology* 79: 33-35.

──── 1944. Optic nerve regeneration with return of vision in anurare. *Journal of Neurophysiology* 7: 57-69.

──── 1945. Central nervous regeneration. *Quarterly Review of Biology* 20: 311-369.

──── 1965. Embryogenesis of behavioral nerve nets. In R. L. Deltaan and H. Ursprung, eds., *Organogenesis*. New York: Holt.

──── 1968. Plasticity of neural maturation. *Developmental Biology, Supplement 2*, 27th Symposium. New York: Academic Press.

STEIN, D. G., and FIRL, A. 1976. Brain damage and reorganization of function in old age. *Experimental Neurology* 52: 157-167.

STEIN, D. G., and LEWIS, M. E. 1975. Functional recovery after brain damage in adult organisms. In F. Vital Durand and M. Jeannerod, eds., *Aspects of Neural Plasticity*. Les colloques de l'INSERM 43: 203-228.

STEIN, D. G., ROSEN, J. J., and BUTTERS, N. 1977. A comparison of two- and four-stage ablations of sulcus principalis on recovery of spatial performance in the rhesus monkey. *Neuropsychologia* 15: 179-182.

STEIN, D. G., ROSEN, J. J., GRAZIADEI, J., MISHKIN, D., and BRINK, J. 1969. Central nervous system: recovery of function. *Science* 166: 528-530.

STENEVI, U., BJÖRKLUND, A., and MOORE, R. Y. 1973. Morphological plasticity of central adrenergic neurons. *Brain, Behavior, and Evolution* 8: 110-134.

STEWARD, O., COTMAN, C. W., and LYNCH, G. S. 1973. Re-establishment of electrophysiologically functional entorhinal cortical input to the dentate gyrus deafferented by ipsilateral entorhinal lesions: innervation by the contralateral entorhinal cortex. *Experimental Brain Research* 18: 396-414.

──── 1974. Growth of a new fiber connection in the brain of adult rats: re-innervation of the dentate gyrus by the contralateral entorhinal cortex following ipsilateral entorhinal lesions. *Experimental Brain Research* 20: 45-66.

STEWARD, O., LOESCHE, J., and HORTON, W. 1977. Behavioral correlates of denervation and reinnervation of the hippocampal formation of the rat: open field activity and cue utilization following bilateral entorhinal cortex lesions. *Brain Research Bulletin* 2: 41-48.

STEWART, D. L., and RIESEN, A. H. 1972. Adult versus infant brain damage: behavioral and electrophysiological effects of striatectomy in adult and neonatal rabbits. *Advances in Psychobiology* 1: 171-211.

STÖECKEL, K., and THÖENEN, H. 1975. Retrograde axonal transport of nerve growth factor: specificity and biological importance. *Brain Research* 85: 337-341.

STONE, L. S. 1944. Functional polarization in developing and regenerating retinae of rotated grafted eyes. *Proceedings of Society of Experimental Biological Medicine* 57: 13-14.

STRYKER, M. P., and SHERK, H. 1975. Modification of cortical orientation selectivity in the cat by restricted visual experience: a reexamination. *Science* 190: 904-906.

SVENGAARD, N. A., BJÖRKLUND, A., and STENEVI, U. 1975. Regenerative properties of central monoamine neurons. *Advanced Anatomical, Embryological, and Cellular Biology* 51: 7-77.

TEUBER, H. L. 1974. Recovery of function after lesions of the central nervous system: history and prospects. In E. Eidelberg and D. G. Stein, eds., *Functional recovery after lesions of the nervous system*. Neuroscience Research Program Bulletin No. 12, pp. 194-209.

———— 1975. Recovery of function after brain injury in man. In *Outcome of severe damage to the central nervous system* (Ciba Foundation Symposium). Amsterdam: Elsevier.

TOLMAN, E. C. 1948. Cognitive maps in rats and men. *Psychological Reviews* 55: 189-208.

TREICHLER, R. F. 1975. Two-stage frontal lesion influences upon severity of delayed response deficit. *Behavioral Biology* 13: 35-47.

TUCKER, T. J., and KLING, A. 1967. Differential effects of early and late lesions of frontal granular cortex in the monkey. *Brain Research* 5: 377-389.

VARON, S. 1975. Nerve growth factor and its mode of action. *Experimental Neurology* 48: 75-92.

VON MONAKOW, C. 1914. Die lokalisation im grosshirn und der abbau der funktion durch korticale herde. Wiesbaden: J. F. Bergmann.

WALBRAN, B. B. 1976. Age and serial ablations of somatosensory cortex in the rat. *Physiology and Behavior* 17: 13-17.

WALL, P.D. 1975. Signs of plasticity and reconnection in spinal cord damage. In *Outcome of severe damage to the central nervous system* (Ciba Foundation Symposium, new series) Amsterdam: Elsevier, pp. 35-63.

WALL, P. D., and EGGER, M. D. 1971. Formation of new connections in adult rat brain after partial deafferentation. *Nature* 232: 542-545.

WEST, J. R., DEADWYLER, S., COTMAN, C. W., and LYNCH, G. 1975. Time dependent changes in commissural field potentials in the dentate gyrus following lesions of the entorhinal cortex in adult rats. *Brain Research* 97: 215-233.

———— 1976. An experimental test of diaschisis. *Behavioral Biology* 18: 419-425.

WIENS, J. A. 1970. Effects of early experience on substrate pattern selection in *Rana Aurora* tadpoles. *Copeia* 3: 543-548.

WIESEL, T. N., and HUBEL, D. H. 1963. Single cell responses in striate cortex of kittens deprived of vision in one eye. *Journal of Neurophysiology* 26: 1003-17.

———— 1965. Comparison of the effects of unilateral and bilateral eye closure on cortical unit responses in kittens. *Journal of Neurophysiology* 28: 1029-40.

WIESEL, T. N., and RAVIOLA, E. 1976. Myopia and eye enlargement after neonatal lid fusion in monkeys. *Nature* 266: 66-68.

WOLSTENHOLME, G. E. W., and PORTER, R., eds. 1968. *Growth of the nervous system*. Boston: Little, Brown and Co.

WOOD, C. C., SPEAR, P. D., and BRAUN, J. J. 1974. Effects of sequential lesions of suprasylvian gyri and visual cortex on pattern discrimination in the cat. *Brain Research* 66: 443-466.

YOON, M. G. 1975. Readjustment of retinotectal projection following reimplantation of a rotated or inverted tectal tissue in adult goldfish. *Journal of Physiology* 252: 137-158.

6 | The Endocrine System
Charles H. Doering

CONSTANCY AND CHANGE as a philosophical notion of duality are illustrated very well by the ontogeny of an individual. These contrasting aspects of duality imply that a being clearly has a certain enduring sameness or lasting identity while various features of it change. Paradoxically one can speak of change only when there is continuity. Growth, development, and personality development are examples of this basic reality. The endocrine system as an important component of the biological substrate of an individual strikingly embodies the dual aspects of constancy and change. A particular homeostasis and level of interaction is bestowed on an individual at the onset of his life along with a multitude of other characteristics in the genetic blueprint. Yet the hormonal system undergoes major changes and readjustments during the individual's life. The interrelated hormonal systems are intimately involved both in the ontogeny of an animal and in the critical stages of differentiation and development.

In recent decades the science of endocrinology has progressed from a description of the chemical nature of hormones and their general biological function to a more detailed understanding of the molecular mechanisms of how hormones act and interrelate. Much of this progress has led to a better understanding of psychoendocrine development. Before discussing aspects of endocrinology that remain unchanged for an individual and discussing the role of hormones in periods of developmental change, this chapter will provide some general background of endocrinology for the subsequent discussions. Chemical and biological details and clinical information on the endocrine system can be found in standard textbooks (Ezrin et al., 1973; Turner and Bagnara, 1976). The direct relationship between hormones and mood and behavior has been reviewed in several excellent publications (Eleftheriou and Sprott, 1975; Levine, 1972; Rose, 1972; Sachar, 1975; Ehrhardt and Meyer-Bahlburg, 1979).

Hormones

Hormones are chemical substances that deliver a message from one part of the organism to another. Typically hormones are synthesized in one organ and affect tissues elsewhere. This system of delivery of messages or transfer of information should be contrasted with the nervous system. Whereas electrical excitations in the nervous system travel in a fraction of a second, hormones must be transported in the circulatory system and take many seconds to reach their target. Once a hormone reaches its destination, the affected tissue must first "recognize" the hormone and then respond. The response times by target tissues to either hormonal or neuronal messages differ even more than the time taken to deliver the message. For neuronal messages the response time might be milliseconds; for hormones the response time is of the order of minutes to hours. If the response to a hormone is the enlargement of a tissue, the time is measured in weeks.

Hormones are very often involved in the homeostasis of an organism; in other words, they help maintain biochemical balance in a changing environment. One example is an organism's ability to control within fairly narrow limits the level of blood sugar in the face of enormous fluctuations of supply due to alimentation. Blood sugar and other vital substances, such as electrolytes, are regulated by elaborate hormonal systems. Hormones are also involved in physiological countermeasures to changes elsewhere in the same organism.

Another prominent area for the action of hormones is development. At every stage of development hormones play an active role. They participate in the critical sexual differentiation prenatally, in maturation and further differentiation at puberty, and they are responsible for the involution of reproductive capacity at menopause.

Hormones are linked to environmental changes not only through chemical sensors but also neuronally. For example, an individual perceives a situation as "frightening," or at least his brain interprets a visual impression as frightening, and automatically and involuntarily certain hormone-producing glands are activated to secrete substances that will be active elsewhere in the body. Since the initial sensory perception is by nature electrical excitation, it is clear that some hormone glands can convert neuronal messages to chemical messages: they are electrical to chemical transducers.

Since hormones are messages, they are themselves subject to control mechanisms. Their concentrations can vary over a broad range through controls on the rate of biosynthesis, the rate of secretion, and the rate of breakdown (catabolism). Additional control mechanisms for the effectiveness of the hormonal message are the transport of the hormone in blood, the conversion of a prohormone to the active hormone in strategic locations of the organism, and the adjustment of sensitivity of certain target tissues for specific hormones.

Many of these regulatory mechanisms are themselves controlled by other hormones. The overall effect is that hormones interact with and influence each other in intricately linked networks or systems. The main interactive mechanisms are control over the metabolism of hormones and competition between hormones in target tissues. There is still much to be learned about the multiple interrelationships.

Hormones are active in very small amounts, and as a result concentrations in the circulation are extremely low. In contrast, protein, sugar, fatty acids, and cholesterol in blood are about 1 million times more concentrated. This difference in concentrations is important: unlike the many blood constituents that are consumed by tissues, hormones are effective in minute amounts because of special potentiating mechanisms of their target tissues. A relatively small number of hormone molecules can trigger a specific physiological response.

Whereas the foregoing has provided a definition of *hormone* and some properties common to most hormones, this section will organize the hormones by their chemical nature. Specific examples will be presented along with typical functions (for a complete listing of hormones refer to a textbook of endocrinology).

Biogenic amines are small molecules derived by the body from certain common amino acids by removal of the carboxyl group and in many cases by additional modifications. Biogenic amines comprise some of the most active compounds, although not all of them are hormones. For example, epinephrine, serotonin, gamma-aminobutyric acid, and dopamine are, or have been postulated to be, neurotransmitters in the central nervous system. Biogenic amines with true hormone properties are epinephrine (also called adrenaline), norepinephrine (noradrenaline), melatonin, and the thyroid hormones triiodothyronine and thyroxine.

The hormonal actions of epinephrine and norepinephrine produced by the adrenal medulla are varied. They respectively either dilate or constrict peripheral blood vessels. Epinephrine additionally enhances the breakdown of liver and muscle glycogen and thus mobilizes the storage form of blood sugar. Melatonin, produced by the pineal gland and derived from the amino acid tryptophan, is a hormone of relatively obscure functions in the human body, although in lower species it is involved in mediating biorhythms.

Much more is known about the thyroid hormones (derived from the amino acid tyrosine). Because of a more efficient transport mechanism, triiodothyronine released by the thyroid gland acts more rapidly than thyroxine. Both hormones stimulate calorigenesis by accelerating the energy metabolism of most tissues and raising the basal metabolic rate. Thyroxine also has important effects on growth and development. It must be present in correct amounts for the normal and full development of the brain in the mammalian embryo; a deficiency leads to mental retardation. The complex control mechanisms of the action of thyroid hormones give rise to a large catalog of genetic abnormalities as well as environmentally induced diseases. In the adult chronic excess of thyroxine can have profound effects on the mind as well as on the body. Hyperthyroid patients are often restless and agitated even to the point of mania. Insufficient thyroxine, on the other hand, leads to severe fatigue and sluggishness of body and mind.

Peptide hormones are compounds consisting of several amino acids linked together in a chain. The particular combination and sequence of amino acids impart the hormone's biological activity. Peptide hormones may consist of from three to about thirty amino acids. The recent discoveries of a number of peptide hormones and peptides active in the brain (neuropeptides) has revolutionized central nervous system endocrinology. β-Endorphins (31 amino acids) and two subunits called enkephalins (5 amino acids each) were found to have powerful opiate-like properties when administered directly to the brain of rats. These peptides appear to be derived from the much larger polypeptide β-lipotropin, discovered and characterized more than a decade before but without any known function until now. These spectacular findings have led to intensive studies of the biological role of the endogenous analgesics, including their possible role in the etiology of mental disease.

One group of peptide hormones called releasing hormones and inhibiting hormones is of hypothalamic origin and acts primarily on the pituitary gland where these hormones regulate the synthesis and release of several pituitary hormones. For example, thyrotropin-releasing hormone (consisting of three amino acids) triggers the release of the thyroid-stimulating hormone; gonadotropin-releasing hormone (ten amino acids) promotes the secretion of both luteinizing hormone, which in turn stimulates gonads to produce steroids, and follicle-stimulating hormone, which in turn stimulates spermatogenesis and follicle growth; and somatostatin (fourteen amino acids) inhibits the release of growth hormone from the pituitary gland. The hormones vasopressin and oxytocin (both consist of eight amino acids of similar sequence) are also produced in the hypothalamus but are stored in the posterior pituitary gland. Vasopressin, the antidiuretic hormone, maintains normal osmotic pressure of plasma by acting on reabsorption of water in the kidneys. Oxytocin, active only during labor and lactation, causes contraction of smooth muscle.

A number of very active peptides with hormonelike properties participate in maintaining electrolyte balance (the angiotensins) and digestion in the gastrointestinal tract (secretin, gastrin, pancreozymin). All the peptides are well characterized chemically and their amino acid sequences are known.

Protein hormones also consist of amino acids but are much larger molecules than the peptide hormones. The exact sequence of amino acids is known for several of the protein hormones, for example, insulin (51 amino acids) and prolactin (198 amino acids). Some protein hormones are considerably more complex, having several subunits and a large carbohydrate component (the latter are called glycoproteins). As a result, the exact structure of some of the latter is not yet known. Luteinizing hormone, follicle-stimulating hormone, thyroid-stimulating hormone, and erythropoietin are glycoproteins.

The actions of this class of hormones are as varied as their structures. Insulin's effect on lowering blood glucose levels is well known; it does so primarily by promoting the glucose uptake mechanism of skeletal muscle cells and of fat tissue cells. In the latter, insulin also promotes the conversion of glucose to stored fat. The actions of growth hormone (or somatotropin) are difficult to summarize. The promotion of growth is most obvious between birth and puberty; during this period the individual seems to show a greater sensitivity to some of the actions of the hormone than adults who have similar concentrations. The major effects of growth hormone on metabolism, in the adult as well as in the child, are to contribute substantially to the maintenance of blood sugar levels and to protect against tissue destruction during fasting and in sleep. These metabolic effects are generally opposite to those of insulin. Growth hormone is released in response to many forms of stress. It seems to counteract and balance some of the effects of cortisol, the stress response hormone of the adrenal cortex.

The clearest action of prolactin is on milk secretion in mammary glands. Since prolactin is present at other times and even in males—often in considerable quantities—additional functions of prolactin will undoubtedly be demonstrated. Prolactin levels are also measured in psychiatric patients as an index of the efficacy of certain drugs, such as haloperidol and chlorpromazine.

Adrenocorticotropic hormone (ACTH), luteinizing hormone, and thyroid-stimulating hormone have much simpler actions. All three are elaborated by the pituitary gland, each controlled by its own hypothalamic releasing hormone, and each has its own single target tissue, which happens to be another hormone gland. ACTH stimulates the adrenal cortex to convert cholesterol to cortisol. ACTH is an important link in the chain of events in the body's response to stress. Luteinizing hormone induces steroid hormone production in the gonads and as such is central in the control of reproductive function. In the ovaries and the corpus luteum it stimulates the conversion of cholesterol to estradiol and progesterone respectively; in the testes it stimulates the conversion of cholesterol to testosterone. The third pituitary hormone in this group, thyroid-stimulating hormone, acts on the thyroid gland by promoting the uptake of iodide and by stimulating the formation and release of thyroid hormones.

Steroidal hormones are small molecules with the characteristic ring system common to cholesterol and related natural products. Unlike the previously listed hormones these are lipids; they have fat-like properties. Steroidal hormones are produced in only a few specialized glands: adrenal cortex, gonads, and placenta.

The chief products of the adrenal cortex are cortisol and aldosterone. Cortisol causes increased breakdown of skeletal proteins and in the liver induces enzymes that convert certain amino acids to glucose. Another effect is to mobilize stored fat to provide fuel for the organism. Aldosterone, on the other hand, regulates sodium, potassium, and water metabolism by acting on kidney mechanisms.

In the adult female the ovaries produce estradiol mainly during the follicular phrase of the menstrual cycle and lesser amounts during the luteal phase. The corpus luteum of the ovary during the luteal phase produces progesterone. While estradiol acts on many different tissues in the body and is responsible for the secondary female sex characteristics, its main effect on the reproductive system is on the uterine lining (endometrium). Progesterone acts on the estrogen-primed endometrium to complete preparation for implantation of a fertilized ovum. It also maintains pregnancies. The placenta, in cooperation with the developing fetus, produces relatively enormous amounts of estrogens and progesterone.

The primary product of the male gonad, the testis, is testosterone; a secondary product is androstenedione. Testosterone acts locally in the testis to maintain spermatogenesis. Having entered circulation, it supports the accessory reproductive structures and secondary male sex characteristics. Testosterone is also an anabolic hormone, which means that it promotes protein synthesis and growth and strengthening of skeletal muscles.

Cortisol, estradiol, progesterone, testosterone, and androstenedione refer to specific hormones (although they are incomplete names of compounds and do not completely specify the chemical structure of the respective compounds). The generic terms adrenocorticoid, estrogen, progestin, and androgen stand for classes of hormones, namely hormones of the adrenal cortex, female sex hormones, hormones with progesterone properties, and male sex hormones.

Vitamin D is an anomaly. It is both a true vitamin, since it is a required trace nutrient for many humans, and a true hormone in its action in the body. Although it is not produced by a special gland it does act on a particular tissue, the small intestine, specifically to promote calcium absorption. It also acts on bone tissue to mobilize calcium, which can be reused by newly forming bone tissue. The body synthesizes the hormone in a remarkable way. Some of the cholesterol formed by the liver enters the intestine in bile and is modified to a cholesterol derivative. The latter is reabsorbed and transported to the skin where, by the action of ultraviolet light, the critical conversion to cholecalciferol (vitamin D) takes place. Cholecalciferol undergoes additional molecular modifications in the liver and then in the kidneys. The final product 1,25-dihydroxycholecalciferol is the true hormone that controls calcium metabolism. With insufficient skin exposure to ultraviolet light, the body depends on a dietary supply of cholecalciferol, or vitamin D.

Prostaglandins are small lipid molecules with high activity in extremely low concentrations. Prostaglandins are derived from certain nutritionally essential fatty acids. Prostaglandins for that reason are analogous to vitamin D. They are synthesized in many different tissues of the body and stimulate smooth muscle, such as the uterus. Their physiological role has to be explored further.

Pheromones are analogous to hormones. They are small molecules secreted typically by a scent gland; however, the "message" that they carry is received by another organism of the same species. The effect in the receiving organism is commonly a change in behavior. Although first explored in insects, for example, the sex attractant of the silk moth, pheromones have now been identified in many species up the phylogenetic ladder. The role of pheromones in human sexual behavior has begun to be explored, and a possible weak effect in some circumstances has been reported (Michael, Bonsall, and Kutner, 1975; Michael et al., 1977). Pheromones are not a single class of compounds, but they generally have the common property of volatility. Often a pheromone is a mixture of compounds, and the particular ratio of concentrations is specific for the species.

Synthesis and Release

Each hormone has its own peculiar life history. As is the case with most body components, hormones are continuously renewed. For hormones to function as carriers of messages, they have to be broken down and eliminated promptly; consequently they need to be resynthesized. The individual biosynthetic steps of many hormones have preoccupied biochemists for decades, and most biosynthetic pathways are known in considerable detail.

The conversion of certain polyunsaturated fatty acids to prostaglandins and of vitamin D to the active hormone controlling calcium metabolism involve relatively few steps located in several scattered tissues. The production of hormones of the biogenic amine type, on the other hand, is much more typical. More steps are required to convert an amino acid to the final hormone, and all the steps are carried out by cells of a specialized tissue, called an endocrine gland. Thyroxine is synthesized in the thyroid gland; epinephrine, in the adrenal medulla. Each individual step of the many chemical modifications requires the participation of a special enzyme as biocatalyst. The enzymes themselves are synthesized by the cells of the hormone-producing gland. The presence of such a special set of enzymes largely accounts for the special function of an endocrine gland (in addition to being responsive to messages to start or to cease hormone production).

The synthesis of peptides with physiological or neuroendocrinological action is being investigated very actively. A fascinating finding is that instead of each peptide's being built up separately from amino acids, a number of active neuropeptide hormones are formed by being split off a single larger protein molecule, a prohormone. As a result, the amino acid sequences of several peptides are closely related. By some unknown mechanism the precursor protein is split at different places to yield the smaller active peptides required by the organism. This arrangement affords exquisite control over the production of these peptides. The protein molecules are presumably cleaved through the action of specific enzymes, the same protein yielding different products with different enzymes. The protein molecules themselves are synthesized in certain neurons, undoubtedly by the same cellular reactions of protein synthesis that are generally applicable to all living systems.

Protein hormones are presumably synthesized by the same general principles as other proteins. Some, such as insulin, ACTH, and parathyroid hormone, are formed from separate larger prohormone molecules. The conversion of prohormone to hormone can be regarded as an activation step. The relatively inactive prohormone is available to the organism for fast response to a physiological need.

Steroid biosynthesis differs in several respects from that of other types of hormones. All hormonal steroids are derived from a single precursor molecule, cholesterol. Cholesterol itself is synthesized in a variety of tissues, predominantly the liver, and is ingested in the diet. In specialized endocrine glands the cholesterol molecule becomes transformed successively by a series of relatively small modifications that drastically alter the physiological properties of the molecule. These molecular modifications are what differentiates, for example, the stress-response hormone, the female sex hormone, or the salt-retaining hormone. Initial reaction steps are common to all hormonal steroids, and from this common pathway branches lead to specific steroid hormones. An outline of the steps is as follows: cholesterol, pregnenolone, progesterone, 17-hydroxyprogesterone, cortisol. A branch pathway from progesterone leads to corticosterone and aldosterone, the salt-regulating hormone. A branch pathway from 17-hydroxyprogesterone leads to androstenedione (and testosterone) and from there to estrone (and estradiol). These are only the main pathways. There are several dozen more intermediate products and corresponding minor interconnecting pathways. Cholesterol undergoes these reactions to the extent that specific enzymes are present and ready to catalyze every single step.

The four steroid-endocrine tissues—ovary, testis, adrenal cortex, and placenta—differ by their relative proportions of enzyme activities. Normally the enzyme activities are such that the chief products of these four tissues are estradiol, testosterone, cortisol, and progesterone, respectively, but most other steroid-metabolizing enzymes are also active to some extent in the same tissues. As a result, the ovaries release small amounts of androstenedione and testosterone, the testes produce minor quantities of estrone and estradiol, and the adrenal cortex contributes several androgens, corticosterone, and other compounds. The placenta produces large quantities of estrone, estradiol, and estriol. One important consequence of the simultaneous presence of separate enzyme systems is that differences in enzyme levels, either induced or genetically determined, result in differences in the levels of circulating hormones and thus in individual characteristics. For example, the degree of hirsutism in women depends to a considerable extent on the adrenal formation of androgens.

The secretion of hormones from the endocrine gland into the blood stream is subject to different kinds of controls. Steroidal hormones are not stored in the gland; they are released as fast as they are formed. The release of steroid hormones is therefore controlled by their rate of production. Peptide and protein hormones, on the other hand, are stockpiled by the producing cells in so-called secretion granules. The granules are transported to the plasma membrane of the endocrine cell, and the hormonal contents are discharged into the circulation. This mechanism allows efficient response by rapid increases of circulating levels.

Circulation

Most hormones are secreted into the blood stream and carried essentially to all parts of the body in very few minutes. Major exceptions are some gastrointestinal hormones and tissue hormones such as prostaglandins. Although they are found in the circulation, they reach their target tissue first in some other manner. A special case of circulation is the portal system between the hypothalamic and the pituitary gland in the brain stem. The hypothalamic-releasing and -inhibiting hormones travel the short distance to the anterior pituitary gland by way of the portal veins; in the peripheral circulation minute amounts can barely be detected with current methods.

All hormones circulate in blood at extremely low concentrations even at moments of peak secretion. The protein hormones prolactin, growth hormone, and luteinizing hormone, when stimulated, reach concentrations in the peripheral blood circulation of 50-150 ng/ml of plasma (1 ng is 10^{-9} or one billionth of a gram). The base levels of the same hormones are about 2-15 ng/ml. ACTH actively stimulates the adrenal gland at concentrations of only 0.1 ng/ml. These peptides and protein hormones are present in blood plasma along with a total protein concentration of about 75 mg/ml, which is 1 to 50 million times more than the hormone concentration. Steroid hormones also circulate in very low concentrations; cortisol in the unstimulated condition is present at 50-100 ng/ml of blood plasma; in normal adult males 4-9 ng/ml of testosterone is sufficient to maintain sexual function; estradiol during the early phase of the female cycle is present at 0.01-0.1 ng/ml; and aldosterone in the range of 0.1-0.5 ng/ml is effective in controlling mineral metabolism. Using the same concentration units for dramatic comparison, we are encouraged to keep our blood cholesterol levels low at around 2,000,000 ng/ml (200 mg/100 ml in medical usage). Blood glucose is around 800,000 ng/ml (80 mg/100 ml). A major achievement of biochemistry and endocrinology in the past decade has been to detect and quantitate with a high degree of specificity such minute amounts.

Another important phenomenon of circulating hormones discovered in recent years is the relatively large fluctuations of most hormones, each with its own distinct pattern. Some hormones appear in peripheral blood in irregular "episodic pulses" throughout the day; others may be nearly undetectable during daytime and appear in large peaks at night. These peaks are high—their amplitude can be 50%-

100% of the mean level—and their interval is typically 30-100 minutes. The existence of these sharp pulses of hormone levels raises important methodological questions in research studies involving single blood collections. Superimposed on the episodic pulses are diurnal fluctuations of some hormones, though with smaller amplitudes of about 10%-50% of mean levels. Finally, cycles with periods of several weeks have been described in both women and men.

Several hormones are transported in the blood tightly bound to specific proteins. Transcortin, for example, binds most of circulating cortisol. Sex steroid-binding globulin has a high affinity for dihydrotestosterone, testosterone, and estradiol. In the adult male about 92% of all plasma testosterone is tightly bound to this protein; in the adult female 98% of circulating testosterone is bound in this manner. Since the hormone has to be released by the protein before it can act, only the small percentage of unbound hormone is physiologically active. The binding proteins are synthesized by the liver and are themselves under hormonal control.

Breakdown and Excretion

Hormones are renewed continuously. They are synthesized and secreted and thus must be eliminated efficiently. For the purpose of "canceling the message" it would suffice to inactivate the hormone by some alteration of the molecule. In actuality hormones are not recycled; they are either modified chemically and excreted or excreted directly. Many degradative steps make hormones more suitable for excretion, particularly in the case of steroids, which are rendered more water-soluble before they are excreted by the kidneys. Typically the liver and the kidneys carry out the degradative steps. Some protein hormones pass the kidneys with only minor changes. Small peptide hormones, on the other hand, seem to be broken down to their component amino acids to a large extent even while circulating in blood.

Efficient breakdown processes result in rapid turnover. The biological half-lives of hormones are rather short. Testosterone has an average half-life of about 20 minutes; gonadotropin-releasing hormone, probably only about 3 minutes. Since only 3% of the original amount is left after five half-lives, it follows that two hours after castration, for example, very little testosterone would be found in the circulation; similarly, 20 minutes after an intravenous administration of gonadotropin-releasing hormone this peptide will have disappeared from the organism. It is therefore understandable that pharmaceutical preparations are often long-acting forms of hormones. Chemical modifications are designed to increase the compound's resistance to the natural breakdown processes and thus to increase its half-life.

Mechanism of Action

The molecular details of how hormones express their effects continue to be under intense study. Findings in this branch of endocrinology go hand in hand with modern molecular biology's discovery of gene expression and protein synthesis. The relevance to psychoendocrinology lies in the expectation that the mechanism of hormone action on the subcellular level is similar whether it occurs in peripheral tissue or in a specific site in the central nervous system. Much of the work is being done in simple model systems, which are tissues that are particularly responsive to hormones, for example, chick oviducts for the action of progesterone, prostate gland for testosterone, and adipose tissue for insulin.

Of the extensive findings, two important and general concepts are receptor proteins in target tissues and gene activation.

Hormones are carried by the circulation to all parts of the body; why, then, do only certain tissues respond in a special way to the presence of hormones? Conceptually the situation is analogous to radio broadcasting, in which a message is radiated in all directions but can be picked up only by specially tuned receivers. All tissues in a body are exposed to the same concentration of estradiol, but only the breasts (in both males and females) and a few other tissues are sensitive to its presence. In the testes only Leydig cells respond to luteinizing hormone; other cell types of the testes are inert to it. Hormone-sensitive cells possess special proteins, called receptor proteins, that bind the hormone very tightly and very selectively; in other words, receptor proteins have a high affinity for a particular hormone. The complex formation of hormone and receptor protein triggers a series of reactions in the cell, culminating in the response of the cell to the hormonal message. A tissue is a target tissue of a hormone when it can react to a hormone in a characteristic manner, and this response requires the initial binding of hormone to a very specific receptor protein.

For most hormones the receptor proteins in target tissues are components of the outer surface of the cell membrane. Circulating hormone is trapped by the specific high-affinity binding sites on the cell surface, which forms the complex between hormone and receptor protein. This complex formation initiates a series of reactions inside the cell and results in the generation of a so-called second messenger, cyclic AMP (adenosine monophosphate), which is the same in a number of different target tissues. The specific response of the target tissue is insured, nevertheless, by the second messenger's activating a part of the genome characteristic for that tissue.

Steroid hormones constitute the major exception to this general mechanism of action. The specific high-affinity receptor proteins are free in the cytosol (soluble portion of the cell) of the target tissue cells. Steroid hormones passively diffuse from the circulation into the target tissue cells and there form the complex by binding to receptor proteins. The steroid-protein complex then enters the cell nucleus and activates a particular gene in the nucleus.

Gene activation, which is central to the mechanism of action of hormones, reveals what a given hormone does. Ultimately a hormone activates a gene, or a group of genes, in the target tissue and the target tissue cells respond by forming one or more proteins, depending on which genes were activated. The activation of specific genes determines the synthesis of specific proteins by following the general principles of molecular biology, namely transcription of activated segments of chromatin material (DNA) and translation of nucleotide sequence (RNA) to amino acid sequence (protein). The protein thus produced in response to a hormone stimulus may be inert—for example, it may be a structural protein—it may be a hormone, or it may have catalytic properties as an enzyme. Increased production of a key enzyme may result in a major shift in metabolism of the target tissue. For example, cortisol can stimulate the liver to shift amino acid metabolism toward greater production of glucose by the enhanced formation of a critical enzyme.

Just how a hormone activates specific genes from the very large genetic content of nuclear chromatin, especially in the cases of hormones acting through second messengers, is not known yet. Sophisticated experiments with model systems are in progress in several laboratories in the attempt to solve the mysteries of this aspect of molecular biology.

The complexity of the hormonal system imparts resiliency to the organism toward perturbations caused by the environment. The myriad interconnections between the hormones, their actions, and their controls may be the bane of a research endocrinologist, but the complexity greatly enhances the organism's adaptability to external and internal changes and safeguards critical functions such as the maintenance of vital blood glucose levels. The complexity of the system also allows for internal compensation. The deficient production rate of a hormone can be overcome by a reduced rate of breakdown, so that the circulating level remains normal. A relatively insensitive or unresponsive target tissue can be partially compensated for by higher circulating levels. The plasma-binding protein important for the transport of one hormone is regulated by another hormone, although the reason for this is not yet clear.

The hormonal system depends directly on the organism's genetic endowment. The concentration of circulating hormones in both the resting and the stimulated condition is partially under genetic control. The detailed chemical structure of hormones, especially of the polypeptide hormones, is under direct genetic determination, just as the hemoglobins are. The nature and the extent of the target tissue's response are under genetic control, as becomes apparent from the mechanism of action of hormones. The genetic variability possible in any of these and other aspects of the endocrine system accounts for individual differences. More extreme individual differences constitute the endocrine pathologies that result in serious disease and require medical intervention. The difference between pathology and idiosyncrasy may be only one of degree.

Permanence of the Individual's Endocrine System

Short of infrequent mutation, an individual's genetic endowment remains constant throughout his life; as a result, the structure and function of the gene product also remain constant.

The function of an active protein (enzyme, hormone, receptor protein) derives from its structure, primarily the sequence of its amino acids and secondarily the spatial arrangement or folding of the amino acid chain. Both the sequence and the spatial arrangement are determined directly by the gene coding for this protein. An alteration in amino acid sequence usually alters the activity of the protein and affects its function. In the extreme case the protein would be completely inactive, a lethal mutation if the protein's function is vital. In many cases the replacement of one amino acid with another results in relatively minor differences of activity. The classical example is hemoglobin, a protein with the vital function of transporting oxygen molecules. Variations of normal hemoglobin are known, with altered properties ranging from insignificant to serious, as in the case of sickle-cell anemia. Although much less explored, similar variations undoubtedly exist in the endocrine system.

An altered structure and function of a component of the endocrine system leads to compensatory levels and dynamics of the components. The homeostatic base levels of an individual thus affected characteristically differ from the norm. Furthermore, his capacity to respond to environmental influences and perturbations may be impaired significantly. Stemming from the genetic endowment, the capacity to respond is a constant trait, expressed only when challenged by the environment.

It is clear, then, that a genetic difference in the endocrine system offers far more possibilities of expression than merely the absence of a particular hormone, which is quite rare because of its lethality. (1) The activity of a hormone, though present in sufficient quantity, may be impaired by altered structure. (2) The activity level of a rate-controlling enzyme may be impaired, resulting in an inadequate supply of an otherwise normally functioning hormone. (3) The effectiveness of a binding protein in the circulation may be reduced, leading to a larger free fraction and consequently to reduced total concentration because the negative feedback control senses the concentration of free circulating hormone. (4) The sensitivity of the specific receptor proteins in the target tissue may be altered, the sensitivity presumably being involved in so-called threshold effects. (The threshold is the minimum concentration of circulating hormone required to achieve a particular effect. Difference in threshold would be an important individual difference.) (5) The program for development of an individual is itself under genetic control, but very little is known about the molecular mechanisms involved. It is apparent that the rate of maturation, both biologically and psychologically, differs from one individual to another, that the difference is familial and must in part be inherited.

It is equally clear that the genetic endowment is permanent for an individual. Internal and external influences, of course, modulate the genetic expressions. Internal compensations may be more or less successful depending on outside influences and challenges. Frequently individual differences can be found only when the organism is stressed.

Genetically determined differences can be so great that they are insufficiently compensated for and thus appear as a clinical condition or disease. Four examples, three mostly from the steroid field, illustrate such conditions.

Adrenogenital Syndrome

The basic defect in the inherited adrenogenital syndrome is the relative deficiency of one or more specific enzymes of the normal biosynthetic pathway of adrenocortical steroids. Some of the enzyme defects lead to death in infancy; others are less severe and can be treated (the disease comes in different forms depending on the precise enzyme defect). In all cases inadequate production of cortisol leads to overstimulation of the adrenal cortex. By negative feedback, hypothalamic releasing hormone causes the pituitary gland to secrete increased amounts of adrenocorticotropic hormone (ACTH), which in turn stimulates the main pathway of steroid synthesis in the adrenal cortex.

The inadequate activity of one enzyme on the main pathway, however, prevents the formation of increased amounts of cortisol. Since other enzymes in adrenal gland pathways are not deficient and the gland as a whole is overstimulated, products of branch pathways "upstream" of the enzyme defect become much more prominent than in the normal gland. Most commonly adrenal androgens appear in excess.

Since this feedback loop becomes established early in fetal life, the genetic defect also shows up early. The excess androgen influences the anatomical development of the genitalia in the male direction, with more obvious and more serious consequences in the case of a genetic female than a male. This condition, although it cannot be cured, is generally controlled by substitution therapy. The regular administration of artificial cortisol prevents the chronically overstimulated adrenal cortex and with it the excess androgen. It is not certain that the excess androgen is completely avoided at all times.

Anke Ehrhardt has reported on two series of studies (Ehrhardt, Epstein, and Money, 1968; Ehrhardt and Baker, 1974). Children were studied in their early teenage years and medical histories obtained. Girls were treated with cortisone from infancy to suppress the adrenal cortex and to avoid the excess androgen production. Generally minor surgery corrected the masculinized external genitalia. Most of the boys were also started on cortisone therapy soon after birth. The remainder began cortisone treatment at age 6 or 7 years when precocious puberty was noted.

In female adrenogenital syndrome patients the clearest and strongest differences compared with unaffected sisters were as follows: (1) The affected girls expended far more intense physical energy in their play and sports. They were not hyperactive; they just played harder. (2) Their preferred playmates were boys. (3) They had little interest in dolls. (4) They were generally characterized as long-term tomboys. Similarly, boys with adrenogenital syndrome differed from unaffected brothers mainly in their high-energy investment in sports and outdoor activities on a long-term basis. There was, however, no difference in fighting behavior between the two groups.

In the medically managed patient the main influence probably occurs only during sensitive embryonic development. Psychological effects are seen years later in childhood and adolescence. Whether these or related psychological attributes persist throughout life is not clear, since this question has not been addressed adequately.

Hormone Binding in Circulation

Several hormones circulate in blood bound fairly tightly to special binding proteins. The degree of binding is important because only the small portion of free hormone is considered physiologically active (for a review see Anderson, 1974). In addition, the breakdown system in the liver acts only on the unbound portion of the circulating hormone. In other words, the metabolic clearance rate is related to the level of plasma binding.

Since there are individual differences in the level of binding, as well as large sex differences, one would expect to find genetically determined clinical cases with extreme differences, such as the complete absence of binding. This situation has not been studied systematically, although Pieter DeMoor states that of some 1,200 human plasma samples examined he has not seen one totally without sex steroid-binding capacity (DeMoor, 1972).

Only a few clinical conditions with abnormal binding have been identified; most are related to or the direct result of other endocrine disorders (Anderson, 1974).

Elevated plasma levels of the binding protein occur in certain hypogonadal men (Vermeulen, Stoica, and Verdonck, 1971). Men with chronic liver disease, such as cirrhosis due to alcoholism, generally have hypogonadism and gynecomastia (enlarged breasts) as a result of increased levels of sex steroid-binding globulin and an associated decrease of unbound circulating testosterone (Galvão-Teles et al., 1973). In another condition high levels of circulating thyroxine (thyrotoxicosis) stimulate the liver to produce abnormally large amounts of the binding globulin. In men such chronically elevated levels of the binding globulin lead to loss of libido, impotence, and gynecomastia. The lower concentrations of free testosterone stimulate greater production of luteinizing hormone through the hypothalamic negative feedback system, which in turn stimulates the testes to produce more testosterone. The additional androgen is ineffective because of the binding in circulation, but the extra estradiol inevitably accompanying the production of testosterone causes the enlargement of breast tissue. In women the main effect of thyrotoxicosis through the sex steroid-binding globulin is loss of regular monthly cycles, apparently due to blunted positive feedback in the hypothalamic-pituitary control (Anderson, 1974). In both men and women the sex steroid-binding globulin is restored promptly to normal levels when thyrotoxicosis is treated.

With low levels of sex steroid-binding globulin, the most serious clinical symptom is hirsutism (excess hair growth) in women. The insufficient amount of binding protein leaves a greater proportion of circulating testosterone and dihydrotestosterone in the free and consequently active form, the target tissue in this case being hair follicles (Rosenfield, 1973). As in so many other diseases, there may be different types of female hirsutism. At least some of them appear to be lifelong and are probably inherited. In a few instances the binding globulin may be defective and may consequently have reduced capacity to bind sex steroids. Low levels of the binding protein also lead to an excess of growth hormone. This relationship has been found both in patients suffering from too much growth hormone (acromegalic men) and in growth-retarded children treated with growth hormone (DeMoor, Heyns, and Bouillon, 1972). This relationship amounts to an important synergistic effect between the growth-promoting properties of growth hormone and the anabolic properties of testosterone.

Androgen Insensitivity Syndrome

Androgen insensitivity, a genetically determined condition, is also called testicular feminization. Individuals with this syndrome are usually reared unambiguously as girls and seek medical advice only after pubertal age because of primary amenorrhea. At this time they have fully developed breasts and female external genitalia but no pubic hair. On examination no uterus, tubes, or ovaries are found, but they have functioning undescended testes and their karyotype is normal male 46,XY. Why do these male pseudohermaphrodites with functioning testes and roughly normal levels of circulating testosterone fail to develop male secondary sexual characteristics? The answer lies in the inability of the target tissues to respond to the male hormone; the defect in the mechanism of action of androgens is apparently uniform in all target tissues. Much has been learned in recent years by the use of certain inbred strains of rats and mice with the analogous genetic defect. In rats and mice androgen insensitivity has been correlated with the virtual absence of the androgen receptor protein in target tissue cells. This correlation has been confirmed in humans by studying the binding of the peripherally potent androgen dihydrotestosterone to skin fibroblasts (Keenan et al., 1974). There was no binding of the hormone in samples taken from androgen-insensitive patients, in contrast with a high degree of binding in samples of normal males.

The complete form of androgen insensitivity syndrome extends also to behavior and gender identity. The girls with the syndrome, although genetically XY males with functioning testes, are reared as girls from infancy; they perfectly fit the stereotypic female role of marriage and parenthood (expecting to become wives and being interested in infant care) and are content with their female identity. None has been described as having been a tomboy during childhood. After adolescence their eroticism and sex behavior are also completely female (Money, Erhardt, and Masica, 1968).

Obviously the condition is lifelong. The female anatomical development and the feminine gender identity indicate its onset early in fetal life. There is no indication that the fetal brain was androgenized, nor is the condition reversible by testosterone substitution therapy later in life.

Stress Response Pattern

The physiological response to an environmental stimulus perceived as threatening or noxious involves a number of hormones and biochemical systems. The hormonal responses are mainly those of the hypothalamus-pituitary-adrenocortical axis (corticotropin-releasing hormone, ACTH, and cortisol) and of the adrenal medulla (epinephrine and norepinephrine). Of the several biochemical responses to the hormones, the changes of the cardiovascular system can typically be sensed by the individual in a stressful situation. The physiological responses are generally considered adaptive, and the ability to cope with the stress may depend on these responses.

There is a strong sex difference in the physiological response to stress, and the response pattern is stable over a considerable span of life. Marianne Frankenhaeuser and her colleagues (1978) recently reported that excretions of cortisol, epinephrine, and a metabolite of epinephrine were significantly greater in young adult males than in females when subjected to severe stress. The females showed relatively small elevations of hormone excretions, while the males had large increases. Similar results were obtained with several other types of stress and over different ages, ranging from 12 years to adulthood (Frankenhaeuser, Dunne, and Lundberg, 1976; Johansson, Frankenhaeuser, and Magnusson, 1973; Johansson and Post, 1974). Since males and females performed equally well on the examination type of stress, the differences lie with the coping mechanisms. Females reported much greater discomfort than males, although their hormones did not respond nearly as much as the hormones in males. These sexually dimorphic response patterns appear to be rather constant in human development. Sexual dimorphism is usually accompanied by individual variation of the measure within the same sex.

Ontogeny of the Individual's Endocrine System

Some of the permanent genetic endowment of an individual is expressed through the endocrine system by a particular homeostatic balance of the hormones. The genetic endowment also provides each individual with a characteristic capacity to respond to environmental changes and stresses. Indeed some individual characteristics are not apparent until the organism is challenged.

In addition to determining the physical and biological end product, the chromatin material also contains the blueprint for the development program. One of the most fascinating problems in modern biology is DNA's encoding of the differentiation of tissues for specific functions, in particular its encoding of the program for an orderly sequence of events. The growth and differentiation of multiple tissues of an embryo must be highly coordinated; errors in the proper sequence lead to drastic consequences. As there are some differences between species, there is opportunity for minor individual differences in the developmental blueprint.

The major developmental periods in which the most important changes take place are the perinatal, pubertal, and menopausal periods. A number of developmental events must occur during these critical periods or they do not take place at all. Examples come from physical and anatomical growth, the establishment of the endocrine system, the nervous system, and psychological development.

Perinatal Changes

Probably the most fundamental aspect of personality development is that of gender identity. Psychological maleness and femaleness have their origins long before birth. Gender identity is initiated not merely by the anatomical differentiation of the embryo (and subsequent reflection on this physical fact) but by direct action of hormones on the developing central nervous system. A gene on the Y chromosome at about the sixth week of embryonic life is responsible for the production of H-Y antigen that acts on undifferentiated gonadal anlagen and promotes their development to become testes (Ohno, 1979). In the absence of the Y chromosome and consequent absence of the critical H-Y antigen, the gonadal anlagen become ovaries. Several weeks later fetal testes produce and release substantial amounts of testosterone.

The embryonic genital or reproductive tract is equally bipotential. A special hormone elaborated by the testes at about the eighth week of gestation causes involution of the müllerian ducts, which would otherwise differentiate to become the female reproductive tract without a requirement for ovarian hormones. The testicular hormone is a medium-sized protein molecule, sometimes called müllerian regression factor. At about the same time the wolffian ducts under the influence of testosterone differentiate to become the male reproductive tract. Testosterone also begins to masculinize external genitalia.

In analogy to anatomical sex differentiation, the brain, too, is a gender-bipotential organ. In the absence of androgens during early fetal life, the central nervous system also develops female. It is responsible for the individual's female gender identity, it contributes to characteristic female behavior patterns, and at puberty it initiates the regular cyclic interplay between hypothalamus, pituitary gland, and gonads. However, at certain critical times well before birth, a relatively brief exposure to testosterone differentiates the central nervous systems in the male direction: male gender identity, male behavior patterns, acyclic hypothalamic-pituitary-gonadal hormonal control.

Sex differentiation is not limited to the reproductive tract and the central nervous system. Rat experiments have shown that even the liver undergoes similar sexually dimorphic differentiation early in development. A single exposure to testosterone during a critical period of only a few days permanently alters the liver metabolism of steroid hormones, particularly of testosterone. The critical period of androgen exposure in the rat lasts a few days at birth, although the difference in metabolism is not seen until puberty. This sex differentiation of the liver is probably only one example of other differentiation. Male and female muscle tissues respond differently to androgens, and this difference may well depend on a critical priming event.

A common theme in sexual differentiation is that maleness is something added to a female biological substrate. The basic tendency of mammals is to develop female, even without hormonal influence. It requires the positive action of androgens to redirect the course of development toward maleness. One natural consequence of this arrangement is that male development is much more subject to error than female development. Arrested or incomplete male development occurs more commonly than the female counterpart. Terry Allen (1976) has reviewed a wide range of biochemical lesions resulting in incomplete sexual differentiation and intersexuality.

In recent years improved analytical methods have simplified the quantitation of a large number of hormones even in small samples. The concentrations of several hormones even in fetal circulation are now known (except for the gestational age of about 25-35 weeks). Entirely consistent with the phenomena of sexual differentiation, originally studied in animal model systems by Alfred Jost (1953), circulating testosterone in the human male fetus reaches a peak concentration in the brief span of about 12-18 weeks gestation (Reyes et al., 1974; Faiman, Reyes, and Winter, 1974). The fetal testes appear to be stimulated by the placental gonadotropin called human chorionic gonodotropin, which reaches very high concentrations just prior to the testosterone peak. In the female fetus the same high levels of the gonodotropin do not stimulate the ovaries, which are known to develop later than the testes. The testosterone concentrations reached in male fetuses are in the normal adult male range (2.5-6.0 ng/ml), while those in female fetuses remain unchanged at low levels (0.1-1.0 ng/ml) (Reyes et al., 1974). After the early peak in the male fetus, testosterone concentration declines gradually and steadily to rather low levels at term, although it remains significantly greater in males than in females as measured in umbilical cord blood at birth (Forest et al., 1974; Doering, unpublished results). Estradiol has been measured during this developmental stage and has been found to be very high, quite variable, and not different for fetal sex. An unexplained very large sex difference, on the other hand, has been found for follicle-stimulating hormone in the fetal circulation. The hormone levels of female fetuses at 20 weeks of gestation reach adult castrate values (Reyes et al., 1974). In the male fetus this hormone remains at a low level.

At birth infants of both sexes experience drastic declines of circulatory estrogens, progesterone, and related steroids with a consequent rebound of the two pituitary hormones: luteinizing hormone and follicle-stimulating hormone. The latter, however, peaks at much higher concentrations and then declines more slowly in girls than in boys, again without any apparent effect on the ovaries. Boys, in contrast, experience a surprising postnatal testosterone peak at 3 months of age, about half of adult male levels (Forest et al., 1974). (Girls have uniformly very low testosterone levels from birth to puberty.) These changes of hormone levels are summarized in figure 6.1.

This second postnatal androgen peak in boys has not yet been explained or interpreted adequately. Perhaps some critical aspect of sex differentiation takes place at this time, but no information on this speculation is yet available.

After this postnatal androgen peak in boys, there is no sex difference in circulating levels of hormones for several years during childhood until the advent of adolescence. At least the sex hormones are uniformly low and the individual experiences no hormonal changes during that span of life.

Growth hormone is of interest because of its role in normal physical development and its reactivity during stress. The human fetal pituitary can synthesize growth hormone from about the ninth week of gestation. Serum concentrations in fetal circulation are several times higher at 20-24 weeks gestation than at term (Kaplan and Grumbach, 1972). This peak of growth hormone is paralleled by electroencephalograph activity. The normal adult relationship between brain waves at the onset of deep sleep and growth hormone secretion may well have its origins at this early stage in development. However, it is not clear that the hormone has any physiological significance for the fetus, since there is an abundance of biologically and chemically similar placental hormone, human chorionic somatotropin.

Although growth hormone responds to stress, the highly variable conditions of birth are not reflected by growth hormone levels in umbilical cord blood. Duration of labor, duration of prenatal distress, Apgar index, infant body weight, and similar parameters did not cor-

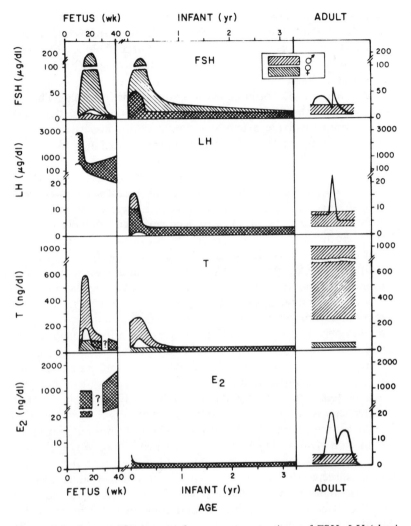

Figure 6.1. *Sex-specific ranges of serum concentrations of FSH, LH (chorionic gonadotropin in the fetus), testosterone (T), and estradiol (E₂) in the fetus, infant, and adult. Gonadotropin concentrations are in microgram LER-907 equivalents/100 ml. T and E₂ concentrations are in ng/100 ml. Adult female data are depicted as typical menstrual cycle values. A question mark denotes an area in which data are especially scanty. (Faiman, Reyes, and Winter, 1974.)*

relate with cord blood levels. Nor was there a difference by fetal sex (von Mühlendahl, Pachaly, and Schmidt-Gollwitzer, 1976). In contrast, 17-hydroxycorticosteroids are elevated in cord blood of the newborn in accordance with the difficulty of the delivery (Franchimont and Burger, 1975).

At birth growth hormone levels again rise above normal. This rise may well be related to the severe metabolic adjustment experienced by the newborn involving a temporary reliance on nonesterified fatty acids for energy, instead of glucose, and high demands for protein synthesis (Franchimont and Burger, 1975).

What are some of the long-range consequences of hormonal changes and interactions at this pre- and postnatal stage in development? Anatomical consequences of various defects of the normal steroid hormone metabolism have been reviewed critically by Allen (1976). He includes consequences beyond the immediate effect at birth by describing further dependent changes at puberty. F. Neumann (1976) similarly describes the intricately programmed sexual differentiation in normal perinatal development, emphasizing the numerous possibilities for interference with this orderly process by the administration of inappropriate sex hormones or antihormones to the pregnant mother. Pharmacological interference results in very similar anatomical aberrations of intersexed individuals, as described by Allen. The interference goes beyond the anatomical. At puberty one important sexual differentiation is the establishment of a cyclical hormonal system in the female and a relatively steady system in the male. The cyclicity is controlled by certain brain centers that establish the female pattern at puberty only if they underwent normal female differentiation *in utero*. The fetal brain is particularly sensitive to androgenic hormones. Even a single exposure to an androgen at the critical time of susceptibility can block cyclicity permanently. Lack of cyclicity in the female means infertility and is thus of grave consequence.

The effects of prenatal differentiation on those brain centers thought to be involved in gender identity and sexually dimorphic behavior patterns are far more difficult to demonstrate. John Money and Ehrhardt (1972) have capitalized on "experiments of nature" and studied the psychological development of patients with certain endocrine abnormalities. It is clear from their work that endocrine events during prenatal development have measurable psychological and behavioral effects much later in life. These effects are subtle in the human but much less so in animals, particularly in lower-ranking species. An extreme exponent of this kind of biological hormonal determinism is Günter Dörner, who believes that humans are profoundly affected by the details of the intrauterine endocrine milieu in their central nervous system control mechanisms (feedback set points), gender identity, gender-specific behavior patterns, and even sexual orientation, for example homosexuality (Dörner, 1977). He also believes that it should be possible to optimize this endocrine milieu prenatally as some form of sophisticated preventive medical intervention.

Additional information of the long-term effects of prenatal hormones comes from studies of the administration of hormones or hormonelike substances to pregnant women. The earlier literature has been reviewed critically by June Reinisch (1974, 1976). When mothers of boys received estrogen-progesterone therapy to avoid pregnancy complications, such boys at the age of 6 and 16 years ranked lower on scales of "masculinity," assertiveness, and athletic ability than boys matched for age and medical condition of mother (Yalom, Green, and Fisk, 1973). This study cannot be interpreted unambiguously because it is confounded both by the medical condition of the mothers (diabetes) and by the administration of progesterone in conjunction with estrogen. The results are, however, at least consistent with findings in animal experiments.

The effects of prenatal exposure to progestins alone (natural and synthetic) have been studied more extensively. The first study included ten girls exposed to synthetic progestins, which have androgenic side effects as evidenced by masculinized genitalia at birth. These girls were characterized by a high degree of tomboyism and, unexpectedly, by much higher than average intelligence (Ehrhardt and Money, 1967). Another study employed teacher ratings to compare 10-year-old boys and girls exposed prenatally to natural progesterone (administered to the pregnant mothers to treat toxemia) with control children. The progesterone-exposed children were ranked much higher in achievement of academic subjects than the control groups. The effect, furthermore, appeared to depend on the total amount of progesterone administered (Dalton, 1968). A recent follow-up of the same population revealed that 32% of the progesterone-exposed children continued their education at the university level, compared with only 6 percent of the control children (Dalton, 1976). Whether Dalton's findings relate to intelligence or to some aspect of personality development is not clear from these studies.

A new study on a larger population with better control showed that neither estrogen nor progestin administered prenatally had a significant effect on intelligence, as measured by the Wechsler IQ test. Nor was there any effect by dose level or sex (Reinisch and Karow, 1977). Results from personality questionnaires, however, yielded significant differences. Children exposed primarily to progestins (with little or no estrogens) before birth were more independent, sensitive, and self-sufficient. Those exposed to large doses of estrogens along with progestins, in contrast, were more group oriented and group dependent. The independent and more self-assured personality of the progestin-treated children may well render them more successful in the school system. This would support Dalton's earlier findings.

Heino Meyer-Bahlburg and Ehrhardt have recently described the effects of the synthetic progestin medroxyprogesterone acetate administered to pregnant mothers, compared with carefully matched controls. Boys, about 11 years old, so treated showed no significant difference relative to controls in energy expenditure of play, in male-specific preferences, or gender identity, although the sample size was small ($N = 13$) (Meyer-Bahlburg, Grisanti, and Erhardt, 1977). Girls of the same age and similarly exposed prenatally to the same drug, on the other hand, registered significantly less tomboyism and stronger preferences for feminine clothes than controls. The girls did not differ in energy expenditure of play or feminine role playing (Ehrhardt, Grisanti, and Meyer-Bahlburg, 1977).

These studies have all been retrospective and are beset with numerous ambiguities and confounding variables, some of which are discussed by Reinisch (1976, 1977). There is yet no published account of a prospective longitudinal study on the association between perinatal endocrine changes and long-term effects on development. However, one such study is in progress, at Stanford University. In this study several endogenous hormone levels of infants at birth have been measured and numerous psychological parameters of the same infants are being assessed longitudinally over several years (Eleanor Maccoby and Carol Jacklin, personal communication; for preliminary results see Maccoby et al., 1979).

Pubertal Changes

Pubertal changes of the endocrine system are at least as profound as those that occur during prenatal development. They mark the first few years of adolescence and affect both boys and girls. For one or two years before puberty, hormones increase very gradually above the earlier childhood levels but then undergo dramatic increases.

The mechanisms controlling the onset of puberty are still not clear. Perhaps a certain critical body mass, appropriate for each individual, must be reached before the pubertal changes are triggered. Most likely, the adrenal cortex and its hormonal output are involved. The main features of the onset of changes are the resetting of the "gonadostat." The negative feedback system of the hypothalamic-pituitary-gonadal axis operates throughout childhood. Before puberty, however, the hypothalamus is sensitive to the very low concentration of circulating gonadal steroids and is not activated to produce the releasing hormone. Puberty appears to be initiated when the hypothalamus loses its sensitivity to low circulating levels of steroids and responds with releasing hormone, which stimulates the secretion by the pituitary of luteinizing hormone (LH) and follicle-stimulating hormone (FSH). The gonads respond soon after to the action of LH by increased production of steroids. The hypothalamus continues to lose sensitivity until a new set point is reached and a feedback system with adult hormone levels is reestablished (Grumbach et al., 1974).

The gonadotropin-releasing hormone produced by the hypothalamus is almost impossible to measure for methodological reasons. Therefore no information is available on changing levels of the releasing hormone. Steroid, LH, and FSH levels, on the other hand, are readily determined.

In girls, sex steroids produced by the adrenal cortex begin to increase in late childhood (Collu and Ducharme, 1975). Dehydroepiandrosterone and androstenedione are weak androgens of adrenal origin that may be involved in the initial development of pubic hair. Some conversion takes place in peripheral tissue from androstenedione to testosterone, which is just detectable in the circulation. Some estrone is released by the adrenal and may act on breast tissue. As a result of these beginning hormone actions, largely due to "adrenarche" (at about 9 years), girls change from the preadolescent stage P_1 (Tanner stage) to stage P_2 (breast budding) at about 11 years of age. At about this age, the pituitary releases more FSH, which promotes ovarian development. Plasma levels of estradiol and testosterone rise. During stage P_3 (further breast and pubic development) LH levels rise significantly. This hormone also acts on the ovaries by promoting estradiol production. By stage P_4 (near-adult breast and pubic hair) both estrogens and both androgens rise precipitously and generally usher in menarche at about 12.8 years (Root, 1973; Winter and Faiman, 1973a; Ducharme et al., 1976; Apter and Vihko, 1977).

When the levels of these hormones are plotted against age, it becomes apparent that beginning at 8-10 years the plasma concentration values spread out and reach enormous ranges by stage P_5 (adult). For example, at stage P_1 estradiol clusters around 0.01 ng/ml, LH around 20 with a standard error of 2 ng/ml, and progesterone around 0.05 ng/ml; at stage P_5 estradiol values range from 0.01 to 0.25 ng/ml, LH from 25 to 350 ng/ml, and progesterone from 0.05 to 13 ng/ml. Several factors contribute to this wide range of cross-sectional data. Individual differences in onset of maturation are the most obvious contribution to the spread. However, the arrangement of values by sex staging or by bone age attenuates the spread only partially. The change in girls from "tonic" to cyclic hormone levels is the main reason for the spread. Jeremy Winter and Charles Faiman (1973b) have presented an excellent illustration of this phenomenon on several hormones, reproduced in figures 6.2 and 6.3. The hourly fluctuations of plasma concentrations of hormones also contribute to the wide range of values. The episodic releases are greater for LH than for FSH and are greater in later stages of puberty than in earlier ones (Penny, Olambiwonnu, and Frasier, 1977). Similar pulsatile fluctuations have been reported for estradiol superimposed on a pronounced circadian cycle in premenarcheal girls (Boyar et al., 1976).

There is a notable lack of longitudinal studies of hormonal changes in human adolescents. Ideally samples should be taken from

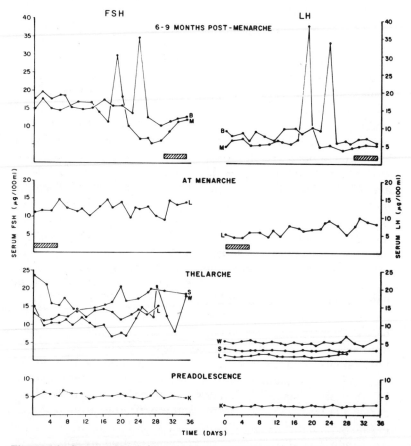

Figure 6.2. *Serum FSH (left) and LH (right) at 2- to 3-day intervals in perimenarchal girls. The hatched bar denotes menses. The cycles of subjects B and M are synchronized about the menses. (Winter and Faiman, 1973b.)*

the same girls at least every three months between the ages of 10 and 15.

The initial prepubertal changes in boys occur about two years later than in girls. These changes also seem to be due to increased output of adrenal steroid hormones (Collu and Ducharme, 1975). Estrone, however, plays a smaller role in boys than it does in girls. The developmental change from Tanner stage P_1 to P_2 (slight enlargement

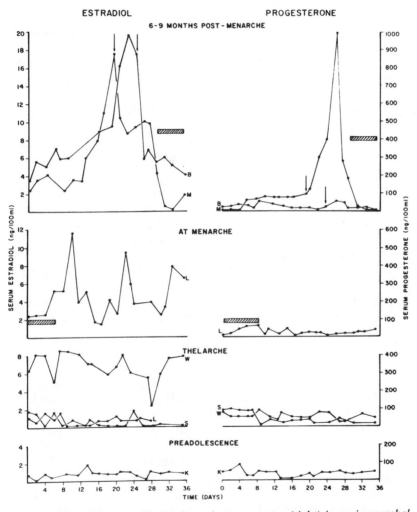

Figure 6.3. *Serum estradiol (left) and progesterone (right) in perimenarchal girls. The hatched bar denotes menses. The arrow shows the time of the LH-FSH peak in the postmenarchal girls. (Winter and Faiman, 1973b.)*

of testes and initial appearance of pubic hair) at about 11.5 years is accompanied by a significant rise in plasma FSH levels. The rise in LH and testosterone levels becomes significant in stage P_3 (further growth of testes, lengthening of penis, moderate pubic and axillary hair) at around 12.8 years. At this stage and into the next, testosterone levels rise most steeply (0.5 to 3 ng/ml). The rise of estradiol and dihydro-testosterone, the latter derived from testosterone in peripheral target tissues, is equally significant (Ducharme et al., 1976; Winter and Faiman, 1972). The comment about spreading hormone values made for girls applies to boys as well. Testosterone concentrations at later pubertal stages have an enormous range of values, largely due to the variation in age of onset of pubertal changes and to individual variations in rate and magnitude of change. The customary presentation of cross-sectional data completely obscures the real changes that a given individual undergoes.

Unlike the situation with girls, a few longitudinal studies of boys have been reported (Knorr et al., 1974; Lee, Jaffe, and Midgley, 1974). Peter Lee and his co-workers have charted the progress of four boys for 4½ years at 6-month intervals and found considerable individual differences. Most striking are the extremely steep rises of testosterone of some, from 0.5 ng/ml to 9 ng/ml in one year. More data of this type were presented by Dietrich Knorr and his co-workers who followed testosterone concentrations of 22 boys for 1-2 years at 3-month intervals. Figure 6.4 shows their data and contrasts the individual rates of puberty with the cross-sectional data (Knorr et al., 1974). The cross-sectional plot shows that testosterone rises gradually from age 10 to adulthood. In the steepest part of the curve testosterone rises by 1.0 ng/ml per year (ages 14-15). Most of the individual plots, however, show that the developmentally important rise from 0.4 ng/ml (average adult female level) to 2.4 ng/ml (third male percentile) is achieved within 10 months.

Episodic fluctuations also contribute to the wide ranges of cross-sectional data. Of the two gonadotropins, LH fluctuates much more than FSH, particularly during later stages of puberty (Penny, Olambiwonnu, and Frasier, 1977; Parker et al., 1975). The interplay between LH and testosterone peaks, and its relationship to wake-sleep cycles is of particular significance in male puberty. To obtain this kind of information requires frequent and regular blood sampling (15-60 min intervals) for at least 24 hours as well as some sleep recordings of electroencephalography. In adult men episodic pulses of LH and testosterone occur throughout day and night, but in pubertal boys these pulses are associated only with sleep (Boyar et al., 1975). In nine boys of pubertal stages P_1-P_4, plasma LH showed large peaks above base-

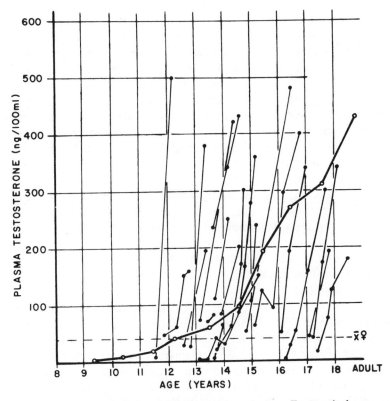

Figure 6.4. *Longitudinal studies of plasma testosterone. Empty circles represent median values of the cross-sectional study. Filled circles indicate individual values of the longitudinal study (N = 22). The range from 40 ng/100 ml to 240 ng/100 ml (third percentile of the adult male) is passed within 10 months. (Knorr, Bidlingmaier, Butenandt, Fendel, and Ehrt-Wehle, 1974).*

line levels synchronous with sleep. These peaks appeared to elevate testosterone secretion substantially—to near adult levels in P_4 boys—during sleep. Testosterone levels declined to the typical baseline levels within a few hours after awakening. The relationship of the augmented hormone production to sleep was confirmed by sleep-wake reversal of a twenty-four-hour day for some of the boys during which the hormone peaks remained associated with sleep. Donal Parker and his colleagues (1975) have confirmed these findings independently and further established the changes of sleep-relatedness with pubertal stages. The most dramatic testosterone increases are seen in mid puberty: 0.6 ng/ml to 2.2 ng/ml within three hours of onset of sleep. These authors believe that their findings suggest "the existence of a fundamental sleep-entrained central nervous system mechanism that plays an important, if not a dominant, role in sexual maturation of boys" (p. 1108).

Fluctuations of plasma concentrations on an hourly or a diurnal basis have serious implications for research methodology. Single blood samples, even when obtained at the same hour of the day (better a fixed time after first awakening in the morning), are subject to substantial uncertainty because of the episodic release of most hormones. To obtain a representative blood sample, one would have to draw several samples during one or two hours and repeat the procedure on two other days. In most cases a practical compromise is struck. The advantage of urine samples is that the kidneys smooth out or integrate the plasma hormone fluctuations over the time span of the urine collection. Carefully controlled urine samples can provide adequate information of certain hormone levels in some circumstances (Kulin et al., 1975), but unfortunately such urine samples are useless for assessing levels of circulating sex steroids. Most steroid metabolites measured in urine are derived over different pathways from more than one plasma hormone.

The plasma sex steroid-binding globulin also undergoes significant changes during this development period. The total binding capacity of this specific globulin in males drops from its highest value of 11.6×10^{-8}M at 6 years of age to its lowest value of 1.7×10^{-8}M at 18 years. The steepest decline is between 13 and 15 years (Horst, Bartsch, and Dirksen-Thedeus, 1977). In other words, the concentration of free testosterone in boys rises even more precipitously than total testosterone does during this age span.

The characteristic growth spurt in puberty raises the question of the role of growth hormone in this growth phenomenon. The secretion pattern of growth hormone may represent the most extreme form of wake-sleep dependence. In prepubescent boys no growth hormone is produced in the awake state, but about 30 minutes after onset of sleep one very large peak appears, followed by one or two minor peaks. In the adolescent or adult male minor peaks appear occasionally during the day, but by far the largest peak is registered within about 1 hour of onset of sleep (Finkelstein et al., 1972). Obviously the role of growth hormone could not be studied by the occasional single blood sample. However, blood samples taken every 20 minutes for an entire 24-hour period revealed that pubertal children (Tanner stages 2-4) secreted significantly greater amounts of growth hormone than either less-developed children or adults (Finkelstein et al., 1972). Using similar techniques, Thompson and colleagues (1972) confirmed that adolescent males tended to have higher growth hormone levels than preadolescent boys and certainly higher levels than adult males. However, they noted that the "integrated concentrations of growth hormone" did not increase along with progressing puberty, with increasing bone age, or with increasing plasma testosterone levels (p. 334). In another study, when boys with familial short stature were contrasted with boys with growth spurt and familial tallness, no correlation was found between the 24-hour mean growth hormone concentration and 24-hour mean testosterone concentration in serum nor between growth hormone and the growth rate of the boys. Testosterone and growth rate, however, did correlate (Butenandt et al., 1976). Thus it appears that the pubertal growth spurt is due not to a change in growth hormone but to the increase of androgen concentration. A synergistic effect between androgens and growth hormone is nevertheless possible.

The pubertal growth spurt is due largely to an increase in muscle mass. Donald Cheek has described a sharp divergence of muscle growth between boys and girls starting at about 9 years (Cheek, 1974). The number of muscle cells (cell nuclei) in boys actually increases in accordance with a cubic equation, whereas in girls the increase continues in linear fashion. With large sex-dimorphic changes there is much opportunity for individual differences as well. The large energy expenditure in outdoor activities and general rough-and-tumble play by tomboys studied by Ehrhardt may well be related to the development of skeletal muscle and perhaps to a heightened responsiveness of muscle tissue to hormonal changes.

Psychoendocrine Relationships

Early adolescence is a developmental phase of rapid behavioral and psychological changes in addition to hormonal changes. Beatrix Hamburg and David Hamburg (1975) write that "Adolescence is the most dramatic example of the complex processes involved in negotiating a critical period of normal development. It illustrates the shifting interplay between biological, psychological, and cultural demands on the individual" (p. 93). The basic biological substrate of an individual is biased prenatally by sexual differentiation of body and mind. During adolescence much of this differentiation becomes activated. The unpredictable moodiness, hostility, and depression typical of adolescents may be related to the significant changes in sex hormones. The relation between these hormone changes on the one hand and aggressiveness, hostility, and sexual behavior on the other are particularly interesting. Can such changes alter the responsiveness to provocative stimulation or lower frustration thresholds (Hamburg and Hamburg, 1975)? Sally Hays (1978) discusses additional possible research questions, particularly as they relate to thyrotropin-releasing hormone, prolactin, and mood states. Reports on these relationships are conflicting, and there are no normative data for adolescents. Ehrhardt and Meyer-Bahlburg (1975) have reviewed psychological correlates of abnormal pubertal development. They discuss problems and important consequences of precocious and delayed puberty as well as problems related to inducing puberty artificially in individuals with genetic defects, such as Turner's syndrome, androgen insensitivity syndrome, and hypogonadisms.

Despite the continuing interest in associating hormone levels with moods or behavior patterns, not a single study has yet been reported on an attempt to relate these drastic hormone changes with any psychological or behavioral variables in normal human adolescence. Very recently, however, such a relationship was described in a longitudinal study of male rhesus monkeys as the first such study in any primate species (Rose et al., 1978). Four male monkeys were followed for about three years spanning adolescence, with monthly determinations of plasma testosterone levels and observations of behavior. Testosterone levels changed from steady low levels during the first observation year to a moderate large peak in the breeding season of the second year and a full adult breeding season peak of testosterone in the third observation year. These changes in male hormone were accompanied by proportional changes in sex behavior and by an inverse relationship to play behavior. However, no important changes in aggressive behavior were observed during this study period and thus did not relate to testosterone. A similar longitudinal study of male adolescent chimpanzees is under way at the Stanford Outdoor Primate Facility (Helena Kraemer, professor and associate director) in collaboration with our laboratory at Stony Brook. Preliminary inspection of data indicates that increases in androgen levels are accompanied by rising levels of agonistic and sexual behavior.

Climacteric Changes

Menopause refers to the involution of ovarian function and to cessation of menstruation. As is the case with menarche in puberty, menopause is a specific event that can be recorded on the calendar, but the process leading up to it is much more diffuse and the hormonal mechanism that controls this process is not fully understood. Samuel Yen (1977) has described menopause as part of a continuing process of aging, which he defines as "the loss of physiologic adaptability to the environment" (p. 287) and a diminished capacity of cells to communicate.

Recent hormone measurements have shown that years before menopause, FSH levels have already begun to rise and by age 45 (still premenopausal) are significantly above the average of age 20-29 (Monroe and Menon, 1977). LH and estradiol generally do not increase until after menopause. Progesterone is lower in women 40-50 years old but not progressively so (Reyes, Winter, and Faiman, 1977). The lack of decline of estradiol before menopause is surprising but might be explained by a lower production rate of estradiol accompanied by lower excretion rate. The rise of FSH without parallel decline of ovarian steroids may be due to an age-related decrease of sensitivity of the hypothalamic feedback mechanism; in other words, it may reflect an involution of target tissue sensitivity. If this is true, this decrease would be an example of the diminished capacity of cells to communicate.

At menopause the ovaries virtually cease to secrete estradiol. Any estrogens found in postmenopausal women are derived from the conversion of androstenedione in peripheral tissues. The androstenedione comes primarily from the adrenal cortex. As a whole, androgen levels are only slightly diminished after menopause.

It is the drastic decline of circulating estradiol that precipitates the symptoms associated with menopause. Secondarily FSH and LH levels become very high. Target tissues of estradiol are also affected, and the resulting vasomotor disturbance of "hot flashes" is still poorly understood but clearly related to estrogen deficiency. Additional symptoms of depression and irritability are probably due to a combination of hormonal and social factors.

In normal aging of men there is no abrupt change in endocrine status. Reproductive fertility can be found in men of advanced age, although potency diminishes gradually. This is in sharp contrast to female development and aging.

A variety of hormones, including several precursors to androgens, and binding globulin have been measured over a broad age range in men. There is a slight and steady decline of total testosterone concentration in plasma from age 20 to 90 (from 8 to 6 ng/ml) while there is an increase of protein-bound testosterone (from 91% to 94%), with a consequent important decline of active free testosterone. Statistically these changes are not significant in men under 60 years old, but men between 61 and 90 differ significantly from younger men. There is no change in FSH levels but a steady slight rise of LH in plasma (Nieschlag et al., 1973; Pirke and Doerr, 1975). Similarly, precursors of androgens on the biosynthetic pathway and related hormonal steroids are significantly lower in men 68-93 years old than in men 19-54 years old, although there is no significant age-related correlation in the younger group (Pirke et al., 1977).

Behavioral endocrinology, or psychoendocrinology, is a young science. Effects and interactions between endocrine and psychological variables are being recorded and cataloged in a rapidly expanding literature. Hypotheses are being tested primarily with animal models, and analogies are continually being drawn between animal models and the human situation, since direct experimentation with human subjects is severely restricted. However, the effect of hormones on certain behaviors seems to become weaker the higher the animal is located in the phylogenetic chain. A clear-cut relationship between hormone and behavior in rodents thus becomes very difficult to demonstrate in primates, especially in the human.

Human evidence derives largely from accidents of nature and from correlational studies in which the association between natural differences in behavior patterns and variations in endogenous hormone levels is tested. The rationale for this correlational work has been reviewed by Frank Beach (1975). The establishment of such an association must in all cases be considered only the first step in this inquiry. It is the search for the particular anatomical and biochemical links between the covarying parameters that is of particular interest to the psychoendocrinologist. Certain regions in the central nervous system involved in behavior patterns have to be identified, and the molecular events of the hormonal interaction have to be studied.

The behavioral effect of hormones is generally a permissive one. Hormones tend to facilitate the occurrence of behavior patterns; hormones do not generate a behavior, as a nerve impulse may. For example, in a rat mother, prolactin and estradiol influence the behavior pattern of pup retrieval (Stern and Mackinnon, 1976; Zarrow, Gandelman, and Denenberg, 1971); the hormones must circulate in a rat mother in adequate concentrations, but a pup must also have left the nest and must release a characteristic high-pitched sound before the mother seeks out the pup and returns it to the nest. Hormones may act by generating the requisite neuronal interconnections, or by providing the proper membrane permeabilities, or by establishing synaptic sensitivities in order to facilitate the appropriate response to an environmental stimulus.

The permissive aspect of the action of hormones is also reflected in their effect on development. The presence of certain hormones is required for specific development to occur. The measurable effect is often delayed considerably, as when prenatal sex differentiation becomes activated much later at puberty. A prenatal excess of androgens in girls appears to result later in a measurable increase of masculine-type play behavior (Ehrhardt and Baker, 1974), whereas the prenatal administration of an artificial estrogen in boys may lead to a degree of feminization (Yalom, Green, and Fisk, 1973). And prenatal progesterone may enhance intelligence or, at least, academic achievement in boys and girls (Dalton, 1968, 1976).

Unfortunately much less is known about the long-term behavioral consequences of hormonal changes at the second major developmental phase, puberty. The normal development at this critical period involves consolidation of personal identity, cognitive processes, coping mechanisms to stresses, and so forth. One hypothesis, amenable to testing in nonhuman primates, is that the learning of distinctive masculine behavior patterns is facilitated by androgens in the adolescent male (D. A. Hamburg, personal communication). A large proportion of the adolescent male's time in a socially integrated group is devoted to intent observation of adult male behavior, which is then imitated and rehearsed cautiously by the adolescent. Female adolescents in the same group pay very little attention to adult male behavior. Yet this is also a period of marked risk for diverse abnormal development, such as homosexuality, schizophrenia, depression, antisocial behavior, and even sleep disorders. It is quite probable that hormones play a significant role in these behavioral or psychiatric "derailments." Much needs to be learned about these possible relationships.

Two additional periods of major hormonal changes have not been explored for possible developmental and psychological consequences. One is the recent discovery of a remarkable rise in circulatory testosterone in the male infant about 2-4 months after birth. At the peak the concentrations of plasma testosterone in male infants are within the range of male adults. The significance of this testosterone surge, which is, of course, entirely absent in the female infant, is not known. At least the anabolic effect of testosterone should be expressed on muscle growth.

The other change is the rapid development of the adrenal cortex in both boys and girls around the onset of puberty. Physical changes such as the first growth spurt and appearance of axillary and pubic hair resulting from increased production of the adrenal androgens dehydroepiandrosterone, its sulfate derivative, 11β-hydroxyandrostenedione, and androstenedione mark "adrenarche" in early adult development. Although the clinical conditions of precocious and delayed adrenarche are well described, their psychological correlates and consequences have not been studied systematically.

The behavior-hormone relationship is a reciprocal one, an important point even when most of the discussion revolves around the psychological or behavioral consequences of hormonal changes. One familiar example is the profound effect that a state of anxiety has on the adrenal gland, both the adrenal medulla (releasing epinephrine) and the adrenal cortex (releasing cortisol). The particular pattern of hormonal response is part of the individual's overall coping mechanism. Frankenhaeuser and her co-workers (1978) were able to demonstrate a significant sex difference in the response pattern to acutely stressful situations. It would be interesting to learn more about when and how these response patterns are established in the early life of an individual. A fascinating question is whether the hormonal response pattern is "learned," perhaps in a series of events in childhood. In a critical review of the extensive body of animal research on the effects of early life experiences on the adrenocortical hormone system, Robert Ader (1975) describes adult rats as less "emotional" and less productive in adrenocortical hormones in response to environmental stimulation if they received extra manipulation in infancy. However, the two effects are not closely related to each other, and their adaptive value is difficult to interpret.

It is clear that more work needs to be done in developmental psychoendocrinology, especially in the area of early adolescence when so many vital hormones first reach and transcend threshold levels. Special attention should be devoted to the permanence or reversibility of psychoendocrine relationships that are being established at this period for a better understanding of long-term consequences.

References

ADER, R. 1975. Early experience and hormones: emotional behavior and adrenocortical function. In B. E. Eleftheriou and R. L. Sprott, eds., *Hormonal correlates of behavior, vol. 1: A lifespan view.* New York: Plenum Press.

ALLEN, T. D. 1976. Disorders of sexual differentiation. *Urology* 7 (no. 4) (supplement): 1-32.

ANDERSON, D. C. 1974. Sex-hormone-binding globulin. *Clinical Endocrinology* 3: 69-96.

APTER, D., and VIHKO, R. 1977. Serum pregnenolone, progesterone, 17-hydroxyprogesterone, testosterone, and 5a-dihydrotestosterone during female puberty. *Journal of Clinical Endocrinology and Metabolism* 45: 1039-48.

BEACH, F. A. 1975. Behavioral endocrinology: an emerging discipline. *American Scientist* 63: 178-187.

BOYAR, R. M., ROSENFELD, R. S., FINKELSTEIN, J. W., KAPEN, S., ROFFWARG, H. P., WEITZMAN, E. D., and HELLMAN, L. 1975. Ontogeny of luteinizing hormone and testosterone secretion. *Journal of Steroid Biochemistry* 6: 803-808.

BOYAR, R. M., WU, R. H. K., ROFFWARG, H., KAPEN, S., WEITZMAN, E. D., HELLMAN, L., and FINKELSTEIN, J. W. 1976. Human puberty: 24-hour estradiol patterns in pubertal girls. *Journal of Clinical Endocrinology and Metabolism* 43: 1418-21.

BUTENANDT, O., EDER, R., WOHLFARTH, K., BIDLINGMAIER, F., and KNORR, D. 1976. Mean 24-hour growth hormone and testosterone concentrations in relation to pubertal growth spurt in boys with normal or delayed puberty. *European Journal of Pediatrics* 122: 85-92.

CHEEK, D. B. 1974. Body composition, hormones, nutrition, and adolescent growth. In M. M. Grumbach, G. D. Grave, and F. E. Mayer, eds., *Control of the onset of puberty*. New York: Wiley.

COLLU, R., and DUCHARME, J. R. 1975. Role of adrenal steroids in the regulation of gonadotropin secretion at puberty. *Journal of Steroid Biochemistry* 6: 869-872.

DALTON, K. 1968. Ante-natal progesterone and intelligence. *British Journal of Psychiatry* 114: 1377-83.

——— 1976. Prenatal progesterone and educational attainments. *British Journal of Psychiatry* 129: 438-442.

DEMOOR, P. 1972. Statement from a recorded general discussion. *Journal of Steroid Biochemistry* 3: 441.

DEMOOR, P., HEYNS, W., and BOUILLON, R. 1972. Growth hormone and the steroid binding β-globulin of human plasma. *Journal of Steroid Biochemistry* 3: 593-600.

DÖRNER, G. 1977. Hormones, brain differentiation and fundamental processes of life. *Journal of Steroid Biochemistry* 8: 531-536.

DUCHARME, J. R., FOREST, M. G., DEPERETTI, E., SEMPE, M., COLLU, R., and BERTRAND, J. 1976. Plasma adrenal and gonadal sex steroids in human pubertal development. *Journal of Clinical Endocrinology and Metabolism* 42: 468-476.

EHRHARDT, A. A., and BAKER, S. W. 1974. Fetal androgens, human central nervous system differentiation, and behavior sex differences. In R. C. Friedman, R. M. Richart, and R. L. Vande Wiele, eds., *Sex differences in behavior*. New York: Wiley.

EHRHARDT, A. A., EPSTEIN, R., and MONEY, J. 1968. Fetal androgens and female gender identity in the early treated adrenogenital syndrome. *Johns Hopkins Medical Journal* 122: 160-167.

EHRHARDT, A. A., GRISANTI, G. C., and MEYER-BAHLBURG, H. F. L. 1977. Prenatal exposure to medroxyprogesterone acetate (MPA) in girls. *Psychoneuroendocrinology* 2: 391-398.

EHRHARDT, A. A., and MEYER-BAHLBURG, H. F. L. 1975. Psychological correlates of abnormal pubertal development. *Clinics in Endocrinology and Metabolism* 4: 207-222.

——— 1979. Prenatal sex hormones and the developing brain: effects on psychosexual differentiation and cognitive function. *Annual Review of Medicine* 30: 417-430.

EHRHARDT, A. A., and MONEY, J. 1967. Progestin-induced hermaphroditism: I.Q. and psychosexual identity in a study of ten girls. *Journal of Sex Research* 3: 83-100.

ELEFTHERIOU, B. E., and SPROTT, R. L., eds. 1975. *Hormonal correlates of behavior, vol. 1: A lifespan view*. New York: Plenum Press.

EZRIN, C., GODDEN, J. O., VOLPE, R., and WILSON, R., eds. 1973. *Systematic endocrinology*. New York: Harper and Row.

FAIMAN, C., REYES, F. I., and WINTER, J. S. D. 1974. Serum gonadotropin patterns during the perinatal period in man and in the chimpanzee. INSERM (Institut National de la Santé et de la Recherche Médicale, Paris) Colloquium 32: 281-297.

FINKELSTEIN, J. W., ROFFWARG, H. P., BOYAR, R. M., KREAM, J., and HELL-
MAN, L. 1972. Age-related change in the twenty-four-hour spontaneous
secretion of growth hormone. *Journal of Clinical Endocrinology and Metabolism* 35: 665-670.

FOREST, M. G., SIZONENKO, P. C., CATHIARD, A. M., and BERTRAND, J.
1974. Hypophyso-gonadal function in humans during the first year of life.
Journal of Clinical Investigation 53: 819-828.

FRANCHIMONT, P., and BURGER, H. 1975. *Human growth hormone and
gonadotrophins in health and disease.* Amsterdam: North-Holland.

FRANKENHAEUSER, M., DUNNE, E., and LUNDBERG, E. 1976. Sex differences
in sympathetic-adrenal medullary reactions induced by different stressors.
Psychopharmacology 47: 1-5.

FRANKENHAEUSER, M., RAUSTE VON WRIGHT, M., COLLINS, A., VON WRIGHT,
J., SEDVALL, G., and SWAHN, C. G. 1978. Sex differences in psychoendocrine reactions to examination stress. *Psychosomatic Medicine* 40: 334-343.

GALVÃO-TELES, A., ANDERSON, D. C., BURKE, C. W., MARSHALL, J. C.,
CORKER, C. S., BROWN, R. L., and CLARK, M. L. 1973. Biologically active
androgens and oestradiol in men with chronic liver disease. *Lancet* i: 173-
177.

GRUMBACH, M. M., ROTH, J. C., KAPLAN, S. L., and KELCH, R. P. 1974.
Hypothalamic-pituitary regulation of puberty in man: evidence and con-
cepts derived from clinical research. In M. M. Grumbach, G. D. Grave, and
F. E. Mayer, eds., *Control of the onset of puberty.* New York: Wiley.

HAMBURG, B. A., and HAMBURG, D. A. 1975. Stressful transitions of adolescence: endocrine and psychosocial aspects. In L. Levi, ed., *Society, stress,
and disease,* vol 2: *Childhood and adolescence.* London: Oxford University
Press.

HAYS, S. E. 1978. Strategies for psychoendocrine studies of puberty. *Psychoneuroendocrinology* 3: 1-15.

HORST, H. J., BARTSCH, W., and DIRKSEN-THEDEUS, I. 1977. Plasma testosterone, sex hormone binding globulin binding capacity and per cent binding
of testosterone and 5a-dihydrotestosterone in prepubertal, pubertal, and
adult males. *Journal of Clinical Endocrinology and Metabolism* 45: 522-
527.

JOHANSSON, G., FRANKENHAEUSER, M., and MAGNUSSON, D. 1973. Catecholamine output in school children as related to performance and adjustment.
Scandinavian Journal of Psychology 14: 20-28.

JOHANSSON, G., and POST, B. 1974. Catecholamine output of males and females over a one-year period. *Acta Physiologica Scandinavica* 92: 557-565.

JOST, A. 1953. Problems of fetal endocrinology: the gonadal and hypophyseal
hormones. *Recent Progress of Hormone Research* 8: 379-418.

KAPLAN, S. L., and GRUMBACH, M. M. 1972. The ontogenesis of hypothala-
mic-hypophysiotropic releasing factor regulation of HGH secretion. In
A. Pecile and E. E. Müller, eds., *Growth and growth hormone.* Excerpta
Medica (Amsterdam) 244: 382-388.

KEENAN, B. S., MEYER, W. J., HADJIAN, A. J., JONES, H. W., and MIGEON,
C. J. 1974. Syndrome of androgen insensitivity in man: absence of 5a-

dihydrotestosterone binding protein in skin fibroblasts. *Journal of Clinical Endocrinology and Metabolism* 38: 1143-46.

KNORR, D., BIDLINGMAIER, F., BUTENANDT, O., FENDEL, H., and EHRT-WEHLE, R. 1974. Plasma testosterone in male puberty. I: Physiology of plasma testosterone. *Acta Endocrinologica* 75: 181-194.

KULIN, H. E., BELL, P. M., SANTEN, R. J., and FERBER, A. J. 1975. Integration of pulsatile gonadotropin secretion by timed urinary measurements: an accurate and sensitive 3-hour test. *Journal of Clinical Endocrinology and Metabolism* 40: 783-789.

LEE, P. A., JAFFE, R. B., and MIDGLEY, A. R. 1974. Serum gonadotropin, testosterone, and prolactin concentrations throughout puberty in boys: a longitudinal study. *Journal of Clinical Endocrinology and Metabolism* 39: 664-672.

LEVINE, S., ed. 1972. *Hormones and behavior.* New York: Academic Press.

MACCOBY, E. E., DOERING, C. H., JACKLIN, C. N., and KRAEMER, H. 1979. Concentrations of sex hormones in umbilical-cord blood: their relation to sex and birth order of infants. *Child Development* 50: 632-642.

MEYER-BAHLBURG, H. F. L., GRISANTI, G. C., and EHRHARDT, A. A. 1977. Prenatal effects of sex hormones on human male behavior: medroxyprogesterone acetate. *Psychoneuroendocrinology* 2: 383-390.

MICHAEL, R. P., BONSALL, R. W., and KUTNER, M. 1975. Volatile fatty acids, "copulins," in human vaginal secretions. *Psychoneuroendocrinology* 1: 153-163.

MICHAEL, R. P., ZUMPE, D., RICHTER, M., and BONSALL, R. W. 1977. Behavioral effects of a synthetic mixture of aliphatic acids in rhesus monkeys (macaca mulatta). *Hormones and Behavior* 9: 296-308.

MONEY, J., and EHRHARDT, A. A. 1972. *Man and woman, boy and girl.* Baltimore, Md.: Johns Hopkins University Press.

MONEY, J., EHRHARDT, A. A., and MASICA, D. N. 1968. Fetal feminization induced by androgen insensitivity in the testicular feminizing syndrome: effect on marriage and maternalism. *Johns Hopkins Medical Journal* 123: 105-114.

MONROE, S. E., and MENON, K. M. J. 1977. "Changes in reproductive hormone secretion during the climacteric and the postmenopausal periods. *Clinical Obstetrics and Gynecology* 20: 113-122.

NEUMANN, F. 1976. Endokrinologische Aspekte der Geschlechtsdifferenzierung. *Gynäkologe* 9: 16-29.

NIESCHLAG, E., KLEY, H. K., WIEGELMANN, W., SOLBACH, H. G., and KRÜSKEMPER, H. L. 1973. Lebensalter und endokrine Funktion der Testes des erwachsenen Mannes. *Deutsche Medizinische Wochenschrift* 98: 1281-84.

OHNO, S. 1979. *Major sex-determing genes.* New York: Springer Verlag.

PARKER, D. C., JUDD, H. L., ROSSMAN, L. G., and YEN, S. S. C. 1975. Pubertal sleep-wake patterns of episodic LH, FSH, and testosterone release in twin boys. *Journal of Clinical Endocrinology and Metabolism* 40: 1099-1109.

PENNY, R., OLAMBIWONNU, N. O., and FRASIER, S. D. 1977. Episodic fluctuations of serum gonadotropins in pre- and postpubertal girls and boys. *Jour-*

nal of Clinical Endocrinology and Metabolism 45: 307-311.

PIRKE, K. M., and DOERR, P. 1975. Age related changes in free plasma testosterone, dihydrotestosterone, and oestradiol. *Acta Endocrinologica* 80: 171-178.

PIRKE, K. M., DOERR, P., SINTERMANN, R., and VOGT, H. J. 1977. Age dependence of testosterone precursors in plasma of normal adult males. *Acta Endocrinologica* 86: 415-429.

REINISCH, J. M. 1974. Fetal hormones, the brain, and human sex differences: a heuristic integrative review of the literature. *Archives of Sexual Behavior* 3: 51-90.

———— 1976. Effects of prenatal hormone exposure on physical and psychological development in humans and animals: with a note on the state of the field. In E. J. Sachar, ed., *Hormones, behavior, and psychopathology.* New York: Raven Press.

REINISCH, J. M., and KAROW, W. G. 1977. Prenatal exposure to synthetic progestins and estrogens: effects on human development. *Archives of Sexual Behavior* 6: 257-288.

REYES, F. I., BORODITSKY, R. S., WINTER, J. S. D., and FAIMAN, C. 1974. Studies on human sexual development. II: Fetal and maternal serum gonadotropin and sex steroid concentrations. *Journal of Clinical Endocrinology and Metabolism* 38: 612-617.

REYES, F. I., WINTER, J. S. D., and FAIMAN, C. 1977. Pituitary-ovarian relationships preceding the menopause. I: A cross-sectional study of serum follicle-stimulating hormone, prolactin, estradiol, and progesterone levels. *American Journal of Obstetrics and Gynecology* 129: 557-564.

ROOT, A. W. 1973. Endocrinology of puberty. I: Normal sexual maturation. *Journal of Pediatrics* 83: 1-19.

ROSE, R. M. 1972. The psychological effects of androgens and estrogens: a review. In R. I. Shader, ed., *Psychiatric complications of medical drugs.* New York: Raven Press.

ROSE, R. M., BERNSTEIN, J. S., GORDON, T. P., and LINDSLEY, J. G. 1978. Changes in testosterone and behavior during adolescence in the male rhesus monkey. *Psychosomatic Medicine* 40: 60-70.

ROSENFIELD, R. L. 1973. Relationship of androgens to female hirsutism and infertility. *Journal of Reproductive Medicine* 11: 87-95.

SACHAR, E., ed. 1975. *Topics in psychoendocrinology.* New York: Grune and Stratton.

STERN, J. M., and MACKINNON, D. A. 1976. Postpartum hormonal and non-hormonal induction of maternal behavior in rats: effects on T-maze retrieval of pups. *Hormones and Behavior* 7: 305-316.

THOMPSON, R. G., RODRIGUEZ, A., KOWARSKI, A., MIGEON, C., and BLIZZARD, R. M. 1972. Integrated concentrations of growth hormone correlated with plasma testosterone and bone age in preadolescent males. *Journal of Clinical Edocrinology and Metabolism* 35: 334-337.

TURNER, C. D., and BAGNARA, J. T. 1976. *General endocrinology,* 6th ed. Philadelphia: Saunders.

VERMEULEN, A., STOICA, T., and VERDONCK, L. 1971. The apparent free testosterone concentration, an index of androgenicity. *Journal of Clinical Endocrinology and Metabolism* 33: 759-767.

VON MÜHLENDAHL, K. E., PACHALY, J., and SCHMIDT-GOLLWITZER, M. 1976. Lack of correlation between clinical data and growth hormone concentrations in cord blood. *Biology of the Neonate* 29: 281-285.

WINTER, J. S. D., and FAIMAN, C. 1972. Pituitary-gonadal relations in male children and adolescents. *Pediatric Research* 6: 126-135.

——— 1973a. Pituitary-gonadal relations in female children and adolescents. *Pediatric Research* 7: 948-953.

——— 1973b. The development of cyclic pituitary-gonadal function in adolescent females. *Journal of Clinical Endocrinology and Metabolism* 37: 714-718.

YALOM, I. D., GREEN, R., and FISK, N. 1973. Prenatal exposure to female hormones: effect on psychosexual development in boys. *Archives of General Psychiatry* 28: 554-561.

YEN, S. S. C. 1977. The biology of menopause. *Journal of Reproductive Medicine* 18: 287-296.

ZARROW, M. S., GANDELMAN, R., and DENENBERG, V. H. 1971. Prolactin: is it an essential hormone for maternal behavior in the mammal? *Hormones and Behavior* 2: 343-354.

7 | Physical Health
Barbara Starfield and
I. B. Pless

APPROACHES TO EXAMINING PATTERNS of constancy or change in physical health differ from those used in the cognitive and psychologic domains. Some manifestations of physical defects or illness can be offset by appropriate treatment, thus making ill health less obvious and less pervasive than is usually the case for psychological phenomena. Moreover, for many physical problems, the basis of the pathology is well known so that the natural history may be interrupted by definitive intervention. Knowledge of the pathogenesis of any problem also makes it possible to better understand the interaction between genetic and environmental factors; thus it is easier to determine what is changeable (with current knowledge) and what is likely to be permanent.

These features complicate the task of determining the relative balance between constancy and change in physical health. If the manifestations of ill health are suppressed by treatment, or if functions that successfully ameliorate a physical disability can be substituted, should we consider the physical problem to be still present? If so, is it changed, or is it constant? As we understand more about genetic predispositions on a molecular level, do we consider a problem that is inborn but is manifested only later in life a constant in physical development because it can be predicted by knowing the genotype? Or is it to be considered a change because it becomes evident only at later ages?

An important distinction is to be made in the ways in which the phenomena of change or constancy are viewed. If the focus is on individuals with a particular condition (hence on the prognosis of the disease), predictions about the outcome apply just to individuals who are known to have the disease. In this approach comparison at two points in time presents only two possibilities: persistent sickness, which may be the same or worse, or improvement. An alternative is to focus on a population of children, some of whom have a disease while the remainder are free of it. When total populations are considered, there are two additional possibilities: children remain well or they become ill.

Because the prognosis of conditions is heavily influenced by the intrinsic biologic nature of the disease, many conditions that commonly affect individuals can be arrayed along a prognosis spectrum, ranging from deterioration (or death) to improvement (or cure). Few disorders can now be classified precisely, although major technological advances may make it possible to do so in the future for some disorders. For example, although the prognosis for cerebral palsy is unlikely to be influenced significantly by the development of new technology, this is not the case for other conditions, such as leukemia or cystic fibrosis. Likewise some disorders are quite homogenous, while many others span a wide spectrum of severity and the prognosis varies accordingly. Illustrative of the latter is asthma which, depending on its severity, can result in serious incapacity or total regression of symptoms.

There is also an important difference between viewing individuals as entities and viewing individuals through particular medical conditions that afflict them. During any specified interval a person may recover from one condition and develop another, unrelated disorder. When conditions alone are considered, the issue of comorbidity is set aside and the individual is assumed to be sick or well depending only on the presence or absence of a particular disease. What is needed to assess the patterns of change in physical health is an index of health status—a composite measure that may reflect levels of well-being, of physical or social functioning, that express the full complement of defects, diseases, or disabilities that an individual may have at any given time, their relative severity, and the manner in which they interact.

Complicating these conceptual difficulties are methodologic problems. Examination of changes in cognitive and psychologic phenomena over time is facilitated by the relative availability of data. Children go to school, and the function of schooling is to promote intellectual and behavioral growth. Assessments of this growth are inherent in all school systems so that considerable information on cognition and behavior becomes an integral part of each child's record. Physical health, on the other hand, is usually a private matter. There exists no institution with sole responsibility or authority to foster it, and there are neither standardized nor widely used instruments for measuring it.

These conceptual and methodologic difficulties are further compounded by the many factors that influence health. Although these influences are not limited to physical derangements, they may be especially important for physical health, particularly when intervening in the natural course of events is possible. Thus, for conditions where medical care makes a crucial difference in prognosis, access to care is a more powerful determinant of constancy or change than it is for conditions where interventions are less efficacious. One of the major determinants of access to care is socioeconomic class. Many studies show the incidence and prevalence of most illness to be highly and inversely correlated with socioeconomic class. Children in lower-class families are more likely than children in middle- and upper-class families to experience many illnesses and less likely to have at least some of their illnesses adequately treated because of reduced access to medical care. It is therefore probable that social class also influences the extent of constancy and change in physical health. Unfortunately, in the United States few data are reported in terms of social class, although reports from the National Center for Health Statistics (the Health Interview Survey and the Health Examination Survey) provide some information according to family income. In Great Britain an administratively defined class structure permits examination of the effects of social class on illness; for this reason and others this chapter draws heavily on British studies.

Reasonably conclusive answers to questions about changes over time can come only from longitudinal studies involving the same persons over long periods. Because of the size and mobility of the American population, such studies are extremely difficult to accomplish in the United States or Canada. In contrast, Great Britain and many Scandinavian countries are much more successful at tracing or keeping track of subjects in longitudinal studies. By American standards their success in this field is remarkable—not only a reflection of geography and sociological differences but a tribute to the tenacity and imagination of investigators and the cooperative spirit of the subjects. Despite their importance, however, longitudinal studies of health and disease rarely provide totally satisfactory answers, particularly for disorders for which major discoveries have led to radical changes in detection, diagnosis, or successful treatment. Today's answers are often acceptable only for yesterday's questions. A good longitudinal study of a cohort of diabetics, for example, reflects only the care provided a decade or two ago, a pattern of care that may no longer be relevant.

Although these conceptual and methodologic difficulties make it difficult to assess the relative contribution of constancy and change in physical health, it is possible to draw tentative conclusions from the relatively few studies that have been done. This chapter includes only those studies which bear on the constancy and change of physical health from childhood to later childhood or to adulthood. The omission of adults alone is not intended to minimize the importance of the subject for later years of life. The rate of development of characteristics is so much greater in children than adults and therefore the counterposition of constancy and change is likely to be most dramatically displayed in childhood. Four types of evidence are examined: evidence from several specific common illnesses, evidence from utilization of health services, evidence from measures of general physical function, and evidence about the relationship between physical health and emotional health. Although no single approach provides definitive answers, the evidence obtained from all four provides important clues about the degree of determinism and flexibility in physical health over time.

Specific Common Illnesses

Many inherited disorders occur regardless of environmental conditions and are not amenable to reversal by known medical means. Examples are cystic fibrosis, sickle cell anemia, and phenylketonuria. For these health problems there is virtual constancy; a child with the genes for the condition is at nearly complete risk of having the condition, having it manifested, and having it permanently. Fortunately these conditions are rare. More common are conditions for which the relative importance of genetic predisposition and environmental influence is unknown and for which there is little firm knowledge about their permanence.

Considerable information on the incidence, clinical manifestations, and treatment of these conditions is available, but little is known about their natural history, partly because it is often difficult to identify them with precision and reliability (Dingle, Badger, and Jordan, 1964, pp. 15-18) and partly as a result of the haphazard organization of most health services, especially in the United States. Apart from the few medical practices that have an identifiable population for which they assume responsibility over a period of time, most health care is discontinuous and episodic, thus virtually precluding any examination of the history of conditions in individual children or in a population of children. Facilities such as academic medical centers, which accumulate large numbers of children with specific diagnoses and follow them over a period of years, generally have such highly selected populations (because they are centers for referral) that the generalizability of their findings is limited.

In this section the more common conditions are presented first. Only evidence derived from studies whose populations were defined either geographically or by specific enrollment are included. The British longitudinal cohorts are important in this regard. In the late 1940s two large groups of children were identified in England, one involving all births during a two-month period in the city of Newcastle upon Tyne (Miller et al., 1974) and one involving all births in England during the first week of March 1947.[1] The Newcastle study followed the children at 10- to 12-week intervals until age 7. Extensive examinations were made at ages 1, 3, and 5 years. From ages 7 to 15 one home visit was made annually, and all school and public health records were available. The 1947 national cohort has been contacted every two years since its inception. Two additional national cohort studies were subsequently initiated, one in 1958 (Fogelman, 1976) and one in 1970. The 1958 cohort obtained information only at ages 7, 11, and 16 and therefore could not describe the occurrence of episodes of short-term common illnesses that would not be well recalled by parents after such long periods of time. Although these studies are longitudinal in the sense that they followed a defined cohort over time, most of the published findings deal with changes in the group as a whole from one age to another in the cohort. Thus it is impossible to determine what happened to the individual children in the cohort as they aged. If the prevalence of a condition increased over time, it is impossible to ascertain whether children who previously had the condition got better and were replaced by newly sick children, or whether the same children remained sick and additional ones became sick. The few analyses of the relationship of early findings to later ones in individual children are informative and important.

Another source of information are the publications of John Fry, a British general practitioner (Fry, 1966; Fry, 1974, p. 44). Fry kept careful records of the care provided to all patients in his practice. There were 1,203 children under age 15 who were in his practice during the first 10 years of their lives. A special follow-up was performed an average of 10 years (varying from 5 to 15 years) after they were initially identified for purposes of these follow-up studies.

Respiratory Problems

Upper respiratory conditions are extremely common in childhood. In 1974-75 in the United States as a whole, there were 124 episodes of upper respiratory problems per 100 children per year under age 6 and 72 per 100 children per year from ages 6 through 16 (U.S.

lems; still, the findings are consistent with those of the prospective British studies.

Ear Infections

Ear infection (otitis media) is one of the most common medical problems seen in pediatric practice. About one in five children enrolled in a prepaid group practice had at least one episode of otitis media in a year (Steinwachs and Yaffe, 1974). In Great Britain about half of all children in Fry's practice experienced at least one episode of otitis media by age 8 (Fry et al., 1969).

Although acute attacks occur predominantly in preschoolers chronic otitis is the major ear problem among school age children. This change in the nature of otitis as children get older suggests that there may be a natural progression from acute to chronic state. However, the extent to which children at greatest risk of chronic otitis in the school-age period are those who had acute episodes earlier is still unknown (Starfield, 1977). The U.S. Health Examination Survey (U.S. DHEW, NCHS, 1972) indicates that children with a history of ear problems are significantly more likely to have abnormalities of the tympanic membrane and poor hearing than other children. The lack of change in prevalence with age, from 6 to 11, suggests that much or most of the damage is probably done before school age. In Fry's practice the 403 children (36% of all those studied) who had attacks of acute otitis media were assessed up to five years after their acute episode. Seventeen percent had a hearing loss of 20 decibels or more in at least two frequencies (Fry, 1974, p. 44). Recurrent attacks occurred in 66%, and an average of 10 years later between 4% and 10% had some loss of hearing (Fry, 1966, p. 47).

Thus there is evidence that children with early episodes of acute otitis media are at high risk of subsequent auditory problems and that perhaps a majority of adults with hearing loss or chronic ear problems had ear problems as children. Firmer conclusions about the magnitude of these effects must await more definitive longitudinal and prospective studies.

In a British study (Peckham and Sheridan, 1976) half of the children with severe unilateral loss at age 7 had recovered normal hearing by age 11. Those who did not were primarily children with other serious defects as well. The frequency of speech problems, motor incoordination, and poor scholastic attainment (which were much more common in these children at age 7 than in the rest of the population) had also fallen to expected levels by age 11. These findings suggest that even severe hearing loss need not produce lasting effects in childhood if prompt medical attention and follow-up are provided. The

DHEW, NCHS, 1977, p. 13). Several studies indicate that children experiencing these symptoms or the "common cold" are more prone to their recurrence than other children. In a study in Cleveland (Dingle, Badger, and Jordan, 1964, pp. 61-66) illnesses in 443 individuals in 86 middle- and upper-class families were observed for a median period of about 6 years. It is not possible to distinguish children from adults in their data. There was a striking amount of variation from individual to individual in the occurrence of respiratory problems and a general downward trend in incidence with increasing age. However, some individuals tended to have either many or few respiratory illnesses over the years. To some extent this is due to intrafamily aggregations of illness resulting from differences among families in reporting illness, recurrent exposure of certain family members to outside sources of illness, or an innate susceptibility or resistance or some other common hereditary or environmental influence.

A survey of 497 families in Westchester County who were visited every 28 days for 3 years indicated that there was considerable constancy in both occurrence of respiratory illness and disability from it in both children and adults (Tucher and Downes, 1953). As table 7.1 indicates, more individuals, both children and adults, had problems in all 3 years than would be expected by chance alone, and fewer had changing illness patterns.[2] As with the Cleveland study, there were

Table 7.1. Constancy and change in disability due to respiratory conditions, Westchester County 1946-1949.

| | Number disabled at some time during the three-year period | | | |
| | Children | | Husbands and wives | |
Illness class	Observed	Expected[a]	Observed	Expected[a]
Disability at some time in all three years	235	211	57	34
No disability in any of the three years	8	2	83	55
Disability some time in only one or two years	124	154	213	264
Chi square	32.18		39.01	
P	less than 0.001		less than 0.001	

Source: Tucher and Downes (1953, p. 146).
a. By chance alone (see note 2).

large intrafamily correlations, which could have been the results of genetic or environmental influences.

A study of 114 families in Baltimore in 1928-1930 (Gafafer and Doull, 1933) concluded that the computed Pearsonian product moment coefficients (.64 with a standard error of .06 for children; .54 with a standard error of .06 for adults) indicate that "there is a tendency for persons to remain in the same cold-number class at least for successive years" (p. 723). Although this family group was not followed for more than two years, a group of medical students in the same geographic area was followed for three successive years. The correlation between the frequency of attacks of colds in the first versus the third year was 0.16 with a standard error of 0.10, implying that over longer periods of time "a single observation indicates no definite tendency for persons to remain in the same class" (p. 723). However, the correlation for these students for two successive years was only 0.41 with a standard error of 0.05 compared with 0.64 with a standard error of 0.06 for the children in the families, thus indicating that constancy is more likely in children in families than in independent adults. However, the families in this study were volunteers and largely upper middle class and the findings might not be generalizable to all types of families. There was greater constancy from year to year in the family study than in medical students studied during the same period of time in the same geographic area; thus it is likely that intrafamily effects on constancy are significant.

In Fry's practice (Fry, 1966, pp. 38-45) 37% of children had acute chest infections during the first 10 years of life. Recurrences occured in 16% of those with such an infection, but 10 years later only 4% were still suffering attacks or had other residual symptoms. Sixteen percent of children in the practice suffered one or more episodes of "acute wheezy chest." Recurrent attacks occurred in 39%, but after 10 years only 4% were still suffering wheezy episodes. (Tonsillitis occurred in 25% of children, and 64% of those had recurrent attacks over the ensuing 10 years.)

Of the children born in one week in 1946 in Newcastle upon Tyne 208 were identified as being at greater risk of continuing respiratory disease because they had had a severe respiratory infection before 5 years of age (Miller et al., 1974, pp. 101-104). These were compared with a control group of 97 standard-risk children chosen from the remainder of the population when they were 15 years old. (Children considered likely to be at high risk were those who had recurrent acute or suspected chronic otitis media (56), frequent or prolonged colds or suspected chronic nasal sinusitis (25), recurrent bronchitis or suspected bronchiectasis (12), recurrent attacks of wheezing (66), pneu-

monia (49), whooping cough associated with radiological changes persisting for more than 6 months (13). Some children had more than one of these conditions.) On follow-up all children were examined with particular attention to the respiratory system. Cytologic examination of nasal material, throat cultures, chest X-rays, and assessment of ventilatory function were performed. The children with early respiratory problems were much more likely to have respiratory problems at age 15 than other children, although about half of this group were completely well (table 7.2).

The significance of these findings is highlighted by a study of chronic cough in young adults in relation to childhood illness. This analysis was based on data obtained from the 1946 birth cohort (Kiernan et al., 1976). For most subgroups (smoking-no smoking, low-high pollution, manual-nonmanual worker) a history of respiratory illness between ages 0 and 2 doubled the risk of having persistent cough a age 25. Of the factors studied, the effect of a history of childhoo respiratory problems was surpassed only by a current history of smo ing. Socioeconomic status (of the individual as a child rather than cu rent status as an adult) was also independently correlated with ad rent status as an adult, for children of manual laborers had higher ra respiratory disease, for children of manual laborers had higher ra of problems as adults than other children.

The Tucson Epidemiologic Study of Obstructive Lung Dise (Burrows, Lebowitz, and Knudson, 1977), which determined the p alence of respiratory problems in a population of adults and t relationship to a history of respiratory disease in childhood, indic that adults with respiratory problems are more likely to report ha had respiratory problems in childhood. The decline with age in r ratory function (determined by objective respiratory function was more rapid if the individual had a history of childhood prol and reported being a smoker. These data should be interprete tiously because the study was retrospective and hence subject to preferential recall of childhood problems by adults with current

Table 7.2. Respiratory disease early in life, Newcastle upon Tyne.

Respiratory problems at age 15	High-risk children (N = 208)	Standard-risk (N = 9
Yes	107	12
No	101	85

Source: Derived from data in Miller et al (1974, pp. 100-104).

contrast between the adequacy of follow-up in the British study and that in a study done in the United States is striking. In a study in Washington, D.C. (Kessner, 1973), fewer than 20% of physicians identified as the child's regular source of care ever tested children for hearing problems, and less than 3% of children had results of hearing tests in their medical records. Only 50% of records with any indication of a past acute ear problem mentioned its subsequent status.

The importance of medical follow-up in influencing the persistence of otitis media and its sequelae has often been stressed (Avery et al., 1976, p. 601). The findings indicating a relatively high constancy of middle ear problems in at least some segments of the U.S. population may therefore be due to a lack of continuity in the U.S. health care system rather than to constancy of some innate biological characteristic.

Asthma, Hay Fever

Asthma and hay fever, two relatively common conditions, are generally considered related to each other because of their allergic basis. Data from the Health Interview Survey (an ongoing household survey of a representative sample of the U.S. population) indicate that 3% of children are reported to have asthma and 3% to have hay fever (U.S. DHEW, NCHS, DA, 1974). Interviews conducted as part of the National Health Examination Survey on children aged 6-11 and youths aged 12-17 (U.S. DHEW, VHS, 1973, p. 13) reveal that the proportion of children with a history of asthma increases from 4% at age 6 to 5% at age 12 and to 7% at age 16. The proportion reporting hay fever also increases substantially with age, from less than 4% among children 6-8 years old to over 10% among those 16-17 years old. One author (Kuzemko, 1976, p. 3) cites eight studies from several Western nations where the prevalence of asthma in childhood varies from 2% to 7%.

Despite the widely held assumption that these conditions are chronic, little is known about the degree to which they persist. Fry states that in most asthmatics, the initial symptoms date from childhood (1966, pp. 75-85). In his practice attacks recurred during a period of 5-10 years after the initial attack, but following this he noted a "natural and spontaneous tendency toward improvement." Only 5%-10% were permanently and severely disabled after 10-20 years.

A recent review (Gordis, 1973) of many studies of the epidemiology of asthma indicates that the results are contradictory and concludes that the natural history of these common and important conditions still requires elucidation.

The extent to which bronchiolitis (a major cause of wheezing in infancy) is associated with subsequent wheezing and asthma is also unclear. Wheezing associated with documented infection with respiratory syncytical virus in 62 children under 2 years of age, seen in a hospital clinic, was followed by further wheezing in 56% (Rooney and Williams, 1971). The period of follow-up is not stated but apparently varied from less than 1 to 5 years. The authors attributed the relative constancy of wheezing to allergic predispositions, as there was a high incidence of asthma in first-degree relatives of those children.

Enuresis

Bedwetting is a common complaint in childhood. In a recent national survey in the United States, 21% of 6-year-olds were reported to be enuretic; at age 11 years the proportion was 10.4% (U.S. DHEW, NCHS, 1971, p. 8). The extent to which a child who fails to achieve dryness in the preschool years is likely to persist in wetting the bed was examined by Peckham (1973). Of the 12,232 children in the 1958 English birth cohort who were examined at age 11, 425 (4%) were enuretic at ages 7 and 11 years, 878 (7%) were enuretic at age 7 but not at age 11, and only 156 (1%) began to wet the bed after age 7. Seventy-three percent of those wetting at age 11 were children who were wetting at age 7; of those wetting at age 7 one-third were still wetting at age 11. Enuresis is therefore characterized by considerable constancy although, as is observed with many other conditions, the majority of children eventually become free of the problem.

Obesity

Evidence is accumulating that the fat infant becomes a fat child and, in turn, a fat adult. The theoretical explanation for this is found in hypotheses about the relative importance of the number and the size of fat cells during growth. The literature indicates that although only a small proportion of obese adolescents were obese in early childhood, a larger proportion of obese youngsters persist in being obese in subsequent years (Weil, 1977). The more overweight the child, the more likely it is that he will be obese later on. The absolute magnitude of these effects differs from study to study, probably because of differences in study design (retrospective data collection versus prospective data collection), differences in the definition or measurement of obesity, and basic population differences (particularly social class).

A study directed at determining the influence of prenatal factors on child development also provided information on obesity at the age of 10 in all 8,000 children born to residents of Newcastle during the years 1960, 1961, and 1962 (Wilkinson et al., 1977). Obesity was defined as weight above the ninety-seventh centile; 161 children (94 girls and 67 boys) fulfilled this criterion at age 10 years. For those whose weights during infancy were available (only about one-third of the total) 50% had been above the ninetieth centile at 6 months and 35% at 12 months. Comparable figures for the nonobese controls at 6 and 12 months were 33% and 25% respectively. More striking suggestions of stability in the pattern of obesity emerged at age 5 years, when it was found that 29% of the boys and 54% of the girls who were obese at age 10 had been above the ninetieth centile for weight, compared with only 4% of the controls. Thus children who are obese later in childhood are more likely than nonobese children to have been obese earlier in childhood.

One example of the association between obesity in adulthood and earlier events is given in the studies of the effects of the Dutch famine of 1944-45 (Ravelli, Stein, and Susser, 1976). This historical cohort study of 300,000 men examined for military induction in 1963-64 at age 19 indicated that those whose mothers experienced famine conditions during the last trimester and first months of their children's lives had significantly lower obesity rates, presumably because the number of fat cells was decreased as a result of the famine. Conversely, however, men with mothers exposed to the famine during the first half of pregnancy had significantly higher obesity rates, possibly because of an effect on the hypothalamus. About 3% of this cohort of 4,300 births were obese—defined as a value of weight for height equal to or greater than 120% of the standard. This figure is double the rate of obesity found among 15,900 births in a control area free of famine, 1.45%. These results, unlike those from studies that have been confounded by effects of social class, were replicated in both manual and nonmanual classes.

Hypertension

Although uncommon in childhood, hypertension is a major and important cause of morbidity and mortality in adults. Whether its antecedents are found in childhood is still unknown.

Only recently have normal blood pressure standards been suggested for children (Lieberman, 1974; TFBPCC, NHLBI, 1977). The actual incidence and prevalence of children with elevated values are still unknown (Loggie, 1977, pp. 1-11); the forthcoming findings from the National Health and Nutrition Survey for persons of ages 6-74 years should provide useful data (U.S. DHEW, NCHS, VHS, 1976).

The majority of children with hypertension have "essential hypertension," that is, there is no known underlying cause. Hypertension has been shown to run in families, and evidence of its hereditary nature is found in reports showing that adopted children resemble their natural parents rather than the parents who adopted them (Mongeau, Bron, and Bertrand, 1977, pp. 39-44). Although constancy in blood pressure measurements might be expected to prevail in childhood, documentation is scant.

Twenty-eight children who were being followed as part of a study of the influence of prenatal and natal complications on birth weight and who had systolic or diastolic blood pressures above one standard deviation from the mean at age 5 were tested eleven years later (Buck, 1973). Their blood pressures were still elevated compared with controls of the same sex from the same class in school. When 20 of the 28 were compared a year later with sex-matched controls drawn from the original group in the larger study, their diastolic pressures were significantly elevated and their systolic pressures elevated to a nearly significant degree.

As a group, 436 young adults in a community sample who had hypertension at ages 15-29 tended to remain hypertensive seven years later (Johnson et al., 1975). To what extent individuals with normal blood pressure at ages 15-29 remained normotensive is unknown, as such individuals were not studied. Therefore the full magnitude of constancy of blood pressure cannot be judged from this study.

Another survey of 549 children (ages 2-14) four years after an initial measurement found that the blood pressures of the children studied were significantly and positively related to the blood pressures obtained four years earlier (Zinner et al., 1974). Preliminary results from a resurvey three to four years after the first resurvey showed that the relationship between early blood pressure levels and more recent ones increases as children age and suggests that some environmental influence might be superimposed on genetic predisposition. The known inverse correlation between hypertension and socioeconomic class may be further evidence of environmental influences (U.S. DHEW, NCHS, VHS, 1976). Thus, although there is evidence of considerable constancy of blood pressure, it is too early to guess the extent to which it prevails in childhood or the extent to which it can be altered by environmental change or medical therapy.

Precursors of Adult Cardiac Disease

Apart from congenital conditions, heart disease is uncommon in childhood. However, there is increasing evidence that precursors of adult heart disease, the major cause of mortality among adults in the United States, are found in childhood (WHO, 1974). No longitudinal prospective studies are available; thus the evidence is inferential. For example, it is known that certain factors, when present in adults, predispose to heart disease. These include high blood cholesterol levels, hypertension, physical inactivity, and smoking. For cholesterol and blood pressure, there is a positive correlation between levels in parents and levels in children. Accordingly, it is presumed that high levels in children predispose to future heart problems. Although these findings appear to be widely accepted, the risk cannot be quantified at the present time.

Children with congenital heart disease represent one of the groups for which therapy strongly influences the pattern of change over time. In this case the therapy is surgery, the results of which are often dramatic. Individuals with tetralogy of Fallot (a congenital cardiac condition for which surgical treatment is efficacious) were followed into young adulthood (Garson, Williams, and Wreckless, 1974). Thirty-seven of 46 patients could be located. Each was assessed for the presence of cyanosis, exercise intolerance, syncope, and growth failure, and a score was devised so that a maximum score of 148 was attainable for the group (37 children each assessed for 4 characteristics). At the time of initial surgery (mean age 6.9 years), the group had a score of 96 out of 129 (19 variables could not be assessed). The 16 who had second surgery (mean age 14.4 years) had a score of 33 out of 58 (6 variables could not be assessed) at the time of survey. At final follow-up (mean age 19 years), the total score was 26 of a maximum possible of 138 (10 variables were not assessed). Thus there was marked improvement over time in these children.

Urinary Tract Infection

Communitywide screening examinations indicate that at least 5% of girls acquire a urinary tract infection during childhood (Kunin, 1970; Dodge, West, and Travis, 1974). Since urinary tract infections are clinically considered to predispose to chronic kidney disease, this finding is important, particularly because two-thirds of all cases are asymptomatic (Kunin, 1976). A cohort of schoolgirls with urinary tract infection was followed for 10 years after initial diagnosis and treatment (Kunin, 1976). Reinfections were common, more so among younger girls than older ones, and more often among white girls than black girls. Over the long term, however, most recurrences abated, so that by three years after discovery of the infection, 95% of girls had attained long-term remissions. However, the rate of recurrence among these girls remained higher than the rate of emergence of urinary tract infection in the general population, 0.3/1,000 per year (Kunin, 1970). Although the effectiveness of treatment of asymptomatic urinary tract infections continues to be debated (Dodge, West, and Travis, 1974), it is widely agreed that adults with urinary tract infections are at increased risk of premature death and that children with urinary tract infections are more likely than other children to have infections during adulthood.

Neurosensory Problems

Ninety percent of the 866 infants born on the island of Kauai, Hawaii, in 1955 and another 116 born in 1956 with moderate to severe perinatal complications were identified (French et al., 1968; Werner, Bierman, and French, 1971). Pediatric and psychologic assessments were carried out at ages 2 and 10 years. One aspect of this study focused on the presence and persistence of congenital defects, acquired handicaps, hearing loss, and visual problems.

The main findings were as follows.

1. Acquired physical handicaps were only half as frequent as congenital handicaps and mental retardation.
2. Over half of the children handicapped at age 2 still had handicaps at age 10.
3. Two percent of children without physical handicaps at age 2 had physical defects at age 10.

The authors stressed the excellence of medical care on Kauai, so children with defects were likely to have received optimal care. In populations exposed to less adequate care the degree of constancy would certainly be greater than was found in this study, particularly for children in low socioeconomic classes.

Of all the neurosensory conditions, those included under the rubric cerebral palsy have been the most extensively studied. As with most other such conditions, little can be said of the "natural" history of this condition because most children receive some form of therapy, usually over long periods of time. In the course of a review of more than 1,800 patients with this disorder seen between 1930 and 1950 at Children's Hospital in Boston, the status of 74 who were "totally untreated" was examined (Paine, 1962). Twenty-three of the 24 with mild spastic hemiparesis had excellent or good gait as did 6 of the 14 with moderate or severe involvement. None of those who originally had mild symptoms developed contractures, and only 4 of those in the most severe group did so. By comparison, the 7 patients with spasticity in all four limbs had poor gait and contractures in later life.

Convulsions (Seizures)

In the Newcastle upon Tyne study, only 2 of the 42 children with seizures in the first 5 years of life had a recurrence during the school years (Miller et al., 1974, p. 131). Six other children had fits for the first time between ages 5 and 15. Fry (1974, pp. 193-198) reported that the outcome in childhood convulsions is good, with attacks ceasing in

95% by the age of 5. Most of these early convulsions are associated with fever, and such febrile seizures rarely have sequelae; only 2% of children with these febrile seizures go on to have epilepsy (Nelson and Ellenberg, 1978). Fry does not address the extent to which major or focal convulsions (known as "epilepsy" in medical terminology) abate by age 5, although he indicates that petit mal epilepsy (which accounts for 10% of nonfebrile convulsions) "tends to cease spontaneously by age 10" (1974, p. 195).

This view is not reflected in the pediatric neurology literature, however, where it is commonly assumed that petit mal persists in a high proportion of adolescents, about 50% or more. Two hundred forty-five Finnish children under age 16 who had epilepsy and who resided in a defined geographic area in the southwestern part of the country were followed at least 7 years (the mean was 10 years); only 5 children were not accounted for at the end of the study interval (Sillanpaa, 1973). At follow-up 44% still had seizures. The rate of remission of the others varied between 3% and 5% per year. Only 27% were free of seizures for 7 years or more.

This study also reported the rate of secondary psychosocial disability associated with childhood epilepsy. More than half (55%) of the children were judged to have neurotic disturbances, 11% were assessed as psychotic, and 33% were thought to display findings characteristic of the hyperkinetic syndrome. Forty-four percent (44%) were totally independent, whereas 14% were slightly to moderately independent, 18% were greatly dependent, and 23% were completely dependent at the time of follow-up. These figures must be interpreted with caution in view of the high frequency of mental retardation found in the study group and in the absence of suitable controls against which the measures of emotional disturbance or independence could be judged.

Another study indicated a similar picture for the prognosis of childhood seizures (Harrison and Taylor, 1976). The original sample consisted of all children from birth to age 14 who were reported as having seizures of any kind in an extensive community survey in the entire Oxford area of England. On follow-up 25 years later, about 10% had died, 6% were confined to institutions, and 7% were invalids at home. Twenty-two percent (24% of the survivors) had seizures on follow-up, and about half of these were in institutions or invalids at home. Thus even though about three-fourths of the children with seizures (most must have been the self-limited type often associated with early childhood fevers) had no residua 25 years later, a sizable minority of individuals continued to have major disability associated with the history of convulsions or from the underlying conditions.

Convulsions appear to be characterized by change rather than constancy. However, this interpretation is confounded by the use of medication to suppress seizure activity; if children are placed on medication before neurologic damage occurs and if the convulsions are not part of a general syndrome of brain damage, the natural history of this condition is impossible to evaluate.

Migraine

A large-population study (Bille, 1973) in Uppsala, Sweden, conducted in 1955 showed the prevalence of migraine among school children to be about 4%. This figure is based on the finding that 347 of the 8,993 school children ranging in age from 7 to 15 years who were studied during 1955 reported having (or ever having had) "paroxysmal headaches separated by free intervals, accompanied by at least *two* of the following four additional diagnostic criteria for migraine—one-sided pain, nausea, visual aura and family heredity." Only 57 children (0.6%) fulfilled all criteria, while 130 others (1.4%) met three of the four criteria. Because both a history of or current problems with these headaches was elicited, the figures reflect the cumulative prevalence of migraine. Accordingly the prevalence in this population is higher in the older age groups than in the younger ones. Two years later, in 1957, 73 children with severe migraine were matched "in pairs" with a comparable group of 73 children free of this disorder. (Details of the matching are not given, but presumably the process involved controlling for age, sex, and socioeconomic status.) The matched groups were followed in 1961, at which time 34% of the migraine group had become free of symptoms while only one child in the control group had developed migraine. A further follow-up ten years later showed that of the original group of 73 with migraine, 41% had recovered completely, 32% had improved, and the rest (27%) had remained the same or become worse. In the control group a total of 11% had developed migraine in the ten-year period. Although the numbers in the follow-up study are small, previous work by the same author suggests that they are fully representative of the population at risk. These results are also of interest because they derive from one of the longest follow-up studies of this disorder.

Juvenile Diabetes

Juvenile diabetes, with an incidence of about 8 per 100,000 annually under age 16 (calculated from data in Wadsworth and Jarrett, 1974) serves as a prototype of conditions for which the natural history can no longer be determined because of the widespread availability of an effective form of therapy. It is typical of many other diseases that can be controlled or contained but not cured. The principle mode of therapy, insulin, lowers the blood sugar, but the extent to which it controls other manifestations of the disease is unknown. Although it is theoretically possible to examine the long-term outcomes of adequate treatment because insulin has been available for many years, most of the long-term longitudinal studies are unrepresentative of the population at large of diabetics.

Children with diabetes seen at the Joslin Clinic in Boston (Hirohata, MacMahon, and Root, 1967) over the period from 1939 to 1959 had no excess mortality in the first 15 years of the disease, whereas in the next decade the excess death rate was between 1% and 2% per year. Moreover, the prognosis for survival was improved for cohorts first seen subsequent to 1944 compared with those seen prior to that time.

The long-term course of juvenile diabetes was examined in 168 individuals whose disease was of more than 15 years' duration and who were treated with the so-called free-diet treatment at the Children's Hospital in Stockholm during the 1930s and 1940s (Larsson and Sterky, 1962). The reporting was unusually complete, and there were few selective biases in this study. The average age at follow-up was 27, and the average duration of follow-up was 21 years. There were 72 patients whose onset of diabetes was earlier than age 5; 60 of these were alive at follow-up. Forty-five of the 60 who had their onset between ages 6 and 10 were still alive at follow-up, as were 21 of the 36 with onset between ages 11 and 15. Almost all the deaths were from causes directly or indirectly related to diabetes. Of the 125 patients who survived and for whom information was available, 80% had full working capacity and 20% had deteriorated so that they were partially or wholly disabled. In the interpretation of these data it is important to remember that the treatment given to these patients (the free diet) is different in approach from the stricter diet usually employed today. Constancy and change are certainly influenced by the availability and type of medical regimens as well as by other environmental and social factors that vary over time.

The gaps in knowledge of the natural history of common childhood disorders is evident from this brief review. Even more striking is the omission of some problems that are common in medical practice, such as abdominal pain and iron deficiency anemia. Gastrointestinal complaints are among the six most frequently given reasons for bringing children to physicians, and large-scale surveys show that one child in seven is anemic. Yet virtually nothing is known about what happens to children with these problems. To what extent are the conditions self-limited? To what extent do they contribute to morbidity, disability, or excess use of services in adulthood? No one knows. The data reviewed in this chapter, although relatively sparse and pertaining only to some conditions, suggest considerable constancy. It would be surprising if this were not also true for conditions for which there are now insufficient data for examination. However, the health problems of many children, and in some instances the majority, become less evident or disappear. The specific factors that predispose to persistence of illness are not generally known; many may be social rather than biological.

Utilization Studies

People seek medical care for many different reasons. They may seek services to obtain advice for and care of a new problem, illness, or injury, for care of a persistent problem, or for prevention (such as check-ups). On the other hand, health practitioners may request patients to return for care of an illness or for a preventive service (as for immunizations). These reasons are all based on a perception of the "need" for care which is generally considered justified by people in a given society. However, the extent to which care is sought for "need" is influenced by other factors, such as the interpretation of the significance of symptoms, financial ability, availability of services, the ability of the health practitioner to deal with the particular problem, and the availability of alternative ways of managing the problem (McKinlay, 1972). Therefore the extent to which services are used has no direct relationship to the presence of morbidity, and the constancy (or lack of it) in use over time may be only imperfectly correlated with the constancy of ill health over time. However, because morbidity is the major determinant of the use of health services, examination of the constancy of use over time can serve as a proxy measure for the constancy of morbidity over time.

The three studies summarized in this section were carried out in prepaid group practices. Unfortunately, such information is unavailable for children who receive their care from other types of facilities (except for individual practices such as those of Fry, 1966; 1974, p. 44) because there is no standard system of data that keeps track of the health care experiences of children, especially if they receive their care from more than one practitioner or health facility.

The HIP Studies

The consistency of utilization among subscribers to a prepaid group medical plan (the Health Insurance Plan of Greater New York) over a three-year period was described in 1959 (Densen, Shapiro, and Einhorn, 1959). Utilization was categorized as low if fewer than 3 visits were made during a year, moderate if 3-9 visits were made, and high if there were 10 or more visits. The major findings were as follows.

1. Although proportionally fewer children than adults were either low or high utilizers, 20% of the children had no visits, and 11% were high utilizers in any single year.

2. Although there was no relationship between size of family and the likelihood of an individual's being a high utilizer, nonutilization decreased as family size increased.

3. Although fewer than half of the children who were high or low utilizers in the first year remained at the same utilization level in the second or third years (table 7.3), the likelihood of individuals' staying at the same utilization level in the three-year period was higher than could be accounted for by chance alone (table 7.4).

4. Limited analyses indicated a tendency for families to have all members at the same utilization level. However, no analyses were done to determine the influence of family size on constancy of utilization over the three-year period.

The report did not provide information on patterns of utilization for age groups within the childhood range. Instead all offspring under age 18 in families of subscribers were combined into one group.

Table 7.3. Utilizers in successive years by children of HIP members, classified by utilization level in 1954.

Utilization	Number of children in year 1 (1954)	Percentage who remain at the same utilization level in years 2 and 3	
		Observed	Expected[a]
Low utilization			
No visits	1,598	27	9
1-2 visits	2,196	14	12
Medium utilization			
3-9 visits	2,191	32	23
High utilization			
10 or more visits	849	17	4

Source: Adapted from Densen, Shapiro, and Einhorn (1959, p. 238).

a. Calculated under the assumption that utilization in a particular year is independent of utilization in prior years. See also note 2.

Table 7.4. Percentage of children of HIP members who were nonutilizers or high utilizers in three successive years (total number of children = 7834).

Children	Initial year	First two successive years		Three successive years	
		Observed	Expected[a]	Observed	Expected[a]
Nonutilizers	20.4	9.0	4.0	5.5	0.7
High utilizers[b]	10.8	3.6	1.0	1.8	0.1

Source: Adapted from Densen, Shapiro, and Einhorn (1959, p. 242).

a. "Expected" calculated under assumption that utilization in a particular year is independent of utilization in prior years.

b. 10 or more visits.

Child Health and Development Studies, Oakland, California

Between August 1959 and April 1967 all children (approximately 19,000 born to members of the Kaiser Permanente Medical Plan of Oakland, California, were enrolled in a longitudinal study to provide information about determinants of health and illness. Information on all medical visits are available for 2,875 children who were born before 1962 and were still enrolled in the plan at age 10. Bea van den Berg, director of the Child Health and Development Studies, analyzed the utilization experiences of these children during three successive periods: birth-2, 3-5, and 6-9 years. Each child was categorized as a low, average, or high utilizer in each of these three periods depending on whether the number of visits was in the lowest third, the middle third, or the highest third of the distribution for the entire cohort of children in that age group. For children aged 0-2, the lowest third comprised children with 13 or fewer visits (low use), the middle third comprised children with 14-23 visits (average use), and the highest third comprised children with 24 or more visits in the three-year period (high use). For children at ages 3-5 and ages 6-9 years, low use consisted of 6 or fewer visits, average use 7-13 visits, and high use 14 or more visits in that three-year period. Table 7.5 gives the number of children in each utilization category during each age period.[3]

Marked change was defined as shifts from high to low or from low to high in any two periods (regardless of the use rate for the third period). Other shifts (average to low, low to average, average to high, high to average) were considered moderate change. Table 7.6 shows the results. The number of children found to be constant in their use of services (consistently high, average, or low) was far in excess of what

Table 7.5. Utilization of outpatient medical care in first 10 years of life of 2,875 children.

Utilization	Number of children		
	0-2 years	*3-5 years*	*6-9 years*
Low	900	977	953
Medium	1,053	946	942
High	922	952	980
Total	2,875	2,875	2,875

Source: Data from the Child Health and Development Studies. University of California at Berkeley. Bea J. van den Berg (personal communication, 1977). See note 3 for method of specifying utilization.

would be expected by chance, and the number of children who showed changing patterns was far fewer than would be expected by chance ($X^2 = 1,828$, p less than 0.001). Of the children who were low users at ages 0-2, 64% were low users at ages 3-5 and of these, 66% remained low users at ages 6-9. Of the children who were high users at ages 0-2, 62% were high users at ages 3-5, and 68% of these remained high users at ages 6-9.

The Columbia Medical Plan

The Columbia Medical Plan is a prepaid group practice in Columbia, Maryland. Records of all face-to-face encounters of patients in the plan have been computerized, with their reasons and disposition, by the Health Services Research and Development Center of the Johns Hopkins Medical Institutions. Because this computerized system has been in operation since 1971, six years of utilization experience were available at the time of this writing. All children whose families were enrolled in the plan through the entire six-year period are included: they range in age from newborn to 14 years old in 1971. The use of health services over three successive two-year periods was examined for each of the 15 cohorts of children. Utilization was defined as low, average, or high in each of the two-year periods depending on whether the number of visits in the period was in the lowest third, middle third, or highest third of the distribution for the entire cohort in that age group. The number of visits separating the low, average, and high groups was similar but slightly higher than for children in the Kaiser-Oakland Medical Plan. Constancy and change were categorized as with the California data. Table 7.7 presents the findings.

Table 7.6. Utilization levels throughout the first 10 years of life in 2,875 children.

| Utilization | Numbers of children in 3 successive age periods: 0-2 years, 3-5 years, and 6-9 years | | | |
| | Observed | | Expected[a] | |
	N	Percentage	N	Percentage
Constant[b]				
Low	381	13.3	101	3.5
Medium	180	6.3	114	4.0
High	391	13.6	104	3.6
Subtotal	952	33.1	319	11.1
Changed[b]				
Moderate[c]	1,479	51.4	1,300	45.2
Marked[d]	444	15.4	1,256	43.7
Subtotal	1,923	66.9	2,556	88.9
Total	2,875	100.0	2,875	100.0

Source: Data from the Child Health and Development Studies. University of California at Berkeley. Bea J. van den Berg (personal communication).

a. If children are distributed randomly into the 27 patterns: 3 constant patterns (LLL, AAA, HHH), 12 moderately changed, 12 markedly changed. The differences between the observed and the expected are highly statistically significant (X^2 = 1828.35, p less than 0.001). See also notes 2, 3.

b. Low in all periods, average in all periods, or high in all periods.

c. Average to low, low to average, average to high, high to average.

d. High to low, low to high.

For each of the 15 cohorts, constancy in patterns of use was much higher and change in use much lower than would be expected by chance alone (X^2 = 453, p less than 0.001). Of the low users in the first two-year period, 54% were low users in the subsequent period, and 54% of these remained low users in the third period. Of the children who were high users in the first two-year period, 56% were high users in the next two-year period and 67% of these remained high users in the third two-year period.

These three studies indicate that patterns of use are more likely to remain constant than to change throughout the childhood years. The proportion of children who had constant patterns of use was 24% in HIP, 33% in Kaiser-Oakland, and 27% in Columbia. This degree of constancy is not likely to be due solely to the presence of children with

Table 7.7. Patterns of utilization of Columbia Medical Plan.

Age periods	Constant pattern[a]			Changed pattern[b]	
	Low	Average	High	Moderate	Marked
0-1, 2-3, 4-5	7	3	10	31	7
1-2, 3-4, 5-6	6	4	10	51	18
2-3, 4-5, 6-7	6	5	6	45	14
3-4, 5-6, 7-8	8	4	16	59	23
4-5, 6-7, 8-9	7	9	14	43	14
5-6, 7-8, 9-10	5	7	13	49	22
6-7, 8-9, 10-11	7	7	16	42	21
7-8, 9-10, 11-12	14	7	21	55	20
8-9, 10-11, 12-13	6	5	12	36	18
9-10, 11-12, 13-14	9	2	10	38	15
10-11, 12-13, 14-15	8	7	7	50	22
11-12, 13-14, 15-16	6	3	8	47	24
12-13, 14-15, 16-17	6	4	6	38	11
13-14, 15-16, 17-18	0	5	3	22	15
14-15, 16-17, 18-19	4	2	6	14	9
Total	99	74	158		
Observed number of children		331		620	253
Expected number of children[c]		136		556	512

a. Low in all periods, average in all periods, high in all periods.

b. Moderate: Average to low, low to average, average to high, high to average; marked: high to low, low to high.

c. If children are distributed randomly into the 27 different patterns: 3 constant patterns (LLL, AAA, HHH), 12 moderately changed, 12 markedly changed. The difference between the observed and the expected are highly statistically significant (X^2 = 452.93, p less than 0.001). See also note 2.

serious illness in the populations under study, for several reasons. First, a large proportion of the constant users in all three facilities were in fact low or average utilizers: 92% in HIP, 59% in Oakland, and 52% in Columbia. Second, the proportion of children with chronic illness for which medical care would be sought frequently is likely to be considerably less than 10% in any general population. This is so because most studies show that the prevalence of these chronic illnesses in childhood is not much more than 10% (Pless, 1968, pp. 760-768) and many of these represent stable conditions for which little medical care is procured. In these facilities constantly high users accounted for only 1.8% of the children in HIP (with high use defined very restrictively—10 or more visits a year), 14% in Oakland, and 13% in Columbia. Accordingly, more children are constantly high users than can be accounted for by children with chronic illness.

Although these cohorts represent general populations of children rather than those characterized by presence of illness, the generalizability of the findings may be limited because all were enrollees of prepaid health plans. Such plans are unlikely to contain a proportionate share of individuals in the lowest socioeconomic classes, since they require either prepayment of premiums or employment in firms that provide a prepaid plan as an insurance benefit. The extent to which a lower-class population would be found to have similar constancy of utilization is unknown. Information about their use of services over time is lacking at least in part because they use multiple sources, thus making data over time unavailable.

General Measures of Health

One problem in interpreting data about the constancy and change in specific conditions is that conditions often coexist in one individual child. Persistence or resolution of one problem may be influenced by the presence of other conditions, and knowledge of the natural history of the problems may give little indication of the constancy and change in overall health of the child with the condition. This difficulty could be surmounted if there were a measure of health that showed the individual components of health and reflected derangements resulting from the variety of disease conditions present in an individual.

For example, a profile of health (figure 7.1) could indicate the degree of present discomfort, dissatisfaction, disability, and underachievement as well as threats to longevity and ill health (Starfield, 1974). Such a profile would make it possible to view the health of children in terms of individuals rather than in terms of diseases and would facilitate observation of change in health over time and as a response to medical and social interventions. The need for such a summarizing measure in this area, in contrast to the undesirability of a similar generalized measure of phenomena such as intelligence, should be clear. Whereas in psychology a general measure of intellect distorts nature, in medicine it is a more accurate reflection of it. Physicians, like psychologists, strive to separate discrete strengths and weakness; nevertheless, both health and illness are manifested functionally and behaviorally in a limited number of ways. These manifestations can be described in several dimensions that should not be averaged; nor, however, can they singly or in combination be equated with a particular illness. A diagnostic label is not equivalent to a meaningful statement of what the child is able to do in any one of several functional

Resilience	Resilient ———————————————— Vulnerable
Achievement	Achieving ——————————— Not Achieving
Disease	Not ——— Undifferentiated — Limited — Persistent Detectable
Satisfaction	Satisfied ————————————— Dissatisfied
Comfort	Comfortable ——————————— Uncomfortable
Activity	Functional ——————————— Disabled
Longevity	Normal ———————————————— Dead Life Expectancy

Figure 7.1 *A profile of health. (From Starfield, 1974.)*

dimensions. For example, a child with severe asthma may be just as unable to participate in athletics as one with rheumatoid arthritis. The reasons and biological mechanisms differ, but the behavioral consequences are the same. The situation becomes even more complex when several disorders coexist, or when they are compounded by emotional or social disorders.

To describe in detail the specific manifestations of each discrete condition in a single child fails completely to describe the health of the child as a whole. Thus, regardless of the causes, summarizing measures of health that reflect the common pathways of dysfunction must be used. The use of discrete descriptions perpetuates the insidious effects of labeling and the other important social implications of systems of classification of children based on their diagnoses rather than on themselves as individuals. It is in an attempt to counteract the powerful impact of the diagnostic label that we espouse the use of not one but a group of summarizing measures of derangement. Until such a profile is developed, constancy and change in the overall health of children must be viewed through a series of diverse and unconnected measures of aspects of health. These include episodes of illness and their severity, individual types of functional disability thought to reflect ill health, and school absences.

The Harvard Studies of Child Health and Development

In 1930, 231 women of American or northern European descent who were receiving prenatal care at the Boston Lying-in Hospital were selected for enrollment in the Harvard Studies of Child Health and Development (Stuart, 1939; Valadian, Stuart, and Reed, 1959). One hundred and thirty-four children in these 231 families were followed from birth to 18 years of age. Information about illnesses was obtained at least once every 6 months during the first 10 years of life, and at least annually thereafter. The 18 years of life were divided into five periods: birth to age 2 (infancy), 2-6 (preschool), 6-10 (school), 10-14 (early adolescence), 14-18 (late adolescence). Two scores were devised for each of the five periods. One score indicated the frequency of illnesses. The overall frequency of illness was considered low if there were fewer than 5 illnesses in infancy and fewer than 9 in each subsequent four-year period. Frequency of illness was considered high if there were more than 8 illnesses in infancy and more than 17 at any subsequent four-year period. Values between these extremes were classified as intermediate. The second score indicated the severity and duration of illness. Severity and duration were determined clinically according to preset rules and combined into a score which was then divided into low, intermediate, and high ranges for the different age periods. The emphasis of this study was on the occurrence and the seriousness of acute illnesses and acute illnesses superimposed on preexisting conditions. Health problems or recurrent complaints were not considered illnesses; neither were localized pathology and deviations from normal in clinical or laboratory findings not associated with clinical symptoms. Thus the following data reflect primarily the occurrence of aberrations from the average state rather than the state of health of the children.

From the published data (Valadian, Stuart, and Reed, 1959) it is possible to categorize constancy and change in the frequency of illness episodes and in their seriousness. Each child was categorized as high (H), intermediate (I), and low (L) separately for frequency of illness and for severity of illness in each of the age periods. Table 7.8 presents the findings when three consecutive age periods (0-2, 3-5, 6-10) were examined. Expected values are derived from the actual proportions of children with high, intermediate, and low scores in each age period for each of the 27 possible combinations of these three levels of scores. There were three combinations indicating constancy (HHH, III, LLL), 12 indicating marked change (high to low, or vice versa), and 12 indicating moderate change (high or low to intermediate, or vice versa). The distributions of frequency of illnesses in subsequent age periods are all close to what might be obtained by chance; although

Table 7.8. Frequency and seriousness of illness in consecutive periods of childhood, 0-2, 3-5, 5-10, Harvard Studies of Child Health and Development.

	Number of children	
Illness	*Observed*	*Expected[a]*
Constant frequency	*19*	15.6
Low in all three periods (LLL)	7	
Intermediate in all three periods (III)	6	
High in all three periods (HHH)	6	
Changed frequency		
Moderate[b]	76	67.9
Marked[c]	39	50.5
Constant seriousness	*37*	24.2
Low in all three periods (LLL)	28	
Intermediate in all three periods (III)	8	
High in all three periods (HHH)	1	
Changed seriousness		
Moderate[b]	68	74.7
Marked[c]	29	35.1

Source: Calculated from data in Valadian, Stuart, and Reed (1959).

a. The differences between observed and expected values for frequency of illness are not statistically significant ($X^2 = 2.25$), but the differences between observed and expected values for seriousness of illness over the successive age periods are significant ($X^2 = 8.49$, p less than 0.015). See also note 2.

b. High or low to intermediate, or vice versa (12 combinations).

c. High to low, or vice versa (12 combinations).

not shown in the table, the distributions increasingly approximate chance distributions as the interval between early observations and later ones increases. The data show that the few (9) children with high scores for frequency of illness in late adolescence were more likely to have had high scores in infancy than children with low scores in adolescence (56% versus 28%). When illnesses are categorized by severity and duration, more children (37) show constancy over the three age periods than would be expected if the illnesses occurred independently from one time period to another. If subsequent age periods (10-14, 14-18) are also included, this constancy (which consists of both constant low scores and constant high and intermediate ones) persists although it does not reach statistical significance largely because the percentage of children with high scores falls with age, from 14% at ages 0-2 to 4% at ages 6-10 to 2% at ages 14-18.

Selective Service Rejection Rates and Childhood Illness

A study of the relationship between physical assessment of children and subsequent results of their medical examinations for the Selective Service System indicated that young children who were likely to have adult health problems could be identified (Ciocco, 1945). More recently, a random sample of 6,425 boys from records of children who finished the eighth grade in 1953-1955 or the ninth grade in 1954-1956 was identified (Densen et al., 1970). Junior and senior high school records of these boys were examined, and 5,863 were found to have no mention of a defect incompatible with subsequent Selective Service acceptance. The material in these 5,863 records was compared with Selective Service medical examination records, which were found for 60%. (An examination of school records of the 40% not found in Selective Service records indicated that no serious bias in the findings was likely to be introduced by their exclusion.)

Table 7.9 shows that individuals with medical conditions noted on their school records were more likely to fail Selective Service examinations than individuals who did not have such conditions noted. Not

Table 7.9. Selective Service rejection rates for examinees with and without childhood illness.

Childhood medical defect associated significantly with rejection	*Percentage rejected, with defect[a]* (1)	*Percentage rejected, without defect[a]* (2)	*Percentage with medical defect* (3)
Uncorrected vision score of 20/25 or worse in better eye	41.2	29.0	12.1
Cardiac condition	54.5	32.4	4.0
Asthma, hayfever	43.5	32.6	6.4
Accidental injury (major)	43.5	32.6	5.3
Health class placement	50.3	31.0	4.9
Behavioral problem	41.2	29.0	38.6
Average annual absence of 30 days or more in grades 1-9	52.3	31.5	9.4

Source: Adapted from Densen et al. (1970, pp. 984; 986).

a. All differences between columns 1 and 2 are statistically significant with p less than 0.01 (chi-square test).

shown in the table is the extent to which failure on the Selective Service examination can be attributed to childhood medical conditions. Of those rejected by Selective Service examinations for medical reasons, 30% had the specific physical conditions listed in table 7.9 noted in their school health records; individuals with these conditions on their medical records composed only 22% of the total population studied. Thus children with certain medical defects are more likely than other children to be rejected by the Selective Service when they reach early adulthood; they also contribute disproportionately to those rejected, even when their defects in childhood are not of sufficient seriousness to mark them as likely to be so impaired. Physical defects not associated significantly with rejection were eye disease without visual defect, hearing loss or chronic otitis, overweight or underweight, orthopedic defects such as flat feet and curvature of the spine, hernia, certain acute childhood diseases, respiratory conditions including chronic tonsillitis, height and weight at ages 6 and 14, and birth weight under 2,501 grams.

In summary, it may be deduced from these data that many conditions display patterns of stability over the period from primary school to the time of Selective Service examination; 40%-50% of children with these conditions still have them as notable problems in early adulthood.

The U.S. Health Examination Survey

During the years 1963-1965 and 1966-1970 the U.S. National Center for Health Statistics conducted a health examination survey on a national probability sample of children 6-11 years old and youths 12-17 years old. By design, a sample of households was revisited during the second survey, so that approximately 2,000 children were examined in both surveys. Neither the interviews nor the physical examinations were identical in the two surveys, although the types of information sought were similar. Five items, all from the interview portion of the examination, appeared to be almost identical. Joan Cornoni-Huntley (1977) of the National Center for Health Statistics arranged for analyses of these items to examine patterns of change in individual children over the interval between surveys. Table 7.10 shows the results.

The prevalence of each of the indicated manifestations of ill health was low for both the children and the youths. Therefore, the number of children free of the problem at both times was very large. In general, a substantial minority of those who had evidence of a health problem at ages 9-11 had it on follow-up at ages 12-15; for example, 40% of those who initially took medicines regularly (4.3% of chil-

Table 7.10. Children with and without health defects at ages 8-11 and 12-15, National Health Examination Survey.

Health problem	Presence in first and second examinations[a]			
	Yes, No	No, Yes	Yes, Yes	No, No
Taking regular medicines	52	90	34	1830
Hearing problems	59	31	33	1853
Walking problems	36	15	14	1947
Restricted activity	14	60	12	1929
School absence for illness	43	78	10	1567

Source: Joan Cornoni-Huntley (personal communication).

a. The kappa statistics for agreement (yes, yes and no, no versus yes, no and no, yes) are statistically significant with p less than 0.01 except for school absences, where p less than 0.05.

dren) still took them three to four years later; 36% of those who initially had hearing problems (4.7% of children) still had them; 28% of the 2.5% with initial walking problems still had them, and 46% of those with initially restricted activity (1.3%) still had it. Even for school absences, 18.9% of the 3.1% of the children initially having frequent absences for illness still had them. Of those who had the problems in the later years, 27%, 52%, 48%, 17%, and 11% respectively had reported them initially. The data can also be viewed in another way. Of those children who had the problem in either period, what proportion had it in both? For school absences, 7.6% of those with problems in either period had it in both. The corresponding figure for restricted activity is 14.0%, for walking problems 21.5%, for hearing problems 27%, and for regular medication 19.3%. Overall, constancy as calculated by the proportion of children who either remain sickly or remain well is much greater than for those who develop one of the conditions or who become free of them. Of those who have the condition at only one time, however, shifts from wellness to illness and vice versa are more likely than not.

British Cohort of 1946

Although no data are yet available on constancy of childhood illness in the British cohort of 1946, the relationship between hospitalizations early in life and later in life was examined (Douglas, 1977). For children in the top 10% for either number of admissions or length of stay from birth through age 6, 8% had high rates of admissions (top

10%) at ages 16-20 and 7% had high rates at ages 21-25. For those with high hospitalization rates at age 7-14, 8% also had high rates at ages 16-20, and 5% at ages 21-25. In comparison, only 3% and 5% of those with hospitalization rates in the "normal" range in childhood had high rates at ages 16-20 and 21-25 respectively. Therefore children with early hospitalization are much more likely than other children to have later hospitalization, even though only a minority of the group with early hospitalization have subsequent hospital stays.

Other Studies

The extent to which the number of school absences in one year was related to the number of absences in the subsequent year was studied in a sample of 1,870 children in the fourth, seventh, and tenth grades of a representative sample of schools in Delaware (Roberts et al., 1969). Pupils who had a low number of absences in the first year tended to have a low number in the following year, while students with a high number of absences in the first year also had many absences in the following year. Follow-up was not continued after one year so the extent of longer-term constancy cannot be determined.

The "Sickly" Child

Is there any relationship between the popular concept of the "sickly" child and what has been considered sickness in this chapter? The popular concept of the sickly child may have some scientific basis. The term is usually used to refer to children who appear to be frequently ill with minor acute illnesses or children who appear ill because they are pale, sallow, or lack energy. Upper respiratory infections involving ears, nose, or throat are the most frequent of the acute illnesses. Many children experience frequent illnesses of this type at some time during childhood, usually when they are expanding their social contacts with other children and hence becoming exposed to new infectious agents. The year following enrollment in day-care nursery or kindergarten is often marked by recurrent episodes of respiratory illness. Overly concerned parents or parents who are unaware that this pattern is to be expected may label their child sickly at these times. The label may also be generated by physicians who themselves fail to recognize the pattern or the anxious parent's response to it.

Rarely, recurrent acute illnesses occur because children have underlying conditions that increase their susceptibility to them. The underlying disorders that increase susceptibility to infection are defects in the immunologic system (which normally protects children from infections through physiological defense mechanisms). Occasionally such immunologic deficiencies are a by-product or side effect of therapy with steroids or other drugs that deliberately suppress the immunologic system in the treatment of malignancies and other disorders. Of course, many children with malignant conditions appear sickly because of the direct effects of the disease or its therapy.

Other diseases that make a child appear sickly are major conditions: anemia, cystic fibrosis, and some nutritional deficiencies. Children with a chronic disorder are, by definition, always sick, yet they usually do not appear sickly. The term is therefore an imprecise one and might most appropriately be applied to a group of children who experience more frequent acute illnesses than would be expected by chance alone when age, social class, or other factors are taken into account.

Accident Proneness

Another popular term that implies constancy is accident proneness. It is widely held that some children are accident prone, with the implication that some constellation of factors or traits, usually a personality characteristic, increase the child's likelihood of having more frequent accidents than his peers. Most studies describing this group of children are open to criticism on methodologic grounds—usually because they are uncontrolled or retrospective or both—and hence cannot establish unequivocably that these characteristics are causally related. Parents whose children have frequent accidents may consciously or otherwise wish to explain this socially undesirable phenomena, and it is therefore reasonable to expect that they would be more likely than other parents to describe repeaters in terms that shift the imputed blame from themselves and the lack of supervision to the child and his "makeup" (which are presumably beyond parental control).

Any study seeking to establish a relationship between one factor and another should include a comparison group of nonrepeaters in which the presence of the same supposedly etiologic factors are sought. Those who seek the information should not know whether the child is accident-prone, in order to avoid allowing prejudices to influence the way the questions are asked. Even more desirable is prospective hypothesis testing, that is, identifying the proposed characteristics before the child's accidents occur. Unfortunately, neither condition is met in most studies. Moreover, investigations usually cover a relatively short time span so that even if the evidence is impressive it cannot determine whether the presumed traits are persistent or transient. There may well be developmental stages during which some children have more accidents than would be expected, for example, when a child whose gross motor development is slower than his peers is struggling to keep up with the peer group in their social and recreational activities. Such children would be unable to manage risk as effectively as others.

A study in Nottingham (Howarth, Routledge, and Repetto-Wright, 1974) confirms the well-documented observation that accidents are more frequent among boys than girls of all ages. The common explanation for the higher frequency of accidents among boys is that they have greater exposure to accident-producing situations and take more risks. In fact, this increased exposure, at least to motor vehicle accidents, is present only before age 8; nor is the higher accident rate of boys due to this increased exposure. Some authors postulate that the higher accident rate among boys is related to their poorer ability to handle the accident-producing situation.

One of the largest studies of accident proneness (Manheimer and Mellinger, 1967) involved 8,874 children ages 8 to 18 years, all enrolled in the Kaiser Foundation Health Plan for at least one age period (0-3, 4-7, 8-11, 12-15), whose ongoing records were available for study. On the basis of their accident history, 684 were selected to represent children of high, intermediate, and low accident liability. The authors were aware that random variation alone might produce a group of children who appeared to be accident-prone and took pains to control for this statistically. Data gathering was carried out ''blind'' (that is, the data collectors did not know which children were accident-prone), and steps were taken to minimize other forms of bias. Boys who were highly accident-liable had an average of 84 accidents per year per 100 boys; those in the intermediate group had 35.2 and those in the low group 4.0. For girls the corresponding figures were 81.6, 26.6, and 0.7.

The results provide strong support for the hypothesis that certain behavioral characteristics thought to be associated with greater exposure to hazards in boys are associated significantly with an increase in the average of frequency of accidents. These are activity level, extroversion, exploring, independence, daring, roughhousing, and athletic proficiency. In girls all these except athletic proficiency, exploring, and independence were also significantly related to higher accident frequency. Another set of psychological attitudes assessed were those thought to influence the child's ability to cope with hazards. Broadly these were conceived as competing motivations, lack of self-control, and other traits such as carelessness and unreliability. Again, for boys significant relationships were found for discipline problems and peer group aggressiveness as well as discipline problems. For girls and boys, peer group aggressiveness was significantly elevated among those with high accident rates and for girls only attention-seeking was also associated, but at a lower level of significance. An additional group of coping measures concerning lack of self-control also showed differences on 6 of the 8 comparisons, all in this expected direction. Therefore, the authors concluded that children who have repeated accidents are both likely to have greater exposure to accident-producing situations and less likely to be able to cope with them. The authors also provide evidence that social and personality maladjustment, independent of the previously described traits, may also be correlated with accident liability—more consistently for boys than for girls. A more recent report also shows a provocative relationship of the same order between accidents among children and the combined effect of social class and depression among mothers (Brown and Davidson, 1978).

Although the authors of these important studies believe their findings to be consistent with earlier smaller-scale "pilot" studies, some authors (Haddon, Suchman, and Klein, 1964) believe the concept of repeatedness to be unsupported scientifically. It is clear that there remains such controversy over this important question—controversy unlikely to be fully resolved until better-designed prospective studies are conducted or intervention trials based on the findings are proven successful. Undisputed, however, is that the concept of proneness or repeaters represents not a dichotomy but a continuum along which the probability of an accident increases. Thus children with fewer accidents differ in degree but not in kind from children who have many accidents or others who have none. However, one cannot conclude from most available studies that proneness is an important explanation for the very large number of accidents seen among children on the whole.

Present knowledge permits few scientifically acceptable assertions about single causal factors. This is certainly the case with respect to accident proneness. It seems certain that any rational attack on the problem of child safety as a whole would have to adopt a multicausal strategy, part of which would obviously be more amenable to intervention than others.

The relative importance of constancy and change varies with the measure used to describe physical health. The health defects listed in table 7.10 are themselves a diverse group. Some may be manifestations of developmental phenomena (walking problems), and some are likely to be secondary effects of other illnesses (hearing problems as a result of middle ear infections). For both conditions, more children lose the condition as they age than acquire them. On the other hand, phenomena that are manifestations of the increasing burden of permanent illness, such as regular medication, restricted activity, and school absence are more likely to increase than to decrease in frequency, and more children will acquire them than will lose them. The Selective Service studies (Ciocco, 1945; Densen et al., 1970) indicate that some physical defects are unlikely to have any measurable impact on health as assessed later on in life. For others (those in table 7.9) the reverse is the case.

The Harvard Child Health Studies indicate that frequency of acute illness early in life is not predictive of later problems, whereas seriousness of illness (or absence of it) is. Moreover, children with high scores in adolescence were more likely to have high scores in their early years than other children. The finding gains added salience from the inclusion of only children thought to be completely normal at birth. The general population would have a greater proportion of children with serious defects manifested early in life and likely to persist. Moreover, the study did not include chronic conditions without superimposed exacerbations of symptoms; these conditions, by definition, are likely to persist.

Thus evidence for constancy and change using general measures of health is generally consistent with evidence from specific health conditions and from utilization studies. As was the case with these other types of evidence, generalizations are hampered by large gaps in our knowledge of the pathogenesis of most illnesses and our poor understanding of their interrelationships, their manifestations, and their sequelae. The unavailability of standardized measures of the effect of illnesses further hampers comparisons between them.

A profile of health such as the one proposed earlier in this chapter would enable both the investigator and the clinician to view the child along dimensions unrelated to a specific medical diagnosis or group of medical diagnoses. What counts for the child is not whether he has a disease designated as diabetes or cerebral palsy but the extent to which his resilience is affected, the effect of the illness on his achievement, whether he is uncomfortable or dissatisfied, and the extent to which normal function is interfered with. Medical thinking tends to grossly oversimplify reality; it ignores the diverse manifestations of disease and almost invariably focuses on liabilities rather than assets, on weaknesses rather than strengths. Achievement and discomfort do not cancel each other; they are each an essential part of the profile of a child's total functioning, no less important than the presence or absence of "disease."

Our concern must be directed as much to assessing the strength of the constancy of these features in the presence of disease as to examining in traditional biological terms the evidence of improvement or worsening.

Emotional Health Problems in Children
With Physical Health Problems

Most illnesses experienced by children are relatively minor. They are usually self-limited and produce no sequelae. Even though the evidence presented so far indicates that sickly children—that is, children who tend to get these minor illnesses—are more likely than other children to be sickly as older children or as young adults, most sickly children have no residua from their acute illnesses.

There are, however, many conditions that affect a smaller proportion of children but have serious impacts. These are the chronic conditions of childhood. By definition they persist for at least three consecutive months; many are rarely cured. These conditions result in persistent disability. It has been variously estimated that between 10% and 20% of children under the age of 18 experience a chronic physical disorder of one kind or another (Pless and Pinkerton, 1975). On one extreme are developmental problems which are common early in life but which usually disappear with time. Chronic diseases also include most congenital abnormalities (often referred to as impairments or disabilities rather than diseases), as well as disorders of a medical nature, those of the special senses, and the subset of mental retardation thought to have a biological basis.

Documentation of the prevalence of individual chronic illnesses is scant. In contrast to the excellent data systems for reporting the causes of death mandated by standard death certificates, there is no reporting of illness in the population—not even serious or life-threatening illness. No one really knows how common most health conditions are. The data in table 7.11 come from the only study of the distribution of chronic illness in a child population. The table shows the approximate frequency of certain medical conditions in children under 16 in Erie County, New York, in the late 1950s. The frequencies given are the cumulative prevalence for children under 16 who, in 1961, were ever diagnosed as having the condition. Only certain chronic conditions were considered in this study. For the most part the conditions considered are biologically permanent and nonfatal. Therefore the prevalences indicate the burden of morbidity accumulated over childhood. One child in 500 has one of these conditions. Not included in this list are the developmental conditions, the congenital anomalies, fatal conditions such as most malignancies (the second most frequent cause of death, after accidents, in childhood), mental deficiency, or the chronic conditions of unclear permanence (such as asthma).

Knowledge about constancy or change in the manifestations of chronic disorders, whether they are lifelong or not, requires data not

Table 7.11. Cumulative prevalence of selected long-term medical diseases in childhood.[a]

Condition		Prevalence
Endocrine conditions		65/100,000
Diabetes mellitus	50	
Cretinism	7	
Adrenal disease	5	
Hypoparathyroidism and pseudohypoparathyroidism	2	
Diabetes insipidus	1	
Blood dyscrasias		50/100,000
Collagen diseases		21/100,000
Juvenile rheumatoid arthritis	20	
Lupus erythematosus	1	
Renal diseases		21/100,000
Nephrotic syndrome	16	
Chronic nephritis	2	
Renal rickets	3	
Peptic ulcer		16/100,000
Inborn errors of metabolism		16/100,000
Histiocytosis X	4	
Phenylketonuria	3	
Albinism	2	
Agammaglobulinemia	2	
Marfan's syndrome	2	
Cystinosis	1	
Glycogen storage disease	1	
Leucine-induced hypoparathyrodism	1	
Neuromuscular genetic conditions		8/100,000
Muscular dystrophy	5	
Amyotonia congenita	2	
Friedreich's ataxia	1	
Bronchiectasis		4/100,000

Source: Adapted from Sultz et al. (1972).

a. Figures are for Erie County, New York, in 1961. Cumulative prevalence is the number of living children on a specific date with a history of one of the conditions per 100,000 children under 16 years of age alive on that date. The prevalence of diabetes in Erie County was 61 per 100,000; as this figure is substantially higher than reported in other studies, a prevalence of 50 per 100,000 is used in this table.

often available in any large-scale, systematic fashion. Conventional wisdom generally substitutes for data about the prognosis of most of these diseases. These statements are based on accumulated clinical experience and little else. Thus the physician caring for a child with a disease may say with some degree of certainty that the prognosis for future functioning, survival, or cure is good or poor, or may even be able to add some statements of probability. Such figures, where they exist at all, are usually based on small samples in which the status of patients has been examined retrospectively. The truth is that we do not know, in most instances, what kinds of symptoms or disabilities will be experienced by most of the children with a chronic disease, or with what frequency.

Clinical impression indicates that the natural history of the chronic diseases is generally toward persistence or gradual worsening of symptoms, with or without medical intervention (figure 7.2). Much less frequently, intervention arrests or successfully controls the manifestations of the disease.

Even where there is relative constancy, however, there may also be change: change relating to the psychological development of the child affected by a disease. As with change in disease state or the use of health services, the body of knowledge pertinent to this phenomenon draws heavily on retrospective or cross-sectional studies. Even the classical cohort studies in Great Britain have presented only a few analyses in which the child is examined as a unit over time, so that it is possible to draw only tenuous inferences about the effects of chronic illness on psychological development.

Over the past fifty years there has been a growing literature docu-

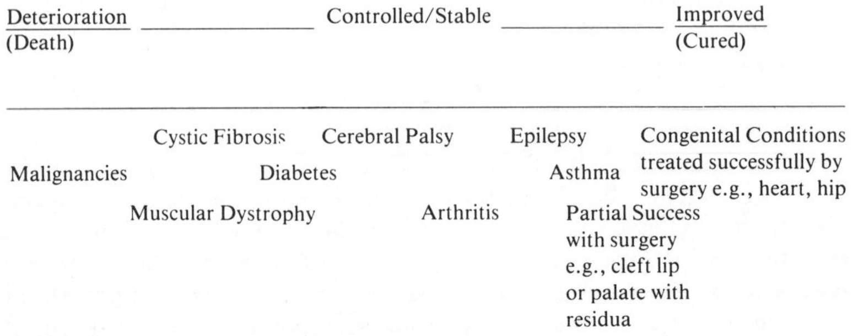

Deterioration		Controlled/Stable		Improved
(Death)				(Cured)

	Cystic Fibrosis	Cerebral Palsy	Epilepsy	Congenital Conditions
Malignancies		Diabetes	Asthma	treated successfully by surgery e.g., heart, hip
	Muscular Dystrophy		Arthritis	Partial Success with surgery e.g., cleft lip or palate with residua

Figure 7.2 *Patterns of constancy and change of selected chronic conditions. Placement of the specific conditions along the spectrum is based on general consensus rather than evidence from longitudinal studies.*

menting the extent to which psychological change occurs among children and adults as a consequence of their experience with a prolonged physical illness or disorder. The inability of these studies to firmly test the hypothesis that physical illness alone may render the child at high risk for psychological disturbance is inherent in the fundamental difficulties of research designs in which a causal sequence is postulated. Truly experimental studies in which children are randomly allocated to disease or nondisease experiences and studied both before and after the onset of the disease are inconceivable. The best that can be done to test the hypothesis is to examine populations longitudinally and to make the best possible comparisons between those who fall ill and those with similar characteristics who do not, controlling as far as possible for other determinants of psychological dysfunction. Such opportunities are infrequent, and for the present the available data must be interpreted with caution.

The basic problems of research design were recognized at the time when this approach received its greatest impetus. A critical appraisal of the literature (Barker et al., 1953) was stimulated by the increased number of persons who, as a consequence of injuries acquired during the Second World War, faced adjustment to a physical handicap. The different points of view were foreshadowed three hundred years earlier in the writings of Burton in *The Anatomy of Melancholy* and those of Sir Francis Bacon (both as cited in Barker et al., 1953, foreword to the first edition, 1946, p. v). Burton wrote that "imperfections of the body do not a whit blemish the soul, or hinder the operations of it, but rather help and much increase it." Bacon, being the better scientist of the two, was more cautious: "Deformed persons are commonly even with nature for, as nature hath done ill by them, so do they by nature, being for the most part void of natural affection, and so they have their revenge of nature."

In addition to reviewing studies, Barker provided a theoretical framework that challenged existing theories and stimulated a new generation of investigators to more searching and precise analyses of the somatopsychologic relationship. We cannot even begin to summarize the related literature published since the early fifties. We can only draw attention to this intriguing and clinically salient question—one that clearly represents another avenue in which constancy or change may be influenced by the presence of a physical illness or disability.

Perhaps one of the simplest examples of this relationship was given in an analysis of some of the psychological correlates of somatic development based on data obtained from the Oakland Growth Study (Jones, 1965). There was considerable attrition in the original sample, first studied in the mid thirties while school children, but the author provides evidence that the adult study members do not differ from the original sample in general intelligence, socioeconomic status, childhood family size, and several selected adolescent personality variables. The striking finding is that the boys in the sample whose physical maturation came early were rated as having superior physique and abilities during adolescence; by the end of high school these boys were rated as more poised, relaxed, good-natured, and unaffected. Administration of the California Personality Inventory administered at age 33 indicated a correlation between psychoneurotic scores and age of maturation, with the early-maturing group appearing to be those more often free of psychoneurotic indicators. The authors concluded that the boy whose physical development is accelerated has a social advantage, and in adulthood the same success pattern continues: he is poised, responsible, achieving in conformity with society's expectations. Whether these associations represent genetic forces or whether they are truly emotional sequelae of physical events cannot be determined from the data presented.

The psychological functioning of a group of adolescents and young adults (ages 13-23 years) was determined by the California Personality Inventory (CPI) administered to children drawn from a 1% sample of the total population of Monroe County, New York (Orr, Satterwhite, and Pless, 1977). The children had originally been studied eight years previously with a battery of other psychological measures, and it was shown that those who had *both* a chronic physical disorder and low scores on the Index of Family Functioning (Pless and Satterwhite, 1973) were at greater risk for psychological maladjustment than those with only physical disorder or poor family functioning or neither. At the time of follow-up the only important predictor of abnormal CPI scores appeared to be the Family Functioning Index scores; those with low scores were more frequently those with abnormal CPI results.

This study also indicated the degree to which the heterogeneous chronic disorders were themselves subject to change. Of the 144 in the original sample of 208 who were successfully traced, 63% of those classified as having a moderate or severe chronic physical disability eight years previously were similarly classified in 1976. Of the less disabled group (those classified as having mild disabilities), 32% were unchanged or worse, and of those with no disability in 1968 (in spite of the presence of a chronic medical condition), 45% were unchanged or worse. Included in the original study group were healthy controls, of whom nearly half had developed some type of disability during the subsequent eight-year period.

Data from the British cohort study of 1946 (Douglas, 1975) indicates the relationship of hospitalizations early in life to subsequent problems. Although the data are generally interpreted as indicating that early hospitalization is causally related to later psychosocial difficulties, it is not inconceivable that the subsequent problem may have been related to the reason for the child's initial hospitalization. This may be particularly true for instability in holding a job. Table 7.12 shows some of the findings.

An important contribution to the intriguing somatopsychological riddle is found in a large-scale retrospective study in which males over the age of 24 who had a hospital record of rheumatic fever or one of six other chronic conditions selected for purposes of comparison (diabetes, tuberculosis, orthopedic, congenital, postpoliomyelitis) were studied to determine the frequency of subsequent psychiatric illness (Wertheimer, 1963). The records of all mental hospitals in New York and Colorado were searched for evidence that psychiatric therapy had been provided to those with a chronic illness or to a matched group of healthy controls. Nearly 600 cases from New York and over 2,000 cases from Colorado were studied. Those children with a chronic disorder during childhood indeed had a higher frequency of psychiatric illness than either the healthy controls or their siblings. The average rate of what was described as functional (as opposed to organic) psychiatric disorder between the ages 12 and 24 years was 2% among the controls and 4% among those with nonrheumatic chronic disorders. For siblings of children with rheumatic disease the rate was 3%, compared with 5% for those with rheumatic fever alone and 7% for those

Table 7.12. Percentage of children with problems in adolescence related to history of hospital admissions in preschool years.

	Admissions at ages 0-5				Length of stay (single admissions)		
Adverse ratings	*None*	*1*	*2*	*3 or more*	*7 days or less*	*1 week to 1 month*	*Over 1 month*
Nervous	15.7	13.1	16.2	8.8	13.0	12.4	17.0
Troublesome	14.8	17.3	21.2	41.2	15.5	19.1	21.3
Poor reading	14.0	15.4	17.9	23.8	11.6	17.4	29.5
Delinquent	12.3	16.8	10.0	19.2	13.1	20.8	25.9
Unstable job	14.5	16.3	31.6	25.9	15.6	15.0	23.8

Source: Douglas (1975).

with rheumatic chorea. The Colorado data showed the rate of psychological disorder in children with rheumatic fever alone to be 6%; those with chorea had a rate of 9%, and siblings showed a rate of 7%—more than three times the rate for the healthy controls and nearly twice that for those with nonrheumatic chronic disorders.

The author concluded that the age-specific psychiatric rates support the belief that pubertal rheumatic disease leads to mental problems. In view of the nearly threefold difference in rate of psychoneurotic disorder when those with nonrheumatic chronic disorders are compared with controls (1.3% versus 0.5%), the results also support a more generic interpretation along the lines suggested by the somato-psychologists, who maintain that the presence of a physical limitation predisposes to psychological problems. Numerous other smaller-scale studies, dealing with either single specific disorders (notably hemophilia, diabetes, or cystic fibrosis) or with categories of disorders (locomotor, nervous system, or special senses), conclude that there is an increased risk of maladjustment following the onset of a chronic physical disorder in childhood (Pless and Pinkerton, 1975). However, some important studies fail to demonstrate such an association. While both camps can be faulted on methodologic grounds, it is likely that the truth lies somewhere between, that subgroups of the chronically ill child population, representing those with special combinations of risk factors, are those most likely to eventually manifest elevated rates of maladjustment.

Clues to the importance of conditions starting in childhood can be obtained by looking for antecedents of conditions found in adults. In the Selective Service rejection study (Densen et al., 1970), 8% of individuals with one or more specific physical problems in childhood (visual defects, cardiac defects, asthma, hay fever, orthopedic defects, major injuries) were rejected by the Selective Service primarily for mental cause, compared with a rejection rate of less than 1% for individuals with no childhood problems. Conversely, 25% of individuals with childhood behavioral problems were rejected by the Selective Service primarily for physical causes ("medical rejection"), compared with a medical rejection rate of 17% for individuals with no childhood problems indicated on their school records. These findings highlight the relationship between childhood physical illness and subsequent mental problems.

A survey of a representative population of adults in an Australian community illustrates the relationship between physical and psychological morbidity using a cross-sectional approach (Andrews, Schonell, and Tennant, 1977). Although such a design leaves unanswered all the questions about the direction of the relationship, this study at least provides a clear estimate of the strength of the association. A simple random sampling of households identified 863 adults aged 20-69 years. Each of the central measures of physical, psychological, and social morbidity were carefully validated. The 0.37 correlation between physical illness and psychological impairment is higher than any of the other relationships examined and is significant at the *p* less than 0.001 level. Of the 46% of the population who reported one or more chronic physical conditions, 14% were also judged to be psychiatrically impaired. However, 24% of the entire population was so judged, and accordingly it may be concluded that psychiatric impairment associated with chronic illness contributes about 58% of all adult mental illness. As the authors caution, this overlap could be an artifact, but after examining several possible sources of bias they conclude that the most likely explanation is that "psychological disability is closely related to the stress of adapting to current life events" and that "prior physical illnesses, both major and minor, has been shown to be among the most significant of life events which predate psychological illness" (p. 328).

A final cautionary note for readers who interpret this discussion as suggesting that chronic disease in childhood may "explain" (in a statistical sense) a substantial part of the riddle of adult mental illness: This is clearly not the case. A longitudinal follow-up study of children with emotional disorders studied in young adulthood (Robins, 1966, pp. 155-156) illustrates the small part played by preceding physical illness in the panorama of adult psychiatric illness. Of the children eventually diagnosed as displaying signs of sociopathic personality during adulthood, a small (but nonetheless disproportionate) percentage had a history of physical defect (37%) or chronic illness (24%) during childhood, and twice as many of these children, as compared with controls (28% versus 14%) chosen from school records, had three or more accidents.

In summary, there is evidence—albeit inconclusive—that one form of change that appears to be more common among those with a chronic physical disorder in childhood than among those who were physically healthy is the change from normal to abnormal emotional or psychosocial functioning. The links are undoubtedly more complex than most investigators realize. Nonetheless, if one examines the accumulated evidence and searches for some common threads, several clues emerge. Characteristics of the disease (such as age of onset, manner of progression, prognosis, type of disability created, and severity of the sociopsychologic and medical disability) clearly have an important but not independent effect on psychological outcomes. The biologic stress created by manifestations of the underlying disease

must be considered in the context of the child's premorbid characteristics, intelligence, personality, coping style, and other special assets,
as well as those of the family. Eventually it may be possible to demonstrate that the family, serving as a buffer against the many stresses
generated by the demands of the illness, is the key link in the chain
that determines whether coping will be effective in diminishing the
likelihood of later psychological sequelae. If this could be demonstrated satisfactorily the implications would be enormous. From the
perspective of constancy and change, findings that bear on relations
between systems, in this case between the physical and the emotional,
provide more accurate and realistic models for the way people function than those in which each element is artifically separated and
examined in isolation.

Many individual children who are sick early in life later become
well and, conversely, many who are well become sick. This observation is not new; it is embodied in the concepts of acute illness and
chronic illness. Acute illnesses are brief, self-limited, or amenable to
treatment, so they generally produce no sequelae. Chronic illnesses are
usually defined as those that persist for at least three months, often
longer and sometimes for a lifetime. If we had examined all chronic
illnesses, which take up the bulk of pediatric textbooks, much more
constancy in the extent of physical health would have been apparent.
Instead we stressed the acute illnesses. There is little point to reviewing
data on typical chronic illness (cystic fibrosis, congenital rubella,
hemophilia, and the like) because they are known to persist and generally to reduce life expectancy. Therefore we addressed the issue
whether illnesses *not* known to persist do, in fact, tend to persist. The
emphasis on acute conditions also explains why it may appear that
more sick children get well over time than well children get sick. Acute
illnesses are very common early in life and become less common with
aging. The reverse is the case with chronic illness. Overall, the magnitude of the health burden increases progressively with age, whether
measured by person-years of illness or extent of physical disability.

Apart from their heuristic value, constancy and change are useful
concepts only if they make it easier to develop rational solutions to
health problems. To convert the findings from these diverse studies
into a potentially useful health planning framework, we may find the
epidemiologic concepts of relative risk and attributable risk helpful.
Relative risk is the extent to which current status determines subsequent status; it is a prospective view. Attributable risk represents the
retrospective view by examining the extent to which a group with a
particular health status had one or more characteristics earlier in life.

The evidence indicates that those who have some of the conditions early in life contribute disproportionately to those having it later (high relative risk). For other conditions, those individuals having the condition later are more likely to have had a predisposing or related condition earlier than might occur by chance alone (high attributable risk). For some conditions, there is both high relative risk and high attributable risk.

Table 7.13 summarizes the findings of studies presented in this chapter within the framework of relative and attributable risk. Because many of the studies are relatively crude and incomplete, this classification should be considered tentative rather than definitive. In terms of developing a rational policy, the important questions are the following.

1. Can individuals with current derangements in health be identified? If so, could or should anything be done if
    a. The derangements are self-limited? If conditions are self-limited, they have a low relative risk: justification

Table 7.13. Common conditions and states with high relative risk or attributable risk.[a]

High relative risk		Low relative risk	High attributable risk
Morbid conditions	Morbid states		
Obesity	School absence due to illness	Convulsions	Enuresis
Uncorrected visual defects	Use of medications		Hearing problems
Cardiac conditions	Restricted physical activity		Respiratory problems
Asthma	Use of medical services		Walking problems
Hay fever (?)	Placement in a special health class		Behavior problems
Major injuries			Urinary tract infections
Severe neurologic and sensory defects			Neurosensory conditions associated with pre- and perinatal insult
Respiratory illnesses			
Behavior problems			
Hypertension			
Otitis media			

a. Categorizations should be considered tentative, as data to quantitate risk are, for the most part, not available.

for intervention would depend primarily on the degree of current impairment.

b. The derangements are not self-limited? If the conditions are not self-limited they have a high relative risk. Justification for intervention here should be related to the degree of current impairment as well as to the likelihood of preventing future impairment.

2. Can the prevalence or impact of current conditions be reduced by intervening *before* they become evident? If so, could and should anything be done if

a. The risk factors are known? These are conditions of high attributable risk and hence intervention could presumably be focused on the susceptible (high-risk) groups.

b. The risk factors are unknown? These are conditions of low attributable risk where any intervention would have to be directed at the whole population.

Our review of this field indicates that the occurrence of many conditions early in life signals problems later in life in a large minority or small majority of children. Unfortunately, it is not often possible to predict which children will suffer handicaps later in life as a result of a current condition. Moreover, a virtually unexplored issue is the extent to which social class influences the relative risk of later handicap. Most conditions occur with greater frequency in individuals in the lower social classes, both in children and in adults (Fry, 1966, pp. 36, 52, 65; Davie, 1972, as cited in Richardson, Peckham, and Goldstein, 1976; Fry, 1974, pp. 47, 74; Miller et al., 1974, p. 123; Kiernan et al., 1976; Sultz et al., 1972, p. 60; Bloom, 1964, p. 184; and Birch and Gussow, 1970, p. 262). What little evidence there is suggests that the existence of many of these conditions in childhood is more likely to presage problems in adulthood in poor individuals than in the non-poor. Whether this is due to persisting environmental insults or to less access to medical care or, as seems more likely, to a combination of these, remains unclear. For some conditions (such as otitis media and associated hearing loss) the evidence strongly suggests that unequal access to effective and continuing medical care contributes heavily to the outcome (compare findings in Peckham and Sheridan, 1976, with those in Kessner, 1973). Studies carried out on middle-class populations show less constancy than those executed in representative community samples (compare Gafafer and Doull, 1933, with Tucher and Downes, 1953). The implications of the effect of social class are powerful, whether conditions are inherited or acquired and whether or not there are medical measures to prevent their occurrence or progression.

The poor are born at increased risk, they continue to be exposed to greater risk, and they are less likely to be reached by interventions that could ameliorate the effects of these risks (Birch and Gussow, 1970). In their words: "Whether or not damage is permanent must be irrelevant in the face of a deprivation which is: the same children whose mothers are ill-fed and unready for pregnancy, who are born into poverty and survive an infancy of hunger and illness, are seldom miraculously saved in the third act" (p. 262).

It is imperative that medical services be provided to detect the existence of problems at the earliest stage at which they can have an effect, especially in populations that are most vulnerable. Because it is not possible to predict exactly which children are at risk, highly targeted interventions are rarely feasible. Instead, a system of discriminating comprehensive health care that allows maximum access to available services is essential. The design of these services must stress early recognition of risk states and must provide for continuity of care over long periods of time. This approach will not only abort serious clinical problems early but will provide better knowledge about the natural progression of disease and its determinants that is so evidently lacking at the present.

Notes

1. There are many publications from these studies. Representative is Pless and Douglas (1971).

2. In all tables, expected values are calculated by assuming that individuals would be distributed in the different categories as they are distributed in the population if no factor other than chance were influencing their distribution otherwise.

3. For tables 7.5-7.7 the proportion of the children who fell in the low, intermediate, and high groups in each of the three age periods was calculated. Because the divisions were made such that approximately one-third of the children were in each, these proportions were close to one-third. There were three age periods, and each had three possibilities (low, intermediate, and high), so there were 27 possible combinations. To calculate the expected value for each combination, the probabilities of occurrence of each of the three were multiplied to determine the probability of the combination of the three. For example, in the Berkeley data the probability of being in the lowest third in the first age period (0-2) was 900/2,875 or 31%; the probability of being in the lowest third in the second age period (3-5) was 977/2,875 or 34%; and the probability of being in the lowest third in the third age period (6-9) was 953/2,875 or 33%. Therefore the probability of being LLL was $0.31 \times 0.34 \times 0.33 = 0.035$, and the number of children expected to have LLL patterns if chance

alone determined the distribution is 0.035 × 2,875, or 101. To determine the probability of constancy, the probabilities of LLL, HHH, and MMM were added. Determination of the probabilities of markedly changing patterns and moderately changing patterns in tables 7.6 and 7.7 was similarly obtained by summing the patterns defined as showing marked or moderate change, respectively.

References

ANDREWS, G., SCHONELL, M., and TENNANT, C. 1977. The relationship between physical, psychological, and social morbidity in a suburban community. *American Journal of Epidemiology* 105:324-329.

AVERY, A. D., LELAH, T., SOLOMON, N., HARRIS, J., BROOK, R., GREENFIELD, S., WARE, J. E., JR., and AVERY, C. 1976. *Quality of medical care assessment using outcome measures: eight disease-specific applications.* Santa Monica, Ca.: Rand, Pub. no. R-2021/2-HEW.

BARKER, R. G., WRIGHT, B. A., MEYERSON, L., and GONICK, M. R. 1953. *Adjustment to physical handicap and illness: a summary of the social psychology of physique and disability.* New York: Social Science Research Council.

BILLE, B. 1973. The prognosis of migraine in childhood. *Acta Paediatrica Scandinavica* Supp. 236:38.

BIRCH, H. G., and GUSSOW, J. D. 1970. *Disadvantaged children: health, nutrition and school failure.* New York: Harcourt, Brace and World.

BLOOM, B. S. 1964. *Stability and change in human characteristics.* New York: John Wiley.

BROWN, G. W., and DAVIDSON, S. 1978. Social class, psychiatric disorder of mother, and accidents to children. *Lancet* 1:378-380.

BUCK, C. W. 1973. The persistence of elevated blood pressure first observed at age 5. *Journal of Chronic Diseases* 26:101-104.

BURROWS, B., LEBOWITZ, M., and KNUDSON, R. 1977. Epidemiologic evidence that childhood problems predispose to airways disease in the adult (an association between adult and pediatric respiratory disorders). *Pediatric Research* 11:218-220.

CIOCCO, A. 1945. Physical growth in childhood and military fitness. *American Journal of Public Health* 35:927-933.

CORNONI-HUNTLEY, J. 1977. Personal communication.

DENSEN, P. M., SHAPIRO, S., and EINHORN, M. 1959. Concerning high and low utilizers of service in a medical care plan, and the persistence of utilization levels over a three-year period. *Milbank Memorial Fund Quarterly* 37: 217-250.

DENSEN, P. M., ULLMAN, D., JONES, E., and VANDOW, J. 1970. Childhood characteristics as indicators of adult health status. *Public Health Reports* 85:981-996.

DINGLE, J. H., BADGER, G. F., and JORDAN, W. S., JR. 1964. *Illness in the home: a study of 25,000 illnesses in a group of Cleveland families.* Cleveland, Ohio: Case Western Reserve University Press.

DODGE, W. F., WEST, E. F., and TRAVIS, L. B. 1974. Bacteriuria in school children. *American Journal of Diseases of Children* 127:364-370.

DOUGLAS, J. W. B. 1975. Early hospital admissions and later disturbances of behavior and learning. *Developmental Medicine and Child Neurology* 17: 456-480.

———— 1977. Personal communication.

FOGELMAN, K. R., ed. 1976. *Britains sixteen year olds*. London: National Children's Bureau.

FRENCH, F. E., CONNOR, A., BIERMAN, J., SIMONIAN, K., and SMITH, R. 1968. Congenital and acquired handicaps of 10 year olds: report of a follow-up study. *American Journal of Public Health* 58:1385-1395.

FRY, J. 1966. *Profiles of disease*. Edinburgh and London: E & S Livingstone

———— 1974. *Common diseases: their nature, incidence, and care*. Philadelphia: J. B. Lippincott.

FRY, J., DILLANE, J. B., JONES, R. F., MCNAB KALTON, G., and ANDREW E. 1969. The outcome of otitis media. *British Journal of the Preventive Society of Medicine* 23:205-209.

GAFAFER, W., and DOULL, J. 1933. Stability of resistance to the common cold. *American Journal of Hygiene* 18:712-726.

GARSON, A., WILLIAMS, R. B., and WRECKLESS, J. 1974. Long-term follow-up of patients with tetralogy of fallot: physical health and psychopathology. *Journal of Pediatrics* 85:429-433.

GORDIS, L. 1973. *Epidemiology of chronic lung diseases in children*. Baltimore, Md.: Johns Hopkins University Press.

HADDON, W., SUCHMAN, E., and KLEIN, D. 1964. *Accident research: methods and approaches*. New York: Harper and Row.

HARRISON, R. M., and TAYLOR, D. C. 1976. Childhood seizures: A 25-year follow-up social and medical prognosis. *Lancet* 1:948-951.

HIROHATA, T., MACMAHON, B., and ROOT, H. F. 1967. The natural history of diabetes. I: Mortality. *Diabetes* 16:875-881.

HOWARTH, C. I., ROUTLEDGE, D. A., and REPETTO-WRIGHT, R. 1974. An analysis of road accidents involving child pedestrians. *Ergonomics* 17(3): 319-330.

JOHNSON, A. L., CORNONI, J., CASSEL, J., TYROLER, H., HEYDEN, S., and HAMES, C. 1975. Influence of race, sex, and weight on blood pressure behavior in young adults. *American Journal of Cardiology* 35:523-530.

JONES, M. C. 1965. Psychological correlates of somatic development. *Child Development* 36:899-911.

KESSNER, D. M. 1973. *Assessment of medical care for children*. Contrasts in Health Status, vol. 3. Washington, D.C.: Institute of Medicine, Panel on Health Services Research.

KIERNAN, K. E., COLLEY, J. R. J., DOUGLAS, J. W. B., and REID, D. D. 1976. Chronic cough in young adults in relation to smoking habits, childhood environment, and chest illness. *Respiration* 33:236-244.

KUNIN, C. M. 1970. The natural history of recurrent bacteriuria in school girls. *New England Journal of Medicine* 282:1443-48.

———— 1976. Urinary tract infections in children. *Hospital Practice* 11(3):91-98.

KUZEMKO, J. 1976. *Asthma in children*. Baltimore, Md.: University Park Press.

LARSSON, Y., and STERKY, G. 1962. Long-term prognosis in juvenile diabetes mellitus. *Acta Paediatrica* (Suppl. 130)51:1-76.

LIEBERMAN, E. 1974. Hypertension in children and youth. *Journal of Pediatrics* 85:1-11.

LOGGIE, J. M. H. 1977. Prevalence of hypertension and distribution of causes. In M. I. New and L. S. Levine, eds., *Juvenile hypertension*. New York: Raven Press.

McKINLAY, J. B. 1972. Some approaches and problems in the study of the use of services: an overview. *Journal of Health and Social Behavior* 13:115-152.

MANHEIMER, D., and MELLINGER, G. 1967. Personality characteristics of the child accident repeater. *Child Development* 38:491-513.

MILLER, F. J. W., COURT, S. D. M., KNOX, E. G., and BRANDON, S. 1974. *The school years in Newcastle upon Tyne*. London: Oxford University Press.

MONGEAU, J. G., BRON, P., and BERTRAND, D. 1977. Familial aggregation of blood pressure and body weight. In M. I. New and L. S. Levine, eds., *Juvenile hypertension*. New York: Raven Press.

NELSON, K., and ELLENBERG, J. 1978. Prognosis in children with febrile seizures. *Pediatrics* 61:720-726.

NIELSON, J., and TSUBOI, T. 1970. Correlation between stature, character disorder, and criminality. *British Journal of Psychiatry* 116:145-150.

ORR, D. P., SATTERWHITE, B., and PLESS, I. B. 1977. Psychosocial effects of chronic illness in adolescents: a follow-up. Paper presented to the Society for Adolescent Medicine.

PAINE, R. S. 1962. On the treatment of cerebral palsy: the outcome of 177 patients, 74 total untreated. *Pediatrics* 29:605-616.

PECKHAM, C. 1973. A national study of child development. *Proceedings of the Royal Society of Medicine* 66:701-704.

PECKHAM, C. S., and SHERIDAN, M. D. 1976. Follow-up at 11 years of 46 children with severe unilateral hearing loss at 7 years. *Child: Care, Health, and Development* 2:107-111.

PLESS, I. B. 1968. Epidemiology of chronic disease. In M. Green and R. Haggerty, eds., *Ambulatory pediatrics*. Philadelphia: W. B. Saunders Co.

PLESS, I. B., and DOUGLAS, J. W. B. 1971. Chronic illness in childhood. Part I: Epidemiological and clinical characteristics. *Pediatrics* 47:405-414.

PLESS, I. B., and PINKERTON, P. 1975. *Chronic childhood disorder and promoting patterns of adjustment*. London: Henry Kimpton.

PLESS, I. B., and SATTERWHITE, B. 1973. A measure of family functioning and its application. *Social Science and Medicine* 7:613-621.

RAVELLI, G.-P., STEIN, Z. A., and SUSSER, M. W. 1976. Obesity in young men after famine exposure in utero and early infancy. *New England Journal of Medicine* 295:349-353.

RICHARDSON, K., PECKHAM, C. S., and GOLDSTEIN, H. 1976. Hearing levels of children tested at 7 and 11 years: a national study. *British Journal of Audiology* 10:117-123.

ROBERTS, D. E., BASCO, D., SLOME, C., GLASSER, J., and HANDY, G. 1969. Epidemiologic analysis in school populations as a basic change in school nursing practice. *American Journal of Public Health* 59:2157-67.

ROBINS, L. 1966. *Deviant children grown up*. Baltimore, Md.: Williams and Wilkins.

ROONEY, J. C., and WILLIAMS, H. E. 1971. The relationship between proved viral bronchiolitis and subsequent wheezing. *Journal of Pediatrics* 79:744-747.

SILLANPAA, M. 1973. Medico-social prognosis of children with epilepsy. *Acta Paediatrica Scandinavica* (Supp. 237):3-104.

STARFIELD, B. 1974. Measurement of outcome: a proposed scheme. *Milbank Memorial Fund Quarterly, Health and Society* 52(1):39-50.

——— 1977. *Middle ear infection*. Harvard Child Health Project, vol. 2. Cambridge, Mass.: Ballinger Publishing Company.

STEINWACHS, D. M., and YAFFE, R. 1974. Developing patterns of primary care: relationships of patterns, process, criteria, and resources. Paper presented at the Operations Research Society of America, Las Vegas, Nevada, November.

STUART, H. C. 1939. Studies from the Center for Research in Child Health and Development, School of Public Health, Harvard University. I: The Center, the group under observation, sources of information, and studies in progress. *Monograph of the Society for Research in Child Development* 4: serial 20, no. 1.

SULTZ, H. A., SCHLESINGER, E. R. MOSHER, W., and FELDMAN, J. G. 1972. *Long-term childhood illness*. Pittsburgh, Pa.: University of Pittsburgh Press.

TASK FORCE ON BLOOD PRESSURE CONTROL IN CHILDREN. National Heart, Lung and Blood Institute. 1977. *Pediatrics* (Suppl.)59(5):797-820.

TUCHER, D., and DOWNES, J. 1953. Disability from respiratory illness. *Milbank Memorial Fund Quarterly* 31:141-148.

U. S. DEPARTMENT OF HEALTH, EDUCATION, AND WELFARE. National Center for Health Statistics. 1971. *Series 11*, no. 108.

U. S. DEPARTMENT OF HEALTH, EDUCATION, AND WELFARE. National Center for Health Statistics. 1972. *Series 11*, no. 114.

U. S. DEPARTMENT OF HEALTH, EDUCATION, AND WELFARE. National Center for Health Statistics. 1977. *Series 10*, no. 114.

U. S. DEPARTMENT OF HEALTH, EDUCATION, AND WELFARE. National Center for Health Statistics, Division of Analysis. 1974. *Statistical data prepared for the Child Health Task Force*, table B5.

U. S. DEPARTMENT OF HEALTH, EDUCATION, AND WELFARE. National Center for Health Statistics. Vital and Health Statistics. 1973. Examination and health history findings among children and youths 6-17 years. *Series 11*, no. 129.

U. S. DEPARTMENT OF HEALTH, EDUCATION, AND WELFARE. National Center for Health Statistics. Vital and Health Statistics. 1976. Advance data HRA 77-1250, no. 1, October 18.

VALADIAN, I., STUART, H., and REED, R. 1959. Patterns of illness experiences.

Pediatrics 24:941-971.

VAN DEN BERG, B. J. 1977. Personal communication.

VAN VOLKENBURGH, V. S., and FROST, W. H. 1933. Acute minor respiratory diseases prevailing in a group of families residing in Baltimore, Maryland 1928-30. *American Journal of Hygiene* 17:122-153.

WADSWORTH, M. E. J., and JARRETT, R. J. 1974. Incidence of diabetes in the first 26 years of life. *Lancet* 2:1172-74.

WEIL, W. B. 1977. Current controversies in childhood obesity. *Journal of Pediatrics* 91:175-187.

WERNER, E. E., BIERMAN, J. M., and FRENCH, F. E. 1971. *The children of Kauai.* Honolulu, Hawaii: University of Hawaii Press.

WERTHEIMER, N. M. 1963. A psychiatric follow-up of children with rheumatic fever and other chronic diseases. *Journal of Chronic Diseases* 16:223-237.

WILKINSON, P. W., PARKIN, J. M., PEARLSON, J., PHILIPS, P. R., and SYKES, P. 1977. Obesity in childhood: a community study in Newcastle-upon-Tyne. *Lancet* 1:350-352.

WORLD HEALTH ORGANIZATION. 1974. Study of atherosclerosis precursors in children. CVD/74.4.

ZINNER, S. H., MARTIN, L. F., SACHS, F., ROSNER, B., and KASS, E. H. 1974. A longitudinal study of blood pressure in childhood. *American Journal of Epidemiology* 100:437-442.

8 | The Course of Schizophrenic Psychosis
Michael J. Goldstein

SCHIZOPHRENIA, in its typical form, rarely appears early in life, so there is little point in tracing its development from birth. Most instances of schizophrenia first appear in late adolescence or early adulthood; thus a different class of developmental issues is relevant than in studies where earlier and later behavior are highly similar. The behavioral precursors of schizophrenia do not necessarily resemble those behaviors that define the adult form of the disorder. There are three broad developmental issues. First, is there evidence for a continuity of development of schizophrenia? Specifically, do behavior attributes observable during childhood or adolescence distinguish the potential schizophrenic from his peers? Second, once a schizophrenic episode has occurred, what changes can be noted over the life span in form and severity of the psychosis? A corollary of this question relates to factors that might be predictive of these variations in the course of the disorder. Third, have recent innovations in the treatment of the psychoses altered the developmental course of psychotic behavior? Do recent developments in pharmacological and psychosocial therapies increase the likelihood of symptomatic remission and social adaptation of schizophrenic patients?

The voluminous literature on schizophrenia could easily demand a separate volume for each of these questions. However, to summarize the more recent state of knowledge for the nonspecialist only representative publications are cited, preference is given to more recent literature, and prospective longitudinal studies receive greater emphasis than retrospective ones. For a more comprehensive review of the earlier literature see the work by Willy Mayer-Gross, Eliot Slater, and Martin Roth (1969).

Schizophrenia has been defined as "a group of disorders manifested by characteristic disturbances of thinking, mood and behavior. Disturbances in thinking are marked by alterations of concept formation which may lead to misinterpretation of reality and sometimes to delusions and hallucinations, which frequently appear psychologically self-protective. Corollary mood changes include ambivalent, constricted, and inappropriate emotional responsiveness and loss of empathy with others. Behavior may be withdrawn, regressive, and bizarre. The schizophrenias, in which the mental status is attributable primarily to a *thought* disorder, are to be distinguished from the major affective illnesses which are dominated by a *mood* disorder" (DSM II, *The Diagnostic and Statistical Manual*, American Psychiatric Association, 1968, pp. 33-35).

This description attempts to delineate the attributes of schizophrenic psychoses and to distinguish them from those of the other major functional psychotic group, the affective disorders (manic-depressive psychosis). This distinction began with the great German psychiatrist Emil Kraepelin, who made it on the basis of differences in continuity over time. Kraepelin believed that schizophrenia resulted in eventual deterioration (dementia) while manic-depressive disorders remitted to preillness levels of social and cognitive functioning. Despite this attempt to differentiate syndromes, studies on the reliability of this broad criterion of schizophrenia (Beck et al., 1962; Kaelbling and Volpe, 1963; Sandifer, Pettus, and Quade, 1964; Schmidt and Fonda, 1956) have been disappointing. These studies used either outpatients or newly admitted hospital patients, among whom the proportion of labeled schizophrenics was relatively low. The probability that two psychiatrists would assign the same diagnosis in the four studies was 53%, 60%, 74%, and 84% respectively. Therefore, much effort has recently been expended in establishing reliable and operationally defined criteria for schizophrenia and manic-depressive disorders (Zubin, 1969; Strauss and Carpenter, 1974; Spitzer, Endicott, and Robins, 1977). These efforts have been designed to clarify the behavioral criteria for diagnosis so that the path between recording of symptoms and diagnostic classification is clearly specified. Examples of one such effort can be seen in appendixes 8.1 and 8.2. Here, diagnostic categories require the presence of key symptoms, which have existed for a minimum length of time and do not coexist with key symptoms of some other known disorder.

One recurring diagnostic issue relates to a syndrome termed schizo-affective disorders, in which a combination of schizophrenic and affective symptoms are observed. One cross-national study

(Cooper et al., 1969) strongly suggests that such behavior patterns are likely to be diagnosed schizophrenic in the United States and manic-depressive in the United Kingdom. Thus attempts to compare rates of recovery from schizophrenia internationally may be hazardous, for the schizo-affective patients—who generally have a better prognosis than other schizophrenic patients—may be included in the statistics for affective disorders in one country and in the schizophrenias in another. The Cooper study verified that a much narrower criterion of schizophrenia has been traditionally used in Western Europe than in the United States. In the definition of schizophrenia taken from DSM II, the central element in the diagnosis of schizophrenia is the presence of thought disorder, which is assumed to be the substrate of delusions and hallucinations. Thus under the traditional American system patients might be diagnosed schizophrenic who showed thought disorder and emotional flattening but no delusions or hallucinations. The narrower European criteria (Langfeldt, 1956; Schneider, 1959) require the presence not only of delusions and hallucinations but also of certain types of delusional or hallucinatory experiences, such as feelings that one's thoughts are being broadcast aloud, that others' thoughts are being placed in one's mind, or that one is under some external control. The definition of schizophrenia offered by Robert L. Spitzer, Jean Endicott, and Eli Robins (appendix 8.1) is a compromise between the traditional European and American conceptions of schizophrenia, but it still requires the presence of some hallucination or delusion.

Despite the development of numerous research diagnostic criteria, there is currently no single criterion for defining schizophrenia that has proven validity. John S. Strauss and Thomas E. Gift (1977) report that the number of diagnosed schizophrenics in a cohort of 272 first lifetime admission cases ranged from 68% to 4% depending on the diagnostic criteria used. They recommend that future researchers collect diagnostic data to allow patients to be classified on all available diagnostic schema so that their relative validity can ultimately be established. While their suggestion is excellent, it does not facilitate the task of tracing the life course of schizophrenia from a literature with varying definitions of the clinical phenomenon.

Progressively narrower research criteria are being developed to define schizophrenia and manic-depressive disorders as entities, leaving many patients between criteria. Ultimately, our understanding of precursors of these disorders and their courses will have to deal with cases that fail to match the diagnostician's ideal template. Ironically, studies searching for etiological clues find that a broad spectrum (the so-called schizophrenia spectrum of disorders consisting of schizophrenia, borderline schizophrenia, schizoid and inadequate personality) of psychopathology is related, whether the search is for genetic (Kety et al., 1968) or familial transmission (Goldstein et al., 1978).

Developmental Precursors

In one sense, a review of behavioral precursors of schizophrenia is inappropriate at this time. Many studies of a prospective nature likely to provide substantial information about precursors are still under way. (For an excellent summary of the issues involved and studies in progress see Norman Garmezy's comprehensive review, 1974a, 1974b, of what has been termed *high-risk research.*) The systematic collection of data before the onset of psychosis will do much to clarify the natural history of the disorder. Still some emerging trends are worthy of note.

The signs and symptoms of schizophrenia represent a major departure from previous functioning. The altered states of consciousness, severe withdrawal, and distorted sensory experiences of the acute episode usually appear over a relatively brief period of a few days or a week. It is natural to ask whether there are earlier signs of the disorder or its precursors that might permit the identification of the potential schizophrenic person. Such identification has important practical implications for early identification and intervention and may ultimately be useful in evaluating etiological theories of the disorder. In this section we shall examine evidence for behavioral attributes which discriminate the potential schizophrenic from his peers, attributes which are sufficiently removed in time from the schizophrenic episode itself to be clearly discriminable from the prodromal phases of the psychotic process. We shall not consider evidence for early signs of neurobiological deficit in pre-schizophrenics as an excellent comprehensive review of this subject has recently appeared (Fish, 1977).

The search for continuity can be pursued from several theoretical positions. The psychological theorist searches for early signs of inadequacy or incompetence forming a continuous and progressive line of social maladaption and culminating in a schizophrenic breakdown. The genetic theorist, on the other hand, may view these same behaviors as subclinical manifestations of the penetrance of the gene for schizophrenia. A search for continuity does not require a choice between these models but merely a quest for empirical regularities. This chapter pursues this quest without theoretical bias as to the ultimate significance of the trends. The search for such continuities has involved a series of questions.

Are potential schizophrenic children discriminably different from other children prior to the onset of their clinical symptoms? The answer to this question involves issues such as the age at which such differences are observable and whether they are discriminable from behavior patterns associated with other forms of psychopathology. Most available data are derived from retrospective studies in which people identified as adult schizophrenics are followed back to early signs of behavioral uniqueness. Typically, these follow-back studies have looked at school records and clinic records for behavioral precursors. In school records investigators have sought personality attributes, such as shyness or abrasiveness, that might herald subsequent schizophrenia. In analyses of clinic records investigators have looked for patterns of childhood or adolescent psychopathology that might increase the likelihood of adult schizophrenia. Each class of retrospective study involves different sampling biases; the school record data are based on samples drawn from a population of all children enrolled in school in a particular area, while clinic record data are taken only from the subsample of children brought to the attention of mental health agencies. Since appearance at a clinic is the result of many complex factors, many children whose school records indicate behavioral disturbances do not appear at clinics during their formative years. Thus we do not know whether clinically disturbed children are always recognizable in teacher reports. Another basis for potential inconsistency between studies involves vague terminology. Shyness in school is not the same as pathological withdrawal and isolation from others seen in clinic cases. Similarly, an abrasive child is not the same as an antisocial child who is challenging the legal structure of society.

Further methodological considerations have clouded the results of analyses of school and clinic records. Often a study is designed to identify attributes that discriminate subsequent schizophrenics from normally developing individuals. Such discrimination, while it may be feasible, does not deal with the issue whether such patterns are precursors of schizophrenia or are as likely to appear in the life history of other psychopathological groups. If we are to understand the critical events in the developmental progression toward schizophrenia, it is helpful to delineate schizophrenia from life courses linked to other patterns of psychopathology.

Many retrospective studies of adult schizophrenics have assumed that a single pattern discriminates potential schizophrenics from other groups. Most studies, especially those designed to test whether schizophrenics manifest schizoid personalities in their earlier premorbid years, present mean differences between future schizophrenics and other life course groups. This search for developmental uniformity ignores a well-established literature relating measures of premorbid psychosocial adjustment to prognosis (Garmezy, 1970). These studies reveal that a wide variation exists within schizophrenic samples in social relationships during late adolescence and early adulthood. Clearly, there is a group of schizophrenics, the so-called poor premorbid group, who show severe withdrawal and social isolation during late adolescence and in some instances in late childhood as well (Gittelman-Klein and Klein, 1969). But many schizophrenics do not manifest this type of asocial history and indicate a good premorbid history with some close peer and heterosexual relationships in adolescence. If one treats all schizophrenics as a group and searches earlier records for personality or clinical attributes that discriminate potential schizophrenics as a group from other groups, there is little likelihood of finding a coherent picture. The mean differences obtained will be a function of the percentages of schizophrenics in the original sample with good and poor premorbid histories. If poor premorbids predominate, then withdrawal may very well show up; if not, then the earlier patterns may be quite different or ambiguous at best. The data on premorbid adjustment strongly suggest that there is more than one developmental route to schizophrenia and that the pursuit of a single path may be fruitless.

Two major studies started with known samples of adult schizophrenics and matched controls and returned to earlier school record data. The study by Eli Bower, Thomas A. Shellhammer, and John M. Dailey (1960) combined school record data with retrospective perceptions from high school teachers of subsequent schizophrenics and controls. This study involved 88 male cases, 44 subsequent schizophrenics and 44 matched controls from the same classroom. These investigators found the potential schizophrenics to be discriminated from matched normal controls during high school by multiple signs of emotional and academic competence. The potential schizophrenics were described as more apathetic, submissive, and less well liked by peers. They also showed a pattern of declining grades over the high school period.

The other major analysis of school records, carried out by Norman Watt and his associates (Watt et al., 1970; Watt, 1972; and Watt and Lubensky, 1976), focused entirely on data available from cumulative records. This study, unlike that by Bower, Shellhammer, and Dailey, involved male ($n = 27$) schizophrenics and female ($n = 27$) schizophrenics and 163 matched controls. This study had the further advantage of considering records from grade school through high school. Males who subsequently became schizophrenic were discriminable from normal controls, but only on information garnered from high school records. The attributes that proved discriminating were different from those identified in the Bower study. Irritability, aggressiveness, and negativistic and defiant behavior were more common in the high school behavior of preschizophrenic males. The Watt data indicate that the control males were becoming more socialized in the classroom while the preschizophrenic males were becoming less so.

Watt identified a subsample of preschizophrenics who manifested a pattern of social withdrawal but noted that this behavior was not as common as abrasive behavior. Thus the Watt and Bower studies concur that preschizophrenic males can be discriminated from normally developing males but disagree on the discriminating attributes. Bower and his colleagues found withdrawal-apathy to be the discriminating attribute; in the Watt study withdrawal-apathy is less common than irritable-abrasive behavior. It is not clear whether differences in the sampling of schizophrenics account for these differences or whether they simply represent failure to replicate. However, a recent report by Sarnoff A. Mednick et al. (1977) from a longitudinal prospective study tends to support the Watt findings; teenagers rated as irritable and aggressive in the classroom appeared much more frequently in his subsequent schizophrenia breakdown group than in the nonbreakdown controls.

These studies suggest that two extreme patterns of social behavior may be related to subsequent schizophrenia—withdrawal-social isolation and abrasive behavior. These patterns could be distinctive developmental paths to subsequent schizophrenia and might be related to other concepts that attempt to distinguish schizophrenic subgroups retrospectively on the basis of preillness psychosocial adjustment or the process-reactive history of the disorder.

While both school record studies discriminate schizophrenics from normals, they have not indicated whether these behavior patterns are unique to schizophrenia or represent patterns of maladaptation common to several later forms of adult psychopathology.

A recurring issue in the school record literature is whether potential schizophrenics manifest lower intellectual functioning on standardized tests during their earlier years. The early reports of Ellen A. Lane and George W. Albee (1964, 1968) suggest that this is the case. More recent studies have supported these findings (Watt and Lubensky, 1976) and have indicated that the lower scores were also manifested in nonschizophrenic siblings as well. Thus schizophrenics, particularly those with gradual onset, may come from families with lower IQ offspring (Lane and Albee, 1970), but low IQ is not specific to schizophrenics, a point also made by Max Pollack, Margaret Woerner, and Donald F. Klein (1970), who found a similar pattern for adults subsequently diagnosed as having personality disorders. A particularly interesting finding of the Watt and Lubensky study was that there was little change in tested IQ of preschizophrenics over the years to support the notion of gradual intellectual deterioration preceding the onset of psychosis.

A series of studies have been carried out on samples of schizophrenic patients who were seen as children or adolescents in child guidance clinics or psychiatric hospitals. Generally the studies have either no control groups or a control group, seen at the same facility at the same time, whose members did not develop schizophrenia. In all such studies the main research question is, Given early signs of psychopathology that warrant contact with a social agency, are there certain specific precursors of subsequent adult schizophrenia?

The no-control studies (Bellack and Parcell, 1946; Friedlander, 1945; Michael, Morris, and Sorokor, 1957) have tested the hypothesis that schizophrenics show a childhood history of schizoid personality manifested by shyness and social withdrawal. Such hypothesis is not consistent with the literature on premorbid adjustment, which suggests a diversity of preillness social patterns, particularly in adolescence. Yet it remains attractive for investigators to search for a single uniform pattern of development. The results of these studies are consistent with the literature on premorbid adjustment in indicating that the majority of subsequent schizophrenics, however defined (introversion, shyness), were not described in clinic records as social isolates. Thus, while many schizophrenics are described as such in retrospective accounts elicited in premorbid adjustment studies, this is not the case for that special sample of child guidance cases seen in clinics during their formative years. Several explanations for this discrepancy are possible—social isolation becomes more intense during adolescence, withdrawn children are less likely to be brought to child guidance clinics than aggressive, irritable children—but there is no obvious way to select one of them.

Two major studies have involved well-designed control groups drawn from the population of child guidance clinic cases. David Ricks and John C. Berry (1970) report a follow-back study using the extensive case records of the Judge Baker Child Guidance Clinic. Male cases who subsequently developed schizophrenia were contrasted with clinic cases who had more favorable outcomes. Within the schizophrenic sample, cases with more chronic outcomes were contrasted with those who had been released after their initial hospitalization.

Ricks and Berry report two patterns of psychopathology observed in adolescence that were more closely associated with subsequent schizophrenic development, a withdrawn pattern and a delinquent pattern. In the delinquent pattern the acting out was directed almost exclusively *at other family members*. The characteristic pattern of delinquency in which the targets of antisocial acts generalized to extrafamilial figures was not noted. The withdrawn pattern was more likely to occur in the chronic outcome sample while the delinquent one was more common in the schizophrenics who had been released.

In the other major study of child guidance records, Lee Robins (1974) used a follow-up rather than a follow-back design. All locatable cases seen at the St. Louis Municipal Psychiatric Clinic were followed up after a thirty-year interval, well within the risk period for schizophrenia. The clinic, closely related to the St. Louis Court System, served clients referred largely for antisocial behavior (73% antisocial behavior referrals). The major purpose of this study was to trace the roots of adult sociopathy. However, a sufficient number of schizophrenic outcomes were found in the sample to permit a search for precursors of this disorder.

The clinic sample was predominantly male (75%), and most of the schizophrenics were found among that group (males 7%, females 3% of their respective samples). An unexplained finding (Robins, 1974, p. 83) is that the reverse was true for the outcomes for the matched controls who had never been seen in a clinic (no males and 8% of females subsequently manifested schizophrenia). These trends are reminiscent of the Watt study data in which preschizophrenic males manifested an abrasive pattern likely to bring them to clinical attention, while preschizophrenic females were not so obviously disturbed.

The Robins sample was subdivided into cases referred primarily for antisocial behavior and those referred for other emotional problems. The relationship to subsequent outcomes depended on the criterion measure used. If hospitalization data were used, then records of psychotic symptoms (delusions, hallucinations, bizarre behavior) were more common in the nonantisocial group. If psychiatric diagnoses based on a compilation of records and personal interviews were used as outcome criteria, then there was no difference in the incidence of diagnosed schizophrenia between antisocial (5%) and nonantisocial referral groups (7%); however, both were significantly higher than the 2% noted for the control group. Unfortunately, there was no further breakdown by sex in these data, despite the notable sex differences in rate of schizophrenia for clinic and control samples.

While the basis for referral to the clinic failed to have predictive value, most preschizophrenics (74%) manifested a significant number of antisocial behaviors but of lesser number and intensity than those manifested by the future sociopath. Robins noted that the antisocial behavior of the preschizophrenic was directed toward relatives or acquaintances, as in the Judge Baker data. Thus in their preschizophrenic, predominantly male samples, the Judge Baker and St. Louis studies support one another in revealing a pattern of aggressive disturbance—best termed "acting in"—in which the targets are family or extended family members.

Results of a Recent Prospective Study

Following the leads of the Judge Baker and St. Louis studies, Eliot H. Rodnick and Michael J. Goldstein (1974) have been carrying out a prospective longitudinal study of a cohort of disturbed adolescents from intact families, following them through the period of risk for schizophrenia. While the study focuses mainly on intrafamilial factors that relate to subsequent early adult psychopathology, the form of presenting problem has been examined as a predictor. The sample has been followed for a five-year period to date; thus they are just entering the period of risk for schizophrenia.

The presenting problems were divided into four groups.

Group I: Aggressive, Antisocial. Characterized by poorly controlled, impulsive, and acting-out behavior. Some degree of inner tension or subjective distress may be present but is clearly subordinate to the aggressive patterns that appear in many areas of functioning—family, school, peer relationships, the law.

Group II: Active Family Conflict. Characterized by a defiant, disrespectful stance toward parents, belligerence and antagonism in the family setting, and often signs of inner distress or turmoil—tension, anxiety, and somatic complaints. There are few manifestations of aggression or rebelliousness outside the family.

Group III: Passive, Negative. Characterized by negativism, sullenness, and indirect forms of hostility or defiance toward parents and other authorities. In contrast to Group II, overt defiance and temper outbursts are infrequent and there is a superficial compliance to wishes of adults. School difficulties are frequent, typically described as underachievement, and with little evidence of disruptive behavior.

Group IV: Withdrawn, Socially Isolated. Characterized by marked isolation, general uncommunicativeness, few friends, and excessive dependence on one or both parents. Gross fears or signs of marked anxiety and tension are often present. Much of their unstructured time is spent in solitary pursuits.

It was hypothesized that Groups II and IV would have higher than average risk for subsequent schizophrenia. With the use of a comprehensive interview and testing procedure at follow-up, blind diagnostic appraisals were placed on a seven-point scale originally used by Paul Wender, David Rosenthal, and Seymour S. Kety (1968) in their genetic research, in which scale points 5-7 represent what they have termed the extended schizophrenia spectrum of disorders (severe personality disorders; inadequate, schizoid, cyclothmic = 5; borderline or probable schizophrenic = 6, definite schizophrenic = 7). Lower scores reflect milder forms of psychopathology; 1 = normal, 2 and 3 = neurotic, and 4 = character disorders. The range 1-4 is considered outside the extended schizophrenia spectrum of disorders and therefore termed nonspectrum diagnoses. Table 8.1 presents the frequency of schizophrenia spectrum and nonspectrum diagnoses observed in the four behavior problem groups in a sample of 28 male cases.

The two groups hypothesized to be at greater risk, Groups II and IV, present a greater number of schizophrenia spectrum disorders at five-year follow-up, with the withdrawn, socially isolated group containing a greater number of "at risk" cases than the group characterized by the "acting-in" pattern noted by Ricks and Berry (1970) and by Robins (1974). However, while cases of borderline schizophrenia, probable schizophrenia, and schizoid personality occur in the withdrawn group, the only cases of definite schizophrenia observed so far have arisen in the active family conflict group.

These data, while only preliminary, support the notion that there

Table 8.1. The relationship between adolescent behavior problem group and five-year follow-up diagnosis for 28 male cases.[a]

	Follow-up diagnosis on 7-point scale	
Problem group	*Nonspectrum (1-4)*	*Spectrum (5-7)*
1. Aggressive antisocial	5	2
2. Active family conflict	4	4
3. Passive, negative	6	1
4. Withdrawn, isolated	2	4
Hypothesized risk groups versus nonrisk groups		
Nonrisk, 1+3	11	3
Risk, 2+4	6	8

a. $X^2 = 2.39$, p less than 0.10.

is more than one developmental route to schizophrenia. One pattern is characterized by severe isolation and few peer relationships during adolescence. The other is characterized by more aggressive behavior localized primarily within the family system.

It is often suggested that the abrasiveness noted by Watt and his associates (1970) in the school record studies conflicts with the studies that indicate a lack of genuine peer relationships among preschizophrenics. In fact, a number of withdrawn males in the prospective study were extremely abrasive, irritable, and odd in their social behavior. They often attempted to initiate social behavior with peers but were rejected, particularly during adolescence. Thus one can become very isolated because teachers and peers turn away from socially unacceptable behavior patterns such as irritability and defiance of authority.

One difficulty in relating earlier symptomatology to subsequent psychopathology is the problem of scaling severity of symptomatology. Some patterns of withdrawal or acting in are part of a constellation of very bizarre attitudes and behaviors while others exist in a context of milder maladjustment. For example, Michael J. Goldstein and James E. Jones (1977) found that when initial severity of adolescent psychopathology was scaled independent of form, a combined index of form and severity greatly sharpened the accuracy of prediction of early adult psychopathology. With the exception of the Ricks and Berry study, few attempts were made to account for the variations in severity within symptom groups so that extreme shyness and severe social isolation from peers are treated as equivalent problems of withdrawal. Possibly, inconsistencies among earlier studies arise from this failure to scale the form and severity of earlier behavior problems.

Although there are clues of behavior problems and traits that differentiate the future schizophrenic from other groups, it is not entirely clear when these attributes begin to possess reliable predictive value. Generally, studies that have relied on characteristics noted in early or middle childhood have not demonstrated continuity with early adult psychopathology. Measures obtained during adolescence (Watt, 1972), on the other hand, reveal greater continuity with later schizophrenia. Whether this result is simply an instance of superior prediction from measures obtained at adjacent time periods or a reflection of the increased demands for autonomy and personal identity in adolescence is difficult to determine. Clearly the pressures on the adolescent to attain acceptance from others may potentiate extreme variations in social behavior, behavior that can be masked by the greater capacity of the nuclear family to meet the emotional needs of the preadolescent than the adolescent. Whatever the explanation, it appears that a process of differentiation begins in adolescence and permits greater delineation of the preschizophrenic from his peers than was true for earlier developmental periods. As suggested earlier by Silvano Arieti (1955), teenage patterns of extreme social isolation or a stormy personality appear to portend greater risk for subsequent schizophrenia than other forms of adolescent psychopathology.

Sex Differences

Most of these findings apply largely to the developmental history of male schizophrenics. However, there are strong signs in the literature that there may be different life histories and precursor signs for female schizophrenics. This difference was first clearly delineated by Watt and his colleagues (1970) in their studies of school records. They found a pattern of progressive introversion for future female schizophrenics but increasing difficulties with impulse control for males.

These differences may be related to sexual status, or they may indicate different temporal courses. Since males tend to break down earlier than females, one could argue that the male patterns reflect disturbances of the immediate premorbid period while the female patterns reflect an intermediate adjustment likely to be followed by greater impulsivity and irritability in their comparable premorbid period, during early adulthood. Since the Watt data extend only through high school, the immediate premorbid period for males, data would be needed from the early twenties for females—their immediate premorbid period—to determine whether these sex differences persist through analogous premorbid stages.

Despite problems of interpretation of the school record data, there are other indications that factors heralding schizophrenic development in males may not be effective predictors for females. Mednick and his colleagues (1977), in large-scale prospective studies in Denmark, followed a large sample of adolescents—some offspring of schizophrenic mothers, others offspring of normal mothers—for ten years. In early reports of this study two factors—a history of pregnancy and birth complications and rapid recovery of skin resistance response to a loud auditory stimulus—observed at the time of adolescent testing predicted cases likely to break down in early adulthood.

In a recent report Mednick and his colleagues (1977) used path analysis (Jöreskog and van Thello, 1972) to determine the most likely direction relationships among variables ordered according to temporal sequence. Path analysis attempts to estimate the most likely causal sequence of events from data so stratified. In these path analyses, factors such as the schizophrenic mother's age of onset, social class, and degree of parent-child separation were considered in addition to complications of pregnancy and birth and a skin resistance index combining reactivity and recovery time (autonomic nervous system variable). Figures 8.1 and 8.2 present the visual representation of the path coefficients for males and females. As with correlation coefficients, the sign of the path coefficient reflects the direction of the relationship. For males there are two independent paths to subsequent schizophrenia. One path is mediated by parental separation; sons of schizophrenic mothers separated from parents at an early age were more likely to break down early in adulthood than those who had not experienced separation. The cluster of circles around the parental separation circle indicates that mothers who broke down early in life and were from lower socioeconomic backgrounds were more likely to be separated from their children. The second path for males reveals that those who had histories of birth complications also showed a combination of marked skin resistance response with rapid recovery to prestimulus level, which in turn predicted schizophrenic breakdown. Thus the data suggest that pregnancy and birth complications relate to schizophrenia through some process related to the autonomic nervous system functioning, which in turn increases the risk for subsequent schizophrenia.

However, the path lines for females are quite different (figure 8.2). It is the mother's age of onset of schizophrenia rather than the

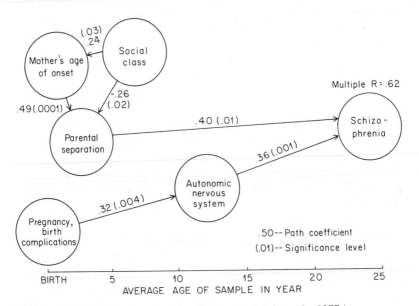

Figure 8.1. *Path diagram for men. (From Mednick et al., 1977.)*

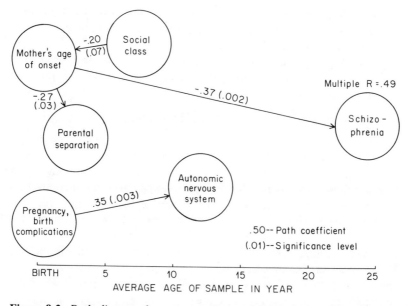

Figure 8.2. *Path diagram for women. (From Mednick et al., 1977.)*

parental separation that is linked statistically with schizophrenia. Of much greater interest is that the path between pregnancy and birth complications and the autonomic variable is still present, but the autonomic variable is no longer predictive of subsequent schizophrenia. The most potent developmental predictor for males does not work for females, and it is difficult to attribute this difference to the use of path analysis. Both the retrospective school record data and the prospective study by Mednick support the notion that these are different life courses for male and for female schizophrenics.

This review of the literature suggests the following conclusions.

1. No single path of development distinguishes the preschizophrenic child from his peers.

2. The life course of the male schizophrenic is distinguishable from that of the female schizophrenic. Males are more likely to appear overtly disturbed to teachers and peers and to appear as applicants for help from child guidance clinics.

3. The social isolation often observed in the adolescent and early adult periods before the onset of acute symptoms of schizophrenia does not appear to be correlated developmentally to shy-

ness or hypersensitivity in childhood. Instead, this isolation appears to be a consequence of abrasiveness and social awkwardness in adolescent social relationships.

4. A pattern of aggressiveness is more common in preschizophrenics than presociopaths and is restricted primarily to family members or close acquaintances.

The Longitudinal History of a Schizophrenic Psychosis

Does one remain schizophrenic once a schizophrenic episode appears, or are there variations in states of remission across the remaining life span? Unfortunately, this question is not as readily answered as one might hope. A number of methodological and conceptual issues require clarification before one examines the existing data.

Data on the long-term course of schizophrenia are available, but not all studies begin with a cohort of patients manifesting their first episodes of schizophrenia. Thus estimates of recovery likelihood are based on an amalgamation of patients who have never recovered from their first episode and are chronically ill, patients who have had multiple episodes interspersed with periods of recovery, and patients having their first episodes. Thus estimates of recovery are confounded by the mix of groups at varying developmental periods in the history of psychosis. Estimating recovery rates in this way is analogous to establishing the predictive validity of an IQ test against adult performance criteria from a cohort ranging in chronological age from 6 months to 16 years. The issue for continuity and change is the nature of the change for a cohort of patients for whom this is the first expression of the disorder. With such data we can estimate the likelihood of freedom from the disorder over the remaining life span.

A second issue is that estimates of recovery rates depend on the criterion of recovery, which ranges from the broad criterion of discharge from the hospital to the highly specific criterion of return to full social functioning. Obviously, estimates of the life course of schizophrenia will vary widely depending on the criterion, for the percentage of recovered patients will be far higher by the discharge criteria. This is a particularly critical issue since almost all schizophrenic patients are discharged from hospitals or community mental health centers but few have recovered symptomatically or socially at the time of discharge.

A third difficulty is that existing studies bridge two major epochs in the treatment of schizophrenia, the pre- and post-phenothiazine drug era. The likelihood of discharge has increased markedly in the phenothiazine era, and some studies represent cohorts preceding this era while others use cohorts from the post-phenothiazine era.

A fourth issue is that diagnosis has undergone a progressive specification and narrowing. Thus twenty or thirty years ago patients were more casually diagnosed schizophrenic than they would be today. Undoubtedly many past schizophrenic patients would be diagnosed as manic-depressive by the research diagnostic criteria of today. Because earlier studies did not specify diagnostic criteria, it is difficult to determine whether the 7% lifetime recovery rate of one study differs from the 36% of another. This is particularly critical in contrasting European and American studies, since a much stricter criterion of schizophrenia has been used in Europe and since a diagnostic differentiation between schizophrenia and schizophreniform psychosis is used by Europeans but not by American psychiatrists.

With these issues in mind, consider the available estimates. Table 8.2 presents relevant statistics from studies that focused exclusively on cohorts of first lifetime admission schizophrenics. Data from the era before drug use and social therapy are considered separately from that obtained after the advent of modern treatment methods. The earlier studies are not consistent among themselves; estimates of total recovery (complete remission of symptoms and resumption of social functioning) range from 7.1% in a study carried out on Prince Edward Island (Beck, 1968) to 30% for two separate Finnish cohorts (Niskanen and Achté, 1974). Beck's data fit more closely with those from another study from the predrug era (Morrison et al., 1973) using mixed cohorts of first- and multiple-admission patients in which only 10% of schizophrenics manifested a total recovery.

The Post-Phenothiazine, Social Therapy Era

The studies following the advent of drug treatments and psychosocial approaches coupled with increased mobilization of community resources present a more optimistic picture of resumption of normal functioning following a schizophrenic episode. The findings by John Kenneth Wing (1966) in England and by Roger C. Bland, Jack H. Parker, and Helene Orn (1976) in Canada are strikingly similar; approximately one in two first-admission schizophrenics makes adequate social recovery for the extended period (five to ten years) after the initial episode.

The Finnish studies (Niskanen and Achté, 1974) do not support such an optimistic view. They estimate an average of 40% fully recovered by the end of the follow-up period, a figure not appreciably greater than estimates derived for a 1930 cohort. What does appear dramatic in the Finnish data is the sharp reduction in the number of chronically psychotic, institutionalized schizophrenics—from 22% in the 1950 cohort to 14% in the 1960 cohort to 10% in the 1965 cohort.

Table 8.2. Outcomes for first-admission schizophrenic cohorts.

Study	n	Hospitalization era	Follow-up period	Results
		Pre-phenathiazine, social therapy era		
Achté (1961)	68	1933-1935	4 years	30% fully recovered
Beck (1968)	90	1930-1932, 1940-1942	20 years	7.1% recovered 4.8% improved 4.8% minimally improved 19.0% unimproved but discharged 64.3% continuously hospitalized
Niskanen and Achté (1972)	100	1950	5 years	37% fully recovered 22% psychotic, working 15% psychotic, not working 22% still hospitalized
		Overlapping samples		
Stephens, Weiner, and Magnum (1970)	102	1948-1951	5-10 years	36% recovered 45% improved 19% unimproved
Stephens, Weiner, and Magnum (1970)	247	1952-1958	5-10 years	24% recovered 51% improved 25% unimproved

Post-phenathiazine, social therapy era

Study	N	Year	Follow-up	Outcome
Wing (1966)	111	1956	5 years	50% recovered 25% moderately ill 25% severely impaired
Niskanen and Achté (1972)	100	1960	5 years	40% fully recovered 28% psychotic, working 13% psychotic, not working 14% hospitalized
Niskanen and Achté (1972)	100	1965	5 years	42% fully recovered 22% psychotic, working 20% psychotic, not working 10% hospitalized
Bland, Parker, and Orn (1976)	88	1963	10 years	*Psychiatric criterion* 58% fully recovered 28% recovery with residual symptoms 8% chronically hospitalized *Social adjustment criterion* 35.2% good 34.1% fair 28.4% poor

The reduction in this chronic, deteriorating form of schizophrenia in the modern treatment era accords well with the observations of Manfred Bleuler (1968) based on his twenty-three-year follow-up study. It is interesting that the two recent studies with the most optimistic outcome figures were done in countries and regions that emphasized community follow-up and care.

While status at the end of a five-year period is an important measure, it is also helpful to have some estimate of a person's likelihood of avoiding a second psychotic episode. In the Bland et al. study (1976) covering a ten-year follow-up period, approximately two-thirds of the patients were readmitted to a psychiatric hospital. In the Wing study (1966) covering a five-year period, 48% of the patients were readmitted, albeit for much shorter stays than their first admission. Thus it appears that despite the relatively optimistic figures for recovery in the modern era, the risk for subsequent breakdown after an initial episode is high.

The data in table 8.2 refer primarily to a relatively short follow-up period, and the lifetime risk for recovery from a first schizophrenic episode is difficult to determine. In the Stephens et al. study (cited in Stephens, 1970), the recovery rate for a ten-year follow-up cohort (24%) was only slightly higher than the figures for a different five-year cohort (22%). These figures in turn are similar to the 25% figure reported by Bleuler (1968) for a cohort studied over a twenty-five-year period. Thus we can estimate that a minimum of 25%-30% of first-admission schizophrenics will make a substantial recovery from their psychosis, a recovery likely to persist over much of their lives. According to the Wing and Bland et al. studies, the short-run prognosis may be higher when the combination of drugs and social therapies is aggressively pursued during and following a relatively brief inpatient period. Whether these short-term advantages affect the lifetime risk for subsequent breakdowns or ultimate recovery is not known at this time.

It has long been recognized that enormous variation exists within schizophrenic patients in their capacity for recovery. Two sets of factors have been examined extensively as predictor variables, premorbid psychosocial adjustment and the clinical picture at the time of the breakdown. There is impressive evidence that variations in preillness social relationships, particularly during late adolescence and early adulthood, are related to subsequent outcome (Phillips, 1953; Garmezy, 1970; Evans, Goldstein, and Rodnick, 1973; Gittelman-Klein and Klein, 1969). Generally these studies are consistent with the suggestion that severe withdrawal and social isolation in late adolescence form one path to schizophrenia, a path associated with poor likelihood of recovery. The pattern for the group with a more adequate premorbid history is clearly favorable but highly variable as a number of good premorbids also show chronic and unfavorable outcomes.

In the case of symptom clusters the significance of affective symptoms such as notable elation, depression, acute confusion, and fear of dying (Stephens, 1970) are consistently mentioned as favorable prognostic signs, and the presence of symptoms such as thought withdrawal, thought broadcasting, thought insertion portends poor outcomes. Since these sets of symptom attributes are often nonoverlapping in the same patient, numerous European psychiatrists (Langfeldt, 1956; Schneider, 1959) suggest that they actually reflect different disorders, termed schizophreniform (or reactive psychosis) and true schizophrenia. Unfortunately, this distinction is often based on premorbid psychosocial history as well as presenting symptoms, so that their relative significance in defining the two syndromes has not been clarified. This amalgamation of history and presenting symptoms is also true of the process-reactive distinction (Wittman, 1941) which overlaps sharply with the true schizophrenic—schizophreniform psychosis distinction. In a comprehensive review of long-term follow-up studies Stephens (1970) summarized the impressive evidence for the difference in recovery potential for true and schizophreniform psychosis (or their counterparts, process and reactive schizophrenics). These studies indicate that only an average of 6%-10% of true (or process) schizophrenics show a full recovery from a schizophrenic episode, while the recovery rate for schizophreniform (reactive) schizophrenia ranges from 30% to 40%.

The apparent replication of these trends noted by Stephens has received a jarring note from a recent study by Alan B. Hawk, William T. Carpenter, and John S. Strauss (1975) as part of the highly sophisticated International Pilot Study of Schizophrenia. In this study carefully diagnosed schizophrenic patients were classified by the symptomatic criteria for true schizophrenia of Gabriel Langfeldt (1956) and Kurt Schneider (1959) and followed for five years. Hawk and his colleagues found that the percentage of full recoveries in patients manifesting the critical signs of true schizophrenia did not differ from those lacking such signs (approximately 40% full recovery in both). Thus either drug treatment tends to limit the value of predictors derived when no effective treatment existed for schizophrenia or these variables predicted because they included psychosocial history factors in the definition of true, or process, schizophrenia.

There is much evidence that the latter explanation possesses considerable validity. Joseph H. Stephens (1977) has recently applied the Elgin Scale (Wittman, 1941) to a sample of 350 schizophrenic patients seen at the Phipps Clinic and followed for up to ten years. The Elgin Scale combines attributes of precipitating factors, symptom patterns, and premorbid psychosocial history. Stephens reports a correlation of 0.61 for the total Elgin Scale and a 3-point follow-up rating. However, when only the items that reflect psychosocial premorbid history are used as predictors, the correlation is 0.62. The addition of items reflecting precipitants or symptoms had little effect on the correlation with outcome. Preillness psychosocial history appears to be the most powerful predictor of the course of a schizophrenic psychosis.

These data are very compatible with the astute observations by Leslie Phillips (1953) that patients with good premorbid histories often reveal known precipitants because their immersion in deep love or work relationships contains the potential for major rejections or losses.

Since the end of World War II, there has been a revolution in the treatment of schizophrenia. With a strong impetus from the psychoanalytic movement, numerous attempts have been to upgrade the hospital treatment of schizophrenics through individual and group psychotherapy as well as through the development of humanistic milieu therapies. With the advent of phenothiazine drugs in the mid 1950s, a remarkable shift toward pharmacological treatment occurred, followed by a declining utilization of psychologically oriented procedures. There is still considerable controversy concerning the relative roles of pharmacological and psychosocial techniques in the treatment of schizophrenia.

During the post-World War II era the number of schizophrenic patients released from hospitals increased dramatically, a process (Stephens, 1970) that appears to have begun gaining momentum before the introduction of the phenothiazine drugs. Not only are more schizophrenic patients released from hospitals, but they are released after shorter stays (Achté, 1961) and in more favorable states of recovery (Stephens, 1970). Contrasts of first-admission schizophrenics treated before and after the advent of phenothiazine drugs (Achté, 1961; Stephens, 1970) reveal a 30% increase in recovered patients at discharge among later cohorts.

These figures, from "mirror-image" studies, have been confirmed by controlled trials (May, 1968; NIMH Psychopharmacology Collaborative Group, 1966) in which patients were randomly assigned to drug and placebo groups. As these studies show, drugs play a significant role in accelerating the likelihood and quality of recovery in a single first-admission episode. This can be seen most clearly in May's data, in which 58% of milieu-only and 65% of psychotherapy-only patients were judged successfully treated in contrast to 95% for psychotherapy plus drug and 96% for drug alone.

But it is much more difficult to estimate the role of drug treatment over the long term. Does drug use reduce the risk for subsequent episodes, or does it enhance the likelihood of full recovery? These are independent questions, worthy of closer inspection. The first question deals with the defensive role of drugs in delaying or reducing the likelihood of future relapses. It does not consider the adequacy of psychiatric or social adjustment of patients who do not relapse. The second question deals with the facilitative role of drug treatment, whether drugs accelerate recovery toward the resumption of normal social functions and interpersonal relationships.

Data concerning the first question are promising for drug treatment. Phillip R. A. May et al. (1976) in a long-term follow-up of his controlled treatment study finds that hospitalized patients treated with drugs subsequently remained unhospitalized significantly longer over a three-year postdischarge period than patients treated by milieu or psychotherapy alone.

The most carefully controlled study of maintenance treatment (Hogarty and Goldberg, 1973) found that when drug treatment was continued after discharge, relapses were significantly less (38%) in the drug-treated than in the placebo-treated (68%) groups. Thus it seems clear that initial drug treatment and subsequent maintenance therapy play an important defensive function in suppressing symptoms.

The data with regard to the facilitative role of drug treatment over the period of the life span are much less clear. In particular, the data for long-term impact of drug treatment for the first-admission patient are murky indeed. Bland, Parker, and Orn (1976) report that half of their full-recovery patients remained on drugs after discharge while the other half did not. In the Hogarty and Goldberg study of chronic patients, continued drug therapy prevented relapse but patients remained marginal in social functioning, rarely went back to work, and often stayed on welfare or disability. The large number of chronically ill patients in this study may have limited the potential for any treatment to facilitate the resumption of social role functioning. While we are just beginning to understand the role of maintenance drug programs in the long-term treatment of schizophrenia, the findings to date are supported by the clinical observations of Manfred Bleuler (1968) and Christian Astrup and Kjell Noreik (1966) that the long-term risk of disabling residual schizophrenia outcomes has been reduced slightly (8% according to the latter source) by drug treatment when compared with data from earlier treatment eras. Whereas the defensive function of drugs over the long term is reasonably well established, it appears that their facilitative role is still unclear.

Phenothiazine drugs increase the likelihood of recovery from an acute schizophrenic episode and enhance the probability of a subsequent recovery. However, there are reports (Astrup, 1975; Hüber, 1966) of an increased incidence of a syndrome during the postpsychotic phase, in German the "reine deficit," characterized by pronounced dysphoria and depletion of vital energy. This syndrome has been more prominent since the advent of phenothiazine drug treatment. Astrup (1975) and Rolf Holmboe, Noreik, and Astrup (1968) report that an increase in the number of remissions has been accompanied by an increase in the number of patients who show this reine deficit, suggesting that drug treatment alters the course and phenomenology of the schizophrenic disorder and results in a major trade-off —chronic deterioration has been reduced at the cost of a residual deficit that limits the level of ultimate recovery. Further evidence on this point comes from Astrup (1975), in which the number of "complete cures" declined from 25% to 9% in a pre- to postdrug series, and in a report by Boris M. Astrachan et al. (1974) that a substantial number of released schizophrenics treated in the drug era showed a substantial number of neurotic and somatic symptoms despite the absence of core schizophrenic symptoms. Thus the continuity of the psychosis has been broken by phenothiazine drugs but their role in generating secondary psychopathology is disquieting.

Interaction of Drug and Social Therapies

Since drugs act primarily to suppress disabling symptoms, it is natural to ask what role psychosocial agents play in the social rehabilitation of schizophrenic patients. Numerous studies of the combination of individual psychotherapy and drugs during the inpatient phase of treatment (see Schooler, 1978, for a careful review of such studies) have not been encouraging. However, attention has recently shifted to the possible interactive role of drugs and social therapies during the posthospitalization period, a critical period indeed since hospitalization itself is now measured in days rather than months or years. In one recent study (Goldstein et al., 1978) the author contrasted patients who received one of two levels of a long-acting injectable phenothiazine drug (fluphenazine enanthate), a minimal level and an adequate level, half of whom also received a crisis-oriented family therapy begun after release from a community mental health center and carried out for a six-week period. Patients who received both the adequate drug and the family therapy had no relapses over the six-week control period or by the time of a six-month follow-up contact. They also manifested a higher level of social and symptomatic functioning, at both points, than groups receiving other combinations of these variables. While there are no long-term follow-up data on these cases, the early trends imply that a combination of drugs and social therapies facilitates the recovery process.

Since good and poor premorbid schizophrenics have different life courses following a first schizophrenic break, it is natural to question whether drugs alone or in combination with social therapies alter these life courses. Stated otherwise, do modern therapies increase the likelihood of a relatively favorable life course in a good premorbid schizophrenic, or are they more likely to raise the prognostic status of a patient with a dim long-term prognosis? A recent review of this issue that focused on the hospital phase of treatment indicated no clear trend (May and Goldberg, 1978). However, the previously cited community maintenance study, combining long-acting phenothiazine and family therapy (Goldstein et al., 1978), found that both premorbid adjustment as evaluated by the UCLA Social Attainment Scale (Goldstein, 1978) and sex were related to status at the six-month follow-up. Males with a preillness history of good peer and heterosexual relationships (good premorbids) had no relapses and a good recovery independent of treatment condition, while males with histories of social isolation (poor premorbids) showed a high relapse rate and limited social recovery when given the minimal amount of drug. Good female premorbids relapsed or deteriorated clinically or socially when no family therapy was offered and showed the best outcome with the combination of adequate drug level and family therapy. Poor female premorbids paralleled the male data; they showed poor response to the low drug level independent of the therapy condition. If these data hold up over longer-term follow-up, they suggest that the continuation of phenothiazine drugs enhances the prognosis for poor-prognosis patients, while good-prognosis patients are either minimally affected or require some form of social therapy for enhanced recovery.

The Laingian position (Laing, 1967; Cooper, 1967) is that drug therapy aborts the psychotic process and thereby interferes with a long-lasting and full recovery. While the Laingian group has advanced persuasive arguments concerning the necessity for use of the psychotic experience as a voyage toward personal integration, they have provided no hard data to support the superiority of the "blow-out" center approach over conventional treatment. Mosher and Menn (1976) have set up an experimental study contrasting a minimal drug use, therapeutic living environment (Soteria House) designed according to Laingian principles with a modern-day drug-present community mental health center program composed of a brief inpatient stay and extensive aftercare in the community. Preliminary data from this study indicate that after a six-week period of treatment, both approaches were equally successful in reducing symptoms. Thus a therapeutic living environment with strong staff support for psychotic expression and minimal drug use (17% of Soteria patients received drugs, contrasted with 100% of control patients) was as effective as the community mental health center program in reducing acute symptoms. At the six-month follow-up the groups were equal in symptom levels, but the Soteria group tended to show a higher level of social functioning in terms of returning to school or work and, most significantly, in moving away from their family of origin. If these gains hold up over a longer follow-up period, this study would provide the first convincing evidence that a psychosis-expressive living environment, in which use of phenothiazine drugs is minimal, facilitates higher levels of personality integration in young schizophrenic patients than obtained with drug treatment. Naturally, the higher levels of social functioning may be due to removal from the noxious family environment, found by Leff and his associates (1976) to precipitate relapse, rather than to the specific program of Soteria House.

Summary

1. The probability of a complete recovery from a first lifetime episode of schizophrenia has increased slightly from the predrug, social therapy era to the present. The most optimistic figures (approximately 50% recovered) arise from studies in which drugs, social therapies, and community rehabilitation programs were aggressively utilized.

2. The best predictor of recovery from a first lifetime episode is some index of preillness psychosocial adaptation. More recent studies have raised doubt concerning the value of specific symptoms or symptom clusters as valid predictors of outcome.

3. The major functions of phenothiazine drugs have been to shorten the period of inpatient stay, increase the likelihood of a social recovery at discharge, and to forestall subsequent relapse when used on a maintenance basis. Their role in facilitating a complete recovery of personal and occupational functioning appears minimal.

4. The clearest achievement of modern treatment methods has been to reduce the incidence of chronic nonremitting episodes of schizophrenia. This achievement has been accompanied by a higher incidence of more phasic courses in which patients manifest a special type of affective syndrome—the reine deficit—during the post-psychotic phases between each episode.

5. Data concerning the facilitative role of social therapies combined with drugs are promising with short-term outcome criteria. There are no good data for the long-run impact of such combined treatment modes or for social therapies used alone.

Appendix 8.1 (From Spitzer, Endicott, and Robins, 1977)
Schizophrenia

There are many different approaches to the diagnosis of schizophrenia. The approach taken here avoids limiting the diagnosis to cases with a chronic or deteriorating course. It includes subjects who would not be considered schizophrenic by many, particularly those subtyped as "acute." However, the criteria are designed to screen out subjects frequently given clinical diagnoses such as: borderline schizophrenia, brief hysterical or situational psychoses, and paranoid states. Subjects with a full depressive or manic syndrome which overlaps active psychotic symptoms are excluded and are diagnosed as either schizo-affective disorder, major depressive disorder, or manic disorder. If the symptoms in A occur only during periods of alcohol or drug use or withdrawal from them, the diagnosis should be unspecified functional psychosis.

A through C are required for the period of illness being considered.

A.   During an active phase of the illness (may or may not now be present) at least two of the following are required for definite and one for probable:

1. Thought broadcasting, insertion, or withdrawal.

2. Delusions of being controlled (or influenced), other bizarre delusions, or multiple delusions.

3. Somatic, grandiose, religious, nihilistic, or other delusions without persecutory or jealous content lasting at least one week.

4. Delusions of any type if accompanied by hallucinations of any type for at least one week.

5. Auditory hallucinations in which either a voice keeps up a running commentary on the subject's behaviors or thoughts as they occur or two or more voices converse with each other.

6. Nonaffective verbal hallucinations spoken to the subject.

7. Hallucinations of any type throughout the day for several days or intermittently for at least one month.

8. Definite instances of marked formal thought disorder accompanied by either blunted or inappropriate affect, delusions or hallucinations of any type, or grossly disorganized behavior.

B. Signs of the illness have lasted at least two weeks from the onset of a noticeable change in the subject's usual condition (current signs of the illness may not now meet criterion A and may be residual symptoms only, such as extreme social withdrawal, blunted or inappropriate affect, mild formal thought disorder, or unusual thoughts or perceptual experiences).

C.   At no time during the *active* period (delusions, hallucinations, marked formal thought disorder, bizarre behavior) of illness being considered did the subject meet the full criteria for either probable or definite manic or depressive syndrome (criteria A and B under major depressive or manic disorders) to such a degree that it was a *prominent* part of the illness.

Appendix 8.2 (From Spitzer, Endicott, and Robins, 1977)
Manic Disorder (may immediately precede or
follow major depressive disorder)

This category is for an episode of illness characterized by predominantly elevated, expansive, or irritable mood accompanied by the manic syndrome. It should also be used for mixed states in which manic and depressive features occur together, or when a subject cycles from a period of major depressive disorder to a period of manic disorder, or the reverse, in which case the duration recorded should refer to the manic symptoms only. The duration of the major depressive disorder would be recorded later. Also the duration of the entire affective episode and the type of cycling is recorded later.

A.   One or more distinct periods with a predominantly elevated, expansive, or irritable mood. The elevated, expansive, or irritable mood must be a prominent part of the illness and relatively persistent although it may alternate with depressive mood. Do not include if apparently due to alcohol or drug use.

B.   If mood is elevated or expansive, at least three of the following symptom categories must be definitely present to a significant degree, four if mood is only irritable. (For past episodes, because of memory difficulty, one less symptom is required.) Do not include if apparently due to alcohol or drug use.

1. More active than usual—either socially, at work, at home, sexually, or physically restless.

2. More talkative than usual or felt a pressure to keep talking.

3. Flight of ideas or subjective experience that thoughts are racing.

4. Inflated self-esteem (grandiosity, which may be delusional).

5. Decreased need for sleep.

6. Distractibility; attention is too easily drawn to unimportant or irrelevant external stimuli.

7. Excessive involvement in activities without recognizing the high potential for painful consequences: buying sprees, sexual indiscretions, foolish business investments, reckless driving.

C.   Overall disturbance is so severe that at least one of the following is present:

1. Meaningful conversation is impossible.

2. Serious impairment socially, with family, at home, at school, or at work.

3. In the absence of (1) or (2), hospitalization.

D.   Duration of manic features at least one week beginning with the first noticeable change in the subject's usual condition (of any duration if hospitalized).

Major Depressive Disorder (may immediately precede
or follow manic disorder)

This category is for episodes of illness in which a major feature of the clinical picture is dysphoric mood or pervasive loss of interest or pleasure accompanied by the depressive syndrome. (Do not include bereavement following the loss of a loved one if all of the features are commonly seen in members of the subject's subcultural group in similar circumstances unless the design of the study calls for their inclusion.) This category is distinguished from less severe disturbances of mood which are not accompanied by the full syndrome. This category should also be used for mixed states, in which the manic and depressive features occur together, or when a subject cycles from a period of mania to a period of depression, or the reverse, in which case the duration of the major depressive disorder should refer to the depressive symptoms only (manic and hypomanic symptoms would be recorded elsewhere). If there has been cycling or a mixed state the entire affective episode should be characterized here.

A.   One or more distinct periods with dysphoric mood or pervasive loss of interest or pleasure. The disturbance is characterized by symptoms such as the following: depressed, sad, blue, hopeless, low, down in the dumps, "don't care anymore," or irritable. The disturbance must be prominent and relatively persistent but not necessarily the most dominant symptom. It does not include momentary shifts from one dysphoric mood to another dysphoric mood, such as anxiety to depression to anger, such as are seen in states of acute psychotic turmoil.

B.   At least five of the following symptoms are required to have appeared as part of the episode for definite and four for probable (for past episodes, because of memory difficulty, one less symptom is required).

1. Poor appetite or weight loss or increased appetite or weight gain (change of 1 lb. a week over several weeks or ten lbs. a year when not dieting).

2. Sleep difficulty or sleeping too much.

3. Loss of energy, fatigability, or tiredness.

4. Psychomotor agitation or retardation (but not mere subjective feeling of restlessness or being slowed down).

5. Loss of interest or pleasure in usual activities, including social contact or sex (do not include if limited to a period when delusional or hallucinating). (The loss may or may not be pervasive.)

6. Feelings of self-reproach or excessive or inappropriate guilt (either may be delusional).

7. Complaints or evidence of diminished ability to think or concentrate, such as slowed thinking, or indecisiveness (do not include if associated with marked formal thought disorder).

8. Recurrent thoughts of death or suicide, or any suicidal behavior.

C.   Duration of dysphoric features at least one week beginning with the first noticeable change in the subject's usual condition (definite if lasted more than two weeks, probable if one to two weeks).

D.   Sought or was referred for help from someone during the dysphoric period, took medication, or had impairment in functioning with family, at home, at school, at work, or socially.

Note

Preparation of this chapter was greatly assisted by NIMH Grant MH-08744 and by a grant from the Foundation for Child Development. Special thanks are due Janet Hubbard-Sonne for her assistance in the literature review.

References

ACHTÉ, K. A. 1961. The course of schizophrenic and schizophreniform psychoses. *Acta Psychiatrica et Neurologica Scandinavica* 36 (Supplement 155).

ARIETI, S. 1955. *Interpretation of schizophrenia*. New York: Robert Bruner.

ASTRACHAN, B. M., BRAUER, L., HARROW, M., and SCHWARTZ, C. 1974. Symptomatic outcome in schizophrenia. *Archives of General Psychiatry* 31: 158-160.

ASTRUP, C. 1975. Classification and prognostic aspects of schizophrenia. *Neuropsychobiology* 40: 1-32.

ASTRUP, C., and NOREIK, K. 1966. *Functional psychoses: diagnostic and prognostic models*. Springfield, Ill.: Charles C. Thomas.

BECK, A. T., WARD, K. H., MENDELSON, M., MOCK, J. E., and ERBAUGH, J. K. 1962. Reliability of psychiatric diagnoses. II: A study of consistency of clinical judgments and ratings. *American Journal of Psychiatry* 119: 315-357.

BECK, M. N. 1968. Twenty-five and thirty-five year follow up of first admissions to mental hospital. *Canadian Psychiatric Association Journal* 13: 219-229.

BELLACK, L., and PARCELL, E. 1946. The pre-psychotic personality in dementia praecox: study of 100 cases in the navy. *Psychiatric Quarterly* 20: 627-637.

BLAND, R. C., PARKER, J. H., and ORN, H. 1976. Prognosis in schizophrenia: a ten-year follow-up of first admissions. *Archives of General Psychiatry* 33: 949-954.

BLEULER, M. 1968. A 23-year longitudinal study of 208 schizophrenics and impressions in regard to the nature of schizophrenia. In D. Rosenthal and S. S. Kety, eds., *The transmission of schizophrenia*. Oxford: Pergamon.

BOWER, E., SHELLHAMMER, T., and DAILY, J. 1960. School characteristics of male adolescents who later became schizophrenic. *American Journal of Orthopsychiatry* 30: 712-728.

COOPER, D. 1967. *Psychiatry and anti-psychiatry*. London: Tavistock Publications.

COOPER, J. E., KENDELL, R. E., GURLAND, B. J., SARTORIUS, N., and FARKAS, T. 1969. Cross-national study of diagnosis of the mental disorders: some results from the first comparative investigation. *American Journal of Psychiatry* 125: 21-29 (April supplement).

EVANS, J. R., GOLDSTEIN, M. J., and RODNICK, E. H. 1973. Premorbid adjustment, paranoid diagnosis, and remission in acute schizophrenics treated in a community mental health center. *Archives of General Psychiatry* 28: 666-672.

FISH, B. 1977. Neurobiologic antecedents of schizophrenia in children. *Archives of General Psychiatry* 34: 1297-1313.

FRIEDLANDER, D. 1945. Personality development of 27 children who later become psychotic. *Journal of Abnormal and Social Psychology* 40: 330-335.

GARMEZY, N. 1970. Process and reactive schizophrenia: some conceptions and issues. *Schizophrenia Bulletin* 2: 30-74.

—— 1974a. Children at risk: the search for the antecedents of schizophrenia. Part I: Conceptual models and research methods. *Schizophrenia Bulletin* 8: 14-92.

—— 1974b. (With the collaboration of Streitman, S.) Children at risk: the search for the antecedents of schizophrenia. Part II: Ongoing research programs, issues, and intervention. *Schizophrenia Bulletin* 9: 55-125.

GITTELMAN-KLEIN, R., and KLEIN, D. 1969. Premorbid asocial adjustment and prognosis in schizophrenia. *Journal of Psychiatric Research* 7: 35-42.

GOLDSTEIN, M. J. 1978. Further data concerning the relationship between premorbid adjustment and paranoid symptomatology. *Schizophrenia Bulletin* 4, no. 2: 236-243.

GOLDSTEIN, M. J., and JONES, J. E. 1977. Adolescent and familial precursors of borderline and schizophrenic conditions. In P. Hartocollis, ed., *Borderline personality: the concept, the syndrome, the patient*. New York: International Universities Press.

GOLDSTEIN, M. J., RODNICK, E. H., EVANS, J. R., and MAY, P. R. A. 1975.

Long acting phenothiazine and social therapy in the community treatment of acute schizophrenia. In M. Greenblatt, ed., *Drugs in combination with other therapies: seminars in psychiatry*, New York: Grune and Stratton.

GOLDSTEIN, M. J., RODNICK, E. H., EVANS, J. R., MAY, P. R. A., and STEINBERG, M. 1978. Drug and family therapy in the aftercare treatment of acute schizophrenia. *Archives of General Psychiatry* 35: 1169-77.

GOLDSTEIN, M. J., RODNICK, E. H., JONES, J. E., McPHERSON, S. R., and WEST, K. L. 1978. Familial precursors of schizophrenia spectrum disorders. In L. C. Wynne, R. L. Cromwell, and S. Matthysse, eds., *The nature of schizophrenia*, New York: John Wiley and Sons, pp. 487-498.

HAWK, A. B., CARPENTER, W. T., and STRAUSS, J. S. 1975. Diagnostic criteria and five-year outcome in schizophrenia. *Archives of General Psychiatry* 32: 343-347.

HOGARTY, G., and GOLDBERG, S. 1973. Drug and sociotherapy in the aftercare of schizophrenic patients. *Archives of General Psychiatry* 28: 54-64.

HOLMBOE, R., NOREIK, K., and ASTRUP, C. 1968. Follow-up of functional psychoses at two Norwegian mental hospitals. *Acta Psychiatrica Scandinanvica* 44: 298-310.

HÜBER, G. 1966. Reine defektsyndrome und basisstadien endogener psychosen. *Fortschritte der Neurologie Psychiatrie und Ihrer Grenzgebiete* 34: 409-421.

JÖRESKOG, K. G., and VAN THELLO, M. 1972. LISREL: a general computer program for estimating a linear standard equation system involving multiple indicators of unmeasured variables. *Research Bulletin* 72-56. Princeton, N.J.: Educational Testing Service.

KAELBLING, R., and VOLPE, P. A. 1963. Constancy of psychiatric diagnoses in readmissions. *Comprehensive Psychiatry* 4: 29-39.

KETY, S. S., ROSENTHAL, D., WENDER, P. H., and SCHULSINGER, F. 1968. The types and prevalence of mental illness in the biological and adoptive families of adopted schizophrenics. In D. Rosenthal and S. S. Kety, eds., *The transmission of schizophrenia*. Oxford: Pergamon Press.

LAING, R. D. 1967. *The politics of experience*. New York: Ballantine Books.

LANE, E. A., and ALBEE, G. W. 1964. Early childhood intellectual differences between schizophrenic adults and their siblings. *Journal of Abnormal and Social Psychology* 68: 193-195.

———— 1968. On childhood intellectual decline of adult schizophrenics: a reassessment of an earlier study. *Journal of Abnormal Psychology* 73: 174-177.

———— 1970. Intellectual antecedents of schizophrenia. In M. Roff and D. F. Ricks, eds., *Life history research in psychopathology*. Minneapolis, Minn.: University of Minnesota Press.

LANGFELDT, G. 1956. The prognosis in schizophrenia. *Acta Psychiatrica Scandinavica*, Supplement 110, pp. 1-66.

LEFF, J. P. 1976. Schizophrenia and sensitivity to the family environment. *Schizophrenia Bulletin* 2: 566-574.

MAY, P. R. A. 1968. *Treatment of schizophrenia*. New York: Science House.

MAY, P. R. A., and GOLDBERG, S. C. 1978. Prediction of schizophrenics response to pharmaco-therapy. In M. A. Lipton, A. DiMascio, and K. F. Killam, eds., *Psychopharmacology: a generation of progress*. New York: Raven Press.

MAY, P. R. A., TUMA, A. H., YALE, C., POTEPAN, P., and DIXON, W. J. 1976. Schizophrenia: a follow-up study of results of treatment. *Archives of General Psychiatry* 33: 481-486.

MAYER-GROSS, W., SLATER, E., and ROTH, M. 1969. *Clinical psychiatry*, 3rd ed. Baltimore, Md.: Williams and Wilkins Company.

MEDNICK, S. A., SCHULSINGER, F., TEASDALE, T. W., SCHULSINGER, H., VENABLES, P. H., and ROCH, D. R. 1978. Schizophrenia in high risk children: sex differences in predisposing factors. In G. Serban, ed., *Cognitive defects and the development of mental illness*. New York: Brunner-Mazel, pp. 169-197.

MICHAEL, C., MORRIS, D. P., and SOROKOR, E. 1957. Follow-up studies of shy, withdrawn children. II: Relative incidence of schizophrenia. *American Journal of Orthopsychiatry* 27: 331-337.

MORRISON, J., WINOKUR, G., CROWE, R., and CLANCY J. 1973. The Iowa 500: the first follow-up. *Archives of General Psychiatry* 29: 678-682.

MOSHER, L. R., and MENN, A. Z. 1976. Dinosaur or astronaut? one year follow-up data from the Soteria Project. *American Journal of Psychiatry* 133 (8): 919-920.

NIMH PSYCHOPHARMACOLOGY SERVICE CENTER COLLABORATIVE STUDY GROUP. 1964. Phenothiazine treatment in acute schizophrenia: effectiveness. *Archives of General Psychiatry* 10: 246-261.

NISKANEN, P., and ACHTÉ, K. A. 1972. *The course and prognosis of schizophrenic psychoses in Helsinki: a comparative study of first admissions in 1950, 1960, and 1965*. Monographs from the Psychiatric Clinic of the Helsinki University Central Hospital, No. 4. Helsinki.

PHILLIPS, L. 1953. Case history data and prognosis in schizophrenia. *Journal of Nervous and Mental Disease* 117: 515-525.

POLLACK, M., WOERNER, M., and KLEIN, D. 1970. A comparison of childhood characteristics of schizophrenics, personality disorders, and their siblings. In M. Roff and D. F. Ricks, eds., *Life history research in psychopathology*. Minneapolis, Minn.: University of Minnesota Press.

RICKS, D. F., and BERRY, J. C. 1970. Family and symptom patterns that precede schizophrenia. In M. Roff and D. F. Ricks, eds., *Life history research in psychopathology*. Minneapolis, Minn.: University of Minnesota Press.

ROBINS, L. N. 1974. *Deviant children grown up*. Huntington, N.Y.: Robert E. Krieger Publishing Company.

RODNICK, E. H., and GOLDSTEIN, M. J. 1974. A research strategy for studying risk for schizophrenia during adolescence and early adulthood. In J. Anthony and C. Koupernik, eds., *The child in his family: children at a psychiatric risk*, vol. 3. New York: John Wiley and Sons.

SANDIFER, M. J., PETTIS, C., and QUADE, D. 1964. A study of psychiatric diagnosis. *Journal of Nervous and Mental Disease* 139: 350-356.

SCHMIDT, H. O., and FONDA, C. P. 1956. The reliability of psychiatric diagnosis. *Journal of Abnormal and Social Psychology* 52: 262-267.

SCHNEIDER, K. 1959. *Clinical psychopathology.* Translated by M. W. Hamilton. New York: Grune and Stratton.

SCHOOLER, N. R. 1978. Antipsychotic drugs and psychological treatment in schizophrenia. In M. A. Lipton, A. DiMascio, and K. F. Killam, eds., *Psychopharmacology: a generation of progress.* New York: Raven Press.

SPITZER, R. L., ENDICOTT, J., and ROBINS, E. 1977. *Research diagnostic criteria RDC for a selected group of functional disorders,* 3d ed. New York: Biometrics Research, New York State Psychiatric Institute.

STEPHENS, J. H. 1977. Personal communication, October 15.

—— 1970. Long-term course and prognosis in schizophrenia. *Seminars in Psychiatry* 2 (4): 464-485.

STRAUSS, J., and CARPENTER, W. 1974. Characteristic symptoms and outcome in schizophrenia. *Archives of General Psychiatry* 30: 429-434.

STRAUSS, J. S., and GIFT, T. E. 1977. Choosing an approach for diagnosing schizophrenia. *Archives of General Psychiatry* 34: 1248-53.

WATT, N. 1972. Longitudinal changes in the social behavior of children hospitalized for schizophrenia as adults. *Journal of Nervous and Mental Disease* 155: 42-54.

WATT, N., and LUBENSKY, A. 1976. Childhood roots of schizophrenia. *Journal of Consulting and Clinical Psychology* 44: 363-375.

WATT, N., STOLOROW, R. D., LUBENSKY, A., and McCLELLAND, D. C. 1970. School adjustment and behavior of children hospitalized for schizophrenia as adults. *American Journal of Orthopsychiatry* 40: 637-657.

WENDER, P. H., ROSENTHAL, D., and KETY, S. S. 1968. A psychiatric assessment of the adoptive parents of schizophrenics. In D. Rosenthal and S. S. Kety, eds., *The transmission of schizophrenia.* Oxford: Pergamon Press.

WING, J. K. 1966. Five-year outcome in early schizophrenia. *Proceedings of the Royal Society of Medicine* 59: 17-23.

WITTMAN, P. 1941. A scale for measuring prognosis in schizophrenia patients. *Elgin State Hospital Papers* 4: 20-33.

ZUBIN, J. 1969. Cross-national study of diagnosis of the mental disorders: methodology and planning. *American Journal of Psychiatry* 125: 12-20 (April supplement).

9 | Cognitive Development in Childhood
Joachim F. Wohlwill

THE REALM of the cognitive functions reveals the essentially paradoxical character of the concept of stability of development. In this area, as in any aspect of growth, the notion of stability is at best an abstraction, since growth, or development, entails change. What, then, can stability mean, in the context of a changing individual?

This question has rarely been confronted in the past. Even the volume by Benjamin Bloom (1964), which represents the most recent comprehensive review of literature on the problem, does not address this question. As Jerome Kagan notes in chapter 2, Bloom equates stability with consistency, which he further identifies with correlation over time, and arrives at the following statement: "Defined in this way, a stable characteristic may be one that is different quantitatively as well as qualitatively at the two time points if the change is *predictable* to some minimal degree" (p. 3, italics added).

This identification of stability with predictability in the test-retest correlation sense has been widely accepted in the literature, partly as a result of the pervasive use of the IQ as the measure of cognitive status. The IQ itself involves an abstraction from change, one that leads to a purely relative index of performance, measured against the norm for a particular age group; it is a measure of individual difference, useful for comparing one child with another rather than for assessing the child's development. Within that frame of reference it is but a short step to equate stability with predictability across time of an individual's performance relative to that of a reference group.

The limitations of this restrictive view of stability from a developmental standpoint have become apparent in recent years, and alternative conceptions of stability and approaches to its study have been proposed (Emmerich, 1966; Kagan, 1971; McCall, 1979a; Wohlwill, 1973b). Two major types of stability should be differentiated.

A basic distinction can be made between stability of an individual and stability of a variable. The former refers to stability as a characteristic in a particular child, whereas the latter concerns a characteristic of a developmental variable considered in a group of individuals. Studies of individual stability include work on the constancy of the IQ or on stability of other measures of cognitive performance, examining longitudinal data for individual children to assess the extent to which any given child retains his relative standing on a particular variable and to determine the correlates of differential constancy or change observed in different children. Studies of the stability of a variable, such as intelligence, on the other hand, provide information on the extent to which performance on that variable for some normative group is stable across age, that is, can be predicted at one age from scores obtained at a prior age. By extension, the stability of different variables in this sense may be compared, in order to answer questions such as whether spatial ability is more stable than musical ability. Similar data—measures of variables across some period of development—are used in both cases, but they are treated differently and used for different purposes.

Individual and group stability are to some degree interdependent. Factors that create instability in individual development, as in the preadolescent growth spurt, for instance, depress group stability in the predictability sense: height in adolescence correlates less strongly with height during childhood than does terminal height. At one extreme, perfect group stability for a variable implies that development for the individuals in that group likewise occurs in a highly predictable fashion. At the opposite end, where group stability approaches zero (for example, predictability of performance on tasks of spatial ability in adolescence from tasks of spatial discrimination in infancy), concern about stability of an individual's development would be pointless, since the identity of the variable in a functional sense would then become moot. (See Emmerich, 1964, for a more thorough analysis of the continuity and stability of psychological variables.)

Although few of the several kinds of stability that can be considered a characteristic of the individual have been studied, it is useful to review them briefly and illustrate their meaning with reference to the cognitive domain.[1]

1. *Absolute invariance.* Consider a typical Piagetian concept— the notion of transitivity: If A is greater than B and B is greater than C, then A is greater than C. The concept is stable in an absolute sense,

that is, children's responses to tasks that involve transitivity relations typically do not change measurably over the first three or four years of life, nor after the acquisition of the concept, perhaps from age 7 on.

2. *Regularity of form of change.* If we chart the progress of change in some given area of mental ability, we may find that a particular child changes in a fairly smooth or regular fashion, while another's progress is marked by jaggedness and reversals. To the extent that development for a given function can be described by a prototypic curve, such as a logarithmic or exponential growth curve (Heinis's mental growth curve, 1926), we can describe the stability of a given child's development in terms of the closeness of the fit of its curve to that prototype. In a more descriptive and less quantitative fashion the Wetzel grid (Wetzel, 1943), though developed primarily for physical growth, has been used in this sense to determine the regularity of a given child's growth pattern.

How does this regularity relate to stability? Clearly we are concerned not with stability in the sense of lack of change but with the stability of the process of change. There is a close relationship between stability in this sense and the predictability criterion suggested by Bloom (1964). Note further that the more regular the growth process is and the closer it conforms to some modal function, the more likely it is that stability, in the sense of the following criterion, will be satisfied: individual differences are preserved over time.

3. *Constancy of relative position.* Of the individual forms of stability only constancy of relative position has received much attention from investigators. Stability in this sense refers to the question, To what extent does a particular child's status relative to some norm remain invariant over age? Thus it uses relativized measures, such as the IQ, and is readily illustrated by studies such as those of the Fels group (Sontag, Baker, and Nelson, 1958), in which changes with age in the IQs of individual children were traced.

4. *Stability of ipsative relations.* Another use of the stability concept is in the ipsative sense, that is, in terms of the pattern of relationship among different traits, abilities, or behavior variables within a given child. Walter Emmerich (1968) has made a persuasive case for an ipsative approach to the study of development as an alternative to both the classical developmental model and the traditional study of interindividual differences, particularly for the study of personality development, although this approach seems equally relevant to the study of the growth of cognitive skills. Thus we might want to know whether children who perform better on verbal than on arithmetical tests in the early grades display the same pattern in adolescence and adulthood. To the best of my knowledge this question has not been

investigated systematically, although certain illustrative studies, of largely methodological interest, touch on it indirectly (Tyler, 1954; Kerlinger, 1954).

With respect to the stability of a variable, an important distinction is that between *stability* and *continuity* (Emmerich, 1964), as well as the related one between homotypic and heterotypic continuity suggested by Kagan (1971). Emmerich uses stability and continuity to differentiate between the preservation of individual differences on measures of a variable taken at two points in time and the preservation of structural relationships among variables, in the factor analytic sense. In a sense, the former presupposes the latter; to the extent that there is a real "developmental transformation" (Emmerich, 1966) in the meaning of a variable, such that the constellation of variables with which the variable is correlated itself changes over time, one would not expect a high degree of stability for that variable over time. One might, however, obtain appreciable correlations between a variable at one time and a different variable at a subsequent time, if the two variables form part of a constant, or continuous, structure. There is reason to believe that this may indeed be the case for prediction of intelligence in childhood from other measures of infant behavior, as contrasted to scores on infant intelligence tests.

Kagan's homotypic versus heterotypic distinction is directly relevant to Emmerich's. Homotypic continuity refers to continuity of an overt behavior despite a change in underlying process. For instance, a child may exhibit a pattern of dependent behavior on the mother in early childhood, because that behavior is rewarded by the mother; at a later age the child may continue to exhibit the same pattern toward other adults or even toward peers, but it is now based on insecurity or fear of failure. The reverse case, that of heterotypic continuity, involves a relationship between two phenotypically different variables X and Y where there is some theoretical reason to postulate a correlation between them across age, that is, X tested at some early age t_1 is a precursor of Y tested at some later age t_2. Such a relationship is presumably based on the kind of developmental transformations that Emmerich considers. It appears to be illustrated by certain relationships between measures taken in early infancy and in early childhood, such as that between rate of habituation to stimuli at 4 months and engaging in play over a sustained period at 2 years of age. Kagan (1971), who reports this finding, considers the two measures to be indicators of a dimension of "conceptual tempo," relating to the individual's capacity to attend to interesting stimuli. Further instances of heterotypic continuity in this sense are reported by Kagan, from his own research and from that of others. Heterotypic continuity is particularly relevant to the study of the stability of cognitive development, because major qualitative changes take place in the manifestation of cognitive activity at different ages. These changes challenge developmentalists to search for evidence of underlying continuity in the relationship between two superficially different variables assessed at different ages.

The Limitations of the IQ

The major issue that needs to be confronted in the measurement of children's intellectual level is that intelligence is a multidimensional construct and can be expressed in terms of a single quantitative index only at the risk of serious distortion. Seen in a developmental context, this multidimensionality has two separable aspects. On the one hand, factor analytic studies of intelligence have consistently indicated that intelligence is not a unitary trait but a constellation of verbal, numerical, spatial, and other abilities, which cannot meaningfully be subsumed under a single construct or assessed in terms of a single index.

This is the horizontal side of the fallacy of unidimensionality implied in the IQ. The vertical side is that cognitive development is characterized by major qualitative changes as children grow from infancy to maturity that make it equally meaningless, at least in a conceptual sense, to define their status in terms of some quantitative index of relative standing such as the IQ. The work of Piaget has underscored the importance of incorporating these qualitative transformations in children's thought into our understanding of intellectual development. These qualitative changes apply across the three major stages of cognitive development (sensorimotor, concrete operational, and formal operational, corresponding to the periods of infancy, early and middle childhood, and preadolescence and adolescence, respectively) as well as within each, further complicating the task of constructing developmental scales of intelligence applicable across a broad segment of the age continuum.

The difficult problems of reconciling a theoretical conception of intelligence such as Piaget's with the tenets of psychometrics that have shaped intelligence testing need systematic attention. Neither developmental psychologists nor those in the field of testing—including the participants of a symposium devoted to this issue (Green, Ford, and Flamer, 1971; Wohlwill, 1972)—have faced these problems. In more recent years there have been encouraging signs of a shift in orientation; these discontinuities are receiving more explicit attention (McCall, Eichorn, and Hogarty, 1977), and attempts have been made to derive ordinal scales of development, particularly for infancy (Uzgiris and Hunt, 1975). But this reorientation has only begun to affect approaches to the study of stability, as in the work of McCall, Eichorn, and Hogarty (1977) and in the work of Kagan (1971) on heterotypic continuity, involving the study of relationships among different though conceptually linked measures of behavior over age.

Apart from the suspect nature of the assumption of unidimensionality and continuity of intelligence, the IQ measure has two further major weaknesses. First, the most commonly used test of intelligence, the Stanford-Binet, bases the IQ on the concept of mental age, which has some dubious characteristics from the standpoint of the scaling and measurement of growth (Wohlwill, 1973b). Mental ages are obtained by assigning to the child some minimum mental age, which means locating that child on the scale of performances considered characteristic of children of a given age, and then adding to that estimate some number of points or month-equivalents based on the number of items passed above that base level; it is thus a mixture of a strict age scale and a point scale. Furthermore, as an age scale it forces mental growth onto a highly artificial and misleading linear pattern, since the change from year to year is necessarily equal; on the average, a child gains a year of mental age for every year of chronological age. This feature raises awkward problems of handling the terminal period of intellectual growth and makes it impossible to determine when, if at all, such growth actually stops; moreover it is clearly inconsistent with general principles of growth, which suggest some negatively accelerated pattern as the norm.

Second, the IQ is a purely relative index based on the ratio of mental age to chronological age. It is thus nondevelopmental; that is, on a purely statistical basis a child's IQ is expected to remain constant from one age to another, on the average. This statistical artifact has been reified into the "hypothesis" of the constant IQ, which starts implicitly from the conception of IQ as a relatively fixed trait that differentiates individual A from individual B in much the same way that one may differentiate them by the color of their eyes. This conception obviously loses sight of the fact that IQ is merely a convenient representation of a child's standing relative to his age group at a particular age, a representation abstracted from the child's actual level of mental development. This statistically based pseudo constancy of the IQ has lent a false plausibility to the hypothesis of stability in intellectual attainment across age. In any event it has encouraged the conception of stability in a quasi-absolute sense, without regard to the abstraction from change that is inherent in the assessment of the stability of a developmental trait. This shortcoming is particularly noticeable in the treatment of stability of a variable—the preservation of individual differences across age with respect to a variable—but it is also evident in the study of individual stability of intellectual development in its quantitative aspect.

Stability of Intraindividual Cognitive Growth

The study of individual cognitive stability and change, that is, of intraindividual consistency in patterns of development, has been confined almost exclusively to standardized intelligence test scores. Yet the study of the growth of intelligence has revealed that a purely quantitative conception of cognitive development, modeled on the accretionary models used to study physical growth (Wohlwill, 1973b), is inadequate. Major qualitative changes appear in the domain of cognitive development. What is the meaning of stability of individual development in the context of such changes? The pertinence of this question becomes particularly evident when we consider Piaget's theory of cognitive development and the place of stability in his theory of stages.

Of the four aspects of intraindividual stability the first, absolute invariance, appears particularly applicable to qualitative change. Absolute invariance was in fact illustrated with respect to an instance of such change, the concept of transitivity. Over extended periods of time, encompassing the period before a concept or cognitive scheme starts to emerge as well as the period following its attainment, little demonstrable change generally occurs; thus, within either of those periods, the child's behavior is perfectly predictable. This aspect of stability is generally trivial, in the sense that it can normally be taken for granted, but it has occasionally become a focus for empirical investigation, in at least two different respects: the "extinguishability" of a concept—whether it is possible for a child to unlearn, or abandon, a concept once it has been formed (Smedslund, 1961)—and the terminal level of a concept—whether a mature individual who appears to have become "fixated" at a particular level of reasoning with regard to a concept can be induced to progress beyond that level. The latter question is relevant chiefly in Piaget's formal operations stage, involving symbolic reasoning, though there is evidence from the study of concepts such as conservation of volume and the water-level problem (Thomas, Jamison, and Hummel, 1973) that it can also become an issue in other areas.

What does the second meaning of intraindividual stability, relating to the form of change, mean in the context of qualitative change? First there is the question whether the responses conform to a stable progression from one level to the next, without reversals to a prior level. In the Piagetian domain, at least, development indeed appears to be marked by considerable consistency by this criterion. This consistency is shown indirectly by the typically high degree of scalability marking progression through Piagetian stages or similar sequences of conceptual response (Davol et al., 1967; Wohlwill, 1960). Scalogram analysis, being cross-sectional, provides at best indirect evidence on the possible occurrence of reversals; thus even more substantial deviation from scalability, such as observed by Kofsky (1966), may reflect error of measurement or differential sequential patterns in different children rather than reversals of a response previously established. More direct evidence on this question comes from longitudinal investigations of the development of Piagetian concepts, but there are few such studies and the results are not wholly consistent. While some research (Benson, 1966; Wohlwill, Devoe, and Fusaro, 1971) found that reversals are rare, another investigation (Almy, Chittenden, and Miller, 1966) encountered them more frequently.

In what is perhaps the only study concerned specifically with instability in the sense of regression of cognitive development, the investigators followed the progress of 65 children, for three years, on diverse Piagetian tasks (Dudek and Dyer, 1972). They found regressions for 10% of the total responses for which regression was possible (that is, excluding the initial set of responses, and those at the lowest level). Only about 1 in 20 of these 10%, however, involved what the authors termed true regressions, from level III, the terminal level of a stage, to level I. They nevertheless focused on a subset of children marked by relative instability in terms of this regression criterion (including both true and partial regressions) and found that they displayed a greater propensity than other children for obsessive response on the Rorschach. Admittedly, this finding tells us little about the functional significance of such cases of instability. If the investigators had had more extensive information about these children and their previous development, the meaning of such instability might have emerged more clearly. But there is no assurance that a search for such correlates would have proved successful. More significant in Dudek and Dyer's work is the concept of developmental instability as a characteristic of a given child, as well as the relative infrequency of instances of such instability compared with the norm of regular stage progression.

Regularity in a different sense is at issue in Piagetian theory with respect to the formation of a stage, regarded as a set of cognitive or conceptual responses linked through some structural bond. The question here is whether concepts that Piaget considered equivalent in terms of underlying cognitive structure—for instance, transitivity and the understanding of conservation of length—are in fact acquired apace, in a determinate synchronous relationship. By Piaget's criterion, the evidence suggests considerable *instability* in the formation of stages, at least during certain phases. Flavell and Wohlwill (1969) have postulated that when a stage-related concept emerges in preliminary form, the child's responses go through a period marked by oscillation and inconsistency among different component responses, followed by a period of consolidation in which these responses are established in their final, determinate, stable form. They reviewed studies by Uzgiris (1964) and Nassefat (1963) that appeared to support such a conception; more recently Moshman (1977) has tested and essentially confirmed the model. In this sense, then, we may say that periods of stability alternate with those of instability in the formation of stage-related concepts—assuming, of course, that the stage concept is considered useful. But only painstaking analysis of patterns of responses at different points in development, preferably through longitudinal research, can provide clear evidence.

The remaining two types of individual stability are less readily applied to qualitative development, since both presuppose the existence of quantitative scales for assessing an individual's standing with respect to some dimension of development. Clearly an individual's standing relative to a group across age can be determined only if it is possible to quantify differences among individuals' attainment with respect to a particular variable. The same point applies to determining ipsative stability, which requires a comparison of an individual's standing for different variables, each measured relative to some reference group. Qualitative change does not seem to allow for measurement of individual differences in this sense—especially since it typically occurs over a limited portion of the age span.

Quantitative Growth in Intelligence

How regular or predictable is the growth of intelligence in the human being? More specifically, is there a prototype form for the developmental function for intelligence? If so, what is it, and to what extent does it represent the broad range of patterns of intellectual development found across variations in environment, culture, family history? In contrast with physical growth, these questions remain unanswered in the domain of intellective development, primarily because of the formidable measurement problems. Indeed, given the inescapable evidence that cognitive functions undergo major qualitative changes over the course of development, the very attempt to suggest a determinate form for the developmental function for growth curves of intelligence is suspect in many quarters. Yet, influenced by the mental test movement and the proliferation of longitudinal and cross-sectional data on intelligence test scores, theorists have proposed approaches to solving the problem of measurement and suggested particular equations or prototype curves to represent the growth curve of intelligence.

Examples are provided by the work of Heinis (1926), Thurstone and Ackerson (1929), Bayley (1956), Dearborn and Rothney (1941), and Freeman and Flory (1937). These theorists, on the basis of empirical and a priori considerations, arrive at somewhat different representations of the mental growth curve. Thurstone and Ackerson, as well as Dearborn and Rothney, suggest an ogival or S-shaped function, changing from a positively to a negatively accelerated curve. In contrast, Freeman and Flory, on purely empirical grounds, arrive at a quasi-linear curve. Bayley's negatively accelerated growth curve may be the most reasonable. But the essential point is that the proposed curves are determined largely by the approach to the problem of defining a *unit* for measuring intellectual growth. Only Freeman and Flory use an essentially raw-score scale, where scores are adjusted only for comparability across subtests. The nearly linear pattern of change found with this scale raises questions about the reliability of their arbitrary scale units for representing mental growth, as the authors admit. But their tests extend only to the eight-year level; thus they are dealing with a sharply truncated portion of the total curve. The other authors work on the basis of synthetically derived quasi-absolute units (Thurstone, 1925; Bayley, 1956), which leaves some doubt about the meaningfulness of the resulting growth curves.

Furthermore, none of these authors has confronted the issue of aggregating individual growth data or relating the composite curve to those for individual children. Thurstone and Ackerman have been prevented from doing so in principle; they not only utilize cross-sectional data but also start from information on pass-fail percentages in groups of children and are thus left without a basis for charting individual development. The other authors work with longitudinal data but lack an analytic model for classifying curves or for expressing individual growth in terms of an overall prototype curve; thus they have nothing more than an impressionistic representation of an individual curve's deviation from the group trend (Dearborn and Rothney, 1941, figures 71-74; Freeman and Flory, 1937, figures 26-33).

Given the equivocal status of generic mental growth curves, attempts to express cognitive development in terms of a given child's conformance to or deviation from a prototype amount to little more than impressionistic representations of acceleration or retardation relative to the norm, or possibly gross idiosyncrasy of pattern of development. These curves may certainly serve purely descriptive purposes, as is illustrated by Leland Stott's representation of the development of two twins, Paul and Sally (figure 9.1). Stott resorted to a straightforward mental-age scale, which necessarily reduces the prototype function in this case to a misleading linear form. However, the patterns reveal the relatively precocious mental growth of the two children as well as their basic similarity.

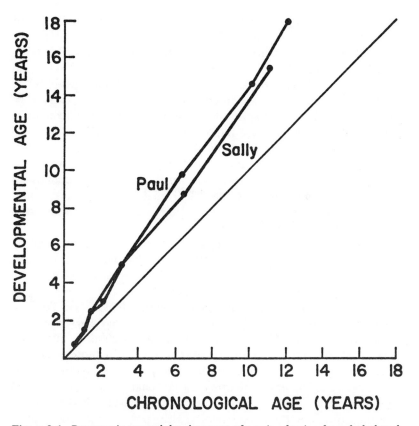

Figure 9.1. *Progress in mental development of a pair of twins from babyhood to age 12 years. (From Stott, 1967.)*

Within the single domain of performance on intelligence tests, a considerable number of studies have looked at the amount of change in a measure of intellectual status relative to the child's age group—the IQ—over two or more ages and attempted to determine correlates of the amount or the direction of change. Most of these studies have been limited to measure of change in IQ score between two ages. As McCall, Appelbaum, and Hogarty (1973) have forcefully argued, this is a severe limitation, since it implicitly imposes a linear model onto such change and utilizes an arbitrary slice of the age continuum as the basis for generalizations about change in IQ. Thus the absence of marked change between two arbitrarily selected age levels may mask considerable change before or after the period over which the change is measured and even within that period itself (a U-shaped pattern of change can occur between two widely separated points in time). In addition, such analyses are prey to all the problems and limitations of change-score analyses—unreliability of change measures, negative correlation of change with initial level, and others (Harris, 1963).

For instance, Honzik, Macfarlane, and Allen (1948) note that 85% of the children in the Berkeley Guidance Study changed in IQ by 10 or more points over the interval between 6 and 18 years, 35% changed by 20 or more points, and 9% showed a change of 30 or more points. While such data are important to counteract naive assumptions about the constancy of the IQ, particularly among parents, teachers, and other laypersons, these frequencies are relative to the age interval taken and constitute information essentially identical to that contained in the stability coefficient, that is, the intercorrelations across age for the group as a whole, at least given a sample whose variability is representative of the population.

The existence of instances of IQ change in appreciable numbers has awakened interest in the problem of change in IQ as such and, more specifically, in the question of the correlates of such change. An early example of work on this problem comes from the studies of genius by Lewis Terman and his colleagues (Burks, Jensen, and Terman, 1930), who examined 54 children from age 10 to age 16 whose mean IQ at age 10 was 148. They separated these 54 children into those whose IQ decreased over the six-year interval and those whose IQ stayed the same or increased. Neither the occupation of the parents nor a rating of the home environment nor changes in family circumstances differentiated these two groups; the only variable that showed any relationship to IQ change was sex; girls showed a mean drop of 17 points, compared with only 3 points for boys.

Wiener, Rider, and Oppel (1963) introduced socioeconomic status (SES) into their study of 39 *S*s matched for initial IQ at 3 to 5 years and retested three years later, finding patterns of increase in IQ associated with higher SES. Concern with this variable recurs in the literature on correlates of IQ and of change in IQ and figures prominently in one of the most comprehensive and ambitious studies of correlates of IQ change, that of Rees and Palmer (1970). These investigators examined data taken from five major longitudinal studies (Fels, Denver Child Research Council, Berkeley Guidance, Berkeley Growth, and Oakland Growth), with specific attention to changes from 6 to 12 years, and from 12 to 17 years. SES showed the typical correlation with IQ level and to a nearly constant degree at ages 6, 12, and 17 (r = .43, .46, and .51 for males; .46, .50, and .38 for females at the three ages). However, Rees and Palmer uncovered an interesting pattern in the relationship between SES and IQ *change*. Children of high SES who scored below the median in IQ at age 6 showed a rising pattern, while children of low SES and with IQs below the median continued to drop in IQ. The authors also found parents' education to be a better predictor of IQ than parents' occupation, but they attributed this to problems of measurement in the scale of occupations. Of particular interest are correlations reported for environmental variables (notably SES) across age, paralleling those for IQ. The correlation between SES of the child's family at birth and at 15 years was .92, pointing to a relative constancy in the environment. This finding is of considerable significance for an evaluation of Bloom's interpretation of stability coefficients (see the next section).

Research of this type, dealing with the correlates of individual changes in intelligence, is subject to a number of severe limitations, relating to the linearity implicit in the use of measures of change between an initial and a final score and to the statistical problems inherent in the use of change scores. The statistical problems were handled in an interesting way by Härnquist (1968), who obtained data on the relationship between changes in intelligence test scores between 13 and 18 years and the youngster's educational level and home background variables. He analyzed these changes by determining gains or losses for individual children measured from the regression line of final on initial scores. In accordance with other findings on the role of education and SES (Honzik, 1940; Rees and Palmer, 1970), children who had attained the highest educational level at age 18 showed positive changes in these relativized gain scores, while those of the lowest educational level showed negative changes. Clearly it is impossible to tease out cause from effect in such a finding, but the method recommends itself for more widespread use.

The linear conception of age changes remains a questionable feature of Härnquist's method. For the age range that he studied (13 to 18 years) one may assume that that problem is minor, but McCall, Appelbaum, and Hogarty's (1973) criticism that this type of research ignores problems of the *patterning* of developmental change remains valid. Information on patterning requires extended longitudinal data like those collected in the major longitudinal studies. For the most part these studies have presented individual patterns of change in intelligence in merely graphic or descriptive form, as in Hilden's (1949) study of cases from the Denver Child Research Council study or Bayley's (1949) reporting of individual cases from the Berkeley Growth Study. Bayley's report supplements these individual cases by quantitative data on "lability" coefficients for individual children, based on the standard deviation of the series of measures for a given child around that child's own mean—a procedure that can be meaningfully applied only to relativized scores such as the IQ or to standardized scores.

Honzik, Macfarlane, and Allen (1948) went a step further in their analysis of cases from the Berkeley Guidance Study. They selected cases marked by instability of intellectual performance over age and attempted to determine some correlates of such instability in the child's experience. This is illustrated in figure 9.2, which shows the developmental history of two cases, in correspondence with fluctuations in their IQ.

A much more systematic attempt to identify possible correlates of shifts in IQ revealed by longitudinal series of measurements was undertaken by Sontag, Baker, and Nelson (1958), using the data of the Fels Longitudinal Study. Their analysis centered on environmental and personality correlates of differential patterns of shifts in IQ. Significantly, the latter proved more successful than the former. The only environmental condition that differentiated children with increasing IQ patterns from those with decreasing IQ patterns consisted of "accelerating" parents who used democratic discipline; this combination characterized the children with increasing IQ during the school years (but not during the preschool period).[2] The two groups were more consistently differentiated on personality traits of the children. At the preschool level children who gained in IQ obtained significantly higher ratings on independence. At the school level a number of traits, such as independence, competitiveness with peers and in school, and self-initiative, differentiated the two groups. These traits were themselves intercorrelated, pointing to an achievement-motive cluster as a likely factor determining the different patterns of IQ change. This finding may be related to the fact that twice as many boys as girls in this sample showed patterns of increasing IQ. Kagan et al. (1958) and Kagan and Moss (1962) report further data from this Fels sample, relating changes in IQ to projective test-derived measures of personality and to measures of achievement striving obtained from interviews with parents, which essentially confirm and extend those presented by Sontag, Baker, and Nelson (1958).

That environmental variables were generally uncorrelated with gross patterns of IQ change in the Fels data is noteworthy; furthermore, a study by J. McCall and Johnson (1972) showed that IQ changes between the ages of 7 and 14 years in a group of 583 children were unrelated to such gross demographic variables as occupational level, family size, and birth order. Neither these demographic variables nor the environmental measures available to the Fels group were necessarily the most appropriate or sensitive ones for this purpose. Yet the findings are not surprising, given the considerable constancy in the environmental circumstances of these children. This constancy applies not only to SES, as in the aforementioned analysis of Rees and Palmer (1970), but also to psychological aspects of the home environment,

The authors proceeded to search for parental behavior correlates of these clusters by means of a multivariate analysis of variance, with ten parental behavior measures as "dependent" variables, and the five clusters as the "independent" factor. The overall significant multivariate F (p less than .001) was attributable primarily to a pair of parental variables, severity of penalties and attempts to accelerate the progress of their children. The relationship of these variables to IQ change is complex. Clusters 2 and 3 are both made up of children showing some tendency to decline in IQ, yet the parents of cluster 2 children were highest in punitiveness while those in cluster 3 were lowest. This result led the authors to suggest that the relationship between parental punitiveness and IQ change is inverted-U-shaped, an intermediate level of punitiveness (as found in clusters 4 and 5) being most conducive to increase in IQ.

IQ change was more directly related to parental acceleration tendency. This was highest for children in clusters 4 and 5, characterized by IQ trends increasing at least to middle childhood, and lowest for those in clusters 2 and 3, showing slight decline in IQ. This outcome confirms the analysis of the same data by Sontag, Baker, and Nelson (1958), based on simple IQ gain scores. But note that clusters 4 and 5 differed markedly in their respective pattern of change in IQ beyond the age of 10, yet they were not significantly differentiated on any of the parental behavior variables. Indeed, cluster 4, with its pattern of decline in IQ after the tenth year, showed the highest mean for parental acceleration.[3] The authors thus speculated that strong accelerational pressures exert a positive influence on the younger child but backfire in adolescence, because of the growing influence of the peer group, and perhaps because the school environment does not motivate children of above-average IQ.

The approach of McCall and his associates, particularly their clustering of cases according to profiles of IQ change, appears an exemplary mode of attack on the problem of individual stability and change within the context of long-term developmental growth in intellectual functioning. It is unfortunate, however, in the light of Sontag, Baker, and Nelson's work (1958) with the same data, pointing to more substantial correlates between changes in IQ and child personality variables, that they made no attempt to examine intercluster differences along some of these personality dimensions. Such an investigation might have clarified the basis for the different patterns shown by members of clusters 4 and 5 in late childhood and adolescence. Admittedly, correlations between child personality and IQ are devoid of causal significance, compared with those involving parental behavior, although the authors rightly note that causal interpretations of parental behavior are also fraught with danger.

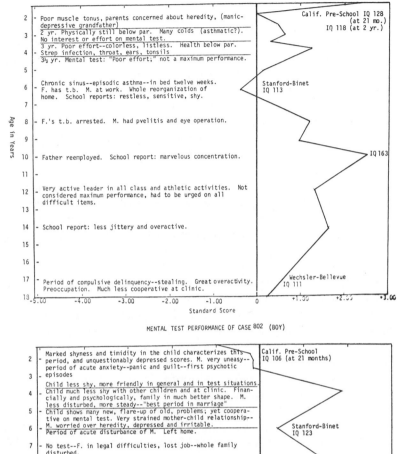

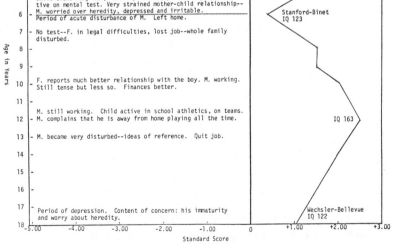

Figure 9.2. *Two cases from the Berkeley Guidance Study, showing changes in IQ correlated with behavior and personality changes and events in the lives of the children. (From Honzik, Macfarlane, and Allen, 1948.)*

such as parent behavior and attitude, for which Hanson (1975) has likewise demonstrated a fair degree of constancy over time. Given such evidence of environmental constancy, one would not expect to find high correlations between particular environmental variables and the extent to which a child's IQ changes over time.

The most ambitious and impressive investigation of individual patterns of IQ change and their possible correlates is contained in the reanalysis of the Fels data by McCall, Appelbaum, and Hogarty (1973). These authors are critical of the focus of prior research on change between two selected points on the age continuum; they are equally critical of the one-sided focus on correlational information (such as that contained in stability coefficients between IQ at two different ages over a group of children), as contrasted with information on mean level of performance and possible changes in means. For instance, they note that preservation of relative position over time (high interage correlations) is typically found at least beyond the preschool level, while at the same time major changes in mean IQ are observed in many studies, particularly those dealing with effects of specific intervention programs or of cultural and educational disadvantage. They thus set out to obtain data on the intellectual development of individual children that retained a maximum of information concerning the child's individual pattern of development and the level of intellectual performance at successive ages. Accordingly, they dealt with profile information, representing the constellation of IQ values at successive ages for each child. They selected 80 cases from the Fels files that permitted the determination of such profiles over the age period from 2½ to 17 years. Applying a combination of trend analysis, based on Tucker's (1966) procedure, and cluster rotation, they arrived at five separable clusters of patterns, along with a set of more idiosyncratic profiles relegated to a "wastepaper basket" category of "isolates." These clusters are shown in figure 9.3.

Not surprisingly, cluster 1, representing patterns of irregular fluctuations in IQ within relatively small limits (for the most part within 10 IQ points on either side of the child's overall IQ) was the most frequent one, while those showing larger and more consistent shifts, such as shown in clusters 4 and 5, were least numerous. In the derivation of these clusters all children are equated in terms of the mean of their several test scores (see the ordinates in figure 9.3, which represent deviations from each subject's mean). The members of the clusters differed in their overall level of intelligence as well: from the age of 4½ years on, and to a marked degree in middle childhood, the means for children in clusters 4 and 5 were above those of the other three clusters.

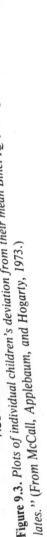

Figure 9.3. *Plots of individual children's deviation from their mean Binet IQ over age for children in each cluster and a group of "isolates." (From McCall, Applebaum, and Hogarty, 1973.)*

One regrettable limitation of this research is the use of the purely relativized measures of IQ in this type of profile analysis, as opposed to some absolute or quasi-absolute measure of performance such as Bayley's 16-D scale or even a simple mental age score. By their resort to the IQ, which does not vary with age on the average, McCall and his colleagues weaken their argument for a developmental analysis based on information about level of performance. Patterns of change in IQ suppress the overall pattern of quantitative and qualitative change in intellectual performance exhibited by all normal children. This point deserves added emphasis in view of the perennial tendency for "consumers" of literature on IQ data to interpret IQ as a measure characterizing the person as an individual, even if subject to change within limits, rather than as a measure of purely relative status compared to some reference group. By the same token, the different profiles uncovered in the work of McCall and his associates are meaningful only in a relative sense, in the context of the norm of a linear pattern of IQ change of zero slope fluctuating around the mean of the reference group; the profiles are thus stripped of developmental significance.

In the aggregate, and despite the ambitious and impressive efforts of investigators such as Rees and Palmer and McCall and his associates, the work on changes in IQ and their correlates has not substantially advanced our knowledge of the influences on the cognitive and intellective development of the child. This disappointing outcome must be ascribed to fixation on the purely relative measure of the IQ, which is in effect an abstraction from developmental change and fails to consider qualitative changes in intellectual functioning. One furthermore wonders why *change* in IQ should be expected to be correlated with variables, whether environmental or behavioral, that play an essentially constant role in the child's experience. In actuality, factors associated with increases in IQ (high SES, achievement motivation) are generally related to high terminal IQ as well; conversely, those less highly related to IQ gains are related to low terminal status. One suspects, therefore, that in many instances IQ change represents a level-seeking phenomenon. For reasons that probably reflect the lack of stability of intelligence itself, the major qualitative changes in its components over development, and sheer measurement error, certain children may undergo marked changes in relative status from early childhood to later childhood or adolescence, and the factors correlated with those changes are also correlated with their eventual status.

If determinants of change in IQ are of intrinsic interest, the indicated strategy would be to look for concomitant changes in the child's experience—due to changed family circumstances, major changes in the physical and social environment of the child, temporary illnesses or emotional strains. Honzik, Macfarlane, and Allen (1948) presented some cases containing information of this kind, if only at a descriptive level. More painstaking and systematic efforts should prove rewarding.

More fundamentally, however, one would welcome intensive analysis of patterns of growth like that of McCall, Appelbaum, and Hogarty (1973), but with reference to measures that have some developmental significance and preferably measures of absolute attainment. One of the few investigations of this type is Bergman's (1973) work on environmental correlates of gains in intelligence test performance measured on an absolute scale, but it is limited to a fairly short age span, from 9 to 12 years. To partial out differences in initial status, Bergman adjusted his scores by analysis of covariance and dealt with changes in these adjusted scores, which were then related to parental education. Even over this restricted age interval he found substantial correlations between amount of growth on his group intelligence measures and parental education, particularly among boys.

Here again we are limited to change in sheer linear terms between two arbitrarily chosen points on the age continuum. This approach might well be extended to a longer period of development and might focus on patterns of absolute change in a manner analogous to McCall, Appelbaum, and Hogarty's work, possibly by recourse to specific parameters of the growth curve relating to rate, form, and terminal level. Such research should provide a more satisfactory picture of the correlates and perhaps the determinants of intellectual development.

From this review of the individual-stability literature, it is clear that the IQ is, to paraphrase *Porgy and Bess*, a "sometime thing," at least in the sense that it is subject to considerable fluctuation over time. The specific determinants of these fluctuations are still far from clear; they may never become fully established, particularly given the changes in the composition of intelligence tests with age, factors relating to the conditions of testing, and other problems. At the same time there is mounting evidence that motivational forces related to achievement needs can accelerate or retard intellectual growth, resulting in a pattern of either increasing or decreasing IQ. The effect of environmental factors is more uncertain, but SES and related variables seem to operate in a level-seeking sense. Children initially scoring below the level expected in terms of their SES will tend to gain in IQ toward that level, and conversely for those starting above the expected level. But these are merely statistical generalizations, which ignore many individual patterns of IQ change that require more detailed attention to the circumstances of the child's life and environment and the changes taking place in them as the child develops.

The Preservation of Individual Differences across Age

The common conception of stability of development is that embodied in the stability coefficient—the correlation between some measure obtained at one age with that obtained at a subsequent one. This amounts to a predictability view of stability: To what extent is it possible to take a measure of a child's intellectual status at one age as indicative of the intellectual status that the child will attain at a subsequent age? Given the relative paucity of longitudinal research, which is required to answer this question, an astounding amount of information has been amassed on it. Indeed, Bloom (1964) has devoted almost an entire volume to a review of data of this type on the stability of physical, intellectual, and educational growth. A volume by Kagan and Moss (1962) is devoted to similar information, drawn from the longitudinal Fels study, concerning a broad array of personality variables but including relationships between different variables across age.

Several points are to be noted concerning the nature of the information contained in such stability coefficients. First, it is inherently nondevelopmental, since correlation coefficients entail discarding all information related to the absolute level of the scores. (In the case of IQ, that information has already been eliminated in the division of mental age by chronological age.) Second, stability coefficients are prone to all the ills to which any correlation coefficient is heir—notably restriction of range—where relatively homogeneous populations are measured. Third, and most important, stability coefficients provide information on the stability of intellectual performance across age for a group of individuals rather than for a given child. To the extent that the group studied is representative of the population, such information may pertain to the variable under study and its "behavior" across age. Indeed, the extensive literature on correlations between IQs obtained over a given age span amounts to a laborious (and for the most part surprisingly successful) effort to establish the robustness of this index as a measure of intellectual attainment relative to a norm that is largely unaffected by gross changes in actual cognitive functioning. But interpreting the magnitude of such coefficients in terms of the relative immutability of intelligence or its impermeability to environmental influences impinging on the child is an entirely different matter. We shall return to that issue following the review of this literature.

Stability of Intelligence Test Scores

Major Longitudinal Studies. Most of the major longitudinal studies of the thirties and forties included lengthy series of intelligence test data, in many cases dating from early infancy and obtained at yearly intervals. These studies provide extensive and complete information on correlations between intelligence test scores over any specified age interval, as typified in Bayley's (1949) data from the Berkeley Growth Study (table 9.1).

These data, and similar ones obtained from the Fels study (Sontag, Baker, and Nelson, 1958), the California Growth Study (Honzik, Macfarlane, and Allen, 1948), and the Brush Foundation Study (Ebert and Simmons, 1943), may be summarized by three propositions, which have become standard in the stability-of-intelligence literature.

1. Measures of cognitive performance in infancy, up to the age of 12 to 18 months, are nonpredictive of later intelligence test scores.

2. Test-retest correlations decrease in direct proportion to the interval between tests.

3. For a constant test-retest interval, test-retest correlations increase with age.

A graphic representation of the first two principles is presented in figures 9.4a and 9.4b, showing test-retest correlations between various ages and age 10 and maturity, respectively.

These curves, especially figure 9.4b for correlations with intelligence at maturity, impressed Bloom with their similarity to growth curves, including curves for the growth of intelligence based on absolute units such as those proposed by Heinis (1926), Thorndike et al. (1927), and Thurstone and Ackerson (1929). Bloom went so far as to present one graph in which the intelligence growth curves proposed in these three papers were superimposed on the intercorrelation curve between IQ at age *x* and at maturity taken from Bayley's data. The fit between Bayley's correlational data and the three growth curves is not as close as Bloom suggests; over the period from birth to age 5, in particular, Bayley's correlations rise much faster than any of these growth curves. Nevertheless, Bloom considers that this match supports an interpretation of the correlation coefficients in terms of percentage of adult intelligence attained at any given age. This interpretation is based largely on Bloom's acceptance of Anderson's (1939) overlap hypothesis, which accounts for the pattern of stability correla-

Table 9.1. Correlation coefficients between age-level standard scores of intelligence.[a]

Average Months / Years	Months							Years				
	4, 5, 6	7, 8, 9	10, 11, 12	13, 14, 15	18, 21, 24	27, 30, 36	42, 48, 54	5, 6, 7	8, 9, 10	11, 12, 13	14, 15, 16	17, 18
1, 2, 3	.57	.42	.28	.10	−.04	−.09	−.21	−.13	−.03	.02	−.01	.05
4, 5, 6		.72	.52	.50	.23	.10	−.16	−.07	−.06	−.08	−.04	−.01
7, 8, 9			.81	.67	.39	.22	.02	.02	.07	.16	.006	.20
10, 11, 12				.81	.60	.45	.27	.20	.19	.30	.23	.41
13, 14, 15					.70	.54	.35	.30	.19	.19	.09	.23
18, 21, 24						.80	.49	.50	.37	.43	.45	.55
27, 30, 36							.72	.70	.58	.53	.46	.54
42, 48, 54								.82	.71	.64	.70	.62
Years												
5, 6, 7									.92	.85	.87	.86
8, 9, 10										.94	.92	.89
11, 12, 13											.96	.96
14, 15, 16												.96

Source: Bayley (1949), table 4. Reprinted by permission of the Journal Press.

a. These scores are the means of standard scores for three consecutive test-ages, months 1, 2, 3; 4, 5, 6; years 5, 6, 7, and so on. The last level is composed of only two test ages, 17 and 18 years. Each child's score is the average of all tests taken by him for the age included in that level.

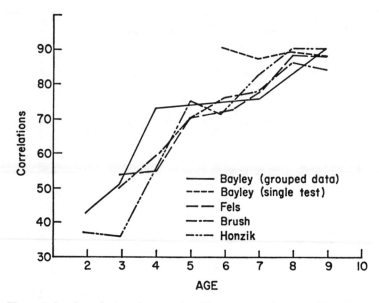

Figure 9.4a. *Correlations between intelligence at each age and intelligence at age 10. (From Bloom, 1964.)*

tions increasing with age in terms of an accretionary model. According to the overlap hypothesis the amount of growth attained at any given age is considered part of that measured at some subsequent age—we are supposedly dealing here with a set of part-whole correlations. Thorndike's curve, on which Bloom relies heavily (see p. 68 of his book), was obtained largely by extrapolation, because no data on the particular intelligence tests on which it is based were available below the age of 10!

That the curve for the magnitude of the correlations from Bayley's data has virtually peaked by age 6 or 7 is significant. It suggests the operation, not so much of a simple accretional growth principle as implied in the overlap hypothesis, but rather of a qualitative change in the composition of abilities tapped by standard intelligence tests, between infancy and early childhood as well as between early and later childhood. Such a three-stage view of cognitive development was originally proposed by Hofstätter (1954) on the basis of a factor analysis of longitudinal Binet intelligence test data. That analysis was justifiably challenged by Cronbach (1967) on the basis of the interdependence between successive measures in a longitudinal series and the simplex structure of a correlation matrix obtained from such data. Yet an essentially similar three-stage view of cognitive development has

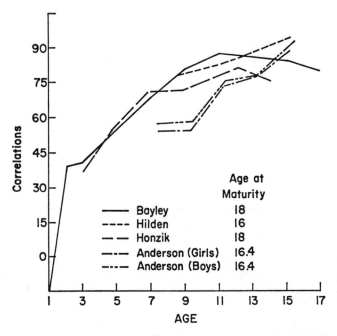

Figure 9.4b. *Correlations between intelligence at each age and intelligence at maturity. (From Bloom, 1964.)*

become widely accepted since that time, largely through the influence of Piagetian theory. The stability coefficient data clearly cannot establish the validity of such a conception of the development of intelligence. But the absence of correlation from infancy to early childhood and beyond, followed by moderate and increasing correlations from early childhood to later childhood and adolescence, and a pattern of stability coefficients approaching the reliabilities of the tests themselves from the early school years onward is consistent with expectations from such a three-stage conception.

In this connection, the data relevant to the third proposition become of interest. Figure 9.5 presents the stability coefficients taken from four of the major longitudinal projects—Berkeley Growth, Berkeley Guidance, Fels, and Brush—separately for specific values of length of the test-retest intervals, from 2 to 5 years, as a function of age at the first test. The values rise consistently between ages 2 and 6 but fluctuate irregularly thereafter. This pattern seems counter to predictions from Anderson's overlap hypothesis, which would entail progressively higher correlations with age as the "part" approached the "whole."

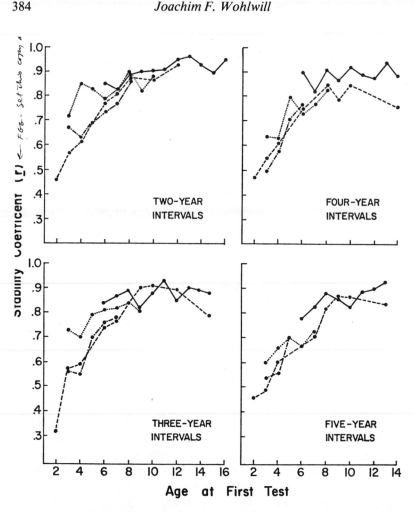

Figure 9.5. *Stability coefficients for specified constant values of the test-retest interval, as a function of age at first test. Data from* ____ *Bayley (1949);* - - - - *Honzik, Macfarlane, and Allen (1948);* . . . . *Sontag, Baker, and Nelson (1958)* _ . _ . _ *Ebert and Simons (1943).*

One major longitudinal study absent from previous literature reviews is the one carried out at the University of Minnesota Institute of Child Welfare (Goodenough and Maurer, 1942). The omission is conspicuous, because this work originated in one of the major centers for child development research of the prewar years, and its senior author is one of the foremost developmental psychologists of that era. In some important respects the data are not consistent with those of the other studies, in particular with the expectations embodied in the second principle, as Goodenough and Maurer themselves emphasize. The data presented in the report are incomplete in comparison with those of the other major longitudinal studies. The chief interest centered on the predictive value of the Minnesota preschool scales of intelligence. Accordingly, the data are limited to intercorrelations between scores on these scales administered at two different ages within the preschool period (between 18 and 66 months),[4] as well as between scores on the Minnesota preschool scales and Stanford-Binet scores from 4½ to 10½ years. Similar correlations are presented with scores on the Arthur performance scale administered between the ages of 5½ and 10½. The curious finding is that the predictive value of the Minnesota preschool scales with subsequent Stanford-Binet scores as a criterion was consistently related to the age at which the Stanford-Binet was administered. That is, the expected decrease in the size of the correlations as the interval between tests increased was not found. Rather, the values fluctuated in an irregular fashion. The same was true for the Arthur scale. Table 9.2 provides a summary of the main findings.

The authors do not offer any satisfactory explanation for the discrepant pattern of their results. The use of the Minnesota preschool scales in this study is not a plausible explanation, since whatever their limitations relative to other tests used during this period, the correlations with Stanford-Binet during the later school years (9 to 11 years) are comparable to those reported in other studies. The items of the

Table 9.2. Correlations between total-score IQs on the Minnesota preschool scales and subsequent Stanford-Binet IQs.

Age at taking Stanford-Binets	Correlations with 1916 Binets (Age at preschool test, in months)			Correlations with 1937 Binets (Age at preschool test, in months)		
	Under 36	36-47	Over 47	Under 36	36-47	Over 47
4½	.75 (31)	.52 (54)	.61 (76)	—	.69 (29)	.76 (29)
5½	.25 (52)	.66 (83)	.48 (127)	—	.66 (29)	.69 (50)
6½	.40 (57)	.55 (67)	.65 (153)	—	.76 (37)	.58 (55)
7½	.48 (65)	.57 (73)	.65 (141)	.26 (26)	.56 (31)	.68 (64)
8½	.45 (47)	.64 (59)	.55 (98)	.22 (24)	.42 (28)	.72 (58)
9½	.30 (28)	.65 (41)	.65 (90)	.15 (21)	.31 (31)	.57 (48)
10½	—	.73 (32)	.58 (70)	.19 (27)	.40 (28)	.70 (47)
11½	—	—	.70 (49)	.45 (22)	.66 (22)	.73 (43)
12½	—	—	.73 (37)	.18 (21)	.61 (28)	.43 (45)

Source: Data from Goodenough and Mauer (1942), tables 19, 20, 21, 24, 25, 26. Reprinted by permission of University of Minnesota Press.

scales are not noticeably different from those used in the Binet at comparable age levels; in some cases they were directly borrowed or adapted from the latter. These findings thus remain a puzzling exception to the rule embodied in the second principle, on which much of our thinking on the stability of intellectual development has been built.

Further data. Many studies have presented information on correlations between intelligence test scores taken at different ages, predominantly over shorter age spans, or limited to just two or three age levels. Some are reviewed in Thorndike (1940) and Bloom (1964). We shall consider only those that appear to be of interest in revealing the role of a factor or influence on stability of intelligence and those that have appeared since Bloom's volume. Most of these more recent studies concern relationships between performance in infancy and early or later childhood (or even beyond); for convenience, these are deferred to the following section.

A series of papers by Bradway and her associates (Bradway, 1944; Bradway, Thompson, and Cravens, 1958; Kangas and Bradway, 1971) presents data on a group of individuals originally tested at age 2 or 3 years and retested successively ten, twenty-five, and thirty-eight years later, thus bringing the stability question into the mature adult period. The correlations from the preschool level to the three later tests drop steadily, as would be expected, from .85 at age 12-15 to .65 at age 27½-32 and .41 at age 40½-45. The two correlations with the 12½-15 scores and the later ones show a similar gradient, though they are of course higher: .85 and .68 with ages 27½-32 and 40½-45, respectively. Finally, the correlation between the two adult ages is .77. It might be tempting to interpret these results as further evidence against the overlap hypothesis, if one accepts the common assumption that growth in intelligence terminates by late adolescence (though that assumption itself is being increasingly questioned). In any event the progressive decrease in the stability coefficients through adulthood would be difficult to explain in terms of that hypothesis, especially since this particular group of subjects increased in their mean IQ. The sample of 111 Ss who were involved in the twenty-five-year retest increased from a mean IQ of 112 at age 12½-15 (essentially identical to their preschool IQ) to 124 at age 27½-32, while the smaller subset of 48 Ss retested again at age 40½-45 achieved a mean IQ of 130 on their last test! These increases are not a function of attrition of the original sample; the effects of retesting cannot be so readily discounted, while secular influences, notably the advent of television, may also have played a part. Whatever the basis for this increase, it is difficult to reconcile with the decrease in the stability coefficients, in terms of the accretionary model underlying the overlap hypothesis.

A curious finding of Kangas and Bradway (1971) concerns a differential pattern of gains in the two sexes. Females with low initial scores as preschoolers gained more than those with high initial scores, as one would predict from regression effects alone. In contrast, the gains for the initially high- and low-scoring males were about the same. The low-scoring group's gains came later, predominantly between their last two tests (covering the third decade of their lives), whereas the high-scoring males appeared to reach their (final) level earlier, by age 27½-32. There is no obvious explanation for these findings, but they demonstrate the importance of attention to means, and changes in means of subgroups, to complement the correlational information, and they reinforce the criticism of the stability literature voiced by McCall, Appelbaum, and Hogarty (1973) on this point.

Two other studies are relevant to the question whether changes in intelligence over age tend to favor those who initially score low, according to a principle of compensation or simple regression to the mean, or whether they tend to magnify initial differences. Pinter and Stanton (1937) tested a sample of 140 Ss on Thorndike's CAVD (Completion, Arithmetic, Vocabulary, Directions) scales at ages 8 and 10, finding a stability coefficient of .76. They found a slight average gain of 2.12 and 1.98 IQ points in the high- and medium-IQ groups, compared with 3.05 in the low IQ group. This result gives limited support to a compensation hypothesis, though it may reflect the operation of a simple regression effect. (Actually this difference was concentrated in the 8- to 9-year age period; the changes over the course of the second year of the study were similar in all groups.) A similar study spanning a wider age range and using the WISC (Wechsler Intelligence Scale for Children) was reported more recently by Klonoff (1972), who retested a sample of 173 children intially aged 5 to 13, twice, at one-year intervals. There was a steady though moderate increase in the stability coefficients over this two-year span, from .72 in the youngest group to .78 in the next-to-oldest group. (For the oldest it reached .87, but that group consisted of only 11 children.) Again, those initially of lower IQ (between 90 and 109) gained more than those initially higher (above 110), in accordance with a compensation principle.

Finally, a longitudinal study by Moore (1967), covering the period from 3 to 8 years was concerned primarily with language development and its environmental correlates but also reported stability coefficients for Binet IQ scores between 3 and 5 years and between 3 and 8 years, separately by sex. The values found are in close accord with those reported previously in the literature: $r_{3,5}$ = .73 and .82 for boys and girls, respectively; corresponding values for $r_{3,8}$ = .67 and .64.

Infant Behavior as a Predictor of Later Intelligence. Much of the more recent research relating to stability of intelligence has concentrated on determining the predictability of intelligence in early or later childhood from performance in infancy, using some recently developed measures and some that cannot be considered indicators of level of cognitive development. This literature has recently been reviewed by McCall (1979a), who makes a plea for a truly developmental conception of stability in the context of change, transcending the limitations of the stability coefficient approach. Since the view is consonant with my own, I shall review only a sampling of the more recent studies on this problem that include follow-up data extending into the preschool period or beyond and that raise issues of special interest for this topic.

A table from McCall's review summarizes the results from nineteen studies, spanning more than four decades of research from 1933 to 1975, in terms of median correlations across combinations of four periods during infancy and three periods of childhood and adolescence (table 9.3). The values in this table provide convincing testimony that measures taken during the first year lack predictive value for later intelligence and, more generally, that the later in infancy or early childhood the predictor measure is taken, the higher its relationship to later intelligence (see progressions along rows). At the same time, the converse is true only to a more limited degree: while correlations with

Table 9.3 Median correlations across studies between infant test scores and childhood IQ.[a]

	Age of infant test (in months)				
Age of childhood test (in years)	1-6	7-12	13-18	19-30	
8-18	.06 (6/4)	.25 (3/3)	.32 (4/3)	.49 (34/6)	.28
5-7	.09 (6/4)	.20 (5/4)	.34 (5/4)	.39 (13/5)	.25
3-4	.21 (16/11)	.32 (14/12)	.50 (9/7)	.59 (15/6)	.40
	.12	.26	.39	.49	

Source: McCall (1979a). Reprinted by permission of J. Wiley.

a. Decimal entries indicate median correlation, the numbers in parentheses give the number of different *r*'s and the number of independent studies used to calculate the median. In the case of more than one *r* per study, the median *r* for that study was entered into the calculation of the cell median. Marginal values indicate the average of the median *r*'s presented in that row or column.

intelligence at ages 3 and 4 are somewhat above those for the two older age levels, the latter two do not differ. Thus by age 5 or so, the structure of tested intelligence has changed to such an extent that the resemblance to its composition in infancy is no greater than it is to its composition even later in life.

To turn to some of the individual studies, one that is worth singling out, if only because it appears to provide more positive evidence of stability from infancy to early childhood, is by Colin Hindley (1965). This investigator obtained Griffiths scale scores at 6 and 18 months along with Terman-Merrill IQs at 3 and 5 years. *All* these scores were significantly intercorrelated; 6-month Griffiths scores correlated to the extent of .40 and .32 with IQ at 3 and 5 years, respectively; these values increased to .54 and .40, respectively, when 18-month Griffiths scores were the initial measures. Whether this finding is indicative of something tapped by the Griffiths scale that may be more intrinsically related to later cognitive functioning than other infant scales such as the Bayley remains an interesting conjecture.

Several studies deal with special genetic, racial, or constitutional groups. The first of these, Ronald Wilson's (1974) study of twins, extends downward only to the upper boundary of the infancy period, including Bayley scale scores obtained at ages 1½ and 2 years along with Binet scores at age 3 and a preschool intelligence scale given at ages 4, 5, and 6 (the numbers at the various ages range from 55 to 260). There is a pattern of steady increase in the means, from the 88.4 and 91.0 values on the Bayley in infancy to the 100.9 value on the WPPSI (Wechsler Preschool and Primary Scale of Intelligence) at age 6. This may of course merely be another manifestation of the invalidity of infant intelligence data, but it seems to point to a significant recovery from a moderately retarded level of development to a normal status. This finding is consistent with the view that twinning is a genetically regressive phenomenon, but one that can be fully compensated for through normal environmental stimulation.

The intercorrelations are likewise of interest because of their relatively high magnitudes. The 18-month Bayley scores correlate .60 with the WPPSI at age 4, and .45 and .46 at ages 5 and 6; correlations for the 24-month Bayley with the same preschool tests are up to .74, .67, and .70, respectively. The author attributes this result, compared with the lower values reported by Bayley on the basis of her longitudinal studies, to improvements in the scales and test administration. But it seems that the use of twins would likewise enhance the correlation because of the interdependence among the members of each pair (on the assumption that some degree of stability exists).

Wilson's most interesting data relate to the comparison of correlations within pairs of twins for monozygous (MZ) versus dizygous (DZ) pairs, based on both overall level and on profile information concerning the pattern of year-to-year changes, as proposed by McCall, Appelbaum, and Hogarty (1973). As shown in table 9.4, the overall level correlations (within pairs) do not differentiate MZ from DZ pairs before the period from 3 to 5 years, whereas the profile data (based on the intraclass correlations obtained from the year-to-year change scores) do so even over the course of the first year. The profile values decrease steadily with age, however, vanishing during the 3- to 5-year period for DZ pairs and by age 6 for the MZ pairs, indicating that neither hereditary nor gross environmental factors (such as would be constant for a DZ pair) appear to control developmental rate of cognitive growth beyond the early childhood period.[5]

Two investigations concern black-white differences as these relate to the predictive value of infant intelligence scores. The first, by Goffeney, Henderson, and Butler (1971), provides data on a large sample of children ($N = 626$) initially tested at 8 months on the Bayley scale and subsequently given WISC and Bender Gestalt tests at 7 years. Separate correlations are reported for three scores obtained from the Bayley (the mental, fine motor, and gross motor scales) and three scores obtained from the WISC (full-scale, verbal, and performance), along with the score on the Bender. While all the resulting 12 correlations were significant at the .01 level for the total sample, these included values as low as .11, and none were above .21. Separation of the groups by sex and race (37% of the sample was black) revealed a number of correlations among females that were substantially higher than the corresponding ones among males, as well as higher among whites than blacks. Thus for the white girls four correlations were between .28 and .35, representing the mental and fine motor scales of the

Table 9.4. Within-pair correlations for MZ and DZ twins for measures of overall level and profile of changes across different periods of infancy and early childhood.

		3-12 months	*1½-3 years*	*3-5 years*	*5-6 years*
Overall	MZ pairs	.90	.88	.90	.88
Level	DZ pairs	.75	.84	.69	.62
Profile	MZ pairs	.75	.67	.47	.10
Data	DZ pairs	.50	.39	.06	.05

Source: Data for 3-12 months are adapted from Wilson (1972); for other periods from Wilson (1974). Measures up to age 2 are from Bayley Scales, at age 3 from Binet, and after age 3 from WPPSI.

Bayley and the full-scale and verbal WISC scores. The authors never-theless stress the overall low predictability of the infant measures obtained from an unselected sample such as they dealt with; the study appears to fall well into the pattern of other data obtained from infant intelligence tests, as discussed by McCall.

The study by Broman, Nichols, and Kennedy (1975) is even more ambitious, both with regard to the unusually large sample sizes—approximately 25,000 whites, 23,900 blacks, and 3,600 Puerto Ricans! —and the conglomeration of 169 environmental, biological, and be-havioral variables used to predict preschool IQ. Correlations between the behavioral measures obtained at 8 months, which included scales of both a motor and a cognitive type, and preschool IQ did not ex-ceed .25 for either whites or blacks, once again confirming the lack of predictive significance of infant behavior measures. Counter to the data of Goffeney, Henderson, and Butler (1971), these correlations provide little evidence of race differences. Race influenced the magni-tude of the correlations of some of the environmental variables with preschool IQ, such as SES and mother's educational level, both of which correlated .38 for whites, but only .24 and .21 for blacks. De-spite the impressive scope of this investigation, the findings in this study are difficult to evaluate. As McCall (1976) has noted, the sample included substantial numbers of children with Down's syndrome and other manifestations of pathological central nervous system function-ing; thus one is uncertain about the meaning of even the modest cor-relations between the 8-month measures and IQ at age 4, which tend to vanish when these children are excluded.

The Role of Environmental Variables. Environmental variables such as parental education and SES are better predictors of childhood intelligence than infant test scores. Thus the failure of the black chil-dren in the research of Broman, Nichols, and Kennedy to show a simi-lar relationship for these variables may be attributed to the reduced variability in that group with respect to these variables. At the same time, parental education and SES are coarse, or in Brunswik's sense distal, variables in terms of their relevance to psychological function-ing. Considerable advances have been made in recent years in measur-ing environments, particularly in infancy research (Caldwell, Heider, and Kaplan, 1966; Wachs, 1976), and these have expanded our under-standing of the influences on development in infancy and the environ-mental correlates of subsequent intellectual status. Broman, Nichols, and Kennedy's investigation has contributed in this direction, but the magnitudes of the correlations for individual variables are small, and the sheer profusion of measures tends to weaken their potential impact for the understanding of environmental correlates of childhood intelligence.

In this respect, the study of Elardo, Bradley, and Caldwell (1975) is superior, even though it is limited to a sample of 77 children. These researchers administered Caldwell, Heider, and Kaplan's (1966) Inventory of Home Stimulation at both 6 and 12 months. This scale measures home stimulation in six areas: responsiveness of the mother and her involvement with the child, absence of restrictiveness and punitiveness, organization of the physical and temporal environment, provision of play materials, and overall variety of stimulation. For the individual variables the correlations with 3-year IQs ranged from .24 to .41 for the 6-month measures and from .24 to .56 for the 12-month ones. The corresponding multiple r's, for the 6-month and 12-month environmental measures as predictors of 3-year IQs are .54 and .59, respectively, attesting to a fair degree of predictive value for these environmental measures. (By way of comparison, Broman, Nichols, and Kennedy report multiple correlations for their arsenal of behavioral and home background variables as predictors of preschool IQ of about .45 for whites, but only .30 for blacks.)

It would nevertheless be a mistake to treat environmental variables, however defined, as direct determinants of the child's intelligence, independent of the child's status in terms of constitutional variables, gross level of behavioral and cognitive functioning, and others. This point is brought out in a study by Willerman, Broman, and Fiedler (1970), which shows an interaction between SES and the predictive values of 8-month Bayley scores for IQ at age 4: In a sample of children with 8-month scores below 80, the typical negligible relationship was found for children of high SES, but it was more substantial for those of low SES. The authors attribute this result to the effect of economic and cultural disadvantage in amplifying IQ deficits in children with incipient indications of below-normal functions.[6] A similar interaction is reported by Ireton, Thwing, and Gravem (1970), formulated in a converse sense: for children scoring low (IQ under 85) on the 4-year intelligence measures, their infant measures were somewhat better predictors of such low intelligence than was SES; precisely the reverse was found for children who achieved high IQs (over 115) at age 4. The fact that 28% of the low-IQ four-year-olds in this study were rated neurologically "suspect" in infancy suggests that a constitutional factor overrides environmental influences in these children.

Yet it would be erroneous to assume that specific neurological or other constitutional problems in infancy are inevitably predictive of subsequent mental deficit. Arnold Sameroff (1975) has reviewed some of this literature and has found essentially no relationship between either anoxia or neurological status at birth and later intelligence.[7] The evidence on the effects of prematurity is more equivocal; some studies show a positive effect, others show none. Sameroff suggests that positive effects may well be mediated by the expectations of the parents and that the mother's behavior toward the infant is elicited by the latter's own behavior. Thus there is a need for a more interactive conception of the relationship between child and environment than has been evident in most of the research in this area.

The complexities in the interaction among constitutional condition and environmental factors in the changing interrelationship among behavioral and intellectual measures from birth to middle childhood are brought out in an extensive longitudinal investigation conducted in Hawaii by Emmy Werner and her co-workers (Werner, Honzik, and Smith, 1968; Werner, Bierman, and French, 1971). This study included measures of perinatal stress involving pre- and neonatal data, scores from the Cattell scale at age 20 months, and intelligence test scores from the WISC administered at 10 years. Not surprisingly, the perinatal stress data failed to correlate with the 10-year IQ measures (as has also been found for Agpar scores at birth related to Binet IQs at age 3; Shipe, Vandenberg, and Williams, 1968). The 20-month Cattell data, on the other hand, correlated with the 10-year measures, the r of .49 being representative of the values reported by previous investigators (table 9.3). More intriguing still are the differences between the groups segregated according to perinatal stress measures on the 20-month Cattell scores. They are negligible for high-SES children, but substantial for those of low SES, just as Willerman, Broman, and Fiedler (1970) had found. This suggests that neurological or other biologically determined deficits may exert potent effects during infancy, though even in this period their expression is modulated by the child's environment. The effects of the conditions associated with perinatal stress appear, however, to dissipate with age. Thus the remarkably high stability between the 20-month and 10-year measures in a subgroup of children of IQ below 80 at age 10 ($r = .71$) is not readily accounted for by the organic factors reflected in the perinatal stress measures.

Notwithstanding the complexities and inconsistencies in the literature on infant behavior measures as predictors of later intelligence, the essential and inescapable point is the marked discontinuity between development during infancy and the subsequent emergence of cognitive development. These discontinuities—there are several—have been most recently documented in impressive fashion by McCall, Eichorn, and Hogarty (1977). These investigators undertook a factor analysis of the scores from birth to age 5 of children in the Berkeley

Growth Study and isolated a set of principal components whose composition underwent demonstrable changes at specific "inflection" points on the age continuum—at ages 2, 8, 13, and 30-36 months. These transition points further determined the pattern of stability coefficients, whose magnitude appeared to undergo marked oscillation (McCall, Eichorn, and Hogarty, 1977, figures 2 and 3), which would be difficult to explain from a continuity view of development and which McCall and his co-workers identify with the transitions across specific stages. These investigators further demonstrate a consistent relationship between the magnitude of the stability coefficients and the number of stage boundaries (zero, one, or two) straddled across the interval over which they are taken (see their table 21).

Genotypic Continuity. The discontinuous character of early cognitive development leaves unresolved an issue of theoretical importance: whether rate of development during infancy is inherently unrelated to later cognitive development or whether there may be genotypic continuities, in Kagan's (1971) sense, that are masked by the phenotypic discontinuities but might be revealed by a more astute choice of behavioral measures in infancy.

The former view is implied by Sandra Scarr-Salapatek (1976) in her evolutionary formulation of development in infancy, in terms of the concept of canalization. This concept is used to denote a process of development during this period that is largely impervious to exogenous forces, thus accounting for the lack of predictive value of measures taken during this period in relation to those taken in later childhood, which are assumed to be much more strongly influenced by environmental stimulation. Scarr-Salapatek's distinction between canalization and a complementary process of developmental adaptation brings to mind Myrtle McGraw's (1935) classical differentiation between phyletic and ontogenetic skills. Yet Scarr-Salapatek seems to stress the former at the expense of the latter, for the period of infancy, while for McGraw the two operate concurrently.

The adequacy of Scarr-Salapatek's case for a semi-insulated process of canalization is difficult to evaluate. At the same time evidence on genotypic continuity, at least for the period from infancy to the end of the preschool years, is scant. Two studies do provide data suggestive of such continuity, however. One is the study by Halverson and Waldrop (1976), who determined relationships between ratings of activity level and measures of social behavior at age 2½ and various cognitive measures at age 7. They found that WISC scores correlated − .38 with activity level at 2½, and − .47 with the social behavior scores. The 2½-year measures relate at best to the upper bound of the infancy period, but given the nature of the activity measures, it should prove worthwhile to obtain them at an earlier age, as well as to relate them to measures of cognitive style, notably reflectivity-impulsivity.

The second study is frankly more startling in its findings. Cameron, Livson, and Bayley (1967) undertook a factor analysis of data for the 115-item California First Year Mental Scale, obtained in the Berkeley Growth Study; testing at one-month intervals permitted the authors to score each item in terms of age at which the item was first passed, thus reflecting *rate* of development with respect to that item. They arrived at six clusters of items. One, represented by vocalizations, showed substantial correlations with intelligence between ages 6 and 26, but only for females. The correlations, for both full-scale and verbal IQs, actually increase with age, and at age 26 reach the improbable values of .75 for verbal IQ and .62 for full-scale IQ (relationships to performance scores are considerably lower). These findings are in marked contrast to the negligible correlations obtained with 10- to 12-month Bayley Mental Scores as the predictor variable. Since the results held only for females and are based on just 39 subjects of that sex, caution is needed in generalizing these findings. The role of SES as a possible mediator of the correlation between vocalization and IQ needs to be borne in mind; unpublished data by Kagan[8] indicate that similar correlations found between infants' vocalization and IQ in childhood vanish when social class is controlled.

Specific Components of Intelligence Tests. To the extent that intelligence is a composite of different abilities, each of which may conform to different developmental patterns, one might expect stability coefficients to be highest for measures of subtests that are unitary with regard to the psychological processes tapped by them, as compared with the far from unitary total intelligence scores that we have dealt with so far. This potential gain due to construct purity is offset by the reduced reliability of the subtest measures, however. The available information suggests that the latter factor contributes more to stability, which is generally higher for total scale than for subscale scores. Hopkins and Bibelheimer (1971) obtained data on the California Test of Mental Maturity in children between grades 3 and 8. For total IQ the median stability coefficients for the six intercorrelations between grades 3, 5, 7, and 8 was .76, but they dropped to .60 and .48 for the language and nonlanguage components of the scale, respectively. The authors attributed these lower magnitudes in comparison with the stability coefficients in the literature reviewed by Thorndike and Bloom to the use of group tests instead of individual tests, but they ignore the fact that their total score stability coefficients are in the .70s and close to the corresponding values for these age levels obtained from individually administered tests such as the Binet.

The lower stability of components of intelligence test performance compared with total scale values is further supported by the findings of Goodenough and Maurer (1942), although in their case only the initial scores obtained from their Minnesota preschool scales are differentiated into verbal and nonverbal components. The differences reported between the total score stability coefficients and those for the verbal and nonverbal scales are generally small, and where the stability coefficients for the two scales at a particular age differ substantially, the total score stability coefficient is sometimes intermediate rather than larger than either.

How does stability compare among particular aspects of cognitive performance? A number of studies show separate values for verbal and nonverbal scales, but the results are mixed. The data of Goodenough and Maurer (1942) show no consistent pattern, although there is a tendency for greater stability for the nonverbal preschool scale (particularly where the 1937 revision of the Stanford-Binet rather than the 1916 version was used at the older age). Further, the nonverbal preschool scores correlate substantially higher with Grace-Arthur performance scores obtained in later childhood than did the verbal preschool scores, testifying to the stability of the verbal-nonverbal differentiation over this age span.

The Hopkins and Bibelheimer study (1971) reports predominantly lower stability coefficients for nonlanguage than for language IQ in the 8-13 age range; Goffeney, Henderson, and Butler (1971) in their study of 8-month-old infants who were subsequently given the WISC at 7 years also report slightly higher correlations from infancy scores to verbal WISC scores than to nonverbal scores, but these differences were small, as were the magnitudes of the stability coefficients.

Several studies report separate stability coefficients for each of the WISC subtests. Osborne and Suddick (1972), tested 204 children in preschool and in grades 1, 3, and 5, finding no substantial difference in stability between the verbal and the performance subtests as a group. The vocabulary subtest had the highest stability, especially over the preschool to grade 5 interval, where the stability coefficient was .67 compared with .52 for information and digit span and .48 for object assembly (the highest value for the five performance subtests). The median stability coefficient from preschool to the three grade-school levels for the individual verbal and performance subtests ranged between .44 and .51, substantially below the values in the .60s and .70s typically found for total intelligence test score stability over comparable age spans.

In a more extensive investigation focused mainly on cognitive-style measures, Holtzman, Diaz-Guerrero, and Swartz (1975) also included certain WISC subtests. This research is noteworthy for being cross-cultural: children from the United States (Austin, Texas) and from Mexico (Mexico City) were compared. Within each culture, data were obtained at yearly intervals over a five-year span from three cohorts aged 7, 10, and 13 at the start of the study. The stability coefficients for the vocabulary subtest scores of the U.S. children are in fairly close agreement with those obtained by Osborne and Suddick for comparable age intervals, but the values for the Mexican children are consistently smaller. (The medians of the 15 correlations reported for each cohort were .66, .61, and .74 in the American groups, compared with .38, .53, and .46 in the Mexican.) No such systematic differences between the two cultural samples were found for any of the other three subtests included in the study: block design, arithmetic, and picture completion, which again showed stability coefficients (for both cultures) similar to those of Osborne and Suddick. The difference in stability between the U.S. and Mexican children on the vocabulary subtest is even more puzzling given that the pattern was reversed on a word association test scored for paradigmatic and syntagmatic associations (to be explained in a later section); here it was the Mexican children who showed the higher stability.

In both Osborne and Suddick's results and Holtzman, Diaz-Guerrero, and Swartz's results the expected age-interval gradient (see proposition 2, p. 380) is curiously absent for any of the subtests. Holtzman and his colleagues provide partial support for proposition 3, since the oldest cohort displays generally higher stability than the two younger ones. Yet the failure of the stability coefficients in these two studies to decrease consistently with increasing age interval remains a conundrum, comparable to that presented by Goodenough and Maurer's (1942) correlations between their preschool scale and later Binet scores.

The general finding from these studies on WISC subtests, that measures of more specialized abilities have lower stabilities than overall performance on intelligence tests, is worth pondering. Yet in the Brush Foundation study (Ebert and Simmons, 1943) stability of scores on two form-board tests, one given at ages 10-14 years, the other at ages 5-11 years, approached the corresponding Binet values, particularly over the 10-14 year span. The suggestion is that stability for more specialized tests increases more slowly with age than is true for wider-ranging intelligence scales, for which the magnitude of stability accel-

erates quickly (figure 9.4b), but that they eventually level off at approximately the same magnitude, presumably asymptotic to their
short-term test-retest reliabilities.

Prediction of Achievement from Childhood Intelligence Scores.
Intelligence test measures from early childhood on appear to predict
scholastic achievement as well as they predict IQ during the school
years. This is the apparent import of the findings of Werner, Honzik,
and Smith (1968) based on correlations between Catell IQs at 20
months and school achievement at 10 years. Not only is the correlation with achievement (.43, averaged over the sexes) slightly higher
than the correlation with IQ (.40, based on the Primary Mental Ability Tests), but children with Cattell IQs below 80 were much more
likely to experience severe school problems at age 10: 19% were placed
in a special class (compared with less than 1% of those above 80 IQ at
20 months), and 33% were below grade for their chronological age
(compared with 7.6% of those above 80 IQ). Ebert and Simmons
(1943) also found achievement test scores between ages 10 and 12 to be
predicted from Binet IQ scores at ages 4 and 6 as well as were IQ
scores at the same ages. In view of the well-known correlation of intelligence with school achievement and SES and given the moderate-sized
stability coefficients for intelligence across the age spans involved in
the two studies, these findings should not be surprising.

A few studies have followed individuals who were given intelligence tests in early or middle childhood and obtained assessments of
their adult occupational statuses or achievements. McCall (1977)
charted correlations, based on the Fels data, between IQ at different
ages and level of education and education attained as adults; these are
reproduced in figure 9.6. Although these curves rise much more slowly
and remain considerably below the level of the correlations with IQ at
age 40, they still attest to the predictive value of IQ for these two
aspects of status at maturity, especially considering that the .50 level
reached by middle childhood corresponds to the correlation between
adult IQ and adult occupational status, as McCall notes. There is also
a differential pattern for the sexes. The lower correlations for the
women in the Fels sample may be ascribed to the role of women in the
culture. In fact, in view of the more restricted opportunities for education and employment for women at the time this sample reached maturity, one would expect an even greater sex difference. Yet the correlations for the women during their early childhood years are actually
higher than those for the men. This higher initial level is probably
related to the higher initial values for the initial-terminal IQ correlations for women. But they do not rise much beyond the 7-year level
(except for the *r* at age 16 with occupation). This might itself be read

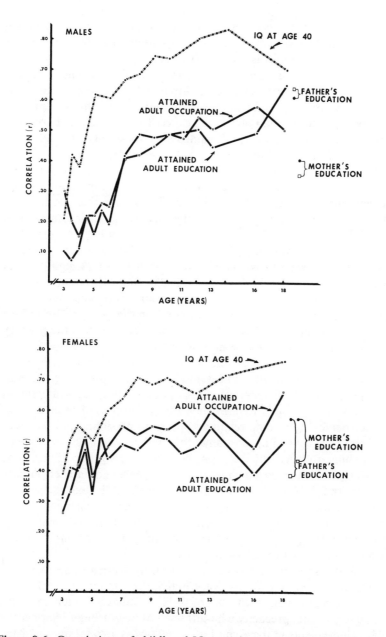

Figure 9.6. *Correlations of childhood IQ at various ages with attained adult educational and occupational status (Fels sample) and with IQ at age 40 years (child guidance sample). Also, correlation of fathers' and mothers' education with offsprings' adult occupational (open square) and adult educational (filled circle) status. (From McCall, 1977.)*

as a reflection of a lesser degree of responsiveness of the educational and occupational system of our society to the abilities displayed by the women of this sample as they neared maturity.

Finally, Terman and Oden (1947), in their twenty-five-year follow-up study of adults who as children had IQs in the genius range found this group to be far more successful in their achievements and occupational status than one would expect for an unselected group of cases (just as their adult IQs remained superior—144, a loss of but 8 points from the childhood mean). Yet cases of less than outstanding achievement as adults were still numerous enough to allow the authors to compare a successful with an "unsuccessful" group, in an attempt to determine possible predictors of lack of success in this select group. Although the two groups differed significantly in their Binet IQ in childhood, that difference amounted to only 5 points. A somewhat greater difference was observed in a concept mastery test administered 18 years later, when these individuals were between 23 and 39 years old (the mean age for both groups was 31). Some differentiation between the groups had appeared in their high school achievement records, but they did not differ in their scores on the Terman Group Test of intelligence administered in high school. It appears that the primary differences between the two groups related to a complex of family-environment, sociocultural, and personality factors, reflected in ratings on certain social adjustment and leadership traits in high school, ratings on traits of self-confidence, perseverance, and integration toward goals as adults. Remarkably, the two groups differed also on certain demographic data relating to parents and siblings; in the high-success group three times as many of the fathers and twice as many of the siblings finished college as in the low-success group. Thus these data suggest that given a high level of intelligence, nonintellectual factors determine the extent to which the potential indicated by the intelligence is realized in educational and vocational attainment. These factors seem to relate to the fostering of education and intellectual pursuits in the family environment and to certain personality traits related to the need to achieve.

Needless to say, this conclusion from the Terman and Oden research cannot be applied to every individual's failure to realize his potential. A poignant case is that of William James Sidis, a man of extreme intellectual precocity who attracted notice through his remarkable achievements in the area of mathematics as a youngster and subsequently went into a state of evident deterioration and decline (Montour, 1977). In the light of Terman and Oden's findings, it is noteworthy that Montour is inclined to ascribe this anomalous development to the seemingly severe pressures for achievement placed on the child by his father.

The preceding review of the literature on the stability of the IQ leaves me with mixed feelings. The sheer bulk of the research on stability of IQ is impressive, particularly considering the need for longitudinal data obtained over extended portions of the individual's growth to maturity. A reasonably coherent picture of the stability of the IQ, over different portions of the age span, and some of the variables affecting it, has emerged from this research.

At the same time the problematical nature of the IQ itself, along with the limitations of the stability coefficients and the problems in its interpretation, leaves one wondering whether this massive expenditure of research time and resources has been as profitable as it might have been. As our understanding of the nature of intelligence evolves, different ways of assessing it are likely to be devised, and the result may well be a major redirection of our mode of attack on the stability issue. Current dissatisfaction on the part of vocal sectors of our society with the IQ, on the basis of the cultural bias built into current intelligence tests, may accelerate this process.

The study of stability for measures of specific cognitive skills and other measures of psychological processes relevant to the child's cognitive development represents an important step in this direction. The following section examines the scattered literature reporting such data.

Other Measures of Cognitive Performance

Three types of measures will be considered: linguistic variables potentially relevant to cognitive processes, such as word associations categorized in terms of their syntactical significance; measures of cognitive style, which involve traitlike dispositions on the part of an individual child revealed in response to perceptual and conceptual tasks; and measures of creativity and originality.

Moran and Swartz (1970) investigated the stability of "cognitive dictionaries" in a combined cross-sectional and longitudinal study of word associations, with children aged 9, 12, and 15 years on initial test, and retested two years later. Over this age span the tendency to respond with a particular semantic class (contrast, predicate, synonym) showed moderate levels of stability, at least in subjects who responded consistently in terms of a particular type of associative set on both tests; for these the stability coefficients (averaged over six semantic classes) ranged from .42 to .59 in the three age groups. For the subjects who did not evince a consistent associative set the values are considerably lower, particularly in the two youngest age groups. Similar results were found in a grammatical analysis of associations falling into either a paradigmatic or syntagmatic type. (Paradigmatic associations are those that are of the same grammatical category as the stimulus word, such as table-chair, red-green; syntagmatic associations are of a different grammatical category from the stimulus word, such as table-eat, red-cherry.)

Moran and Swartz's study formed part of an extensive longitudinal cross-cultural investigation by Holtzman, Diaz-Guerrero, and Swartz (1975). These latter authors report stability coefficients for proportions of noun-noun and for a combinaton of verb-verb plus adjective-adjective paradigmatic associations and for syntagmatic associations (without differentiating subjects into set versus nonset). These values were somewhat higher than those of Moran and Swartz, particularly for the oldest group. More noteworthy, however, is that generally higher values were found for the Mexican sample than for the American. The median two-year stability coefficient (for nine values reported for the combinations of three age groups and three types of associations) was .61 for the Mexican children, compared with .52 for the American, while the means differed even more sharply: .59 versus .44. This finding may reflect an interesting difference between the two languages, particularly if it could be established that the shift with development from paradigmatic associations (say, adjective to noun) to syntagmatic associations (noun to noun) found for American children (Entwisle, 1966) either does not apply to Spanish-speaking children or occurs either much later or much earlier. Unfortunately, data on this point were not reported by Holtzman, Diaz-Guerrero, and Swartz; means were given only for syntagmatic associations, which occur more frequently among the Mexican children in the two younger age groups, while in the oldest group they occur more frequently among the American children.

The concept of cognitive style has been applied in different senses by different investigators, but it refers basically to individual difference of response to cognitive tasks, that is, to consistent tendencies on the part of a given individual to organize stimuli or concepts or to structure spatial or temporal experience in a fashion that is different from that of other children. Kagan and Kogan (1970) have reviewed the extensive developmental literature on this topic, which deals with such diverse traits as analytic versus perceptual approaches to object classification, dependence on field- versus self-based cues in spatial orientation, impulsiveness or reflectivity in problem solving, and others. While the unitary nature of these dimensions of cognitive style remains to be established in many cases, this body of research has contributed significantly to our understanding of diverse qualitative aspects of cognitive development. The study of the stability of these traits over age is particularly important in verifying that they are a stable characteristic of the developing child, but considerable gaps remain in our knowledge.

The most comprehensive set of data on stability of cognitive style, comprising three dimensions of cognitive style, is contained in the recent monograph by Kogan (1976). Kogan reports on an extensive partially longitudinal investigation of the precursors of some commonly studied aspects of cognitive style in early childhood and, in the case of one dimension, goes back to infancy. Most of the stability data reviewed in this volume (some obtained by other investigators) cover no more than a 12-month period and are thus hardly comparable to the intelligence test data considered previously. Kogan deals with measures for the Preschool Embedded Figures Test (PEFT), for reflection-impulsivity, based on a test of matching familiar figures (MFF), and for breadth and style of categorization, based on measures obtained from the Sigel Object Sorting Test (SOST). Twelve-month stability for the PEFT is of the order of 0.50 between ages 3 and 4, while a study correlating PEFT measures at age 4 with CEFT (Children's Embedded Figures Test) scores at age 5 found fair stability (.43) for boys, but a negligible value for girls (.14). These data are taken from an unpublished study by Jean and Jack Block, who likewise report stability data for the MFF between ages 3 and 4, which attained significance in the case of error scores ($r = .44$), but not for latencies. Kogan cites further data from a study by William Ward extending over a three-year period, which were of similar magnitude. Finally, style of categorization was found (again by the Blocks) to show significant stability for two of the three response categories, descriptive and categorical, for girls but not for boys, while an accuracy score derived from the SOST also showed a significant degree of stability for both sexes combined ($r = .37$); breadth of categorization, however, failed to exhibit significant stability. Kogan also cites data of Block and Block on McReynold's Concept Evaluation Test from ages 4 to 5, showing a stability coefficient of .50.

In view of the uncertain reliabilities of these tests, particularly at these early ages, these stability values are probably as high as one should expect, and given the relatively short interval between tests they are perhaps more appropriately treated as reliability values than as indicators of stability in the long-range sense. Unfortunately, information based on longer-term research in this area is sparse, with the exception of work relating to the dimension of field independence studied by Witkin and his colleagues (Witkin et al., 1962).

A very recent study by Rusch and Lis (1977) on the rod-and-frame test, in which the subject is asked to adjust a luminous line appearing within a luminous rectangle tilted to the vertical (in the dark), contains test-retest data covering a three-year span for children between 7 and 10 years of age at initial test. The stability coefficients for the most part range in the .50s, but a highly anomalous result is contained in those for the 8-year-olds retested at 11. The girls in this group showed a test-retest correlation (for total scores, combining left and right tilt) of .90; by contrast, the correlation for boys is but .26. The confusion is compounded by the finding of higher stability for the 7- to 10-year-old boys, although that difference is confined largely to the left-tilt data (where the male and female values are .50 and .08, respectively). The well-known sex differences in measures of field dependence were confirmed: girls showed much larger mean errors than boys at all ages. Yet given the failure to find any sex differences in stability in the two older groups and the greater stability in boys in the youngest group, the anomalous finding in the 8- to 11-year group remains a result of doubtful generalizability. The overall magnitude of the stability coefficients, particularly in the two older groups of boys and girls, where it ranges from .57 to .62, is reasonably high, especially since data cited by the authors show test-retest correlations of only .48 to .61 over a span of one to two months in a group of 5- to 7-year-olds.

Further stability data related to the field dependence dimension but covering a broader age interval were obtained by Witkin, Goodenough, and Karp (1967). These investigators found a correlation of .72 and .62 for errors on the rod-and-frame test, in males and females respectively, tested at ages 10 and 17. A more convincing demonstration of the stability of this measure, combining information on means and individual differences, is shown in a comparison between the seven most field-independent and the seven most field-dependent males over the period from 10 to 24 years. The age curves for both groups clearly show the overall decrease up to late adolescence in errors of field dependence, while the almost perfectly parallel shapes of the two curves brings out the stability of this trait (in the individual difference sense).

Similar data were obtained by Faterson and Witkin (1970) on a measure of adequacy of the body concept, based on the degree of articulation of body parts in the child's drawing. The 10- to 17-year stability correlations for males are very close to those for the rod-and-frame test: .74; for females, however, the values were higher, .86. Stability held up on a further retest of males at age 24; in fact, both the 10- to 24-year and the 14- to 24-year correlations exceeded (by 4 points) the corresponding correlations with scores for age 17.

The study by Holtzman, Diaz-Guerrero, and Swartz (1975) includes measures of cognitive style, along with the WISC and verbal association data mentioned previously, and other measures based on the Holtzman Inkblot Test which because of its uncertain relevance to the study of cognitive processes will be omitted from consideration here. Stability coefficients for the Embedded Figures Test (EFT) show the expected gradients (decrease with test-retest interval, increase with age on first test) for the U.S. children and are generally of substantial magnitude for both reaction time and number of correct items; however, these data are confined to the two oldest groups. Thus, $r_{10,12} = .66$ and .67 for these two measures, respectively; the corresponding values for $r_{10,14} = .53$ and .50. The equivalent values in the Mexican sample are considerably lower: $r_{10,12} = .59$ and .45; $r_{10,14} = .32$ and .20. There was an even wider gap in the stability coefficients for the two cultural groups obtained from the scores on a Perceptual Maturity Scale, which is a test of preference for designs taken from the Welsh Figure Preference Test, and scored in terms of inferred developmental level. These measures were obtained only for the last three years of the study, when the children in the three cohorts were aged 9 to 11, 13 to 15, and 17 to 19. The median of the resulting nine test-retest correlations (three per group) was .63 for the U.S. children and only .16 for the Mexican children. Since this pattern of greater stability in the U.S. children did not apply across the board—the WISC performance tests and the Harris-Goodenough figure drawing test showed no consistent difference between the two groups, while for the word association data the values were substantially higher for the Mexican children—any simple interpretation in terms of better test-taking orientation or rapport or other reliability-related factors on the part of the U.S. children is ruled out. No easy explanation suggests itself for these differences, but their existence emphasizes the importance of cultural and other environmental influences as modulators of developmental stability.

Results from the Object Sorting Test in this same investigation are available only for the first three years of the study. Even over this limited time span they failed consistently to attain values above .50 among the U.S. children, except at the high-school level. Again the values for the U.S. were higher than those for the Mexican children, although on only one of the three measures (number of groups constructed) was this difference a substantial one.

Two studies are available in which tests of creativity first administered in the preadolescent period were readministered after a five-year interval, in late adolescence. Cropley and Clapson (1971) administered two tests of creativity to children at ages 12 and 17, one of "consequences" (invention of unusual outcomes of a hypothetical situation related to the subject) and one of "circles" (originality of designs created from a circle). Along with an overall substantial increase in creativity, they report stability coefficients of 0.37 and 0.44 for these two tests. On both measures males showed substantially higher stability than females (.50 versus .27 for consequences and .48 versus .33 for circles), even though the two sexes were not significantly differentiated in their means. The authors consider the extent of stability on these tests to be of comparable magnitude to those that Cropley (1964) reported for subtests of the WISC, but these values are lower than one would expect from other data for these same measures. On the other hand, Cropley and Clapson's values are closer to those found by Kogan and Pankove (1972), who administered the Wallach-Kogan tests of creativity to children at age 11 and again at age 16, at least for values for boys in one of the two schools in which the study was carried out. There was a curious interaction between school and sex. Boys showed greater stability in school B than in school A, while the opposite was true of the girls. Although school B was much larger, the authors attribute this anomalous finding to the fact that in school B the tests were group administered, while in school A they were given individually. They suggest that as boys reached adolescence they reacted more unfavorably to the individual examiner. The girls, on the other hand, responded negatively to the depersonalized context in school B. The number of cases tested in school A was small, so the generalizability of these findings is moot, but they alert us to the potential importance of situational factors in the assessment of cognitive performance.

Hutt and Bhavnani (1972) have contributed a study that is of interest in dealing with measures of play and exploratory activity in preschool children—relatively neglected aspects of child behavior until recently—and relating these to measures of creativity obtained during the primary school years. The number of children included in this study is small, especially given the differential patterns found once again for the sexes, but the results are nevertheless suggestive. The authors divided the group of children into nonexplorers (NE), explorers (E), and inventive explorers (IE), on the basis of their response to a new toy in preschool (between 3 and 5 years). Among the boys these three groups displayed increasing levels of creativity four years later, based on the originality scores obtained from the Wallach-Kogan tests of creativity; their means were 24.5, 44.9, and 76.3, respectively. Here the E group differs significantly from both the NE and the IE group, indicating that exploration of a novel stimulus per se was predictive of later creativity. For girls, on the other hand, the corresponding means for those in the NE, E, and IE groups were 36.2, 39.8, and 61.5, respectively; the E group differed significantly only from the IE group. In nursery school there was a noted sex difference in response to the novel toy; three times as many girls as boys were classified as nonexplorers, and four times as many boys as girls were classified as inventive explorers. Yet for the longitudinal sample there appeared little overall difference in creativity four years later.

This report by Hutt and Bhavnani, for all its brevity, is particularly noteworthy because it considers precursors at the nursery school level of later creativity in terms not only of a different mode of expression of creativity (inventive play) but of an altogether different type of response (exploration of novel stimuli). In this respect the study is clearly related to the more extensive and systematic work by Kagan (1971) on heterotypic continuity, based on relationships between measures of attention, exploration, and vocalization to stimuli in infancy and other cognitive and behavioral measures in early childhood. The field of cognitive development needs more work of this type, especially given the major qualitative shifts in the manifestation of cognitive activity at different periods of development.

The Interpretation of Stability Coefficients

This review of the proliferating literature on stability of cognitive development based on test-retest correlation coefficients raises some major questions concerning the conclusions that may be drawn from such data and their limitations as evidence on the stability issue.

A few problems are essentially statistical. First, stability coefficients are only extensions of reliability coefficients, in the test-retest sense. The assumption is, of course, that lack of stability of a test score over a very brief interval represents a defect in the measuring instrument, whereas over an extended period of time it reflects an intrinsic change in the individual. The boundary between these two alternative conceptions is arbitrary, and even when stability coefficients are obtained over an extended period of time, they are obviously affected by lack of reliability of the measuring instrument at both the initial and the terminal level. Frequently, stability data have been corrected for the test's lack of reliability but it is questionable whether such manipulation yields values that are valid measures of a variable's "true" stability.

A real question arises whether the data concerning lack of stability of intelligence as measured from infancy to later childhood can be attributed simply to the well-known intraindividual variability of infant behavior and the resulting lack of reliability of measures obtained from infants. Undoubtedly problems of reliability of a set of measures limit the size of stability coefficients based on them, yet reliability by itself cannot account for the patterns of decreasing correlation from infancy to early and later childhood as the interval between tests is increased (table 9.3). Nor can it explain why intercorrelations within the period of infancy decrease with increasing interval (table 9.1) when reliability is presumably increasing with age.

Stability coefficients are subject to all the shortcomings of the correlation coefficient. Among these the most serious is probably their dependence on the amount of variability in the measures. Less stability is to be expected in a highly homogeneous population than in an unselected one, not because the variable involved "behaves" differently in the two groups, but because evidence on stability in the sense of the preservation of individual differences within a group depends on the extent of variability present in that group. This seemingly trite conclusion is worth emphasizing because the magnitudes of stability coefficients are thus devoid of meaning in any absolute sense and more fundamentally because their use presupposes that variability remains approximately constant across the period of development under study. This means, for instance, that stability of the development of simple arithmetic skills could be usefully determined only for a very restricted portion of the age scale: before the age of 5 the skill is largely nonexistent, and variability is thus close to zero; after the age of 12 or so most children have become so proficient in it that variability should again be curtailed. Many dimensions conform to this model of individuation emerging at some point during development and increasing over a period of time, only to converge toward a terminal level at which differences are either eliminated (except for cases of major abnormality or severe retardation) or greatly attenuated in amount. More generally, stability in this sense must be considered in relation to the overall pattern of differentiation over the course of development characterizing a particular variable. (For a fuller treatment of this issue, see Wohlwill, 1973b, chapter 12.)

A related property of correlation coefficients is their insensitivity to changes in means. Bearing in mind that stability in the individual difference sense is abstracted from change with respect to level, let us recall the observation of McCall (1979a) that a focus on individual differences as contrasted to overall changes in level may provide different answers to questions about the relative influence of environmental and genetic factors, the role of particular environmental influences, and the meaning of concepts such as stability and continuity. In effect, stability coefficients tell us as much about the meaning of a particular measure as an expression of a hypothetical developmental variable as they tell us about the process of developmental change in that variable. For example, if some measure of physical fitness showed low stability from early childhood to adolescence, the reason might be that the individual developmental timetables for physical fitness are highly variable, so that some who are relatively low on this dimension in early childhood are relatively high as adolescents. Alternatively, the low stability could reflect a change in the construct of fitness itself, in terms of the measures used to operationalize it at the two ages. This problem would not exist for a variable with a more determinate definition, such as height or strength; similarly it does not apply to narrowly defined psychological variables such as verbal fluency and perceptual field dependence unless these variables are interpreted as reflections of broader cognitive or personality processes. But, in the absence of a precise definition of intelligence, it is clear that the information derived from stability coefficients for IQ scores is fundamentally ambiguous in this respect.

Thus Bloom's interpretation of such coefficients in his comprehensive survey of the literature (1964) becomes questionable. Two specific aspects of his interpretation may be challenged: the interpretation of stability coefficients in terms of percentage of mature intelligence attained, and the conclusion that the rapid rise in such coefficients points to a lessened influence of the environment with increasing age.

The notion that stability coefficients can be translated directly into percentage of adult status attained at a given age seems to be based, first, on the assumption that the overlap hypothesis formulated by Anderson (1939) to account for the rise in stability coefficients with age applies and, second, on the seeming correspondence (figure 9.4b) between the developmental function for stability coefficients and for quasi-absolute scales of intelligence. The overlap hypothesis is based on an accretionary model of growth originally intended for physical variables such as height and certain similar psychological variables such as vocabulary development, motor abilities, and the like. It does not seem applicable to a variable such as intelligence which, as the tests themselves show, undergoes marked qualitative changes in the mode of its manifestation with age. Besides the similarity between the growth curve for intelligence and for stability coefficients based on intelligence test scores is more apparent than real. The discrepancy is particularly marked over the early period of development, in which these coefficients rise much faster than would be predicted from the growth curves.

Probably the more important issue, however, concerns Bloom's conclusion that the rapid increase in stability of IQ with age, and its attaining a value well above .50 after early childhood (with maturity taken as the terminal point), indicates that intelligence is relatively impervious to environmental influences after that point. This conclusion would be valid only if one assumed a highly changeable environment over the course of development (McCall, 1979b). Conversely, given a perfectly constant environment, the low degree of stability early in life would be devoid of significance for the role of environmental factors during that period. Stability coefficients are equivocal in their bearing on the role of environmental factors, at least in the absence of some independent assessment of the constancy or lack of it in the environment.

On this critical point there is little information. Bloom noted that psychology had neglected the problem of devising adequate measures of environmental forces relevant to the development of the child. Although work on this problem goes back several decades, most of the early work is either limited to a particular age group, such as Van Alstyne's (1929) scale for the home environment of nursery school children (see also Wellman, 1940) or intended primarily for the study of personality development, such as Baldwin, Kalhorn, and Breese's (1949) scales for the measurement of parental behavior and Kagan and Moss's (1962) assessment of maternal variables. Bloom refers to a study by Wolf (1966), which deals more broadly with environmental stimulation in the home relevant to the developing child, and more recently a variety of similar instruments have been developed, although mainly for use with infants. Such scales have rarely been used on a sufficiently long longitudinal basis to provide information on the degree of constancy in the child's environment, on which Bloom's interpretation of stability coefficients is predicated.

A partial exception is a study by Hanson (1975), reporting measurements of home environments for 110 children from the Fels Longitudinal Study over the period from birth to age 10. The stability of the environment for a rural town such as Yellow Springs, Ohio, may not be representative of that generally experienced by children in this country, but this study is significant because so much of our stability information has come from the Fels data. It included a large number of environmental variables but focused on seven that were correlated with IQ at one or more of three age levels (3, 5½, and 9½ years). These seven dealt primarily with parental behavior that fostered or stimulated the child's intellectual activity, through direct teaching of language, allowing the child to engage in verbal expression, and other similar means. The variables were found to load on one of two factors, one concerned with the child's verbal expression and with parental involvement with the child, the other with encouraging the child's achievements and providing models for the child. Stability coefficients were obtained for the environmental variables, both individually and for certain composite indices derived from them, over three periods, from birth to age 3, from 4 to 6, and from 7 to 10. For the two adjacent pairs the stability values ranged from .31 to .56; for the correlation between the first and third periods (0-3, 7-10) the values were somewhat lower, ranging from .16 to .49. Values for the two composite indices for these factors were higher, however, ranging from .48 to .62 for the two adjacent periods; for the first and third periods, the values were .32 and .55. These data corresponded closely to values reported by Kagan and Moss (1962, p. 209) for the stability of parental behavior, along dimensions such as restriction and acceleration.

Hansen's study thus seems to demonstrate considerable constancy in the quality of the child's home environment, along dimensions relevant to intellectual growth. To that extent his results raise questions about the validity of the inference that Bloom and others have drawn from the high stability coefficients for intelligence from middle childhood period onward—that with increasing age environmental factors play a diminishing role in the child's intellectual development. On the other hand, Hansen limited himself to the *home* environment. In a purely ecological sense, and perhaps in a more fundamental sense as a primary influence in the child's mental development, the home undoubtedly decreases in importance as the child goes to school and is exposed to diverse environments in the community (Wright, 1956). To the extent that these environmental changes are institutionalized, however, their role in stability of intelligence in the individual-difference sense may be a subsidiary one. If they exerted a constant effect on all children, they clearly would not affect stability. But this is undoubtedly an oversimplistic assumption, since one must consider the interaction of a new environmental experience with the child's level of development, home background variables, and other factors. This point is demonstrated by the differential response of children in different cultural groups to the school and the stimulation it offers.

The whole stability-coefficient approach comes to an impasse at this point, if we are interested in determining whether particular environmental variables stimulate or inhibit the child's mental development. What is needed here is obvious: information on children's response to a major change in their environment, of a kind that can be assumed to be relevant to their intellectual functioning. Evidence on this question is scanty and provides little information on the child's long-term cognitive development. But the available evidence deserves to be examined in detail, especially since it has not been related to the stability issue.

Effects of Environmental Change

Evidence available on the effects of environmental change is of three types: effects of intervention programs to compensate for sub-optimal early environmental stimulation in early childhood; effects of placement in foster homes to compensate for early institutionalization; and effects of migration from one environment to another assumed to be either more or less favorable for cognitive development.

The rather unwieldy literature on intervention has been reviewed by Horowitz and Paden (1973) and by Bronfenbrenner (1974). Much of the work in this area encompasses too limited a time span, notably in terms of obtaining follow-up data, to provide information pertinent to our purposes. However, two studies that include such data by Kirk (1958) and by Klaus and Gray (1968) (see also Gray and Klaus, 1970), are significant because of their careful design and their extended follow-up work.

Samuel Kirk's study, although carried out with children diagnosed as mentally retarded, was predicated on a rationale similar to that which inspired the subsequent Head Start programs. In fact, as Clarke and Clarke (1976a) note in their brief review of major intervention research, closer attention to Kirk's study and its implications could have helped to place the Head Start program on a sounder footing. Kirk essentially dealt with two variables in interaction: the role of institutional versus community environment for his preschool children (about a third of whom were institutionalized at the beginning of the study) and the effects of an experimental program of nursery school experience given to about half of the children in each of the two groups. Overall there was a significant increase in IQ of 11 points in the children given nursery school training, although the change for individual children varied between a gain of 33 points and a loss of 17 points. Further the ameliorative effect appeared to be more pronounced in children who did not suffer organic impairment. The interpretation of this effect is clouded by the finding of a similar, smaller gain, averaging 7 points, in the community Control group over the same period, which contrasted with a loss of the same magnitude in the institutionalized Control group. Thus for the group as a whole the nursery school experience largely "inoculated" the children against the loss of IQ that they would have experienced in their institutionalized environment. This interpretation is strengthened by the finding that after a year of elementary school the difference between the Experimental and Control children raised in the community became even further attenuated, presumably because of the Control children's positive response to the school experience. These effects appeared to depend in part, however, on the quality of the home and the extent of deprivation to which the children from the community groups were subjected. Kirk's major conclusion—it is hardly surprising—was that the accelerated mental growth of these (initially) retarded children was roughly proportional to the amount of environmental change that they experienced. This change was greatest for those institutionalized children given preschool training and subsequently released from the institution, as well as for those from inadequate homes who were placed in a foster home.

The Klaus and Gray project likewise involved children in four groups but limited itself to black children in small southern cities whose mean IQs on initial testing ranged between 85.4 and 92.5. The intervention treatment was limited to ten-week summer programs of preschool training (as provided for in the Head Start program), along with weekly visits from a specially trained paraprofessional to the child's home during the regular year. (This visitor's main function was to support the parents rather than to work directly with the children.) This treatment was given to two groups, T_1 over a three-year period and T_2 over a two-year period. There were two control groups, T_3 from the same city and T_4 from a different city, to control for the possible effects of diffusion of the intervention program to the children in group T_3, who lived close to the children in the intervention groups. Intelligence tests were administered to all groups at the beginning and at the end of the first three summers of the study and at intervals of one, two, and four years following the end of the intervention period. The results, in terms of the children's mental ages, are shown in figure 9.7. (The Stanford-Binet, on which these data are based, was not given at the start of the summer of the third year of the program.)

The graph shows a consistent and significant superiority on the part of the two intervention groups (the two-year group was superior to the three-year group from the very beginning of the study, though not significantly), but with a clear tendency for the Control group from the same community to catch up to the intervention group eventually. The finding that the "distal" Control group appears to fall increasingly behind the others, including the T_3 group, might suggest that some diffusion of the effects of the study to the local control group (T_3) had taken place. Several factors argue against such a hypothesis, however. First, it seems implausible that such diffusion effects would attain their maximum potency after the termination of the intervention program, which is when the Stanford-Binet scores of the T_3 group began to accelerate. Furthermore, on several other measures of intelligence, including the Peabody Picture Vocabulary Test and the WISC, no significant differences appeared between T_3 and

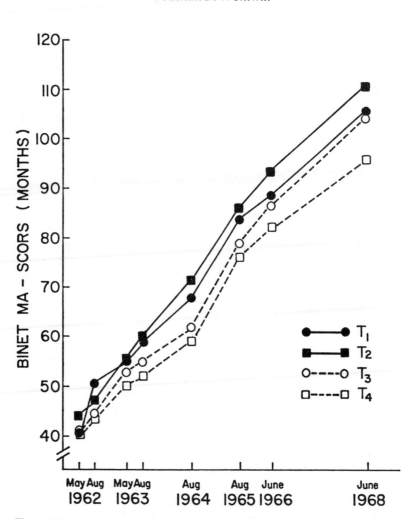

Figure 9.7. *Mental ages for two intervention and two control groups on the Stanford-Binet Test. (From Gray and Kraus, 1970.)*

T_4; they did, however, appear on several measures of school achievement, suggesting that the school environment may have had a more favorable impact on the children in the distal control group.

That the effect of the intervention program was nevertheless real is shown in two further findings. The analysis of the WISC subtests shows that on every subtest except arithmetic the two experimental groups were significantly superior to the Control groups (for all administrations combined), whereas the two Control groups differed only on the information subtest. The second, even more suggestive, finding relates to the vertical diffusion that appears to have taken place from the children in the experimental groups to their younger siblings: the latter differed significantly in intelligence from those in the two Control groups as well.[9] The authors, plausibly enough, attribute this diffusion more to the effect of the home visits on the mother, generalizing to her behavior toward the younger children, than to direct diffusion of the summer intervention program to which the older siblings in the experimental groups were exposed.

Both the Kirk and the Klaus and Gray studies clearly indicate that intelligence in retarded or culturally disadvantaged children can be modified through focused and suitably designed intervention programs during the preschool years, but they also suggest that if intervention is not continued into the school years, such effects are likely to become attenuated over time. This is hardly a surprising result: the environments of all children undergo a marked change as they enter school; thus, except for the institutionalized children, the environment of the children in Kirk's study became fairly similar, whether or not they participated in the intervention programs. It is thus understandable that the effect of the school should override that of the previous intervention.[10]

Several other studies of intervention effects with culturally disadvantaged children have likewise encompassed a span of several years; they tend to emphasize intervention through the mother rather than direct educational experiences through a preschool program. Representative of this approach is the work of Heber and Garber (1975), which entailed extensive intervention in the lives of inner city children and their mothers. Although their procedures resulted in some dramatic increases in intelligence, these effects became progressively attenuated over time (Clarke and Clarke, 1976a). This finding weakens the force of Bronfenbrenner's (1976) emphasis on the potential positive impact of radical alterations in the child's ecological environment (as opposed to limited intervention through a structured program of preschool experience, for instance), though it does lend implicit support to his argument for intervention programs involving the family and sustained over a considerable period of time. Even at latest report (Clarke and Clarke, 1976a), the children in Heber and Garber's project still exhibited above-average IQs; from a high of about 120 at the end of the intervention period at age 6, the mean IQ declined only to 106 three or four years later.

Kirk's study (1958) has become known chiefly for its attempt to counteract mental retardation in young children through a special program of preschool activities. Yet about half of the children were institutionalized, and some were later released from their institutions.

Their subsequent development to a near-normal level is thus a joint function of the intervention program and the marked change in their environment. The role of environmental change is more directly demonstrated in studies of the effects of institutionalization on children who at some age (typically in early childhood) were placed in foster homes.

These studies have become well known and widely discussed and reviewed (Casler, 1961; Yarrow, 1961; Clarke and Clarke, 1976b). The studies can be roughly divided into those that stress the lasting effects of institutionalization (Goldfarb, 1943; Dennis, 1973) and those that emphasize their reversibility (Clarke and Clarke, 1959; Skeels, 1966; and Tizard and Rees, 1974). Yet this distinction is somewhat artificial, since workers on both sides report that the severity of the effects depends on the age at which the children were adopted (for example, before or after two years of age). In particular, this is true of the studies of Dennis and Tizard and Rees. Indeed, the inevitable lack of control over this factor, and the problem of selective factors that relate to the age at which a child is adopted, plagues much of this research and makes it hazardous to draw any but highly tentative conclusions from them. On the basis of this literature the following statement seems warranted: The effects of early institutionalization are reversible in principle, but the extent to which a particular institutionalized child overcomes that handicap (notably in regard to intellectual functioning) depends on the interactive effects of two factors: age at adoption or placement in a foster home (that is, amount of the child's early life spent in the institutionalized environment) and the adequacy of the foster home's physical and psychosocial care and resources. These two factors interact. Given an excellent quasi-institutional environment such as the Israeli kibbuzim and the residential nurseries of Tizard and Rees's sample, few adverse effects may result, regardless of the length of time the children stay there. The children in Tizard and Rees's sample who were still institutionalized at age 8 had a mean IQ of 105—below that of the group adopted before the age of 4½, which was 116 but certainly far from subnormal. The lowest average IQ in their report, 98.2, was for children who were restored to their original working-class parents and surroundings. This pattern was reversed in the WISC scores, however; thus the safest conclusion—especially in view of the small numbers in these groups—is that the effectiveness of the institution was roughly equivalent to that of the home environment of this latter group.

In any event, both of these two factors are important. It seems questionable to try to explain away the results of Goldfarb (1943) and Dennis (1973) as due entirely to selective factors operating in favor of the early-adopted children (that is, the children remaining in the institution were of inferior intelligence to begin with), as Clarke and Clarke (1976b) attempt to do. Although the results of Goldfarb and Dennis's studies remain equivocal, a more reasonable suggestion is that resilience in recovering from early adverse environments is relative: the more severe the adverse conditions, and the longer they operate, the less likely it is that the child will be able to overcome them through a change in environment.

A shortcoming of this literature is that it frequently lacks adequate information about the postinstitutional environments of the children and the comparability of these environments for the institutional versus the noninstitutional or for the early- versus the late-adopted children. The very fact that late-adopted children tend to be of below-average intelligence when they are released from the institution is likely to affect the quality and the adequacy of their care in their adopted homes; we are likely to find a positive-feedback process operating here, such that the effects of the early adversity becomes cumulative. Such a phenomenon appears amply documented in the well-known study by Skeels (1966), which has generally been interpreted as indicating the extent to which special care in early childhood can counteract the effects of adverse institutional upbringing. In fact, the children in the contrast group either remained institutionalized until adulthood or grew up under conditions that in many cases perpetuated their environmental adversity.

Effects of Migration

Children are subjected to frequent and sometimes drastic changes in their environment, through migration of their parents from farm to city, from city to suburb, from snowbelt to sunbelt, to mention only some of the most common demographic movements in the United States over the past several decades. Yet psychologists, particularly child psychologists, have displayed a lack of interest in the psychological impact of such moves, so that we have very little information concerning the effects of these changes in environment on the child's development.

Much of this type of environmental change may be of limited interest for our purposes, since it is frequently difficult to compare the old and the new environment with regard to the quality, amount, and type of stimulation for cognitive growth. However, a few studies of children moving from country to city or from one region to another started from the premise that such moves represented a change to a more stimulating environment.

Otto Klineberg's (1935) study of 12-year-old black children who had migrated from the South to New York City at different ages found a steady rise in their mean intelligence scores with length of residence in the city. Klineberg's main aim was to demonstrate the efficacy of the host environment in counteracting the prior less favorable environment, as opposed to a selective migration hypothesis according to which the brighter children were more likely to become migrants. While Klineberg emphasizes length of time spent in the host environment of the city, a developmental psychologist might be tempted to interpret his findings in terms of the *age* at which the child left the presumably depriving environment. These two factors are necessarily confounded in Klineberg's study, since children at only a single age were included. Furthermore, two similar investigations reported by Klineberg in this same monograph yielded less consistent results. Nevertheless, his main conclusions have been borne out in a more satisfactory study by Everett Lee (1951), who examined longitudinally the IQs of black children who had moved to Philadelphia from the South at different ages, so that information was available on the effects of both age at migration and length of time in the new environment. The results are summarized in table 9.5.

The data in this table testify to the importance of the factor stressed by Klineberg, amount of time spent in the northern city envi-

Table 9.5. Mean IQs on Philadelphia tests of mental and verbal ability.

Group	N	1A	2B	4B	6B	9A
Philadelphia-born who attended kindergarten	212	96.7	95.9	97.2	97.5	96.6
Philadelphia-born who did not attend kindergarten	424	92.1	93.4	94.7	94.0	93.7
Southern-born entering Philadelphia school systems in grades						
1A	182	86.5	89.3	91.8	93.3	92.8
1B-2B	109		86.7	88.6	90.9	90.5
3A-4B	199			86.3	87.2	89.4
5A-6B	221				88.2	90.2
7A-9A	219					87.4

Grade in which test was taken

Source: Lee (1951), table 1. Values for σ omitted. Reprinted by permission of American Sociological Association.

ronment. The values decrease within each column, indicating that for children in any given grade, the earlier they had come to Philadelphia, the higher their IQ. Similarly, the values increase steadily within each row; for any given cohort, the child's IQ rises with increasing duration of their exposure to the Philadelphia environment. There is little evidence that age at migration has an effect, since values along the diagonals, representing approximately constant intervals of time since arrival in the city, are equivalent. The fact that the Philadelphia-born children show no rise in IQ with grade level further supports the interpretation of the horizontal increase in values in terms of amount of time spent in the new environment.

The findings of Klineberg and Lee lead one to wonder what a replication of this work at the present would show. In view of the deterioration of the northern black ghettos and their school systems, it is by no means certain that similar beneficial results of such migration would be found today. But the broader question raised by these studies concerns the nature of the environmental change responsible for the improvement in the children's mental performance following their move to the North. The effect probably results from a combination of factors: improvement in the families' socioeconomic conditions, better schooling, the move from total segregation to at least partial integration, and a change in general stimulation associated with rural-urban migration. On this last point, both studies are disappointing in their lack of precise data. Lee provides no information on the children's communities of origin or to what extent they came from rural rather than urban areas. Klineberg concerns himself with this question, noting that many of the children had undoubtedly moved from farms to cities within the South before coming North but that there was no information on their prior history. He was nevertheless able to differentiate a group of girls from his larger sample into those who had been born in urban (defined as cities of population over 5,000) and those born in rural areas. Significantly, the retardation of the rural children on first testing in the Philadelphia schools was considerably more marked, and the slope of the function showing their progressive approximation to the IQ of the northern-born children was correspondingly steeper, so that after seven to eight years in the North the urban and rural groups were no longer separable in IQ. The total number of children in the rural group was quite small ($N = 40$), so the results should be interpreted with caution, especially since Klineberg notes that another investigator obtained much more inconclusive differences between the two groups.

A less ambitious and extensive study of a similar nature carried out in Italy is unique in presenting data on effects of migration on performance on Piagetian conservation tasks. Nicola Peluffo (1962) compared three groups of 9- to 11-year-old children in Genoa. One group was native to that city, a second group had migrated to Genoa from "underdeveloped" regions of southern Italy within the past year, and a third had originated in the same rural region but had lived in Genoa for longer than three years. On tests of conservation of weight, the group native to Genoa was superior to the two migrant groups at ages 9 and 10, but by age 11 the three-plus migrant group had caught up to the native group (converging on 100% success), while only 60% of the more recent migrants exhibited conservation. The results for the (more difficult) problem of volume conservation were even more dramatic: the native group was markedly superior to the recent migrant group at all ages, with little evidence of age change, but the three-plus group, while comparable to the more recent migrants at age 9, had seemingly caught up with the native children by age 11; at age 10 they were intermediate between the other two.

The evidence from the migration literature is thus consistent with the research on intervention and recovery from institutionalization. It demonstrates the beneficial impact of change in environments and of the associated quality of stimulation (and probably education) for children of school age. Since these effects occurred at a later age than that for which recovery from severe effects of institutionalization has been demonstrated, they tend to support the resilience view of response to early deprivation conditions espoused by Kagan and Klein (1973) and by Clarke and Clarke (1976b).

Finally, a study by Watson (1973), although modest in scope, points to the issue of adaptation in children's response to a new environment. Watson dealt with a small group of West Indian children who had migrated to England and who had scored below 80 on the WISC upon their initial arrival. When retested after 1½ to 2½ years they exhibited a mean rise in IQ of 8 points. While this shift is equivalent to that found by Lee in his study of black migrants to Philadelphia, Watson is inclined to view it as a manifestation of adaptation to the new environment rather than the beneficial effect of that environment on the child. To establish this interpretation would require data on the children's intelligence before their move. Yet the point is consonant with the emphasis on this element of adaptation to environmental change by Fuller (1967) in his reinterpretation of the role of stimulus deprivation on problem-solving skills at the animal level.

The Cumulative Deficit Hypothesis

An issue that complements the preceding discussion of the impact of environmental change and provides a link with the earlier focus on stability concerns the impact of conditions assumed to be unfavorable to the child's cognitive functioning, when they are sustained over an extended period. In principle an equivalent question could be formulated for the long-range impact of especially favorable conditions, but apart from the fact that we can be more certain of what constitutes a deprivation environment than an enriching one, the long-range effects of an enriching environment are of less practical concern. Thus research has been directed largely at testing the hypothesis that children raised in an environment lacking adequate stimulation for mental growth will exhibit progressively increasing retardation in their mental development, relative to the norm, evidenced in a decrease in IQ with age (Stinchcombe, 1969).

An impressive body of literature demonstrates just such a phenomenon. Among the earliest reports of such a cumulative deficit is an account of children living on canal boats in England, with virtually no schooling, which was published by the London Board of Education and has been attributed to Hugh Gordon, an inspector of schools (Gordon, 1923). An abbreviated version, focusing on the portion dealing with these children's test performance, was subsequently published (Gordon, 1972); it presents data on 76 children ranging from 5:1 to 14:0 years, with a mean IQ of 69.6. For these children there was a correlation of $-.76$ between IQ and age; thus the older the child, the lower the IQ.

Similar trends of intelligence steadily decreasing with age were found in several early studies of children growing up under fairly severe cultural isolation in Appalachia (Asher, 1935; Sherman and Key, 1932; Wheeler, 1932; 1942). Further evidence comes from Skeels and Fillmore's (1937) study of children admitted to institutions, at different ages, after having spent their early years in their own homes under conditions of deprivation and neglect. Here again, age was found to be negatively correlated with IQ.

More recent research has failed to corroborate this phenomenon. Instead, studies have generally either failed to find any relationship between IQ and amount of time spent in a depriving environment or found more selective effects, along with some evidence of actual reversal of the early deficit at least in certain aspects of intellectual functioning.

Thus Elfriede Hoehn (1974), reviewing studies of canal boat children in contemporary Germany, reports a deficit in verbal intelligence subtest scores of the WISC at the first-grade level but none on performance tests. At the fourth-grade level even the former deficit had become insignificant. Similarly, studies of children growing up in isolated farms in northern Norway (Haggard, 1973; Hollos and Cowan,

1973) show that farm children and children growing up in small towns are equal on Piagetian tasks, as well as on diverse aspects of intelligence test performance; the major deficit found in the farm children occurred for tests of role-taking ability. Hollos (1975) has reported similar data for Hungarian children.

These latter studies are relevant to the cumulative deficit hypothesis to only a limited degree since no apparent general deficit was found for the isolated children, although Haggard reports some initial deficit on certain of the WISC subtests, which was reduced in the older children. The broader significance of these recent replications of Gordon, Sherman, Key, and others, however, is that contemporary Western societies appear to be able to provide the degree and diversity of stimulation and educational experience for their children that will counteract deprivation effects. That is, neither the material nor the cultural deprivation experienced by the children in Norway and Hungary on isolated farms is comparable to the conditions of Appalachian children of the 1930s. Similarly, contemporary canal boat children in Germany are undoubtedly exposed to environmental stimulation far superior in quality, and to improved educational experience (since they do attend school), than were the English canal boat children in the 1920s.

The cumulative deficit hypothesis has been most typically applied to the culturally disadvantaged child, especially the black child; this literature has been thoroughly reviewed by Arthur Jensen (1974). Unfortunately, Jensen's review focuses on race per se—on differences between whites and blacks—and the question whether these differences increase with age when some measure of relative status (such as the IQ, or scores expressed in standard deviation units) is employed. The evidence appears decidedly mixed. Kennedy, Van De Riet, and White's (1963) study of eighteen hundred black children in five southeastern states shows mean IQs declining from 86 to 51 between the ages of 5 and 16; other studies, notably Baughman and Dahlstrom's (1968) and Osborne's (1960) of southern blacks and whites, showed no consistent changes with age in differences between the two groups, but rather an essentially constant gap between them. Jensen makes several valid methodological criticisms of much of this literature: he points to the equivocal nature of cross-sectional data as evidence on developmental processes (for example, in the face of possible secular trends confounding the role of the age factor), to selective factors inherent in grade placement (within any given grade there will be a spread of ages, with the youngest being biased toward the high-intelligence end and the oldest toward the low-intelligence end) and to other problems.

Jensen (1974, 1977) further presents contrasting data from two studies. The first, carried out in the schools of Berkeley, California, yielded evidence that seemed to oppose the cumulative deficit hypothesis while the second, on children from rural Georgia, tended to confirm it. To avoid some of the problems of traditional cross-sectional age-group comparisons, particularly when age groups are selected on the basis of grade in school, Jensen examined differences between siblings, to determine whether older children scored lower on the average than their younger siblings, and whether that difference was correlated with the number of years separating them. The findings from the Berkeley study were essentially negative, but the study in rural Georgia revealed substantial correlations between intrasibling pair differences in IQ and the age differences separating them. This evidence remains cross-sectional, and the assumption that the differences between sibs are equivalent to the age changes that would have been found upon longitudinal measurement remains untested. Furthermore, it is possible that systematic differences favor older siblings and thus mask the age decrement. Jensen (1974) demonstrates a negligible correlation between birth order and IQ for his Berkeley data and a lack of any interaction between birth order and race, but age was not controlled in the tests for a possible effect of birth order, which leaves this question moot.

Taken at face value, Jensen's findings might well be interpreted as indicating that, under the relatively advantageous conditions of the Berkeley environment (and of the schools of that community in particular), in comparison with children from more extreme deprivation environments such as Harlem or the rural South, deficits do not seem to increase after the children enter school. Such an outcome is compatible with an environmentalist's interpretation of deficits increasing with age, where such an increase occurs, in terms of the cumulative deficit hypothesis. The critical factor appears to be the environmental conditions of the locality. In his review Jensen (1974) cites data suggesting that the phenomenon is a highly selective one, appearing under conditions of a highly depriving environment but not under conditions of lesser deprivation. For instance, the Coleman report (Coleman et al., 1966) gives evidence that the gap between blacks and whites increases with age in nonmetropolitan areas of the South but not in metropolitan areas of the North, just as Jensen's data appear to indicate.

If this literature permits a generalization, then, it is that cumulative deficit appears to occur only under marked and sustained environmental deprivation. Most of the negative evidence cited by Jensen, along with evidence on recovery from effects of institutionalization and other unfavorable environments reviewed by Clarke and Clarke

(1976a, b) can thus be ascribed to either less severe or shorter deprivation. The same appears to apply to the effects of severe malnourish-
ment during the first two years, as studied by Richardson, Birch, and
Yoder (1972), which show no consistent age trends in the intellectual
deficits encountered in their subjects.[11]

Is there any evidence of the opposite phenomenon, of a compensatory process that substantially attenuates or cancels effects of
early deprivation, in the absence of specific intervention to produce
such an effect? In the realm of physical growth the operation of such
"catch-up" processes has been documented, notably among children
subjected to temporary severe forms of undernourishment or anorexia
(Tanner, 1963). Kagan and Klein (1973) believe that they have established a similar process among children from poor, isolated Guatemalan communities, who in their early years displayed a substantial
degree of retardation which decreased markedly with age. Kagan's
data are cross-sectional, and the role of possible secular factors cannot
be ruled out. More to the point, however, the village environment of
these children could not be said to be extremely depriving. Rather, the
early signs of apparent retardation reflected the restriction of movement and the lack of varied perceptual experience to which the parents
subjected their infants. In this sense, Kagan's results are comparable
to those found for children in other cultures that severely restrict the
movement of their infants, such as the Hopi (Dennis, 1940) and the
peasants of Albania (Danzinger and Frankl, 1934). Kagan's stress on
the resilience of development must be viewed in the specific context of
the counteraction of deprivation experienced *in infancy*. While the
data counter the views of psychoanalytically disposed writers, such as
John Bowlby, regarding the primacy of infant experience, they are
readily assimilated into the research that has demonstrated a lack of
relation between rate of development in infancy and cognitive status
in later childhood or adolescence—a basic discontinuity in cognitive
development between infancy and subsequent development.

Toward a Feedback Model of Individual Variation

This review of the research on stability and change of cognitive
and intellectual development cries out for a broader integrative framework. If we are to come to grips with the individual differences in cognitive functioning and to conceptualize them in the context of the
developmental changes within which these differences unfold, a more
dynamic model than that represented by the essentially static concept
of stability coefficients is required.

Let us start with a simplistic assumption, that a child's environment—along whatever dimensions may be relevant to the child's cog-

nitive development, including physical stimulation, parental and other interpersonal influences, and broader social and cultural forces— remains constant with age. This assumption is at best only partially correct and is thus offered here mainly for the sake of the argument to follow. Important changes occur in children's effective environments, both for children as a whole, as in the change from a home-centered to a school- and peer-centered life, and differentially for individual children, as a result of changing family conditions, moves, and the like.

Let us make three further, more reasonable assumptions. One is that cognitive development is a function of children's interaction with their environment, in three specific senses. First, children select particular stimuli or elements from their environment (Kessen, 1968). Second, the child's response to incoming information is a function of the cognitive schemata formed in his prior cognitive growth; compare Hunt's (1963) hypothesis of the match and Dember and Earl's (1957) hypothesis of pacer stimuli based on the level of complexity attained in the organism's past experience. Third, the child appears to be particularly responsive to stimuli or objects that respond in turn to the child, and thus create a feedback loop. These include, first and foremost, other human beings, as well as animals, and toys with a built-in feedback feature (Wachs, 1976; Wohlwill, 1973a; Yarrow, Rubenstein, and Pedersen, 1975, pp. 96ff).

A second assumption is that there are important differences in the quality of the environments in which children grow up, in terms of variety of stimulation and consequently opportunity for selection (Heft, 1976) and in terms of the environment's responsiveness to the child.

Third, children are assumed to differ in their own tendency or ability to select information from the environment, to form schemata, and to act responsively to stimuli and objects that respond to the child (see the review by Parke, 1978).

Once we accept these assumptions, along with the assumption of a constant environment, we are led to a positive-feedback model according to which any small differences in rate of cognitive development that are present at some specified point early in life become progressively magnified during the course of a child's further development. This occurs simply because the level of development attained determines the child's response to further environmental stimulation and information, for this level governs the selection of information from the environment, the assimilation of information compatible or slightly discrepant with preexisting schemata, and the elaboration of behavior in reaction to responsive stimuli related to the child through feedback loops. This process is undoubtedly reinforced in many cases by differential expectancies of success and failure on the part of parents and teachers, which similarly feeds on incipient differences in ability and achievement.

The result of such a progressive magnification of individual differences is a strong tendency for relative individual status on any scale of mental ability to be preserved, a tendency for *stability*. Counter to Bloom's suggestion that increasing stability with age reflects decreasing influence of environmental stimulation, this model accounts for stability in terms of the continuing and sustained influence of some constant set of environmental conditions.

One interesting and testable implication of the model is that individual differences should increase steadily with age. This has been found true for aspects of physical growth such as weight and strength (Carron and Bailey, 1974), where similar positive-feedback mechanisms may be assumed to be operating, as well as for aspects of mental growth measurable in constant absolute units (Jensen, 1974). This phenomenon is not generally evident from standardized intelligence test data, for the simple reason that care is generally taken in the standardization process to ensure that the standard deviation remains approximately constant with age—a dubious procedure from a developmental perspective. Freeman and Flory (1937) found a clear pattern of standard deviations increasing with age over the period from 8 to 13 years, for the raw scores on the VACO (Vocabulary-Analogics-Completion-Opposites) tests of specific verbal abilities. The standard deviations later decline again, resulting in an overall inverted-U pattern. But that decrease is entirely attributable to two of the subtests, completion and opposites, which (whether because of poor test construction or because of the nature of these abilities) showed a pattern of convergence toward an asymptotal value common to all children, just as one would probably find for tests of arithmetic. For the vocabulary and analogies portions of the test, on the other hand, there was an essentially linear increase of standard deviation with age.

Such a positive-feedback process of individuation, according to which experience "feeds" on any incipient differences that may be present at some early stage and magnifies them through cumulative action, undoubtedly represents a widespread phenomenon that accounts for a broad range of individual differences in abilities, skills, or aptitudes, from one individual to another and from one group to another. Athletic ability, though outside our purview of cognitive development, may be proposed as a prototype. The child who, through some combination of constitutional and environmental factors, shows an early propensity and aptitude for athletic activity will seek out such activity and obtain intrinsic as well as extrinsic rewards from engaging in it, thus developing that aptitude increasingly above the norm. At the group level, the consistent differences between the sexes in athletic ability, which become increasingly obvious with age (though reinforced by the physical changes and increased cultural pressures at adolescence) illustrate this process even more vividly.

Yet the positive-feedback model is at most a partial one; it needs to be supplemented by certain other processes to provide a comprehensive account of the development of individual differences in behavior. One is a complementary process of negative feedback, one that tends to counteract and possibly reduce individual differences once they have appeared. This process involves the activation of some compensatory force that may be introduced from outside the system or may be of a more spontaneous nature. To return to our analogue from the realm of athletics, individuals of either sex often compensate for some childhood infirmity or weakness by becoming involved at times to an almost compulsive extent in physical activity or the development of some athletic proficiency. The phenomenon is epitomized by the legendary case of Theodore Roosevelt but is duplicated in athletes such as Wilma Rudolph, who overcame an early severe condition of polio to achieve success as a track star in the Olympics. More generally we can consider the growing encouragement of athletic activity in girls from grade school to college as a deliberate effort to apply the brakes to the unchecked operation of positive feedback and to the resulting extreme differentiation between the sexes that the society has come to recognize as dysfunctional.

We know relatively little about the factors that set such compensatory forces in motion spontaneously in individual cases (childhood polio is not a typical precursor of adult athletic success!) nor to what extent these forces may operate in the realm of cognitive development. They may be activated through some subtle shifts in a child's environment (the arrival of a younger sibling, the influence of a new teacher), that alter the child's motivational state and create a new challenge or need for achievement. At the same time the community or society may provide such compensatory experiences, through ideological commitment or through a sense of responsibility for environmental conditions that may have inhibited optimal cognitive development. Or the society may simply recognize the necessity for a counteractive force to ensure that a disadvantaged child will be able to respond to the normal educational process and eventually acquire the information and skills required for survival in contemporary society.

This raises anew the question of the efficacy of such compensatory efforts, which Jensen and other critics of the compensatory education movement have debated. As Jensen (1974) points out, the "cumulative deficit" characterizing the groups at which these efforts are directed entails an increasing lag of a group behind the norm, or some other referent group, expressed in relativized or standardized measures such as the IQ. In other words, the group mean is falling steadily behind some norm, not just in an absolute sense, but in a relative sense as well. One presumes that this happens where the positive-feedback process has run amok, where the combination of unfavorable conditions for development progressively retards growth relative to the norm. The virtual impossibility of identifying conditions associated with a pattern of IQs or similar relativized measures progressively *increasing* above the norm suggests that these cases of cumulative deficits represent an inhibition of normal growth processes carried to an extreme.

Under these circumstances the prospect for reversing this escalated manifestation of the ordinary positive-feedback cycle is not bright and should become less so the longer the cycle has run its course. On the other hand, if intervention is applied sufficiently early, more positive results may be possible, depending on two factors: the magnitude of the preexisting differential and the potency of the external forces fueling the positive-feedback cycle. A temporary program of intervention, operating for 10 or 12 weeks of a summer for a limited portion of the day during the preschool years, can hardly be expected to have any long-term effect on the growth-retarding processes that act on the typical inner city child. At the same time, the apparent success of some of the programs that have tried to involve mothers in the educational process is reasonable, insofar as these programs may introduce a longer-term corrective force in the child's environment. Urie Bronfenbrenner (1976) has emphasized both intensity and continuity of early intervention programs and the reciprocity between mother and child such that "the mother not only trained the child, but the child also trained the mother" (p. 250). A recent report by Falender and Heber (1975) provides some empirical backing for the potential value of intervention programs directed at creating a more effective reciprocal relationship between mother and child. According to the present model, such an experience would be required to alter the processes that produce the cumulative deficit typically operating for the children for whom these programs are intended.

Such programs, what Bronfenbrenner has called "ecological intervention," reduce original deficit according to a true compensatory model and must be distinguished from cultural and societal influences that have a seeming constant influence on the children's experience— the most obvious being the school. This influence, if it is constant from child to child, might be thought to act as an equalizer, counteracting initial differences and thus representing a compensatory force. Experience is interactive, however; children respond differentially to a constant educational experience, depending on their own prior development, the stimulation of their home environment, and their motivation. Furthermore, the school is ordinarily a far from constant factor; it is as likely to reinforce as to oppose the positive-feedback processes that retard the intellectual growth of some children while accelerating those of others. We hardly need to document the marked differences between the physical resources, teaching personnel, and general learning atmosphere in the typical school of the upper-middle-class suburb and those of the inner-city school.

How is our two-part model of the development of individuation of mental abilities and cognitive performance related to the issue of the stability of cognitive development? There is an apparent paradox here. The positive-feedback processes appear as the instruments for stability, in the sense that they preserve relative status, despite the disequilibrium connotation of positive-feedback systems, while compensatory forces introducing negative feedback would in a statistical sense act to reduce stability. The contradiction rests on a shift of reference from absolute differences among individuals to relative status of children in a group. The positive-feedback processes control differential rates of growth in different children, which when maintained over a period of time promote the stability of the relative standings of the children in their group. Conversely, the negative-feedback process embodied in compensatory mechanisms diminishes and may eliminate or even reverse earlier individual differences and thus reduces stability in the group sense. The negative-feedback model is not intended to suggest a system in equilibrium, since the correction or compensation is superimposed on a system undergoing change and affects the rate of such change rather than the restoration of some earlier state. Indeed, as Ludwig von Bertalanffy (1950) has persuasively demonstrated, equilibrium models are in principle incompatible with the nature of growth processes.

One may still ask whether the positive-feedback or difference magnification model, alone or in conjunction with the counteractive effect of compensatory processes, can account for the data relating to stability. To the extent that increased variability inherent in the positive-feedback process results in a concomitant increase in the reliability of the measures obtained, some increase in stability coefficients with age (as are found for constant test-retest intervals) would be expected. That is, early in life, where absolute standings for a group of children are compressed into a narrow range of some measured variable, individual differences should be subject to more unreliability due to the fallibility of measurement than is true later in life after the individual values have spread further apart. The same principle predicts that adult status will be more highly correlated with status in middle childhood than in early childhood. Yet it is doubtful that this reliability factor can do justice to the situation.

The positive-feedback model is based on one assumption that is at best a poor approximation to the truth—namely, that the environmental circumstances in which the cognitive development of a child takes place remain constant. While there is sufficient constancy in such environments to raise questions about Bloom's proposed interpretation of the changing magnitudes of stability coefficients, changes in environmental stimulation must be reckoned with, in two senses. First, for particular children, the quality and quantity of stimulation at home, for instance, may indeed undergo drastic change as a result of changes in the composition of the household, moves from one environment to another, encounters with a changing peer group, and the like. Presumably the departure from stability commonly observed throughout childhood, and in particular the differential patterns of cognitive growth found in studies of change in IQ and analyzed most incisively by McCall, Appelbaum, and Hogarty (1973), are related at least in part to such environmental change. More important, major changes occur in the environmental stimuli impinging on the child at different ages, both in a general ecological sense, that is, with regard to the behavior settings frequented by the child (Wright, 1956), and in terms of aspects of stimulation specifically relevant to cognitive development. Any inventory of the toys, games, and books considered appropriate at different age levels would be sufficient reminder of this point, which limits the applicability of this positive-feedback model, with its implicit assumption of continuity of environmental stimulation in the qualitative sense.

This discontinuity in quality of environmental stimulation across the period of development is reinforced by the even more salient discontinuities in the nature of cognitive development itself. The major discontinuities discovered by McCall and others, which are in accordance with Piaget's stages of cognitive development and have been more recently reformulated by Uzgiris (1976) and others, would depress stability values over this interval and would require substantial modification in the positive-feedback model. Nor is the problem of qualitative transitions limited to infancy; there is accumulating evidence that the preschool years represent another sharp transition period (White, 1965), and there may well be others, such as that in preadolescence marking the transition from operational to formal thought (Nassefat, 1963). Thus the fanning out of interindividual variation suggested by our positive-feedback model represents but a first approximation to a vastly more complex reality, in which broad individual differences in cognitive skills arise from more specific cognitive processes, some of which run their course over limited time spans. For these (illustrated in the Piagetian domain), individual differences are largely nonexistent up to some specified age and vanish again some years later when the development of the process in question has been completed for virtually every child; thus individual differences exist mainly in terms of *rate* of development through this period, or age of attainment of a given concept (Loevinger, 1966; Wohlwill, 1973b, figure 13-4, Model I). It should be clear that in the perspective of this stage conception of cognitive development the determination of gross stability coefficients becomes an exercise verging on the meaningless.

Conclusion

This review and analysis of the literature casts the question of the stability or continuity of cognitive development in a different light, once the premises of the analysis are accepted. The question we are asking entails removing the individual difference aspect of a child's status from the context of the developmental changes that occur in the child's cognitive processes. What is left is an abstraction of limited interest for the developmentalist. Although this horse remains very much alive, it seems pointless to flog it further, since the matter has already been extensively argued (Wohlwill, 1973b; McCall, 1979a,b). It will be more useful to consider some of the changes in our conceptions and strategies of research that are needed to arrive at a more satisfactory picture of the differential aspect of cognitive development, and thus of the problem of continuity and stability in the context of change.

First, this problem brings out the value of the developmental function approach to the study of development that both McCall (1979b) and I (Wohlwill, 1973b) have espoused. Only by examining the quantitative as well as the qualitative changes that occur in some aspect of behavior under some specified normative set of conditions can we hope to describe, let alone understand, the individual variations in the operation of developmental processes that are at the heart of the issue of continuity and stability. Thus the finding of a stability of .50 between two ages with respect to some measure of cognitive performance can have different meanings. It may reflect basic differences among children in their rate and pattern of development superimposed on overall cognitive change, as is the case with measures of mental age obtained from standard tests. Alternatively, it may involve an aspect of cognitive performance that runs its course over a restricted portion of the age span in a predictable manner, starting from the same point and converging to some higher point with consistent differences across individuals in rate of change occurring over that age span. If the initial and final ages over which the correlation is taken fall at approximately the times at which this development starts and finishes, a value for stability of the order of .50 could well result. Finally, a moderate-sized stability coefficient may reflect certain qualitative changes in the processes that underlie the measure in question, as in correlations between intelligence scales administered in later infancy and early childhood. Such discontinuity would cause infancy test scores to be of little value as a predictor of later intelligence.

Second, we need new methods and approaches to replace the fruitless and limiting linear models of developmental change (as embodied in the stability coefficient) and of the interplay of endogenous and exogenous factors (as represented in heritability coefficients or figures on percentage of variance accounted for by heredity and environment). Sameroff (1975) has argued persuasively for an interactive model of development, in which nonaddivity of internal and external influences results from the manner in which children interact with, and indeed alter, their social and physical environments. Such an interactive view underlies the preceding account of positive- and negative-feedback processes proposed and at a different level it animates the interpretation of intervention effects on the part of Bronfenbrenner (1976) and of parent-child relations more generally (Bell, 1968).

Third, we need further work on the construction of instruments to measure the quality and type of environmental stimulation, physical and social, impinging on the child (Wohlwill, 1973a; Wohlwill and Heft, 1977). Considerable progress has been made in this area for infant development, but in view of the discontinuities between development in infancy and later childhood, such efforts need to be extended. The work of Hanson (1975), though confined mainly to variables relating to interaction between mother and child, represents a useful beginning in this direction; Moore's (1968) measures of environmental correlates for language and intellectual development are somewhat broader, and the results achieved with them are promising. But a more painstaking ecological analysis of the changes in the child's interaction with its environment is needed in order to encompass the range of stimuli and forces that constitute the functional environment for the child and the changes in them over the course of development.

Fourth, a more imaginative and theoretically inspired effort seems necessary to identify possible heterotypic continuities in development, as defined by Kagan (1971), particularly given the qualitative changes in the nature of intellectual functioning that take place with age and the evidence for changes in factorial structure. What is called for here is probably not so much the stab-in-the-dark approach that seems to have led to findings like that of Cameron, Livson, and Bayley (1967) of a correlation between vocalization in infancy and adult IQ, but rather more conceptually based searches for instances of heterotypic continuity, such as Hutt and Bhavnani's (1972) demonstration of a relationship between exploration of novel stimuli at the preschool level and creativity in middle childhood.

Finally, a major reorientation seems to be in order in our shopworn approaches to assessment of cognitive functioning. This review leaves one with a strange sense of culture-lead: All about us we hear a clamor for the revision, if not abandonment, of our reliance on standard intelligence tests and on the IQ, on the grounds that they are culture- and class-biased, that they have a racist effect when used to identify children for inclusion in special programs for the retarded. Such criticisms reflect a healthy mistrust of the conceptual validity of the notion of intelligence on which our standard tests are based, and this mistrust is reinforced by the synthetic and ultimately arbitrary content of these tests. Yet in our research on intelligence, we continue to spew forth, and analyze ad nauseam, data on IQ.

There are hopeful signs that an evolutionary process is under way, one that may bring us from the stone age of the Binet, through instruments such as the Wechsler and the Primary Mental Ability tests that recognize the differentiation of mental abilities, to those that will eventually allow us to encompass qualitative and quantitative changes in one package—undoubtedly influenced by, if not specifically based on, the seminal thought of Jean Piaget. In the process our quantitative information on the stability of intelligence and our concept of stability itself will undergo marked revision. But such a reformulation of the problem and of the approaches to its study is bound to lead to a conception of stability in the context of developmental change that can be incorporated into the empirical and theoretical corpus of knowledge on processes of cognitive development, and that promises to lead to a true integration of the differential and developmental views of the cognitive functioning of the child.

Notes

I am indebted to Paul Baltes and Robert McCall for a critical reading of an earlier draft of this paper and for valuable comments and suggestions. The assistance of Philip Davidson in the literature search and review phase of this paper is gratefully acknowledged.

1. These distinctions correspond partially to those proposed by Kagan in chapter 2. The first two types of stability in his classification correspond

directly to the first and third variants, absolute invariance and stability of ipsative relations. Kagan's last two types in the present treatment represent aspects of the stability of variables to be discussed in the following section.

2. Kagan (personal communication) indicates that children in the Fels study with patterns of rising IQ tended to come from families of above-average SES, just as Rees and Palmer (1970) had found.

3. The ratings of parental behavior were averages of a set of ratings obtained at approximately yearly intervals between 3 and 13 years. No indication is given of their constancy or lack of it, but since these ratings were more frequently missing during the earlier years, they are said to be more representative of the older than of the younger ages.

4. Goodenough and Maurer do not provide any more precise information on the actual ages at which their preschool scales were administered.

5. We are not concerned here with the import of Wilson's data for the heritability issue. This matter is discussed extensively by McCall (1977b).

6. In a subsequent report, Willerman and Fiedler (1974) confirm the lack of relationship between 8-month Bayley scores and 4-year IQ for a group of 4-year-olds of superior intelligence (IQ above 140).

7. This conclusion is reinforced by the findings of Levine et al. (1977), which indicate that the diagnosis of neurological dysfunction and other similar signs of at-risk status is highly unstable in infancy; only about half of the children so diagnosed at 2 months remain in that category at 6 months. This result is consistent with the findings of Werner, Bierman, and French (1971), which show that measures of perinatal stress are unrelated to 20-month Cattell scores.

8. Personal communication.

9. The picture is complicated by the apparent difference between the older and younger siblings in the Control groups; this difference may reflect low reliability of the tests at the younger levels or more unfavorable environments for the younger child due to neglect by the mother, which might have been counteracted in the Experimental families through the home visits by the paraprofessional. The superiority of the older siblings in the Control groups goes counter to Jensen's (1974) data, used as a basis for a test of the cumulative deficit hypothesis, to be discussed in the following section.

10. These studies of effects of early intervention parallel the classical work of the thirties on effects of nursery school attendance on IQ. These effects, whatever the final verdict on the real or artifactual nature of the effects observed, were likewise evanescent, as was to be expected, given the normal range of intelligence of the children included in this research and the lack of any attempt to provide experiences in the nursery school specifically aimed at accelerating cognitive growth.

11. We are concerned here with effects of adverse environmental conditions that persist over time, rather than with effects of intervention or other environmental change that may reverse early deprivation conditions. Thus with respect to the role of malnutrition, Winick, Meyer, and Harris (1975) have shown that Korean children who were adopted into homes in the United

States by age 3, even though severely malnourished in infancy, attained normal status in height and weight, as well as in intelligence, in later childhood.

References

ALMY, M., CHITTENDEN, E., and MILLER, P. 1966. *Young children's thinking: studies of some aspects of Piaget's theory.* New York: Teachers College Press.

ANDERSON, J. E. 1939. The limitations of infant and preschool tests in the measurement of intelligence. *Journal of Psychology* 8: 351-379.

ASHER, E. J. 1935. The inadequacy of current intelligence tests for testing Kentucky mountain children. *Journal of Genetic Psychology* 46: 480-486.

BALDWIN, A. L., KALHORN, J., and BREESE, F. H. 1949. The appraisal of parent behavior. *Psychological Monographs* 63 (4, Whole No. 299).

BAUGHMAN, E. E., and DAHLSTROM, W. G. 1968. *Negro and white children: a psychological study in the rural South.* New York: Academic Press.

BAYLEY, N. 1949. Consistency and variability in the growth of intelligence from birth to eighteen years. *Journal of Genetic Psychology* 75: 165-196.

———— 1956. Individual patterns of development. *Child Development* 27: 45-74.

BELL, R. Q. 1968. A reinterpretation of the direction of the effects in studies of socialization. *Psychological Review* 75: 81-95.

BENSON, F. A. M. 1966. An examination over an eight-month period of Piaget's concept of number development and the presence or absence of certain interrelated tasks in a group of first-grade children. Ed.D. dissertation, University of Oregon.

BERGMAN, L. R. 1973. Parents' education and mean change in intelligence. *Scandinavian Journal of Psychology* 14: 273-281.

BERTALANFFY, L. V. 1950. The theory of open systems in physics and biology. *Science* 111: 23-29.

BLOOM, B. S. 1964. *Stability and change in human characteristics.* New York: Wiley.

BRADWAY, K. P. 1944. I.Q. constancy in the revised Stanford-Binet from the preschool to the junior high school level. *Journal of Genetic Psychology* 65: 197-217.

BRADWAY, K. P., THOMPSON, C. W., and CRAVENS, R. B. 1958. Preschool I.Q.s after twenty-five years. *Journal of Educational Psychology* 49: 278-280.

BROMAN, S. H., NICHOLS, P. L., and KENNEDY, W. A. 1975. *Preschool IQ: prenatal and early developmental correlates.* New York: Wiley.

BRONFENBRENNER, U. 1974. *A report on longitudinal evaluations of preschool programs,* vol. 2. Washington, D.C.: U.S. Department of Health, Education, and Welfare. Publication No. OHD 74-25.

———— 1976. Is early intervention effective? Facts and principles of early intervention: a summary. In *Early experience: myth and evidence,* ed. A. M. Clarke and A. D. B. Clarke, New York: Free Press, pp. 247-258.

BURKS, B. S., JENSEN, D. W., and TERMAN, L. 1930. *The promise of youth.*

Genetic studies of genius, vol. 3. Stanford, Calif.: Stanford University Press.

CALDWELL, B. M., HEIDER, J., and KAPLAN, B. 1966. The inventory of home stimulation. Paper presented at meeting of American Psychological Association, New York, September 1966.

CAMERON, J., LIVSON, N., and BAYLEY, N. 1967. Infant vocalizations and their relationship to mature intelligence. *Science* 157: 331-333.

CARRON, A. V., and BAILEY, D. A. 1974. Strength development in boys from 10 through 16 years. *Monographs of the Society for Research in Child Development* 39 (4, Whole No. 157).

CASLER, L. 1961. Maternal deprivation: A critical review of the literature. *Monographs of the Society for Research in Child Development* 26 (2, Whole No. 80).

CLARKE, A. D. B., and CLARKE, A. M. 1959. Recovery from the effects of deprivation. *Acta Psychologica* 16: 137-144.

——— 1976a. Some contrived experiments. In *Early experience: myth and evidence*, ed. A. M. Clarke and A. D. B. Clarke, New York: Free Press, pp. 213-228.

——— 1976b. Studies in natural settings. In *Early experience: myth and evidence*, ed. A. M. Clarke and A. D. B. Clarke, New York: Free Press, pp. 69-96.

COLEMAN, J. S., ET AL. 1966. *Equality of educational opportunity*. Washington, D.C.: U.S. Office of Education.

CRONBACH, L. J. 1967. Year-to-year correlations of mental tests: a review of the Hofstaetter analysis. *Child Development* 38: 283-289.

CROPLEY, A. J. 1964. Differentiation of abilities, socio-economic status, and the WISC. *Journal of Consulting Psychology* 28: 512-517.

CROPLEY, A. J., and CLAPSON, L. 1971. Long-term test-retest reliability of creativity tests. *British Journal of Educational Psychology* 41: 206-208.

DANZINGER, L., and FRANKL, L. 1934. Zum Problem der Funktionsreifung. Erster Bericht über Entwicklungsprüfungen an albanischen Kindern. *Zeitschrift für Kinderforschung* 43: 219-254.

DAVOL, S. H., CHITTENDEN, E. L., PLANTE, M., and TUZIK, J. 1967. The conservation of continuous quantity investigated as a scalable developmental concept. *Merrill-Palmer Quarterly* 13: 191-199.

DEARBORN, W. F., and ROTHNEY, J. W. M. 1941. *Predicting the child's development*. Cambridge, Mass.: Sci-Art.

DEMBER, W. M., and EARL, R. W. 1957. Analysis of exploratory, manipulatory, and curiosity behavior. *Psychological Review* 64: 91-96.

DENNIS, W. 1940. Does culture appreciably affect patterns of infant behavior? *Journal of Social Psychology* 12: 305-317.

——— 1973. *Children of the crèche*. New York: Appleton-Century-Crofts.

DUDEK, S. Z., and DYER, G. B. 1972. A longitudinal study of Piaget's developmental stages and the concept of regression. *Journal of Personality Assessment* 36: 380-389, 468-478.

EBERT, E., and SIMMONS, K. 1943. The Brush Foundation study of child growth and development. I: Psychometric tests. *Monographs of the Society of Research in Child Development* 8 (2, Whole No. 35).

ELARDO, R., BRADLEY, R., and CALDWELL, B. M. 1975. The relation of infant home environments to mental test performance from six to thirty-six months: a longitudinal analysis. *Child Development* 46: 71-76.

EMMERICH, W. 1964. Continuity and stability in early social development. *Child Development* 35: 311-332.

———— 1966. Continuity and stability in early social development. II: Teacher ratings. *Child Development* 37: 17-27.

———— 1968. Personality development and concepts of structure. *Child Development* 39: 671-690.

ENTWISLE, D. R. 1966. *Word associations of young children*. Baltimore, Md.: Johns Hopkins University Press.

FALENDER, C. A., and HEBER, R. 1975. Mother-child interaction and participation in a longitudinal intervention program. *Developmental Psychology* 11: 830-836.

FATERSON, H. F., and WITKIN, H. A. 1970. Longitudinal study of the development of the body concept. *Developmental Psychology* 2: 429-438.

FLAVELL, J. H., and WOHLWILL, J. F. 1969. Formal and functional aspects of cognitive development. In *Studies in cognitive development: essays in honor of Jean Piaget*, ed. D. Elkin and J. H. Flavell. New York: Oxford University Press, pp. 67-120.

FREEMAN, F. N., and FLORY, C. D. 1937. Growth in intellectual ability as measured by repeated tests. *Monographs of the Society of Research in Child Development* 2 (2, Whole No. 9).

FULLER, J. L. 1967. Experiential deprivation and later behavior. *Science* 158: 1645-52.

GOFFENEY, B., HENDERSON, N. B., and BUTLER, B. V. 1971. Negro-white, male-female, eight-month developmental scores compared with seven-year WISC and Bender test scores. *Child Development* 42: 595-604.

GOLDFARB, W. 1943. The effects of early institutional care on adolescent personality. *Journal of Experimental Education* 12: 106-129.

GOODENOUGH, F. L., and MAURER, K. M. 1942. *The mental growth of children from two to fourteen years*. Minneapolis, Minn.: University of Minnesota Press.

GORDON, H. 1923. *Mental and scholastic tests among retarded children*. Education Pamphlet 44, London Board of Education. London: H.M.S.O. Reprinted in abbreviated form in *Historical readings in developmental psychology*, ed. W. Dennis. New York: Appleton-Century-Crofts, 1972.

GRAY, S. W., and KLAUS, R. A. 1970. The early training project: a seventh-year report. *Child Development* 41: 909-924.

GREEN, D. R., FORD, M. P., and FLAMER, G. B. 1971. *Measurement and Piaget: proceedings of the CTB/McGraw-Hill conference on ordinal scales of cognitive development*. New York: McGraw-Hill.

HAGGARD, E. A. 1973. Some effects of geographic and social isolation in natural settings. In *Man in isolation and confinement*, ed. J. Rasmussen. Chicago: Aldine, pp. 99-144.

HALVERSON, C. F., JR., and WALDROP, M. F. 1976. Relations between preschool activity and aspects of intellectual and social behavior at age 7½. *Developmental Psychology* 12: 107-112.

HANSON, R. A. 1975. Consistency and stability of home environmental measures related to I.Q. *Child Development* 46: 470-480.

HÄRNQUIST, K. 1968. Relative changes in intelligence from 13 to 18. *Scandinavian Journal of Psychology* 9: 50-64, 65-82.

HARRIS, C. W., ED. 1963. *Problems in measuring change*. Madison, Wisc.: University of Wisconsin Press.

HEBER, R., and GARBER, H. 1975. Progress report II: an experiment in the prevention of cultural-familial retardation. In *Proceedings of the third congress of the International Association for the Scientific Study of Mental Retardation*, vol. 1, ed. D. A. Primrose. Warsaw: Polish Medical Publishers, pp. 34-43.

HEFT, H. 1976. An examination of the relationship between environmental stimulation in the home and selective attention in young children. Ph.D. dissertation, Pennsylvania State University.

HEINIS, H. 1926. A personal constant. *Journal of Educational Psychology* 17: 163-186.

HILDEN, A. H. 1949. A longitudinal study of intellectual development. *Journal of Psychology* 28: 187-214.

HINDLEY, C. B. 1965. Stability and change in abilities up to five years: group trends. *Journal of Child Psychology and Psychiatry* 6: 85-99.

HOEHN, E. 1974. Schifferkinder: Eine Untersuchung über die Auswirkung eingeschränkter Umwelterfahrungen in früher Kindheit. *Psychologische Beiträge* 16: 254-276.

HOFSTÄTTER, P. R. 1954. The changing composition of intelligence: a study in T-technique. *Journal of Genetic Psychology* 85: 159-164.

HOLLOS, M. 1975. Logical operations and role-taking ability in two cultures: Norway and Hungary. *Child Development* 46: 638-649.

HOLLOS, M., and COWAN, F. A. 1973. Social isolation and cognitive development: logical operations and role-taking abilities in three Norwegian social settings. *Child Development* 44: 630-641.

HOLTZMAN, W. H., DIAZ-GUERRERO, R., and SWARTZ, J. D. 1975. *Personality development in two cultures: a cross-cultural longitudinal study of school children in Mexico and the United States*. Austin, Tex.: University of Texas Press.

HONZIK, M. P. 1940. Age changes in relationship between certain environmental variables and children's intelligence. *Thirty-ninth yearbook of the National Society for the Study of Education*. part II, pp. 185-205.

HONZIK, M. P., MACFARLANE, J. W., and ALLEN, L. 1948. The stability of mental test performance between two and eighteen years. *Journal of Experimental Education* 17: 309-324.

HOPKINS, K. D., and BIBELHEIMER, M. 1971. Five-year stability of intelligence quotients from language and nonlanguage group tests. *Child Development* 42: 645-649.

HOROWITZ, F. D., and PADEN, L. Y. 1973. The effectiveness of environmental intervention programs. In *Review of Child Development Research*, vol. 3, ed. B. M. Caldwell and H. N. Ricciuti. Chicago: University of Chicago Press, pp. 331-402.

HUNT, J. McV. 1963. Motivation inherent in information processing and action. In *Cognitive factors in motivation and social organization*, ed. O. J. Harvey. New York: Ronald.

HUTT, C., and BHAVNANI, R. 1972. Prediction from play. *Nature* 237: 171-172.

IRETON, H., THWING, E., and GRAVEM, H. 1970. Infant mental development and neurological status, family socioeconomic status, and intelligence at age four. *Child Development* 41: 937-945.

JENSEN, A. R. 1974. Cumulative deficit: a testable hypothesis? *Developmental Psychology* 10: 996-1019.

——— 1977. Cumulative deficit in IQ of blacks in the rural South. *Developmental Psychology* 13: 184-191.

KAGAN, J. 1971. *Change and continuity in infancy*. New York: Wiley.

KAGAN, J. and KLEIN, R. E. 1973. Cross-cultural perspectives on early development. *American Psychologist* 28: 947-961.

KAGAN, J., and KOGAN, N. 1970. Individual variation in cognitive process. In *Carmichael's manual of child psychology*, 3d ed., vol. 1, ed. P. H. Mussen. New York: Wiley, pp. 1273-1365.

KAGAN, J., and MOSS, H. A. 1962. *Birth to maturity: a study in psychological development*. New York: Wiley.

KAGAN, J., SONTAG, L. W., BAKER, C. T., and NELSON, V. L. 1958. Personality and IQ change. *Journal of Abnormal and Social Psychology* 56: 261-266.

KANGAS, J., and BRADWAY, K. 1971. Intelligence at middle age: a thirty-eight year follow-up. *Developmental Psychology* 5: 333-337.

KATZ, E. 1941. The constancy of the Stanford-Binet IQ from 3 to 5 years. *Journal of Psychology* 12: 159-181.

KENNEDY, W. A., VAN DE RIET, V., and WHITE, J. C., JR. 1963. A normative sample of intelligence and achievement of Negro elementary school children in the southeastern United States. *Monographs of the Society for Research in Child Development* 28 (6, Serial No. 90).

KERLINGER, F. N. 1954. The statistics of the individual child: the use of analysis of variance with child development data. *Child Development* 25: 265-275.

KESSEN, W. 1968. The construction and selection of environments. In *Environmental influences*, ed. D. C. Glass. New York: Rockefeller University Press, pp. 197-201.

KIRK, S. A. 1958. *Early education of the mentally retarded*. Urbana, Ill.: University of Illinois Press.

KLAUS, R. A., and GRAY, S. W. 1968. The early training projects for disadvantaged children: a report after five years. *Monographs of the Society for Research in Child Development* 33 (4, Whole No. 120).

KLINEBERG, O. 1935. *Negro intelligence and selective migration*. New York: Columbia University Press.

——— 1938. The intelligence of migrants. *American Sociological Review* 3:

218-224.

KLONOFF, H. 1972. IQ constancy and age. *Perceptual and Motor Skills* 35: 527-534.

KOFSKY, E. 1966. A scalogram study of classificatory development. *Child Development* 37: 191-204.

KOGAN, N. 1976. *Cognitive styles in infancy and early childhood.* Hillside, N.J.: L. Erlbaum Associates.

KOGAN, N., and PANKOVE, E. 1972. Creative ability over a five-year span. *Child Development* 43: 427-442.

LEE, E. S. 1951. Negro intelligence and selective migration: a Philadelphia test of the Klineberg hypothesis. *American Sociological Review* 16: 227-233.

LEVINE, M. D., PALFREY, J. S., LAMB, G. A., WEISBERG, H. I., and BRYK, A. S. 1977. Infants in a public school system: the indicators of early health and educational need. *Pediatrics* 60: 579-587.

LOEVINGER, J. 1966. Models and measures of developmental variation. *Annals of the New York Academy of Sciences* 134: 585-590.

McCALL, J. N., and JOHNSON, O. G. 1972. The independence of intelligence from family size and birth order. *Journal of Genetic Psychology* 121: 207-213.

McCALL, R. B. 1976. Predicting four-year IQ. Review of S. H. Broman et al., *Preschool IQ: prenatal and early developmental correlates. Contemporary Psychology* 21: 181-182.

——— 1977. Childhood I.Q.'s as predictors of adult educational and occupational status. *Science* 197: 482-483.

——— 1979a. The development of intellectual functioning in infancy and the prediction of later IQ. In *Handbook of infant development*, ed. J. D. Osofsky. New York: Wiley.

——— 1979b. Qualitative transitions in behavioral development in the first three years. In *Psychological development from infancy*, ed. M. H. Bornstein and W. Kessen. Hillsdale, N.J.: L. Erlbaum.

McCALL, R. B., APPELBAUM, M. I., and HOGARTY, P. S. 1973. Developmental changes in mental performance. *Monographs of the Society for Research in Child Development* 38 (3, Whole No. 150).

McCALL, R. B., EICHORN, D. H., and HOGARTY, P. S. 1977. Transitions in early mental development. *Monographs of the Society for Research in Child Development* 42 (3, Whole No. 171).

McGRAW, M. B. 1935. *Growth: a study of Johnny and Jimmy.* New York: Appleton.

MONTOUR, K. 1977. William James Sidis: the broken twig. *American Psychologist* 32: 245-254.

MOORE, T. 1967. Language and intelligence: a longitudinal study of the first eight years. Part I: Patterns of development in boys and girls. *Human Development* 10: 88-106.

——— 1968. Language and intelligence: a longitudinal study of the first eight years. Part II: Environmental correlates of mental growth. *Human Development* 11: 1-24.

MORAN, L. J., and SWARTZ, J. D. 1970. Longitudinal study of cognitive dictionaries from ages nine to seventeen. *Developmental Psychology* 3: 21-28.

MOSHMAN, D. 1977. Consolidation of stage formation in the emergence of formal operations. *Developmental Psychology* 13: 95-100.

NASSEFAT, M. 1963. *Étude quantitative sur l'évolution des opérations intellectuelles*. Neuchatel: Delachaux and Niestlé.

OSBORNE, R. T. 1960. Racial differences in mental growth and school achievement: a longitudinal study. *Psychological Reports* 7: 233-239.

OSBORNE, R. T., and SUDDICK, D. E. 1972. A longitudinal investigation of the intellectual differentiation hypothesis. *Journal of Genetic Psychology* 121: 83-89.

PARKE, R. B. 1978. Children's home environments: social and cognitive effects. In *Children and the environment*, Human behavior and environment, vol. 3, ed. I. Altman and J. F. Wohlwill. New York: Plenum, pp. 33-81.

PELUFFO, N. 1962. Les notions de conservation et de causalité chez les enfants provenant de differents milieux physiques et socio-culturels. *Archives de Psychologie (Geneva)* 38: 275-291.

PINTER, R., and STANTON, M. 1937. Repeated tests with the C.A.V.D. scale. *Journal of Educational Psychology* 28: 494-500.

REES, A. H., and PALMER, F. H. 1970. Factors related to change in mental test performance. *Developmental Psychology Monograph* 3 (2, Part 2).

RICHARDSON, S. A., BIRCH, H. G., and YODER, E. G. 1972. Intellectual levels of school children severely malnourished during the first two years of life. *Pediatrics* 49: 814-824.

RUSCH, R., and LIS, D. 1977. Reliability and trend for field independence as measured by the portable rod and frame. *Perceptual and Motor Skills* 44: 55-61.

SAMEROFF, A. J. 1975. Early influences on development: fact or fancy? *Merrill-Palmer Quarterly* 21: 267-294.

SCARR-SALAPATEK, S. 1976. An evolutionary perspective on infant intelligence: species patterns and individual variations. In *Origins of intelligence: infancy and early childhood*, ed. M. Lewis. New York: Plenum, pp. 165-198.

SHERMAN, M., and KEY, C. B. 1932. The intelligence scores of isolated mountain children. *Child Development* 3: 279-290.

SHIPE, C., VANDENBERG, S., and WILLIAMS, R. D. 1968. Neonatal Apgar ratings as related to intelligence and behavior in preschool children. *Child Development* 39: 861-866.

SKEELS, H. M. 1966. Adult status of children from contrasting early life experiences: a follow-up study. *Monographs of the Society for Research in Child Development* 31 (3, Whole No. 105).

SKEELS, H. M., and FILLMORE, E. A. 1937. The mental development of children from underprivileged homes. *Journal of Genetic Psychology* 50: 427-439.

SMEDSLUND, J. 1961. The acquisition of concepts of substance and weight in children. III: Extinction of conservation of weight acquired "normally" and by means of empirical controls on a balance scale. *Scandinavian Jour-*

nal of Psychology 2: 85-87.

SONTAG, L. W., BAKER, C. T., and NELSON, V. L. 1958. Mental growth and personality development: a longitudinal study. *Monographs of the Society for Research in Child Development* 23 (2, Whole No. 68).

STINCHCOMBE, A. L. 1969. Environments: the cumulation of events. *Harvard Educational Review* 39: 511-522.

STOTT, L. H. 1967. *Child development: an individual longitudinal approach.* New York: Holt, Rinehart and Winston.

TANNER, J. M. 1963. The regulation of human growth. *Child Development* 34: 817-848.

TERMAN, L. M., and ODEN, M. H. 1947. *The gifted child grows up: twenty-five years follow-up of a superior group.* Stanford, Calif.: Stanford University Press.

THOMAS, H., JAMISON, W., and HUMMEL, D. D. 1973. Observation is insufficient for discovering that the surface of still water is invariantly horizontal. *Science* 181: 173-174.

THORNDIKE, E. L., BREGMAN, E. O., COBB, M. V., and WOODYARD, E. 1927. *The measurement of intelligence.* New York: Teachers College, Columbia University.

THORNDIKE, R. L. 1940. "Constancy" of the IQ. *Psychological Bulletin* 37: 167-186.

THURSTONE, L. L. 1925. A method of scaling psychological and educational tests. *Journal of Educational Psychology* 16: 433-451.

THURSTONE, L. L., and ACKERSON, L. 1929. The mental growth curve for the Binet tests. *Journal of Educational Psychology* 20: 569-583.

TIZARD, B., and REES, J. 1974. A comparison of the effects of adoption, restoration of the natural mother, and continued institutionalization on the cognitive development of four-year-old children. *Child Development* 45: 92-99.

TUCKER, L. R. 1966. Learning theory and multivariate experiment: illustrations by determination of generalized learning curves. In *Handbook of multivariate experimental psychology*, ed. R. B. Cattell. Chicago: Rand McNally, pp. 476-501.

TYLER, F. T. 1954. Organismic growth: *P*-technique in the analysis of longitudinal growth data. *Child Development* 25: 83-90.

UZGIRIS, I. C. 1964. Situational generality of conservation. *Child Development* 35: 831-841.

———— 1976. Organization of sensorimotor intelligence. In *Origins of intelligence*, ed. M. Lewis. New York: Plenum, pp. 23-263.

UZGIRIS, I. C., and HUNT, J. McV. 1975. *Assessment in infancy: ordinal scales of psychological development.* Urbana, Ill.: University of Illinois Press.

VAN ALSTYNE, D. 1929. *The environment of three-year-old children.* (Teachers College Contributions to Education, no. 366). New York: Teachers College, Columbia University.

WACHS, T. D. 1976. Utilization of a Piagetian approach in the investigation of early experience effects: a research strategy and some illustrative data. *Mer-*

rill-Palmer Quarterly 22: 11-30.

WATSON, P. 1973. Stability of IQ of immigrant and non-immigrant slow-learning pupils. *British Journal of Educational Psychology* 43: 80-82.

WELLMAN, B. 1940. The meaning of environment. *Thirty-ninth yearbook of the National Society for the Study of Education*, part 1, pp. 21-40.

WERNER, E. E., BIERMAN, J. M., and FRENCH, F. E. 1971. *The children of Kauai: a longitudinal study from the prenatal period to age 10*. Honolulu, Hawaii: University of Hawaii Press.

WERNER, E. E., HONZIK, M. P., and SMITH, R. S. 1968. Prediction of intelligence and achievement at ten years from twenty-months pediatric and psychologic examinations. *Child Development* 39: 1063-75.

WETZEL, N. C. 1943. Assessing physical fitness in children. III: The components of physical status and physical progress and their evaluation. *Journal of Pediatrics* 22: 329-361.

WHEELER, L. R. 1932. The intelligence of East Tennessee mountain children. *Journal of Educational Psychology* 23: 351-370.

———— 1942. A comparative study of the intelligence of East Tennessee mountain children. *Journal of Educational Psychology* 33: 321-334.

WHITE, S. H. 1965. Evidence for a hierarchical arrangement of learning processes. *Advances in Child Development and Behavior* 2: 187-220.

WIENER, G., RIDER, R. V., and OPPEL, W. 1963. Some correlates of IQ changes in children. *Child Development* 34: 61-67.

WILLERMAN, L., BROMAN, S. H., and FIEDLER, M. F. 1970. Infant development, preschool IQ, and social class. *Child Development* 41: 69-77.

WILLERMAN, L., and FIEDLER, M. F. 1974. Infant performance and intellectual precocity. *Child Development* 45: 483, 486.

WILSON, R. S. 1972. Twins: early development. *Science* 175: 914-917.

———— 1974. Twins: mental development in the pre-school years. *Developmental Psychology* 10: 580-588.

WINICK, M., MEYER, K. K., and HARRIS, R. C. 1975. Malnutrition and environmental enrichment by early adoption. *Science* 190: 1173-75.

WITKIN, H. A., DYK, R. B., FATERSON, H. F., GOODENOUGH, D. R., and KARP, S. A. 1962. *Psychological differentiation*. New York: Wiley.

WITKIN, H. A., GOODENOUGH, D. R., and KARP, S. A. 1967. Stability of cognitive style from childhood to young adulthood. *Journal of Personality and Social Psychology* 7: 291-300.

WOHLWILL, J. F. 1960. A study of the development of the number concept by scalogram analysis. *Journal of Genetic Psychology* 97: 345-377.

———— 1972. And never the twain did meet. Review of D. R. Green, M. P. Ford, and G. B. Flamer, eds., Measurement and Piaget. *Contemporary Psychology* 17: 334-335.

———— 1973a. The concept of experience: S or R? *Human Development* 16: 90-107.

———— 1973b. *The study of behavioral development*. New York: Academic Press.

WOHLWILL, J. F., DEVOE, S., and FUSARO, L. 1971. *Research on the development of concepts in early childhood*. Final report for NSF Grant G-5855.

WOHLWILL, J. F., and HEFT, H. 1977. Environments fit for the developing child. In *Ecological factors in human development*, ed. H. McGurk. Amsterdam: North-Holland, pp. 125-138.

WOLF, R. 1966. The measurement of environments. In *Testing problems in perspective*, ed. A. Anastasi. Washington, D.C.: American Council on Education.

WRIGHT, H. F. 1956. Psychological development in Midwest. *Child Development* 27: 265-286.

YARROW, L. J. 1961. Maternal deprivation: Toward an empirical and conceptual re-evaluation. *Psychological Bulletin* 58: 459-490.

YARROW, L. J., RUBENSTEIN, J. L., and PEDERSEN, F. A. 1975. *Infant and environment: early cognitive and motivational development*. Washington, D.C.: Hemisphere Publishing.

10 | Cognitive Development in Adulthood
John L. Horn and Gary Donaldson

W HEN WE LOOK back over eighty years of research on human abilities, we are struck by the similarity of the issues raised then and now, by the concordance of the results, and by indications that the same principles are used to account for the organization and development of cognitive processes. Although principles may be timeless, it is still surprising that current generalizations were identified in the work of previous periods. Each generation enters history at different points. There have been dramatic and massive changes in our culture—in education, travel, communication, social organization, work, control over one's destiny, the physical environment. Surely the manifestations of human cognitive capacities in 1975 should be quite different from those in 1935 or 1905. Yet the Binet-Simon (1905) discussion of memory and Spearman's (1904) analysis of reasoning could, except for some quaintness of writing style, appear alongside current treatments of these topics and not be detected as notably different. Indeed, a heartening feature of the study of human abilities is the architectonic growth of the discipline; the graduate students of each new generation need not unlearn, or avoid learning, material developed in previous generations; new material can be based on a broad foundation of previous learning.

But continuity in the development of theory says nothing about continuity in the development of the individual. Here again, however, much of what we see through the lens of present evidence is gradual change through accretion, consolidation, stability, and attrition.

In this century, at least in this country, there has been a notable increase in the belief that one can change substantially. Many anecdotes have portrayed adults dramatically changing their life-styles.

But we find little to indicate dramatic, within-person improvement in adult intelligence, even when anecdote and fiction are considered. (Daniel Keye's *Flowers for Algernon*, perhaps better known as the movie *Charley*, being a notable exception.) When we look at the evidence from research to alter major cognitive capacities in adulthood (Labouvie-Vief, 1976; Plemons, Willis, and Baltes, 1978), we are surprised and dismayed to find the changes small, the generalizations narrow, and so many functions seemingly unalterable. There are discontinuities, but these are often decrements, as when severe brain injury decreases the level of intelligence. Such changes portray the extreme of a common occurrence, for much of the story of adulthood development of abilities is a tale of gradual decline. This story threatens the optimism that often seems to accompany the view that there are, or at least can be, great discontinuities in human intellectual development.

There are many problems with the evidence on adult development and with the continuity interpretations imposed on it. Much of the evidence is not directly relevant to the issue of stability in the ipsative sense, as discussed by Wohlwill in chapter 9 and first introduced by Cattell (1946). Interpretations may be misleading in the sense that researchers have been unable to resist the constraints pressed on them by a world view (Brim, 1966). Perhaps we have been forced into theory characterized by continuity because we have been limited by the data gathered and the questions asked of the data. Perhaps discontinuity is the rule, but investigators have not looked for the evidence of this rule.

Continuity and discontinuity are parts of theories pertaining to how we regard developmental processes. Brim and Kagan noted in chapter 1 that theory is needed to provide a framework for understanding. For example, substantive theory is necessary to deal with the problems to which Wohlwill referred in chapter 9. In this respect it is important to recognize that theory is dynamic, even as the laws that one attempts to incorporate in a theory are stable. Theory need not be discarded simply because some of the evidence is inconsistent with, or does not derive from, the theory. For a good theory to be properly overthrown, there must be a better theory. A major theory is rarely discarded in toto; a new theory is usually a modification of an old one. Thus to study intellectual development is to study theory about this development even though we know that all current theory is wrong in major respects.

In recognition of these facts about theory, this chapter has been organized in accordance with major features of several currently well accepted theories about intellectual development. Rather than review each of many theories separately, however, we have tried to put all theories together in a single account of theory. Elsewhere we have considered and compared different theories (Horn, 1972, 1977a, b, 1978b).

Our emphasis on theory might be decried by some. Let the facts speak for themselves, they might say, in " 'theory-free' inductive interpretations" (Baltes and Schaie, 1976). But facts do not speak for themselves. There is always a set of assumptions—a theory of sorts, although it may not be explicit—underlying interpretations of observations. This is the position developed not only in the analyses of logical empiricists, such as Hempel and Nagel, but also in the writings of those philosophers, such as Hanson, Kuhn, and Toulmin, who stress "world view" aspects of scientific thought.

The very definition of intelligence depends critically on theory. Statements such as "intelligence is the capacity to process information" or "intelligence is what intelligence tests measure" do little to provide an understanding, or even a meaning, of intelligence. We suggest that intelligence, like any theoretical concept in science, can be given only a partial interpretation through logical connections between statements about intelligence and statements having empirical content. The scientific meaning of intelligence consists of the specification of lawful relationships between intelligence, other scientific concepts, and observable phenomena. Such a view is incompatible with a "definition" of intelligence as "what intelligence tests measure."

A theory about adulthood development of intelligence is needed for two concrete reasons that may be more compelling than philosophical requirements. First, throughout this century there has been a proliferation of paradigms, tests, and studies designed to reveal the nature of cognitive processes and the development of these processes. Without theory to organize the findings, this proliferation leads to chaos. Second, two kinds of research have been conducted: research based on observations of individual differences and research on average behavior in which these differences are regarded as part of error variability. Theory is needed to provide a basis for integrating the findings from these different approaches.

It is important to distinguish individual differences research from a form of research we are referring to, for lack of a better term, as averaging research (see also Carroll, 1976; Hunt, 1978; Underwood, 1975). The difference between these two kinds of research has been referred to in several ways; perhaps the best known treatment is that of Cronbach (1957, 1975), who characterized it as a distinction between response-response (RR) and stimulus-response (SR) research. It is useful also to see that individual differences (ID) research is based on tests and averaging research (AV) is based on paradigms.[1]

The idea of a paradigm is illustrated by some well-known procedures developed by Sternberg (1967). In this work a subject was asked to press a lever to indicate that he saw a particular word among a set of other words. The number of words in the identification set was varied. A set size of 5 words, for example, might represent the words *dog, cat, mouse, hole, cheese.* The subject's reaction time to ascertain that the word *mouse* was among thise set was recorded in milliseconds. Sternberg demonstrated that the amount of time a person needed to decide whether an item was embedded in the list is an increasing and linear function of the number of items in the list. The top part of figure 10.1 provides a representative picture of this function.

In the design for this kind of (averaging) study subjects are typically assigned randomly to groups in which all subjects deal with a given feature of the paradigm (a given set size), and the average (for example, of reaction time) for one group is compared with the averages for other groups. There are many designs for AV studies, but their important feature is that individuals within each group are treated as replications of each other. The individual differences are not of primary concern. In contrast, an essential feature of ID research is that the stimulus conditions are standardized—each subject is exposed in the same way to the same set of conditions—and analyses are directed at comparing individuals.

Many differences that are important for theory follow from the differences between AV and ID research. For example, the treatment of individuals as replications of each other (in AV research) is based on an implicit assumption that the same process is observed in each individual and that the differences between individuals represent mainly errors in observing the process. In ID research, by contrast, the assumption is that differences between individuals represent mainly nonerror magnitudes of a process or, in some cases, nonerror differences in processes. AV studies using the Sternberg paradigm assume that all individuals exposed to a set size of 5 process the information in much the same way, the only differences being errors within them and errors associated with the observation procedures.

These descriptions of AV and ID research point to the extremes. Much psychological research, particularly that on human development, is a mixture, partly AV and partly ID. It is useful to see the extremes in order to appreciate the relative emphasis on AV or ID in the hybrids.

A good example of mixed AV-ID study is Anders and Fozard's (1973) use of the Sternberg paradigm (see the bottom part of figure

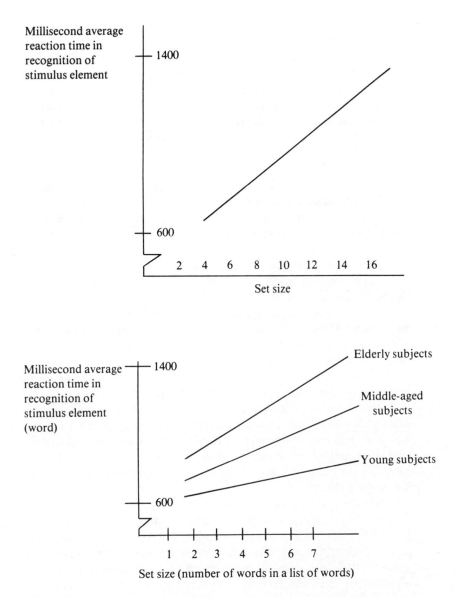

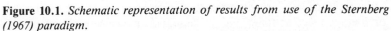

Figure 10.1. *Schematic representation of results from use of the Sternberg (1967) paradigm.*

10.1). They first classified people as young, middle-aged, and old. Age is a variable of individual differences, so in their classification Anders and Fozard employed a crude measure of this variable. The same standardized conditions were used for all subjects in obtaining these measures, and the same standardized conditions were used for all individuals to obtain reaction times for each of several different set sizes. When conditions of observation are the same (as nearly as possible) for all individuals, the result is often referred to as a test. Within each age group, Anders and Fozard treated individuals as replications of each other. In their analyses, individual differences in reaction times among the young, for example, were treated as error. The results from this study, as depicted in figure 10.1, suggest that in a task similar to the one developed by Sternberg the rate (slope) of increase in reaction time per unit increase in set size is greater for older than for younger subjects. Mixed AV-ID studies such as the Anders and Fozard study are common in developmental psychology.

The Sternberg procedure is one example of a paradigm. Paradigms discussed in recent work have been developed by Posner, Sperling, Wickens, Atkinson and Shiffrin, Chase and Clark, Bransford and Franks, Mandler, Broadbent, Murdock, Butterfield and Belmont, and Glanzer and Cunitz, to mention only a few. The number of paradigms for studying cognitive processing is already large, and is growing ever larger. Theory is needed to provide a framework for interpretation of phenomena indicated by these paradigms.

Paradigms are often ingenious, and the phenomena that they reveal can be interesting. However, they often pertain only to a narrow aspect of behavior. Psychological tests, on the other hand, often provide information about fairly broad segments of behavior. This is probably the major distinction between paradigm and test; formally the two are similar.

When a task is called a test and used in ID research, each subject is exposed to a variety of similar stimulus conditions (the same variety for every subject), the average of a coding for responses over all items for each subject is taken as the measure, and then individuals are compared on these measures. In a test based on the Sternberg paradigm, for example, each subject might be asked to recognize words in the same series of set sizes. One measure of the subject might be the sum or average reaction times over all sets. This measure is thus based on items that are somewhat different and might be called information processing efficiency. Such a measure might seem a bit too gross, an inadequate representation of the concepts of Sternberg's studies. To obtain a measure that could be better, one might compute the average reaction times separately for several sets of each size and determine the slope, for each individual, on a line of relationship between set size and average reaction time. The results of Anders and Fozard suggest that such a slope measure correlates positively with age (the larger the slope, the older the individual).

Thus paradigms and tests can refer to similar aspects of behavior. Usually, however, when the focus is on paradigms, individual differences are ignored. The aim is to demonstrate how the behavior of the "typical" individual indicates laws of functioning that apply to all individuals (sometimes even including nonhumans). On the other hand, ID research is usually directed at demonstrating processes, and laws of functioning that make a difference in individual differences. Something that characterizes all individuals is of at most minor interest in such research.

The Sternberg paradigm provides information about processing times at different stages in recognition memory. Much ID research has studied recognition memory (whether one recognizes or not) in company with other kinds of memory and as an aspect of intelligence. Existing evidence suggests that all forms of short-term memory represent only a small part of intelligence, small both in terms of the proportion of the variance that memory has in common with intelligence measures and small in terms of the extent to which it is implicated in intellectual development. Such evidence suggests that it can be a long leap from the observations provided by a paradigm to an indication of how these observations pertain to intelligence and its development. The slopes for the lines in figure 10.1 are interpreted as indicating rate of search through memory, but there is little to indicate how, and to what extent, this rate is related to what is customarily identified (with tests) as intelligence.

ID research with tests has indicated broad patterns of organization among abilities, and these broad patterns may eventually be understood in terms of the narrower processes that have been demonstrated using paradigms in averaging research. Performance on memory tests, for example, can be analyzed in terms of primary and secondary memory, as these have been distinguished by paradigm research (Horn, 1978c), but it is reasonable to suppose that this performance can also be understood in terms of other processes that have been distinguished, in several different ways, in averaging research. An age difference in memory might be attributed (in part) to any one process or to any of several possible combinations of distinct processes. It is important to be able to step down the abstraction ladder from the gross behavior revealed by tests to the more finely grained analyses provided by the paradigms. Thus AV and ID research are complementary in several respects, even as the methods, assumptions, results, and theories that have grown up with one approach are often distinct from comparable elements of the other approach. We have been examining the differences between the two approaches. Our conclusion is that under many conditions the two approaches can lead to the same laws (see also Underwood, 1975).

It is probably not fruitful to regard AV and ID research as representing entirely different disciplines. Important aspects of cognitive-intellectual functioning and development have been revealed by both lines of research. There is need to put the findings and theory of each approach in the purview of the other (Horn, 1968).

Our objectives in this chapter are to look at the research deriving from the AV and the ID approaches and to discuss results within a common theoretical framework. Our strategy is to use the literature rather than to cite it in detail. We have tried to understand essential implications of the studies bearing on an issue and to convey the general sense of these implications without citing chapter and verse for each clause of an assertion. Similarly, we have tried to convey the sense of controversies in the field without developing each nuance of the contestants' positions.

With this general orientation in mind, let us first consider some information organized in terms of theory deriving from individual-differences research, then look at some of the ideas deriving from averaging research on cognitive processing, and along the way see how the two seem to fit together.

Research on Individual Differences

Research on individual differences provides the principal theoretical orientation of the chapter. This orientation specifies a hierarchy of the processes of human intelligence. The principal evidence for the theory derives from four main sources, namely studies of achievement and social class correlates of ability test performances, the structure of interrelationships among abilities, age differences and age changes in abilities over the entire life span, particularly in adulthood, and physiological differences that are correlated with age or with injury and illness. Much of this evidence has been reviewed elsewhere (Botwinick, 1977; Bloom, 1964; Buss and Poley, 1976; Carroll and Maxwell, 1979; Cattell, 1971; Green, 1974; Horn, 1972, 1975, 1976a,b, 1977a,b, 1978a,b; Hunt, 1961; Matarazzo, 1972; Resnick, 1976); some of the evidence, such as that pertaining to achievements and childhood development, has been considered by Featherman (chapter 14) and by Wohlwill (chapter 9). Thus for much of the material only major points need be considered here.

Achievement and Social Class

Some tests and abilities relate more highly to social class and school achievement than others. As shown in figure 10.2, results can be arranged in a fan of relevancy coefficients (to be interpreted as validity coefficients or correlations with a criterion) for predicting academic achievement. Results from many studies (see reviews by Anastasi, 1958; Bloom, 1964; Buss and Poley, 1976; Cronbach, 1970; Featherman, chapter 14; Tyler, 1965) indicate that tests of verbal comprehension, general knowledge, and information have the highest correlations with academic achievement and socioeconomic class, with relevancy coefficients of the order of 0.5 to 0.6. Tests that tap spatial reasoning (matrices) have lower correlations with academic

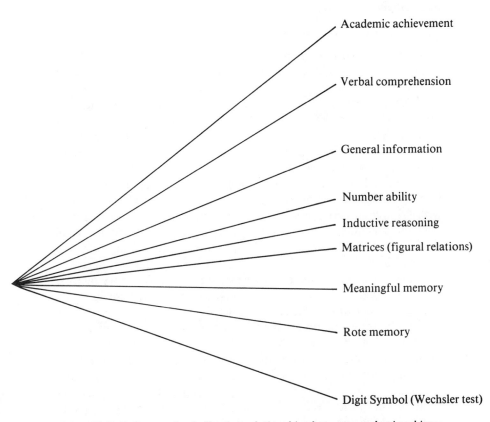

Figure 10.2. *Relevance fan indicating relationships between academic achievement and performances on various kinds of tests. Size of angle between achievement and test is inversely proportional to magnitude of relationship.*

achievement, on the order of 0.35 to 0.45. Still lower are the correlations involving tests of memory (correlations in the range of 0.25 to 0.35). These are the abilities that Jensen (1971) refers to as as Intelligence I (in contrast to Intelligence II). At the lowest end of the fan of relationships are very simple perceptual tasks, such as the digit symbol task of the Wechsler test of intelligence.

While the tests in the fan may be said to reflect a vital aspect of intelligence, the relevancy fan indicates that such intelligences relate in different ways to school achievement and to socioeconomic class (when class is specified either in terms of parental characteristics during childhood or achievement and occupation in adulthood). The results of these studies indicate that different tests of intelligence have different construct validities. The tests point to distinct subprocesses of intelligence.

Intercorrelations among Abilities

If good performance on task A typically correlates with good performance on tasks B, C, and D (which in turn covary), it is reasonable to suppose that each of the four performances depends on a common capacity. Research directed at developing such conjunctive concepts, often called factors, has been accumulating in the study of abilities for roughly eighty years. We shall speak of two levels of factors, primary and second order. The factors reflect the principal constructs of the hierarchy of mental processes.

From well over one hundred studies, in which many kinds of ability tests have been factor analyzed in a variety of ways (but usually with a simple structure model), the factors in table 10.1 have emerged. A factor is included in this table only if it has been identified in several studies, usually conducted by different investigators using different methods in different decades of this century. In order to appreciate this kind of empirical evidence, consider some of the memory factors.

In one sense almost all thinking involves memory, but when psychologists speak of memory, they are usually referring to recall or, less commonly, to recognition that occurs a few seconds or a few minutes after presentation of the material to be remembered. The factors of section E of table 10.1 represent memory in this sense of the word.

Many normative studies have established that what one remembers and how much one remembers depend on features of content and context. One recalls related words better than amorphous spatial forms, and the conditions under which memory is enhanced are different for these two kinds of memory. In ID research the correlations among scores on memory tests having different contents (such as numbers, words, pictures, and abstract designs) are typically of the

Table 10.1. Primary mental ability factors.

Factors	Symbols used by		
	J. W. French (1963)	*J. W. French (1951)*	*J. P. Guilford (1967)*
A. Factors involving (primarily) figural content			
1. Visualization	Vz	Vi	CFT
2. Flexibility of closure, gestalt flexibility, visual cognition	Cf	Gf	NFT
3. Speed of closure, gestalt perception	Cs	GP	CFU
4. Spatial orientation, spatial relations	S	SO	CFS
5. Perceptual speed, speed of symbol discrimination	P	P	ESU
6. Figural adaptive flexibility	Xa		DFT
7. Semantic redefinition	Re		NMT
8. Spatial scanning, perceptual foresight	Se		CFI
9. Length estimation	Le	LE	
10. Figural relations			CFR
11. Figural classification			CFC
12. Speed of alternating reversals, figural spontaneous flexibility		PA	DFC
B. Factors involving (primarily) symbolic content			
13. Induction, symbolic correlates	I	I	NSR
14. Symbol cognition			CSU
15. Cognition of symbolic classes			CSC
16. Symbolic relations			CSR
17. Convergent production of symbolic systems			NSS
18. Symbolic identification			ESU
19. Symbol manipulation			ESR
C. Factors involving (primarily) semantic content			
20. Verbal comprehension	V	V	CMU
21. Mechanical knowledge, mechanical information	Mk	ME	

(*continued*)

Table 10.1 continued

Factors	*J. W. French (1963)*	*J. W. French (1951)*	*J. P. Guilford (1967)*
22. General reasoning, deduction	R	D	CMS
23. Syllogistic reasoning, logical evaluation	Rs	D	
24. Sensitivity to problems	SEP		EMI
25. Judgment		J	EMT
26. Semantic relations			CMR
27. Experiential evaluation			EMS
28. Conceptual classifications			CMC
29. Penetration			CMI
30. Conceptual classifications			CMI
31. Concept naming			NMU
32. Convergent production of semantic classes			NMC
33. Semantic correlates			NMR
34. Ordering			NMS
35. Semantic redefinition			NMT
D. Semantic fluency factors			
36. Ideational fluency	Fi	IF	DMU
37. Word fluency	Fw	W	DSU
38. Associational fluency	Fa		DMR
39. Expressional fluency	Fc	FE	SSS
40. Spontaneous flexibility	Xs		DMC
41. Originality	O		DMT
42. Semantic elaboration			DMT
E. Memory factors			
43. Associative memory, rote memory	Ma	N	MSR
44. Memory span	Ms	Sm	MSU
45. Meaningful memory	Mm		MMR
46. Memory for ideas			MMU
47. Visual memory			MFU
48. Memory for spatial order			MFC
49. Memory for temporal order			MMS
F. Miscellaneous			
50. Number facility, number	N	N	NSI
51. Carefulness		C	
52. Schooling		Sc	

Source: Horn (1977b).

order of 0.3 to 0.8, even though reliabilities would permit correlations of the order of 0.7 to 0.9 (Horn, 1978c; Guilford, 1967; Kelley, 1964; Underwood, Boruch, and Malmi, 1978). Similarly, the correlations between different kinds of memory tasks, such as paired associate and serial learning tasks, are not as large as the reliabilities of the tests.

Thus in a sense each memory test represents a different kind of memory. But the factors of table 10.1 indicate that such apparently different tasks nevertheless have stable features in common. This factoring research also suggests that the low correlation between different tests may represent little more than peculiar features of the tests rather than important memory processes.

Kelley's (1964) study illustrates the factoring research that has revealed primary abilities of memory. This study, based on data gathered from 442 Air Force pilot trainees, consisted of 27 memory tests chosen to represent different features of memory—verbal and nonverbal, visual and auditory, recognition and recall, meaningfully associated and nonsensically related, paired associates and serial. The results of Kelley's analyses suggested the following: (1) of the 27 tasks 13 have a single quality in common and thus covary to indicate the associative memory primary ability (number 43 in table 10.1); (2) another 7 tasks indicate the span memory factor; (3) yet another 7 tasks point to a meaningful memory primary ability. These three factors account for about 75% of the reliable variance of most of the memory tests. Thus although each of the 27 tests could measure a form of memory specific to the task, this specific represents a smaller part of what the test measures than is represented by the three primary abilities of memory. Since some of the reliable specific variance is due to systematic features of motivation and attention that are external to memory, it is reasonable to suppose that the major qualities of memory revealed in Kelley's tests are well represented by the concepts symbolized as Ma, Ms, and Mm in table 10.1.

It is in this sense that each of the primary abilities represents covariance among tests, implying that some common processes and variation in such processes are responsible for individual differences in the ways that intelligences are developed and expressed. In addition to several kinds of memory abilities, there are language abilities, spatial abilities, reasoning capacities, and abilities pertaining to knowledge systems, such as those of mathematics (factor N) or mechanical principles (factor Mk). The primary abilities also measure cognitive styles, as indicated by the gestalt closure tests (factor Cf) and the Embedded Figure tasks (factor Cs). Tests of the latter factor have been used most frequently to represent Witkin's (1973) concept of field dependence.

The research on primary abilities has involved all the subtests of major, well-known intelligence tests. Moreover, the primary abilities account for almost all that is reliably measured in IQ tests. Indeed, the available research has shown that widely used intelligence tests measure only a few of the well-established primary abilities.

While it is reasonable to suppose that the primary abilities identified in table 10.1 represent basic processes that are important for understanding intellectual performance and development, no study has been done, or is likely to be done (Undheim and Horn, 1977), to establish that all the primary abilities are independent. Several analyses have suggested that the number of established, independent primary abilities is less than the 54 listed in table 10.1 (Buss and Poley, 1976; Ekstrom, 1973; French, Ekstrom, and Price, 1963; Hakstian and Cattell, 1974; Horn, 1970b; Horn and Knapp, 1973, 1974; Undheim, 1976; Undheim and Horn, 1977). As many as 25 primary abilities are probably needed to account for the reliable variance in tests that can be accepted as indicants of intelligence.

The naming of primary abilities accomplishes little more than specifying items in a catalog. Table 10.1 is therefore rather like a list of Volkswagen parts without instructions for assembling them or a description of what the parts look like when assembled and what the machine does if the parts are put together correctly. While the system of primary abilities is an improvement over the chaos represented by a large number of tests, it is still too cumbersome and too atheoretical. Hence efforts have been devoted to defining organization among abilities at a more general level than is represented by the primary abilities (Cattell, 1941, 1957, 1963, 1971; Horn, 1967, 1968, 1970a, 1972, 1974, 1978a,b, 1979). Studies based on the logic of conjunctive concepts and using factor analysis have been designed to determine the structural interrelationships among the primary abilities. The design for these studies has derived from the idea of obtaining a representative sample of primary abilities to reveal broad concepts. Some results from this work are summarized in table 10.2 (see Horn, 1968, 1972a, for detailed, historical review).

The procedures in early studies in this line of research involved selecting a broad sample of the well-established primary mental abilities, each measured with two or three tests. The scores on two or three marker tests of the primary factor were summed to provide a measure of the primary ability. Primary abilities were then intercorrelated and factored in accordance with the criteria for simple structure that are specified in analytic, objective procedures (Horn and Knapp, 1973, 1974). The individual tests were then correlated with the second-order factors to determine how well a single test represented a primary abil-

Table 10.2. Summary of results indicating the nature of Gf and Gc and related functions.[a]

Abilities measured in	Intellectual factor							
	Gc	Gf	Gv	TSR	SAR	Gs	DS	Ga
Broad range vocabulary	70							
Common word discriminations	60	30						
Remote associations	60			30				
General information	70							
Verbal analogies	50	20						
Common word analogies	30	30						
Esoteric word analogies	60							
Syllogistic reasoning	30	30						
Word problem reasoning	30	30						
Mechanical knowledge	50	20	20					
Tools	50		20					
Mechanical principles	30	30	30					
Meaningful association memory	30	30			40			
Letter series	20	40						
Matrices		40	20				20	
Paper folding		30	40					
Hooper visual organization		40	20					
Gestalt closure		20	40					
Embedded figures		50						
Associations for a word	20			60				
Uses for objects	20			60				
Things fitting a definition				60				
Finding letter *a*						60		
Comparing numbers						60		
Matching forms						60		
Span memory (backward)	20	30			40			
Primacy	30	20			60			
Recency		30			50			
Permuted clustering recall		30		20	50			
Slow writing		30			50			
Sorting prior to recall	30	30			60			
Question-asking efficiency	30	30			30			
Quickness, correct response							60	
Quickness, incorrect response	30						60	
Speech perception under distortion								60
Auditory cognition of relations								55
Discriminate between sound patterns								55

a. Numbers are rough averages representing factor correlations obtained over several studies.

ity in defining the second-order dimension. In later studies this evidence was used to design studies in which tests alone, rather than tests combined to measure primary factors (as described above), were used to provide the basis for demonstrating the second-order factors. This procedure was used to save time for trying out new ideas about variables that could elucidate the nature of the second-order factors. Second-order factors are described by Horn and Cattell (1967) and by Horn (1968, 1972a, 1977b, 1978a).

The second-order factors represent latent attributes that are only imperfectly indicated by the fallible variables of any particular study. For example, the first factor in table 10.2 is identified with a concept labeled crystallized intelligence, or Gc. Although the Gc factor has been indicated by the conjunction of many different kinds of tests, the concept itself refers to a much broader domain of behavior. The concept refers to a universe of abilities that are highly valued in a culture and are believed to be important for maintaining the culture. Such abilities are systematically imparted to the members of the culture through acculturation.

Some of the abilities that exemplify Gc are the following:

Verbal comprehension: The ability to decipher a written or spoken communication, extract the main ideas, and retain these for further use.

Experiential evaluation: The ability to use social conventions, and the knowledge and nature of a culture, in making reasonable decisions for which the information is relevant.

Formal reasoning: The ability to deal with problems in ways that are more or less formalized within a culture, as in rendering a quasi-legal decision.

Technical proficiency: The abilities invoked in everyday calculations and related adjustments, as in using percent thinking, solving problems such as making change, balancing a checkbook, figuring out how much gasoline to buy to get from x to y.

The universe of the abilities of Gc is huge; the sampling of abilities that have indicated the factor in existing studies is minuscule by comparison and is no doubt biased in numerous, unknown ways.

The concept and empirical manifestation of crystallized intelligence is distinguishable from the latent variable referred to as fluid intelligence (Gf), represented in the second column of table 10.2. Like Gc, it also involves many of the basic processes of intelligence—abstracting, problem solving, reasoning, concept attainment, the eduction of relations, the drawing of inferences. But the abilities that define Gf form a different set. Some variables that exemplify Gf are the following:

Series reasoning with abstract elements. In letter series, for example, the subject must figure out which letter comes next in a series of this form.: A C F J O U.

Identifying optional classifications. Suppose that 36 objects can be classified in a large number of ways—by color, by shape, by use —but some systems allow classification of all objects into, say, 5 categories, while other systems require more categories; then the subject's task is to find systems that require the fewest categories. Verbal materials or other materials that are part of the culture can be used for such a task, provided the categorization itself is not greatly aided by acculturation.

Completing visual patterns. In a well-known test of visual patterns a pattern is indicated in a 3 by 3 matrix by variations across rows and down columns, and one must determine what should be in the cell in the lower-right corner of the matrix.

These variables represent qualities of intelligence that are only loosely tied to formal education. The Gf abilities seem to be imparted by influences other than those included in the systematic process of acculturation. Many features of acquisition are not systematized in acculturation. For lack of a better term these are referred to as casual learning influences.[2] Gf is an outcome of mixtures of such experiential determiners and other influences that directly affect the physiological structures and processes on which intellectual development is most fundamentally based.

One major difference between Gc and Gf relates to the extent of acculturation. There is much acculturation in Gc development, little in Gf. Fallible measures of Gc indicate how well one has incorporated into one's own system all the knowledge and skill that is transmitted systematically as the wisdom of a culture. Gf, on the other hand, represents qualities of thinking, reasoning, and problem solving that are acquired under casual learning conditions. These are the qualities most immediately affected by changes in the physiological structures that support the maintenance, development, and expression of intelligence.

The Gf-Gc distinction may also reflect differences in the strategies that control acquisition and use of knowledge. Gf is characterized by the development of idiosyncratic strategies, while Gc is characterized by the adoption of strategies that have become a part of cultural knowledge. To estimate the amount of cement needed for an oval patio, for example, a person with highly developed Gc might use algebra, whereas a person who relied primarily on Gf might use his own system of estimation.

In a sense the distinction between Gf and Gc can be said to represent a difference between process and product, or between analytic and achievement tasks (Cattell and Horn, 1978; Guttman, 1965; Horn, 1972). However, in most usages, these concepts probably refer to phenomena somewhat different from those characterized by the Gf-Gc distinction.

Process or analytic ability is usually characterized by the idea that in some intellectual tasks one must form a concept or work out a strategy. With a product or achievement, on the other hand, one merely demonstrates knowledge of a strategy or concept that has been attained earlier. These distinctions are probably important, but one problem with using them to characterize the difference between Gf and Gc is that both Gf and Gc are based on products, that is, achievements (of casual and acculturational learning, respectively), and both are indicated by tasks in which one must work out new concepts or strategies. For example, a task that enabled a subject to use algebra to develop a new concept—say one of reliability—is likely to indicate largely individual differences in Gc. On the other hand, in a letter series task that is mainly indicative of Gf, subjects use the products of their own previous efforts to develop ways of coping with seriation problems. It is probably true, however, that as measured there is more product than process in Gc and more process than product in Gf.

The broad visualization (Gv) and broad auditory (Ga) second-order factors of table 10.2 represent latent structure organizations in the processes of seeing and hearing. The visualization factor pertains to perceiving how things change as they move in space, keeping visual configurations in mind, and achieving gestalt closure. Similarly, auditory organization represents processes of detecting subtle sound differences, identifying a pattern in sounds embedded within noise, and achieving temporal and relational integration of sounds. It seems that the Gv and Ga functions operate to prepare information for the eductive-deductive-abstracting thinking that is represented by fluid and crystallized intelligence.

The short-term acquisition and retrieval factor (SAR) of table 10.2 and the tertiary storage and retrieval dimension (TSR) also represent major processes of support for fluid and crystallized intelligence. They are not themselves highly characteristic of the features of intelligence that are most uniquely human, but they are important adjuncts to Gf-Gc functioning. It is necessary to have enough short-term memory to keep the elements of a reasoning problem in awareness, but two people who are equally good at retaining the fundaments of a problem may nevertheless differ in their reasoning with these elements. SAR represents abilities of retrieving and maintaining awareness of stimulus elements over relatively short periods of time; TSR indicates ability in recalling information from the relatively distant past (of one's own development) and bringing it to bear in solving a problem.

The broad speediness (Gs) and decision speed (Ds) columns in table 10.2 do not represent well-replicated factors (although factors of the indicated form have been found) as much as they represent that quickness in performance on intellectual tasks is often largely independent of (but positively correlated with) correctness of response. Quickness factors have been found in several studies, but it is not clear that they are replications of and thus indicative of the same latent variables. At least two and possibly three broad speed functions appear to be prominent in commonly studied intellectual tasks.

The best replicated of the second-order speed factors is identified by quickness in writing and printing, reading, and scanning an array of symbols to find a particular symbol. In early studies this factor was referred to as "general speediness," Gs (Horn and Cattell, 1966). It is now clear that the factor is not general in the sense that all forms of speed on intellectual tasks indicate the factor. In particular, quickness in choosing answers is a separate factor. Speed in arriving at wrong answers correlates as much with this factor as quickness in choosing correct answers. The factor seems to represent an aspect of decision speed. The third possible broad dimension of speediness is defined primarily by measures of quickness in abandoning items (providing neither right nor wrong answers), referred to as quit decision speed (QDS) (Horn, 1978c).

Although the mutual independence of these factors of intellectual speediness has not been established, their emergence in some studies suggests that correctness of response is not usually indicated by quickness of response.

In a sense each of the well-replicated second-order factors described in the previous section represents a kind of intelligence. But different aspects of intelligence are indicated by each factor, and some of the factors exemplify the sine qua non of human intelligence more nearly than others. For example, mammals other than humans have fairly good short-term memories, and several species of the great apes show good organization of visual processes. It seems that the second-order factors represent organizations at different levels of intellectual functioning. Such organizations extend from basic sensory detection of stimuli to abstract analyses of complex awarenesses. There are no clear demarcations between levels, and even the extremes are not always clearly distinguished, but existing knowledge can be usefully organized in terms of the five levels identified in figure 10.3.

Performance on almost any ability task depends on functioning at every level, but in some tasks the performance is more nearly char-

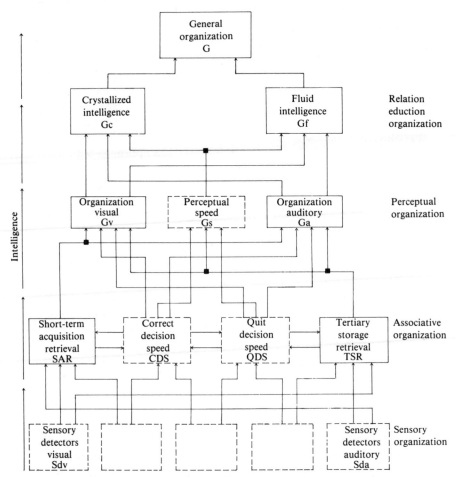

N.B. Interpret arrows developmentally rather than as at-time-of-measurement determination.

Figure 10.3. *Schematic representation of intellectual functions.*

acteristic of functioning at one level than at another. If an ability task is merely to find a particular spatial form embedded in a set of lines, then it is likely to be more indicative of perceptual organization than organization at the level of eduction of relations. So it is with other tasks; they can involve functioning at a particular level to a greater or lesser degree.

Processes thought to exist at different levels of intellectual function are nevertheless identified at the same second-order level in structural analyses. Thus level in factor analysis (first-order, second-order) need not correspond to level of function, as represented in figure 10.3.

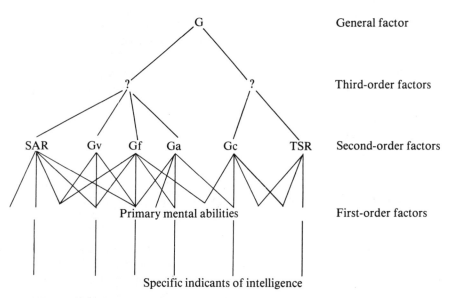

Figure 10.4. *Hierarchy of intellectual factors.*

Figure 10.4 shows the kind of hierarchy that has been suggested by results from factor analytic research. This hierarchy includes factors at the second order that appear at different levels in the functional hierarchy of figure 10.3. Question marks at a third order in figure 10.4 represent a hypothesis based on a very few analyses of the second-order factors.

A General Factor of Intelligence?

Figures 10.3 and 10.4 assume that almost all intellectual processes are related and organized at a general level as general intelligence (G or IQ). Theories of general intelligence have been considered by Featherman (chapter 14), Wohwill (chapter 9), and Horn (1978a,b) and thus need not be considered in any detail here. However, brief mention of such theories is needed to provide a perspective for the concepts that are considered in some detail.

Despite arguments against the usefulness of a concept of G, there is considerable evidence for its utility (Humphreys, 1979; Humphreys, Parsons, and Park, 1979; Jensen, 1979). One major form of evidence is a well-replicated finding of positive correlation among almost all abilities that involve thinking, abstracting, and reasoning, even when the ability measurements rely on different test materials (figural, semantic), and different abilities measured at widely separated points in development (Horn, 1970a). The correlations are not large but they are positive. The only notable exceptions to these generalizations are (1) findings that highly speeded performance on tasks of very low difficulty have a near-zero or perhaps negative correlation with completely unspeeded, or power, performances on tasks involving considerable difficulty of eduction of relations and correlates (reasoning tasks), and (2) results indicating that measurements obtained with infant tests (before children age 2) have near-zero or perhaps negative correlations with measures of intelligence obtained at older ages.

The evidence for positive correlations among abilities (referred to as positive manifold) has been questioned by some. Guilford (1964) presented results suggesting that roughly 15%-20% of the intercorrelations among ability measures are not significantly different from zero. There are several problems with interpreting Guilford's results as indicative of an absence of positive manifold (Horn, 1970a,b). For example, the measures involved in some of the near-zero correlations may not be measures of abilities. Reaction time measures are particularly suspect on these grounds. Evidence of reliability was not presented for some of the tests with low correlations. Unreliable measures are expected to correlate near zero. The samples of subjects on which some near-zero correlations were based were homogeneous with respect to age and several other variables. Correlations can be very much reduced by sample selectivity that reduces the range of observed performances.

The evidence of positive manifold should not be accepted as unequivocal support for a hypothesis of a general factor of intelligence. Such a hypothesis must be supported by results in addition to those provided by studies of ability intercorrelations. Even when only intercorrelations are considered, the hypothesis requires stronger evidence than merely positive manifold. Theories that do not posit a single factor of intelligence can account for positive manifold, as was pointed out by Godfrey Thomson (1939) and Truman Kelley (1928). The G hypothesis requires, at a given order of analysis, evidence that one and only one general factor fully (except for error) accounts for the intercorrelations. A finding that one factor accounts for a large proportion of the reliable variance among abilities is not equivalent to a finding of one and only one factor at a given level of analysis. This latter condition is extremely demanding. Data must fall precisely into a particular form if the one-and-only-one hypothesis is to be retained.

Thus, while the verifiable evidence of positive manifold is consistent with theories that hypothesize a general factor of intelligence, this evidence is also consistent with other theories. Nevertheless, most modern theories about intellectual abilities either state or assume a concept of general intelligence, often rather implicitly as in Piaget's well-known writings (1960), or make no statements designed to account for the evidence of positive manifold, as in Guilford's (1967) influential theory. In general, therefore, the general factor assumption in figures 10.3 and 10.4 well represents present-day evidence and theory pertaining to the organization among human abilities.

Learning and Inheritance of Intellectual Abilities

Even very elementary abilities, such as those of simple memory tasks, require a considerable amount of learning (although this learning could have occurred at a young age). But it does not necessarily follow that observed individual differences in the ability are explained in terms of differences in learning. Consider a simple example.

Suppose that the ability to throw a spear is valued in a given community and that all boys and girls are intensively trained in this ability throughout childhood. Indeed, suppose that all boys and girls are given precisely the same training in throwing spears. It does not follow that at maturity all young adults will be able to throw spears equally well. To the contrary, any individual differences due to heredity, nutrition, injury, or other factors that interfere with or enhance spear throwing, not training, will be reflected in the ability.

At the root of the long-standing debate about the heritability of intelligence are differences in the assumptions about acquisition conditions. This debate should not obscure awareness of the fact that most of the behavior taken to indicate intelligence, Gf as well as Gc, depends very much on learning. Thus the Gf-Gc distinction does not necessarily reflect a separation of inherited and acquired aspects of intelligence, although it may be discussed this way. Gf may be said to represent inherited determinants of intelligence to a greater extent than does Gc, which in turn is said to represent environmental determinants more surely than genetic determinants. Such reasoning seems to follow from recognition that many of the abilities of Gc require learning, whereas some of the abilities of Gf (span of apprehension) seem to depend very little on learning. But the implication of the hypothesis is that individual differences in Gf reflect mainly individual differences in genetic endowment and that individual differences in Gc indicate mainly environmental influences (associated with learning). This implication is problematical; existing evidence does not provide strong support for the hypothesis that Gf reflects genetic differences more than Gc. Results from studies of the heritabilities (h^2) of the primary abilities that define Gf and Gc, for example, do not indicate that the h^2 for the primary abilities of Gf are notably larger than the h^2 for those of Gc (Ashton and Polovina, 1977; Bock and Vandenberg, 1968; DeFries, Kuse, and Vandenberg, 1979; Vandenberg, 1965).

Although behavioral (psychological) concepts of intelligence are based on learned abilities, individual differences in such abilities may nevertheless reflect genetic differences. One should not, at this time in history, conclude that either the Gf or Gc form of intelligence provides a better basis than the other for identifying a hereditary component of intelligence. One should be wary of claims that intelligence of either form, or any behavioral variable, is determined mainly by hereditary or mainly by environmental influences. There are many problems with the research on which such conclusions might be based (Horn, 1974, 1976a; Loehlin, Lindzey, and Spuhler, 1975).

Adulthood Age Differences in Abilities

Many studies have provided a wealth of information about differences between the performances of older and younger adults.[3] Recent reviews of this information have been prepared by Botwinick (1977) and Horn (1970a, 1972, 1975,a,b, 1978a).

We should mention a controversy before we get into a review of results. This is a debate over the meaning of results from longitudinal and cross-sectional studies. These results have been regarded as contradictory. A question of concern, therefore, is whether we need to consider two separate and contradictory lines of evidence. In principle, longitudinal and cross-sectional forms of data can be sensitive to different influences and could thus yield different results, yet the results from existing studies need not lead to different conclusions. It will be shown later that the results are not contradictory if one takes into account the difference between Gf and Gc and attends to matters of statistical power. Our summary therefore is based on the evidence of both kinds of studies.

Some of the intellectual abilities that have been found to decline with age in adulthood are indicated in figure 10.5. The evidence for this decline derives from studies in which primary abilities, or single tests, were used. It is consistent with evidence in which the Wechsler test was used to indicate performance IQ (Matarazzo, 1972).

The Wechsler tests (for children as well as adults) consist of ten to twelve subtests that represent either verbal IQ or performance IQ. Several of the subtests that are said to indicate performance IQ are similar to the marker tests for Gf, and several of the verbal IQ subtests are measures of Gc. Thus in a rough way the distinction between performance IQ and verbal IQ represents the distinction between Gf and Gc. Quite a number of aging studies based on the Wechsler scales have indicated decline in performance IQ—that is, Gf abilities.

Curves summarizing age differences in short-term acquisition and

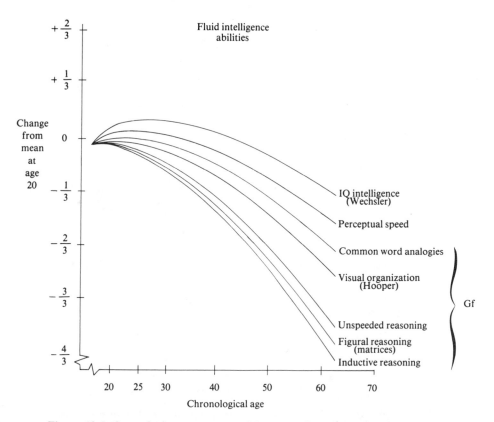

Figure 10.5. *Smoothed curves summarizing several studies indicating aging changes for fluid intelligence.*

retrieval (SAR) abilities (figure 10.6) are similar to the curves shown in figure 10.5 for fluid abilities. Yet the two sets of abilities are distributed independently, as indicated by the evidence of higher-order factoring. The correlations between elements of one construct (SAR) and the elements of the other construct (Gf) are less than the internal correlations among the elements of each construct. The correlations between the abilities of SAR and those of Gf are about 0.3, while the correlations among the subtests of SAR and among the Gf abilities are about 0.5 or higher (see Hundal and Horn, 1977, for review). The aging curve for one construct is not accounted for (predicted by) measures of the other construct, implying that the subjects who show notable decline in Gf do not necessarily show comparable decline in SAR and vice versa. The subsamples of subjects exhibiting decline in

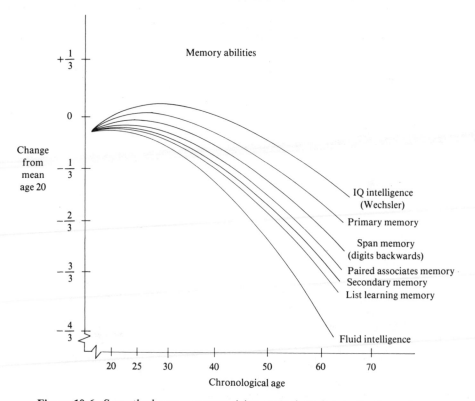

Figure 10.6. *Smoothed curves summarizing several studies indicating aging changes in short-term acquisitions and retrieval (SAR) abilities.*

SAR are somewhat different from the subsamples exhibiting decline in Gf. Moreover, controlling for differences in the memory functions of SAR does not eliminate the aging decline of Gf. In general, there is a loss of fluid intelligence with age that is not best described as a loss of memory, and there is loss of memory that is not accompanied by comparable loss of fluid intelligence. The curves in figures 10.5 and 10.6 thus represent different processes although the two curves are similar in forms.

   Many studies have found that in the same samples of subjects in which the abilities of Gf and SAR are seen to decline, the abilities that have their principal correlation with Gc do not decline or even improve with age during adulthood (figure 10.7). Another set of abilities for which the evidence suggests little or no decline with aging are those

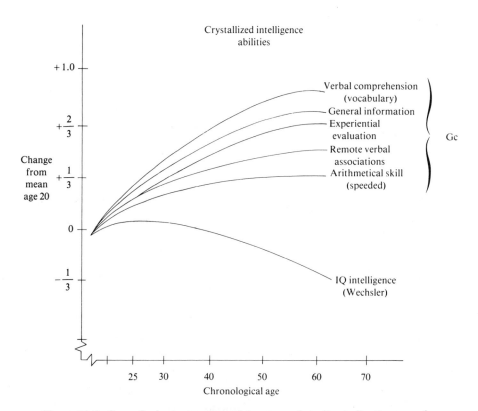

Figure 10.7. *Smoothed curves summarizing several studies indicating age effects associated with crystallized intelligence.*

of the factor indicating tertiary storage and retrieval (TSR). Age difference curves for some abilities are summarized in figure 10.8.

As with the distinction between Gf and SAR, the age difference curves for Gc and TSR are similar, but two reliably independent processes are indicated. Individuals who improve with age in the "knowledge" abilities of Gc are not generally the same people who improve with age in the fluent-expressive abilities of TSR. Many of the TSR tasks are speeded, so the evidence of no aging decline or age-related improvement in these tasks supports a hypothesis that slowing of performance is not a general characteristic of aging.

The data in figures 10.5-10.8 represent a sampling of classes of performance, not a detailed account of findings obtained with particular tests and paradigms. Some test findings are not consistent with

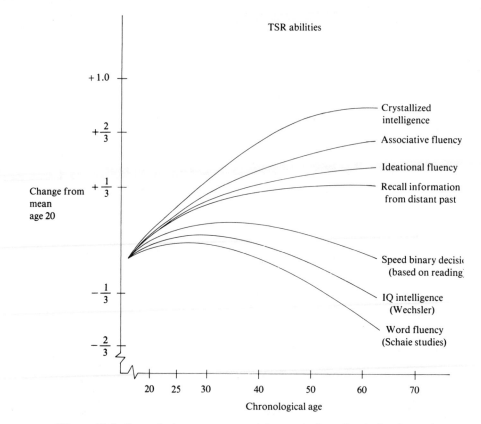

Figure 10.8. *Smoothed curves summarizing several studies indicating aging changes in tertiary storage and retrieval (TSR) abilities.*

this summary, and there are many possible reasons for such inconsistencies: tests yield different results in different investigations; particular forms of a test can be appropriate for one sample of subjects but not for another; the sampling of subjects in one study can yield anomalous results. Thus the data in the figures represent a smoothing of many studies.

Improvements and lack of decline in Gc and TSR abilities have been found in the same samples as those in which notable decrements in Gf and SAR abilities have been indicated. Since it is impossible to have samples of younger and older subjects that are truly representative of all people at these ages, a finding of only a decrement in Gf abilities might be parsimoniously interpreted as due to a cohort difference. For example, in this century older people have had less formal education, on the average, than younger people. But when decrements in some of the abilities of intelligence are accompanied by increments in other abilities, in general when rates of change are different for different tasks, then it is more difficult to argue that education, or a similar cohort factor, is responsible for both changes in intelligence.

Learning in Relation to Aging

The decline of some abilities and the lack of decline of other abilities needs explanation. In forming an explanation the role of learning is paramount.

Since much of what is measured in both Gf and Gc is learned material, established principles of acquisition and retrieval are appropriate for understanding the development of intelligence (whether or not one chooses to believe that most of the variance in manifestations is determined by heredity). A person forgets and loses coherence of learned material in accordance with these principles over the entire life span, not just in adulthood.

For example, existing evidence suggests that the curve for forgetting over months and years has the same negatively accelerated form as the curves for retrieval loss over seconds, minutes, or hours (Riegel, 1972). The amount of learned information that a person of any age can recall at any given moment is inversely related to the time elapsed since having learned or used the material (figure 10.9); one is constantly losing and replenishing elements of the knowledge base.

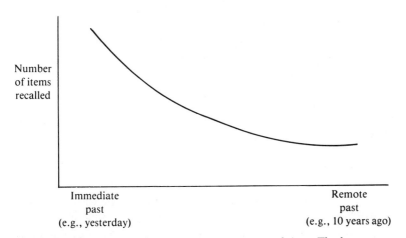

Figure 10.9. *Recall memory after varying amounts of time. The largest proportion of the tertiary memory store of a person of any age is from the immediate past, and events more remote are less well recalled. (After Riegel, 1972.)*

Decline and improvement are thus always resolutions of vectors of anabolic and catabolic forces. Thus at any age a major portion of the learned content of intelligence was acquired, or at least reinforced, in the recent past. If this recent-past development and maintenance is poor, the affected abilities will decline. This is true for Gc as well as for Gf.

If a particular test measures information or a skill that an individual has not used for a long time, that individual's performance is likely to be low relative to past performance. This conclusion needs to be qualified in several ways. For example, the amount by which performance is depressed depends on the quality and kind of initial learning or most recent rehearsal. Retention of learned material is a function of many factors operating when the material was learned. Material that is organized and therefore understood well is usually retained much better and for longer periods of time than material learned by rote practice. The spacing and the number of learning trials also influence the amount retained and the length of retention. A large number of such factors operate and interact to determine retention (Arenberg and Robertson-Tchabo, 1977; Craik, 1977; Craik and Lockhart, 1972; Horn, 1978a,b; Kintsch, 1970; Nelson, 1977). The important point is that the conditions operating during initial learning and rehearsal (if any) affect the amount retained. Thus, while most of what one knows at a given time is largely material that was learned or rehearsed in the recent past, some was learned in the more distant past because the quality of this early learning was quite good.

Considerations of this kind complicate possible explanations for the differences in the aging curves of Gf, Gc, SAR, and TSR. There is some suggestion that the abilities that do not decline are well consolidated in initial acquisition and are (perhaps in consequence) frequently rehearsed throughout adulthood. Some of the evidence that is consistent with this view has been provided in the studies of Botwinick and Storandt (1974) and Warrington and Sanders (1971). The "shape" of these results is depicted in figure 10.10.

The basic finding represented in figure 10.10 is that individuals of different ages can recall relatively more of some information learned (it seems) in late adolescence and young adulthood than comparable information learned (it seems) in the more recent past. In the Botwinick and Storandt studies, for example, tests of knowledge were constructed from questions about events that occurred in each of several historical periods of this century. A person could be compared with himself (in an ipsative fashion) to determine how much he remembered of events that were current when he was 15-20, 20-25, 25-30 years old. The results of such a comparison suggest that people can

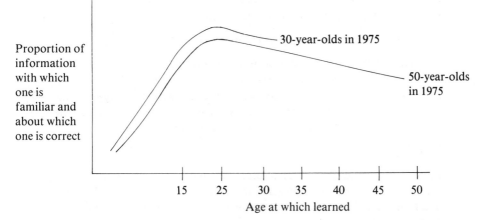

Figure 10.10. *Age of learning for material recalled some years later. A large proportion of what one can retrieve was learned in late adolescence and young adulthood, between the ages of 15 and 25, independent of the age at which recall is measured. (After Botwinick and Storandt, 1974; Warrington and Sanders, 1971.)*

recall relatively more information that was current when they were 20-25 years old than information that was current at other periods of their lives. Thus a person who was 30 years old in 1975 does relatively better on tests about events that occurred between 1965 and 1970, and a person who was 50 years old in 1975 performs best on tests dealing with events that occurred between 1945 and 1950.

One interpretation of these results is that between 20 and 30 years of age the peak in Gf is reached and other conditions are such that the quality of learning is maximized. For example, during this period one is called on to prepare for, or assume, an occupational role, to make sexual and mating adjustments—in general, to move from the category "child" to the category "adult." Under such conditions the motivation to acquire information and to understand can be quite high. Thus it may be that a relatively large proportion of the content of intelligence that persists at later ages is acquired in young adulthood.

It may be, too, that one tends to rehearse and re-rehearse this content of intelligence. This explanation is consistent with a law of inertia of our knowledge base. We tend to retain and build on what we already know rather than discard and revamp this material. The abilities that are expressions of this organized knowledge system do not decline with age; if properly measured, they probably improve over much of adulthood. The knowledge that is acquired in young adulthood is at the core of this structure of knowledge.

Neurological Correlates of Ability Decline

The abilities that are not well integrated into our rehearsed knowledge structure may decline for no other reason than because they are not well rehearsed. However, there is evidence to suggest that other influences reduce some of our intellectual capacities. Prominent among these are the influences associated with neurological structure and functioning. Some of the evidence that links physiological, principally neurological, changes to performance on ability tests is direct, in the sense that the physiological and the psychological measurements are obtained on the same persons and concomitant variations in these measurements are recorded. Other evidence in this area is indirect: averages in physiological measures and averages in measures of ability performance are recorded for different age groups, but each kind of average is based on a different sample of subjects.

There is little research evidence of a direct relationship between neurological dysfunction due to aging and corresponding loss of intellectual abilities. There are clinical reports and commonsense observations that suggest relationships, particularly between onset of an age-associated neurological disease, such as Alzheimer's, and decline in global intelligence. There are correlational studies and before-and-after studies of relationships between brain damage and performance on ability tests. The effects of brain damage in these cases are neurologically and behaviorally similar to some of the effects associated with aging (Horn, 1970a).

The evidence on brain damage in relation to human intellectual behavior is difficult to interpret. This is not surprising; one cannot arrange damages of neatly calibrated amounts to occur in carefully designated areas of the human brain. Given the widely variable amounts and locations of damage, it is extremely difficult to discern a replicable pattern of effect using post hoc procedures. Such conditions for research provide fertile ground for propounding hypotheses. Indeed, ideas about how brain malfunction might be manifested in behavior abound (see those mentioned by Royce, Yeudall, and Bock, 1976, for example). Of the many ideas, Hebb's (1942) have perhaps been most influential in shaping present-day theory about the organization of human abilities as seen in factor analytic results.

Hebb's evaluation of the evidence indicated that if brain damage occurs in adolescence or adulthood (not childhood), then the effects on some of the abilities that are readily identified as involving intelligence are different from the effect on other abilities. Performance on most tasks is depressed immediately following brain injury, but some performances later recover to a point where the person performs nearly as well as he did before the injury. Performance on other tasks does not return to a preinjury level. For nonaphasic injuries the performances that recover are those of Gc, whereas those of Gf and SAR do not.

These conclusions, particularly those concerning the aphasias, need to be qualified. Language comprehension is a prominent feature of Gc. Loss in the knowledge system that is coded in language is loss of Gc. The aphasias represent the fact that language loss occurs as a result of brain injury. Moreover, the language abilities that are affected do not always return to preinjury levels. In a sense, then, measures of Gc abilities can be as sensitive to brain injury as measures of Gf abilities.

There are two ways in which this qualification needs to be added to the generalization that Gc abilities tend to recover after brain injury and Gf abilities do not: (1) If the injury is sufficiently massive, then both Gc and Gf abilities are affected adversely and do not return to preinjury levels. (2) Injuries to particular parts of the brain affect particular features of language ability, and if a measure of this feature of language is included in a multiple measure of Gc, then Gc can be as much affected by brain injury as Gf. The provisional clause in the second statement is needed because with some aphasias it is possible to measure comprehension of language without introducing decrements associated with the aphasia. For example, understanding of words can be measured in a manner that does not introduce variance due to an inability to speak, or to speak the intended words (anarthria). Indeed, in the typical verbal comprehension measure, used to measure an aspect of Gc, this separation in measurement is probably achieved. Under such conditions the anarthria need not produce a decline in Gc following injury.

Thus when brain injury is severe enough to produce aphasia, the question whether Gf and Gc decline by different amounts becomes complicated by considerations of which primary ability components and which test measures of Gf and Gc may be affected by the injury. In general it seems that Gf is affected adversely by brain injury no matter where this injury is localized, whereas some components of Gc may be considerably more affected than others, depending on the location of the injury.

The evidence on lateralization also complicates generalization. We do not yet know precisely how to integrate the lateralization evidence into broad theory about intellectual functioning. One possibility is that in right-dominant people—right-handed, right-eyed, right-eared people—the left hemisphere of the brain is specialized for the language abilities that are prominent in Gc, but the other abilities of Gc are not so localized. Another possibility is that all the abilities of Gc tend to be left-brain localized in right-dominant people. Similarly, the functions supporting expressions of Gf may tend to be localized in the right hemisphere of right-dominant people; alternatively, only visualization (Gv) and/or auditory (Ga) organizations may be thus localized. These and other hypotheses are compatible with the existing evidence. The issues in this regard become even more complicated when one introduces consideration of left-dominance, sex differences, and modes of using a writing implement (Harnad et al., 1977; Dimond and Beaumont, 1974; Levy and Reid, 1976).

With these refinements and qualifications, we can conclude that Gf is more pervasively and permanently affected by brain damage in adulthood than is Gc. This conclusion follows from considerable research (Halstead, 1947; Hebb, 1942, 1949; Crown, 1951; Reitan, 1958, 1964; Meyer, 1961; Payne, 1961; Willett, 1961; Pribram, 1971). It seems that Gf decrement is roughly proportional to the amount of loss of central nervous system (CNS) structure. The loss of ability appears immediately after brain damage and, for the most part, persists. Damage in the frontal areas of the brain may have a greater influence than damage elsewhere, consistent with some well-known theories (Luria, 1969; Warrington, 1969) but even fairly localized damage in areas remote from the frontal sections produces notable Gf decrements (Meyer, 1961; Royce, Yeudall, and Bock, 1976; Willett, 1961).

The direct evidence suggesting that brain injury affects Gf and Gc in different ways may be indicative of the ways in which Gf and Gc are affected by aging. In particular, with advancing age there may be an accumulation of brain injuries, each rather minor in itself, each too small to produce an effect on behavior that is large enough to detect with our usual behavioral measures, that together can eventuate in ability changes comparable to those seen when there is brain injury and a consequent loss of intellectual ability. This reasoning is based on several assumptions, any one of which might be unwarranted. In particular, the reasoning is based on the assumption that aging is associated with physiological and neurological changes that are in some respects the same as brain injuries. Is the evidence consistent with this assumption?

There are many problems with the evidence pertaining to aging effects. There are no direct demonstrations that a given change in neural structure due to aging leads to corresponding changes in intellectual ability. All that has been shown is that the average performances on Gf and SAR tasks decline with age and that there are changes, again as recorded in averages, in neurological structure or function. The standard deviations for these variables are large. The distributions for different ages overlap, in some cases substantially. A particular individual may not be affected by influences that produce the average. In much of the research on neurological aspects of aging, the samples have been small and atypical. There are often problems with the observation techniques. There are usually several possible interpretations of a given type of observation. The evidence has many flaws.

One must draw conclusions with caution. Given this proviso, however, one is led by the existing evidence to a conclusion that with age there is a loss of the neurological base for intellectual functions and that this loss is probably reflected most notably in Gf. Between about 20 and 60 years of age, for example, the averages, based on samples that have been gathered, suggest that the following changes occur:

Decrease in brain weight from about 1,400 grams to 1,250 grams, about a 12% loss.

Decrease, up to 50% in some areas of the brain, in total number of functional neurons (cortical atrophy).

Corresponding increase in water content of brain.

Decrease in neuronal conduction rate (conflicting evidence).

Decrease in cerebral blood flow, that is, increase in cerebral arteriosclerosis (Meier-Ruge et al., 1975).

Increase in width of brain fissures, ventrical size.

Increase in inert waste products—for example, Lipofuscin—in the neuron cells (Sekhon and Maxwell, 1974; Brizzee, Ordy, and Kaack, 1974), perhaps having a detrimental effect on cell motility (Murray and Stout, 1974).

Increase in neurofibrillary tangles and senile plagues, with loss of neuron function (Matsuyama, Namiki, and Watanabe, 1966; Terry and Wisniewski, 1972, 1975).

Loss of integrity of cell nuclei (Andrews, 1956).

Increase in Nissl substance abnormalities (Kuhlenbeck, 1954; Ellis, 1920).

Increase in atypical morphological characteristics of cellular organelles (Andrews, 1956).

Loss of suporting structures of the brain.

Decrease in RNA, in half-life of ribosomal protein (Hyden, 1960; Menzes and Gold, 1972).

Change in protein-DNA ratio (van Hahn, 1970).

Increase in oddities of synaptic transmitter substances (Robinson et al., 1972).

This list is no more than a sample. Although some recent evaluations of this literature are more optimistic than some earlier evaluations (Bondareff, 1959, 1977), the balance of the indirect evidence supports the hypothesis that there is deterioration with aging, at least in averages, in some of the physiological structures and functions believed to provide a basis for intellectual performances.

The empirical evidence indicates that the abilities of Gf are more permanently affected by loss of brain tissue than are the abilities of Gc, but it is by no means clear why this should be true. Our view is that Gc is a better indicator than Gf of the wholistic totality of an individual's knowledge structure. This knowledge structure is analogous, perhaps, to a fully constructed building that can stand and even appear to be fully intact when in fact there are bricks lost here, shingles blown away there, perhaps even whole rooms lost to function due to water damage (analogous to the aphasias). Such a structure is said to be overdetermined. In the case of Gc an overdetermined structure seems to be brought about by integrative learning, in which parts are welded into the whole of a knowledge system. Such learning is said to be well consolidated. The skills that result from such learning tend to be those that one uses again and again. They are maintained through use.

The neurological equivalent of behavioral overdetermination is elaboration of and redundancy in neural networks referred to as cell assemblies and phase sequences (Hebb, 1949). If 100 neurons can interact in any of 10 ways to produce recall of a word, this retrieval is overdetermined relative to a recall in which 10 neurons must interact in only 1 way. If there is substantial overdetermination in a skill, then notable amounts of neural tissue can be lost without loss of the skill. This neural overdetermination characterizes the knowledge structure that is Gc.

An analogy that characterizes Gf without misleading is difficult to specify. In his early statements of Gf-Gc theory Cattell (1957) had likened Gc to coral and Gf to the polyps that build such structures. This analogy is a bit misleading because it suggests that Gc is a dead residue whereas the abilities that define Gc are quite active in enabling an individual to adapt and elaborate the knowledge system. However, the analogy is useful in suggesting that Gf is a complex of several functions, a complex that grows and expands with development and yet such that a detriment in the health of any one of its systems affects the functioning of the system as a whole. This latter represents a condition of interdependency among the separate components of a complex structure. Whereas Gc is characterized by overdetermination, Gf appears to be characterized by interdependency.

A recent review of neurological function in relation to psychological abilities (Hyden, 1973) suggests a biochemical and electrical basis for the distinction between Gf and Gc. On the one hand, long-term mnemonic storage is based on biochemical structural alterations of neuronal synapses. These alterations correspond to encoding memory traces in some exceedingly complex fashion, perhaps facilitated by some macromolecular code (Hyden, 1973). If, as seems to be the case, such information is encoded diffusely throughout the brain, then this diffuse encoding can be a neurological representation of the overdetermination underlying Gc. On the other hand, the evidence indicates that some behavioral functions are sustained by the predominantly electrical, evanescent networks of neuronal firing. Perhaps Gf depends on such functions, based in some gross fashion on the total number of available, functional neurons in the cortical mass.

Integration of Averaging and Individual Differences Research

Broadbent (1966), Keele (1973), Kintsch (1970, 1974), and Norman (1970, 1977) provide definitive and integrated reviews of verified findings pertaining to information processing, learning, and related processes. This will be referred to as cognitive processing research. Craik (1977) and Arenberg and Robertson-Tchabo (1977) provide excellent reviews of much of this evidence as it pertains to adulthood development. The generalizations of this section derive primarily from these sources.

The concepts pertaining to adult development that derive from cognitive (information) processing theory are similar in several respects to the ideas already mentioned in this chapter. The words used to tag concepts are sometimes different, the operational definitions may not be precisely the same, and there are some fundamental differences; but the phenomena discussed by ID researchers and those discussed in mainstream cognitive psychology have much in common, including the following points of similarity.

1. Recognition that to a considerable extent the cognitive processes observed in adulthood reflect a history of learning. Thus the acquisition, maintenance, and expression of such processes (skills or abilities) should be understandable, in part, in terms of established principles of learning.
2. Recognition that age changes may reflect changes in
   a. Knowledge—crudely, the content of long-term memory.
   b. Processes—crudely, the means by which the elements of memory are acted on (accessed, maintained). Processes are often characterized as either automatic (not requir-

ing attention) or controlled (requiring active investment of attentional resources).
c. Production systems (Newell and Simon, 1972) and strategies for carrying out information-processing strategies.
3. Use of similar forms of analysis to indicate development. Most extant research is based on cross-sectional data gathering, but longitudinal observations have been obtained occasionally.

Here we shall emphasize these common features rather than point to differences. In the spirit of emphasizing what is common, we continue to use terms specified earlier in the chapter rather than adopt the terminology that is most frequently used in cognitive processing and other averaging research. For example, the term SAR will be used rather than the expression short-term memory (STM), even though the latter would be more readily understood by mainstream cognitive processing researchers.

Before we consider results, as such, it will be useful to look briefly at a methodological problem that has eroded the usefulness of much research on cognitive processing in relation to aging. This is the problem of reliability of measurement. It is our view that the conclusions of many studies should not be accepted because the evidence for reliability is not sufficient to support the claims on which the conclusions are based.

If reliability of measurement is low, it is difficult to show a difference between groups on the measurements in question. In some research this is not important because absence of an effect is failure to support a hypothesis. In aging research, however, a hypothesis of principal interest may be one that stipulates no notable age differences. If a conclusion is to be compelling, there must be sufficient reliability to allow for demonstration of an effect.

A study by Walsh and Baldwin (1977) provides an example of how problems of reliability are neglected. Walsh and Baldwin provided a well-reasoned basis for using a paradigm developed by Bransford and Franks (1971) to study adulthood age differences in linguistic integration. The idea of this paradigm is that people report that they have been previously exposed to sentences even when they have not if the semantic structure of the sentences is quite consistent with ideas to which they have been exposed. The occurence of such false positive recognitions is said to indicate linguistic abstraction or integration. In a comparison of 20 young (average age 18.7 years) and 18 old (average age 67.3 years) adults, Walsh and Baldwin found no significant difference between the age-group means for measures intended to represent this form of integration. From this finding they concluded that elderly subjects are as accurate as young subjects in retaining integrated representations of semantic information.

There are several problems with this conclusion. For example, there is the logical problem of dealing with contrasts between groups that differ in many respects. There is also the problem of accepting the null hypothesis as true (particularly when sample sizes are small). But the fundamental problem we emphasize here is that Walsh and Baldwin presented no basis for evaluating whether the measure of integration was sufficiently reliable to detect a difference between means if such a difference was of about the same magnitude as has been found for other measures of cognitive ability. A useful way to think about this question of reliability is to code the groups 0 and 1 (to represent young or old) and to recognize that the test of significance between group means is a test of the significance of difference from zero of a point of biserial correlation between the 0, 1 codes and the measure of integration. When the test is expressed in this way, one can immediately recognize that the upper limit for the correlation (and hence its significance level) is the reliability of the integration measure. One can also recognize that with small sample sizes this reliability, and hence the correlation, should be large to show significance. In studies of adult development of abilities such correlations are typically of the order of 0.3—the aging effects are not very large. To demonstrate significance for such effects one needs highly reliable measures or large samples (for there is a trade-off between reliability and sample size; Horn, 1979c).

This example illustrates a common problem in the study of aging from a background of cognitive processing. In cognitive processing research typically powerful manipulated conditions are imposed to demonstrate an effect; thus high reliability is not usually needed and reliability is not considered. The investigator then fails to consider reliability and power when age is a principal variable and high reliability is required. The null hypothesis is then inappropriately accepted as true. This error of reasoning occurs all too frequently.[4]

Analyses

Turning now to some results, consider again the organizational scheme represented in figure 10.3. Here it is recognized that paradigm manipulations reflect roughly five kinds of functional organization: sensory detection, perceptual pattern recognition (Gv and Ga), associative acquisition and retrieval (SAR and TSR), eduction of relations and correlates (Gf and Gc), and general organization (G). Performance on any particular task (paradigm) involves all of these functions but may reveal more about one level of functioning than about the other levels.

Levels of functions are of particular interest in the study of capacities that seem to decline with aging because it is reasonable to suppose that apparent deficits at the highest levels of intellectual functioning are reflections of losses at lower levels. These losses are often considered to be easily correctable (as with hearing aids, spectacles) whereas losses of eductive[5] or associative powers have been regarded as much less correctable. It is depressing, however, that the research results lend little support to the view that aging deficits in higher functions are reflections of losses of lower functions. While there are indeed aging losses of sensory and perceptual functions, there also seem to be losses of associative and eductive capacities that are not reflections of losses of the former.

One principal finding of research on sensory processes is that the human is capable of being momentarily aware of a large proportion of the surrounding events. For very brief periods of time a person may be immediately aware of many distinct new elements in his environment (Broadbent, 1958, 1966; Keele, 1973; Sperling, 1960). This memory is sometimes referred to as iconic (for visual awareness) or echoic (for auditory awareness). It lasts only a second or two, although perhaps a bit longer if echoic than if iconic. Typically, the memory is organized in terms of the sensory organ that detects the information rather than in terms of meaning of the information. Thus a number is represented iconically in terms of its shape, not in terms of its numerical properties.

The evidence for detector functions makes it reasonable to suppose that they might undergo aging losses and that these losses would be reflected in declines in abilities that indicate intelligence. Perhaps the breadth of sensory detection becomes narrower as we get older and we consequently become less able to solve problems that are believed to measure eductive or associative capacities but also involve breadth of awareness. Matrix problems, for example, might have this quality. If older persons have greater difficulty than younger persons in becoming aware of the totality of the stimulus array presented, then by partialling out the variance associated with sensory awareness measures in the relationship between age and performance on matrix problems, the aging decline indicated for performance would be reduced, perhaps eliminated, and thus be shown to reflect a sensory awareness deficit. This hypothesis is reasonable, but the evidence gives scant support for it.

Research reviewed by Botwinick (1977), Bromley (1974), Craik (1977), Horn (1970a, 1975, 1976), and Welford (1958) suggests that there are aging decrements in sensory detector functions. Representative of this evidence is a recent study by Walsh and Thompson (1978), in which the mean duration of iconic memory was found to be 15% greater for the young (mean 24 years) than for the old (mean age 67 years). Such sensory memory decrements seem to be small (Craik, 1977; Walsh, 1975), however; most important, they do not seem to account for changes observed in intellectual tasks.

Some results from recent studies are illustrative (Horn, 1976b, 1978c). Paradigms invented by Sperling (1960) and Broadbent (1954, 1958) were converted to individual differences measurements and used in partial covariance analyses with test measures of Gf, Gc, and other intellectual abilities. Two major conclusions were indicated by the analyses: (1) Sensory detector measures have only low correlations with Gf and aging differences in adulthood. In particular, they do not account for aging decline in Gf. (2) Sensory detector measures correlate relatively higher with short-term memory than with Gf and Gc indicants of eductive processes. It seems that with decrease in meaningful association in memory there is increase in correlation with sensory detection.

The conclusion is that sensory detector functions decline with aging, but the decline of these functions is not responsible for the aging decrements of fluid intelligence. In units in which a standard deviation is 15 points, the decline in sensory detector functions seems to be of the order of 2 points per decade between age 30 and age 50. There are low correlations between these measures and Gf—relationships of the order of 0.15 to 0.20. But the correlations of sensory detector measures with measures of short-term memory are about 0.35 to 0.40, and when memory is partialled out, the correlations between sensory detector measures and Gf approach a point at which one would not want to regard them as indicating functional dependence, even with corrections for unreliability.

There is no clear line between sensory detector functions and perceptual organization, nor between the latter and associative processes. Operational definitions of perceptual organizations are indicated very crudely by the Gv and Ga factors. These involve complex visual and auditory performances but are independent of the factors based on association tasks and those emphasizing eduction of relations and correlates. These operational definitions are useful, but they reveal little about the essential underlying processes. Fortunately, several lines of cognitive processing research have yielded some insights into the nature of these processes.

One promising way of distinguishing between awarenesses at different levels of organization—sensory, perceptual, associational, eductive—is in terms of a combination of the amount of information retained in awareness and the amount of time over which it can be retained. There is considerable evidence that these two features of retention are a function of the goodness of organization achieved for the retained information (Mandler, 1967; Kintsch, 1970).

The term *organization* in this context can have several meanings. Generally it pertains to the way and the extent to which a person makes sense of information. In the organization achieved at the level of sensory detection, however, the retained elements are not well related to one another; one remembers in terms of locations, order in time, and the sense organ through which awareness is achieved. The scope of such awareness can be large, but the time over which retention is maintained is short, only a second or two. At the other extreme, when eductive processes are used to explicate a poem or work out a chess strategy, many details can be retained over extended periods of time, months and years. Between these extremes of sensory detection and eduction of meaning are perceptual organizations characterized by awareness of patterns and associational organizations characterized by semantic relationships. A perceptual organization is illustrated by retention of a melody. A melody can be remembered more completely and for a longer period of time than a random set of notes because one perceives a pattern among the notes. The memory of melody can occur even when one cannot represent the melody in the semantic units of any language. Perceptual organization in this sense is distinguishable from associational organization, although the line between the two processes is often fuzzy.

The evidence suggests that fallible measures of perceptual organization (as in Gv and Ga) are correlated about 0.4 with Gf and a bit lower with Gc, when reliabilities of measurement are in the neighborhood of 0.8. This evidence also indicates that neither Gv nor Ga nor the two in combination are responsible for adulthood decline in Gf. In the Horn-Cattell (1967) study when Gv was controlled by covariance analysis, the relationships between Gf and age remained essentially unaltered. Other analyses have demonstrated that Gv and Gf have different relationships with age (Horn and Cattell, 1966). Similarly, in a recent study (Horn and Stankov, 1979) Ga was found to have no notable effect on the relationship between age and Gf.

These results should be regarded as suggestive rather than definitive. More work is needed to elucidate the ways in which perceptual organizations can be independent of associational and eductive organizations and to indicate adult development of these functions. At present, however, it seems that if eductive processes are controlled, perceptual organizations will not be highly associated with aging decline in Gf.

Language provides a powerful means for organizing information. When an echoic or iconic image is transformed into meaningful language, there is an important gain in awareness, which can be elaborated by talking about it, either internally or externally. The information can thus be retained in a way that is not possible when only perceptual or sensory awareness is involved. However, there is a clear continuum in such awareness, extending from that based on little semantic elaboration to that involving a great deal. This continuum is represented by a distinction between primary memory and secondary memory, a distinction that has been indicated in several ways in cognitive processing research (Broadbent, 1954; Glanzer and Cunitz, 1966; Yntema and Trask, 1963; Waugh and Norman, 1965; see Kintsch, 1970, for review) and has been supported by ID research as well (Horn, 1976b; 1978c). More important for present purposes, the distinction pertains to a stable feature of adulthood development.

Primary memory is analogous to a temporary holding store. The concept differs from that of sensory detection in that a small number of elements are retained for periods of time that are somewhat longer than two or three seconds; one to four distinct elements can be retained in immediate awareness for periods of up to about 20 seconds without there being association among the elements or rehearsal.

Secondary memory is retention over seconds or minutes, or longer, in which meaningful organization among the elements is recognized or imposed. For example, in remembering a telephone number long enough to dial it, primary memory might keep 3 or 4 of the digits in awareness, and secondary memory could aid by grouping the digits in sets of 3 or 4 or by interrelating the digits mathematically or in terms of a historical date or the like. Through the operation of primary memory and secondary memory the average person can retain a seven-digit telephone number in immediate awareness for 5 to 30 seconds, considerably longer than sensory detection lasts.

While aging in adulthood is often thought to be accompanied by loss of short-term memory, this loss seems to occur not so much for the very short term memory of sensory detection or primary memory as for secondary memory. One must be cautious about overgeneralizing the existing results, but aging decline in primary memory seems to be less marked, less consistent, and less related to decline in Gf than the aging deficit in secondary memory (Craik, 1968, 1971, 1977; Horn, 1970a,b, 1978a,b,c; Hulicka and Weiss, 1965; Muenster, 1972; Wimer and Wigdor, 1958). The age relationships for primary memory are similar to those for sensory detectors—the decline is small and only weakly related to indicants of Gf or Gc (Anders and Fozard, 1973; Botwinick and Storandt, 1974; Bromley, 1958; Craik, 1968, 1971, 1977; Horn, 1976b, 1978a,b,c).

When secondary memory does not occur, the result can be viewed as a failure to organize (to make sense of) the information at the encoding stage (Craik, 1977; Horn, 1976a,b; Hultsch, 1969, 1971a,b, 1974; Laurence, 1967). This failure to organize can be a result of failure to educe relationships. A loss of secondary memory function thus seems to reflect, in part, a loss of eductive processes, and vice versa.

Other results suggest that short-term memory becomes related to the eductive processes of intelligence and to Gf aging decline as demands for dividing attention in the memory task are increased. Such results were perhaps first adduced in the pioneering work of Welford and his co-workers (Welford, 1958). They have since been supported in several ways in other studies (Botwinick and Storandt, 1974; Broadbent and Herron, 1962; Roth as reported in Eysenck, 1967; Horn, 1970a, 1978c; Hunt, 1976, 1978). Hunt suggested that memory does not require intelligence (as measured with eductive tasks) until a notable demand of attentional processes is added.

Also related are findings based on a form of incidental memory. The term *incidental memory* has several operational and theoretical definitions (Estes and DaPolito, 1967; Horn, 1970a; Postman, 1964). In this context it refers to tasks in which subjects are asked to recall or recognize material that they have not been asked to remember. The material might be episodes of a movie (Jones, Conrad, and Horn, 1928, events staged during testing (Horn, 1978a,c), or words that subjects were asked to sort but not to memorize (Horn, 1978a,c; Mandler, 1968). Older persons tend to score lower than younger persons in such tasks, and their poorer performance seems to be related to aging decline in Gf. In the pioneering studies of Jones, Conrad, and Horn (1928) and Willoughby (1927, 1930) memory for events that occurred several minutes before testing for recall, when no instructions to remember had been given, dropped steadily with age in adulthood.

Recognition memory should be distinguished from recall. There is evidence to suggest that unfamiliar, low-association, infrequently occurring information is recognized under conditions in which such material is not recalled. It seems, also, that recognition memory either does not decline with aging or it declines less than recall memory (Craik, 1977; Hultsch, 1971a,b; Schonfield, 1965; Walsh and Baldwin, 1977). There is a problem with this interpretation of the findings, however. Since recognition tasks are less difficult than recall tasks, perhaps the different decline curves for recognition and recall memory indicate only that decline occurs primarily when tasks become difficult.

The distinction between SAR and TSR factors indicates that the processes of memory over periods of seconds and minutes are independent (to some extent) of processes of remembering things learned months and years before. The existing evidence suggests that there is aging decline in many of the processes that are interrelated in SAR, and that this decline becomes more pronounced and more related to Gf decline as memory requires recognizing or imposing organization. It might seem, therefore, that the long-term memory of TSR should show severe aging decline, since it seems to depend on recognizing or imposing organization on the material to be remembered. The evidence does not support this view, however, although the relation of the results to the hypothesis as stated is questionable.

The evidence in question is based on two kinds of tasks: those in which subjects are required to produce words or ideas that relate to a particular word or idea and those in which subjects are required to recognize an item of information that was presumably learned some years before. There appears to be no aging decline for either type of task; if anything, it seems older persons perform better on such tasks than younger persons (Botwinick and Storandt, 1974; Craik, 1977; Horn, 1970a; Horn and Cattell, 1967).

A problem with interpreting such performances as indicative of long-term memory, as such, is that memory, exposure, rehearsal, and other aspects of response are inextricably confounded. An older person may remember more words similar in meaning to the word *warm* because he has learned more such words, because he has had more practice in using such words, because he has less demanding criteria for similarity. He may be better able to recall or recognize the name of an ambassador because he has better learned or more frequently rehearsed such items, not because his long-term memory has not declined.

TSR may represent mainly retrieval functions that do not decline with age once information has been adequately encoded. The abilities that decline most with age are largely those in which encoding is a prominent feature of the ability. On the other hand, some findings suggest that older adults do as well as, if not better than, younger adults after they have properly encoded information, for example in learning of the kind required in college or university studies (Horn, 1970a, for review). However, differences in motivation, as well as factors associated with sample selection, may be the major influences in these results. Nevertheless, the findings suggest that once an older adult achieves a meaningful association among items of information, he retains this information for long periods of time as well as a younger person.

This section is only illustrative of a large body of work. More research has been done on memory processes than on any other aspect of intelligence; this is true also of research on adulthood development. Other summaries of this work are provided by Arenberg and Robertson-Tchabo (1977), Carroll (1978), Carroll and Maxwell (1979), Craik (1977), Horn (1970a, 1978a,b,c,d), Hunt (1978), and Sternberg (1977).

Next consider Gf and Gc. What is it that distinguishes the processes of these factors from the associative and perceptual processes that define SAR, TSR, Ga, and Gv? At this stage of study we can only point to behaviors that seem to be indicative of the eductive processes of intelligence; we cannot specify the sine qua non of these processes.

At a general level, Gf and Gc represent capacities for becoming aware of complex relationships among items of information, for construing these relationships in ways that are useful for retention and communication, and for drawing reasonable (logical) inferences. These processes are not well described simply as those of analyzing in terms of the formal logic discussed by philosophers, although such thinking is probably an important part of Gf-Gc intelligence. Many of the solutions reached in Gf and Gc tests, as well as in real-life exercise of intelligence, are not, strictly speaking, logical (Hoffman, 1964; Riegel, 1973b).

Gf and Gc represent, in part, capacities for attaining a comprehension that enables one to retain information over relatively long periods of time. Carroll (1972, 1976) distinguishes this kind of comprehension from memory in much the same way that we have distinguished Gf-Gc forms of intelligence from the SAR-TSR functions that support intelligence. Again, however, there is more to Gf and Gc than merely the processes that enable one to retain awareness for extended periods of time.

The distinction between Gc and Gf is mainly a distinction between eductive processes that stem from an overdetermined structure of knowledge built up largely through acculturation and an interdependent set of reasoning processes that have derived from casual learning. (Both forms of intelligence are based on inherited determiners.) The Gf abilities decline first and most markedly with age in adulthood.

Summary

Human intellectual capacity, as outlined in this chapter, consists of the primary mental abilities, each exhibiting some features of intelligence as this concept has been described verbally. There are in addition patterns of interrelationships among the primary abilities. Two of these are referred to as fluid and crystallized intelligence, Gf and Gc. Other abilities, SAR, TSR, Gv, and Ga, are important aspects of intelligence, but they do not constitute the essence of adult human intelligence.

The Gf, Gc, SAR, TSR classes of abilities are independent not only in the sense that individual differences in one do not predict individual differences in the others but also in the sense that they have different patterns of relationship with several nonbehavioral variables. In particular, the sets of abilities are separate, because they manifest different relationships with age. This suggests that the latent attributes represented by the manifest ability measurements have different developmental histories. The patterns of differences between means for adults grouped according to age are similar for Gf and SAR, but independence in the development of these two classes of abilities is suggested by findings that the reliable age differences in one class are not accounted for by the reliable variance of the other class. Similarly, Gc and TSR have similar patterns of mean differences for subject groupings based on age, but the two sets of differences are not highly predictable from each other.

Figure 10.11 depicts some of the influences and outcomes in the development of intellectual abilities. The curves represent accumulations of effects. The one labeled Gc-TSR is intended to suggest that capacities represented by the fallible indicants of Gc and TSR are enhanced and expanded by the experience, learning, restructuring, practice, refining, tuning, that can occur throughout adulthood. Much of this is culture-directed learning, here described as acculturation. Differences in acculturation account for much of the observed variation in Gc and TSR. The capacities represented by Gf and SAR are also enhanced and expanded by learning, but learning defined as casual.

Table 10.3 is a summary of major cognitive processes associated with ability decline and improvement in adulthood. The ideas of this table have been developed in previous sections of this chapter.

Intellectual achievements in adulthood are a function of both Gf and Gc. In fact, of course, such achievements are a result of many factors that are not indicants of intelligence in any usual sense of the word —motivation, social circumstances, luck (as indicated in the recent studies of Jencks et al., 1972; Lundberg, 1968; Mayeski et al., 1973; Mosteller and Moynihan, 1972; Zajonc, 1976, for example).

Results from research relating intellectual achievement to test scores hint that some kinds of achievement may depend more on Gc than on Gf, or vice versa. For example, Lehman's research (1964) on the achievements of several kinds of intellectual professionals suggests that in some fields—mathematics, music, chemistry, poetry—outstanding work was produced at a relatively early age and thus may be most dependent on Gf, while in other fields—history, astronomy, philosophy, fiction writing, psychology—major achievements occur later in life and may be relatively more dependent on Gc than on Gf. Table 10.4 is a summary of results from this line of research.

These hypotheses need to be qualified in several ways. The analy-

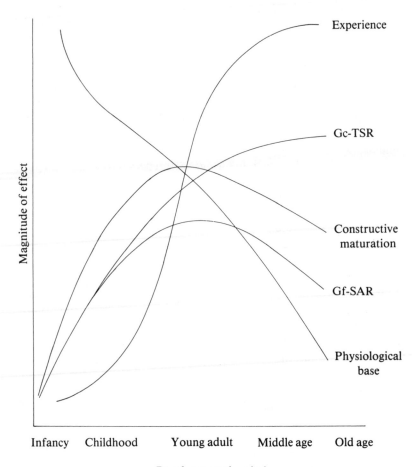

Figure 10.11. *Cumulative influences and developmental outcomes over the life span.*

ses of Dennis (1956, 1968), for example, suggest that Lehman's results could represent mainly cohort and historical time effects rather than individual life-span trajectories.

The evidence for aging loss at several levels of functioning suggests that decline of intelligence in adulthood is characterized by loss of ability to comprehend possible relationships among items of information, to form the best possible organizations of information, to form concepts, and to draw the best possible implications. These inabilities show up primarily when the established concepts of a culture or cultural aids cannot be used effectively to solve a problem. The

Table 10.3. Decline in abilities, processes, and capacities.

Adulthood decline	*No adulthood decline*
Relation education functions	
Gf	Gc
Eduction of novel relationships	Store of available concepts
Drawing novel inferences	Use of well-learned, frequently used
Elaboration of hypotheses	strategies
Use of complex, infrequently used	Eduction of relations that depend
strategies	on breadth of knowledge
Direct concept attainment	Hypothesis development based on
	breadth of knowledge
Associative organization	
SAR	TSR
Secondary memory	Long-term tertiary memory
Attentional capacity	
Incidental memory	Recognition memory
Recall memory	
Perceptual organization and sensory detector functions	
Gv, Ga	
Sensory detectors	Primary memory

inabilities may be due to a loss of capacity for maintaining close attention to features of complex problems, particularly when attention must be divided between several aspects of a task.

Issues and Outcomes Illustrated with a Recent Study

The material summarized so far provides a basis for conducting studies that might shed light on the nature of adulthood development of intellectual abilities. One such study provides results that are useful in integrating the material discussed so far and illustrates methods and methodological issues of general relevance for the study of human development.

The subjects of the study were 147 male volunteers at the Colorado State Penitentiary. The sample was chosen to represent midlife aging rather than the entire adulthood period. The age range was 20 to 50 years, but most of the men were between 25 and 40 years old. The study thus pertains to development in what some regard as the early phases of adulthood. The age range of the subjects makes this study

Table 10.4. Intellectual achievements in relation to age.

Rate of output of chemists highest at 30-34, drop by 40-44.
  Highest level chemical contributions peak at 30.
For music composed between 1912 and 1932, a rise in production to age 35,
  level off until age 70.
Poets peak at age 25-29.
Writing *output* steady through to old age, but author's one best book peak at
  age 35, decline thereafter. Superior novels a bit later; age 40-44.
Philosophy 35-39 best ages for quantity and quality, decline after.
  Metaphysics a bit later, 40-49 age peak.
Psychologists peak at age 35-39, then decline.
Astronomers peak at age 40-45, then decline.
Film directors' major contributions at about age 35-39, decline slowly to age 55,
  then rapidly.
Men and women similar in most of these kinds of findings.
Average starting age of chemists who produced only one outstanding paper was
  36. Chemists producing over 20 major contributions, started at age 22. Thus
  the more *prolific* started earlier. They also finished their creative output *later*.
Peak years for *largest* earnings in most fields is age 50-55.
Largest proportion of people earning large incomes is age 60-64.
Military highest rank reached by age 40-44 (Naval leaders may be somewhat
  later).
Age distribution for *successful* U.S. Presidential candidates, compared with
  unsuccessful ones, suggests that youth helps, but both successful and unsuccessful are 45 or over, and the mean age for an elected President is in the
  neighborhood of 55.

Source: Lehman (1964).

different from most other studies of adult development. Most such
research has been based on samples of the elderly (those over age 65)
and on contrasts between young (college students) and elderly adults.
Schonfield (1972) has pointed out some severe limitations of this latter
kind of sampling when the objective is to describe normal aging.

Table 10.5 describes the variables used in the study. The analyses
are not described in detail, but referring to this list of variables when
examining figures should enable one to understand the major results
of the study. More complete descriptions can be found in Horn
(1978c).

Figures 10.12-10.15 provide a means for communicating results
from the analyses of the study. In each of these figures a heavy line
represents the Gf or Gc age differences before any control was introduced. The performance variables (factors) were scaled to have means

Table 10.5. Variables representing major independent factors of intelligence.

Factor (variable) name	Symbol	Description and test scores combined	Internal consistency (r_{xx})
A. Core factors			
1. Fluid intelligence	Gf	Number correct: Letter series (LS), matrices (MAT), visual organization (VOG), and paper folding (PF)	0.77
2. Crystallized intelligence	Gc	Number correct: vocabulary (EV), esoteric analogies (EA), remote associations (RAT)	0.71
3. Short-term acquisition, retrieval	SAR	Serial list recall in several kinds of lists	0.84
4. Tertiary storage, retrieval	TSR	Number responses: things (THG), uses (USE), and associations (ASC)	0.75
B. Other composite variables			
5. Speediness in Gf tasks	SPGf	Complement of average time-to-correct in MAT, PF, and LS	0.33
6. Speediness in Gc tasks	SPGc	Complement of average time-to-correct in EA, CA, EV	0.63
7. Speediness to wrong	SPw	Complement of average time-to-incorrect in EV, CA, EA, RAT, LS, GES	0.59
8. Carefulness	CAR	Complement of number incorrect in EV, CA, EA, RAT, LS, MAT, GES	0.83
9. Secondary memory	SM	Short primacy and short slope	0.66
10. Attention division	ATD	Marking a's on several tasks interpolated between a spoken discourse and a recall trial	0.82
11. Canceling numbers	CN	Similar to task 10 but not necessary to anticipate upcoming recall trial	0.77
12. Syllogisms: requiring logical flexibility	RRF	Either the conclusion required followed from the premises but was nonsensi-	

(continued)

Table 10.5 continued

Factor (variable) name	Symbol	Description and test scores combined	Internal consistency (r_{xx})
		cal or the conclusion did not follow but was sensible	0.46
13. Recency primary memory	PM	Recall of last word presented in serial learning lists	0.64
14. Obvious conventional clusters	OCC	Clusters in recall when words of conventional categories are presented together (in clusters)	0.47
15. Incidental memory	ICM	Recall of rather minor events staged throughout the testing period	0.70
16. 20-questions hypothesis testing	HYP	Goodness of questions that if answered truthfully enable one to determine thing in 20-questions game	0.92
17. Concept attain: eliminate irrelevant	E	In successive indications of what one professes to attend to in a concept formation task, elimination of irrelevant characteristics	0.77

of 100 and standard deviations of 15, so the units along the ordinates in the figures correspond to IQ units in popular tests. The magnitude of an effect is thus indicated in IQ units along the vertical axes. The decline of Gf is approximately 4.9 IQ units per decade, and there is a corresponding rise in Gc of about 4.8 units per decade. A light line in the figures represents the age differences after the linear effects associated with a particular variable have been controlled in Gf or Gc by part correlation (the partialling was not applied to age).[6] If the slope for a Gf curve becomes less steeply negative as a consequence of part correlation control, the result can be interpreted as indicating that the controlled variable represents a process involved in the aging decline of Gf. If this slope becomes more steeply negative with control, then the controlled variable can be interpreted as representing an influence that disguises aging decline of Gf. Similar interpretations follow from changes in the slope for the Gc curve in consequence of controlling by part correlation (Horn, 1978c).

This kind of control is based on assumptions similar to those in matched-group control, but it has several advantages. Power is not lost by discarding subjects. Instead of assuming that two different scores are the same, as is usually the case in matched-group control, the control is based on scores actually obtained on the control variable and the relationships between these scores and the dependent variable scores.

Control that removes an influence disguising an aging trend is illustrated by partialling out Gf in Gc and partialling out Gc in Gf. The results are depicted by the outermost curves in figure 10.12. When Gc is thus controlled in Gf, there is an increase in the decline, from about 4.9 to about 6.8 units per decade. Removal of the influence of Gf in Gc raises the increase of Gc from about 4.8 to 6.8 units per decade. Such results suggest that the measures of Gf and Gc are not pure, that each contains some variance in common with the other. For example, the measure of Gf probably represents some variance in acculturation that should be in Gc alone.

The control in these cases is probably excessive. It yields an age trend for a controlled Gf that has zero correlation with Gc. Yet in theory even if Gf were purged of all spurious variance associated with Gc, it would still be expected to correlate positively with Gc because both forms of intelligence should be determined in part by the same set of genetic factors.

Neither speed in obtaining correct answers nor speed in obtaining wrong answers has any substantial effect on the age relationship for Gf and Gc. This finding supports previous results indicating that speed per se is not responsible for Gf decline.

Earlier studies (Horn and Bramble, 1967; Horn and Cattell, 1966) demonstrated that the decline for Gf that is revealed by power tests (in which all subjects attempted all items) is essentially the same as the decline indicated by tests in which the rate of obtaining only correct answers is the measure. Subsequent studies (Horn, 1978c) provided evidence that controlling for speed did very little to alter Gf decline. These are the kinds of results indicated by the SPw and "other SP" curves in figure 10.12.

These results are not inconsistent with the established evidence indicating that speed in performing intellectual (and other) tasks declines with age (Birren, 1955, 1965, 1974; Botwinick, 1977; Horn, 1970a). There is little doubt that speed on many tasks declines with age, but this loss of speed need not be associated with the aging decline

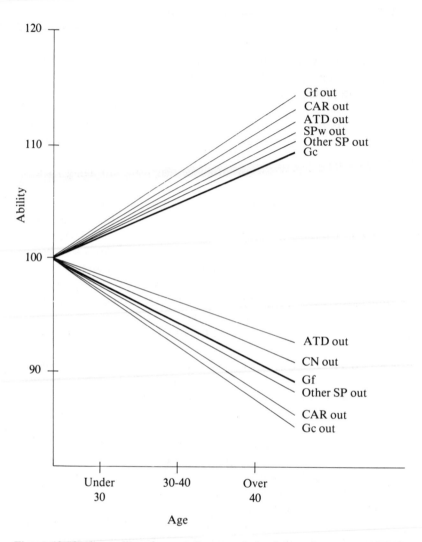

Figure 10.12. *Controlling for speediness and carefulness in cross-sectional assessment of development of Gf and Gc.*

of Gf. The evidence suggests that speed is not the core process in this decline.

These results do not necessarily conflict with studies showing that if an investigator scores the first part and the last part of an ability test separately, decline can be found for the latter and not for the former (Lorge, 1936; Ghiselli, 1957; Birren, 1965; Cunningham, 1976). If a time limit is imposed, a subject who solves problems slowly, for whatever reason, will attempt fewer of the items or rush carelessly near the end of a test. Scores in this section of the test will be reduced as a result. Scores in the early part of the test need not be lowered, however, particularly if the items in the first part of a test are easy enough that most people can deal effectively with them if given enough time. On many of the problems of intelligence tests, older adults work more slowly than younger adults. This does not necessarily mean that lack of speed is the core process. If an older subject finds it difficult to solve problems and works more slowly for this reason, his score near the end of a test could be depressed, but the score in the first part of the test would not necessarily be low. Such an interpretation of the results is consistent with findings showing that when all subjects attempt all problems, older adults solve fewer problems correctly than young adults. This interpretation is also suggested by the results indicating that controlling for the average speed of solving problems effects very little change in the decline curve.

Some slowing in intellectual test performances may reflect a loss of ability to maintain divided attention. This seems to be related to loss of capacity, or inclination, to concentrate on the details of tasks.

Controlling for carefulness, however, increases the absolute value of the age-Gf and the age-Gc correlations. That is, it makes the difference between the age-related curves for Gc and Gf more pronounced (upward for Gc, downward for Gf). This effect is similar to the one often sought with scoring corrections for guessing in ability tests. Such corrections, penalizing for wrong answers, are typically justified on grounds that they improve validity. Such improvement is indicated here in two relationships with age. The carefulness variable is the complement of the number of wrong answers given in several tests. When it is controlled, the effect is analytically similar to subtracting the number of wrong answers in corrections for guessing. Hence the finding in this study can be viewed as supporting a hypothesis that validity of measurement is enhanced by penalizing for guessing or careless responding and thus rewarding carefulness. This result replicates a previous finding (Horn, 1976b).

As in previous studies, short-term acquisition and retrieval (SAR) accounts for some of the decline in Gf, but not all of it (see figure 10.13). Controlling SAR also raises the Gc-age correlation. The effect is to account for about 1 IQ unit of decline in Gf and to indicate an additional Gc improvement of about 2 IQ units per decade.

None of the components of SAR, treated alone, brings about the magnitude of change produced by the broad SAR measure. Neither secondary memory alone nor primary memory alone produces the effect. Indeed, only when some aspects of organization in memory are

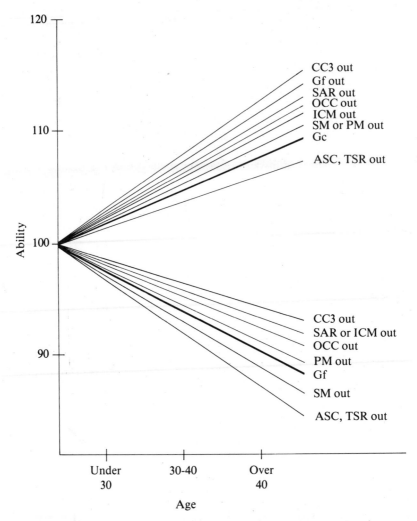

Figure 10.13. *Controlling for encoding and retrieval in cross-sectional assessment of development of Gf and Gc.*

brought into the control do the short-term memory variables have notable effects on the age-intelligence relationships. The clustering-in recall measure OCC (modeled on the work of Bousfield and Bousfield, 1966) accounts for much of the age-intelligence difference. The measure of incidental memory does even better.

These findings suggest that encoding rather than retrieval is the principal process involved in Gf decline. The most consistent shifts in the age-intelligence curves are associated with the measures designed to represent organization at the stage of encoding. The CC3 measures derive from Mandler's (1967, 1968) demonstrations that good recall results even when one is not instructed to remember but does the work of organizing (at the level of encoding). These measures account for a major part of the manifest decline in intelligence.

Thus it seems that the aging problem in intellectual functioning is not so much retrieval memory as the effective encoding of the material that one is ultimately called on to remember. Changes in short-term memory do not account for intellectual decline with age to any great degree.

Of interest in this regard are some results from a study by Botwinick and Storandt (1974) suggesting that a capacity for focusing concentration is involved in effective encoding and retrieval (hence Gf). A simple task of drawing as slowly as possible was found to be correlated with short-term memory and aging decline of this memory. This task does not seem to involve memory but does call for concentration. The work of Marx (1970) suggests that this capacity for concentration is spontaneous rather than willed.

The behavior represented by TSR involves retrieval in verbal fluency tasks that are sometimes regarded as measures of creativity. Such measures can reflect several influences in addition to storage and retrieval. Given only the data of these measures, the TSR factor might as well be regarded as a kind of verbal productive thinking, a term used to identify the behavior in several earlier studies. However, structural analyses have suggested that the essential processes involved in this fluency are also involved in encoding and retrieval over periods of time as short as a minute (Horn, 1978c). On this basis, the factor has been interpreted as reflecting ease of associating dissimilar things. This ease of association facilitates organization and recall in the short run and enables one to fluently gain access to material learned in the distant past.

The TSR factor is somewhat more highly correlated with Gc than with Gf. In control by part correlation TSR thus produces effects similar to those produced when Gc is treated as a control variable. The aging decline indicated for Gf is increased, for example. The greater fluency of older persons relative to younger ones can be seen to represent the longer period over which acquisition, rehearsal, consolidation, and other depth of processing occurs.

Hypothesis testing and concept formation controls are depicted in figure 10.14. The 20-questions game is related to intelligence and aging decline. When measures based on this game are controlled in the present data, the curve for Gc is raised about 1 IQ point per decade, and the decline in the Gf is reduced by about 0.6 unit per decade. Simi-

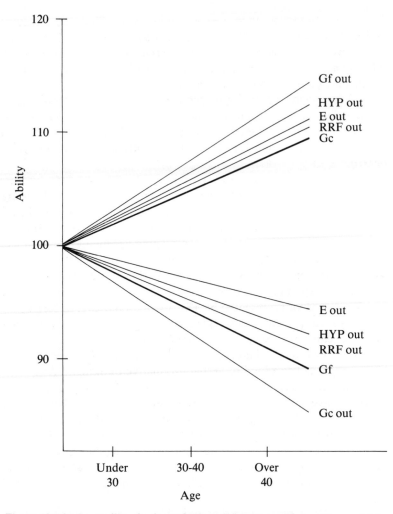

Figure 10.14. *Controlling for hypothesis testing, concept formation variables, in cross-sectional development of Gf and Gc.*

lar effects are produced by an E-measure of concept formation, a measure of ability to eliminate irrelevant attributes in forming concepts. A measure of attending to relevant attributes did not account for Gf decline in the present data.

The 20-questions and concept formation variables involve behavior that is similar to that which Denney and Denney (1973) and Denney and Lennon (1972) found to be important in describing age differences in intellectual performances. Their results indicated that older adults relative to younger ones do not formulate hypotheses that lead efficiently to clear conclusions. Also the older person more often repeated observations that did not add information in concept attainment (or problem solving).

The overall results of our study are summarized in figure 10.15. These results suggest that the processes that enable one to avoid attending to irrelevant aspects of problems are most strongly implicated in Gf decline. Next in importance are the encoding functions associated with sorting tasks. The 20-questions measure of ability to form hypotheses also represents an aspect of the central processes implicated in decline. The aging loss in memory itself seems to be associated primarily with encoding problems and incidental memory. Collectively these central processes account for about 2 IQ units of Gf decline per decade and thus leave about 2.9 units to be described.

Controlling for processes in the age changes for Gc suggests that this latent attribute improves over the vital years from age 20 to age 50 by perhaps as much as 8 points per decade.

Control for educational differences in Gf-age relationships tends to increase, not decrease, the rate of decline (Horn, 1976b). The effects are similar to those shown in the study under review by control of carefulness. Thus the findings from our previous work suggest that controlling for educational differences in the present study would not greatly alter the general picture.

It is interesting to consider how the analytic controls of this study may relate to the controls brought about in commonsense assessments of intelligence, as in personnel decisions or in evaluating politicians or teachers. Systematic work on this theme has yet to be done.

Interpretation of these findings in terms of more fundamental aspects of cause may go in several directions. Charitable interpretations might stress that the accumulation of information with age can produce overload effects. The older person can have more on his mind and more available in retrieval, and this abundance can interfere with problem solving. With more alternative hypotheses to consider, there are more ways to organize any information. Hence, not to take the simple hypothesis, not to eliminate all possibly irrelevant hypotheses, and not to use simple organizational schemes may merely reflect the functioning of a system that has become more complex as a function of development. Such interpretations might also argue that experience teaches one to realize that in real life the seemingly less relevant possibility sometimes becomes the realized fact. Thus the better part of truly mature human intelligence might be represented in a tolerance for the irrelevant and the bad hypothesis. Riegel (1973) argued persua-

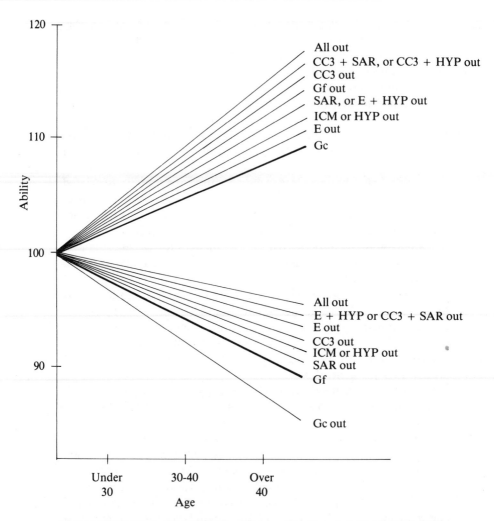

Figure 10.15. *Controlling for encoding organization, hypothesis formation, eliminating irrelevancies, and memory in cross-sectional development of Gf and Gc.*

sively that the highest refinement of human intelligence is seen in capacity to deal with and accept contradictions.

Less sanguine interpretations of the findings might point to evidence suggesting aging loss in the neural basis for intellectual processing. Losses of neural tissue can produce "holes" in the physiological system for comprehension. More elaboration on fewer neurons is required to produce a synthesis. To circumvent neural tissue "holes" requires increased repetition in order to comprehend what is relevant; there is less efficiency in eliminating the irrelevant, less ability to see through the haze of irrelevancies and ask the most clarifying question.

The available evidence is not sufficient to force a choice between these kinds of alternatives. Both should be kept open as a basis for design of further research.

Evaluating the Evidence

One can be skeptical of the evidence and the arguments presented so far. We have given a few valid reasons for such skepticism. Now we need to consider these matters more fully. In particular we need to consider the reasons for doubting conclusions that an increase in age is accompanied by increased loss of the physiological and neurological structures that support intellectual functioning and by consequent decrease in important features of intelligence. The studies on which the evidence is based suffer from a number of serious defects. We need to recognize that losses might occur for some individuals but not for all, and that aging deficits have not been found in some studies, particularly studies using longitudinal designs. Prominent researchers in the field of aging have argued that the decline in adult intelligence is a myth (Baltes and Schaie, 1974, 1976; Schaie, 1974). How should one evaluate skepticism about the evidence and the arguments that intellectual abilities decline with age?

We should be careful to identify the particular age deficit hypothesis under scrutiny, for there are several, and it may be reasonable to reject one and retain another. For example, there are two important interpretations of phrases such as "changes that result from aging, per se." One meaning is that the change is an aspect of maturation. The age at which change occurs might vary with genetic endowment, injury or illness, use of drugs, or favorable circumstances, but the ultimate occurrence is inevitably determined by the genetic structure of the organism. A second meaning is probabilistic. The change occurs for a population of individuals. Such changes may be associated with illnesses or injuries for which there are probabilities of occurrence that operate over one's life span. The longer one lives, the more likely it is that one will suffer the illness or injury.

While these different conceptions of an aging effect are logically distinct, they are not easily distinguished in the design of studies. In fact the results from most studies can be interpreted under either assumption. It is useful to retain the distinction, however, to understand some discussions of aging differences. Disagreements about the evidence may actually be due to differences in these views about an aging effect. One investigator might produce a very old person who had none of a defect that occurred with considerable frequency and regularity in the peer group and on this basis argue that the deficit was not an outcome of aging per se. This evidence is relevant for rejecting a hypothesis that derives from the first meaning of aging but is not convincing for hypotheses based on the second concept.

Arguments Pertaining to Decline Interpretations

An example of the argument that decline occurs only probabilistically is the death-drop hypothesis (Jarvik and Blum, 1971; Riegel and Riegel, 1972). Support for this idea is found in evidence indicating that among individuals measured at time A and then again at time B— say two to five years later—after which it is determined who among the sample died within the next two to five years, the decline between A and B is associated primarily with those who died in the period following B. Since older cohorts contain proportionally more individuals likely to die in a short time span, the mean scores for these cohorts will be depressed by death-drop influences relative to the mean scores for younger cohorts. Thus decline that seems to occur gradually in all individuals may be only decline for a few individuals whose scores notably affect the averages. This death-drop effect can be part of what is meant by "average aging decline" (Botwinick, 1977; Horn, 1976).

It is sometimes argued that a hypothesis of universal decline is false (Baltes and Schaie, 1976; Schaie, 1974). This argument might represent acceptance of the first assumption, that the effect is not intrinsic to the structure of the individual, but it can also be a statement that change or difference in averages can hide the fact (if it is a fact) that not every individual is affected by the same influences. If particular injuries to the central nervous system are responsible for decline in abilities, but some individuals do not experience these injuries, the curve for averages will not represent the unaffected individuals. A few individuals experiencing large losses could set a trend line for an average curve that would not represent most individuals. Universal decline, for all individuals, is thus not unequivocally indicated by average age differences or changes (whether based on cross-sectional or longitudinal data).

Rejection of the claim that intelligence declines with age may also reflect the belief that the evidence pertains only to parts of intelligence and that aspects of intelligence seen at one age are replaced by other aspects at a later age. This argument is an application of an alternative mechanism idea that has been used to help explain other aspects of intellectual phenomena (Horn, 1968; Horn and Cattell, 1966). Basically, the notion is that the capacities of intelligence can be manifested in different ways, much as energy can be expressed in the form of heat or kinetic energy or chemical energy. Some expressions of intelligence represent developmentally appropriate behaviors that can seem inappropriate if judged by the criteria of the wrong stage of development. For example, a measure of conservation appropriate for 5-year-olds might mislead if it is used with 14-year-olds who can distinguish between logical necessity and empirical demonstration. Thus if one concluded that a 14-year-old did not understand the concept of conservation because he questioned empirical evidence that the amount of liquid remained the same when the liquid was poured from one container to another, then criteria appropriate to an earlier stage of development would have been inappropriately used to assess the later stage.

Ability might seem to have declined when in fact no decline occurred. Similarly, age differences in tasks that depend on classification may represent only different developmental stages in the manner of conceptualizing relationships (Kogan, 1973). The totality of intelligence, or the underlying basic capacity, need not have declined with these changes.

It is sometimes contended that the evidence of adult decline merely reflects a fact that tests developed to measure the abilities of children are not good measures of intelligence manifested in adulthood. What seems to be a decline in adult intelligence is merely a shift from developmentally primitive expressions, measured with existing tests, to developmentally advanced expressions that are not measured with these tests (Riegel, 1973a).

Also important are arguments that the evidence indicates primarily generational cohort differences (Schaie, Labouvie, and Buech, 1973; Schaie and Labouvie-Vief, 1974; Schaie and Strother, 1968). In these arguments it is likely to be claimed that decline cannot be indicated in cross-sectional studies but only in studies based on follow-up designs (Schaie, 1973, 1974). In cross-sectional study, subsamples of different ages, born at different periods of history, are compared. The argument is that the differences between the subsamples indicate only differences between generations—for example, the fact that education, quality of health care, and degree of exposure to culture through mass media have increased in almost every decade of this century. To bolster such an argument, those who hold this view may cite studies in which no age differences were found, in particular studies based on repeated measures of the same individuals, as in longitudinal data gathering, or repeated measures of the same cohorts but different individuals, in what can be referred to as a quasi-longitudinal design.

Usually the cohort difference arguments have referred only to experiential factors and to corresponding behavioral differences, but the arguments can apply to physiological differences as well. For example, age differences in intellectual abilities may indicate only that health care was, on the average, less adequate for older than for younger individuals when the respective cohorts passed through particular formative periods, say infancy and early childhood.

These are but a few of the many arguments that can be marshalled against statements that intelligence declines with age in adulthood. For each of these arguments, however, there is a counter argument (or several such). For example:

It is wishful thinking to suppose that any substantial number of individuals will escape the illnesses and injuries that afflict others.

Although the samples in studies indicating aging deficits are not representative, there are many studies and collectively they include exemplars of most kinds of people.

Even the findings obtained with abnormal individuals are likely to indicate lawful relationships that apply to normal people, albeit in milder form.

Although there are many missing links in the chain of relationships between physiological function and psychological process, the evidence for both kinds of aging change is reasonably convincing, and there are many good reasons to suppose that the two forms of change are related.

While some of the tests that have indicated adult differences might produce cohort-specific variance, other tests pertain instead to capabilities that are part of the expression of intelligence for any cohort. If decrements occur in such capabilities, these seem likely to affect the totality of intelligence, even granting that some compensatory abilities would be developed.

While it is reasonable to argue that existing tests are not appropriate for measuring adult intelligence, it is difficult to describe— and even more difficult to devise—more appropriate tests. Efforts to develop such tests have not been impressive in indicating either new aspects of adult intelligence or qualities that are different from those measured with existing tests.

In some respects the educational and physical (physiology-affecting) features of environment have been superior for older compared with younger cohorts. For example, there was considerably less smog and carbon monoxide in the Denver air of 1930 to 1950, in which a Denverite who is now 50 years old would have developed from birth to age 20, then in the air in which a Denverite who is now 20 years old would have developed. Inhalation of carbon monoxide, if there is enough of it, destroys neurons.

Similarly, exposure to certain drugs that are harmful to the nervous system has become more widespread in this century. And while the number of years of formal education has increased throughout this century, it does not follow that the quality of education, or education that is best for development of intelligence, has increased in every decade over this period. More people may have read more books in earlier periods of this century than in more recent decades, for example. There are results suggesting that college entrance exam scores have declined over the last decade. Thus there are several reasons to question the assumption that the environment for the development of intellectual abilities has been better for younger persons than it was for older persons.

Some of the age differences that occur are not those predicted from a theory that younger cohorts have been better educated than older cohorts. For example, the Gc abilities are, to a large extent, fostered by good education, but older persons perform as well as or better than younger persons in these abilities.

If major decrements are brought on by illnesses that eventually produce death, so, too, would decrements be expected when these or similar illnesses do not produce death in the short run, and the likelihood of illnesses of various kinds increases with age in adulthood (Bromley, 1974). Hence the evidence that indicates death drop can also point to a gradual drop to be expected on a statistical basis (Botwinick, 1977; Horn, 1976a,b).

Problems of selectivity and interpretation seriously undermine arguments that the results from longitudinal and cross-sequential studies support the view that cross-sectional age differences reflect primarily cohort differences (Horn and Donaldson, 1976, 1977).

Many of these plausible positions have been developed in readily available writings (Baltes, 1973; Botwinick, 1977; Buss, 1973; Horn, 1970a, 1976a; Horn and Donaldson, 1976, 1977; Schaie, 1973; Wohlwill, chapter 9, 1970). However, some misunderstandings about longitudinal data and about intervention studies should be examined because they are prevalent and misleading, and have not been discussed elsewhere.

Perspectives on Longitudinal Data

It is often stated that longitudinal and cross-sectional studies have provided grounds for different conclusions about aging decline of intelligence. In particular, it is argued that the cross-sectional results suggesting decline are indicative mainly of cohort differences and that results from longitudinal studies have demonstrated no notable aging decline in intelligence. When one examines longitudinal and cross-sectional studies closely, however, one finds that these conclusions are not well supported. The results from the two kinds of studies are not contradictory (Horn, 1970a). Several issues need to be considered in arriving at this conclusion. Tables 10.6 and 10.7 help illustrate these issues.

The numbers in the two tables refer to calculations on intelligence test scores that have been scaled (or rescaled) to have a mean of 100 and a standard deviation (sigma) of 15. This scaling was used to provide a common basis for comparing results of different tests. IQ tests are typically scaled in this manner, and people are accustomed to thinking about intelligence in terms of IQ tests. The units of measure are referred to as IQ units in some of the discussion that follows.

Table 10.6 provides a summary of several frequently cited longitudinal studies indicating that follow-up results contradict the findings from cross-sectional studies. The data pertaining to predicted change and net change in this table are averages derived from cross-sectional studies, as shown in some detail in table 10.7.

A number in the first or third row of table 10.7 is the average change over the five-year period represented in a column heading. For example, the average decline of Gf from age 40 to age 45 is 2.3 IQ units. The average Gc rise for this period is 1.5 IQ units. The sum of these two averages is a decline of 0.8 units. This is the amount of decline estimated if test variance reflects Gf and Gc about equally. If a test were a fairly pure measure of Gc, decline would not be expected and a rise comparable to that estimated for Gc would be expected over the five-year span.

The numbers in the second and fourth rows of table 10.7 are cumulative changes from age 20 (or younger) up to the older of the two ages indicated in a column heading. Thus a 13 in row 2 under the 50-55 heading indicates that for cross-sectional data there is an average decline in Gf of about 13 IQ points from age 20 to age 55.

A difference in two cumulative sums estimates the change from one age period to another. For example, the difference between the 13 in row 2 under the 50-55 heading and the 7.0 in row 2 under the 40-55 heading indicates that from age 45 to age 55 a decrease of 6 units in Gf is expected. To obtain estimates of changes for ages that fall within categories, as in the "change predicted" columns of table 10.6, linear interpolation was used. Thus to estimate the Gc change expected from age 28 to age 42 for the Bayley-Oden study of table 10.6, cumulative

Table 10.6. Summary of longitudinal studies often cited as contradicting cross-sectional studies.

Authors	Tests	Factor measure	Approximate age		Change predicted IQ-units			Change reported	Sample size		Reported vs. predicted difference	Difference significant
			Young adult	Old adult	Gf	Gc	Net		Obtained	Pooled		
Bayley and Oden (1955)	Vocabulary	Gc	28	42	0	5.1	5.1	7.5	70		2.4	No
	Analogies	Gc	28	42	0	5.1	5.1	7.3	70		2.2	No
Bradway and Thompson (1962)	Stanford-Binet IQ	Gc + Gf	15	30	-1.0[a]	10.8	9.8	10.8	111	212	1.0	No
Jones (1959)	Terman	Gc + Gf	16	33	-1.9	12.3	10.4	7.5	83		-2.9	No
Bayley (1966)	Wechsler P[b]	Gf	21	36	-2.9	0	-2.9	-6.7	54	63	-3.6	No
	Wechsler V[c]	Gc	21	36	0	7.6	7.6	6.8	54	63	-0.8	No
Owens (1953)	Army Alpha	Gc	20	51	-10.6	13.0	2.4	10.0	127	363	7.6	.01
Owens (1966)	Army Alpha	Gc + Gf	51	62	-6.6	1.7	4.9	-2.0	97	127	-6.9	.05

a. Minus sign indicates that reported change suggests more decline than does predicted change.

b. P = Performance.

c. V = Verbal.

Table 10.7. Expected age differences estimated as the median shift over several studies (expressed in sigma = 15 units).

Item	Age interval							
	20-25	25-30	30-35	35-40	40-45	45-50	50-55	55-60
Expected Gf decline	0.0	1.0	1.5	2.2	2.3	3	3	3
Cumulative expected decline	0.0	1.0	2.5	4.7	7.0	10	13	16
Expected Gc rise	3.8	3.0	1.5	1.5	1.5	1.5	0.8	0.8
Cumulative expected Gc rise	3.8	6.8	8.3	9.8	11.3	12.8	13.6	14.4
Net gain or loss	3.8	2.0	0	−0.7	−0.8	−1.5	−2.2	−2.2
Cumulative net gain or loss	3.8	5.8	5.8	5.1	4.3	2.8	0.6	−1.6

Source: Horn (1970a), in which results from several studies were averaged.

change to age 28 was estimated to be 3.8 (the cumulative change to age 25) plus 3/5 of 3 (the cumulative change from 25 to 30), this total being 5.6. Cumulative change to age 42 was estimated to be 9.8 plus 2/5 of 1.5, or 10.7. Thus the difference between the totals, 10.7 − 5.6 = 5.1, was calculated to indicate the expected Gc rise.

For present purposes these estimates do not have to be highly accurate. The important point is that there is relatively little change in either Gf or Gc from one decade to another and that these changes tend to cancel each other in omnibus IQ tests, where mixtures of Gf and Gc are obtained. Thus in evaluating the results of a (longitudinal, for example) study, it is important to note whether the N is large enough to show the change that can be expected and to consider whether the test used to measure intelligence should indicate mainly decline (if Gf) or rise (if Gc) or neither (if Gf and Gc are about equally represented). It is also important to notice whether the first measures are obtained before peak performance is expected.

In the study by Bayley and Oden (1955) no decline in ability is expected because the Concept Mastery test used to indicate intelligence is mainly a measure of Gc. The measures were obtained in a period when Gc is expected to rise. The Concept Mastery test consists of two subtests, vocabulary and esoteric analogies. Both subtests are fairly pure measures of Gc. The subjects were from Terman's Stanford Study of the Gifted, individuals of upper social class who scored quite high on the Stanford-Binet when they were young and most of whom have demonstrated high levels of educational achievement and motivation throughout their lives (Oden, 1968). The rise of 7.5 units from age 28 to age 42 in this study is more than the average Gc rise for cross-sectional studies, but it is not a remarkable deviation from the average. The measures are highly reliable and appear to be sensitive to the learning effects that can be expected in a study in which individuals are selected because of a high motivation to develop Gc abilities.

Similar considerations apply to the studies of Bradway and Thompson (1962) and Jones (1959), who measured intelligence with the Stanford-Binet test. At the age levels in question (see table 10.6) this test is very heavily weighted with verbal comprehension and thus with Gc (Jones, 1954). Average score on the test could thus be expected to rise, consistent with findings from cross-sectional studies. Perhaps more important in accounting for the apparent rise, however, is that the early measurements were obtained before peak performance would be expected and that the later measurements were obtained before any notable decline in Gf would have occurred. Results from cross-sectional studies suggest an increase in Gf as well as in Gc from the age of 15 or 16 (when the first measures of these studies were obtained) to age 20. The expected increase is 4 IQ units. In the Bradway-Thompson study this increase can be added to a 6.8-unit Gc rise and a 1.0-unit Gf drop between ages 20 and 30. Thus the change expected from consideration of cross-sectional results is of the order of 9.8, similar to the 10.8 increase that was reported. Similarly, in the Jones study an increase of 10.4 units is predicted from cross-sectional results, an increase of 2.9 units more than was obtained in the longitudinal study. Thus for these studies there is no fundamental difference between longitudinal and cross-sectional results.

The findings from the study by Bayley (1966) (sometimes called the Berkeley Growth Study) are also consistent with outcomes from cross-sectional studies. The sample in this study was small, so statistical significance for change is difficult to demonstrate. Different tests were used—the Wechsler-Bellevue test at the young age and the Wechsler Adult Scale at age 36. Nevertheless, the patterns of changes found in this study are similar to those found in cross-sectional studies. The performance subscale of the Wechsler tests provides a rough measure of Gf (Horn, 1970a; Matarazzo, 1972), and scores on this component dropped about 6.7 units from age 21 to age 36, indicating a decline of 3.6 units more than has typically been found for Gf. The verbal component of the Wechsler scales similarly provides an estimate of Gc; the rise found for this measure is similar to that estimated on the basis of cross-sectional studies.

The two Owens studies (1953, 1966) are based on measures obtained when the subjects entered college; the average age was 20. Of 363 subjects in the original sample, 201 were located and 127 cooperated in a second testing conducted when the subjects were approximately 51 years of age. Over the 31-year period there was a significant rise of approximately two-thirds of a sigma (10 IQ units) in tests of general information, vocabulary, disarranged sentences, and practical judgment. These tests are indicative of Gc. There were no significant differences between the means at the two ages for tests of following directions, arithmetical reasoning, verbal analogies, and number series. Eleven years later Owens (1966) again tested 97 of the 127 subjects who had cooperated in the second testing. None of the averages for individual tests changed significantly over this period. When tests were combined to measure primary factors and adjustments were made in accordance with estimates of cultural changes, Owens found significant improvement in verbal comprehension and significant decline in reasoning. Thus the results indicate that some abilities (namely those of Gc) tend to improve from age 20 to age 62 and that other abilities (those of Gf) decline, but the age period in which the decline is found to be statistically significant occurs later than in some other studies.

The first measures in the Owens study were obtained a bit before the peak in Gf would be expected. Thus any decline that might have occurred would probably have been underestimated. Also, attrition may have been nonrandom: the sample obtained for the second and third testings could be expected to have contained a small proportion of the subjects whose scores declined notably from the first testing. The estimates of Gc improvement and no decline for the Gf-Gc mixture in the mid years of adulthood might be high relative to what they would have been if no sample selectivity had occurred.

The results reviewed here also agree with the longitudinal findings of Burns (1966), Nisbet (1957), and Tuddenham, Blumenkrantz, and Witkin (1968). In general, the results from longitudinal studies lead to essentially the same conclusions as those found in cross-sectional studies. For development between the ages of 20 and 60 both kinds of evidence indicate either improvement with age or no decline in Gc abilities and no notable decline for measures consisting of mixtures of Gf and Gc subtests. When relatively pure measures of Gf are obtained, decline is demonstrated.

Longitudinal data are often assumed to provide more valid indications of "pure" aging functions than cross-sectional results. This assumption is based on the view that "pure" aging is to be understood in terms of changes determined in the structure of the organism rather than in the structure of the environment. This assumption is probably false, as indicated by several statements of the relative merits of data-gathering procedures for studying aging (Schaie, 1965; Baltes, 1968; Buss, 1973; Horn and Donaldson, 1976). These considerations are summarized in table 10.8, where the sampling procedures known as cross-sectional, longitudinal, and quasi-longitudinal (different members of the same cohort measured for each occasion) designs are compared on the basis of several criteria.

In this table an X indicates that a design is deficient with respect to the corresponding criterion. Following the terminology of Baltes (1968), selective sampling refers to the bias generated when one must depend on volunteers for a study; selective dropout refers to the change in the composition of the sample as subjects drop out in a nonrandom fashion over time; selective survival describes the nonrandom change in the composition of the population, as well as in the sample, as a function of death-ability correlations. Briefly, the remaining criteria are confounding (whether a factor other than age is associated with the observed variation in the dependent variable), retest effects (whether previous testing occasions systematically affect later measurements), and limitation of generalization (whether sampling only one time or one cohort limits the generalizability of the results).

An inspection of table 10.8 reveals that only the longitudinal design is deficient with respect to each criterion. Since these influences generally bias longitudinal data in a positive direction—leave the means for older individuals greater than for younger individuals, as a function of the bias—one should be particularly cautious about interpreting longitudinal results as indicating no aging decline even when the problems discussed in reference to table 10.6 do not occur.

These considerations of longitudinal data should not lead one to discount the virtues of this form of data gathering, particularly if attrition can be kept low and the other problems can be minimized. However, such considerations should lead one to question the belief that longitudinal data gathering is necessarily preferable and should

Table 10.8. Bias in different data-gathering designs.

Item	Cross-sectional	Longitudinal	Quasi-longitudinal
Selective sampling	X	X	X
Selective drop-out		X	
Selective survival	X	X	X
Confound	X	X	X
	(cohort)	(time)	(time)
Retest effects		X	
Limitation of generalization	X	X	X
	(particular time)	(particular cohort)	(particular cohort)

warn one against uncritical acceptance of results from longitudinal data gathering. Other issues related to these methods have been considered by Horn and Donaldson (1976, 1977).

Perspectives on Intervention Research

Considerable research has been designed to demonstrate that intervention can improve abilities thought to decline with aging (Baltes, 1968; Baltes and Labouvie, 1973; Plemons, Willis, and Baltes, 1978). This work has been advocated not only on the grounds that it may demonstrate procedures for correcting ability losses, but also on the grounds that it can support hypotheses that the affected abilities do not decline (Labouvie-Vief 1976; Plemons, Willis, and Baltes, 1978). The logic of this second basis is dubious.

The design of these intervention studies has been one in which a group of older individuals is provided with training intended to improve performance on intellectual tasks for which there has been the suggestion of a decline with aging. Such improved performance, if obtained, is then interpreted as representing modification of the latent ability assessed by the test. The appropriateness of this interpretation depends on the satisfaction of several design conditions of adequacy (Donaldson, 1979).

One condition is that improvement must be of sufficient breadth to warrant the conclusion that an ability, not merely test performance, has been modified. This can normally be accomplished by obtaining measurements on enough tests to define an ability at the primary factor level or higher and by demonstrating improvement on mean factor scores or, alternatively, on mean scores for tests defining the factor, as a function of the intervention.

A second condition is that motivation and other possible extraneous influences must be controlled in order to reliably demonstrate that an ability per se is improved by intervention. In general, intervention studies require the same attention to controls that is advocated for controlled experimental research.

To demonstrate that improvement in Gf invalidates the view that decline is normal, an intervention study must use younger controls. Thus sampling of different cohorts is required, and all the problems of obtaining comparable samples are raised. If an adequate sample of youthful controls is not obtained, there is no basis for concluding that improvement in aged subjects would not have been matched (or exceeded) by improvements in younger subjects had they received the intervention treatment. None of the intervention studies mentioned previously included youthful controls; thus the results do not support an inference that an observed effect is inconsistent with a hypothesis of normative decline.

Intervention studies can be useful for demonstrating that a specified age trend is not immutable. However, the assumption that traits such as Gf must display invariant age trends, or that such traits must resist modification, is almost certainly false (Botwinick, 1977; Donaldson, 1979; Horn, 1970, 1975; Horn and Donaldson, 1976, 1977).

These criticisms are not intended to suggest that intervention research is not valuable or that it can be of no help in improving intellectual deficits. There are excellent reasons for urging that such research be vigorously pursued. Indeed, we hope that future studies may be strengthened by incorporating some of these design suggestions.

Notes

We are grateful to Earl Hunt, Jerome Kagan, Orville Brim, Jr., Eric Wanner, Robert Engstrom, Jan Keenan, and George Potts for a number of very helpful criticisms and suggestions that materially shaped this chapter. These friendly critics should not be held responsible for weaknesses of the chapter, much as some of the good features of the writing stem from their thinking.

Preparation of the chapter was aided by support from the National Institute of Aging, grant number 1 RO1 AG00583-01. Our empirical research summarized in this chapter was supported not only by this grant but also by grants from the National Science Foundation, GB-41452, and the Army Research Institute, DAHC 19-76-G-0019. We thank George Levy, prison psychologist, the staff of the prison, and volunteers for enabling us to do this research.

1. Several of our friendly critics urged us to retain established terminology in this regard, by referring to the distinction between experiments and correlational studies, or the like. We persisted in our efforts to break away from prior designations, however, mainly because we believe them to be misleading (for reasons elaborated in Horn, 1973). The term *correlation* should be used to designate methods of analyzing data, not to indicate study design; these methods are as appropriate for controlled-manipulative (referred to as experimental) studies as for concomitant variational studies. Many studies that are said to be experimental in the sense of controlled-manipulative design are not; they are simply concomitant variation (correlation) studies in which one concomitant variable is dichotomized or trichotomized to form a basis for contrast of group means. As Humphreys (1978) has shown recently, this can be an inefficient way of analyzing the data of a concomitant variational study (see also Horn, 1979c).

2. In previous writings these were referred to as "incidental" learning influences. As Earl Hunt noted in a personal communication, this is a poor term, because incidental learning has a quite different meaning within cognitive psychology. Thus our use of this term might confuse more than it communicates. "Casual learning" is a bit misleading, too, but seems the least evil of several possible terms.

3. In the interest of conciseness, the word *change* (and its variants) is used throughout this chapter to refer to age differences whether these are truly changes (within particular persons) or only differences between means for dif-

ferent groups of people of different ages.

4. Indeed one can identify a variety of other problems that should not but do occur in research on the development of intellectual abilities. A recent sermon on such matters might be of interest to some readers (Horn, 1979c).

5. The term *eductive processes*, or the like, is used in what follows as a shorthand way of referring to the processes of eduction of relations and correlates.

6. Part correlation rather than partial correlation was used in these analyses in order to subtract behavioral variance from other behavioral variance, not from a status variable such as age, though "partial" sometimes appears.

References

ANASTASI, A. 1958. *Differential psychology*, 3d ed. New York: Macmillan.

ANDERS, R. T., and FOZARD, J. L. 1973. Effects of age upon retrieval from primary and secondary memory. *Developmental Psychology* 9: 411-415.

ANDREWS, W. 1956. Structural alterations with aging in the nervous system. In *The neurologic and psychiatric aspects of the disorders of aging*, Proceedings of the Association for Research in Nervous and Mental Disease, vol. 35. Baltimore, Md.: Williams and Wilkins.

ARENBERG, D., and ROBERTSON-TCHABO, E. A. 1977. Learning and aging. In *Handbook of the psychology of aging*, ed. J. E. Birren and K. W. Schaie. New York: Van Nostrand Reinhold.

ASHTON, G. C., and POLOVINA, J. 1977. Path analysis of familial relationships of 15 tests of cognitive ability and four derived factor scores. *Behavior Genetics* 7: 42-43.

BALTES, P. B. 1968. Longitudinal and cross-sectional sequences in the study of age and generation effects. *Human Development* 11: 145-171.

—— 1973. Life-span models of psychological aging: a white elephant? *Gerontologist* 13: 458-492.

BALTES, P. B., and LABOUVIE, G. V. 1973. Adult development of intellectual performance. In *The psychology of adult development and aging*, ed. C. Eisdorfer and M. P. Lawton. Washington, D.C.: American Psychological Association.

BALTES, P. B. and SCHAIE, K. W. 1974. The myth of the twilight years. *Psychology Today* 40: 35-38.

—— 1976. On the plasticity of intelligence in adulthood and old age: where Horn and Donaldson fail. *American Psychologist* 31: 720-725.

BAYLEY, N. 1966. Learning in adulthood: the role of intelligence. In *Analyses of concept learning*, ed. H. J. Klausmeier and C. W. Harris. New York: Academic Press.

BAYLEY, N., and ODEN, M. H. 1955. The maintenance of intellectual ability in gifted adults. *Journal of Gerontology* 10: 91-107.

BINET, A., and SIMON, T. 1905. New methods for the diagnosis of the intellectual level of subnormals. *L'Anné Psychologique* 11: 191-244. Translated by E. S. Kline in *The development of intelligence in children*. Vineland, N.J.: Training School No. 11, 1916.

BIRREN, J. E. 1955. Age changes in speed of simple responses and perception and their significance for complex behavior. In *Old age in the modern world*. London: Livingston.

———— 1965. Age changes in speed of behavior: its central nature and physiological correlates. In *Behavior, aging, and the nervous system*, ed. A. T. Welford and J. E. Birren. Springfield, Ill.: Thomas.

———— 1974. Psychophysiology and speed of response. *American Psychologist* 29: 808-815.

BITTERMAN, M. E. 1965. The evolution of intelligence. *Scientific American* 212: 92-100.

BLOOM, B. S. 1964. *Stability and change in human characteristics*. New York: Wiley.

BOCK, R. D., and VANDENBERG, S. G. 1968. Components of heritable variation in mental test scores. In *Progress in human behavior genetics*, ed. S. G. Vandenberg. Baltimore, Md.: Johns Hopkins University Press.

BONDAREFF, W. 1959. Morphology of the aging nervous system. In *Handbook of aging and the individual*. Chicago: University of Chicago Press.

———— 1977. The neural basis of aging. In *Handbook of the psychology of aging*, ed. J. E. Birren and K. W. Scaie. New York: Van Nostrand Reinhold.

BOTWINICK, J. 1977. Aging and intelligence. In *Handbook of the psychology of aging*, ed. J. E. Birren and K. W. Schaie. New York: Van Nostrand Reinhold.

BOTWINICK, J., and STORANDT, M. 1974. *Memory, related functions, and age*. Springfield, Ill.: Thomas.

BOUSFIELD, A. K., and BOUSFIELD, W. A. 1966. Measurement of clustering and of sequential constancies in repeated free recall. *Psychological Reports* 19: 935-942.

BRADWAY, K. P., and THOMPSON, C. W. 1962. Intelligence at adulthood. *Journal of Educational Psychology* 53: 1-14.

BRANSFORD, J. D., and FRANKS, J. J. 1971. The abstraction of linguistic ideas. *Cognitive Psychology* 2: 331-350.

BRIM, O. G. 1966. Socialization through the life cycle. In *Socialization after childhood: two essays*, ed. O. G. Brim and S. Wheeler. New York: Wiley.

BRIZZEE, K. R., ORDY, J. M., and KAACK, B. 1974. Early appearance and regional differences in intraneuronal and extraneuronal lysofusion accumulation with age in the brain of a nonhuman primate (Macaca mulatta). *Journal of Gerontology* 29: 366-381.

BROADBENT, D. E. 1954. The role of auditory localization in attention and memory span. *Journal of Experimental Psychology* 47: 191-196.

———— 1958. *Perception and communication*. London: Pergamon.

———— 1966. The well ordered mind. *American Educational Research Journal* 3: 281-295.

BROADBENT, D. E., and HERRON, A. E. 1962. Effects of a subsidiary task on performance involving immediate memory in younger and older men. *British Journal of Psychology* 53: 189-198.

BROMLEY, D. B. 1958. Some effects of age on short-term learning and remembering. *Journal of Gerontology* 13: 398-406.

—— 1974. *The psychology of human aging*, 2d ed. London: Penguin.

BURNS, R. B. 1966. Age and mental ability: retesting with 35 years interval. *British Journal of Educational Psychology* 36: 116-120.

BUSS, A. R. 1973. On extension of developmental models that separate ontogenetic change and cohort differences. *Psychological Bulletin* 80: 466-479.

BUSS, A. R., and POLEY, W. 1976. *Individual differences: traits and factors*. New York: Gardner.

CARROLL, J. B. 1972. Defining language comprehension: some speculations. In *Language comprehension and the acquisition of knowledge*, ed. R. O. Freedle and J. B. Carroll. New York: Wiley.

—— 1976. Psychometric tests as cognitive tasks: a new "structure of intellect." In *The nature of intelligence*, ed. L. B. Resnick. Hillsdale, N.J.: Erlbaum.

—— 1978. How shall we study individual differences in cognitive abilities? Methodological and theoretical perspectives. *Intelligence* 2: 87-115.

CARROLL, J. B., and MAXWELL, S. E. 1979. Individual differences in cognitive abilities. *Annual Review of Psychology*, in press.

CATTELL, R. B. 1941. Some theoretical issues in adult intelligence testing. *Psychological Bulletin* 38: 592 (abstract).

—— 1957. Personality and motivation structure and measurement. New York: World Book.

—— 1963. Theory of fluid and crystallized intelligence: a critical experiment. *Journal of Educational Psychology* 54: 1-22.

—— 1971. *Abilities: their structure, growth, and action*. Boston: Houghton-Mifflin.

CATTELL, R. B., and HORN, J. L. 1978. A check on the theory of fluid and crystallized intelligence with description of new subtest designs. *Journal of Educational Measurement* 15: 139-164.

CRAIK, F. I. M. 1968. Short-term memory and the aging process. In *Human aging and behavior*, ed. G. A. Tolland. New York: Academic Press.

—— 1971. Primary memory. *British Medical Bulletin* 27: 232-236.

—— 1977. Age differences in human memory. In *Handbook of the psychology of aging*, ed. J. E. Birren and K. W. Schaie. New York: Van Nostrand Reinhold.

CRAIK, F. I. M., and LOCKHART, R. S. 1972. Levels of processing: a framework for memory research. *Journal of Verbal Learning and Verbal Behavior* 11: 671-684.

CRONBACH, L. J. 1957. The two disciplines of scientific psychology. *American Psychologist* 12: 671-684.

—— 1970. *Essentials of psychological testing*, 3d ed. New York: Harper and Row.

—— 1975. Beyond the two disciplines of scientific psychology. *American Psychologist* 30: 116-127.

CROWN, S. 1951. Psychological changes following prefrontal leucotomy: a review. *Journal of Mental Science* 97: 49-83.

CUNNINGHAM, W. R. 1976. Fluid intelligence vs. the intellectual speed hypothesis. Paper presented at the American Psychological Association Annual

Meetings. New York, August 31-September 6.

DeFries, J. C., Kuse, A. R., and Vandenberg, S. G. 1979. Genetic correlations, environmental correlations, and behavior. In *Theoretical advances in behavior genetics*, ed. J. R. Royce. Alphen aan den Rijn, The Nederlands: Sijthoff and Noordoff (forthcoming).

Denney, D. R., and Denney, N. W. 1973. The use of classification for problem solving: a comparison of middle and old age. *Developmental Psychology* 9: 275-278.

Denney, N. W., and Lennon, M. L. 1972. Classification: a comparison of middle and old age. *Developmental Psychology* 7: 210-213.

Dennis, W. 1956. Age and productivity among scientists. *Science* 123: 724-725.

———— 1968. Creative productivity between ages twenty and eighty years. In *Middle age and aging*, ed. B. Neugarten. Chicago: University of Chicago Press.

Dimond, S. J., and Beaumont, J. G., eds. 1974. *Hemisphere functions in the human brain*. London: Elek.

Donaldson, G. 1979. Condition of adequacy for abilities intervention studies as applied to a particular case. *Journal of Gerontology*, in press.

Ekstrom, R. B. 1973. *Cognitive factors: some recent literature*. Princeton, N.J.: Educational Testing Service, PR-73-30.

Ellis, R. S. 1920. Norms of some structural changes in the human cerebellum from birth to old age. *Journal of Comparative Neurology* 32: 1-34.

Estes, W. K., and DaPolito, F. 1967. Independent variation in information storage and retrieval processes in paired-associate learning. *Journal of Experimental Psychology* 75: 18-26.

Eysenck, H. J. 1967. Intelligence assessment: a theoretical and experimental approach. *British Journal of Educational Psychology* 37: 81-98.

French, J. W., Ekstrom, R. B., and Price, L. A. 1963. *Manual and kit for cognitive factors*. Princeton, N.J.: Educational Testing Services.

Ghiselli, E. E. 1957. The relationship between intelligence and age among superior adults. *Journal of Genetic Psychology* 90: 131-142.

Glanzer, M., and Cunitz, A. R. 1966. Two storage mechanisms in free recall. *Journal of Verbal Learning and Verbal Behavior* 5: 351-360.

Green, D. R., ed. 1974. *The aptitude-achievement distinction*. Monterey, Calif.: CTE/McGraw-Hill.

Guilford, J. P. 1964. Zero intercorrelations among tests of intellectual abilities. *Psychological Bulletin* 61: 401-404.

———— 1967. *The nature of human intelligence*. New York: McGraw-Hill.

Guttman, L. 1965. A faceted definition of intelligence. *Scripta Hierosolymitana* 14: 166-181.

Hakstian, A. R., and Cattell, R. B. 1974. The checking of primary ability structure on a broader basis of performance. *British Journal of Educational Psychology* 44: 140-154.

Halstead, W. C. 1947. *Brain and intelligence*. Chicago: University of Chicago Press.

Harnad, S., Doty, R. W., Goldstein, L., Jaynes, J., and Krauthamer, G., eds. 1977. *Lateralization and the nervous system.* New York: Academic Press.

HEBB, D. O. 1942. The effects of early and late brain injury upon test scores, and the nature of normal intelligence. *Proceedings of the American Philosophical Society* 85: 275-292 (abstract).

――― 1949. *The organization of behavior: a neuropsychological theory.* New York: Wiley.

HOFFMANN, B. 1964. *The tyranny of testing.* New York: Collier.

HORN, J. L. 1967. Intelligence: why it grows, why it declines. *Trans-Action* 5: 23-31.

――― 1968. The organization of abilities and the development of intelligence. *Psychological Review* 75: 242-259.

――― 1970a. Organization of data on life-span development of human abilities. In *Life-span development psychology*, ed. L. R. Goulet and P. B. Baltes. New York: Academic Press.

――― 1970b. Review of J. P. Guilford's *The nature of human intelligence.* *Psychometrika* 35: 273-277.

――― 1972. The structure of intellect: primary abilities. In *Multivariate Personality Research*, ed. R. M. Dreger. Baton Rouge, La.: Claitor.

――― 1973. Research proposal to study speed, power, carefulness, and short-term learning components of intelligence. Army Research Institute, Grant Number DAHC 19-74-5-0012.

――― 1974. The prima facia case for the heritability of intelligence and associates. A review of A. R. Jensen's *Educability and group differences.* *American Journal of Psychology* 87: 546-551.

――― 1975. Psychometric studies of aging and intelligence. In *Genesis and treatment of psychologic disorders in the elderly.* Aging, vol. 2, ed. Samuel Gershon and Allen Raskin. New York: Raven.

――― 1976a. Human abilities: a review of research and theories in the early 1970s. *Annual Review of Psychology* 27: 437-485.

――― 1976b. *Report on a study of speed, power, carefulness, and short-term learning components of intelligence.* Army Research Institute Research Grant Number DAHC 19-76-G-0019.

――― 1977a. Personality traits and concepts of ability. In *International encyclopedia of neurology, psychiatry, psychoanalysis, and psychology*, vol. 8, ed. B. B. Wolman. New York: Aesculapius Press and Van Nostrand-Reinhold.

――― 1977b. Personality and ability theory. In *Handbook of modern personality theory*, ed. R. B. Cattell and R. M. Dregar. New York: Hemisphere.

――― 1978a. Human ability systems. In *Life-span development and behavior*, vol. 1, ed. P. B. Baltes. New York: Academic Press.

――― 1978b. The nature and development of intellectual abilities. In *Human variation: the biopsychology of age, race, and sex*, ed. R. T. Osborne, C. E. Noble, and N. Weyl. New York: Academic Press.

――― 1978c. *Final report on a study of speed, power, carefulness, and short-term learning components of intelligence and changes in these components in adulthood*. National Science Foundation Grant Number GB-41452-1978.

————— 1979a. The rise and fall of human abilities. *Journal of Research and Development in Education* 12: 59-78.

————— 1979b. Intelligence and age. Symposium de la clinique psychiatrique. Bel-Air de l'Université de Génève. September 20-22.

————— 1979c. Some correctable defects in research on intelligence. *Intelligence* 3: 307-322.

HORN, J. L., and BRAMBLE, W. J. 1967. Second-order ability structure revealed in rights and wrongs scores. *Journal of Educational Psychology* 58: 115-122.

HORN, J. L., and CATTELL, R. B. 1966. Refinement and test of the theory of fluid and crystallized intelligence. *Journal of Educational Psychology* 57: 253-270.

————— 1967. Age differences in fluid and crystallized intelligence. *Acta Psychologica* 26: 107-129.

HORN, J. L., and DONALDSON, G. 1976. On the myth of intellectual decline in adulthood. *American Psychologist* 31: 701-719.

————— 1977. Faith is not enough: a response to the Baltes-Schaie claim that intelligence does not wane. *American Psychologist* 32: 369-373.

HORN, J. L., and KNAPP, J. R. 1973. On the subjective character of the empirical base of Guilford's structure-of-intellect model. *Psychological Bulletin* 80: 33-43.

————— 1974. Thirty wrongs do not make a right: a reply to Guilford. *Psychological Bulletin* 81: 502-504.

HORN, J. L., and STANKOV, L. 1979. Auditory abilities in relation to marker tests for Gf and Gc. In preparation.

HULICKA, I. M., and WEISS, R. L. 1965. Age differences in retention as a function of learning. *Journal of Consulting Psychology* 29: 125-129.

HULTSCH, D. 1969. Adult age differences in the organization of free recall. *Developmental Psychology* 1: 673-678.

————— 1971a. Adult age differences in free classification and free recall. *Developmental Psychology* 4: 338-342.

————— 1971b. Organization and memory in adulthood. *Human Development* 14: 16-29.

————— 1974. Learning in adulthood. *Journal of Gerontology* 29: 302-308.

HUMPHREYS, L. G. 1978. Doing research the hard way: substituting analysis of variance for a problem in correlational analysis. *Journal of Educational Psychology* 70: 873-876.

————— 1979. The construct of general intelligence. *Intelligence* 3: 105-120.

HUMPHREYS, L. G., PARSONS, C. K., and PARK, R. K. 1979. Dimensions involved in differences among means of cognitive measures. *Journal of Educational Measurement* 16: 63-76.

HUNDAL, P. S., and HORN, J. L. 1977. On the relationships between short-term learning and fluid and crystallized intelligence. *Applied Psychological Measurement* 1: 11-22.

HUNT, E. B. 1976. Varieties of cognitive power. In *The nature of intelligence*, ed. L. B. Resnick. Hillsdale, N. J.: Erlbaum.

———— 1978. Mechanics of verbal ability. *Psychological Review* 85: 109-130.

HUNT, J. McV. 1961. *Intelligence and experience.* New York: Ronald Press.

HYDEN, H. 1960. The neuron. In *The Cell,* vol. 4, ed. J. Brachet and A. Mirsky. New York: Academic Press.

———— 1973. RNA changes in brain cells during changes in behavior function. In *Macromolecules and behavior,* ed. G. B. Ansell and P. B. Bradley. Baltimore, Md.: University Park Press.

JARVIK, L. F., and BLUM, J. E. 1971. Cognitive declines as predictors of mortality in discordant twin pairs: a twenty-year longitudinal study. In *Prediction of life span,* ed. E. Palmore and F. C. Jeffers. Lexington, Mass.: D.C. Heath, Lexington Books.

JENCKS, C., SMITH, M., ACLAND, H., BANE, M. J., COHEN, D., GINTIS, H., HEYNS, B., and MICHELSON, S. 1972. *Inequality: a reassessment of the effect of family schooling in America.* New York: Harper and Row.

JENSEN, A. R. 1971. A theory of primary and secondary familial mental retardation. In *International review of mental retardation,* ed. N. R. Ellis. New York: Academic Press, pp. 33-105.

———— 1979. G: outmoded theory or unconquered frontier? *Creative Science and Technology* 11: 16-29.

JONES, H. E. 1959. Intelligence and problem solving. In *Aging and the individual,* ed. J. E. Birren. Chicago: University of Chicago Press.

JONES, H. E., CONRAD, H. S., and HORN, A. 1928. Psychological studies of motion pictures. II: Observation and recall as a function of age. *University of California Publications in Psychology* 3: 225-243.

JONES, L. V. 1954. Primary abilities in the Stanford-Binet, age 13. *Journal of General Psychology* 84: 126-147.

KEELE, S. W. 1973. *Attention and human performance.* Pacific Palisades, Calif.: Goodyear.

KELLEY, H. P. 1964. Memory ability: a factor analysis. *Psychometric Monographs* 11. Chicago: University of Chicago Press.

KELLEY, T. L. 1928. *Crossroads in the mind of man.* Stanford, Calif.: Stanford University Press.

KINTSCH, W. 1970. *Learning, memory, and conceptual processes.* New York: Wiley.

———— 1974. *The representation of meaning in memory.* New York: Wiley.

KOGAN, N. 1973. *Categorizing and conceptualizing styles in younger and older adults.* Princeton, N.J.: Educational Testing Service.

KUHLENBECK, H. 1954. Some histological age changes in the rat's brain and their relationship to comparable changes in the human brain. *Confinia Neurology* 14: 329-342.

LABOUVIE-VIEF, G. 1976. Toward optimizing cognitive competence. *Educational Gerontology* 1: 75-92.

LAURENCE, M. W. 1967. Memory loss with age: a test of two strategies for its retardation. *Psychonomic Science* 9: 209-210.

LEHMAN, N. C. 1964. The relationship between chronological age and high level research output in physics and chemistry. *Journal of Gerontology* 19: 157-164.

LEVY, J., and REID, M. 1976. Variations in writing posture and cerebral organization. *Science* 194: 337-339.

LOEHLIN, J. C., LINDZEY, G., and SPUHLER, J. 1975. *Race differences in intelligence*. San Francisco, Calif.: Freeman.

LORGE, I. 1936. The influence of the test upon the nature of mental decline as a function of age. *Journal of Educational Psychology* 27: 100-110.

LUNDBERG, F. 1968. *The rich and the super-rich*. New York: Lyle Stuart.

LURIA, A. R. 1969. Frontal lobe syndromes. In *Handbook of clinical neurology*, ed. P. J. Vinken and G. W. Bruyn. Amsterdam: North Holland.

———— 1973. *The working brain*. London: Penguin.

MANDLER, G. 1967. Organization and memory. In *The psychology of learning and motivation: advances in research and theory*, vol. 1, ed. K. W. Spence and J. T. Spence. New York: Academic Press.

———— 1968. Organized recall: individual functions. *Psychonomic Science* 13: 23-236.

MARX, D. J. 1970. Intentional and incidental concept formation as a function of conceptual complexity, intelligence, and task complexity. *Journal of Educational Psychology* 61: 297-304.

MATARAZZO, J. D. 1972. *Wechsler's measurement and appraisal of adult intelligence*. Baltimore, Md.: Williams and Williams.

MATSAYUMA, H., NAMIKI, H., and WATANABE, I. 1966. Senile changes in the brain in the Japanese: incidence of neurofibrillary change and senile plaques. In *Proceedings of the Fifth International Congress of Neuropathology*, ed. F. Luthy and A. Bischoff. Netherlands: Excerpta Medica, series no. 100, pp. 979-980.

MAYESKI, G. W., OKADA, T., BUSOR, A. E., COHEN, W. M., and WESLER, C. E. 1973. *A study of achievement of our nation's students*. Washington, D.C.: U.S. Government Printing Office.

MEIER-RUGE, W., ENZ, A., GYGAX, P., HUNZIKER, O., IWANGOFF, P., and REICHLMEIER, K. 1975. Experimental pathology in basic research of the aging brain. In *Aging*, vol. 2, ed. S. Gershon and A. Raskin. New York: Raven.

MENZES, R. A., and GOLD. P. H. 1972. The apparent turnover of mitochondria, ribosomes, and sRNA of the brain in young and aged rats. *Journal of Neurochemistry* 19: 1671-83.

MEYER, V. 1961. Psychological effects of brain damage. In *Handbook of abnormal psychology*, ed. H. J. Eysenck. New York: Basic Books.

MOSTELLER, F., and MOYNIHAN, D. P., eds. 1972. *On equality of educational opportunity*. New York: Vintage Books.

MUENSTER, P. A. 1972. Learning and memory in relation to age. *Journal of Gerontology* 27: 361-363.

MURRAY, M. R., and STOUT, A. P. 1974. Adult human sympathetic ganglion cells cultivated in vitio. *American Journal of Anatomy* 80: 225-273.

NELSON, T. O. 1977. Repetition and depth of processing. *Journal of Verbal Learning and Verbal Behavior* 16: 151-171.

NEWELL, A., and SIMON H. 1972. *Human problem solving*. Englewood Cliffs, N.J.: Prentice-Hall.

NISBET, J. D. 1957. Intelligence and age: retesting with twenty-four years interval. *British Journal of Educational Psychology* 27: 190-198.

NORMAN, D. A., ed. 1970. *Models of human memory.* New York: Academic Press.

────── 1977. Research considerations in the assessment of the (impaired) elderly. Paper presented at the Conference on Cognition and Aging. Battelle Research Center, Seattle, Washington, January.

ODEN, M. H. 1968. The fulfillment of promise: 40-year follow-up of the Terman gifted group. *Genetic Psychological Monographs* 77: 1, 3-93.

OWENS, W. A., JR. 1953. Age and mental abilities: a longitudinal study. *Genetic Psychology Monographs* 48: 3-54.

────── 1966. Age and mental abilities: a second follow-up. *Journal of Educational Psychology* 51: 311-325.

PAYNE, R. W. 1961. Cognitive abnormalities. In *Handbook of abnormal psychology*, ed. H. J. Eysenck. New York: Basic Books.

PIAGET, J. 1960. *Psychology of intelligence.* Peterson, N.J.: Littlefield Adams.

PLEMONS, J. K., WILLIS, S. L., and BALTES, P. B. 1978. Modifiability of fluid intelligence in aging: a short-term longitudinal training approach. *Journal of Gerontology* 33: 224-231.

POSTMAN, L. 1964. Short-term memory and incidental learning. In *Categories of human learning*, ed. A. W. Melton. New York: Academic Press.

PRIBRAM, K. H. 1971. *Languages of the brain: experimental paradoxes and principles in neuropsychology.* Englewood Cliffs, N.J.: Prentice-Hall.

REITAN, R. M. 1958. Qualitative versus quantitative mental changes following brain damage. *Journal Psychology* 46: 339-346.

────── 1964. Psychological deficits resulting from cerebral lesions in man. In *The frontal granular cortex and behavior*, ed. J. M. Warren and K. A. Akert. New York: McGraw-Hill.

RESNICK, L. B., ed. 1976. *The nature of intelligence.* Hillsdale, N.J.: Erlbaum.

RIEGEL, K. F. 1972. The changing individual in the changing society. In *Determinants of behavior development.* New York: Academic Press.

────── 1973a. The recall of historical events. *Behavioral Science* 18: 354-363.

────── 1973b. *Dialectic operations: the final period of cognitive development.* Princeton, N.J.: Educational Testing Service.

RIEGEL, K. F., and RIEGEL, R. M. 1972. Development, drop and death. *Developmental Psychology* 6: 306-319.

ROBINSON, A. J., NIES, A., DAVIS, J. N., BUNNEY, W. E., DAVIS, J. M., COLBURN, R. W., BOURNE, H. R., SHAW, D. M., and COPPERN, A. J. 1972. Aging, monamines, and monamine oxidase levels. *Lancet* 1: 290-291.

ROYCE, J. R., YEUDALL, L. T., BOCK, C. 1976. Factor analytic studies of human brain damage. I: First and second-order factors and their brain correlates. *Multivariate Behaviorial Research* 11: 381-418.

SANFORD, A. J., and MAULE, A. J. 1973. The concept of general experience: age and strategies in guessing future events. *Journal of Gerontology* 28: 81-88.

SCHAIE, K. W. 1965. A general model for the study of developmental problems. *Psychological Bulletin* 64: 92-107.

―――― 1973. Methodological problems in descriptive developmental research on adulthood and aging. In *Life-span developmental psychology: methodological issues*, ed. J. R. Nesselroade and H. W. Reese. New York: Academic Press.

―――― 1974. Transitions in gerontology—from lab to life: intellectual functioning. *American Psychologist* 29: 802-807.

SCHAIE, K. W., LABOUVIE, G. V., and BUECH, B. U. 1973. Generational and cohort-specific differences in adult cognitive functioning: a fourteen-year study of independent samples. *Developmental Psychology* 9: 151-166.

SCHAIE, K. W., and LABOUVIE-VIEF, G. 1974. Generational versus ontogenetic components of change in adult cognitive behavior: a fourteen-year cross-sequential study. *Developmental Psychology* 10: 305-320.

SCHAIE, K. W., and STROTHER, C. R. 1968. A cross-sequential study of age changes in cognitive behavior. *Psychological Bulletin* 70: 671-680.

SCHONFIELD, D. 1965. Memory changes with age. *Nature* 208: 918.

―――― 1972. Theoretical nuances and practical old questions: the psychology of aging. *Canadian Psychologist* 13: 252-266.

SEKHON, S. S., and MAXWELL, D. S. 1974. Ultrastructural changes in neurons of the spinal anterior horn of aging mice with particular reference to the accumulation of lipofuscin pigment. *Journal of Neurocytology* 3: 59-72.

SHEPARD, R. N. 1967. Recognition memory for words, sentences, and pictures. *Journal of Verbal Learning and Verbal Behavior* 6: 156-163.

―――― 1978. The mental image. *American Psychologist* 33: 217-225.

SMITH, I. M. 1965. *Spatial ability: its educational and social significance.* San Diego: Knapp.

SPEARMAN, C. 1904. "General intelligence" objectively determined and measured. *American Journal of Psychology* 15: 201-292.

SPERLING, G. 1960. The information available in brief visual presentation. *Psychological Monographs* 74: 498.

STERNBERG, R. J. 1977. *Intelligence, information processing, and analogical reasoning: the componential analysis of human abilities.* Hillsdale, N.J.: Erlbaum.

STERNBERG, S. 1967. Two operations in character recognition: some evidence from reaction-time measurements. *Perception and Psychophysics* 2: 45-53.

TERRY, R. D., and WISNIEWSKI, H. M. 1972. Neurofibrillary tangle and senile plaque. In *Aging and the brain,* ed. C. M. Gaitz. New York: Plenum Press.

―――― 1975. Structural and chemical changes of the aged human brain. In *Aging*, vol. 2, ed. G. Gershon and A. Raskin. New York: Raven.

THOMSON, G. H. 1939. *The factorial analysis of human ability.* London: University of London Press.

TUDDENHAM, R. D., BLUMENKRANTZ, J., and WILKIN, W. R. 1968. Age changes on AGCT: a longitudinal study on average adults. *Journal of Consulting Clinical Psychology* 32: 659-663.

TYLER, L. E. 1965. *The psychology of human differences.* New York: Appleton-Century-Crofts.

Underwood, B. J. 1975. Individual differences as a crucible in theory construction. *American Psychologist* 30: 128-134.

Underwood, B. J., Boruch, R. F., and Malmi, R. A. 1978. Composition of episodic memory. *Journal of Experimental Psychology: General* 107: 393-419.

Undheim, J. O. 1976. Ability structure in 10- to 11-year-old children and the theory of fluid and crystallized intelligence. *Journal of Educational Psychology* 68: 411-423.

Undheim, J. O., and Horn, J. L. 1977. Critical evaluation of Guilford's structure-of-intellect theory. *Intelligence* 1: 65-81.

Vandenberg, S. G. 1962. The hereditary abilities study: hereditary components in a psychological test battery. *American Journal of Human Genetics* 14: 220-237.

—— 1965. Multivariate analysis of twin differences. In *Methods and goals in human behavior genetics*, ed. S. G. Vandenberg. New York: Academic Press.

Van Hahn, H. P. 1970. Structural and functional changes in nucleoprotin during the aging of the cell. *Gerontologia* 16: 116-128.

Walsh, D. A. 1975. Age differences in learning and memory. In *Aging: scientific perspectives and social issues*, ed. D. S. Woodruff and J. E. Birren. New York: Van Nostrand Reinhold.

Walsh, D. A., and Baldwin, M. 1977. Age differences in integrated semantic memory. *Developmental Psychology* 13: 509-514.

Walsh, D., and Thompson, L. 1978. Age differences in visual sensory memory. *Journal of Gerontology* 33: 383-387.

Warrington, E. K. 1969. Constructional apraxia. In *Handbook of clinical neurology. Vol. 4: Disorders of speech, perception and symbolic behavior*, ed. P. J. Vinken and G. W. Bruyn. Amsterdam: North-Holland.

Warrington, E. K., and Sanders, H. I. 1971. The fate of old memories. *Quarterly Journal of Experimental Psychology* 23: 432-442.

Waugh, N. C., and Norman, D. A. 1965. Primary memory. *Psychological Review* 71: 89-104.

Welford, A. T. 1958. *Aging and human skill*. London: Oxford University Press.

Willett, R. A. 1961. The effects of psychosurgical procedures in behavior. In *Handbook of abnormal psychology: an experimental approach*, ed. H. J. Eysenck. New York: Basic Books.

Willoughby, R. R. 1927. Family similarities in mental-test abilities. *Genetic Psychological Monographs* 2: 235-277.

—— 1930. Incidental learning. *Journal of Educational Psychology* 21: 12-23.

Wimer, R. E., and Wigdor, E. T. 1958. Age differences in retention of learning. *Journal of Gerontology* 13: 291-295.

Witkin, H. A. 1973. The role of cognitive style in academic performance and in teacher-student relations. Princeton, N.J.: Educational Testing Services. RB-73-11.

Wohlwill, J. F. 1970. Methodology and research strategy in the study of developmental change. In *Life-span developmental psychology*, ed. L. R. Goulet and P. B. Baltes. New York: Academic Press.

Yntema, D. B., and Trask, F. P. 1963. Recall as a search process. *Journal of Verbal Learning and Verbal Behavior* 2: 65-74.

Zajonc, R. B. 1976. Family configuration and intelligence. *Science* 192: 227-236.

11 | Longitudinal Study of Personality Development
Howard A. Moss and Elizabeth J. Susman

A LONG-STANDING, pervasive assumption held by lay persons and psychologists alike is that an individual's behavior is generally predictable across a variety of situations and over time. It is assumed that one needs only a certain basic familiarity with individuals and a modest sampling of their behavior to make reasonable predictions about individuals' concurrent or future responses in comparable situations and modalities of functioning. Many life decisions and interpersonal actions are predicated on the deep-rooted and universally held conviction that one can anticipate the probable responses and actions of different individuals. Indeed, the very concept of personality implies a differentiated and organized hierarchy of psychological sets and behavioral dispositions that are manifested as consistent and enduring patterns in denoting the uniqueness of the individual. William James (1950) reflects this universally endorsed point of view concerning the consistency of personality in the following elegant statement from his lecture on habit.

> . . . Already at the age of twenty-five you see the professional mannerism settling down on the young commercial traveller, on the young doctor, on the young minister, on the young counsellor-at-law. You see the little lines of cleavage running through the character, the tricks of thought, the prejudices, the ways of the "shop" in a word, from which the man can by-and-by no more escape than his coat sleeve can suddenly fall into a new set of folds. On the whole, it is best he should not escape. It is well for the world that in most of us, by the age of thirty, the character has set like plaster, and will never soften again (p. 121).

E. Lowell Kelly (1955) noted, in his presidential address to the American Psychological Association, that the belief in the consistency of personality is the one issue on which there appears to be the greatest unanimity among the diverse psychological theories represented in the profession. He summarizes this view by observing, "Whether one is an extreme hereditarian, an environmentalist, a constitutionalist, or an orthodox psychoanalyst, he is not likely to anticipate major changes in personality after the first few years of life" (p. 659).

To put Kelly's view in perspective it is important to note that some psychologists have recently presented thoughtful and vigorous arguments against an unequivocal acceptance of the notion of consistency of personality characteristics (Mischel, 1969; Nesselroade and Baltes, 1974). As one would expect, challenging the belief in consistency of personality has resulted in a lively controversy in which the dissenters, in turn, have been challenged about the validity of their contentions (Block, 1977; McCall, 1977; McCall, Eichorn, and Hogarty, 1977). It is not within the scope of this chapter to attempt to resolve the existing controversies, but it would be useful to identify the main issues or reservations that have been raised concerning the consistency of aspects of personality over different ages so that these issues can be considered to understand and evaluate critically the longitudinal data on personality that will be presented.

Walter Mischel (1968, 1969) argues that the view that personality is consistent across situations and stable over time is overstated and likely to be incorrect. His position is that behavior is specific to situations and much more influenced by the vicissitudes of social learning conditions than by enduring psychological predispositions. He makes the distinction between intellectual and cognitive functioning, which he feels shows high levels of consistency and stability, and personality traits, which he contends lack cross-situational or longitudinal generality. Mischel's conclusion is based on his review of the empirical evidence which shows that correlation coefficients for personality variables rarely exceed 0.30 across situations and therefore accounts for less than 10% of the variance. Mischel's review of the literature (1968) is not comprehensive and, as one dissenter (Block, 1977) stated, Mischel's negative review is "a vehicle to illustrate his perspectives and conclusions on the issues involved albeit in a highly distilled form. Obviously, Mischel's conclusion, whatever its degree of correctness, cannot be truly supported by so brief, selective, and undetailed a literature presentation" (p. 13).

Mischel (1969) resolves the discrepancy between his view of the lack of evidence for continuity of personality and the strongly held convictions of many others that this continuity exists by the following line of reasoning.

There is a great deal of evidence that our cognitive constructions about ourselves and the world—our personal theories about ourselves and those around us—often are extremely stable and highly resistant to change. Studies of the self-concept, of impression formation in person perception and in clinical judgment, of cognitive sets guiding selective attention—all of these phenomena and many more document the consistency and tenacious continuity of many human construction systems. Often these construction systems are built quickly and on the basis of little information. But, once established, these theories, whether generated by our subjects or ourselves, become exceedingly difficult to disconfirm. (p. 1012)

Mischel discounts arguments that the limited success of investigators in finding greater stability and consistency in behavior is a function of imprecise and often crude measurement procedures and inadequate research design. His position is "that the observed inconsistency so regularly found in studies of noncognitive personality dimensions often reflects the state of nature and not merely the noise of measurement" (p. 1014). Yet reliability coefficients of personality measurements tend to be about 0.70, whereas intelligence tests usually yield reliabilities about 0.90. The attenuation associated with reliabilities of 0.70 would have a pronounced effect on the stability coefficients of personality variables.

Mischel's position is provocative and challenging. It provides the initiative for a self-conscious reappraisal of longitudinal research on personality and stimulates a critical attitude about the nature of stability of behavior, which heretofore had been taken for granted. This is not to say that stability is no longer a tenable characterization of human development, but only that we should be open to alternative paradigms for viewing and monitoring personality development.

John Nesselroade and Paul Baltes (1974) as well as Warner Schaie (1965) have also strongly criticized the validity of findings from longitudinal studies of personality. Their criticism stresses methodological flaws in the research; if their criticisms are valid, these flaws would severely undermine the substantive contributions of many longitudinal findings on personality. In general they are pessimistic about longitudinal research because of their conclusions that age, year of measurement, and year of birth are hopelessly confounded and that the effects of repeated testing and selective attrition further bias and distort longitudinal findings. They contend that past longitudinal studies have not paid enough attention to the differential experience of various samples and populations of subjects. They argue that the historical period in which individuals live has a prepotent influence on their attitudes, feelings, and general style of psychological functioning. Cultural events and circumstances change dramatically during different epochs (even short time periods), and the contemporary milieu in which the individual is functioning is considered to have a major impact on the way he behaves and develops. This concern with historical and cultural conditions in the shaping of personality parallels Mischel's assertion that situational factors are the major determinants of psychological behavior.

Nesselroade and Baltes (1974) conclude that the large potential variability from sample to sample makes it difficult to generalize from longitudinal studies, which are restricted to one sample. To test their assertion that historical and cultural factors and secular changes have a dominant effect on personality dimensions, they administered Cattell's High School Personality Questionnaire and Jackson's Personality Research Form to four adolescent cohorts born in 1954, 1955, and 1956, and 1957, respectively. Each cohort was administered these tests on three occasions: in 1970, 1971, and 1972. This design permitted them to compare mean scores for each chronological age, studying developmental changes for each cohort and analyzing for similarity of scores for each historical period (year of assessment) across cohorts (different age groups). They found that the year in which the measurement was made accounted for more variance between groups than the age of the subject at the time of the assessment. For example, "all adolescents (largely independent of their age) showed a significant decrement in super-ego-strength, social-emotional anxiety, and achievement from 1970 to either 1971 and/or 1972 and an increase in independence during the same time interval" (p. 69). Based on these data they suggest that findings from simple cross-sectional or longitudinal studies yield limited descriptive information concerning development. Instead, they recommend "that future descriptive research on ontogeny employ sequential strategies (cross-sectional and longitudinal sequences) with appropriate controls for various aspects of internal and external validity." Furthermore, they urge that research models be developed to "explicitly deal with the interaction between individual and historical change." As a caveat their research was based on questionnaire data, thus limiting generalization from these findings to actual behavior. Since questionnaire responses also are susceptible to response sets, one should be cautious in interpreting yearly vicissitudes in mean scores; fluctuations in reference group values could spuriously accentuate or depress certain response tendencies in answering questionnaire items.

Robert McCall (1977) disagrees with the conclusions of Nesselroade and Baltes (1974) and Schaie (1965) concerning the fallibility of the traditional longitudinal design. He maintains that the longitudinal approach is the sine qua non for studying developmental changes and patterns of growth and contends that this approach is necessary for tracing developmental phenomena. McCall acknowledges that age changes might be confounded with extraneous variables but feels that this problem is not a sufficient basis for discarding the one methodology uniquely suited to studying intraindividual growth patterns. One would find it difficult to identify any methodology used in personality assessment that does not make some assumptions concerning the effect or control of extraneous variables. McCall points out that proposed alternative research designs are impractical; as an example he describes the following implications of a design suggested by Schaie, which includes separate cohorts born in different years. Based on a minimum design proposed by Schaie a longitudinal study using yearly assessments over a forty-year period would require several thousand subjects, take eighty years to complete, and would be prohibitively expensive.

Two distinctly different research objectives have been emphasized in longitudinal studies of personality. One involves the search for stability or consistency of personality characteristics over time, and the other focuses on change in personality across different developmental stages. Walter Emmerich (1964, 1968) has conceptualized the distinction between stability and change and has described some of the theoretical issues and methodological considerations involved in pursuing either of these longitudinal objectives. He refers to evaluating consistency of personality as the study of stability-instability and to the investigation of change as the study of continuity-discontinuity. Stability reflects the degree to which an individual retains the same relative position on a dimension over time, and continuity is concerned with whether the quality or meaning of a behavior remains the same with development. A finding that infants who cry a great deal are irritable as school-aged children would be interpreted as evidence for stability. However, crying diminishes greatly from infancy to childhood, and crying that occurs later is in a different behavioral context; this is evidence for discontinuity. Some investigators have adopted the distinction between stability and continuity, as proposed by Emmerich, whereas others use the words stability and continuity interchangeably for describing what Emmerich labels stability.

Bernice Neugarten (1977) discusses the divergence of different theoretical orientations in their perspectives on constancy of personality. Some theories emphasize stability, whereas other theories are based on a developmental model oriented toward change. The distinction between the study of stability and the study of change is important for putting methodological issues and criticisms in proper perspective. Clarifying the distinction between stability and change is relevant for judging the capability and usefulness of the longitudinal approach for personality research. Although most investigators who conduct longitudinal studies acknowledge the distinction between stability and change, they tend to emphasize only one of these in discussing the significance of their findings. Thus those who emphasize stability tend to be positive about the longitudinal method for studying personality, whereas those who emphasize the study of change are inclined to be pessimistic about the usefulness of this methodology. The statistical methods currently available lend themselves readily to the study of stability but are not so well designed for measuring change. Furthermore, the conceptual assumptions associated with the study of stability are more straightforward and easier to define than those associated with the study of change.

Nesselroade and Baltes (1974) focus on change in their longitudinal study of adolescent personality. Because of their finding that age, cohort, and year of assessment (historical time) were confounded in measuring change, they conclude that the straight longitudinal design is unsatisfactory for studying development. However, as a secondary aspect of their research they present stability coefficients for ten factor scores across three age periods (at yearly intervals) for the four cohorts that they studied. They reported average correlations between 0.39 and 0.72 with a median correlation of 0.59. These results indicate a respectable degree of stability over time and support a different conclusion about the value of longitudinal research than the one they reached by focusing on the information yielded from studying change scores. The stability coefficients that Nesselroade and Baltes report are about twice as high and account for approximately four times the variance that Mischel claimed was typical of longitudinal studies of personality.

The normative search for stability of personality characteristics over time asks whether individuals maintain the same relative position on a personality dimension during different age periods. Stability can also be studied ipsatively by evaluating whether different personality characteristics retain the same hierarchial position or salience within the individual over time. The focus here is on the degree of constancy in the measurement of individual differences over time. Stability is evaluated by examining the magnitudes of correlation coefficients. This strategy is similar to that used for obtaining reliability coefficients but involves relating measurements separated by longer time spans. The assumption for reliabilities is that less than perfect correlation is due to error of measurement, whereas for studies of stability a lower correlation is interpreted as reflecting change in the individual's relative position on a personality dimension. Obviously the measurements used for assessing stability are also subject to the attenuating effect of imperfect reliabilities. Correcting for attenuation, which is ordinarily not done, would thus provide a more accurate and higher estimate of stability. Jack Block (1971) has stressed the need for incorporating this statistical adjustment in longitudinal research.

McCall (1977) and Joachim Wohlwill (1973) have suggested that since development implies change, the proper concern of developmental psychologists is the study of behavioral changes within individuals across time. It is intuitively obvious that individuals exhibit change as well as stability in aspects of personality over the life span. McCall (1977) states that "a behavior can increase or decrease in frequency or amount across age, or one behavior can replace, supplement, or grow out of another with development" (p. 338). There is consensus over the meaning of stability, but not over ways to conceptualize change. The assessment of change can be based on shifts in mean scores on a psychological dimension, or low stability coefficients, or reorganization in the interaction of attributes within the individual. The use of low stability coefficients can be dismissed as an acceptable method for judging change, since such a procedure would be tantamount to accepting the null hypothesis. Thus instances of instability cannot be interpreted as evidence of change because to do so would violate a basic assumption of statistics. Studies of changes in the organization of attributes within the individual tend to be based on qualitative analyses and idiographic reports, although the Q-sort has been used effectively as a quantitative method for assessing intraindividual change. An additional measure of change, which could also be construed as a form of stability, is seen when a particular attribute at one age is predictive of a phenotypically different but theoretically reasonable attribute at a later age. This situation could be viewed as either a derivative developmental transformation or a later manifestation of an earlier and underlying genotype. Jerome Kagan (1971) has given the label heterotypic continuity to these types of transformations and the label homotypic continuity to manifestations of stability between phenotypically similar attributes. Richard Bell, George Weller, and Mary Waldrop (1971) have defined correlations between disparate characteristics as metamorphic relations and correlations between similar characteristics as isomorphic relations. Thus change can be construed as shifts in the importance of a dimension at different developmental stages, shifts in individual differences on a dimension over time, or derivative developmental transformations.

The issue of personality change is more complicated than it appears. When we study stability there are fairly clear guidelines about what we are predicting. In longitudinal studies of stability we are seeking to identify consistencies in behavior over time. In studies of change, however, the theoretical guidelines about what is being predicted are not as well established. Three somewhat independent approaches to the study of change are to investigate the occurrence and nature of invariant sequences of behavior, to measure growth, and to identify empirically important heterotypic (or metamorphic) relations.

The view that personality change should be determined by evaluating transitions through invariant developmental sequences has no doubt been popularized by the seminal contributions of Piaget and his co-workers in their use of a sequential stage model for the study of cognitive development. To test or construct a sequential stage model of personality development, from longitudinal data, would require that specific information related to the theory be obtained on subjects at different ages. Large-scale longitudinal research programs have not collected data according to a format that would be consonant with a developmental stage theory of personality. Moreover, the few developmental stage theories of personality that exist (Freud, 1968; Erikson, 1963; Kohlberg, 1969) use variables that are not of interest to many developmental psychologists (Freud, 1968), cover broad periods of the life span that would be impractical to study longitudinally (Erikson, 1963), or deal with a single aspect of personality (Kohlberg, 1969). Thus although a sequential stage approach appears to be a sensible and laudatory framework for evaluating personality change, the current status of developmental theories of personality severely restricts this approach in longitudinal research.

Attempts to study personality change as growth are ostensibly patterned after the models and methodology used for studying physical growth. However, the instruments used for measuring personality variables, and the circumstances surrounding these measurements, are not comparable to those used in the measurement of physical growth. Personality tests are not based on equal-interval scales; the measurement of personal characteristics is influenced by the social and psychological context in which the behavior is assessed; and assessments of personality are defined differently for individuals at different ages.

Bloom (1964) attempted to measure growth of personality by studying the percentage of variance accounted for in correlations of personality measurements between adjacent age periods. Increases in the amount of variance for correlations at older age periods were interpreted as growth, and the age at which further increases were no longer observed was defined as the leveling off point for the growth of that characteristic. However, such relations, in fact, do not reflect absolute change but are simply restatements of normative stability. Bloom's abortive approach exemplifies the dilemma that psychologists face in attempting to measure personality change.

Personality theory has progressed slowly and has been burdened with innumerable problems in developing a comprehensive and scientific understanding of personality. Donald Fiske (1978) in his overview of the state of the personality field concludes that "the discipline of personality as currently studied is and will remain prescientific" (p. 20). He bases this conclusion on the limited consensus about data and theory among students of personality, the extensive use of interpretive judgments, the lack of agreement about the meaning of words (descriptions and definitions), and the use of broad rather than specific units of behavior. It is not possible to study the ontogenesis of personality without using the guiding framework of some theory of personality. Thus the longitudinal study of personality is necessarily subject to the same general problems besetting personality theory. The tenuous status of personality theory has undermined efforts to study personality longitudinally because of the different ways in which personality variables are defined and measured across the life span. Moreover, personality theory does not specify the links between personality variables at different developmental periods.

A frequently made assumption is that what is being measured at one age is in some way "equivalent" to what is being measured at a later age. This assumption is made credible by the use of the same personality labels across age groups, regardless of differences in underlying operational definitions. Differences in the definition of a personality variable tend to become progressively pronounced as the age interval between measurement increases. These differences in definition are particularly evident when ratings are the basis of measurement.

There is no consistent or rigid way to define any personality variable so that it applies equally across the life span. A definition of any personality variable changes across different age periods in order to be consonant with the behavioral repertoire, the age-related psychosocial demands, and the shifting social context that are present and salient at different developmental stages. Thus physical fighting among preschoolers, verbal insults among school-aged children, social rejection by teenagers, and ruthless business dealing among adults might all be defined as aggression. The same label is used to define disparate behaviors.

The greatest disparity in definitions of personality occurs for definitions of infant and adult personality. The study of personality in infancy is not well established as a systematic area of inquiry. Social scientists have attributed personality characteristics to infants, but most of the information that has been gathered, and the concepts that have been formulated, have been shaped by concerns with adult personality. The study of adult personality emphasizes the evaluation of individual differences in emotions, motives, and defenses and focuses on the effects that differences in these psychological characteristics have on interpersonal relations. On the other hand, studies of infancy tend to emphasize evaluating response capacities or learning potentials. Most personality theories tend to stress the individual's symbolic life and rely heavily on interview data in order to assess personality functioning. Since the infants' repertoire of symbols is limited, their personalities are not yet well formed and not accessible to study. Most efforts at evaluating personality variables during infancy have relied on assessing behaviors (such as activity level, reaction to stimulation, and time spent in different states), which are presumably precursors of later personality functioning. Consequently, longitudinal relations between infancy and later stages of development are by definition heterotypic. Partly for the reasons already discussed and partly because of practical considerations, longitudinal studies of personality stress the use of ratings (or codings) of observed behavior for younger subjects and base assessment of older subjects on the use of self-report inventories.

The use of both rating scales and self-report inventories in longitudinal research is influenced by the tendency to define personality variables somewhat differently at different ages. Rating scales have sliding definitions, so the same scale can accommodate different age groups. For example, a rating scale definition used to assess aggression longitudinally incorporates different descriptive statements so that the same scale can be used flexibly for different age groups. The same point could be made for Q-sort techniques in which a series of items is used to classify individuals at different ages. In the Q-sort, however, the changing definitions of items are implicit, since they require judges to modify their frames of reference about the meaning of a behavior in order to accommodate different age groups. Thus studies of stability may appear to deal with stability mainly because the same label is used to classify different behaviors at different ages. Psychologists simply impose conceptual stability on behaviors that may be dissimilar. An analysis that is more behaviorally oriented might dispose one to regard some of the evidence for stability as evidence of change. The same line of reasoning could be applied in evaluating the meaning of heterotypic relations. A longitudinal correlation between two phenotypically different behaviors is regarded as evidence of heterotypic continuity. However, in certain instances, shifting from a somewhat specific to a more general or inclusive conceptual label could make it reasonable to reconstrue a relationship as homotypic and reflecting stability rather than heterotypic and reflecting change. There is an advantage to conceptualizing variables so that homotypic relations can be studied, for such analyses imply the testing of a developmental hypothesis and thus the results can be accepted with greater certainty. Heterotypic findings tend to be discovered empirically by selection from a large intercorrelation matrix and are usually given post hoc developmental interpretations. Unpredicted heterotypic relations need to be buttressed by strong evidence of internal validity or through replications in order to avoid the risk of accepting chance findings.

As instruments for measuring longitudinal change, self-report personality inventories have the same built-in limitations as rating scales. Personality inventories are typically designed and standardized to measure the functioning of a specific age group. That is, items tend to be selected and scales developed so that they are valid only for individuals at a particular developmental stage. An inventory is usually designed for children, for adolescents, or for adults. Thus the same personality inventory cannot be used appropriately in longitudinal studies spanning these developmental periods. Because of this constraint some longitudinal studies have been limited to readministering the same personality inventory two or more times to a sample of subjects only while they remain within the same developmental period (childhood, adolescence, or adulthood). Moreover, some studies that cover a time interval during which only minimal changes are expected, such as the one by Nesselroade and Baltes (1974), have nonetheless emphasized change measures in their analyses and in their results. It seems somewhat paradoxical to stress change when the repeated measurements cover a relatively narrow age period during which developmental changes are not likely to occur. Nesselroade and Baltes's finding that cultural and historical factors accounted for more change than the age of the subjects might be explained by the restriction of their longitudinal assessment to a fairly homogeneous developmental period.

Longitudinal studies of change that are based on evaluating shifts in the mean level of a behavior or attribute or those based on correlational patterns imply normative developmental transformations that all individuals are expected to pass through. Other theories (Murphy, 1964; Escalona and Heider, 1959), however, consider developmental change to be a highly individualized matter. Investigations based on these theories are concerned with the intraindividual dynamics and interactions of personality attributes as forces for change. They focus on the emergence and shaping of attributes as a function of the continuous effort to adapt to the internal and external demands that act on the individual. Although certain modal changes are expected, the focus is on observing and understanding the idiosyncratic changes that emerge in order to meet the unique needs and circumstances of the individual. This information is idiographic, and most of the work using this approach has consisted of case studies and anecdotal reporting. The nonsystematic and qualitative information coming from these idiographic analyses does not readily lend itself to integrative summaries of personality.

Whether the focus is on stability or change, what remains important is acknowledging the proper role and usefulness of the longitudinal method for testing and forming hypotheses and advancing a developmental theory of personality. A statement that stability or change occurs is limited in meaning. Of greater significance is determining the malleability of personality and identifying the antecedent conditions and sociopsychological dynamics that maintain or alter patterns of behavior.

In interpreting and predicting the findings of longitudinal studies of personality it is helpful to be able to identify factors likely to minimize or maximize the observation of constancy and continuity of personality. Two major classes of factors could strongly affect whether stability or change is observed: (1) factors based on the methodology of the study (sample, time interval between measurement, age of subjects, variables studied, assessment procedure) and (2) factors associated with changes in the psychosocial conditions experienced by different subjects (such as moving to a different environment). These two classes of factors may not be independent, since certain methodologies could either capitalize on or minimize the influence of psychosocial conditions.

The primary methodological factors that could affect whether stability or change is observed for different personality variables are the nature of the sample, the time interval between measurements, the ages at which the subjects are studied, the particular variables studied, and the type of measuring instruments used to assess personality.

If a sample is relatively homogeneous, the lack of variability among subjects could make it difficult to find stabilities because of the restricted range of scores. Even when there is an apparent range in scores, this range may result because raters are being asked to make finer discriminations within a narrow band and thus are not actually sampling the entire theoretical range of scores. The finer the discrimination that a rater has to make, the greater the room for error, resulting in potentially lower measurement reliability. This lowered reliability would of course attenuate stability coefficients. The manner in which long-term longitudinal samples are recruited and maintained increases the risk that they may include a particularly homogeneous population. Long-term longitudinal samples are subject to attrition, which could alter the composition of the samples and thus affect longitudinal results in unknown ways. If attrition is greater among subjects who might potentially exhibit the most change, an impression of greater stability might be created based on those cases who remained. On the other hand, if the initially most extreme subjects stopped participating in the study, the homogeneity of the sample could increase, thus making it more difficult to demonstrate stability.

The greater the time interval between measurements, the greater the opportunity for change. Also the age of the subjects at the time they were studied might affect whether stability or change were evident in the data. One expects greater stability among older subjects, particularly when the correlated measurements were obtained within the same developmental period in which the developmental tasks and life circumstances remained relatively constant. Measurements of older subjects might exhibit greater stability because psychological experiences have a cumulative effect and because developmental stages (as they are conceptualized) span greater periods of time as one gets older. An important related issue is deciding how to define and conceptualize the age periods to be studied. This decision is a major problem for integrating longitudinal findings, because there is considerable variation among longitudinal studies in the time units and because there is no consensually accepted theoretical model for determining meaningful periods for study. Neugarten (1977) points out that "age itself is an empty variable, for it is not merely the passage of time, but the various biological and social events that occur with the passage of time that have relevance for personality change" (p. 633). She distinguishes between life time (chronological age), social time (structuring by different societies of age periods with their concomitant psychological demands), historical time, and psychological time (subjective time). She argues for designing longitudinal personality research in terms of the impact of major life events and the transition associated with developmental tasks.

Personality variables might be differentially susceptible to external influences; thus certain variables might be more likely than others to exhibit change. It is important that longitudinal reports not overgeneralize about stability and change in personality based on a sampling of a subset of variables; instead they should qualify their interpretations in terms of the nature of the variables studied.

There is no basis for assuming that the different instruments or measurement procedures used in longitudinal assessments of personality will yield equivalent information. On the contrary, some of the inconsistent or conflicting findings could be reasonably explained in terms of variations in assessment procedures. Block (1977) has discussed the ways that different classes of data, categories originally outlined by Cattell, affect the likelihood of obtaining positive longitudinal findings concerning the stability of personality. Block designates these classes O-, S-, and T-data. O-data involve summary evaluations made by an observer, S-data are based on the individual's judgment of his own personal characteristics, and T-data are derived from standardized, objective tests or experiments.

Block (1977) reviews several longitudinal studies to determine the relative effectiveness of these types of data or assessment procedures for identifying longitudinal relationships. For personality variables he concludes that O- and S-data yield stronger and more consistent findings than T-data. Block attributes Mischel's negative evaluation of longitudinal studies of personality partly to the fact that in his review he relied heavily on studies consisting of T-data.

Longitudinal findings on stability or change are occasionally discussed as if they represent a discovery of an invariant and irrevocable developmental truth. Thus, for example, if a study demonstrates stability for individual differences on "aggressive behavior" it is tempting to proclaim that aggression is stable (as an absolute phenomenon) without considering the relative nature of this finding and all the contingent and contextual factors that might alter or dilute it. Longitudinal findings such as these should be viewed not as conclusive facts but as information that, when interpreted or examined in the context of the life events and prevailing conditions for the subjects being studied, could enhance a developmental theory of personality. Much of the stability that is observed is probably a function of the individual's living in a stable environment while maintaining a psychological equilibrium. However, a crisis or a major change in environment (milieu) could dramatically alter a personality and could affect certain patterns of behavior more than others. Furthermore, some individuals might be more susceptible to change than others. If a behavior pattern is serving a strong protective function in maintaining the psychological well-being of an individual, the individual may resist relinquishing this behavior pattern even when there is strong pressure to change. Furthermore, individuals who exhibit attributes that are highly approved of might be expected to have little incentive to change, whereas those who have attributes that are viewed negatively might be more motivated to change. Thus stability or change in personality is not necessarily an inherent aspect of development but is influenced by the prevailing psychosocial conditions. Although stability coefficients are a summary statistic, much variability usually remains as to whether stability or change happens to be the case for the individual.

Some of the investigators who have conducted longitudinal research have observed differences among their subjects in stability of various personality variables (Block, 1977; Murphy, 1964; Clausen, 1964). Daryl Bem and Andrea Allen (1974) have shown, in addition, that there are individual differences in cross-sectional consistency. Block (1977) has utilized this observation in his analyses by comparing subjects who are stable over time with those who are not. John Clausen (1964), based on his observations of subjects in the Oakland Growth Study, states that "certain individuals show marked change because of the development both of the individual's resources and of unexpected contingencies in the environment. Such contingencies led to the crystallizations of new goals and self-images for some subjects and the dissolution of goals for others" (p. 169).

The observation that certain individuals exhibit personality consistency for different variables and others do not offers an opportunity for advancing developmental theory by identifying and explicating the contingencies that contribute to stability or change. Such a strategy goes beyond simple description by providing a further understanding of these phenomena and thus for gaining greater insight into the nature of personality development. The challenge then is to identify variables that can predict which individuals might show stability or instability for particular personality attributes and to determine the functional basis behind this differential stability. Variables used to classify subjects into groups that might show different patterns of behavior or consistency in response to a set of conditions have been referred to as moderator variables by Michael Wallach and Nathan Kogan (1965). These investigators have used moderator variables to great advantage in their cross-situational studies of risk-taking behavior. Moderator variables have also been used in several longitudinal studies of personality. Some examples are studies showing different patterns of personality consistency for males and females (Kagan and Moss, 1962), consistency in early maternal behavior for the better-educated half of a longitudinal sample (Moss and Jones, 1977), and the finding that certain personality attributes were associated with later increases and decreases in IQ scores (Kagan, Sontag, and Baker, 1958). The continued search for moderator variables in longitudinal studies of personality should prove highly useful both for disclosing continuities and stabilities that might otherwise be masked through the pooling of disparate groups and for developing a conceptual framework for understanding longitudinal results.

Theoretical and methodological factors underlying the study of longitudinal stability and change have received increasing consideration (Emmerich, 1964; Block, 1971; Baltes, Reese, and Nesselroade, 1977; Nesselroade and Reese, 1972). Prior to the 1960s longitudinal consistency and change in development were evaluated primarily by studying individuals from a single age group repeatedly over a specified period of time, although Raymond Kuhlen (1940) earlier warned of the risks in generalizing from one cohort sampling. Recent studies and analyses have challenged the utility of using only one cohort, since age-related changes are purported to be confounded with cohort differences. With few exceptions (Martin, 1964; Nesselroade and Baltes, 1974), most of the studies reviewed assessed consistency and change within one cohort.

In search for consistency and change the research questions have mandated the use of certain statistics. Stability was generally evaluated by correlating a particular characteristic at time 1 with the same characteristic at time 2. Change was generally evaluated by comparing means at time 1 with means at time 2. Deviations from these basic statistical approaches have varied in complexity and scope.

A detailed description of the data base, sample characteristics, and methodologies of the major longitudinal studies conducted in the United States that have investigated personality consistency and change is available in Kagan (1964). Included in the major longitudinal studies are hundreds of variables designed to assess personality from infancy to adulthood. Variables vary in (1) the specificity of the unit of analysis, for example, galvanic skin responses versus clinical ratings of personality trait; (2) the degree of inference needed to quantify the variable, for example, observation of overt aggressive behavior versus ratings of hostile motives inferred from interview statements, and (3) the methods used to generate and define the variables, for example, frequencies, rank orderings versus factor scores. These three considerations in the construction of variables, in addition to the vast number of variables, impose a prodigious organizational task on those interested in integrating the findings on longitudinal stability and change in personality throughout the life span. The major longitudinal studies included assessment of many common personality dimensions. For instance, assessment of some aspect of achievement motivation has consistently been included in the major longitudinal studies (Block, 1971; Kagan and Moss, 1962; Kelly, 1955; Martin, 1964; Sears, 1977).

The longitudinal studies on personality included in this review are presented in chronological order. Since some studies cover longer time periods than others, there is some overlap in the chronological ordering of these studies. Figure 11.1 shows the sequence of presentation of the studies reviewed in this chapter and the age periods spanned by

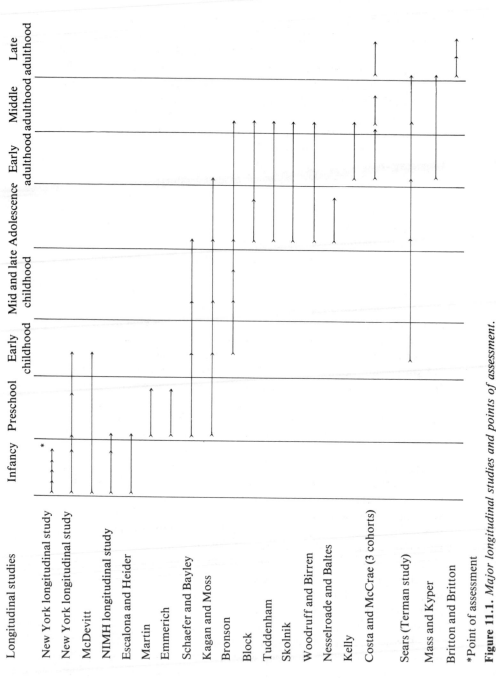

Figure 11.1. *Major longitudinal studies and points of assessment.*

each. The line across age periods indicates the age span of each respective study and the arrowheads indicate ages at which assessments were conducted.

Stylistic differences in behavioral reaction to internal and external stimulation have been regarded as the earliest manifestation of individual differences among infants. Because the emergence of these differences in initial response tendencies precedes any apparent environmental influences, there has been a tendency to regard these behaviors as originating in the biological makeup of the infant. However, since the evidence for constitutional determinism has been indirect, investigators have been cautious in taking a definite position on the origin of these behaviors. The study of these initial reaction patterns is of considerable importance, for they may have a significant influence on personality in later stages of development. Infant research has been dominated by the study of these initial reaction patterns, although little work has been done to trace these patterns longitudinally.

The New York Longitudinal Study is the most extensive study of the temperamental development from infancy through early childhood. The investigators did two analyses of their data, one covering the first two years of life (Thomas et al., 1963) and the other covering years 1-5 (Thomas and Chess, 1977). The primary data of the NYLS came from a series of interviews with the parents that emphasized the child's behavior in specific situations. Special attention was given in the interviews to determining the quality of the child's first contact with a new stimulus and his response to the same stimulus on subsequent exposures, until a consistent long-term pattern of response had emerged. The NYLS group stresses that only behavioral data were used for scoring these interviews. Nine categories of initial characteristics of reactivity (which they label as temperament in their later work) were derived, and each was scored on a 3-point scale for each of the parental interviews. These categories of reactivity or temperament are activity level, rhythmicity, approach or withdrawal, adaptability, intensity of reaction, threshold of responsiveness, quality of mood, distractibility, attention span, and persistence.

The NYLS researchers divided the period from 3 months to 2 years into five periods and studied the stability of the nine temperamental variables across these five periods. The initial assessment was delayed until the infants were about 3 months old, based on the assumption that infant behavior is too variable over the first few months of life to yield reliable data. They analyzed their data in several ways in order to test for stability with each of the methods they used. Each of the methods they used yielded different results. In general, the greatest stability was found for mood, adaptability, approach behavior, and intensity, and the least stability for activity level and distractibility. Seventy-eight of the 80 children included in this analysis maintained a statistically reliable rank pattern over the first two years in four or more of the nine categories. Higher correlations tended to occur for adjacent ages and among the younger age periods.

The follow-up study conducted by the New York Longitudinal Program (1977), which spanned the first five years of life, dealt with the same nine temperamental variables used in the earlier study. Summary scores were derived from the interview ratings for each of the first five years and interyear correlations were calculated for each of the nine variables. The greatest stability obtained from this analysis occurred for activity, rhythmicity, and adaptability and the least for approach or withdrawal, distractibility, and persistence. The first year of the assessment was not predictive of behavior during the fifth year for any of the variables. As the time span between measurement of variables was increased, the number of significant correlations decreased. A number of statistically significant correlations were obtained, but as was the case for the analysis dealing with the first two years of life, the magnitudes of these relations were modest and accounted for little variance. For instance, the mean stability correlations for activity, rhythmicity, and adaptability were 0.26, 0.22, 0.33 respectively. Even though these are the most stable of the nine categories, the correlations were still too low to have any predictive utility for individual cases. There was little consistency in the findings from the two analyses. The only overlap was that adaptability was stable and distractibility unstable in both studies. Results for males and females were not reported separately.

Sean McDevitt (1976) used the nine categories developed by the NYLS to assess the stability of temperament on a sample of 187 children, from infancy through early childhood. Rather than rely on personal interviews with the parents he used questionnaires, which he administered to the mothers through a home mailing. The questionnaires were filled out twice, once when the child was 4-8 months old and again when these children were 3-7 years of age. Different versions of the questionnaire (Carey, 1970; McDevitt and Carey, 1979) were developed for the infancy and childhood assessments so that the questions that were asked of the mothers could be designed to be appropriate to the age of the child. The sample at the 3-7 year evaluation was dichotomized into more homogeneous age groupings of 3-5 and 5-7, and the infancy temperament scores were related to the temperament scores at each of these two childhood assessments. There was low to moderate stability from infancy to the 3-5 year age period for activity level, adaptability, threshold, and intensity for both sexes. Approach-withdrawal and mood were stable only for males, and rhythmicity was stable only for females over these years. The stability coefficients dropped considerably when predicting from infancy to the 5-7 year age periods. Over this time span activity level was moderately stable and persistence and mood slightly stable for males, whereas none of these stability coefficients was statistically significant for the female sample. As in the case of most longitudinal reports, even the correlations that were statistically significant were of insufficient magnitude to justify predictive statements about individual cases.

McDevitt further analyzed his data according to the model suggested by Emmerich (1966) in which two types of constancy are explored: continuity, in which behavior retains similar meaning at different stages, and stability, which reflects constancy in individual differences. McDevitt evaluated continuity by factor analyzing the questionnaire data at 4-8 months, 3-5 years, and 5-7 years of age. He extracted four factors at each of the three age periods studied and found that a sociability-adaptability and a vigor-intensity factor showed continuity from infancy to the 3-5 period and that sociability-approval, vigor-approach, and vigor-intensity factor pairs reflected continuity from infancy to the 5-7 year interval. The analysis of the infancy to 3-5 period revealed a correspondence between the continuity and stability findings, but for the longitudinal results dealing with the 5-7 age group there were instances of stability-continuity and stability-discontinuity. The stability discontinuity findings are an example of what Kagan refers to as heterotypic relations.

A longitudinal program recently carried out at the National Institute of Mental Health (NIMH) (Halverson, Moss, and Jones, 1977; Moss and Jones, 1977; Yang and Moss, 1978) focused on the determinants and stability of social and temperamental variables over the early years of life. In this program families were studied longitudinally, at different developmental stages, in order to evaluate the convergence of environmental and biological factors in determining child behavior. This longitudinal program included a preliminary series of short-term, delimited adjunct studies, in preparation for the study of a primary longitudinal cohort. The study of the primary cohort has only recently been completed. Data were collected at four developmental stages in order to assess the respective contribution of environmental and biological factors in the ontogeny of behavior. The prospective parents were studied early in the marriage (prior to the birth of the infant) to determine the psychological environment they were likely to provide for their child, and infants born to these parents were studied at the newborn stage to evaluate their initial response tendencies (biological makeup) before there was any real opportunity for parental influences. Studies of mother-infant interaction at 3 months and child behavior in a nursery school at 3 years served as criterion phases to evaluate the separate and conjoint effects of probable environmental influences, based on parental characteristics of the couple and the biological predisposition (temperament, tempo, and the like) of the child, as judged from the newborn assessment. The marriage data was collected at the newlywed stage and consisted of a series of interviews, questionnaires, and experimental conflict situations. The newborn data were collected at 2 days of age and consisted of 5 hours of autonomic recordings during undisturbed periods and during 1 hour of behavioral testing. When factor analyzed, these data yielded three stable dimensions: reactivity-irritability, maturity, and reflexive and discriminative sucking. The 3-month mother-infant study consisted of 12 hours of home observations during which behaviors were coded and rated; when factor analyzed, these data yielded three dimensions for males (tonic-active, social, and clarity) and four for females (active-social, tonic, positive vocalizations, and clarity). The 3-year-old data were based on time sampling of behaviors from observations in a 4-week research nursery school. The four factors derived from these data were general activity level, impulsive behavior, positive social interaction, and assertive "busy" play behavior.

The cross-stage findings from this research showed that both biological and environmental factors contribute to the evolution of behavior. In certain instances both factors combined in shaping behavior, whereas in other instances the effects of either the environmental or biological influences seemed prepotent. In general, over the early years of life, biological characteristics seem more predictive for males, whereas environmental forces appear more effective in shaping the behavior of females. Behaviors that seem to be related to temperamental predispositions, such as activity level and tempo, show greater stability and organizational properties for males, whereas variables reflecting social responsiveness toward environmental stimuli seem better able to account for the ontogenesis of female behaviors.

One analysis from this research consisted of relating the newborn and the 3-month factors (Yang and Moss, 1978). The main findings emerging from this analysis was a positive relation between newborn maturity (gestational age, body size, and respiratory rate) and tonic-active behavior (vocalizations, visual alertness, muscle tonus, and kicking and thrashing behavior) at 90 days of age for males. These results were interpreted as reflecting greater endogenous stability for males and suggesting that females may be more reactive than males to environmental influences during early infancy. The 3-month factor scores were also correlated with the 3-year nursery school factors (Halverson, Moss, and Jones, 1977). For males there was substantial predictability between the behaviors at 3 months and the behaviors at 3 years of age. Social behavior for males at 3 months (mutual gazing, vocalizing, and smiling) was positively related at the preschool age to the general activity level and to positive social interaction. On the other hand, the 3-month tonic-active factor was negatively related to the 3-year activity and social behavior factors for males. This result parallels the inversion of intensity findings reported by Bell, Weller, and Waldrop (1971) which found, in an adjunct study of the NIMH program, that newborn measures of high arousal (high respiratory rate, low tactile threshold, quick and intense reaction to interruption of sucking) were related to low-intensity social behavior in the nursery school 2½ years later. A comparable newborn-to-nursery school analysis for the main cohort did not replicate this relation (Halverson and Waldrop, 1976; Yang and Halverson, 1976), so the status of this inversion of intensity finding is uncertain. The findings of Halverson and his co-workers relating the 3-month behavior to the 3-year behavior were interpreted as suggesting that measures of social behavior at 3 years for girls may reflect the influence of both mother and child in an interaction while the scores for boys may reflect relatively more variance attributable to the child's own endogenous tendencies.

Additional evidence for this pattern of differential predictors of early development for males and females comes from an analysis of the ontogeny of vocal behavior carried out as part of the NIMH longitudinal program (1977). Variables associated with the instigation and constancy of infant vocal behavior were studied using data from pregnancy through 3 years of age. The sources of data for this analysis were ratings of maternal interviews, newborn observations, 3-month home and 3-year nursery school observations, and behavior in a vocal conditioning procedure at 3½ months of age. Variables selected for this analysis dealt with probable social and endogenous (biological) contributors to vocal behavior. The primary finding was that both social and endogenous factors were associated with the emergence of vocal behavior but that the social factors tended to be stronger for the females and the endogenous factors more salient for the male infants. As an illustration, male newborn arousal measures were related to vocalizing and the kick-and-thrash scores at 3 months and to vocalizations during vocal conditioning at 3½ months. In addition, the male infants' 3-month vocalization scores in the home were predictive of their vocalizing in the conditioning procedure and in the nursery school approximately 3 years later. On the other hand, for females, a measure of the mother's contingent vocalizations from the home observations and maternal interview ratings on interest in social interaction with infants were strongly related to the girls' vocalizations during vocal conditioning at 3½ months and frequency of vocal behavior and vocabulary scores at 3 years of age in the nursery school. Thus this research provides evidence of both biological and environmental antecedents of vocal behavior, with the variance related to these correlates being different for the sexes. That is, measures of the infant's arousal (activity) level were more predictive of vocal behavior for males, whereas the mother's interest in social behavior toward infants was more effective in contributing to the constancy of vocal behavior and language skills in females.

Further evidence from the NIMH program for different developmental patterns for the sexes was demonstrated from a newborn assessment of minor physical anomalies which were found to be predictive of impulsive, aggressive, and inattentive behavior of 3-year-old boys and predictive of withdrawn and low expressive behavior in girls. In either case these correlates of minor physical anomalies imply that biological factors contribute to the emergence and constancy of certain personality characteristics. Results from other adjunct studies conducted as part of the NIMH longitudinal program were consistent with these sex differences in endogenous and environmental contributors to the constancy of behavior. Female visual behavior (fixation time to two-dimensional stimuli) at 3½ months of age was related to earlier measures of contingent and positive social interactions with the mother (Moss and Robson, 1968), whereas visual behavior for the males at 3½ months was related to the amount of time they spent at an optimal level of arousal for assimilating visual stimuli in their home environment during the early weeks of life (Moss and Robson, 1970). Other adjunct studies included in the NIMH longitudinal program have shown stability for both sexes on measures of arousal and activity level during infancy and over the childhood years. Moderate stability coefficients were obtained on measures of irritability, drowsiness, and vocalizations from 3 weeks to 3 months of life (Moss, 1967), and children observed in a five-week nursery school at 2½ years of age and again in free play at 7½ showed considerable stability over this five-year period of measures of activity level (Halverson and Waldrop, 1976).

Although the NIMH longitudinal project was designed to study child behavior, repeated measurements of the mother made it possible to assess the stability of maternal attitudes and behaviors. Stability was found for maternal attitudes across early marriage, pregnancy, and to the time that the children were infants and 3-year-olds in the nursery school. That is, women who expressed positive attitudes toward infants and toward the maternal role early in their marital careers continued to express similar attitudes and behaviors consistent with these attitudes through the time that their children were at the preschool stage. Social class appeared to be a powerful moderator variable in identifying the constancy of maternal behavior; much stronger relations were found across stages for mothers who formed the upper half of the educational distribution of the sample (Moss and Jones, 1977). In one analysis maternal behaviors toward both first-born and second-born infants were measured when the children reached 3 months of age (Jacobs and Moss, 1976). Mothers spent significantly less time in social, affectionate, and caretaking interactions with their second-born children than they had with their firstborns, although they still exhibited a high level of stability in these maternal behaviors toward their two infants, whose average age difference was about two years. As an illustration, mothers kissed their second-born infants substantially less frequently than the first-borns ($t = 3.70$, p less than 0.001). Yet the stability coefficient for this variable with first-borns and second-borns was 0.72 (p less than 0.001). Ordinarily this type of finding would be regarded as an example of discontinuity with high stability. However, discontinuity is usually interpreted as a reflection of reorganization of behavior or decreased salience of a developmental function because of a shift in the developmental appropriateness of that behavior. But regarding this type of maternal change as evidence of discontinuity seems enigmatic, since maternal affection seems relevant to maternal behavior with all offspring. A corollary of this finding might be that not all instances of change are evidence for discontinuity.

Sibylle Escalona and Grace Heider (1959) predicted personality characteristics of preschool children from observations made when these children were between 4 and 32 weeks of age. Descriptive summary data were available on 31 children at both infancy and at the preschool period from two separate studies conducted with this sample at the Menninger Foundation. One of the investigators read through detailed descriptive accounts of each infant's behavior and then, based on subjective impressions, attempted to predict personality characteristics approximately 2½ to 5 years later. The accuracy of the infant predictions was then checked against the descriptive information collected on these subjects from the preschool study. These predictions did not involve phenotypic continuities but consisted of clinical judgments about the early origins of later complex behavior patterns.

Some of these predictions were made from the behavior of children as young as 4 weeks of age. About two-thirds of the total of 882 predictions were judged correct. It is not possible to determine the chance level of accuracy for these predictions, so it is difficult to evaluate the significance of the findings. The predictions were classified into 44 content areas, and the success rates of the predictions ranged from 38% to 95%. The most successful predictions were made for sex role behavior, interest patterns, motor functioning, activity pattern, and expressive behavior, and the lowest level of confirmation was obtained for predictions concerning response to unfamiliar situations, achievement needs and competitiveness, relationship with mother, shyness, response to frustration, and basic attitudes toward themselves and the world. Thus predictions seemed more successful for stylistic characteristics and less successful for variables pertaining to complex psychological states and interpersonal behavior. The variability in predictive success among the children was considerable, ranging from 33% to 92%. The infant predictive descriptions and the preschool outcome data were both rated on a series of items, and correlations between these two sets of ratings were computed for each child. These ipsative correlations ranged from 0.67 to -0.27 with a median correlation of 0.47, again reflecting considerable variability in predictive success for different children. This evidence of variability among subjects in the continuity of behaviors is consistent with the findings of other longitudinal studies. For this research, however, there is some reason to assume that methodological factors contributed to the observed variability. This research illustrates the use of the clinical method in the longitudinal study of personality. Unfortunately, the highly private and idiosyncratic procedure of relying on subjective impressions for making the predictions does not provide sufficient information for identifying the conceptual basis for the predictions or the findings.

The evidence for stability over the early years of life is modest. The magnitude of stability coefficients over this period tends to be from low to moderate, with many instances of contradictory or negative findings. As the time interval between measurements during infancy increases, many of the reported stabilities diminish. One conclusion that could be drawn from these sparse findings is that behavior remains plastic during the early years and that infants are not captives of crystallized behavior patterns. On the other hand, exceedingly difficult methodological problems are associated with attempting to investigate complex psychological phenomena during infancy, and the sparsity of findings could be a function of the lack of suitable methodologies for studying personality variables during this period. Much of the data on infant behavior patterns has come from qualitative reports and information provided by untrained observers (parents).

The developmental course and significance of activity level has particularly interested investigators of infancy and early childhood. Activity level may receive special attention because this variable is relatively easy to measure, is evident in the behavior of children at all ages (so that it can readily be studied longitudinally), and because it seems theoretically related to important dimensions of personality (extraversion-intraversion, assertiveness, social interactions, and tractability). The stability data concerning activity level are somewhat inconsistent and ambiguous during the early years, although there is some evidence for stability of this behavior, from infancy to early childhood, from studies in which the data are based on direct observations of behavior. The use of sex as a moderator variable appears to be important in identifying stabilities during the early years. Longitudinal investigations of this age period have limited themselves to studying links with contiguous developmental periods, so that there are no existing data that attempt to connect characteristics in infancy to personality variables at middle childhood or older.

The preschool period is the time at which personality variables are first conceptualized and defined in terms that are consonant with their descriptions throughout the rest of the life span. Of course, there is considerable inconsistency in the prominence with which specific variables are emphasized in the study of different developmental stages. This seems to be a function of variations in the behavioral salience of different variables at different age periods and of variations in the life circumstances, making certain variables more or less functional at different stages.

Nursery school settings provide the opportunity for incorporating two desirable features into a developmental study: first, a short-term longitudinal perspective because children are usually enrolled for two to three years; second the study of multiple cohorts because new children are enrolling each year. Both design features were incorporated into the Purdue Longitudinal Study by following four preschool cohorts for two years. Martin (1964) assessed both normative and ipsative stability and change in a sample of 53 children when they were between 2 and 5 years of age. Observations of free play were used to time-sample frequencies of dependency, nurturance, aggression, control dominance, autonomous achievement, avoidance-withdrawal, and friendship-affiliation behavior. Assessments were made for each of four consecutive semesters. Normative findings showed that in all four cohorts the mean frequency of these behaviors tended to increase with time and the increases became more apparent with time. In addition, the degree of stability in all four cohorts, based on rank-order correlations, was impressive. Children tended to manifest the same relative amount of aggression and control-dominance over two years, and three of the four cohorts also showed evidence of stability on dependency, autonomous achievement, and friendship-affiliation behaviors. Only nurturance and avoidance-withdrawal showed no evidence of stability.

Ipsative longitudinal trends were also assessed through the study of continuity and change in behavior profiles. The behavior profiles were derived by calculating the proportion of each behavior from the total frequency of all behaviors for each child. This procedure made it possible to characterize each child in terms of the relative salience of the various behaviors that were sampled. The results revealed highly significant, well-articulated individual behavior profiles among the children in the sample. Moreover, these individual profiles proved highly stable, since only 9 of the 53 children showed a significant change in their behavior profile over the two-year period of the study. Correlation coefficients summarizing the stability of each child's behavior profile over the two-year period ranged from 0.64 to 0.97. The normative and ipsative stability observed for this sample is impressive during a period "in the life span when instrumental behavior is demonstrable, changing in response to modifications in individual capabilities and social expectations" (Martin, 1964, p. 465). On the other hand, these results might be partially attributable to the short term of the study, which spanned only one developmental period within which there may be less reordering on a particular dimension than if stabilities were assessed across contiguous or noncontiguous developmental stages.

Whereas most investigators use the terms *continuity* and *stability* interchangeably, Emmerich (1964, 1968) defines them differently. He uses continuity-discontinuity to describe whether a particular behavior or dimension continues to characterize psychological functioning at different ages. In this context discontinuity would be equivalent to change. Stability on the other hand, is used as it is by other investigators, to signify whether an individual retains the same position in relation to others on a dimension over time. Utilizing the Purdue Longitudinal sample, Emmerich sought to study the combined effects of continuity and stability over a two-year period (four semesters) for a set of 31 social behaviors. He factor analyzed time-sampled scores on these behaviors for the same children in each of four consecutive semesters and then used the resulting factors to develop three bipolar scales: (1) interpersonal versus impersonal orientation (similar to an extraversion-introversion dimension), (2) positive versus negative attitude (similar to an evaluation dimension), (3) active versus passive mode (similar to a potency or activity dimension).

The degree to which each dimension continued to account for behavioral variance across the four semesters was interpreted as reflecting the continuity or discontinuity of that dimension. By this criterion the positive-negative attitude dimension showed discontinuity (declined in variance accounted for) whereas the other two dimensions manifested persistent continuity over the two-year period. In addition, the interpersonal-impersonal orientation was highly stable over the four semesters. Emmerich concluded that an interpersonal-impersonal orientation, a dimension similar to introversion-extraversion, is a fundamental organizer of social behavior during the preschool years.

There was also evidence for a developmental transformation "in which there is change of meaning over time on factors which also maintain the ordering of individual differences in the network" (Emmerich, 1964, p. 329). Interpersonal children who tended to be negative in attitude during the first year of nursery school became poised, while impersonal children who tended to be positive in attitude became socially insecure. Despite the stability of behavior in the sample as a whole (Martin, 1964), the transformation of behavior, from negative attitude to poised behavior, attests to the qualitative changes that occur even within brief developmental periods.

In addition to assessing stability of child behaviors from infancy to adolescence, Earl Schaefer and Nancy Bayley (1960, 1963) also studied the relation of mothers' behavior to the social and emotional development of their children. Observations of maternal behavior during infancy, interviews with the mother when the children were 9 to 14, and ratings of child behavior from infancy to adolescence formed the data base. The sample included mothers and children (27 boys and 27 girls) who were participants in the Berkeley Growth Study.

Schaefer and Bayley (1960) addressed the question whether nurturant behavior of mothers toward their infants is a predictor of similar behavior toward their children during preadolescence. A two-dimensional organization of maternal behavior was identified. The first dimension, love versus hostility, included such variables as cooperativeness, positive evaluation of the child, egalitarianism, expression of affection, ignoring, irritability, punishment, punitiveness, perception of the child as a burden, use of fear to control the child, strictness, positive mother-child relationship, and rejection of the homemaking role. Correlations between the scales at infancy and preadolescence showed that the love versus hostility dimension of maternal behavior was stable over time ($r = 0.68$) and was consistent toward both sexes. The second dimension, autonomy versus control, included autonomy, excessive contact, intrusiveness, and fostering dependency. Autonomy versus control in maternal behavior was not stable from infancy to preadolescence for the sexes combined or for boys, but for girls positive and significant correlations in maternal behavior were found between the two periods.

Behavior ratings on the children included ratings for four age periods; 10-36 months (infancy), 27-96 months (early childhood), 9-12 years (late childhood), and 12-18 years (adolescence) to determine both short- (within age periods) and long-term (between age periods) consistency of child behavior patterns. Only the long-term trends are reviewed. The ratings for each age period were organized in circumplex order, that is, variables were arranged in sequence according to the proportion of shared variance within each developmental period.

For boys, rapidity and activity, behaviors assumed to be related to extraversion and responsiveness to persons during infancy, were negatively correlated with task-oriented behaviors during early and late childhood. These infant behaviors were not predictive of social or emotional behavior during adolescence. For girls, rapidity and activity during infancy were not related to preschool behavior but were negatively correlated with task-oriented behaviors in late childhood and with introverted behavior at adolescence and positively correlated with extraverted, hostile behavior at adolescence. Happy, calm, and positive behaviors of girls during infancy showed few correlations with later behavior; for boys, happy, calm and positive behavior during preschool was positively correlated with task-oriented behaviors during early and late childhood.

Behavior ratings during early childhood were related to behavior ratings during late childhood, especially for boys. Boys showed high stability on friendliness and cooperativeness and behaviors pertinent to test taking such as attentiveness. There were few significant correlations between behavior ratings at preschool and adolescence. The correlations were lower for girls than for boys.

Behavior ratings of friendliness during early childhood were positively related to friendly social and independent behavior during adolescence and negatively related to timid and reserved behavior for boys. The rating for girls at early childhood and adolescence did not reveal a pattern of consistency. On the other hand, correlations between ratings made at late childhood and adolescence were high for the girls but not for the boys. That is, ratings of not shy, friendly, cooperative, interested, exerts efforts, attentive, and not being distractible were consistent across these age periods for girls.

Schaefer and Bayley (1963) point out that three general trends can be gleaned from the large number of findings between the four developmental periods. The short-term behavior ratings showed inconsistency during the early period, consistency during latency, and inconsistency during adolescence. Second, the correlations were higher for contiguous than for noncontiguous periods of development. Third, consistency of behavior did not emerge until early childhood for both social and task-oriented behavior. The pattern of consistency evolved somewhat earlier in this sample than in the Fels sample.

Personality development from birth through adulthood was the focus of the longitudinal project conducted at the Fels Research Institute (Kagan and Moss, 1962). Eighty-nine white children were included in the study. Visits to the homes of the participants were made twice yearly from birth until the children were 6, and narrative summaries described the child's behavior and experiences. Each child when between 2½-6 years of age participated in the Fels experimental nursery school. A summary of the child's behavior and a series of personality ratings were made, based on observations of the child during each of the nursery school sessions. The children also attended the Fels Day Camp each year when they were 6-12 years, and summaries of the child's behavior and personality ratings were made that were similar to the nursery school ratings. Interviews were conducted with many of the subjects when they were 6-12 and during adolescence. Seventy-one of the subjects, when they were young adults, participated in an intensive assessment program consisting of five hours of interviews and a battery of personality tests. Personality ratings were made from tape recordings of these interviews.

The primary data for the Fels study consisted of two sets of correlations derived from ratings of personality variables. A set of variables relevant to the first 14 years of life (child variables) was defined. The longitudinal material for the childhood years was divided into four age periods: 0-3 (infancy), 3-6 (preschool), 6-10 (middle childhood), and 10-14 (early adolescence). A second set of variables, similar to the child variables, were derived from adult interviews. The primary goal of the research was to investigate stability of behavior from childhood through early adulthood.

In the Fels study passive and dependent behavior in childhood was assessed on the following variables: passive reaction to frustration, dependency on female adults, independence, and anxiety over loss of nurturance. Passivity was highly stable for boys and girls over the first ten years of life, and the greatest degree of stability was evidenced in contiguous age periods. A dependent orientation to adults showed a moderate degree of stability over the first ten years of life. Independence was stable for females over the eleven-year span from 3 to 14 while independence was stable for males only from middle childhood to adolescence.

Passive and dependent variables for the adult period included dependency on love object, dependency on parents, dependency on parent substitute figures and friends, withdrawal from stressful situations, conflict over dependency, and seeking dependent gratifications in vocational choice. Girls who were dependent on female adults during middle childhood established a dependent and passive relationship with males during adulthood. Dependency during the childhood years in boys was not predictive of dependency on love object during adulthood.

Dependency on parents during adulthood followed a pattern similar to dependency on love object. Girls who were passive and dependent during middle childhood and adolescence were dependent on their families during adulthood. The middle childhood correlations were only suggestive, whereas the adolescent to adulthood correlations provided evidence of moderate stability for these variables. Dependency on friends during adulthood was not consistently related to similar behaviors during childhood for women. The correlations reversed directions for females. That is, the independent school girl became dependent on friends in adulthood. The dependent male during adolescence exhibited emotional dependence toward friends as an adult.

Withdrawal from stressful situations, conflict over dependency, and dependency in vocational choice (for example, job security versus avoidance of job risk) showed sex differences in stability. For women, but not men, passivity and dependency during middle childhood was a reliable predictor of withdrawal from stress, of minimal conflict over dependency, and of concern for job security in adult women.

In summary, the stability of passive and dependent behaviors appears to be related to cultural expectations for independence in males and females. Independence and dependency are both tolerated in females, and in the absence of negation of either type of behavior, consistency in early behavior persists into adulthood. The cultural expectation of independence for males may contribute to the instability of early patterns of passivity and dependency.

Aggression in the Fels study referred to a response aimed at inflicting psychological or physical injury to a person or person surrogate (Kagan and Moss, 1962). Aggression variables included aggression to mother, physical aggression to peers, indirect aggression to peers, behavioral disorganization (temper tantrums, crying, or destructive behavior, conformity to adults, dominance to peers, and competitiveness).

Childhood aggression to mother showed moderate stability from preschool to middle childhood and from childhood to adolescence. In contrast, physical aggression to peers was highly stable over the first ten years of life. Indirect aggression to peers, such as verbal attacks, was stable from the preschool years through adolescence. Behavioral disorganization during the first three years of life showed no relationship with similar behavior during the subsequent eleven years. Behavioral disorganization was stable, however, for boys across the preschool, middle childhood, and adolescent years. Conformity to authority was stable between the contiguous preschool and school-age periods but was unstable over the longer period 3-14 years of age. Dominance of peers and a competitive attitude were both stable over the span from preschool to adolescence.

Aggression in adulthood was defined as the individual's tendency to retaliate with direct verbal aggression or blatant resistance, ease of anger arousal, competitive behavior, aggressive conflict, and criticism of parents. Aggression was more stable for males than for females from childhood to adulthood. Aggression to mother, behavioral disorganization, and dominance during middle childhood and adolescence predicted adult retaliation for men but not for women. Peer-directed aggression during childhood did not predict retaliation in adult men. For women, there was a negative relationship between peer aggression during childhood and adult aggressive behavior. Girls who were physically assaultive with peers until age 6 were the least likely to be retaliatory as adults.

Ease of anger arousal in adulthood was associated with aggression to mother and behavior disorganization during middle childhood and adolescence for men but not for women. In males, competitiveness during adulthood, a socially effective modality for expressing hostility, was also associated with aggression to mother, behavioral disorganization, and both direct and indirect aggression to peers. Competitiveness during middle childhood predicted adult female competitive behavior.

Aggressive conflict during adulthood was related to absence of aggression to mother and to a high degree of conformity during middle childhood for both men and women. Behavioral disorganization during childhood and adolescence was also negatively related to adult anxiety and repression but only for men. A conforming and nonaggressive attitude toward mother and adults during the early years remained with the individual through young adulthood and was predictive of anger, repression, and inhibition of aggression.

In summary, aggression was more stable for males than for females from childhood to adulthood. The absence of stability in aggression for females may be a result of more intense aggressive conflict because aggressive behavior in girls is punished more consistently than similar behavior in males.

Achievement was defined in the Fels study as "behavior aimed at satisfaction of an internal standard of excellence" (Kagan and Moss, 1962, p. 120). The goal of recognition behavior was assumed to be some positive reaction from other people or a social acknowledgment of the individual's skills. Achievement and recognition during childhood were rated by the following variables: general achievement-mastery behavior, intellectual achievement, mechanical achievement, athletic achievement, recognition behavior, competitiveness, expectancy of task failure, general withdrawal, and withdrawal from task situations.

Achievement behavior during the preschool period was associated with intellectual achievement behavior during the adolescent period for both sexes. Mechanical achievement was more stable than athletic achievement particularly from middle childhood to adolescence. Achievement during the first three years of life was unrelated to achievement behavior during later periods.

Intellectual achievement from the preschool and middle childhood periods to adolescence was more stable than athletic or mechanical achievement over comparable periods. Competitiveness was moderately stable during childhood. Fear of failure was stable from 6 to 14 while withdrawal from potential failure situations was stable only for girls. In summary, all the achievement behaviors were relatively stable during the childhood years.

Achievement and recognition behavior in adults was highly related to achievement behavior at age 10 and was equally stable for both sexes. Similarly, achievement at age 10 and concern with intellectual competence during adolescence were highly predictive of concern with intellectual competence during adulthood. Adult fear of failure was negatively related (moderately) to achievement behavior during middle childhood for both males and females; however, the relationship between withdrawal in adulthood and achievement, fear of failure, or withdrawal in childhood were related for women but negligible for men.

In general, achievement by age 10 was a good predictor of adult achievement behavior for males and females. Intellectual achievement showed the highest stability over time, whereas involvement in athletics during childhood was unrelated to adult achievement.

Heterosexual behavior and sex role interests were assessed in the

Fels study in relation to social interaction with members of the opposite sex and adoption of traditional sex-typed interests and behavior. Heterosexual interaction was aimed at evaluating the frequency and quality of interaction with members of the opposite sex during middle childhood and adolescence. Opposite sex role activity was defined in the Fels study by the child's interest in the practice of activities that are traditionally associated with the opposite sex. Interest in athletics, mechanical objects, and highly competitive activities were regarded as masculine interests, whereas involvement in gardening, music, cooking, and noncompetitive activities were viewed as feminine interests.

Amount of contact with opposite sex peers during middle childhood was not predictive of similar behavior during adolescence. The degree to which sex role activity remained masculine or feminine was stable throughout the preschool and adolescent period. That is, boys and girls who exhibited a penchant for either traditionally masculine or feminine activities during the preschool years continued to exhibit these preferences into the adolescent years.

During adulthood, the interview variables relevant to sexuality assessed erotic behavior and anxiety over sexuality, as well as opposite sex activities. Boys who avoided dating during adolescence were less likely to establish intimate heterosexual relationships or engage in erotic activity during adulthood. Boys who failed to adopt masculine behavior during the preschool or middle childhood period demonstrated high sex anxiety in adulthood. Heterosexual interaction and opposite sex activity during childhood were not predictive of erotic behavior and anxiety over sexuality at adulthood for females. Opposite sex interests, however, were stable from childhood to adulthood for both sexes, with this relation being greater for males.

Furthermore, the sex role content of the boys' play as early as age 3 was predictive of adult sex role interests. That is, involvement in mechanical, gross motor, and aggressive games were predictive of sex role activities twenty years later. Sex role interests during childhood were not related to adult sexual anxiety in females.

In general, heterosexual behavior was unstable within childhood while sex role interests were stable during childhood and were predictive of adult heterosexuality, particularly for males. Failure to adopt masculine behavior during childhood predicted high sexual anxiety in adult males. Fairly rigid behavior patterns are dictated for males by traditional sex role stereotypes which, if not adopted early, lead to anxiety about sexuality. Females are allowed more flexibility in their appropriate sex role behavior patterns throughout child and adulthood.

Social interaction anxiety, or the perception of threat in interpersonal situations, was evaluated in relation to the degree of spontaneity or inhibition that accompanies interaction with others. During childhood, social anxiety was assessed on anxiety in novel situations, social spontaneity, expectancy of peer rejection, and withdrawal from social interaction. Situational fear and inhibition (anxiety with the Fels visitor and in novel situations) during the first six years of life were moderately stable for boys but not for girls. Social spontaneity (the inverse of social anxiety) showed moderate stability for boys over the first ten years and for girls over the first six years while spontaneity was stable for both sexes after age 10. Expectancy of rejection, which was rated only at 6-10 and 10-14, was stable across these periods for boys and girls.

Social interaction anxiety during adulthood was assessed by inhibition in social situations or the degree to which an individual approached interaction with strangers with caution and apprehension due to expectancy of rejection. For boys, the beginnings of anxiety in adulthood were suggestive during early childhood, while for girls, this relationship did not emerge until middle childhood. That is, unspontaneous behavior and social withdrawal during middle childhood and adolescence were predictive of adult social anxiety.

Physical harm anxiety was rated during the childhood period on anxiety over bodily harm, irrational fears, and avoidance of dangerous activity. Fear of bodily harm was relatively stable over the first ten years of life. Fear of harm during the preschool years was predictive of avoidance of potentially dangerous activities during adolescence. Presence of irrational fears was more stable for girls, whereas avoidance of dangerous activities was more stable for boys. There were no specific interview variables that assessed physical harm anxiety in adulthood.

Nurturance compulsivity, hyperkinetic behavior, and introspectiveness were also evaluated in the Fels study during the childhood and adult period. Nurturance was not stable across any of the childhood periods, and no specific adult interview variable was analogous to the childhood nurturance variable. Compulsivity evaluated children's concern with neatness, cleanliness, order in their environment, and preciseness in working with materials. Compulsive habits were stable over all the childhood periods for boys. For girls, compulsivity was stable only from preschool to middle childhood and from middle childhood to adolescence. Compulsive habits in childhood were not related to caution or compulsivity in adulthood.

Hyperkinetic behavior was used to describe children unable to inhibit impulse to action, especially aggressive outbursts. Hyperkinetic behavior was stable across the preschool, middle childhood, and adolescent years, and no specific interview variables evaluated hyperkinesis in adulthood.

The variable introspectiveness described the individual's ability and willingness to discuss motives, goals, conflicts, and anxiety during interviews by the Fels staff. Introspectiveness was stable from adolescence to adulthood. Thus compulsivity and hyperactivity were stable during childhood, while only introspectiveness was predictive of a similar tendency during adulthood.

Longitudinal personality research has emphasized correlations in the same behavior over several time periods. This type of analysis has been referred to as *homotypic* continuity (Kagan, 1971). A second type of analysis, *heterotypic* continuity, assesses the degree to which the overt character of behavior changes over time while individual differences remain stable across different developmental periods. This type of continuity has been interpreted to imply that one continuous disposition underlies each of the different behavioral manifestations and that the developmental function is phenotypically discontinuous but genotypically continuous. Kagan and Howard Moss (1962) suggested that a specific variable might not be predictive of a phenotypically similar behavior in adulthood and yet may be associated with a behavior that was theoretically consistent with the early behavior. These conceptually related adult responses are viewed as derivatives of early behavior. In the Fels study selected childhood variables were correlated with adult variables to determine the degree to which childhood behavior was predictive of genotypically similar behavior in adulthood. Derivatives of passivity and dependency, aggression, and achievement during childhood were evaluated.

Passivity among males during at least one childhood period was predictive of noncompetitiveness, nonmasculine interests, avoidance of sexual behavior, and apprehension in social situations. Passivity among girls during middle childhood predicted low dependency conflict, noncompetitiveness, feminine interests, and repression of sexual motives in adulthood. Dependency during childhood, in contrast to passivity, was less predictive of adult behavior.

Aggression during childhood was predictive of a similar constellation of behaviors in adulthood for males but was predictive of more derivative behaviors in adulthood for females. Boys who were aggressive toward their mother during the first ten years of life were aggressive as adults and adopted traditional masculine attributes. Girls who were aggressive toward their mother became women with a high fear of failure, feminine sex role interests, and low strivings for social recognition. Verbal aggression to peers, among boys, was predictive of adult behavior characterized by frequent sexual episodes, low sexual anxiety, and competitiveness. Peer-directed aggression among girls predicted ease of anger arousal and low sex anxiety in adulthood. Behavioral disorganization in middle childhood among boys predicted overt aggression in adult males, while behavioral disorganization among girls was predictive of intellectual mastery, dependency conflict, and masculine interests.

Derivatives of achievement behavior were noted in both sexes. Among the Fels women achievement during childhood was associated with a cluster of behaviors outside the achievement domain. Girls who were achievement oriented became adults who were counterphobic in problem situations, competitive, masculine in their interests, and self-confident.

An alternative approach to evaluation of heterotypic continuities was used in a reanalysis of the Fels data (Ryder, 1967). By means of principal axes and canonical correlation, two clusters of attributes that related childhood variables to those of adolescence and adulthood were identified. Indirect competitiveness and task persistence during childhood and adolescence were related to adult achievement orientation. Furthermore, direct aggression, physical adventurousness, sociability, and nonconformity to adult standards in childhood were related to adult sexual behavior. Thus one dimension between childhood and adulthood is competitiveness and achievement orientation, and the other is adventurousness, ease in social relationships, and sexual activity.

In summary, the overt character of passivity and dependency, aggression, and achievement changed from childhood to adulthood, but these behaviors were predictive of socially acceptable derivative behaviors in adulthood. This trend is particularly evident in behavior associated with traditional definitions of sex roles for both sexes. Behavior that is incongruent with traditional sex roles, such as passivity in males, is expressed in a socially acceptable behavior in adulthood, such as noncompetitiveness. Unfortunately, a theoretical framework for conceptualizing heterotypic continuity has not been articulated; thus it is difficult to interpret the many statistical relationships found among clusters of variables across different developmental periods.

Although the stability of the major socialization variables—passivity and dependency, aggression, achievement, and sexuality—varied across the childhood periods and from childhood to adulthood, a pattern of impressive stabilities emerged, mainly by middle childhood. This pattern relates to cultural expectations held for appropriate sex role behavior. If a pattern of early childhood behavior is consistent with cultural expectations, there is a high probability that the behavior will remain stable over time. Passivity, for instance, an acceptable behavior for females but not for males, was stable from childhood to adulthood only for females. Achievement, an acceptable behavior for males and females, was stable for both sexes across contiguous and noncontiguous childhood periods and from childhood to adulthood. Furthermore, assessment of heterotypic development showed that behavior that is incongruent with traditional sex role definitions in childhood may be expressed in adulthood in a socially acceptable behavior.

Longitudinal patterns of behavior were investigated by Wanda Bronson (1966) on a sample of 85 boys and girls who were participants in the Berkeley Guidance Study. Annual personality ratings based on interview material were available for these children when they were between 5 and 16 years of age. These ratings were summarized into four age groupings (5-7, 8-10, 11-13, and 14-16) and then were analyzed to determine the internal structure of the variables within each group as well as to evaluate the stability of personality over time. The measures were found to cluster into three dimensions: expressiveness versus withdrawal, placidity-controlled versus reactivity, and passivity versus dominance. The first two dimensions were relatively independent of each other whereas the dimension passivity versus dominance tended to overlap with the other two dimensions. Expressiveness-withdrawal was the most stable dimension over the four age periods, with a mean correlation of 0.73 for boys and 0.65 for girls. The other two dimensions showed moderate mean stability coefficients for both sexes, with correlations among age periods ranging between 0.43 and 0.55. These results are consistent with those of other longitudinal research projects which show, as summarized by Schaefer (1964) in his review of consensus findings among longitudinal studies, consistent evidence of long-term stability for "active, expressive, extroverted behavior."

Bronson (1967) carried out a follow-up study with these subjects when they were about 30 years old in order to explore the range of continuity in personality development. This follow-up study utilized for antecedent data the measures on the dimensions of expressiveness versus withdrawal and placidity-controlled versus reactivity that were derived from the four childhood age periods. The adult evaluation consisted of a series of interviews dealing with problems and satisfactions related to coping with life. These adult interviews, which were part of another adolescent-to-adult longitudinal assessment planned by Block, were quantified on the 100-item California Q-set. The expressive dimension at all four childhood periods was significantly associated for males with phenotypically similar adult behavior, that is, they continued to be gregarious, expressive adults. For the males, this childhood dimension was also predictive of adult interview responses indicative of warmth, self-acceptance, and productivity. Expressiveness during the childhood years for the females was also related to similar adult behaviors. That is, the expressive girls were as adults outgoing, talkative, and assertive in interpersonal situations, and they tended to dramatize and be open about their needs and impulses and exhibited a rapid personal tempo. In addition, there was a domineering quality to their adult behavior. Thus for both males and females expressiveness during childhood was related to sociability and a lack of reserve in adulthood. The placid-controlled dimension also showed continuity into the adult years for both sexes. For males this dimension was predictive of overly controlled, inhibited, constricted, rigid, and humorless behavior as adults, whereas for females being placid-controlled as a child was related to calmness, self-satisfaction, openness, dependability, and a smooth comfortable adjustment as an adult. Thus the controlled aspect of this dimension tended to characterize continuities for males, and the placid component was reflected in the continuities for females. For both males and females there was some variation as to which childhood period was predictive of a given adult behavior. For instance, only the placid-controlled versus reactive ratings obtained for the 11-13 age period for females were correlated with their adult measures.

One of the most ambitious and comprehensive longitudinal studies on personality development was carried out by Block (1971). He combined the data from the Oakland Growth Study and the Berkeley Guidance Study in order to assess longitudinal patterns of development from early adolescence to middle adulthood. This sample consisted of 170 cases from these two longitudinal programs. There was reasonably full archival information for these subjects for the junior high and high school period. In addition, Block conducted an extensive (12-hour) interviewing and testing program with his subjects when they were in their mid 30s. This project involved both the normative (nomothetic) and ipsative investigation of continuities and changes among these subjects over three different life periods (junior high, senior high, and middle adulthood). It took about thirty years to collect these data, and the adult assessment and collating of the findings covered another ten-year period.

The Oakland Growth and Berkeley Guidance studies had accumulated an impressive quantity of diverse information on their subjects. However, there were problems of incomplete information and changes in procedures and in conceptual foci over the course of the longitudinal data collection. Block faced the problem of merging the two samples and the problem of quantifying abundant naturalistic data from uncontrolled life situations. A Q-sort multiple-judge rating procedure was chosen (California Q-set) as a means of overcoming these methodological problems. The Q-sort procedure consists of a set of rules for scaling a group of personality-descriptive variables (Q-items) for a particular individual (Block, 1971). Judges assign Q-items into a designated number of categories with a prescribed number of items in each category. At one end of the judgmental continuum are the items most characteristic of the person being described and at the other end are the items least characteristic of that person. The final ordering of the Q-items represents the judge's formulation of the individual's personality. The personality variables for the adult subjects consisted of a modified version of the California Q-set. The adolescent variables consisted of a further modification of the adult Q-set and a second Q-set (interpersonal Q-set) emphasizing interpersonal behaviors of adolescents. From these Q-sorts several hundred items were scaled for each individual in the study. The Q-sort procedure allows for testing changes in the salience (means) and range (standard deviations) of personality attributes over time and permits correlational analyses. Judges, in Q-sorting a subject, employ an ipsative frame of reference. That is, the set of Q-items is ordered by the judge with respect to the comparative salience of these variables for the individual being evaluated. Although each Q-rating was developed ipsatively, within the context of other variables describing a subject, one can treat these ratings in the normative way. Thus normatively treated Q-variables make it possible to compute both correlations and mean comparisons for Q-sorts obtained at different time periods.

The findings from this study often consist of exhaustive listings and detailed reporting of a myriad of facts, emanating from the large number of items used for describing and comparing subjects and from the variety of analyses that were employed. We have attempted to summarize these findings by discussing them in terms of concepts that subsume larger numbers of items and by selecting findings that appear to be representative, salient, and reflective of conceptually cohesive themes. Block has facilitated this summarizing process by factor analyzing the Q-sort results in an attempt to organize and structure the large number of items used to evaluate the subjects.

Personality continuity was based on statistically significant correlations between Q-sort items at different age periods. From junior high to senior high school and from senior high school to adulthood, both males and females showed stability in maintaining an intellectual (cognitive-reflective) orientation toward themselves and their world. Both sexes also showed continuities between the junior high and senior high years in being expressive and responsive and in being effective and comfortable in their interpersonal relations. The males, in addition, exhibited stability over the adolescent years in maintaining a positive attitude about themselves and in their ability to control their own lives. The females, between early and middle adolescence, were stable in their personal adjustment, social sensitivity, inclination to be other directed, and in their sexual interests. From senior high to adulthood the males exhibited great stability with respect to dependability and impulsivity. The females, over this same period, showed evidence of persistence of a dimension reflective of a passive conforming femininity at one end and as expressive-aggressive autonomy at the other end.

Personality changes were based on statistically significant differences in mean level between Q-sort items administered at different age periods. Thus both stability (relative ordering) and change (mean level) may occur for the same item or cluster of items. Changes from junior high to senior high school showed that both the males and females increased in intellectual-reflective concerns, in searching for meaning in life, and in their heterosexual interests. The males, over the adolescent years, also became more self-conscious and outwardly controlled, less dependent, and more self-confident. The females, over the same period, became more cynical, distant, hostile, and less spontaneous and less positive in their interpersonal relations. Between adolescence and adulthood, both the males and the females changed in the direction of becoming more like the adult prototypes in our culture. The males became more integrated and assured in their personal lives, exhibited greater self-control and self-confidence while becoming more serious, stolid, and bland individuals. The males also exhibited a decrease in their need for reassurance and in being concerned about comparisons with others as they reached the adult years. As the female subjects moved from adolescence to adulthood, they showed an increase in culturally conventional femininity (eliciting nurturance, sympathetic, protective, submissive, warm, and less power oriented), became more psychologically minded, exhibited greater social ease and security, became more dependable and less self-centered, and manifested a decreased emphasis on sexuality. Within both the male and female samples subjects tended to become more like one another (showed less variability) for motives that were salient during the adolescent years, for example, interests in physical attractiveness and concern over sexuality.

The correlational analyses provided highly convincing evidence in favor of continuity of personality, particularly between the junior high and senior high years. As an indication of the pervasiveness of the findings in favor of continuity, Block reports that for men and women, respectively, 96% and 89% of the junior high to senior high Q-items were significantly correlated beyond the 0.05 level and 59%, and 60% of the senior high to adult Q-item correlations achieved the 0.05 level of significance.

Block notes that some individuals stabilize their character early whereas others change considerably over the years. That is, stability and change do not occur in a consistent way for all individuals. Psychological, environmental, physiological, and sociohistorical factors may influence the degree to which stability or change in personality characterizes different individuals for different stages in life. Block was interested in determining the variability among individuals in the stability that they exhibited over different age periods and in identifying and determining the influence of moderator variables as factors leading to stability or change for different individuals.

To assess the variability among individuals in their personality consistency over time, Block correlated each subject's Q-sorts between junior high and senior high periods and between the senior high and adult assessments. This resulted in correlations for each individual that reflected the stability of their composite personality picture, as rated from the Q-sort procedure, across these age periods. Block found average across-time correlations of 0.77 and 0.75 for the junior high to senior high interval and 0.56 and 0.54 for the senior high to adult interval for men and women, respectively. This is strong evidence for personality consistency, with higher stabilities for the shorter interval between the two adolescent assessments than for the longer interval between middle adolescence and adulthood. Nonetheless, Block found extreme variation among individuals in the degree of personality consistency exhibited across the age periods studied. Thus the personality consistency correlations from junior high to senior high ranged from -0.02 to 1.00 for different individuals and the correlations from senior high to adulthood ranged from -0.49 to 0.99. Block interprets this extremely wide range of Q-correlations as showing that the high mean Q-correlations characterizing the sample as a whole are uninformative about any particular subject. As a corollary to this finding, Block attempted to ascertain the factors or conditions that characterized changes and nonchanges.

Individuals whose correlations between their Q-sorts for different age periods fell below the mean correlation of the group were classified as changers; those who had Q-correlations above the mean were classified as nonchangers. There was no association in the degree of change that occurred between the junior high and senior high years and the change that occurred between senior high and adulthood. Males who changed between junior and senior high school were found to be insecure, dependent, fearful, vulnerable, and lacking self-confidence. Male nonchangers over this same period were observed to be uncomplicated, self-confident, nonintrospective, adaptable individuals. Males who changed between the senior high and adult years were characterized as being insecure, defensive, other directed, immature, lacking in direction, self-centered, undercontrolled; they exhibited poor coping skills and were oriented toward the peer culture. Nonchangers over these years, on the other hand, were described as being mature, productive, alert, diligent, thoughtful, introspective, self-assured, adult oriented, and fluent individuals who exhibited the cultural values of striving toward intellectual goals and behaving responsibly toward others. These variables are just a sampling of a larger pool of adjectives found by Block to characterize these two groups. It is difficult to extrapolate a series of personality dimensions from the lengthy list of descriptors distinguishing male changers from nonchangers. However, an underlying theme seems to be that changers are experiencing disequilibrium and tension both within themselves and in relation to established adult society and values, whereas nonchangers appear to be relaxed, effective individuals who were comfortably pursuing culturally valued goals while achieving an idealized adaptation to the world about them.

Females who changed from junior to senior high school saw their parents as old-fashioned, were assertive and hostile toward peers, valued independence, and showed occupational interests ordinarily characterized or reflecting aggressive masculinity. The female nonchangers, from junior to senior high school, on the other hand, were described as dependent, submissive, held positive attitudes and feelings toward their family, and were accepting of stereotyped feminine sex-typing. From senior high to adulthood, females changers were described as being defensive, insecure, erratic, rebellious, distrustful, negativistic, hostile toward adults, and they saw their parents as old-fashioned. Female nonchangers, over this period, had positive perceptions of and relations with adults and parents, were satisfied with self, productive, favored the status quo, were submissive, conservative, and seemed to have an easier and less stressful adaptation to emerging developmental tasks than did the changers. Our sampling of the variables that described these two female groups showed, as with the males, that there was more evidence of disequilibrium, tension, and dissatisfaction among the female changers than among the nonchangers. The tension exhibited by the changers seemed to be both internal and in relation to others. Furthermore, the female changers appeared to be adamantly resistant to the values and status of their prior generation. The nonchangers, on the other hand, appeared to have a calm acceptance of themselves and their world; they seemed to assimilate comfortably the values of their culture and were acquiescent in accepting traditional role prescriptions. For both male and female changers, then, life was a struggle with a force toward change, whereas for the nonchangers it was a smooth process.

Block extended his investigation of factors associated with continuity or change by classifying his subjects by personality type and then analyzing the data to determine whether personality continuity varied among these different personality types. The personality types were derived by means of an inverse factor analysis that shows communalities among individuals rather than among variables. The data for this factor analysis consisted of the pooling of the 90 Q-items from the junior high and the 90 Q-items from the adult California Q-sort procedures that were common to the evaluation of these two age periods. This analysis resulted in five factors, or personality types, for the male sample and six for the female sample.

The personality types in the male sample were:

1. *Ego resilient:* shows "long standing characterological integrity or resourcefulness."

2. *Belated adjusters:* "signifies growth and competence after a troublesome and unpromising adolescence."

3. *Vulnerable overcontrollers:* "indicates excessive constriction characterizing their personality added to an adulthood with developing failure of ego defenses."

4. *Anomic extroverts:* "conveys the valuelessness and the absence of innerlife that has so essentially characterized them."

5. *Under-controllers:* "indicates the pervasive impulsivity within these individuals" and the fact that by the mid-thirties they "have not yet fixed upon their niche in life."

Those in the female sample were:

1. *Female prototype:* "these individuals have manifested the qualities our culture prescribes as appropriate for its females."

2. *Cognitive copers:* "to signify the essentially intellectual way they have applied throughout life as a means of processing encounters with the world."

3. *Hyperfeminine repressives:* "the essence of their personality is a repressive but unarticulated character structure, fitful emotionality alternating with blandness and sexuality that is both unwilling and deliberate."

4. *Dominating narcissists:* "indicates the self-absorption of these women and the aggressive interactions they employ to advance their desires."

5. *Vulnerable undercontrollers:* "a label conveying their unmodulated impulsivity of action and reaction together with the poignant and plaintive submissiveness that prepares the way for their exploitation of others."

6. *Lonely independents:* "to indicate the highly motivated assertiveness and desire for autonomy of these individuals together with the interpersonal unconnectedness that characterizes them."

The Q-sorts were correlated between junior and senior high and between senior high and adulthood for each of the personality types in order to determine whether personality type predicted differential continuity. The correlations between junior and senior high were substantial, ranging from 0.50 to 0.62 for correlations uncorrected for attenuation and from 0.79 to 0.93 when corrected for attenuation. There seemed to be little evidence, however, of differential stability for the various personality types, for males and females, across the adolescent years. The uncorrected correlations between high school and adulthood ranged from 0.11 to 0.55 (0.17 to 0.78 when corrected for attenuation), with most of the correlations greater than 0.35 or 0.50, for uncorrected or corrected correlations respectively. There was no stability from high school to adulthood for the male belated adjusters, and minimal stability for the male anomic extraverts and the female hyperfeminine repressives. The remaining personality types, both male and female, showed moderate stability over this period.

Block had available information on the families of his subjects, and he found that parental personality and family atmosphere were highly related to the individual's personality structure. Overall his findings provide strong and pervasive evidence of personality continuity. Particularly impressive and elucidating is the ipsative data that show that many individuals tend to maintain similar internal ordering and organization of personality characteristics over time. Of equal significance is the finding that despite the evidence for continuity, there is still substantial variability among individuals in the consistency of personality over time.

Read Tuddenham (1959) studied the stability of a large number of personality variables, from adolescence to mid adulthood, on a sample of 72 subjects who were members of the Oakland Growth Study. These subjects were rated on observational material collected during early adolescence and then again approximately nineteen years later, when they averaged about 33 years of age. The adult ratings were based on two follow-up interviews, each about 1½ hours long. Fifty-two of the subjects studied by Tuddenham were also included in the sample studied by Block, although they conducted separate follow-up interviews and used a different methodology for evaluating the adolescent material. Tuddenham found average correlation coefficients between adolescence and adulthood of 0.27 for men and 0.24 for women. He concludes that although these correlations are too low to permit individual prediction, there is clearly significant temporal stability across the developmental span from early adolescence to adulthood. Aggression was the most stable variable rated for men, and social prestige was the most stable variable rated for women with stability coefficients of 0.68 and 0.67, respectively. A cluster of variables that showed continuity for the males involved self-assertiveness versus self-effacement, whereas for the females a group of variables on masculinity-femininity exhibited stability. Several stylistic variables dealing with expressiveness and expansive spontaneity versus inhibition were stable for both sexes. Ratings of attractiveness and self-confidence lacked stability across the age periods studied. Unlike the findings of some other longitudinal studies spanning the adolescent to adult years (Block, 1971; Kagan and Moss, 1962) a measure of drive for achievement was found by Tuddenham to be unstable for both sexes.

Arlene Skolnik (1966) studied the continuity of responses to the Thematic Apperception Test (TAT) of the Oakland Growth Study sample over a twenty-year period. Subjects were administered the TAT at age 17 and again at age 37. Their responses were scored for motives of achievement, aggression, affiliation, and power. Significant stability coefficients were obtained for men on the measures of power and aggression and for the women on affiliation and achievement imagery. Although these correlations were statistically significant they were of a low order of magnitude (correlations ranged between 0.21 and 0.34). However, these findings gain further credibility from their consistency with the results obtained in other longitudinal studies that utilized observational data.

Diana Woodruff and James Birren (1972) suggest that life span studies reporting personality test scores have been based on cross-sectional or longitudinal designs while little attempt has been made to distinguish between age differences and age changes and to use sequential strategies to separate ontogenetic (age changes) from generational components (age differences). Consequently, discrepancies exist concerning the magnitude of age changes in personality test scores. Longitudinal study of personality shows small age changes while cross-sectional study of personality shows substantial age differences in personality. Citing Schaie (1965), Woodruff and Birren suggest that longitudinal studies measure maturational changes while cross-sectional studies assess generational change. Thus their study was an attempt to clarify this issue.

Adolescents tested in 1944 on the California Test of Personality were retested twenty-five years later (1969) when they were middle-aged adults (1924 cohort). The adults were first asked to describe themselves (self-scores). They were then asked to answer the inventory a second time as they thought they had answered it in 1944 (retrospective scores). To provide cohort comparisons, high school (1953 cohort) and college students (1948 cohort) were also tested in 1969 on the California Test of Personality.

For the within-1924 cohort comparison, 1944 self-scores were compared with 1969 self-scores. There were no significant age changes in mean personality test scores. When the retrospective scores were compared with the actual scores achieved in 1944, adults scored lower (negative image) when they described themselves as students than they had actually scored when they were students.

For the between-cohort comparisons on the self-scores, the cohort of 1924 scored significantly higher than the combined mean for the cohorts of 1948 and 1953 whether they were adolescents or adults. When the retrospective scores of the 1924 cohort were compared with the self-condition scores of the 1948 and 1953 cohorts, the adults describing themselves as students had higher mean scores than the contemporary students. The conclusion was that age changes in personality are small from adolescence to middle age while age differences in personality are great. This statement may be somewhat overstated because age changes could be evaluated only in relation to one cohort. To validate that age differences are more important than age changes, Nesselroade and Baltes (1974) suggest employment of sequential strategies consisting of serial cross-sectional and longitudinal comparisons that make it possible to estimate the relative significance of individual and historical change components.

Nesselroade and Baltes (1974) included eighteen hundred 13- to 18-year-olds, four cohorts born in 1954, 1955, 1956, and 1957, in a sequential longitudinal design. The study focused on examining ontogenetic (individual) and sociocultural (historical) change in adolescent personality. Subjects were tested at three points during a two-year period on the Cattell High School Personality Questionnaire and Jackson's Personality Research Form. Ten factors or personality dimensions were extracted from the test scores.

One- and two-year stability coefficients for the personality dimensions ranged from 0.06 to 0.81, with a high average magnitude of 0.57. Stability increased with age and decreased as the interval between testing increased, a pattern frequently observed in other longitudinal research.

Developmental change was reported to be more influenced by the cultural movement (time effects) than by age changes. Adolescents decreased in superego strength, achievement motivation, and social-emotional anxiety independent of their age. Adolescents increased in independence during the same period. The changes were interpreted as evidence that simple longitudinal designs are inadequate for describing developmental change in light of the preponderance of findings relating to cultural change rather than age change. The studies by Woodruff and Birren (1972) and Nesselroade and Baltes (1974) are important for their methodological contribution to separating the generational and maturational components of change. However, the focus of these investigations was on measuring change versus stability. Thus these methodological innovations are relevant primarily to assessing change.

In the majority of longitudinal studies reviewed thus far, personality factors within the individual have been considered in relation to consistency and change, although some attention was given to the influence of cultural influences on stability (Kagan and Moss, 1962). The dialectic between personality characteristics and societal and cultural demands has been made more explicit in the design of longitudinal studies of the adult years. In addition to personality factors, sociocultural influences or extrinsic sociological variables such as social norms are generally incorporated into these assessments, although some studies include only psychological variables. Social or cultural demands hereafter will be referred to as *extrinsic* factors, while psychological factors will be referred to as *intrinsic* factors.

Alex Inkeles and David Smith (1974) were interested in the contribution of external cultural factors to the process by which people move from traditional to modern personalities. Since this study only approximates a longitudinal design, we shall not review its findings; however, an aim of the study was to discover whether factory work had a modernizing influence on men in developing countries whose experience was formerly limited to agricultural and related pursuits in a traditional village. Similarly, in a cross-sectional study of adult personality, Elaine Cummings and William Henry (1964) developed a disengagement theory of aging to explain the process by which the old person becomes less involved in the performance of social roles secondary to changes in interaction with others.

Melvin Kohn and Carmi Schooler (1978) have investigated the

relation between intellectual flexibility and occupation, both cross-sectionally and longitudinally, over a ten-year period and have found a high degree of stability for their measure of intellectual flexibility. They are currently studying the longitudinal relations for aspects of personality functioning in regard to occupational structure.

External factors influencing personality have also been considered a microcosm of the larger culture, that is, the family as an external influence on the continuity of personality. Kelly (1955) assessed consistency and change within marital dyads as well as within the individual husbands and wives themselves. As husband and wife, each individual was presumably subject to common social forces.

Three hundred couples were initially contacted when they were engaged. The initial assessment program took place on the first anniversary of their marriage. A twenty-year follow-up was conducted in 1953-54. The original measures consisted of the Strong Vocational Interest Inventory, the Allport-Vernon Scale of Values, Otis Self-Administering Test of Mental Ability, the Bernreuter Personality Inventory, the Bell Adjustment Inventory, and two of Remers' Generalized Attitude Scales. In addition, a 36-trait personality rating scale was developed and administered. On the twenty-year follow-up, retesting was done on 227 couples on all measures except the Otis and Bell inventory.

Changes over the twenty-year period showed both continuity and discontinuity. On the Allport-Vernon Scale of Values, the largest and most significant changes reported were an increase in religious values and a downward shift in aesthetic values for women and an equally divided downward shift for aesthetic and theoretical values for men.

On Remers' Generalized Attitude Scales attitudes toward marriage, church, child rearing, entertaining, and gardening became more favorable while attitudes toward housekeeping became less favorable. Few changes were noted on the Strong Vocational Interest Blank or the Bernreuter Personality Inventory. While there was no essential sex difference in the original sample on the Bernreuter, women on the follow-up study showed a statistically significant shift toward greater self-confidence. When self-ratings made by the subjects at a median age of 25 were compared with self-ratings twenty years later, few of the comparisons were significantly different. Men and women at 45 rated themselves somewhat less peppy, less neat in dress, and somewhat less broad in their interests than they did twenty years earlier.

Kelly reasoned that the absence of mean change on some variables could have resulted either from little or no changing in individuals or from the cancelling of increases and decreases in the scores of individuals. Retest correlations over the twenty-year time span were compared with retest correlations on the same measures for relatively short time intervals, for example, 12-month test-retest correlations. The pattern of higher short-term than long-term stability coefficients, corrected for attenuation, was similar to other assessments of personality consistency. The stability of five domains of variables fell into three distinct levels: (1) Values and vocational interests were the most stable, with average correlations of about 0.50. (2) Self-ratings and the other personality variables were somewhat less consistent, with correlations of about 0.30. (3) The lowest consistency was for attitudes, which tended to have stability correlations of less than 0.10. This pattern was interpreted as indicating that values and vocational interests are deeply ingrained motivational patterns that do not change during middle age whereas attitudes are more malleable. "The relative changeability of attitudes is probably a function of their specificity and the fact that alternative attitude objects can be substituted one for the other in the service of maintaining an individual's system of values" (Kelly, 1955, p. 675).

Kelly used the fact that married couples are members of a close diadic group and share a similar social environment. A question was whether there was any systematic relationship between the changes in one spouse and the original scores of the other member of the pair. Correlations were computed between each set of change scores and the original scores of the spouse on all the personality variables. For both cross-spouse comparisons the correlations were relatively low, indicating that neither spouse tended to change toward the original score of the other. Thus these data did not support the old adage that husbands and wives become more like each other throughout marriage. In fact, correlations between husband and wife variables showed small significant shifts in the direction of decreasing similarity over the twenty years. Kelly concluded that husbands and wives can establish and maintain a cohesive relationship without the need to become more alike. The diversity of roles that husbands and wives must fulfill in a marriage perhaps mandates that disparate forces operate in order for the partners to fulfill their respective roles.

Kelly (1955) asked the question whether change on one personality variable is relatively specific or likely to be accompanied by changes on other variables. In contrast to the method of correlating scores on the same variable at two points in time, as in the Fels study, Kelly used intercorrelations of the differences between scores at time 1 and time 2. Change scores are indicative of the direction of the changes. The values of the intercorrelations tended to be low and similar for both sexes. Less than 20% of these correlations were significant at the 1% level. Changes on approximately half of the variables were found to be unrelated to changes on the other variables. Kelly concluded that the relative specificity of the changes is inconsistent with a global notion of personality.

In conclusion, Kelly's research demonstrated that despite the long time period between assessments and the fallibility of the tools used, much consistency was found for certain personality variables over the twenty years studied. But considerable instability and change were also found in many of the variables. The changes were shown to be specific rather than global. Attitudes showed the least stability, perhaps because they are more subject to influence by changing cultural and societal influences.

Intrinsic personality factors are the focus of the Normative Aging Study which consists of a longitudinal assessment of normal health and aging (Bell, Rose, and Damon, 1972) in 2,000 male volunteers screened for physical and psychiatric health at time of entry into the study. Because the primary focus of the study was originally on physical health and aging, a regular cycle of psychological measurement was not incorporated into the study. Instead psychological measurement consisted of a one-time battery of tests administered to 1,100 subjects between 1965 and 1967; included were the Sixteen Personality Factor Questionnaire (16PF), the Strong Vocational Interest Blank (SVIB), the Allport-Vernon-Lindsay Scale of Values (AVL), and the General Aptitude Test Battery (GATB) (Costa and McCrae, 1978).

Between 1975 and 1977 follow-up personality assessment procedures were administered to the participants which included a revised version of the 1962 edition (Costa and McCrae, 1978). Over the ten-year period, personality traits as measured by the 16PF showed remarkable stability of individual differences. Stability coefficients were generally greater than 0.40 for most of the sixteen factors. To assess change during the same period, repeated measures analysis of variance on all sixteen scales, with three age cohorts (25-34, 35-54, 55-82) as an additional classifying variable, showed cohort differences for conscientiousness, tendermindedness, and liberal thinking, with an increase in all three with increasing age groups. Longitudinal changes were seen for brightness and independence, with both measures showing an increase over time.

Nine-year longitudinal stability for anxiety and extraversion was also examined in the adult males (Costa and McCrae, 1977-78). Intercorrelations were computed for the 1966 and 1976 anxiety and extraversion cluster scores, derived from a cluster analysis of the 16PF (Costa and McGrae, 1976) and the Eysenck Personality Inventory (EPI-Q) Extraversion and Neuroticism Scale for the three age groups. Correlations between the 16PF measures over a nine-year period range from 0.58 for the anxiety cluster in the youngest group to 0.84 for the extraversion cluster in the oldest group. Stability coefficients from the Eysenck measures of similar constructs range from 0.41 in the youngest group to 0.54 in the middle age group. These high coefficients are evidence of the enduring quality of anxiety and extraversion within different cohorts.

In this study of adult males stability is a primary characteristic of adult personality while personality change is negligible. Costa and McCrae (1978) suggest that lack of evidence for substantial maturational change can be attributed to an inherent weakness in longitudinal research. Cross-sectional designs can compare individuals across the full range of the adult life span while longitudinal studies typically cover only a few years, and changes within such short intervals may be too small to detect. This criticism may be accurate for later periods in the life span when change is not as rapid as in early periods (Bloom, 1964), but other studies reviewed earlier (Martin, 1964) show that change is indeed detectable even within brief time intervals at other points in the life span.

In a study that combined the samples from the Oakland Growth Study and the Berkeley Guidance Study, the interaction between personality and social demands was considered in relation to the relevance of early adult life-style and personality-to-personality functioning during the later years (Maas and Kuypers, 1975). The questions addressed included these: What are personality and life-style sequences between early adulthood and old age? Under what circumstances do changes and continuity occur in late adult life? The subjects included 142 parents (95 mothers and 47 fathers) of the children in the Oakland Growth Study and the Berkeley Guidance Study. The parents were interviewed when the children entered the study in the 1920s and at subsequent intervals until the 1960s when the children were 40 and the parents ranged in age from 60 to 82.

The parents were interviewed to obtain information on home and neighborhood, work and retirement, and leisure activities, parenting, grandparenting, siblings, marriage, friendship, membership in organizations, health, death, important persons in their lives, recreational activities, and perspectives on past life. These data were rated to assess the life-styles of and the environmental and health conditions under which the parents currently were living. Personality assessments were made by use of Q-sort items and ego-defense scales.

James Maas and Joseph Kuypers (1975) evaluated life-style during late adulthood in many arenas of daily living—home, work, leisure, marriage, parenting, and grandparenting. Life-style was further conceptualized in terms of interaction, involvement, satisfaction, and perception of change. These later aspects of life-style were examined in relation to arenas of daily living to identify distinguishable life-style clusters. Four father and six mother life-style clusters were identified by factor analyzing 88 components of life-style. Each life-style is described in terms of components that distinguish the cluster of fathers or mothers from all other fathers or mothers combined. Maas and Kuypers provide extensive descriptions of each life-style cluster. Some dominant characteristics of each cluster are summarized here. The children of these parents involved in the original longitudinal study are referred to as Child-S.

Family-centered father: High involvement as a marital partner, sees children and grandchildren frequently, and relationship with Child-S improved with age.

Hobbyist father: Engages in solitary recreational pursuits, sees children infrequently, and relationship with wife has an instrumental orientation.

Remotely sociable father: Socially busy; not very involved in relationships with Child-S or marital partner.

Unwell-disengaged father: Poor health and self-perceived withdrawal from the world; sees grandchildren infrequently and has low marital satisfaction.

Husband-centered wife: Daily life is spouse centered and marital satisfaction is high; involvement with children and grandchildren is low.

Uncentered mother: Few recreational activities, no involvement with work or social groups, has no marital partner, and sees children and grandchildren frequently.

Visiting mother: Highly involved as hostess and guest, and with children and friends; marriage is not a central concern.

Employed (work-centered) mother: Highly involved as worker and satisfied with work situation; not married; sees children and grandchildren often.

Disabled-disengaging mother: Dissatisfied with many things including marriage but particularly her health; low involvement with grandchildren and Child-S.

Group-centered mother: High involvement as group member and as citizen; marriage is not important; exerts parental control over her children.

The question addressed by Maas and Kuypers was whether antecedent measures, ratings on the parents when they were in their thirties, were relevant to life-styles in old age. The antecedent ratings for subjects manifesting each life-style cluster were compared with the ratings of all remaining parents of the same sex.

Early adult life had more relevance for the aging life-styles of the fathers than for the mothers with the exception of the family-centered fathers. The hobbyist fathers, earlier as well as later in life, were the healthiest of all fathers and were also the lowest in socioeconomic status. The early salience of religion appeared in old age as frequent church attendance while lack of warmth in the hobbyist's early marriage was reflected in later marriage by instrumentality in the marital relationship. The discontinuity with the past was reflected in an increase in recreational activities.

The unwell-disengaged fathers were characterized in both early and late adulthood by their ill health, social withdrawal, and marital conflict. Absence of a close bond with children as young parents was reflected in disapproval of children's visiting and child-rearing practices as aged parents.

The remotely sociable fathers demonstrated both continuity and change. Early adult high income and lack of financial strain coincided with high occupational status in the later years. Their early cool and aloof interpersonal style was reflected in old age as a marked noninvolvement with others. The change noted in these fathers was in an early good parental relationship that dissipated over the years.

Change rather than continuity of life-style into old age characterized the mothers. The exceptions were the visiting mothers and husband-centered wives, for whom antecedent measures had little relevance for later life-styles. The work-centered mothers, who were the lowest in energy and least satisfied with their lot during early adulthood, were marked by high energy, good health, and life satisfaction in their aging years. Radical changes for the better were seen in these mothers. Similarly, the group-centered mothers' early life-style pattern of low marital compatibility and disapproving stance toward their children was replaced in old age with a closer relationship with Child-S and a greater investment in social, church, and civic affairs.

In contrast to the positive changes seen in the work-centered and group-centered mothers, the uncentered mothers' changes were in a more negative direction. The family-centered, healthy, and happy mothers moved into a style of living characterized by few friends and few leisure-time or recreational interests. Nothing seemed to replace their early-adult family-centered interests.

The disabled-disengaging mothers exhibited both continuity and change. Like their male counterparts, these mothers had health problems in early and later life. A poor relationship with their children also spanned the forty-year period. Change is evident in these mothers in two domains. Their style of attacking versus withdrawing in the face of conflict was replaced by disengagement during old age. Marriage in early adulthood as an area of conflict became a positive arena in late adulthood.

Thus continuity of life-style into old age was more characteristic of the mother than the fathers. For the mothers there was little variability in their contexts in the early adult years. The primary role of a mother during the 1930s was that of wife and mother. During the later years the mothers were released to pursue occupational and recreational activities, therefore creating change in their lives. For the fathers, the continuities were associated with few changes in their lives except for retirement.

In addition to distinguishing life-style clusters, Maas and Kuypers (1975) identified seven personality dispositions among the parents. Varimax factor analysis of the California Q-sort (Block, 1971), an ipsative assessment procedure, was used to define the personality groups.

Person-oriented mothers: Giving, sympathetic, warm, talkative, social poise, and responsive to humor in others.

Fearful-ordering mothers: Uncomfortable with uncertainty and complexity, vulnerable to real or fancied threat, anxious, and overconcerned with her own adequacy.

Autonomous mothers: Attempts to keep others at a distance, values her own independence and autonomy, hostile to others, and high aspiration level.

Anxious-asserting mothers: Rapid personal tempo, talkative, histrionic, assertive, and concerned with comparisons between herself and others.

Person-oriented fathers: Warm, sympathetic, giving, enjoys being with others.

Active-competent fathers: Critical, rebellious, personally charming, and expresses his ideas well.

Conservative-ordering fathers: Conventional, moralistic, overcontrols his needs, values power.

Early adult antecedent ratings were found to be relevant to variations in personality forty years later. The early roots of personality in late life were more apparent for the mothers than the fathers. For the fearful-ordering mothers 31% of the 68 personality, health, and social-interaction antecedent measures distinguish these mothers from the other mothers, while 30% of the measures distinguish the anxious-asserting mothers. The percentages refer to significant differences (p less than or equal to 0.10) between groups of parents.

The fearful-ordering mothers in early and late life were depressed in mood and activity level, low in adaptive capacity and sense of self-worth, and had health and economic disadvantages. For the anxious-asserting mothers, anxiety, tension, and assertiveness were features characteristic of early and late life. Low personal satisfaction and self-doubt were also common features of early and late life.

For the other personality groups the percentage of statistically significant differences that distinguished the groups was substantially lower. The diversity of life-styles and personality in this group of parents indicates that the aged cannot be viewed in a monolithic way. These diversities are mediated by sex differences, contexts of daily life, health, and personality characteristics. The finding that stability in personality is characteristic of older persons high in anxiety and ego disorganization (fearful-ordering and anxious-asserting mothers) supports other empirical findings indicating the persistent stability of aberrant patterns of behavior throughout the life span.

The longest longitudinal study of personality undertaken so far grew out of an investigation with a different original purpose. Terman's well-known longitudinal study of gifted children was originally intended to examine how they differed from other children, in general, and to follow the course of their intellectual development. The sample consisted of grade school boys ($N = 857$) and girls ($N = 671$) with an IQ of 135 or higher (Sears, 1977). For fifty years subjects have been evaluated at successive intervals by a combination of questionnaires, personality tests, interviews, and ratings scales. A questionnaire follow-up of the men conducted in 1972, focused on delineating developmental antecedents of life satisfaction with occupation and family life, determining degree of work persistence into the 60s, and finding whether they remained married or divorced.

Three types of variables were included as potential predictors of occupational life satisfaction: achievement variables, objective events such as health and education, and feeling-expressive variables such as enjoyment of and satisfaction with work. Occupational life satisfaction was predictable, as far back as three decades, from the individuals' expressions of feelings about their lives. Path analysis of predictor variables for occupational life satisfaction showed that ambition, liking one's work and satisfaction with it early in adulthood, a feeling of having lived up to one's potential, good health, and a feeling at age 30 of having chosen an occupation rather than having drifted into it were all predictive of final occupational life satisfaction. Sears concludes that some continuing affective quality, such as an optimism about life, an enjoyment of occupational challenge, and a feeling of self-worth, that characterized satisfied men at 30 persisted over three decades.

Occupational persistence versus retirement was related to more objective facts of life: education, occupational status, and career success from age 30 to 50. Men who continued to work had thirty years earlier judged themselves to be persistent and integrated in their work and had 12 years earlier described themselves as more ambitious than most men. Furthermore, they reported having more vitality than their retired counterparts and having liked their work during mid life.

Predictors of family-life satisfaction were identified in very early developmental periods of the Terman men. Good mental health in 1940 and in 1960 and scores on the marital aptitude and marital happiness scale were both related to family-life satisfaction. Good social adjustment as early as 1922, sociability in high school, and feminine tastes and interests were slightly predictive of satisfaction in family life.

A comparison of the lives of men who had unbroken marriages with those who had experienced divorce or separation showed that the factors predictive of family-life satisfaction were also predictive of unbroken marriage; these factors included marital aptitude and marital happiness measures for the husbands at age 30, good mental health, and affectional bonds toward parents. The more masculine a boy was at age 10, the more likely he was to have an unbroken marriage at age 62.

Impressive stabilities of personality development were noted in the Terman males. The relatively high degree of consistency over the fifty-year period may be accounted for by a precocious maturity that minimized instabilities thereafter. Two findings that have been associated with stability in other studies appear to be operative in this assessment. Self-ratings, in contrast to more objective personality measures, showed impressive stability in this study as well as in studies reviewed earlier (Block, 1977; Kelly, 1955). The finding that the highest stability coefficients diminished in magnitude as the time interval between measurement increased was also reported in other assessments of personality continuity and change.

Only subjects 65 and over were included in Joseph Britton and Jean Britton's (1972) longitudinal study of consistency and change in personality and adjustment. One of the aims of the investigation was to determine the consistency and change in personality and adjustment of older adults over time and to identify factors related to consistency or change.

The sample at the start of the study in 1956 consisted of 59 male and 87 female residents of a rural village and surrounding township. Because of death and other factors affecting experimental mortality, 17 men and 29 women were available for three testing and interviewing sessions over a nine-year period. Subjects were interviewed to obtain descriptive data on social norms and expectations for the behavior of older people and to allow the interviewer to rate the subjects on their ability to communicate and interact with others. Psychometric measures included the Chicago Activity Inventory, Chicago Attitude Inventory, Personality Relations and Sociability Scale, Opinion Conformity Scale, and Thematic Apperception Test.

This over-65 group of men and women tended to rate their health as remaining stable over the years even though individuals may have experienced important changes in health. Over the years, both men and women reported seeing their families less frequently; however, the older subjects reported no increase in feelings of neglect. They reported their economic position as remaining stable even though the income of men decreased. Number of friends decreased over the years while leisure-time activities increased.

Overt activity and scores on the Attitude Inventory decreased over the years, the latter decrease indicating that aging individuals find decreasing satisfaction in the ordinary affairs and activities of life and in feelings of happiness and usefulness. Similarly, the judges' ratings of adjustment in terms of primary relationship and emotional security declined over time. There were few changes over the years in satisfaction with personal relations or sociability. The number of responses to the TAT increased in men. Interviewers' ratings of interviewees' ability to be attentive and to interact and cooperate in that situation declined over the years.

In summary, the descriptive findings provide evidence that aging is accompanied by a decrease in adjustment as evidenced by their decreasing satisfaction with the ordinary affairs of life and feelings of happiness. However, even though friends and contact with families decline, there is no decrease in feelings of neglect or satisfaction with available social contacts. Perhaps it is the constriction of work and familial roles that leads to a perception of lack of uselessness.

Interyear correlations were computed to determine the extent to which the ranking of individuals on the measures at one point corresponded to their ranking at a later point. The interyear correlations ranged from -0.06 to 0.90 and were higher for men than for women. As reported in other longitudinal studies, the shorter the time period between testing, the higher the correlations.

A longitudinal trend score (LTS) consisting of the product-moment correlation between the three years or times of assessment (1956, 1962, 1965) as one variable and the individual's scores on a measure for those years as the other variable was used to measure individual change. Longitudinal trend scores were interpreted as a correlation coefficient showing direction and degree of individual change over the nine-year period.

The distribution of LTS was divided into thirds; those $+0.50$ and higher indicated an improvement over the years, -0.49 to $+0.49$ indicated no real change, and -0.50 and higher indicated decline. Improvement, maintenance, and decline were evidenced for all the measures. The mean longitudinal trend score provides a summary of the directionality of change. No subject showed markedly positive change on measures of personality and adjustment, but a fifth of the men and a third of the women appeared in the markedly negative change categories. The majority were stable on the personality and adjustment measures. Factors associated with positive and negative change could not be identified in this aging sample. Unlike the persons in Block's (1971) sample, those who changed in a positive direction were indistinguishable from those who changed in a negative direction.

From these findings, one can conclude that although change may occur in a negative direction, change still occurs even in a group of individuals as old as 95 years. Britton and Britton (1972) proposed that although the community environment in which the sample resided was characterized by relative stability, changes in the environment are continually occurring and may have "affected personal and social characteristics in adults during their most rapid period of decline or during periods of transition in either the individual or his life situation" (p. 168). Changes in life situations are frequently imposed by the changing physiological status of elderly individuals. Such changes may also force the individual into a new environment. That is, the interaction between changing physiological and environmental variables affect the individual to an unknown extent. Finally, the subjects' subjective ratings indicated stability on issues related to health and finances when, in fact, there was objective change. This finding raises the question whether less objectively verifiable personality characteristics such as anxiety are also likely to be perceived by the individual as stable when more objective assessment might reveal change.

Certain classes of aberrant behavior are obstinately stable. Psychopathology, neurosis, and recidivism among felons are not only highly stable but also highly resistant to change. The immutability of antisocial and psychopathological behavior patterns is attested to by their tendency to remain unchanged despite extreme social pressure to change, the persistent efforts of many professional workers to modify them, and the obvious pain and suffering inherent in these maladaptive patterns of functioning. Hospital, clinic, and court records are replete with longitudinal (albeit nonsystematic) information concerning these extreme or aberrant forms of behavior. However, in the clinical and societal context, immutable behavior is referred to as chronicity, poor prognosis, and recidivism rather than as stability or consistency of personality. The resistance of many psychological symptoms to prodigious psychotherapeutic efforts and the proclaimed futility of many prison rehabilitative programs provides compelling evidence for personality stability. The evidence for stability among socially or psychologically disturbed individuals can contribute to our understanding of personality stability.

Clinical studies reveal striking individual differences in the potential for and the occurrence of change among individuals who exhibit antisocial or maladaptive patterns of behaving. Change in an individual can occasionally be forecasted on the basis of prior knowledge of the individual's circumstances and psychosocial status, whereas in other instances the basis for change can only be speculated on after the fact. In either case recognition that complex individual dynamics allow for change in certain instances and rigidly resist change in other instances emphasizes the necessity of including idiographic studies in the longitudinal assessment of personality. These individual differences in the "potential" for change also argue for searching out relevant moderator variables that might be predictive of these differences.

There are various theoretical explanations for the resistance to change of certain psychological symptoms. O. Hobart Mowrer's (1950) discussion of the "neurotic paradox" and Wilhelm Reich's (1972) writings on "character armor" are but a few of the theoretical attempts to explain how symptoms are retained to protect the individual from relentless and often overwhelming states of anxiety. Both environmental and biological interpretations have been proposed to explain the durability of antisocial behavior. For instance, Glueck and Glueck (1950) stress that individuals with certain somatypes seem predisposed to antisocial functioning. More recently attempts have been made to identify characteristic genotypes among chronic felons. Irving Goffman (1961) has described the way that institutional life helps perpetuate the behavioral patterns of inmates. He regards institutions as bureaucratic settings that control the handling of many human needs. The staffs of these institutions are concerned with surveillance and the inmates with conformity; this conformity is often essential for survival with the system.

Data on readmissions and time spent in mental hospitals can be regarded as indirect evidence of the stability of extreme personality characteristics that underlie mental disorders. However, one must not draw such a conclusion too quickly because, as Goffman (1961) and others have indicated, continued hospitalization of mental patients can be a function of acquiescence to a system and a product of subjugative hospital practices, as well as the result of chronic mental disturbance. Nonetheless, the effects of coercive environmental conditions on maintaining the stable psychological status of mental patients are no less relevant than the perhaps more subtle but prevailing environmental forces that contribute to stable personality patterns among normal individuals. Data on readmissions and time spent in mental hospitals is not readily available because the mental health professions are oriented more toward recording recovery from mental disorders than toward recording the longevity of these conditions. The recent emphasis on the development and use of the psychiatric case register, however, should increase the opportunities to obtain longitudinal data on psychiatric populations. The psychiatric case register of Monroe County, New York, has been in operation since 1960 and records contracts, demographic data, diagnosis, services provided, and additional information on all public and private psychiatric patients seen in the county. Some illustrative longitudinal findings obtained from this register are that within 100 months after discharge from a hospital approximately 50% of schizophrenic patients were readmitted, and a seven-year follow-up of psychotically depressed individuals showed that about half of those who received treatment had no recurrent depressive episode (Babigian, 1972).

Longitudinal work on the stability of psychological disorders suggests that severe disturbances tend to be long-standing whereas isolated symptoms and mild reactions tend to be transitory. This difference in the persistence of severe and mild reactions may be based on the probability that severe disturbances are likely to reflect a fundamental and pervasive personality problem that is tied to the psychobiological history of the individual. Isolated symptoms are more likely to reflect temporary stress reactions to passing situations and ephemeral developmental demands.

To anticipate and empirically document the consistency of human personality is one aim of psychology. To some degree this exalted aim has been realized in the longitudinal study of consistency and change in personality variables. Consistency is most obvious for personality characteristics that are endowed with positive cultural and societal valences. Achievement motivation, a socially valued characteristic, was found to be a stable trait across contiguous and noncontiguous developmental periods for both sexes. Similarly, culturally prescribed appropriate sex role behaviors and interests were stable from middle childhood to adulthood. Attitudes, which are susceptible to changing cultural values, were one of the least stable personality characteristics. Thus both the modifiability and consistency of personality can be partially understood within the context of social and cultural norms. Stylistic behaviors such as expressiveness, intraversion-extraversion, and activity level show stability beginning at the preschool years and continuing throughout the developmental span, whereas evidence for stability of motivational characteristics first emerge, to an appreciable degree, by middle childhood. Studies using an ipsative strategy are effective in demonstrating stability and change, since their emphasis on the organization of characteristics within the individual allows one to trace longitudinally complex behavioral patterns and avoids some of the measurement problems associated with normative longitudinal studies of personality. The use of moderator variables such as sex, social class, and personality types was proved useful for identifying and explicating continuities.

A second aim in the longitudinal study of personality is to identify factors that are likely to minimize or maximize the observation of consistency and change in personality development. The time interval between measurements is an important factor in influencing consistency of personality during the early years; as the time interval between measurement increases, the evidence of stability decreases. During later developmental periods, the interval between measurements becomes a less significant influence on consistency (Sears, 1977). Similarly, age at time of assessment influences consistency of personality; the younger the organism at time of measurement, the higher the probability of detecting inconsistency and change. The instabilities and changes associated with the time interval between measurements and age at time of assessment are a function of a singular developmental phenomenon. Children pass through many different developmental periods in the early years, while adult developmental periods span a greater number of years. Because of the broader time intervals characterizing developmental stages in adulthood, change within these years may occur at a slower rate than change during earlier periods. Age per se, however, may not be wholly responsible for inconsistencies in personality across different points of the life cycle. Many of the variables in longitudinal studies of the early years include social interaction variables that are susceptible to ephemeral environmental influences, while studies of the adult years usually include variables designed to assess motivational or affective traits that are less susceptible to fluctuating environmental conditions. With the extension of the longitudinal study of personality to all periods of the life span, one is confronted with the challenge of identifying additional factors that may minimize or maximize consistency and change for different phases in the life cycle.

References

BABIGIAN, H. M. 1972. The role of psychiatric case registers in the longitudinal study of psychopathology. In M. Roff, L. N. Robins, and M. Pollack, eds., *Life history research in psychopathology*, vol. 2. Minneapolis, Minn.: University of Minnesota Press.

BALTES, P. B., REESE, H. W., and NESSELROADE, J. R. 1977. *Life-span developmental psychology: introduction to research methods*. Monterey, Calif.: Brooks/Cole.

BELL, B., ROSE, C. L., and DAMON, A. 1972. The normative aging study: an interdisciplinary and longitudinal study of health and aging. *Aging and Human Development* 3: 5-17.

BELL, R. Q., WELLER, G. M., and WALDROP, M. 1971. Newborn and preschooler: organization of behavior and relations between periods. *Monographs of the Society for Research in Child Development* 36 (1-2, Whole No. 142).

BEM, D. J., and ALLEN, A. 1974. On predicting some of the people some of the time: the search for cross-situational consistencies in behavior. *Psychological Review* 81: 506-520.

BLOCK, J. 1971. *Lives through time*. Berkeley, Calif.: Bancroft Books.

———— 1977. Advancing the science of personality: paradigmatic shift or improving the quality of research? In D. Magnusson and N. S. Endler, eds., *Psychology at the crossroads: current issues in interactional psychology*. Hillsdale: N.J.: Lawrence Erlbaum Associates.

BLOOM, B. 1964. *Stability and change in human characteristics*. New York: Wiley.

BRITTON, J. H., and BRITTON, J. O. 1972. *Personality changes in aging: a longitudinal study of community residents*. New York: Springer.

BRONSON, W. C. 1966. Central orientations: a study of behavior organization from childhood to adolescence. *Child Development* 37: 125-155.

———— 1967. Adult derivatives of emotional expressiveness and reactivity control: developmental continuities from childhood to adulthood. *Child Development* 38: 801-817.

CAREY, W. B. 1970. A simplified method for measuring infant temperament. *Journal of Pediatrics* 77: 188-194.

CLAUSEN, J. A. 1964. Personality measurement in the Oakland Growth Study. In J. E. Birren, ed., *Relations of development and aging*. Springfield, Ill.: Charles C. Thomas.

COSTA, P. T., and MCCRAE, R. R. 1976. Age differences in personality structure: a cluster analytic approach. *Journal of Gerontology* 5: 564-570.

———— 1977-78. Age differences in personality structure revisited: studies in validity, stability, and change. *International Journal of Aging and Human Development* 8: 261-275.

———— 1978. Objective personality assessment. In M. Storandt, I. C. Siegler, and M. F. Elias, eds., *The clinical psychology of aging*. New York: Plenum.

CUMMINGS, E., and HENRY, W. E. 1961. *Growing old: the process of disengagement*. New York: Basic Books.

EMMERICH, W. 1964. Continuity and stability in early social development. *Child Development* 35: 311-332.

—— 1966. Stability and change in early personality development. *Young Children* 21: 233-243.

—— 1968. Personality development and concepts of structure. *Child Development* 39: 671-690.

ERIKSON, E. H. 1963. *Childhood and society*, 2d ed. New York: W. W. Norton.

ESCALONA, S., and HEIDER, G. 1959. *Prediction and outcome*. New York: Basic Books.

FISKE, D. W. 1978. *Strategies for personality research*. San Francisco: Jossey-Bass.

FREUD, S. 1968. *The standard edition of the complete psychological works of Sigmund Freud*, vol. 7. London: Hogarth Press and the Institute of Psychoanalysis.

GLUECK, S., and GLUECK, E. G. 1950. *Unravelling juvenile delinquency*. New York: Commonwealth Fund.

GOFFMAN, E. 1961. *Asylums*. Garden City, N.Y.: Doubleday.

HALVERSON, C. F., MOSS, H. A., and JONES S. J. 1977. Longitudinal antecedents of preschool social behavior. National Institute of Mental Health, Bethesda, Md.

HALVERSON, C. F., and WALDROP, M. F. 1976. Relations between preschool activity and aspects of intellectual and social behavior at age 7½. *Journal of Developmental Psychology* 12: 107-112.

INKELES, A., and SMITH, D. H. 1974. *Becoming modern: individual change in six developing countries*. Cambridge, Mass.: Harvard University Press.

JACOBS, B. S., and MOSS, H. A. 1976. Birth order and sex of sibling as determinants of mother-infant interactions. *Child Development* 47: 315-322.

JAMES, W. 1950. *The principles of psychology*. New York: Dover Press.

KAGAN, J. 1964. American longitudinal research on psychological development. *Child Development* 35: 1-32.

—— 1971. *Change and continuity in infancy*. New York: Wiley.

KAGAN, J., and MOSS, H. A. 1962. *Birth to maturity*. New York: Wiley.

KAGAN, J., SONTAG, L. W., BAKER, C. T., and NELSON, V. L. 1958. Personality and IQ change. *Journal of Abnormal and Social Psychology* 56: 261-266.

KELLY, E. L. 1955. Consistency of the adult personality. *American Psychologist* 10: 659-681.

KOHLBERG, L. 1969. Stage and sequence: the cognitive developmental approach to socialization. In D. A. Goslin, ed., *Handbook of socialization and theory and research*. Chicago: Rand McNally.

KOHN, M. L., and SCHOOLER, C. 1978. The reciprocal effects of the substantial complexity of work and intellectual flexibility: a longitudinal assessment. *American Journal of Sociology* 84: 24-52.

KUHLEN, R. G. 1940. Social change: a neglected factor in psychological studies of the life span. *School and Society* 52: 14-16.

MAAS, H. S., and KUYPERS, J. A. 1975. *From thirty to seventy*. San Francisco:

Jossey-Bass.

MARTIN, W. E. 1964. Singularity and stability of profiles of social behavior. In D. B. Stendler, ed., *Readings in child behavior and development*. New York: Harcourt, Brace, and World.

McCALL, R. B. 1977. Challenges to a science of developmental psychology. *Child Development* 48: 333-344.

McCALL, R. B., EICHORN, D. H., and HOGARTY, P. S. 1977. Transitions in early mental development. *Monographs of the Society for Research in Child Development* 42 (3, Whole No. 171).

McDEVITT, S. C. 1976. A longitudinal assessment of longitudinal stability in temperamental characteristics from infancy to early childhood. Ph.D. dissertation, Temple University.

McDEVITT, S. C., and CAREY, W. B. 1979. The measurement of temperament in 3 to 7 year old children. *Journal of Child Psychology and Psychiatry*, in press.

MISCHEL, W. 1968. *Personality and assessment*. New York: Wiley.

————1969. Continuity and change in personality. *American Psychologist* 24: 1012-18.

Moss, H. A. 1967. Sex, age, and state as determinants of mother-infant interaction. *Merrill-Palmer Quarterly* 13: 19-36.

Moss, H. A., HALVERSON, C. F., YANG, R. K., and JONES, S. J. 1977. Developmental contributors to vocal behavior. National Institute of Mental Health, Bethesda, Md.

Moss, H. A., and JONES, S. J. 1977. Relation between maternal attitudes and maternal behavior as a function of social class. In P. H. Leiderman, S. R. Tulkin, and A. Rosenfeld, eds., *Culture and infancy, variations in human experience*. New York: Academic Press.

Moss, H. A., and ROBSON, K. S. 1968. Maternal influences in early social visual behavior. *Child Development* 39: 401-408.

———— 1970. The relation between the amount of time infants spend at various states and the development of visual behavior. *Child Development* 41: 509-517.

MOWRER, O. H. 1950. *Learning theory and personality dynamics, selected papers*. New York: Ronald Press.

MURPHY, L. B. 1964. Factors in continuity and change in the development of adaptational style in children. *Vita Humana* 7: 96-114.

NESSELROADE, J. R., and BALTES, P. B. 1974. Adolescent personality development and historical change: 1970-1972. *Monographs of the Society for Research in Child Development* 39 (1, Serial No. 154).

NESSELROADE, J. R., and REESE, H. W. 1973. *Life-span developmental psychology: methodological issues*. New York: Academic Press.

NEUGARTEN, B. L. 1977. Personality and aging. In J. E. Birren and K. W. Schaie, eds., *Handbook of the psychology of aging*.

REICH, W. 1972. *Character analysis*. New York: Farrar, Straus, and Giroux.

RYDER, R. G. 1967. Birth to maturity revisited: a canonical reanalysis. *Journal of Personality and Social Psychology* 1: 168-172.

SCHAEFER, E. S. 1964. An analysis of consensus in longitudinal research on personality consistency and change: discussion of papers by Bayler, Macfarlane, Moss and Kagan, and Murphy. *Vita Humana* 7: 143-146.

SCHAEFER, E. S., and BAYLEY, N. 1960. Consistency of maternal behavior from infancy to preadolescence. *Journal of Abnormal and Social Psychology* 61: 1-6.

———— 1963. Maternal behavior, child behavior, and their intercorrelations from infancy through adolescence. *Monographs of the Society for Research in Child Development* 28 (3, Serial No. 87): 1-127.

SCHAIE, K. W. 1965. A general model for the study of developmental problems. *Psychological Bulletin* 64: 94-107.

SEARS, R. R. 1977. Sources of life satisfactions of the Terman gifted men. *American Psychologist* 32: 119-128.

SKOLNICK, A. 1966. Stability and interrelationships of thematic test imagery over twenty years. *Child Development* 37: 389-396.

SMITH, M. E. 1952. A comparison of certain personality traits as rated in the same individuals in childhood and fifty years later. *Child Development* 23: 161-180.

THOMAS, A. and CHESS, S. 1977. *Temperament and development*. New York: Brunner Mazel Publ.

THOMAS, A., CHESS, S., BIRCH, H. G., HERTZIG, M. E. and KORN, S. 1963. *Behavioral individuality in early childhood*. New York: New York University Press.

TUDDENHAM, R. D. 1954. The consistency of personality ratings over two decades. *Genetic Psychology Monographs* 60: 3-29.

WALLACH, M. A., and KOGAN, N. 1965. *Modes of thinking in young children*. New York: Holt, Rinehart, and Winston.

WOHLWILL, J. F. 1973. *The study of behavioral development*. New York: Academic Press.

WOODRUFF, D. S., and BIRREN, J. E. 1972. Age changes and cohort differences in personality. *Developmental Psychology* 6: 252-259.

YANG, R. K., and HALVERSON, C. F. 1976. A study of the "inversion of intensity" between newborn and preschool-age behavior. *Child Development* 47: 350-359.

YANG, R. K., and MOSS, H. A. 1978. Neonatal precursors of infant behavior. *Developmental Psychology* 14: 607-613.

12 | Values, Attitudes, and Beliefs
Norval D. Glenn

THERE IS little disagreement that persons typically experience considerable change during their lifetimes in at least some of their attitudes, values, and beliefs. There is disagreement, however, concerning whether specific changes typically occur at specific stages of the life span in response to aspects of biological, social, and psychological aging. Nor is there agreement whether aging birth cohorts become less responsive to influences for change other than the influences associated with aging.

This chapter assesses evidence concerning the degree and the kinds of change in attitudes, values, and beliefs that typically occur at different stages of the life span. Since most of the evidence considered here pertains to the United States in the past few decades, I refrain from generalizing beyond this society during this brief period. However, most of the relevant theory leads one to expect a great deal of intersocietal continuity in lifetime patterns of change, at least in modern, industrialized societies.

Attitudes, values, and beliefs are psychological phenomena, and psychologists are deeply involved in research designed to assess the potency of different influences in bringing about attitude change, but much of the work on aging and attitudes has been done by sociologists and political scientists. As a sociologist with an interest in political phenomena, I am more inclined to draw on the work of sociologists and political scientists than on the work of psychologists, and I employ the concepts and analytic tools favored by the former. Although all students of aging and life span development face essentially the same logical and methodological problems, some of the problems are more salient in some disciplines than in others. The concepts and especially the terminology vary by discipline, thus making effective interdisciplinary communication difficult.

The term *attitude*, in common with many terms used in the social and behavioral sciences, has been defined in a variety of ways. For this essay, I define an attitude simply as an evaluation of an object, a definition consistent with most attitude measures used in social scientific research. The term *object*, in turn, refers not only to material things but also to persons, categories of people, institutions, organizations, ideas, practices, and the like. For instance, the object of an attitude might be premarital sexual intercourse, abortion, marriage, communism, the Catholic Church, psychology, or Italian-Americans. Defined in this way, an attitude is similar to an opinion, as that term is commonly used.

Some definitions of attitude include a cognitive component, or a belief about the nature of the object, in addition to the evaluation. Although cognition and evaluation of an object usually occur together, no evaluation is inextricably linked to any particular cognition, and thus it seems preferable to conceive of the two separately and to refer to the cognition as a belief rather than a component of an attitude.

Some authors try to make a clear distinction between attitude and value, whereas others do not. When an attitude is defined as an evaluation of an object, an unambiguous distinction between an attitude and a value does not seem possible. Some authors say that a value is more abstract than an attitude, but this distinction is hard to apply, since the objects of attitudes can be highly abstract and general. It therefore seems more useful to define a value as a special kind of attitude—one with a highly abstract and general object. Values, in other words, are highly abstract ideas about what is good or bad, right or wrong, desirable or undesirable. Although I define a value as a special kind of attitude, in order to avoid awkward phrasing I use the term *attitude* without a modifier to refer to attitudes that are not values.

The distinctions between attitude, belief, and value can be made clearer by illustration. Consider the following two statements.

Personal freedom is good.

The law recently passed by the legislature is good because it enhances personal freedom.

The first statement expresses a value, since it gives an evaluation of the highly abstract concept of personal freedom. The second statement expresses both an attitude ("the law is good") and a belief ("the law enhances individual freedom''). In this case the value, the belief, and the attitude bear a distinctive logical relationship to one another, so that they can be arranged into a loose, imperfect syllogism:

> Major premise (the value): Personal freedom is good.
> Minor premise (the belief): The law enhances personal freedom.
> Conclusion (the attitude): The law is good.

Of course, this is not a true syllogism; not everyone who accepts both premises must necessarily accept the conclusion, since several different values and beliefs may influence the attitude toward the law. However, the logical relationships illustrated by this imperfect syllogism are important to understanding how changes in values, attitudes, and beliefs can be and often are interrelated.[1]

The broad enterprise of attitude research often deals with values and beliefs, as I have defined them, as well as with the more specific attitudes. For instance, questions that ask respondents to predict whether there will be a third world war or to state whether they believe in God are loosely referred to as attitude questions, even though they ask about beliefs. The distinctions between attitude, value, and belief are sometimes theoretically important, but where the distinctions are not important I use terms and phrases such as *attitude research* and *attitudes and aging* in their more general sense.

Much recent research concerning aging and attitudes has used a strategy called cohort analysis. Cohort analysts employ a number of specific research techniques, and they have their own concepts and their own distinctive perspective on the logical problems of studying life span development.[2]

The term *cohort*, as it is used by cohort analysts, refers to people within a geographically or otherwise delineated population who experienced the same significant life event within a given period of time. The given period of time may be of any length and may begin at any arbitrarily selected point in time, but it is usually a period of from one to ten years. The significant life event is more often than not birth, in which case the cohort is a birth cohort.[3] When cohort is used without a modifier, the implied modifier is almost always birth. However, there are other kinds of cohorts, defined by events such as marriage, divorce, birth of the first child, retirement, completion of high school, and so forth.

The term *cohort analysis* usually designates a study in which there are measures of some characteristics of a cohort (birth or otherwise) at two or more points in time. The simplest cohort analysis, according to this definition, would be a comparison of the characteristics of one cohort at two points in time. For instance, persons born in 1920-1924 might be studied in 1940, when they were 16-20 years old, and in 1945, when they were 21-25 years old. In other words, this would be a study of change in the cohort from one point in time to another, or a simple intracohort trend study. Such a simple study might be useful for some purposes, but the utility for understanding life span development is minimal unless there are data for more than one cohort or for more than two points in time.

An intracohort trend study is similar to a panel study. The difference between the two is that in a panel study the same specific individuals are studied at two or more points of time and the total amount of individual change—including changes that offset one another in the aggregate data—is measured, while in an intracohort trend study, samples of individuals are independently drawn from the cohort at time 1 and at time 2 (and at any subsequent points in time), so that there is no measure of change at the indivdual level. For instance, suppose that 20% of the members of a birth cohort were Republican in 1960 and that 20% were also Republican in 1970. This lack of net change in the percentage of Republicans does not mean that there was no movement into and out of the Republican category from 1960 to 1970—only that movements in the two directions were equal. A panel study will reveal how many individual changes in party identification occurred, but an intracohort trend study will reveal only the net effect of those changes.

Typically a cohort analysis involves data on trends in more than one cohort and involves cross-sectional, intercohort comparisons as well. Frequently it also entails data on trends at each age level as one cohort replaces another. All these comparisons are possible from the standard cohort table, in which the intervals between the points in time for which there are data are uniform and correspond with the time intervals used to delineate the cohorts. Such a table is constructed by juxtaposing cross-sectional data for two or more points in time so that cross-sectional comparisons can be made by reading down the columns, intracohort trends can be traced by reading down and to the right, and trends at each age level can be traced by reading across the rows. (See tables 12.8 and 12.9 for examples of standard cohort tables.)

The differences among the cells of a standard cohort table have four distinct classes of sources (in addition to sampling error, in the case of data from survey samples): age effects, cohort effects, period effects, or compositional effects according to their presumed sources. Age effects result from influences associated with various aspects of biological, social, and psychological aging; cohort effects result from the unique situations and formative experiences of each cohort; period effects result from the influences associated with each period of time; and compositional effects result from changes in the kinds of people remaining in a cohort as cohort members die and as living people move into and out of the delineated population.

The term *age effects*, as it is used by cohort analysts, is often misunderstood. When data on chronological age are used to infer an age effect, it might seem that causation is being attributed to chronological age. In fact, social scientific students of aging agree that chronological age, by itself, is unlikely to have a direct effect on attitudes or other variables of interest to social scientists. Rather chronological age is used as a convenient surrogate for the several dimensions of biological, social, and psychological age, all of which are at least moderately correlated with chronological age.[4] To label a phenomenon an age effect is therefore to attribute it to one or more influences associated with chronological age. Of course, the phenomenon is not truly "explained" or "understood" until the specific influence or influences responsible for it are identified.

The variable *cohort* is also used in cohort analysis as a surrogate for a number of specific influences associated with it. Members of different cohorts have different formative experiences because of differences in child-rearing practices at different times and due to differences such as those in economic conditions during their early years. Furthermore, there are some lifelong differences in cohort situations, for instance, those growing out of the number of persons in the cohort relative to the numbers in older and younger cohorts. For example, in the United States members of the relatively small birth cohort born during the period of low fertility of the 1930s have had uniquely favorable job opportunities (Harter, 1977).

Period likewise is a variable used as a surrogate for a large number of specific influences, namely, all those influences that vary through time. For instance, period influences change with changes in economic conditions, as wars commence and cease, and as social and cultural change occurs.

Compositional effects are of a different nature from age, cohort, and period effects. As a birth cohort grows older, its membership suffers attrition due to mortality, and if the population is not closed— that is, if living people move into and out of it—some living cohort members will leave the population and other persons not among the original cohort members will come into the population and appear in cohort samples. In fact, mortality probably has very little effect on most cohort analyses of attitude data, because few attitudes seem to be correlated to an important degree with longevity. Furthermore, the population of the United States is sufficiently near to being closed that immigration and emigration presumably have little effect on most cohort analyses with U.S. national data. However, when the population used for cohort analysis is a portion of the total national population, and when movement into and out of that population is possible, compositional effects are likely to distort the results. For instance, a cohort analysis with data from the southern United States is likely to be affected to an important degree by the fact that many relatively prosperous older people move into the region to retire. To give an example with cross-sectional data, the positive correlation of age and job satisfaction among employed women in the United States (see Glenn, Taylor, and Weaver, 1977) may be largely a compositional effect. Many women who do not enjoy working outside the home may quit working by the time they are middle-aged, thus leaving in the labor force at the older ages primarily the women who enjoy working.

The study of developmental processes is an unusually difficult kind of research. A consideration of how the different kinds of effects are confounded with one another in a standard cohort table will illustrate why the research is so difficult. At least two of the four kinds of effects that account for the differences in the tables are confounded with one another in each column, in each cohort diagonal, and in each row. Age, cohort, and compositional effects are confounded in each column (and in each set of cross-sectional data that is not part of a cohort table); age, period, and compositional effects are confounded in each cohort diagonal; and cohort and period effects are confounded in each row. Furthermore, it is logically impossible to unconfound the age, cohort, and period effects through statistical analysis (Glenn, 1976, 1977). Since age is a perfect function of cohort and period, since cohort is a perfect function of age and period, and since period is a perfect function of cohort and age, it is impossible to hold two of these variables constant and vary the third. Cohort analysts are therefore faced with a classic example of the identification problem (Blalock, 1966, 1967), which obtains when two or more independent variables of theoretical interest are interrelated in such a way that their effects cannot be statistically separated. It is not logically impossible to separate compositional effects from the other effects, but the researcher rarely has all the information needed to do that.

Because of the identification problem, neither the cohort analyst nor the student of aging who examines cross-sectional, panel, or retrospective data is ever able to arrive at conclusive proof of cause and effect through the analysis of the data,[5] which are always susceptible to more than one interpretation. However, the researcher who uses theory and information from outside the data set (what Converse, 1976, calls "side information") to aid the interpretation can arrive at some rather confident conclusions about what causes what.

The Aging-Stability Thesis

A thesis that appears frequently in the social scientific literature on aging and attitudes is that attitudes, values, and beliefs tend to stabilize and to become less likely to change as persons grow older. This thesis is stated explicitly by Karl Mannheim (1953), Norman B. Ryder (1965), Gosta Carlsson and Katarina Karlsson (1970), S. N. Eisenstadt (1971), and Ronald Ingelhart (1977), and it is at least implicit in numerous other publications. For instance, all references to "formative experiences" and to a "formative stage" imply an early stage of high malleability followed by a stage of relative stability. That young people tend to change and that older people are less likely to change is a part of the folk wisdom that most people would never challenge. "Everyone knows" that people older than young adults tend to become "set in their ways" and that middle-aged and older persons are very likely to take their prejudices and preconceptions to their graves.

The social scientific statements on the topic are similar to but more sophisticated than the folk wisdom. For instance, Ryder (1965) states that "the potential for change is concentrated in the cohorts of young adults who are old enough to participate directly in the movements impelled by change, but not old enough to have become committed to an occupation, a residence, a family of procreation or a way of life" (p. 848). Carlsson and Karlsson (1970) describe and provide a formalized quantitative version of what they call a "fixation model." They write: "With increasing age people become less likely to change; in its later life each birth cohort reflects, therefore, largely the conditions prevailing during its early formative years. Changing conditions will become visible most directly and most quickly in the behavior of young people, late cohorts, and much less in the behavior of earlier cohorts, that is, among middle-aged or old people" (pp. 710-711). Although Carlsson and Karlsson speak of behavior, it is clear from their examples that their fixation model applies to attitudes as well. The quantitative version of the model, derived from data from a Swedish voting study, shows a monotonic decrease in change-proneness after ages 20-24 but the steepest decline from ages 25-29 to ages 30-34.

Most other statements of the aging-stability thesis imply that the decline in change-proneness is monotonic through adulthood but is nonlinear, because the decline is especially steep right after the earliest stage of adulthood. Some authors seem to think that the decline is continuous after early childhood, but others, including Ryder (1965), seem to think that persons in late adolescence are more likely to change than younger persons.

With a few exceptions, the statements of the aging-stability thesis in the social scientific literature seem to be based more on common-sense notions and the folk wisdom than on scholarly theory or on systematic examination of relevant evidence. However, as Ryder points out, the thesis is consistent with much of the literature on socialization and human development, which at least until recently tended to posit an early crystallization of "basic values" and a "basic personality structure." The view, once implicit in much of the literature on child development, that development ceases with the attainment of adulthood, is no longer considered tenable; nevertheless, there are still some apparently sound reasons for expecting values and attitudes to tend to stabilize after young adulthood.

One of the major reasons for this expectation is the dense spacing of significant life events in early adulthood and the wider spacing of those events thereafter (Browning, 1968). During a period of a few years beginning in late adolescence, the person typically experiences important status changes, assumes important new roles, and changes many social relationships. Leaving home, completing formal education, choosing and entering an occupation, marriage, and becoming a parent all typically occur within a very small proportion of the total life span. Both geographic and social mobility characterize early adulthood in modern societies and are much less frequent in the later years. The status transitions and assumption of new roles by young adults entail a great deal of resocialization, including presumably the adoption of new values and attitudes and the modification of old ones. Furthermore, the rapid succession of changes in circumstances and social relationships is likely to produce much attitude change that is not an aspect of resocialization.

This explanation does not posit a decline in the inherent changeability of the individual—only a decline in exposure to influences for change. There are also some reasons for believing that inherent changeability may decline with aging. For instance, Carlsson and Karlsson (1970) suggest that the physiological changes of aging may lead to rigidity in attitudes and behavior, and they cite some of the literature on age and intelligence. The relevant evidence is much more complex than Carlsson and Karlsson imply (see chapter 10 by Horn and Donaldson and chapter 9 by Wohlwill in this volume), but it is possible that biological aging brings a tendency toward rigidity.

Other authors believe that stabilization of values, attitudes, and beliefs comes about through attempts at adjustment (Ryder, 1965). According to this point of view, once the person arrives at a constellation of attitudes and beliefs that gives a sense of understanding and being able to deal with reality, the person tends to resist influences that would change those attitudes and beliefs and perhaps lead to feelings of dissonance. Some authors seem to believe in an "attitude inertia," by which attitudes, once established, tend to perpetuate themselves. It is almost as though established attitudes are thought to have an incumbency advantage over competing attitudes, analogous to the advantage of incumbent political officeholders over their challengers. Furthermore, long-held, publicly espoused attitudes are thought to be more fixed than recently acquired and privately held ones. A related view is that existing attitudes are the products of accumulated experience and that their resistance to change varies directly with the amount of experience that has produced and reinforced them. Glenn (1974) tries to convey the essence of this point of view through deliberate oversimplification:

> To illustrate how this change [increase in attitudinal stability] may occur, let us assume an oversimplified model of attitudinal development whereby one's attitude on a controversial issue is determined by the mean of all of the pro and con stimuli to which the person has been exposed. The second or third stimulus may change the mean considerably, but the twentieth or fiftieth can have relatively little effect. In fact, attitudes do not develop in such a simple fashion. Yet, there may be a tendency for the effects of stimuli to diminish with the number of preceding relevant stimuli. If the number and intensity of stimuli and experiences do not vary appreciably from one year to another, the effect of a year of living on one's attitudes may be roughly a function of the proportion of the time the person has lived which that year constitutes. If so, each subsequent year will tend to have somewhat less effect than the year before. (pp. 180-181)

One of the major problems with this oversimplified model is that the person is not a passive receptacle of influences, as the model implies, but rather has needs and dispositions that make him receptive to some influences and resistant to others. Hence prolonged and strong positive influences, for instance, may be offset by brief and weak negative influences if taking a negative position on some controversial issue is consistent with the person's needs and dispositions. However, this modification of the model does not change the prediction of increased attitude stability with aging, assuming that the person's needs and dispositions remain fairly stable. If even weak influences can lead a person to adopt attitudes consistent with his needs, by the middle adult years the person is likely to have acquired a large number of need-consistent attitudes that will be highly resistant to change.

The literature on the aging-stability thesis ostensibly deals with values, attitudes, and beliefs "in general," but there are reasons to expect differing average degrees of change and of stability for values, attitudes, and beliefs. Furthermore, some values are likely to be more stable than other values, some attitudes are likely to be more stable than other attitudes, and some beliefs are certainly more stable than other beliefs. At the stable end of the stability-malleability continuum should be the values emphasized during childhood socialization, the so-called deeply ingrained values concerning religion, the family, marriage, and such abstractions as love, freedom, democracy, and communism. At the malleable end of the continuum should be beliefs about the nature of changeable and tangible objects. The normal person of any age who has not suffered a sharp loss of perceptual acuity will change his beliefs about the nature of such an object if he attends to it as it changes. Beliefs with more abstract objects have much greater potential for stability, and some, such as a belief in God, may be as stable as the more stable values. In general, however, values should be relatively stable and beliefs should be relatively changeable. Attitudes should be highly variable, some being almost as changeable as the most changeable beliefs. For instance, attitudes with relatively changeable and tangible objects are likely to be quite changeable, even if the values that provide the standards of evaluation remain stable. An example is the approval by the people of the United States of the performance of a president. The expectations for his performance may remain stable, but the level of approval will fluctuate with changes in perceptions of the nature of his performance.

Since the changeability of such attitudes throughout all or almost all of the life span is hardly problematic, they are not appropriate for testing the aging-stability thesis. Rather one must seek measures of attitudes that tend to reflect "basic values," and these are generally attitudes with stable or highly abstract objects. These attitudes should tend to stabilize beyond young adulthood if the aging-stability thesis is correct.

Evidence concerning the inherent changeability of individuals must come from experimental research, in which the influences for change are controlled, or from research that measures and thus allows statistical control of the influences for change to which individuals are exposed. Unfortunately, such research designed to study age and attitude changeability has been very rare. A good many studies of attitude change have incorporated age into the research design in some way, but since the researchers have had no more than an incidental interest in the aging-stability thesis, they have not designed their research to test this thesis. For instance, they have not dealt with ceiling and floor effects, and the subjects have generally been few and lacking in the needed diversity in age.

Although Ryder (1965) and several other authors believe that greater attitude change is likely to occur in late adolescence and in young adulthood than at earlier stages of the life span, they attribute the difference to greater influences for change rather than to increased inherent changeability. Therefore the Ryder version of the aging-stability thesis is not contradicted by experimental studies, which have generally found greater attitude change in response to a controlled stimulus among younger than among older preadults (Guest, 1964; Vornberg and Grant, 1976; Roberts, 1969).

The few experimental studies that have compared adults of different ages have also generally found a negative relationship between age and degree of attitude change (Clos, 1966). Thus the experimental evidence, considered as a whole, suggests a monotonic decrease through the life span in attitude changeability. However, in view of the limitations of the evidence, this conclusion must be very tentative.[6]

There are numerous reports of experimental panel studies in the large literature on attitude change, but the studies in general have not been properly designed, and their data have not been properly analyzed, to shed light on the aging-stability thesis. The typical report of such studies focuses on test-retest correlations of attitudes measured at two points in time, the period between the two measurements sometimes being as long as 30 years. Test-retest correlations over periods of 20 to 30 years are typically small to moderate, thus indicating considerable change in attitudes.[7] However, the respondents were usually no older than young adults when the first measurement was taken, and the data do not show whether the attitudes tended to stabilize as the respondents grew older. Panel data have rarely been analyzed to compare the attitude change of older and younger respondents, but at least one such study has shown greater change among younger respondents than among older ones (Hoge and Bender, 1974).

The evidence of greatest interest comes from cohort studies, and of course it deals with aggregate change in birth cohorts rather than with the inherent changeability of individuals. Although several cohort studies have been designed at least in part to test the aging-stability thesis, some of them share weaknesses with the other kinds of studies; the most important is a failure to deal with ceiling and floor effects.

All measures of attitudes are sensitive to change only to a certain point in either direction, and since some respondents or subjects begin closer to that point than others, some have greater potential for measurable change than others. For instance, if evaluation of an object is indicated on a 10-point scale varying from 0 for very negative to 9 for very positive, a person who initially gives an evaluation of 8 has less potential for change in a positive direction than one who gives an initial rating of 5. Or, if the attitudes of entire categories of people are being compared, a category with 90% "approve" responses to an opinion question can move less in the direction of approval than a category with 30% "approve" responses.

An example with real data should make the issue clearer. A national survey of adults in the United States conducted in 1972 (the General Social Survey conducted by the National Opinion Research Center) found that 20% of the white females of ages 20-29 and 46% of those of ages 30-39 said that premarital sexual intercourse is "always wrong." Thus the potential for decline was 46 percentage points in the older of the two birth cohorts but only 20 percentage points in the younger cohort. By the time a similar survey was conducted in 1975, the indicated percentage had declined by 4 points in the younger cohort and by 12 points in the older one. Does the greater change in the older cohort indicate greater change-proneness in that cohort? Quite aside from problems of sampling error, the answer must be not necessarily, since a floor effect probably prevented the younger cohort from experiencing as much measured change as the older one. In fact, the younger cohort may have experienced a greater increase in sexual permissiveness than the older one, but beyond a certain point, such change would not be reflected in a decrease in the "always wrong" responses.

This illustration shows that simple comparisons of measured change in two categories are not always good bases for inferring relative degrees of change-proneness.[8] Furthermore, since most ceiling and floor effects are artifacts of the method of measurement rather than the result of empirical limits on the range of variation in attitudes, failure to take the effects into account can vitiate even descriptive comparisons of degrees of change.

However, if the compared categories are initially at about the same level for the attitude measured, or if the levels are different but all fairly near the floor (or ceiling) and moving away from it, then ceiling and floor effects are not a problem. For instance, if the initial percentages of respondents in three compared categories who chose a certain alternative to an opinion question are 15, 20, and 25, ceiling effects are unlikely to be responsible for any substantial differences in increases in the percentages.

The most important of the published evidence that tends to support the aging-stability model comes from two cohort studies of tolerance for nonconformity. Both studies use data collected by Samuel Stouffer in 1954 for his famous study reported in *Communism, Conformity, and Civil Liberties* (1955), and both use comparable data collected early in the 1970s.

Clyde Z. Nunn, Harry J. Crockett, and J. Allen Williams, Jr. (1978) did a full-scale replication of the Stouffer study with data collected in a national survey in 1973. The report of their study includes the data shown in table 12.1, which trace attitudes in three birth cohorts from 1954 to 1973. The attitudes used for this study are appropriate for testing the aging-stability thesis, because attitudes toward civil liberties and nonconformists are typically acquired in childhood and adolescence and are widely believed to be highly resistant to change after young adulthood.

Since the percentages for 1954 are all fairly low and not very different, ceiling effects should have had little or no impact on the amount of measured change in the different cohorts. The monotonic decrease in degree of change from the youngest to the oldest cohort is therefore consistent with the aging-stability thesis. The indicated amount of change is no more than moderate for any of the cohorts and is quite small for the one that was 40-49 years old in 1954 and 59-68 in 1973.

However, these data are not unambiguous evidence in support of the aging-stability thesis. Nunn, Crockett, and Williams do not report the size of their cohort samples, but the sample from the oldest cohort in 1973 was probably small.[9] Since the greatest indicated difference is between the oldest cohort and the two younger ones, sampling error in the oldest cohort could account for most of the negative relationship between change and age. Furthermore, if the data accurately reflect the intracohort changes in the total population, the greater change in

Table 12.1. Birth cohorts and political tolerance, 1954 and 1973.

Born in	Age in		Tolerance scale: percentage more tolerant			Listening in on conversations: percentage should not[a]		
	1954	1973	1954	1973	Change	1954	1973	Change
1925-33	21-29	40-48	41	56	+15	32	49	+17
1915-24	30-39	49-58	37	48	+11	31	45	+14
1905-14	40-49	59-68	31	33	+2	29	35	+6

Source: Reprinted with permission from Nunn, Crockett, and Williams (1978), p. 84.

a. Data pertain to attitudes about government investigators listening in on the conversations of communists.

the younger cohorts than in the oldest one could be a cohort effect rather than an age effect. That is, any greater change-proneness of the younger cohorts could be a lifelong difference, resulting perhaps from an early socialization that encouraged a more tentative commitment to values. Or, the higher educational attainments of the younger cohorts could make them more change-prone.

However, the other cohort study of tolerance for nonconformity indicates that differences in the change-proneness of the cohorts were not strictly the result of differences in education. Stephen J. Cutler and Robert L. Kaufman (1975) conducted a cohort analysis by using the Stouffer data and a few of the Stouffer items that were asked on the 1972 General Social Survey. Through use of multiple classification analysis, they controlled amount of education, race, and gender; thus differences in education among the cohorts could not account for any differences in amount of change in attitudes. In four ten-year birth cohorts, ranging in age from 20-29 to 50-59 in 1954, the indicated degree of change between 1954 and 1972 varied inversely and monotonically for a nine-item scale measuring general tolerance of ideological nonconformity and for three-item scales measuring tolerance of civil liberties for atheists, socialists, and communists. On the average, the amount of change for the oldest cohort was less than half the amount for the youngest cohort, and the variation between was approximately linear. A replication of the study with comparable data from the 1973 General Social Survey yielded very similar results.[10]

The similarity of the findings of these two cohort studies suggests that the intercohort pattern of change found by Nunn, Crockett, and Williams did not result solely from sampling error in the 1973 survey, since Cutler and Kaufman used different surveys conducted in the 1970s. The data from both studies, considered together, provide strong support for the aging-stability thesis, but of course one still cannot be certain that the intercohort differences in change were not cohort effects.

A third study that supports the aging-stability thesis is reported by Glenn (1974). A U.S. Gallup survey conducted in 1954 revealed that very few people of any age expressed approval of admission of Communist China to the United Nations, the percentage of approval responses varying from five to eight among five ten-year birth cohorts. By 1964 the indicated approval had increased moderately in the younger cohorts and very little in the older ones, the increase in percentage points, from the youngest to the oldest cohorts, being 13.9, 10.4, 8.9, 3.3, and 4.4. Although the cohort sample sizes were rather small, it is improbable that sampling error would produce such a nearly monotonic pattern of change.

Again, the indicated differences could be cohort rather than age effects, but these data on a different kind of attitude and from different samples combine with the data on tolerance of nonconformity to lend credence to the aging-stability thesis. However, the data from the three studies do not support the version of the thesis that states that there is a steep decline in change-proneness after the earliest stages of adulthood and a less steep decline after that. Rather, the Cutler and Kaufman and the Glenn data suggest an almost perfectly linear decline. The Nunn, Crockett, and Williams data suggest a possible non-linear pattern in any decline in change-proneness, but the steepest rate of decline seems to be between ages 30 and 40 rather than during the 20s.

Not all the relevant published data support the aging-stability thesis. A cohort analysis of political party identification by Norval Glenn and Ted Hefner (1972) found no systematic intercohort differences in the change when shifts in party identification in the United States occurred between 1945 and 1969.[11] Some data that Glenn and Hefner employed to help discern between cohort and age effects are shown in table 12.2. They assumed that the change during each four-year period in party identification in the 21-29-year-old life stage was a rough measure of the strength of period influences for change, and they reasoned that if change-proneness in each cohort declined as it grew older, the ratio of change in it to change in the 21-29 life stage would decline. Therefore, if the aging-stability thesis were correct, there should be a monotonic decrease in the ratios, both across the rows and down the columns in table 12.2. On the other hand, a de-

Table 12.2. Ratio of index of dissimilarity[a] (between adjacent dates) for cohorts to index of dissimilarity for the 21-29 life stage.

Cohort (date of birth)	1945-49	1949-53	1953-57	1957-61	1961-65	1965-69
1916-1925	1.16	0.83	0.14	1.19	0.76	1.06
1906-1915	1.02	0.40	0.33	0.49	0.30	0.75
1896-1905	0.40	0.20	1.36	0.47	1.47	1.15
1886-1895	1.60	0.26	1.36	0.68	1.52	0.49
Mean	1.05	0.42	0.80	0.71	0.93	0.71

Source: Reprinted with permission from Glenn and Hefner (1972), p. 45.

a. The index of dissimilarity is the percentage of individuals at either of the compared dates who, by changing identification, would have equalized the distributions for the two dates.

crease down the columns but not across the rows would indicate cohort but not age differences in change-proneness. Obviously, neither
of these systematic patterns of variation appears in the table.

However, Glenn and Hefner point out a peculiar pattern in the
data. In periods marking the beginning of a trend in the 21-29 life
stage (1949-1953, 1957-1961, and 1965-1969),[12] the ratios, and thus the
degree of change, averaged higher in the younger two cohorts than in
the older ones. Conversely, during periods in which a trend continued
(1953-1957 and 1961-1965), the change was greater in the older two
cohorts than in the younger cohorts or the 21-29 life stage. Only limited confidence can be placed in these data, since they are subject to
sampling error, but they seem to suggest that the influences that produced change in the younger cohorts produced change of a similar
magnitude in the older cohorts about four years later. If so, the delayed response to influences for change in the older cohorts could be
either an age or a cohort effect, but the data suggest that a modified
version of the aging-stability thesis may apply in this case.

The negative evidence concerning party identification should not
lead one to conclude that the simple form of the aging-stability thesis
is not generally correct. Party identification has been shown by panel
studies to be much more stable among adults than issue-related attitudes (Knoke, 1976), and in general, party identification seems to
behave differently from most other attitudes. Perhaps party identification tends to reach such a high level of stability early in the life span
that little increase in stability can occur later. In other words, a kind of
ceiling effect may prevent an appreciable increase in the stability of
party identification during the adult years.

The published evidence seems to support the aging-stability thesis,
on balance, but it deals with a very restricted range of attitudes, and
since the data are subject to sampling error, not much confidence
should be placed in evidence from only a few surveys. However, some
heretofore unpublished evidence adds to the volume of data and lacks
some of the weaknesses of the earlier evidence.

First, consider a reanalysis of the evidence on attitudes toward
admission of Communist China to the United Nations. The data in
Glenn (1974) are from one Gallup survey conducted in 1954 and one
conducted in 1964. It is possible to add data from a second survey
conducted in 1954 and from three other surveys conducted in 1964-65.
The resulting increase in the cohort sample sizes lessens the problem of
sampling error and produces a set of data in which one can have more
confidence (table 12.3).

The intercohort pattern of change shown by the enlarged data set

Table 12.3. Change in reported approval of admission of Communist China to the United Nations in five ten-year birth cohorts, U.S. national data, 1954 to 1964-65.[a]

Cohort			Percentage approving (N)		Change	Education-adjusted change[b]
			1954	*1964-1965*		
1	Age	20-29	30-39		15.0	13.2
		9.4 (645)	24.4 (1,246)			
2	Age	30-39	40-49		10.4	10.9
		8.8 (797)	19.2 (1,380)			
3	Age	40-49	50-59		8.6	10.2
		7.9 (646)	16.5 (1,144)			
4	Age	50-59	60-69		7.3	8.6
		7.2 (431)	14.5 (973)			
5	Age	60-69	70-79		8.5	8.3
		3.6 (318)	12.1 (492)			

Source: American Institute of Public Opinion (American Gallup) Surveys 533, 534, 684, 701, 706, and 721.

a. Data are standardized to a sex ratio of 100.

b. Data are standardized to an educational distribution with equal proportions of people with (1) no high school diploma, (2) high school diploma but no college, (3) some college but no degree, and (4) one or more college degrees.

is still generally consistent with the aging-stability thesis (third column of table 12.3), but there is little indicated difference in the change in the oldest three cohorts. These data, taken at face value, seem to indicate an important decline in change-proneness prior to age 40 but little or no decline after that.

Any intercohort differences in change-proneness could result from differences in amount of education, since there are reasons to believe that highly educated persons tend to be unusually attentive and responsive to influences for change. To see whether the intercohort differences in change shown in table 12.3 resulted from differences in education, I standardized the data from all cohorts to the same educational distribution. The education-adjusted changes shown in the fourth column of the table fall into a perfectly monotonic pattern consistent with the aging-stability thesis, and thus differences in education seem to account for little of the variation in amount of change. Of course, controlling for education does not necessarily remove all cohort effects, but the education-adjusted data lend credence to an aging interpretation.

The next body of evidence deals with racial, ethnic, and religious tolerance and intolerance, which are presumably among those "deeply ingrained" attitudes that become highly resistant to change by the middle adult years. Civil rights workers during the 1960s often discounted older whites, especially those in the South, and proclaimed that the hope for the future lay with youth. The belief that "older people aren't going to give up their prejudices" partly accounted for the shift in strategy early in the 1960s away from attempts to reduce prejudice to direct attacks on discrimination.[13]

In view of the prevalence of the belief in the futility of trying to reduce the prejudice of older people, the data in tables 12.4-12.6 are of special interest. On an American Gallup survey in 1959 and again in 1969 respondents were asked whether they would vote for a qualified black, Jew, and Catholic for president.[14] During that decade the responses changed substantially, and the data in tables 12.4-12.6 show that there was an important amount of change in the older birth cohorts as well as in the younger ones. The oldest cohort consistently changed the least, but otherwise there was no consistent tendency for the younger cohorts to change more than the older ones.

These data seem to be evidence against the aging-stability thesis, at least in the form that posits a linear decline in change-proneness or in the form that posits a steep decline after the earliest stage of adulthood. However, the data are subject to distortion by ceiling effects, since in 1959 the proportion who said they would vote for a minority candidate for president was considerably higher among younger adults than among older ones. Some of the percentages in the younger cohorts were as high as 75 and thus could increase by only about 25 points.

Methods for taking ceiling effects into account are controversial; since it is not known precisely how the effects operate, there can be no precise correction for them. However, most of the suggested corrections would yield rather similar results if used on the data in tables 12.4-12.6. One transformation simply expresses the measured change in each cohort as a percentage of the potential change (fourth column). This correction is based on the assumption that if the cohorts have equal change-proneness, they will move equal proportions of the distance to the ceiling. Another transformation converts the complement of each percentage to its common logarithm (fifth column). Use of the complement changes ceiling effects to floor effects, and the log transformation takes into account that as the floor is approached, movement toward it will decelerate; as the percentage drops toward zero, decrements of a percentage point become progressively larger on the log scale. If the deceleration due to floor effects is accurately taken into account by the log transformation, then cohorts with equal change-proneness should change the same amount on the log scale.

Table 12.4. Change in reported willingness to vote for a black for president, whites in five ten-year birth cohorts, U.S. national data, 1959-1969.[a]

Cohort	Percentage willing to vote for a black (N)		Change	Change as percentage of potential change	Change in log of complement	Education-adjusted[b]		
	1959	1969				Change	Change as percentage of potential change	Change in log of complement
1	Age 20-29 59.4 (201)	30-39 71.5 (293)	+12.1	29.6	−0.16	+10.3	22.8	−0.17
2	Age 30-39 50.9 (285)	40-49 64.7 (295)	+13.8	28.1	−0.14	+8.3	17.6	−0.08
3	Age 40-49 39.3 (292)	50-59 63.8 (244)	+24.8	40.4	−0.22	+22.5	37.4	−0.20
4	Age 50-59 39.0 (240)	60-69 57.9 (201)	+18.9	31.0	−0.17	+20.4	34.3	−0.18
5	Age 60-69 36.2 (199)	70-79 46.1 (124)	+9.9	15.5	−0.07	+15.7	25.2	−0.12

Source: American Institute of Public Opinion (American Gallup) Surveys 622 and 776.

a. Data are standardized to a sex ratio of 100.

b. Data are standardized to an educational distribution with equal proportions of people with (1) no high school diploma, (2) high school diploma but no college, (3) some college but no degree, and (4) one or more college degrees.

Table 12.5. Change in reported willingness to vote for a Jew for president, non-Jewish persons in five ten-year birth cohorts, U.S. national data, 1959-1969.[a]

Cohort		Percentage willing to vote for a Jew (N)		Change	Change as percentage of potential change	Change in log of complement	Education-adjusted[b]		
		1959	1969				Change	Change as percentage of potential change	Change in log of complement
1	Age	20-29 78.1 (225)	30-39 92.2 (330)	+14.1	64.4	-0.45	+14.6	57.4	-0.37
2	Age	30-39 75.1 (319)	40-49 87.7 (304)	+12.6	50.6	-0.31	+9.8	37.7	-0.20
3	Age	40-49 71.1 (308)	50-59 83.9 (248)	+12.8	44.3	-0.25	+12.3	43.2	-0.24
4	Age	50-59 66.4 (250)	60-69 82.1 (209)	+15.7	46.7	-0.28	+14.4	46.3	-0.27
5	Age	60-69 67.7 (209)	70-79 72.0 (130)	+4.4	13.6	-0.06	+7.4	26.1	-0.13

Source: American Institute of Public Opinion (American Gallup) Surveys 622 and 776.

a. Data are standardized to a sex ratio of 100.
b. Data are standardized to an educational distribution with equal proportions of people with (1) no high school diploma, (2) high school diploma but no college, (3) some college but no degree, and (4) one or more college degrees.

Table 12.6. Change in reported willingness to vote for a Catholic for President, non-Catholic persons in five ten-year birth cohorts, U.S. national data, 1959-1969.[a]

Cohort	Age	Percentage willing to vote for a Catholic (N)		Change	Change as percentage of potential change	Change in log of complement	Education-adjusted[b] Change	Change as percentage of potential change	Change in log of complement
		1959	1969						
1	Age 20-29 30-39	73.4 (174)	93.7 (243)	+19.4	75.5	−0.61	+18.4	69.2	−0.51
2	Age 30-39 40-49	69.0 (223)	88.6 (212)	+19.6	63.2	−0.43	+20.7	61.8	−0.42
3	Age 40-49 50-59	65.2 (238)	82.8 (136)	+17.6	50.6	−0.30	+18.1	51.4	−0.32
4	Age 50-59 60-69	55.9 (202)	80.3 (171)	+24.4	55.3	−0.35	+25.3	60.1	−0.39
5	Age 60-69 70-79	54.8 (177)	69.6 (114)	+14.8	32.7	−0.18	+13.7	31.3	−0.16

Source: American Institute of Public Opinion (American Gallup) Surveys 622 and 776.

a. Data are standardized to a sex ratio of 100.

b. Data are standardized to an educational distribution with equal proportions of people with (1) no high school diploma, (2) high school diploma but no college, (3) some college but no degree, and (4) one or more degrees.

Therefore the aging-stability thesis predicts that the transformed change measures will vary inversely with the age of the cohorts.

In tables 12.5 and 12.6, the transformations bend the data almost into the predicted pattern. The indicated change decreases monotonically from the youngest to the oldest cohorts, except that the indicated change in cohort 4 is greater than in the next younger cohort. This one deviation from the expected pattern could easily have resulted from sampling error. In contrast, the transformed data in table 12.4 do not support the aging-stability thesis, except that the smallest indicated change is in the oldest cohort. The greatest indicated change is in cohort 3, which was 40-49 years old in 1959 and 50-59 years old in 1969.

Standardizing the data to the same educational distribution (the last three columns of tables 12.4-12.6) tends to move them away from the pattern predicted by the aging-stability thesis and indicates that an important amount of any greater change-proneness of the younger cohorts was due to their higher educational attainments. The data in table 12.4 no longer support the aging-stability thesis, and the data in table 12.5 support it only insofar as the smallest indicated change is for the oldest cohort and the greatest change is for the youngest one. Only the data in table 12.6, on voting for a Catholic for president, still are in the negative monotonic pattern, except for the deviant cohort 4.

Overall, the data in table 12.4-12.6 provide only limited support for the aging-stability thesis. Since those data come from only two surveys and from rather small cohort samples, it would be a mistake to conclude that they are important negative evidence. However, they do suggest that the aging-stability thesis is not categorically correct, that change-proneness in regard to all kinds of attitudes reflecting basic values does not always decline as cohorts age through the adult stages of the life span. Perhaps the most important implication of the data is that older adults can and do change their responses to questions designed to measure racial and ethnic prejudice.[15]

The failure of the data on voting for a black for president to support the aging-stability thesis deserves special attention. If this failure did not result from sampling error, it may reflect the fact that whites aged 40 and older, who seemed generally to have been more responsive than younger people to influences for change, had less reason than the younger whites to feel threatened by the intensified black drive for equality during the 1960s. Middle-aged whites were usually already well established in their occupations and were in little danger of suffering economic and occupational losses as a result of black gains.[16] If this explanation is correct, the case of white attitudes toward blacks during the 1960s may be unusual but hardly unique, since there should be other occasions when the self-interests of young adults tend to make them more resistant than older adults to influences for change. Even if younger birth cohorts are generally more susceptible than older cohorts to attitude change, the perceived self-interests of the cohort members may, in addition to this general susceptibility, determine how a cohort reacts to specific influences for change.

In spite of the theoretical and practical importance of the aging-stability thesis as it applies to values, attitudes, and beliefs, research to test it is only in its infancy. Any conclusions about the validity of the thesis must therefore be quite tentative.

On balance, the available evidence supports the thesis, the most important negative evidence being in regard to political party identification and expressed attitudes toward a hypothetical black presidential candidate. The most reasonable tentative conclusion seems to be that the general change-proneness of cohorts declines in an approximately linear fashion after adolescence or young adulthood but that differences in perceived self-interests occasionally lead older cohorts to respond more than younger ones to period influences for change. Furthermore, some attitudes, such as political party identification, may be so stable in young adulthood that there can be little increase in stability as a birth cohort grows older.

An alternative explanation for all the evidence supporting the aging-stability thesis is that each birth cohort that has matured into adulthood in recent decades has been more change-prone than the cohort before it, as a result of changes in early socialization that have led to a more tentative commitment to values and attitudes. There is no fully satisfactory research strategy to provide evidence on which to base a choice between this explanation and the aging-stability thesis. (Of course, both could be correct.) However, the most fruitful approaches are likely to be those that trace cohorts through major portions of the life span and compare the intracohort changes at each life-span stage with estimates of period influences, similar to the procedure used by Glenn and Hefner (1972).

Additive Effects of Aspects of Aging

Only one thesis guides the discussion of the possible effects of aging on the responses of birth cohorts to period influences.[17] However, there are dozens of propositions concerning possible effects of various dimensions of biological, social, and psychological aging at various stages of the life span. Some of the propositions derive from theory and the folklore; others come from examination of cross-sectional data. Space limitations preclude discussion of a large proportion of the propositions, and the few topics that are presented to illustrate the nature of the evidence reflect my personal interests; but they have all received much attention in the social scientific literature.

Liberalism-Conservatism

Perhaps the most widely held belief about the effects of aging on attitudes is that aspects of the aging process tend to produce conservative attitudes. The meaning of the term *conservative* varies among the authors who use it, but the conceptions of conservatism are broadly similar and include such elements as a high valuation of social order, emphasis on authority and obedience, a restrictive rather than tolerant and permissive attitude toward human behavior, and opposition to egalitarianism. In addition, conservatism is often identified with opposition to humanitarian social and political movements and with the interests of the more privileged segments of society (Glenn, 1974).

According to the folklore, the liberalism of youth tends to give way to conservatism in the middle adult years. Proponents of the aging-conservatism thesis generally do not posit monotonic change in a conservative direction from early childhood on. Rather they assume that children typically accept the conservative values of their parents and reject some or all of those values during late adolescence and young adulthood. Then, according to this view, the trend toward conservatism during adulthood is largely a matter of reacceptance of the values rejected during late adolescence. Some authors seem to think that the trend during adulthood is approximately linear, but most state or imply that the greatest rate of change is during young adulthood.

Passage from the earliest to the early-middle stages of the adult life span by way of marriage and childbearing, an aspect of social aging, may tend to lessen devotion to humanitarian ideals and thus to lessen the specific attitudes that derive from humanitarian values. Although individuals vary along a general dimension from altruism to self-centeredness, they may vary as much or more in the focus of their altruistic concerns. This latter variation may depend to a large extent on the stage of social aging. Any altruistic impulses of the unmarried young adult or adolescent are likely to be diffuse, perhaps directed to racial and ethnic minorities or to disadvantaged people in general. With the assumption of family responsibilities, however, any general humanitarianism is likely to be overshadowed by concern for specific others. If one's family is not among the disadvantaged, there will be some conflict between the interests of the family and those of the disadvantaged. Faced with this conflict, the person is likely to favor the interests of the family.

To the extent that persons become successful, either in terms of "worldly" accomplishment or simply in terms of attaining a fairly high level of psychological well-being, they have interests at stake in the status quo and may be motivated to resist social and political change. To the extent that success, broadly defined, increases with age, then growing older should be accompanied by an increase in conservatism.[18]

Some conservatives believe that experience tends to lead to more accurate and realistic views of human nature and society and thus to acceptance of conservative tenets. For instance, if—as one kind of conservatism would have it—people are by nature evil and must be restrained by law and other social institutions, then accumulative exposure to incompletely restrained human nature should tend to convert one to conservatism. Of course, only a conservative is likely to believe that any conservatism associated with aging is simply an aspect of wisdom born of experience.

An abundance of cross-sectional data relate age to many of the dimensions of conservatism. This evidence should not be ignored, although its meaning is inherently ambiguous. Table 12.7 presents a fairly representative selection of recent cross-sectional data from U.S. national surveys.

These data, like most of the cross-sectional data, generally show a positive monotonic relationship of age to conservatism, although there are exceptions. For instance, traditional religious beliefs were just as characteristic of the younger respondents as of the older ones, although a slightly larger percentage of the older respondents said that religion can answer most of today's problems. Political and economic conservatism varied moderately and moral conservatism substantially by age—the greatest age differences in responses being to questions about premarital sexual intercourse and legalization of the use of marijuana.

Overall the responses varied more between the youngest and middle age levels than between the middle and oldest levels: the average of the conservative percentages across the 22 questions was 44 for under age 30, 53 for ages 30-49, and 56 for age 50 and older. This pattern is consistent with the belief that there tends to be a sharp shift toward conservatism after the youngest adult stage of the life span. However, there are reasons to suspect that the pattern results, partly or entirely, from a sharp cohort difference between people who became adults before the mid 1960s and those who became adults during the tumultuous late 1960s and early 1970s.

Analysis of cross-sectional data can never provide a definitive choice between the cohort and aging explanations. However, some clues can be derived from controlling amount of education—a cohort

Table 12.7. Percentage of conservative responses to selected attitude and belief questions, U.S. national samples, by age.

	Age		
Question	Under 30	30-49	50 and older
Think that premarital sexual intercourse is always wrong (whites only, 1972)	18	41	52
Oppose legalization of abortion through third month of pregnancy (1974)	36	52	57
Oppose legalization of use of marijuana (1974)	54	79	83
Oppose the Equal Rights Amendment (1974)	17	22	27
Would not vote for a woman for president (1969)	35	39	41
Oppose busing to achieve better racial balance in the schools (1974)	55	70	70
Disapprove of marriage between whites and blacks (1972)	44	60	72
Disapprove of marriage between Jews and non-Jews (1972)	9	13	17
Disapprove of marriage between Protestants and Catholics (1972)	7	14	17
Believe that religion can answer most of today's problems (1974)	55	64	66
Believe in life after death (1968)	71	73	75
Believe in God (1968)	97	98	99
Believe in heaven (1968)	84	84	88
Believe in hell (1968)	66	67	65
Believe in the devil (1968)	60	61	60
Consider themselves conservative (1972)	29	44	48
Would prefer the conservative party if the two major parties were liberal and conservative (1974)	29	44	40
Think the federal government should reduce spending for social programs (1974)	22	35	43
Oppose a 5% surtax on family incomes over $15,000 to help pay for programs for poor and unemployed (1974)	50	64	52

(*continued*)

Table 12.7 continued

| | Age | | |
Question	Under 30	30-49	50 and older
Oppose cut in defense spending (1974)	44	43	47
Oppose reestablishment of diplomatic relations with Cuba (1974)	30	39	40
Favor the death penalty for persons convicted of murder (1974)	52	66	71

Source: Various issues of the *Gallup Opinion Index*, except for the data on attitudes toward premarital sexual intercourse, which are from the 1972 General Social Survey.

characteristic. In general, well-educated persons are less conservative than persons with less education, and thus it might seem that the lower educational attainments of the older cohorts could account for their greater conservatism.

Controls for education do generally reduce age differences in conservatism, but rarely if ever do they completely remove them. Typical is the case of attitudes toward premarital sexual intercourse. Standardizing the responses from each age level to the same educational distribution results in "always wrong" responses of 20% for under age 30, 39% for ages 30-39, and 47% for age 50 and older. In other words, the difference between the youngest and middle levels is reduced from 23 to 19 percentage points, and the difference between the middle and oldest levels is reduced from 11 to 8 points. It is clear that the differences in education were not responsible for most of the differences in conservatism.

Nevertheless, a cohort explanation is generally more appealing than an aging explanation for the cross-sectional relationship of age to various dimensions of conservatism. If the aging-stability thesis is correct, then influences for change will affect the cohorts differently according to their age and will produce age differences in attitudes. At any one time, younger adults will differ from older people in the direction of recent change, and the magnitude of the age differences will vary directly with the magnitude of the recent change. In general, the data in table 12.7 fall into this pattern. According to trend data from U.S. national surveys, religious beliefs in this country have changed little in recent decades, and any age differences in religious beliefs are minimal. The trend data show a moderate decrease in many kinds of political and economic conservatism, and the age differences in political and economic conservatism are moderate. The trend data show a substantial decrease in recent years in such dimensions of conservatism as opposition to premarital sexual intercourse, opposition to legalization of use of marijuana, and opposition to interracial marriage. The age differences on these variables are substantial.

Another reason for favoring the cohort interpretation is a general failure of panel and cohort data to support the aging-conservatism thesis. Individuals and cohorts seem generally to have become more liberal rather than more conservative as they have aged during the past few decades (Greeley and Spaeth, 1970; Cutler and Kaufman, 1975; tables 12.1, 12.3, 12.4-12.6). Of course, these observed changes are primarily if not entirely period effects, and effects of aging could have been masked by stronger period effects in the opposite direction. If so, however, the age effects could not have been very great.

To my knowledge, only one cohort study has provided any definite support for the aging-conservatism thesis. A cohort analysis of liberal-conservative self-identifications has shown a trend toward conservatism within aging cohorts without a corresponding trend in the total adult population (Evan, 1965). However, the fact that the aging persons apparently came to view themselves as more conservative does not mean that they became more conservative according to any constant definition of conservatism. As the society as a whole has become less conservative, aging cohorts apparently have not changed to a corresponding extent (as the aging-stability thesis predicts) and thus have become more conservative relative to other people in the society. In other words, social definitions of conservatism have changed, so that persons whose attitudes have remained the same or have become only slightly more liberal have apparently come to view themselves, and perhaps to be viewed by others, as having become more conservative.

One set of previously unpublished cohort data relating to aging and conservatism is shown in table 12.8. Since the 1940s, the American Gallup Poll has periodically asked its respondents the following question:

Which of these three policies would you like to have President _____ follow?
  a. Go more to the Left, by following more of the views of labor and other liberal groups.
  b. Go more to the Right, by following more of the views of business and conservative groups.
  c. Follow a policy halfway between the two.

Table 12.8. Percentage of respondents who said they would like for the federal administration to "go to the Right," by age, U.S. national data, 1945, 1955, and 1965.[a]

Age	1945 (N)		1955 (N)		1965 (N)	
20-29	10.1	(737)	14.9	(256)	17.6	(590)
30-39	15.2	(984)	15.2	(320)	13.8	(621)
40-49	16.6	(979)	15.7	(296)	16.5	(677)
50-59	20.7	(753)	18.4	(209)	16.9	(598)
60-69	26.3	(411)	24.3	(147)	16.4	(537)
70-79	19.9	(158)	17.6	(69)	15.7	(268)
Total	16.9	(4,022)	16.9	(1,297)	16.2	(3,291)

Source: American Institute of Public Opinion (American Gallup) Surveys 353, 362, 701, and 721.

a. Data are standardized to a sex ratio of 100.

This question is superior to a liberal-conservatism self-identification question, since it identified Left with the interests of labor and Right with the interests of business rather than leaving the terms undefined. However, the wording is ambiguous, since "more to the Left" and "more to the Right" might seem to imply a comparison with the current policies of the president. Thus the responses may reflect not only the values of the respondents but also their perceptions of the current policies of the president. Nevertheless, the percentage of "go to the Right" responses provides a rough measure of the degree of conservatism in each cohort. In the absence of any trend in the total population or any apparent period influences toward conservatism, consistent increases in conservative responses in the aging cohorts would suggest an age effect.

The conservatism data are arranged in standard cohort table format (table 12.8); each cohort can be traced through time by reading diagonally down and to the right. Although five of the indicated intracohort changes from one date to the next are in a conservative direction, four are in the opposite direction and one percentage remained virtually stable. Among the four cohorts that can be traced through the entire twenty-year period, the trend in conservative responses was distinctly up in one and distinctly down in another, and the remaining two experienced little net change, according to the data. Therefore the intracohort trend data fail to support the aging-conservatism thesis.

However, it is possible that a one-time age effect had disappeared by 1965. According to the data, a distinct positive relationship between age and conservatism existed in 1945, was weaker in 1955, and had disappeared by 1965. Although the meaning of this trend is unclear, it may reflect a disappearing age effect.

Political Party Identification

Closely related to the aging-conservatism issue is the debate about age effects on political party identification in the United States. Some authors have hypothesized that a tendency for aging individuals to become more conservative has led to an increase in Republican party identification in aging cohorts. John Crittenden (1962) published a widely cited and highly influential article reporting a cohort analysis which he claimed indicated an aging effect toward Republican identification, and for several years this conclusion was generally accepted as correct.

However, Crittenden's data show only that during the period covered by his study (1946-1958), Republican identification did not decline as much in the aging cohorts as it did in the total adult population. Therefore the aging cohorts became more Republican in a relative sense but not in an absolute sense. Furthermore, since much of the decline in Republican identification in the total adult population resulted from mortality in the heavily Republican older cohorts (Glenn and Hefner, 1972), not all the influences producing the trend in the total adult population impinged on the aging cohorts. The failure of the aging cohorts to follow the general trend away from Republicanism is thus not evidence for an aging effect toward Republican identification or conservatism. The high percentage of Republicans in the older cohorts, who received their early socialization during the Republican era prior to the Great Depression, was apparently a cohort rather than an age effect.

Critiques of the Crittenden aging-Republicanism thesis by Neal Cutler (1969-70), Glenn and Hefner (1972), and Philip E. Converse (1976) have apparently led to its rejection by most political scientists and political sociologists concerned with the issue. It is not certain that aging has not exerted some influence toward Republican identification, but there appears to be no credible evidence for such influence. Some tentative evidence suggests that a trend toward Republicanism in the white-collar portions of the aging cohorts may have been offset by a trend away from Republican identification in the blue-collar portions (Glenn, 1973).

Another hypothesis concerns a possible age effect on the strength of party identification and on political independence. Angus Campbell and his colleagues (1960) concluded on the basis of cross-sectional data that strength of party identification tends to increase with age. More recently, Converse (1976) conducted careful cohort analyses which provide persuasive evidence that from about 1945 to 1965 the aging of each adult birth cohort in the United States led to a decrease in political independence in it and to an increase in the mean strength of the party identification of the identifiers. The evidence is quite persuasive because (1) independence decreased and strength of party identification increased in the aging cohorts and (2) a lack of a trend in party identification in the entire adult population suggests that there were no period influences that could account for the intracohort trends. However, the magnitude of the apparent age effects is not great, and virtually everyone who has examined the data apparently agrees that the sharp age differences in independence that have appeared since 1966 are cohort rather than age effects (Glenn, 1972b; Converse, 1976; Abramson, 1975, 1976).

Persuasive evidence of age effects in the past does not necessarily mean that the effects will persist. Age effects may change through time, or, stated differently, there may be age-period interactions. In some cases once-persuasive evidence becomes less persuasive when it is viewed in light of more recent data. An example is the case of possible age effects on interest in politics.

Interest in Politics

In the United States, as well as in many other countries, voter turnout has been lowest among young adults (Glenn and Grimes, 1968; Tingsten, 1937; Crittenden, 1963; Schmidhauser, 1958; Campbell et al., 1960), and cohort analyses have established that voter turnout has increased in birth cohorts in the United States as they have aged from young adulthood to middle age (Glenn and Grimes, 1968). There are several possible reasons for the low turnout among young adults, but since cross-sectional data have also shown low interest in politics and low knowledge of political events and personalities among young adults, it might seem that the age differences in voting have resulted to a large extent from differences in interest in politics (Glenn and Grimes, 1968; Glenn, 1969, 1972a). The low interest in politics of young adults, in turn, may result from the dense spacing of significant life events in young adulthood, which distracts young adults from politics. If so, there is an effect of social age on interest in politics.

However, recent data show that age differences in reported interest in politics had virtually disappeared by the late 1960s (table 12.9), while age differences in voter turnout persisted (U.S. Department of Commerce, 1972). The complicated pattern of the data in table 12.9 suggests no simple interpretation. The data indicate that from 1960 to

Table 12.9. Percentage of respondents who reported "a great deal" of interest in politics, by age, U.S. national data, 1952, 1960, and 1968.[a]

Age	1952 (N)	1960 (N)	1968 (N)
21-28	19.0 (1,555)	18.4 (447)	18.7 (249)
29-36	22.0 (1,756)	22.3 (619)	17.4 (241)
37-44	24.1 (1,527)	24.8 (655)	17.0 (251)
45-52	28.6 (1,281)	21.7 (498)	20.5 (248)
53-60	30.7 (1,035)	28.7 (451)	19.0 (204)
61-68	33.8 (779)	27.8 (450)	18.9 (150)
69-76	37.3 (431)	30.0 (240)	23.0 (101)
Total	25.7 (8,364)	24.2 (3,360)	18.9 (1,444)

Source: American Institute of Public Opinion (American Gallup) Surveys 502, 503, 504, 636, 757, and 758.

a. Data are standardized to a sex ratio of 100.

1968 reported interest in politics declined in all the cohorts (the largest changes occurred in the two oldest cohorts), probably due to period influences, and yet reported interest did not decline at the youngest adult age level, as would be expected if there had been strong general period influences toward less interest in politics. The effects of age may have changed during the period, or some complicated combination (and perhaps interaction) of age, period, and cohort effects may account for the pattern of the data in table 12.9. At any rate, there is a lesson to be learned—namely, that relationships between age and attitudes may change rapidly.

Vocationally Related Interests

Vocationally related interests are among the attitudes for which there is considerable evidence for age effects. Much of the evidence is summarized by David P. Campbell (1971) and is from a number of longitudinal studies of responses (of males only) to the Strong Vocational Interest Blank.[19] The data from a number of panel studies covering overlapping age ranges provide reasonably good evidence of changes in expressed interests from age 15 to about age 50. The data confound age and period effects, but there is little reason to believe that most of the attitudes tapped by the Strong instrument have been subject to appreciable period effects. It is therefore reasonable to assume that the observed changes reflect primarily age effects.

A fairly large number of the Strong items evinced an important relationship to age, and they were combined to form the Age-Related

Interest Scale. The scale scores increased very steeply, in the longitudinal data, from age 15 to age 20 and then increased at a decelerating rate until the change virtually ceased beyond age 40. The items on the scale are varied, but the one with the largest positive weight (its selection increased with age) measured interest in "raising flowers and vegetables," and the item with the largest negative weight measured interest in "climbing along the edge of a precipice." Many of the negatively weighted items involve physical activity and risk taking. The greatest changes in expressed interests were among the most highly educated respondents.

These data are probably the strongest available evidence for any kind of age effect on attitudes, and they are unusual in covering attitude changes from late adolescence to young adulthood. One must not generalize from these attitudes to others, because the vocationally related interests, unlike most other kinds of attitudes, could be directly affected by the biological changes of aging. Nevertheless, it is important that the greatest changes in vocationally related interests were observed prior to adulthood—a fact suggesting that studies restricted to the adult years may often fail to detect the most pronounced age effects on attitudes.

Job Satisfaction

Longitudinal studies of job satisfaction and attitudes toward work have been rare (a notable exception is Hoppock, 1960),[20] but cross-sectional data relating age to job satisfaction abound (Wright and Hamilton, 1978; Gibson and Klein, 1970; Herzberg et al., 1957; Hulin and Smith, 1965; Saleh and Hyde, 1969; Quinn, Staines, and McCullough, 1974; Campbell, Converse, and Rodgers, 1976). Most of the studies deal only with males, but a few of the recent studies deal with females in the United States (Glenn, Taylor, and Weaver, 1977). The studies consistently show a positive relationship, which, while not large in an absolute sense, is stronger than most other observed relationships with job satisfaction. The usual explanation of the relationship is that it is an age effect, that workers tend to become more satisfied with their work as they grow older, perhaps because job changes eventually result in a better fit between workers and jobs (Wright and Hamilton, 1978). The plausibility of this interpretation is enhanced by the fact that the relationship has been observed in the United States over a period of more than fifteen years, during which time the overall level of job satisfaction has changed very little. Presumably, if the relationship were a cohort effect, by which workers in each successively younger cohort tended to enjoy work less than those in the older cohorts, then the exit of older cohorts from the labor force through death and retirement and the entry of new cohorts would lead to a steady decline in overall job satisfaction.

However, two other credible interpretations of the data lead to the conclusion that there has been no persuasive evidence of important age effects on job satisfaction. First, there are possible, and even probable, offsetting period and cohort effects that could account for the approximate stability in the age-job satisfaction relationship and in the overall level of job satisfaction. Successive cohorts that have matured into adulthood in recent years may have been less inclined to enjoy work, especially if there has been a decline in the Protestant work ethic and in commitment to work, as much impressionistic literature would have it (Whyte, 1956). However, the effects of this inter-cohort trend on overall job satisfaction may have been offset by changes in modal styles of supervision and by the various attempts of management to enhance job satisfaction.

Second, much of the variation by age in job satisfaction may be compositional effects; that is, it may result from movements of different kinds of persons into and out of the labor force within birth cohorts as aging occurs. In this regard it is useful to examine the recent data on age and job satisfaction in table 12.10. The female data are especially instructive, since labor force participation of women is more often voluntary than that of men and thus is more likely to be selective of persons who enjoy working outside the home. However, labor force participation is often virtually mandatory for young, unmarried women and for young wives whose husbands are still in school or for some other reason have not become well established as breadwinners, and it is often necessary for middle-aged and elderly widows if they are to avoid poverty. It is revealing, therefore, that the women workers with the lowest job satisfaction were those under age 30 and those age 60 and older. The difference between the youngest and the middle-aged workers is especially likely to be a compositional effect, since the women most likely to stop working after they have husbands capable of supporting them are the women least inclined to enjoy working outside the home.

The male data do not so clearly suggest compositional effects. However, the higher aggregate reported satisfaction of workers age 60 and up than of middle-aged workers could reflect a tendency for the men who enjoy working the least to retire early. Or it could partly reflect higher mortality among men who do not enjoy their work (for some suggestive evidence, see Palmore and Jeffers, 1971). The difference between the youngest and the middle-aged males is not very likely to be a compositional effect and may result from the increase in extrinsic job rewards that typically occurs after young adulthood (Glenn,

Table 12.10. Reported job satisfaction of white workers employed full-time, by sex and age, pooled data from U.S. national surveys conducted in 1974, 1975, and 1976.

	Males				Females			
Age	Percentage satisfied	Percentage satisfied	Mean satisfaction score[a]	(N)	Percentage satisfied	Percentage satisfied	Mean satisfaction score[a]	(N)
18-29	82.8	44.7	2.22	(291)	80.6	43.5	2.20	(191)
30-39	87.5	55.3	2.38	(257)	94.4	65.6	2.58	(125)
40-49	90.9	57.3	2.45	(220)	92.4	59.3	2.50	(118)
50-59	91.1	59.6	2.47	(224)	96.0	67.0	2.63	(100)
60 and over	97.7	73.9	2.72	(88)	83.7	65.1	2.44	(43)
Total	88.5	55.2	2.40	(1,081)	88.9	57.2	2.44	(577)

Source: The 1974, 1975, and 1976 General Social Surveys conducted by the National Opinion Research Center (James A. Davis, principal investigator).

a. Very dissatisfied = 0; a little dissatisfied = 1; moderately satisfied = 2; very satisfied = 3.

Taylor, and Weaver, 1977) or from adjustive job changes during the first few years in the labor force (Wright and Hamilton, 1978).

The case of age and job satisfaction illustrates that a very large amount of research devoted to a topic does not necessarily assure the existence of evidence on which to base confident conclusions of cause and effect. With the exception of a few recent publications (Glenn, Taylor, and Weaver, 1977; Wright and Hamilton, 1978), the authors of research reports on the topic have not recognized the logical problems involved in discerning between age and cohort effects, and thus they have not analyzed their data in ways that provide the best clues as to the nature of effects. To my knowledge, this chapter is the first publication to consider that the age-job satisfaction relationship may be largely a compositional effect.

Global Happiness

A related topic on which there is also much evidence but about which no confident conclusions can be made is age and global happiness and satisfaction. According to the folklore, aging beyond young adulthood (or even beyond adolescence—"the best years of life") typically leads to a decline in happiness.[21] Survey data gathered in the 1940s and 1950s tended to support this belief, insofar as there was a moderate negative relationship between age and reported happiness and satisfaction (Gurin, Veroff, and Feld, 1960). However, data gathered in the late 1960s and in the 1970s fail to show the earlier negative relationship and in some cases show a slight positive relationship (Campbell, Converse, and Rodgers, 1976; Andrews and Withey, 1976; Glenn, 1975). Recent changes in the relationship to age of two measures of global happiness are shown in table 12.11 and 12.12. The data in the two tables are not comparable, because the Gallup question (table 12.12) elicits a larger percentage of "very happy" responses than the National Opinion Research Center question (table 12.11).[22] However, the two sets of data show similar trends. For both sexes combined, the NORC data in table 12.11 show a shift from a slight negative relationship in the early 1960s to a slight positive relationship in the early 1970s, and the Gallup data in table 12.12 show a change from a distinct negative relationship in the 1940s and 1950s to virtually no relationship in the 1960s and 1970s. Except for the 1946-1948 Gallup data, all the data show male-female differences in the age pattern of reported happiness. The negative relationships shown by the earlier data are stronger for females than for males, and even the later data show no positive relationships for the females.

The meaning of these data for possible age effects on happiness is uncertain. The optimistic interpretation is that an earlier negative ef-

Table 12.11. Percentage of white persons who said they were "very happy," by sex and age, U.S. national data, 1964-1965 and 1972-1974.

Age	Males		Females		Both sexes	
	1964-1965 (N)	1972-1974 (N)	1964-1965 (N)	1972-1974 (N)	1964-1965 (N)	1972-1974 (N)
18-39[a]	34.3 (475)	28.2 (780)	40.0 (575)	39.3 (886)	37.4 (1,050)	34.1 (1,666)
40-59	28.7 (547)	38.2 (628)	35.6 (491)	41.0 (692)	32.0 (1,038)	39.7 (1,320)
60 and older	31.9 (329)	39.3 (433)	30.3 (244)	38.7 (434)	31.2 (573)	39.0 (867)
Total	31.5 (1,351)	34.2 (1,841)	36.6 (1,310)	39.8 (2,012)	34.2 (2,661)	37.1 (3,853)

Source: National Opinion Research Center Survey Research Service Surveys 630 and 857 and the 1972, 1973, and 1974 General Social Surveys conducted by the National Opinion Research Center (James A. Davis, principal investigator).

a. Age range is 21-39 for 1964-1965.

fect has disappeared, that people in the United States once did, but no longer do, typically become less happy as they age beyond young adulthood. It seems more likely, however, that in recent years cohort effects have come to mask negative age effects. The birth cohorts now and recently in young adulthood are large, in numbers of people, relative to older cohorts, and they have had unusual difficulty in finding jobs and attaining a degree of economic and occupational success commensurate with their expectations and with the status of their families of orientation. Moreover, conservative critics of these cohorts believe that many of the cohort members are products of overly permissive child rearing which has left them deficient in coping ability, and many of them had parents who divorced during the "divorce boom" following World War II. For these and similar reasons, these cohorts may have an unusually low propensity to be happy.

Furthermore, there are probably compositional effects in the cross-sectional data relating age to reported happiness and satisfaction that could obscure a negative age effect. There is some evidence that chronically unhappy people typically die at a younger age than happier people (Palmore and Jeffers, 1971), and any such differential mortality tends to increase aggregate happiness and satisfaction at the older ages.

Unless such effects of differential mortality are appreciably greater for males than for females, the data in table 12.11 and 12.12 indicate that any negative age effect on happiness is greater for females than for males. It is unlikely that a gender difference in the mortality effect largely accounts for the male-female differences in the

Table 12.12. Percentage of white persons who said they were "very happy," by sex and age, U.S. national data, 1946-1948, 1953, 1956-1957, 1963-1966, and 1973.

Age	1946-1948 (N)	1953 (N)	1956-1957 (N)	1963-1966 (N)	1973 (N)
Males					
20-39	44.3 (1,228)	47.5 (545)	53.6 (890)	47.0 (883)	54.8 (513)
40-59	37.9 (1,055)	42.6 (530)	50.5 (1,021)	45.2 (823)	52.3 (440)
60 and older	36.2 (519)	41.0 (312)	49.4 (595)	48.7 (556)	53.7 (335)
Total	40.4 (2,802)	44.2 (1,387)	51.4 (2,506)	46.8 (2,262)	53.7 (1,288)
Females					
20-39	44.2 (1,396)	57.2 (701)	63.5 (1,266)	54.0 (912)	61.6 (606)
40-59	39.1 (983)	49.0 (488)	52.8 (1,034)	49.6 (981)	56.8 (493)
60 and older	34.2 (401)	41.6 (214)	46.7 (424)	45.7 (618)	55.4 (276)
Total	40.9 (2,780)	52.0 (1,403)	56.8 (2,724)	50.2 (2,511)	58.6 (1,375)
Both sexes					
20-39	44.3 (2,624)	53.0 (1,246)	59.4 (2,156)	50.6 (1,795)	58.5 (1,119)
40-59	38.5 (2,038)	45.7 (1,018)	51.7 (2,055)	47.6 (1,804)	54.7 (933)
60 and older	35.3 (920)	41.3 (526)	48.3 (1,019)	47.1 (1,174)	54.5 (611)
Total	40.7 (5,582)	48.1 (2,790)	54.2 (5,230)	48.6 (4,773)	56.2 (2,663)

Source: American Institute of Public Opinion (American Gallup) Surveys 369, 410, 425, 508, 570, 571, 580, 675, 735, 736, 867, and 868.

data, since the greatest of these are in the differences in reported happiness between young adults and middle-aged persons—ages at which neither males nor females have suffered substantial mortality. A more probable reason is the "double standard of aging," whereby aging from young adulthood to middle age leads to a greater loss in resources and in the bases of self-esteem for females than for males (Sontag, 1972). Females are also at a disadvantage because they are less likely than males to remain married as they grow older. Females are more likely to be widowed, and if they are widowed or divorced, they are less likely than males to remarry (Carter and Glick, 1976). This is a crucial disadvantage, since being married is one of the strongest positive correlates of reported happiness which has been identified (Campbell, Converse, and Rodgers, 1976; Glenn and Weaver, 1979).

The evidence considered here concerning possible age effects on conservative attitudes, political party identification, interest in politics, vocationally related interests, job satisfaction, and global happiness is in no case conclusive. However, one can be fairly confident that there have been some age effects on some vocationally relevant interests and on strength of party identification. All other conclusions must be more tentative, but there is little credible evidence that aging beyond young adulthood tends to produce conservative attitudes or identification with the Republican party. Evidence concerning possible age effects on interest in politics, job satisfaction, and global happiness is ambiguous; thus any confident statements about such effects should be viewed with skepticism until more evidence is in.

This treatment of a few possible kinds of age effects demonstrates how difficult it is to investigate age effects and how little is currently known about any kind of age effects on values, attitudes, and beliefs. However, I do not wish to imply that studying age effects is so difficult that little will ever be known about them. On the contrary, carefully conducted research aided by theory and various kinds of "side information" can lead to conclusions in which one can have high confidence. Few confident conclusions can now be made only because the needed work has not been done. Available longitudinal data and national survey data appropriate for cohort analysis provide enormous opportunities for research concerning age effects on attitudes, and it is likely that knowledge of this aspect of life span development will grow rapidly in the next few years.

This discussion of change and constancy through the life span in values, attitudes, and beliefs raises many questions and answers few. The main conclusion to be drawn from the survey of evidence from U.S. studies is that little is known and much remains to be learned, even though there apparently is more evidence for the United States than for any other society.

It is now known that changes in attitudes in the United States in the recent past have often been greater in the younger adult birth cohorts than in the older cohorts, the pattern being approximately linear. However, it is not known how nearly universal this pattern of change has been, nor is it known whether any greater change-proneness of the younger cohorts is an age effect or a cohort effect. Virtually nothing is known about the change-proneness of the attitudes of preadults.

It is also known that several of the changes in attitudes that seem to reflect basic values have been substantial in birth cohorts aging into their 60s and 70s, although the change was usually greater in the younger cohorts. Even elderly people seem to have the potential to participate in major value shifts in the society.

Much of the evidence concerning possible age effects on values, attitudes, and beliefs is negative; some of the positive evidence is convincing, but none of it is conclusive. Little is known about possible age effects on preadults, the major exception being in regard to some vocationally related interests covered by the Strong Vocational Interest Blank. Some attitudes that once varied systematically by age no longer did so in the recent past, either because onetime age effects disappeared or because of some complex combination or interaction of age, period, and cohort effects. In any event these rapid changes emphasize the need to limit conclusions concerning age effects to the period in which the data were gathered. Of course, conclusions for the United States should not be generalized to other societies.

This aspect of life span development is an almost virgin area for research, which beckons the investigator equipped with the proper concepts, methods, and understanding of the logical problems of studying life span development. The social scientific data archives have vast amounts of already collected data which can be analyzed to cast light on the life span development of attitudes (Glenn and Frisbie, 1977). Cross-cultural research in this area is yet to be begun, although many survey data sets appropriate to the task are waiting to be exploited. Let us proceed with the work that needs to be done.

Notes

1. The statement that attitudes are a function of values and beliefs does not mean that each individual's attitudes can be deduced from his values and beliefs. An individual may learn an attitude from other people without learning the values and beliefs from which it could be deduced. Furthermore, different individuals may have the same or similar attitudes but may have arrived at them from different sets of values and beliefs. For instance, persons who express the same degree of approval of the U.S. president's performance may have arrived at that degree of approval for quite different reasons.

2. For a more detailed treatment of cohort analysis, see Norval D. Glenn (1977).

3. Unfortunately, a few authors refer to birth cohorts as "age cohorts" rather than consistently using the significant life event that defines the cohorts to designate the kind being discussed.

4. The conceptual distinctions among biological, social, and psychological age are treated at various places in the literature, including in two of my publications (Glenn, 1974, 1977). Of course, chronological age is simply the length of time since birth.

5. Age and period effects are confounded in the data from both panel and retrospective studies. The typical panel study, with a small sample not representative of the national population, provides fewer clues than most cohort studies to help the researcher tentatively unconfound the age and period effects. For instance, a panel study showing that a sample of the 1950 graduates of X College experienced a certain change in attitudes from 1950 to 1960 is of virtually no value for understanding developmental processes. The observed change may have resulted from influences unique to the period or even unique to the graduates of X College.

6. Carl I. Hovland and Irving L. Janis (1959) provide a good summary of the earlier evidence (largely from experimental studies) on the relationship between age and "persuasibility." They write: "Even at the purely descriptive level, we have only a fragmentary picture of how persuasibility changes with chronological age" (p. 247). More recent reviews of the evidence on attitude change (Oskamp, 1977) have a dearth of references to age and thus suggest that Hovland and Janis's conclusion made twenty years ago is still correct.

7. For instance, Capel (1967) reports test-retest correlations over a 30-year period for a sample of 100 women ranging from 0.43 to 0.68 and averaging 0.55 for eight attitude objects (war, law, birth control, and so on). E. Lowell Kelly (1955) retested 368 subjects after 20 years and found test-retest correlations ranging from 0.06 to 0.35 and averaging 0.25 for six attitude objects (church, marriage, and so on).

8. The term *change-proneness*, as it is used here, is not synonymous with the inherent changeability of individuals. It refers instead to the likelihood that a cohort, as a whole, will change. The change-proneness of a cohort at a given stage of the life span therefore depends on the influences for change characteristic of that stage as well as on the inherent changeability of the cohort members.

9. The total number of people of all ages was 4,932 in the 1954 sample and 3,546 in the 1973 sample.

10. Cutler and Kaufman do not deal with ceiling effects and do not report raw percentages, so it is impossible to know to what extent their findings were affected by ceiling effects. However, the scale scores do not approach the theoretical upper limit even for 1972, so it is unlikely that ceiling effects were very important.

11. Neither ceiling nor floor effects were likely to have distorted the finding of this study very much, since none of the percentages is very near 0 or 100.

12. The beginnings of trends were identified from data not shown here. A shift to Republican identification began between 1949 and 1953, a shift to Democratic identification began between 1957 and 1961, and a shift away from Democratic identification (but not toward Republican identification) began between 1965 and 1969.

13. This change in strategy was apparently wise, even if this rationale for it was faulty.

14. The wording of the three questions is, "If your party nominated a generally well-qualified man for president and he happened to be a Negro (Jew, Catholic), would you vote for him?"

15. One may suspect, with good reason, that some prejudiced respondents chose the "nonprejudiced" response alternative to avoid the disapproval of the interviewer—an example of the "social desirability effect" (Phillips, 1973). It seems improbable, however, that any such bias accounts for the fairly substantial amount of measured change in the older cohorts.

16. One of the major explanations for racial prejudice, stated in incomplete and oversimplified form, is that prejudice exists to justify discrimination, which in turn exists because benefits from it accrue to the dominant race (Dollard, 1937; Glenn, 1966).

17. "Effects of aging," as the phrase is used here, does not refer to effects of chronological aging; it is a shorthand way of referring to "effects of influences associated with chronological aging."

18. On the average, earnings and occupational prestige increase after the early 20s. However, many persons fail to attain the degree of worldly success to which they aspire, and one might think that awareness of failure would cause many people to turn away from conservatism in middle age. On the other hand, middle-aged "failures" may tend to refocus their ambitions on their children and grandchildren and to continue to support the existing structure of opportunities.

19. The interests measured by the Strong instrument are not explicit interests in occupations but interests in activities and objects related to the tasks of various occupations.

20. The Hoppock twenty-seven-year panel study of job satisfaction shows an average increase in job satisfaction. Although this finding is consistent with the thesis that there is a positive age effect on job satisfaction, it does not prove the thesis. Period effects are confounded with age effects in the panel data, and workers who became less rather than more satisfied with their work may have dropped out of the panel and perhaps even out of the labor force.

21. As is often the case, the folklore on this topic is not entirely consistent.

22. The NORC question is, "Taken all together, how would you say things are these days—would you say that you are very happy, pretty happy, or not too happy?" The Gallup question has two versions, which apparently elicit the same percentage of "very happy" responses (Glenn, 1977, p. 29). The versions are (1) "In general, how happy would you say you are—very happy, fairly happy, or not very happy?" (2) "In general, how happy would you say you are—very happy, fairly happy, or not at all happy?"

References

ABRAMSON, P. R. 1975. *Generational change in American politics.* Lexington, Mass.: D. C. Heath.

——— 1976. Generational change and the decline of party identification in America: 1952-1974. *American Political Science Review* 70: 469-478.

ANDREWS, F., and WITHEY, S. B. 1976. *Social indicators of well-being: Americans' perceptions of life quality.* New York: Plenum Press.

BLALOCK, H. M., JR. 1966. The identification problem and theory building: the case of status inconsistency. *American Sociological Review* 31: 52-61.

——— 1967. Status inconsistency, social mobility, status integration and structural effects. *American Sociological Review* 32: 790-801.

BROWNING, H. L. 1968. Life expectancy and the life cycle: some interrelations. In R. N. Farmer, J. D. Long, and G. J. Stolnitz, eds., *World population: the view ahead.* Bloomington, Ind.: Indiana University Bureau of Business Research.

CAMPBELL, A., CONVERSE, P. E., MILLER, W. E., and STOKES, D. 1960. *The American voter.* New York: John Wiley and Sons.

CAMPBELL, A., CONVERSE, P. E., and RODGERS, W. L. 1976. *The quality of American life*. New York: Russell Sage Foundation.

CAMPBELL, D. P. 1971. *Handbook for the Strong vocational interest blank*. Stanford, Calif.: Stanford University Press.

CAPEL, W. C. 1967. Continuities and discontinuities in attitudes of the same person measured through time. *Journal of Social Psychology* 73: 125-126.

CARLSSON, G., and KARLSSON, K. 1970. Age, cohorts and the generation of generations. *American Sociological Review* 35: 710-718.

CARTER, H., and GLICK, P. C. 1976. *Marriage and divorce: a social and economic study*. Cambridge, Mass.: Harvard University Press.

CLOS, M. 1966. Evaluation of mental health workshops in Kentucky. *Journal of Educational Research* 59: 278-281.

CONVERSE, P. E. 1976. *The dynamics of party support: cohort-analyzing party identification*. Beverly Hills, Calif.: Sage.

CRITTENDEN, J. 1962. Aging and party affiliation. *Public Opinion Quarterly* 26: 648-657.

———— 1963. Aging and political participation. *Western Political Quarterly* 16: 323-331.

CUTLER, N. E. 1969-70. Generation, maturation, and party affiliation: a cohort analysis. *Public Opinion Quarterly* 33: 583-588.

CUTLER, S. J., and KAUFMAN, R. L. 1975. Cohort changes in political attitudes: tolerance of ideological nonconformity. *Public Opinion Quarterly* 39: 63-81.

DOLLARD, J. 1937. *Class and caste in a southern town*, 3d ed. New York: Doubleday-Anchor.

EISENSTADT, S. N. 1971. *From generation to generation*, 2d ed. New York: Free Press.

EVAN W. 1965. Cohort analysis of attitude data. In James M. Beshers, ed., *Computer methods in the analysis of large-scale systems*. Cambridge, Mass.: Joint Center for Urban Studies of the Massachusetts Institute of Technology and Harvard University.

GIBSON, J. L., and KLEIN, S. M. 1970. Employee attitudes as a function of age and length of service: a reconceptualization. *Academy of Management Journal* 13: 411-425.

GLENN, N. D. 1966. White gains from Negro subordination. *Social Problems* 14: 159-168.

———— 1969. Aging, disengagement, and opinionation. *Public Opinion Quarterly* 33: 17-33.

———— 1972a. The distribution of political knowledge in the United States. In Dan D. Nimmo and Charles M. Bonjean, eds., *Political attitudes and public opinion*. New York: David McKay.

———— 1972b. Sources of the shift to political independence; some evidence from a cohort analysis. *Social Science Quarterly* 53: 494-519.

———— 1973. Class and party support in the United States: recent and emerging trends. *Public Opinion Quarterly* 37: 1-20.

———— 1974. Aging and conservatism. *Annals of the American Academy of Political and Social Science* 415: 176-186.

———— 1975. The contribution of marriage to the psychological well-being of males and females. *Journal of Marriage and the Family* 37: 594-600.

———— 1976. Cohort analysts' futile quest: statistical attempts to separate age, period, and cohort effects. *American Sociological Review* 41: 900-904.

———— 1977. *Cohort analysis*. Beverly Hills, Calif.: Sage.

GLENN, N. D., and FRISBIE, W. P. 1977. Trend studies with survey sample and census data. In Alex Inkeles, James Coleman, and Neil Smelser, eds., *Annual Review of Sociology, 1977*. Palo Alto, Calif.: Annual Reviews.

GLENN, N. D., and GRIMES, M. 1968. Aging, voting, and political interest. *American Sociological Review* 33: 563-575.

GLENN, N. D., and HEFNER, T. 1972. Further evidence on aging and party identification. *Public Opinion Quarterly* 36: 31-47.

GLENN, N. D., TAYLOR, P. A., and WEAVER, C. N. 1977. Age and job satisfaction among males and females: a multivariate, multisurvey study. *Journal of Applied Psychology* 62: 189-193.

GLENN, N. D., and WEAVER, C. N. 1979. A note on family situation and global happiness. *Social Forces* 57: 960-967.

GREELEY, A. M., and SPAETH, J. L. 1970. Political change among college alumni. *Sociology of Education* 43: 106-113.

GUEST, L. 1964. A longitudinal study of attitude development and some correlates. *Child Development* 35: 779-784.

GURIN, G., VEROFF, J., and FELD, S. 1960. *Americans view their mental health*. New York: Basic Books.

HARTER, C. L. 1977. The "good times" cohort of the 1930s. *PRB Report* 3: 1-4.

HERZBERG, F., MAUSNER, B., PETERSON, R., and CAPWELL, D. 1957. *Job attitudes: review of research and opinion*. Pittsburgh, Pa.: Psychological Services of Pittsburgh.

HOGE, D. R., and BENDER, I. E. 1974. Factors influencing value change among college graduates in adult life. *Journal of Personality and Social Psychology* 29: 572-585.

HOPPOCK, R. 1960. A twenty-seven year follow-up on job satisfaction of employed adults. *Personnel Guidance Journal* 38: 489-492.

HOVLAND, C. I., and JANIS, I. L. eds. 1959. *Personality and persuasibility*. New Haven, Conn.: Yale University Press.

HULIN, C. L., and SMITH, P. C. 1965. A linear model of job satisfaction. *Journal of Applied Psychology* 49: 209-216.

INGELHART, R. 1977. *The silent revolution*. Princeton, N.J.: Princeton University Press.

KELLEY, E. L. 1955. Consistency of the adult personality. *American Psychologist* 10: 659-681.

KNOKE, D. 1976. *Change and continuity in American politics*. Baltimore, Md.: Johns Hopkins University Press.

MANNHEIM, K. 1953. The sociological problem of generations. In P. Kecskemeti, ed., *Essays on the sociology of knowledge*. New York: Oxford University Press.

NUNN, C. Z., CROCKETT, H. J., JR., and WILLIAMS, J. A., JR. 1978. *Toler-

ance for nonconformity. San Francisco: Jossey-Bass.

OSKAMP, S. 1977. *Attitudes and opinions*. Englewood Cliffs, N.J.: Prentice-Hall.

PALMORE, E., and JEFFERS, F. C. 1971. *Prediction of life span*. Lexington, Mass.: D. C. Heath.

PHILLIPS, D. L. 1973. *Abandoning method*. San Francisco: Jossey-Bass.

QUINN, R. P., STAINES, G. L., and McCULLOUGH, M. R. 1974. *Job satisfaction: is there a trend?* Washington, D.C.: U.S. Government Printing Office.

ROBERTS, D. F., JR. 1969. A developmental study of opinion change: source-orientation versus content-orientation at three age levels. *Dissertation Abstracts* 29: 4107.

RYDER, N. B. 1965. The cohort as a concept in the study of social change. *American Sociological Review* 30: 843-861.

SALEH, S. D., and HYDE, J. 1969. Trends in job satisfaction along the age dimension. *Experimental Publication System, American Psychological Association* 1, ms. 33.

SCHMIDHAUSER, J. 1958. The political behavior of older persons. *Western Political Quarterly* 11: 113-124.

SONTAG, S. 1972. The double standard of aging. *Saturday Review: The Society*, October, pp. 29-38.

STOUFFER, S. A. 1955. *Communism, conformity, and civil liberties*. Garden City, N.Y.: Doubleday.

TINGSTEN, H. 1937. *Political behavior*. London: King.

U.S. DEPARTMENT OF COMMERCE, BUREAU OF THE CENSUS. 1972. Voter participation in November 1972. *Current Population Reports*, Series P-20, *Population Characteristics*, no. 244.

VORNBERG, J., and GRANT, R. 1976. Acquaintance experiences and ethnic group attitudes. *Adolescence* 11: 601-608.

WRIGHT, J. D., and HAMILTON, R. F. 1978. Work satisfaction and age: some evidence for the "job change" hypothesis. *Social Forces* 56: 1140-58.

WHYTE, W. H., JR. 1956. *The organization man*. New York: Simon and Schuster.

13 | Criminal Behavior over the Life Span
Hugh F. Cline

CRIMINAL BEHAVIOR has been a major topic of investigation in the social and behavioral sciences, but it has rarely been studied from the perspective of life span development. It is generally assumed that criminal behavior occurs more frequently during late adolescence and early adulthood. Most official statistics on arrest, prosecution, and incarceration reinforce these widely held notions. Children who commit criminal acts are less frequently arrested, and they are usually remanded to their family or to a social welfare agency. Our society does not recognize criminality among children. Regardless of behavior, one is rarely classified as a criminal until adolescence.

Almost two-thirds of those arrested in the United States are between the ages of 13 and 30, and more people are arrested at age 16 than at any other age (Federal Bureau of Investigation, 1977, table 32). But very little is known about the dynamics of the rising arrest rates during adolescence and the steeply declining rates after the age of 30. Although this pattern of age distribution of arrest rates is true for all offenses combined, it breaks down for specific offenses, such as prostitution, arson, homicide, or gambling. Offense rates vary across age groups in systematic and potentially revealing ways.

Deviant behavior has been given a wide variety of definitions in the social science research literature. Ideally, this chapter should take a comprehensive definition of its subject matter and include all types of deviant behavior—both criminal and noncriminal. Unfortunately, this is not possible, for the available empirical data are quite meager. Most researchers in this field have focused on a particular type of deviant behavior, such as juvenile delinquency, homicide, or white-collar crime. Because these behaviors tend to be age specific, little effort has been made to look at deviance across different phases of the life course. A few longitudinal or panel studies have attempted either to predict adult criminal behavior from patterns of delinquency or to assess programs to prevent delinquency, rehabilitate recidivists, or treat drug addicts. Because of the paucity of data, the focus of this chapter is limited to illegal behaviors, as defined by federal, state, or local statutes.

Pulling together the data on patterns of criminal behavior throughout the life course raises questions that have important theoretical as well as policy implications for our criminal justice systems. For example, what happens to the very large number of adolescents who come within the purview of the criminal justice system early in life and never again appear in official crime statistics? Of those who commit white-collar crimes in middle age, what proportion were earlier adjudicated as delinquents? No one knows the answers to such questions. Both theory and research have been framed in such a fashion that efforts have not focused on a life span perspective. For the most part, our knowledge of criminal behavior throughout the life span is based upon case histories and anecdotes.

Theoretical Perspectives

Social and behavioral scientists have always had great difficulty in defining deviant behavior. Part of this difficulty stems from the fact that deviance is usually defined in contrast with expected or normal behavior. However, what is considered normal changes over time and from one social setting to another. Norms that become accepted are formally codified as laws, but normative consensus is frequently unstable. For example, both norms and laws have recently changed in areas such as prohibitions against the use of alcoholic beverages and nonaddictive drugs, homosexual behavior, abortions, as well as discriminatory behavior based on sex, race, or age. Many social theorists have pointed out that deviance is frequently a source of innovation and change in society. Behavior that was once considered unacceptable and deserving of negative sanction frequently becomes more widely accepted and eventually elicits positive sanctions. In addition, in certain subcultures criminal acts are uniformly rewarded positively.

It is possible to classify the theoretical explanations for deviant behavior into three major categories: individual or psychological theories; group, collectivity, or sociological theories; and social interaction or social psychological theories. The individual-level theories include biological and psychophysiologically oriented perspectives (Lombroso, 1876; Sheldon, 1949; Landau et al., 1972; Shah and

Roth, 1974; Mednick and Christiansen, 1977). Individual-level theories also include the perspectives represented by the psychodynamic theorists (Abrahamsen, 1952; Alexander and Staub, 1956; Hallock, 1967). Although these perspectives cover a wide variety of causal mechanisms in explaining deviant and criminal behavior, they all focus at the individual level. They tend to emphasize the more stable behavioral patterns resulting from genetic, physiological, or psychological characteristics. They frequently stress early developmental experiences that determine personality characteristics, which presumably dictate behavior patterns throughout life. For this reason, all the individual-level theories tend to emphasize constancy of behavior patterns and tend to overlook change. From this perspective one might expect the incidence of deviant behavior to remain fairly constant for an individual over the life span.

The second category of explanations, the group or collectivity theories, focus on the macrosociological characteristics of the social milieus or the disjuncture between individual motivations and the social environment as the basic causes of deviance. The collectivity theories include the work of the opportunity structure school (Merton, 1938; Cohen, 1955; Miller, 1958; Cloward and Ohlin, 1960) as well as the social conflict group (Turk, 1969; Quinney, 1970; Chambliss, 1974). Social environments change throughout the life span, and often dramatically at particular transitions: for example, leaving school, marriage, parenthood. The group-level theories focus on changes in behaviors and tend to place less emphasis on constancy. From this perspective one might expect to find a relationship between the incidence of deviant behavior and the prevalence of salient characteristics of the social environment.

The third group of theories is both more eclectic in perspective and more heterogeneous in its inclusion of a wider variety of forms of deviant behavior. These theories focus on the microsociological level, which is concerned with social interactions that create criminal behaviors rather than individual characteristics or social environments that create criminals. The major theory in this group is the differential association theory (Sutherland and Cressey, 1970). Differential association posits that criminal behavior is learned in interaction patterns that favor violation of laws. As learned behavior, it is subject to change depending on the frequency, duration, priority, and intensity of subsequent interaction patterns. This theory has been extended to the psychological learning and reinforcement models (Akers, 1973; Bandura, 1973). It is also related to the labeling theories (Becker, 1964, 1973; Kitsuse and Cicourel, 1963; and Lemert, 1972) and includes the more recently proposed microsociological perspective that focuses on the relationships between offenders, victims, and the structural contexts of deviant behavior (Goode, 1970; Curtis, 1975). The social interaction theories thus incorporate features of both the individual and the collectivity levels, and, therefore, more broadly encompass both constancy and change.

Criminal behavior is a subset of deviant behavior. If detected or alleged, criminal acts are negatively sanctioned by the criminal justice system. But the processes of detection, prosecution, and incarceration operate differentially along a number of sociological dimensions, including class, race, sex, and age. According to the life span perspective, the social interaction level is a more promising theoretical perspective for further research and theory development in the area of criminal behavior. The earlier work at both the individual and the group level has been most fruitful; but as one thinks of developing a more comprehensive theoretical framework for future research, the social interaction level demands higher priority. It incorporates the perspective that inherent characteristics, early learning experiences, and the relationship between the individual and structural features of the society are necessary for examining both constancy and change in criminal behavior over the life span.

Arrest Rates by Age Groups

Available data on individual criminal behavior over the life course are meager. However, it is possible to raise some interesting questions by examining arrest statistics for criminal offenses grouped by age category. The *Uniform Crime Reports*, compiled and published yearly since 1930 by the Federal Bureau of Investigation, are the only available source of nationwide indicators of criminal behavior. Despite their many substantive and methodological problems, these data reveal interesting patterns of arrests by age groups.

The data in table 13.1 are adapted from the 1977 *Uniform Crime Report*, which summarizes reports from over ten thousand local police agencies and covers almost 200 million people. The arrest data are grouped into six age categories and eighteen offense categories ordered by median age at arrest. Traffic, less serious motor vehicle code violations, and other minor offenses such as loitering, runaway, and curfew violations are excluded from the table. As the total column shows, the distribution of the total number of offenses is uneven. Property crime, with over 1.4 million arrests, is the largest category, and drunkenness is the second largest, with 1.2 million arrests. The rates then decrease substantially, to only 16,000 arrests for arson.

The age distribution of arrests for all offenses combined, as reported in the top row of the table, is also uneven. Arrests peak in ado-

Table 13.1. Reported arrests by age groups, 1977.

		Percentage						
Arrests	*Median age*	*12 and under*	*13-19*	*20-29*	*30-39*	*40-49*	*50 and over*	*Total*
Total arrests	23.9	2.6	32.7	33.9	14.1	8.9	7.8	9,021,845
Adolescence								
Vandalism	16.9	15.8	54.6	19.8	5.8	2.5	1.5	196,426
Motor vehicle theft	17.7	1.9	65.0	24.2	5.9	2.1	0.9	135,097
Arson	18.0	17.1	41.9	22.5	9.9	5.1	3.5	16,510
Liquor laws	18.0	0.3	63.2	23.3	5.5	3.9	3.8	321,188
Property[a]	18.3	6.9	51.8	26.9	7.7	3.5	3.2	1,460,082
Young adulthood								
Stolen property	20.0	2.4	46.0	34.9	10.2	4.2	3.3	104,356
Narcotics	21.2	0.3	42.0	46.1	8.4	2.2	1.0	568,767
Violence[b]	23.7	1.6	31.5	40.0	15.4	6.9	4.6	386,649
Disorderly conduct[c]	23.9	1.9	30.4	40.1	13.8	7.6	6.2	668,529
Prostitution	24.3	0.1	19.9	62.8	10.8	3.7	2.7	77,032
Assault	24.9	2.4	26.6	39.3	17.6	8.7	5.4	399,541
Weapons	25.2	0.9	26.6	39.7	17.1	8.9	6.8	136,119
Sex offenses	25.9	2.1	25.0	35.9	18.7	9.9	8.4	60,938
White collar[d]	26.4	0.9	17.5	46.2	22.2	9.0	4.2	290,962
Family[e]	27.8	1.8	12.2	43.2	26.8	11.5	4.5	53,344
Middle age								
Drunkenness	34.7	0.0	11.2	28.9	19.2	18.9	21.8	1,207,804
Drunk driving	35.4	0.0	9.8	37.3	22.1	16.2	14.6	1,103,552
Gambling	37.2	0.0	8.4	24.3	22.6	20.6	24.1	52,410

Source: Adapted from Federal Bureau of Investigation, 1977 *Uniform Crime Reports*, table 32. See pages 304 and 305 for detailed definitions of offenses.

a. Includes burglary and larceny theft.

b. Includes murder, forcible rape, robbery, and aggravated assault.

c. Includes vagrancy.

d. Includes forgery, fraud, and embezzlement.

e. Includes offenses of nonsupport, neglect, desertion, or abuse of family and children.

lescence and young adulthood, 32.7% and 33.9%, respectively; and the median age of arrest is 23.9 years. But for specific offenses one can discern a pattern of variable incidence at different phases throughout the life span. The offenses are ordered by median age and are grouped in three categories: adolescence, young adulthood, and middle age.

The first group of offenses, which are more prevalent among adolescents, consists of vandalism, motor vehicle theft, arson, violations of liquor laws, property crimes, which include burglary and larceny theft. The median age of arrest for each of these offenses is below 20 years. Both vandalism and arson show relatively high proportions of arrest before the age of 13, 15.8% and 17.1%, respectively. Motor vehicle theft and liquor law violations are especially concentrated among adolescents, 65.0% and 63.2%, respectively. It is clear that these crimes are more prevalent among adolescents and pre-adolescents. These offenses also show a pattern of rapid decline in the proportion of arrests in the older age categories.

The second group of offenses, which are more prevalent in young adulthood, ages 20-29, includes possession of stolen property, violations of narcotics laws, violent crime (including murder, forcible rape, robbery, and aggravated assault), disorderly conduct (including vagrancy), prostitution, assault, possession of deadly weapons, sex offenses (excluding forcible rape and prostitution), white-collar crimes (including forgery, fraud, and embezzlement), crimes against the family and children (including nonsupport, neglect, desertion, and abuse). These crimes are committed by adults whose median age is between 20 and 29 years, and the rates for these offenses decline after the age of 30. Although some of these offenses have relatively high incidences during adolescence, they all have median arrest ages in the 20-29 category. Prostitution is especially prevalent in the young adult group, with 62.8% of all arrests occurring between the ages of 20 and 29. It comes as no great surprise that prostitution is an age-related behavior, but examining arrest data by age categories reveals that generalizations about crime rates can be misleading unless broken down by type of offense.

Arrest rates for violations of narcotics laws are very high in adolescence and young adulthood and very low beyond the age of 30. This pattern suggests a cohort effect, first identified by Norman B. Ryder (1965) and later discussed by Matilda White Riley and her colleagues (1972). A cohort effect is an event or phenomenon associated with a particular time in history which has an influence on a specific age group cohort. For example, drug use has only recently become widespread among adolescents and young adults in our culture, and the 1977 arrest data indicate that almost 90% of the arrests for violations of narcotics laws involved individuals under the age of 30.

The third group of offenses, which includes drunkenness, drunk driving, and gambling, are crimes of the middle-aged. Although the highest incidence occurs in the 20-29 age group, the proportions of arrests in the older age categories are much greater than the proportions for the offenses identified as adolescent or young adult offenses. Particularly drunkenness and gambling persist quite strongly in even the oldest age category.

In many respects the patterns shown in table 13.1 are not surprising. Many of the offenses included in the adolescent and young adult categories require substantial physical strength. Of course, some of the offenses are age-specific by statute; for example, most of the arrests for violation of liquor laws occur during adolescence, among individuals purchasing or using alcoholic beverages before the legally permissible age. Furthermore, few adolescents have the opportunity to engage in the white-collar crimes of forgery, fraud, or embezzlement. The age distribution of arrests for gambling is consistent with the popular notion that it is older individuals who are participants or facilitators of gambling activities.

Data revealing the patterns of arrests by age distribution are most useful for raising questions concerning constancy and change in criminal behavior over the life span. For example, when all the individuals who accounted for 1977 arrest data have aged by ten, twenty, or thirty years, will similar patterns appear? Some insight into this question can be gained by looking at the age distributions in earlier arrest reports. Similar analyses of the 1975 and 1976 CCR data show that, for the most part, there are only minor differences in the age distributions of offenses.

Society's norms and laws will continue to change, and this shift could produce different patterns. Laws concerning the possession and use of marijuana have already changed, for example, and certain behaviors are no longer considered deviant and illegal. Perhaps a cultural change similar in scope to the emergence of the drug culture may produce a new category of offenses that could become prevalent among adolescents or even the elderly. Alternately, continued change in society's values concerning sexual behavior may affect the incidence of prostitution and other sex offenses. Or our conceptions concerning neglect or desertion of family and children may change as different family and child-rearing patterns emerge.

The more interesting questions from the perspective of the life span concern the past and future behavior of the individuals included in table 13.1. Using the patterns identified from the data in the 1977 *Uniform Crime Report*, one may pose questions relevant to the constant and varying nature of criminal behavior throughout the life span. For example, what proportion of those who committed offenses in 1976 in the age category 13-19 will appear in another age column of a future *Uniform Crime Report?* Do young arsonists persist into their middle years in destroying property by fire? The arrest rates clearly decline with age, suggesting that not all of them do. Are there constant patterns associated with a particular age cohort? What proportion of the adolescents arrested in 1977 will subsequently be arrested for the offenses that seem more prevalent in young adulthood? What happens to young shoplifters as they enter middle age? Do they become involved in white-collar crime or gambling? What happens to prostitutes after the age of 30? What patterns of deviant or criminal behavior characterize the earlier lives of those arrested for drunkenness or drunk driving? What do we know about the earlier behaviors of individuals who commit offenses against their families and children? Is there a consistent or constant set of behaviors that these individuals persist in throughout their lives, or do they shift from one type of criminal behavior to another? Is there anything in our theoretical conceptions of delinquency and crime to suggest a progression from, let us say, vandalism or property crimes in adolescence to violent crimes or illegal possession of weapons in young adulthood and then to white-collar crimes in middle age?

Serious methodological problems are involved in the use of the arrest data from the *Uniform Crime Report*. Official arrest statistics are very poor substitutes for data on the incidence of criminal behavior. Arrest rates reveal only a small, and as yet unknown, proportion of the total incidence of criminal acts. Of those criminal acts which come to the attention of the police, only a small proportion are cleared by an arrest.[1] Criminal victimization studies, which ask a sample of people whether they have been the victims of crimes during the past six months, reveal that 90% of all robberies and burglaries, but only about 30% of petty household larcenies, are reported (Law Enforcement Assistance Administration, 1976). From a methodological perspective, therefore, an even more difficult question is what proportion of those arrested in 1977 will commit offenses in the future, regardless of whether they are arrested.

Three additional points should be mentioned when one is using arrest data to investigate constancy and change in criminal behavior. The first point concerns the recent declines in crime rates. The Federal Bureau of Investigation reported that during the first three months of 1978, property and violent crimes decreased by 4% from the same period in 1977, a 9% decrease from 1976.[2] Falling crime rates are attributed primarily to the maturing of the nation's population. As the age cohort of the post-World War II baby boom passes through the crime-prone adolescent and young adult years, the rates begin to decline. If this explanation of declining crime rates is correct, further decreases can be expected as the number of adolescents and young adults continues to decrease through the 1990s (Fox, 1976).

Second, the biases that operate within the criminal justice system may result in the arrest, conviction, and imprisonment of disproportionate numbers of poor, male, minority group members. Is it possible that these biases in our social control agencies operate against the young as well? Many critics have claimed that criminal behavior is rampant among middle-aged, affluent people but that these offenders have more resources to avoid detection and prosecution as well as greater access to ameliorative programs. Unfortunately, there is insufficient evidence to support or to refute this charge; the position is based primarily upon a large number of partially documented and unsubstantiated cases.

Finally, one important aspect of crime distinguishes it from most of the other topics treated in this volume, namely, the extent to which the actions of others determine whether a behavior is defined as criminal. The policies and practices of criminal justice agencies significantly influence crime rates. For example, if school violence is perceived as an important problem, the deployment of additional police and truant officers to schools may heighten the salience of the issue and result in more arrests. If, on the other hand, adolescent acting out is viewed as a normal part of the developmental process, it might be underplayed or ignored. In recent years both public opinion and criminal agency response to white-collar crime has changed dramatically. The behavior of white-collar offenders, who are mostly in their middle years, may not have changed in the past ten or twenty years, but the official agency response has, and these different responses will result in higher arrest rates and a modified perception of constancy and change in criminal behavior over the life span.

In theory at least one can construct standard measures of growth, pathology, cognition, attitudes, or personality characteristics and document stability or variation for representative samples over time. Change in these areas can be assumed to have occurred in the subjects being examined. But in the area of crime, and perhaps mental illness as well, the change may well be in the social control agencies that respond to the individual behaviors. The complex interaction between the criminal and the control agency is a problem that plagues the interpretation of official statistics on crime across all age levels.

Research Design

This discussion of an ideal design for studying constancy and change in criminal behavior departs from the usual procedure in schol-

arly writing, in which one typically reviews the literature before proposing a research agenda. In this instance it seems preferable to first
provide a paradigm for a longitudinal study and then to compare existing studies with the proposed design. My intent is not simply to criticize earlier work but to make programmatic statements about the
work that is needed to address the constancy and change issue.

Suppose that we had a large nationwide sample of adults over the
age of 40 and that we could assign them to one of the eight patterns
identified in figure 13.1 depending on whether they committed any of
the crimes listed in table 13.1 during adolescence, young adulthood, or
middle age. For the moment, ignore the question whether we could
obtain valid information on criminal acts from such a sample. We
shall assume that we have accurate data on felonies, regardless of detection, arrest, prosecution, or conviction, and we examine the resulting patterns.

Both pattern 1, representing involvement in criminal behavior in
all three periods of the life span, and pattern 8, representing no criminal behavior in any period, are examples of constancy—no change in
behaviors with respect to violations of criminal law. Most individuals
in the sample would probably be assigned to pattern 8, for both offi-

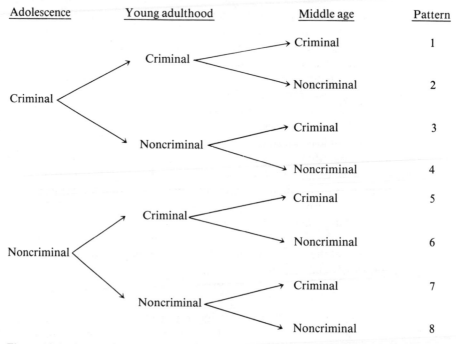

Figure 13.1. *Criminal career progressions.*

cial arrest data and the longitudinal studies discussed below indicate that the majority of people in any age cohort do not engage in criminal behavior at any time in their lives. These data corroborate the common assumption that most people are law-abiding and that noninvolvement in crime is essentially constant. However, in recently completed criminal self-report surveys a majority of the respondents indicated that they had committed at least one felony in their lives, suggesting greater rates of change in criminal behavior over the life span (Wallerstein and Wylie, 1967). The need for more refined and definitive data is now becoming abundantly clear.

Assigned to pattern 1, which corresponds to criminal behavior in all three periods in the life span, would be individuals typically referred to as habitual offenders or recidivists. Although the absolute number of individuals in this category would probably be small they apparently account for a large number of crimes and place a heavy load on our criminal justice systems. Unfortunately, very few data are available to give an accurate estimate of either the size of the habitual offender group or the costs of processing them by the police, courts, and correctional institutions. A recent Rand Corporation report describes a study of 49 inmates with previous sentences, who were then serving time for armed robbery in a medium-security prison in California. These felons reported committing a total of over 10,500 crimes in an average criminal career spanning a twenty-year period, approximately half of which was spent in prison. This works out to almost one major crime committed every ten working days while not in prison (Petersilia, Greenwood, and Lavin, 1977).

All other patterns in figure 13.1, patterns 2-7, represent change in criminal behavior over the life span. For example, a pattern 4 person was a delinquent during adolescence but did not commit any subsequent criminal acts as an adult. There is some evidence to suggest that this is a fairly common pattern, as is pattern 2, which characterizes the individual who engages in criminal behavior as an adolescent and as a young adult but "goes straight" on reaching middle age. The changes reflected in patterns 2 and 4 represent a progression from involvement to noninvolvement in crime, the traditional goal of treatment programs aimed at reducing recidivism. The social science literature is replete with accounts of these efforts, usually stressing small and short-term successes. With a few exceptions, most of this research has focused on individuals who have criminal records. There is very little data on undetected crime, for it is costly and difficult to study the criminal behavior of those who do not come to the attention of criminal justice agencies. Consequently, existing social science research has tended to study primarily those in patterns 1, 2, and 4.

The remaining patterns—3, 5, 6, and 7—also represent some

change in involvement in major crimes across the three periods of life included in the hypothetical research design. But they all involve a movement from noninvolvement to involvement in crime from at least one period to the next. One might regard the individuals assigned to these patterns as anomalies, for they represent a regression rather than a progression. But this view assumes that maturity promotes a decreasing involvement in crime, an assumption that corresponds to the widely accepted notions about criminals and to the declining arrest rates beyond age 30. However, interesting deviations from that general pattern appear when arrest rates are examined by age for specific offenses, such as gambling, white-collar crime, and prostitution. For example, prostitution may correspond to pattern 6; or white-collar crimes may fit pattern 7.

Now to return to the research design, suppose that we had accurate information on the nature and the time of each criminal offense committed by every individual in the sample. Using the three groupings of offenses employed in table 13.1, we could then characterize each period for each member of the sample in one of the following four categories: (1) no criminal behavior; (2) adolescent crimes; (3) young adulthood crimes; and (4) middle-age crimes. We would have to devise an appropriate method for classifying the modal offense for those individuals who committed multiple offenses in several categories during the same life-span period.

With four categories over three periods in the life span, there are sixty-three patterns of criminal careers and one pattern of consistent noninvolvement in crime ($4 \times 4 \times 4 = 64$). This design allows us to examine in far greater detail the constancy and change patterns in criminal behavior over the life course. First, we could determine the relative frequency or occurrence of each of the sixty-four patterns and identify the more and less common progressions. We could answer all the questions we raised after examining table 13.1. In addition, if we had also collected other data concerning the backgrounds of those in the sample, we could examine causal hypotheses generated from the three theoretical perspectives discussed above. With appropriate multivariate statistical analyses, we could begin to estimate the relative salience of causal factors in criminal behaviors at the individual or psychological level, the social milieu or sociological level, and the social interaction or social psychological level.

This design is still seriously flawed, for it represents an attempt to generalize on the basis of findings from a single age cohort. The design must be expanded to include replications of the same analyses on successive cohorts, for many social conditions change over time. For example, factors affecting criminal behavior for individuals who were adolescents during the depression and young adults during World War

II may be very different from factors affecting those who were adolescents during the politically and socially turbulent 1960s and young adults during the economic instabilities of the 1970s. In addition, the activities and programs of criminal justice agencies are continually changing; and successive cohorts of juvenile delinquents and adult offenders are exposed to different penal philosophies and treatment programs. For example, the widespread use of residential treatment programs for juvenile delinquents in the post-World War II period is now giving way to a preference for decarceration and community-based treatment programs. All these changing conditions affect causal relationships in explaining criminal behavior, and it is therefore essential that successive cohort studies be completed.

Finally, enormous problems remain to be resolved in such a successive cohort longitudinal study design. There are the extremely difficult questions of collecting valid and reliable data on behaviors that many people would have very little inclination to reveal. It would not be possible to get data on all criminal acts. But a carefully administered longitudinal design using a combination of official records and repeated personal interviews with respondents who participate in the study throughout large segments of their lives would elicit sufficiently valid and reliable data to justify the enormous effort and expense of such research. It would not be a single research project, but a long-range, continual collection and analysis of data involving several panels of respondents at any given time. Unless such an effort is undertaken, we shall never be able to untangle the issues of constancy and change in criminal behaviors; and public policy determination in the criminal justice field will continue to operate on an inadequate knowledge base. Given the annual expenditures of $24 billion in 1978 to maintain our current system of police, criminal courts, legal services, public defense, and corrections (Law Enforcement Assistance Administration, 1980), the investment in such a research facility would not be excessive.

We have presented this extended discussion of an ideal research design as a preface to our review of the existing empirical data on constancy and change in criminal behavior over the life course to provide both a paradigm against which to compare previous research as well as a conceptual context into which the reader can place a rather substantial amount of detailed information. Of the studies on which we shall report none has all the characteristics of our hypothetical design, but each has some important parts included.

Survey of Longitudinal Studies

To be reviewed in this section, a study had to provide data that spanned at least two major phases in the lives of the subjects, ranging through adolescence, young adulthood, and middle or older age. The studies are grouped into three categories: (1) studies that contain longitudinal data concerning primarily adolescent criminal behavior; (2) studies that report data on both adolescent and young adult criminal behavior; and (3) studies that include data on behavior in adolescence, young adulthood, and middle age. My primary purpose is to glean from these investigations information on consistent or varying patterns of criminal behavior across two or more phases in the life course. I am not attempting to summarize findings with respect to the etiology of deviant and criminal behavior nor to explore the efficacy of various prevention or treatment programs.

Adolescence

One of the earliest studies to focus on preadolescent and adolescent behavior was done by Thomas Ferguson (1952) in Scotland. Ferguson collected data on a cohort of 1,349 boys in Glasgow who completed grammar school in 1947. The data reported their home situation, school performance, and delinquency records between their eighth and seventeenth birthdays. Through this period 12.2% of the boys had been convicted, primarily for theft and burglary offenses. Over the ten-year period this small proportion of the boys accounted for 268 convictions. In analyzing the relation between delinquency and environmental factors, Ferguson reported a number of characteristics that pertained to preadolescent behavior. He pointed out that the 66 boys who had multiple convictions before the age of 18 were usually underdeveloped physically, came from broken homes, did not attend church or belong to any organized youth group, had fathers who were unskilled laborers and frequently unemployed, usually had a record of truancy in elementary school, lived in a low-income housing area, and usually came from a large and unstable family. Unfortunately, Ferguson did not make any comparisons with the boys in his cohort who received no convictions; nor did he have any data on behavior beyond 18 years of age.

Glenn Mulligan and his colleagues (1963; Douglas et al, 1966) followed a sample of 5,362 children born in England in 1946. Two studies of delinquency have been completed from this sample. One followed 2,402 boys in the sample who were still living in England in the early 1960s and found that 12% of these boys had come to the attention of the police and 2.8% had multiple convictions. The second study focused on aggressive behavior and compared boys who had been convicted of at least one offense with nondelinquents. Both studies report findings similar to Ferguson's concerning family and home situations and evidence of preadolescent antisocial and aggressive behaviors.

In a study of almost 500 boys and girls in the sixth grade in a midwestern U.S. city, Robert Havighurst and his colleagues (1962) found that 39% of the boys and 8% of the girls had had some contact with the police during adolescence. Most of these offenses were minor, including truancy, speeding, and minor property damages. This study examined a wide variety of developmental questions for the cohort between the ages of 11 and 20, and delinquent behavior was only one of many issues examined. The investigators concluded that the first signs of delinquent behavior appear in preadolescence and are usually related to failure in school, most frequently a failure to read as well as peers. Reading failure in this cohort was usually accompanied by aggression or withdrawal. By the age of 12 or 13, about 15% of the cohort were showing signs of maladjustment and failure in school. The investigators concluded that these children tried to attain the standards promoted by their teachers and supported in the community, but if they were unable to succeed by legitimate means, they were likely to turn to delinquency. This group of children came from all social classes in the community but disproportionately more from the lower-middle class.

An investigation, which is still under way in a working-class area of London, is under the direction of David Farrington and Donald West of the Institute of Criminology, Cambridge University (West, 1969; West and Farrington, 1973, 1977). The study involves 411 males and was initiated in 1962 when the boys were 8 years old. Each boy was given a battery of psychological tests and interviews every two years from ages 8 until 14. These data were supplemented with parent interviews and records from the central Criminal Record Office. Interviews with the boys were repeated at ages 18 and 21. The major aim of the project was to explore factors contributing to delinquency, which occurred in 20% of the sample. In this study delinquency was defined as being found guilty in court of any criminal offense. The majority of the offenses were thefts and burglaries, especially of motor vehicles. Approximately half of the delinquents were convicted of multiple offenses. As with the other studies cited, the delinquents came from poor families, had lower IQs, and were characterized as having cruel, passive, or neglecting parents. Their mothers tended to have both mental and physical health problems, and their fathers usually had unstable employment patterns. In addition, the delinquents were physically less well developed than their peers and performed poorly on psychomotor tests.

Probably the best-known longitudinal study of a cohort is Marvin Wolfgang's investigation of almost 10,000 boys who were followed through adolescence in Philadelphia, Pennsylvania (Wolfgang, Figlio, and Sellin, 1972). Data were obtained from school records and police department files. Approximately 35% of the boys were delinquent and had a record of some type of police contact. Of these delinquents 29% were white and 50% were nonwhite. Twenty-seven percent of the upper socioeconomic group and 45% of the lower socioeconomic group were delinquent. The authors concluded that race and social class were most strongly related to delinquency. The investigators further divided the delinquents into one-time offenders, 46%, and recidivists, 54%. They found that recidivists had greater residential mobility, lower IQ scores and achievement levels, and dropped out of school at an earlier age. The proportion of boys engaged in property offenses increased steadily from ages 10 to 16, at which point a gradual decrease occurred. The likelihood of violent crimes increased steadily up to age 18. This observation corresponds with speculations, based on the *Uniform Crime Reports*, that property crimes were more characteristic of adolescents and violent crimes more characteristic of young adulthood.

Figure 13.2 reproduces Wolfgang's cumulative probabilities from age 7 to age 30 for at least one index offense (an offense listed in *Uniform Crime Reports*). The observed data are taken from the cohort study up to age 17, and the predictions are extensions of the observed curve. Wolfgang is continuing this study and following the cohorts, so it will be possible to check the predicted probabilities up to age 30 (Collins, 1977). By age 17, almost 13% of the cohort had committed at least one offense. If the probabilities follow the predictive model, 15% of the cohort will have committed at least one index offense by age 30. The curve shows a steep rise from early adolescence through about 22 or 23 years and then begins to flatten very quickly.

These major longitudinal studies of juvenile delinquency reveal little about postadolescent behavior. However, there are some clues concerning preadolescent behaviors and characteristics. These studies reveal that delinquent children are likely to come from disadvantaged positions—characterized by lower socioeconomic status, unstable parental figures, inconsistent control devices during child rearing, poor academic performance, and aggressive or withdrawal behavior. Now the question most relevant from the perspective of constancy and change is the stability of these factors and their relation to criminal behaviors. Much inconclusive empirical research has attempted to assess the relative weights of family and social class characteristics. The two are strongly correlated, but an important social policy issue concerns a youth's capacity to overcome their consequences as he ages. Fortunately, Wolfgang will be able to address some of these issues in his report on the follow-up study of the cohort.[3]

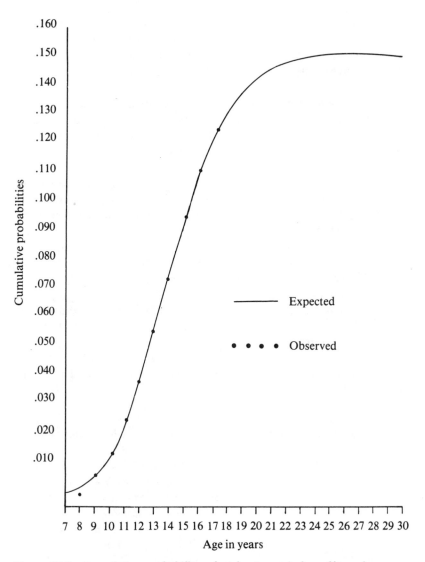

Figure 13.2. *Cumulative probability of at least one index offense by age. (From Wolfgang, Figlio, and Sellin, 1972.)*

Adolescence to Adulthood

Several studies report on behavior patterns spanning adolescence and young adulthood. Foremost of these are the investigations of Sheldon Glueck and Eleanor Glueck. Their research reports published between 1930 and 1972 cover four major studies of delinquents and

one comparative study of delinquents and nondelinquents in the Boston area. The studies included follow-up data covering periods from
five to fifteen years of adolescent and adult behavior. The major focus
of these investigations was the etiology of criminal behavior.[4]

One of their studies collected follow-up data on 1,000 boys adjudicated as delinquents. Data were gathered at three successive five-
year intervals from adolescence to approximately 30 years of age.
They found that 41% of the boys had been subsequently arrested for
felonies and 32% for misdemeanors; the remaining 27% had no arrest
records. Table 13.2 presents the arrest offenses for the group in the
original and three follow-up periods. The pattern of arrest offenses
reported by the Gluecks is consistent with the pattern in table 13.1, the
1976 *Uniform Crime Report*. The most common offenses in early
adolescence (ages 11-15) were property offenses, 62.9%; fifteen years
later property offenses accounted for only 18.2% of the total arrests.
During the period 26-30 years of age drunkenness was the most common offense, accounting for 42.0% of the arrests. Disorderly conduct
remained fairly constant, around 20% in all four periods, with a slight
increase in early young adulthood (ages 21-25). Crimes of violence increased from 2.5% to 6.8% from the first to the last period, but they
remained at a fairly low level throughout. Offenses against family and
children, sex offenses, and violations of narcotics laws all showed
consistent increases; but they never exceeded 5% of the total arrests in
any period.

Table 13.2. Arrest offenses for 1,000 delinquents in Glueck and Glueck's
study (percents).

Offense	Early adolescence (11-15)	Late adolescence (16-20)	Early young adulthood (21-25)	Late young adulthood (26-30)
Property	62.9	48.7	24.6	18.2
Disorderly conduct	21.7	22.2	30.3	22.5
Violence	2.5	4.4	7.3	6.8
Drunkenness	0.0	9.3	29.0	43.0
Family and children	0.0	0.5	1.6	3.3
Sex	0.3	1.6	2.4	2.6
Narcotics	0.0	0.1	0.3	0.6
Other	12.6	13.2	4.5	3.0
Total arrests	1,333	2,719	2,547	2,195

Source: Adapted from Glueck and Glueck, 1940, p. 310.

In early adolescence the 1,000 delinquents accounted for 1,333 arrests, a rate of 1.33 arrests per boy. As they approached age 30, 270 had no further arrest records; and the remaining 730 accounted for 2,195 arrests, a rate of 2.92 arrests per person. Although the number of arrests per person increased dramatically, there is a marked change in the type of offenses: a large decrease in property offenses, a large increase in drunkenness, and smaller increases in all other offenses. Glueck and Glueck separately analyzed the follow-up data for the 748 delinquents who committed more serious property and violent crimes. For this group they also report a notable change in the character of offenses. By age 30, 35% were property offenders, 16% had become chronic alcoholics, and smaller proportions were involved in offenses against family, sex offenses, and assault. For the serious offenders as well as the entire group Glueck and Glueck report a decrease in the seriousness of offenses.[5]

In comparing the behavior of a group of 500 delinquents with a matched control group of 500 nondelinquents, Glueck and Glueck report that until age 30 there were significant differences not only in criminal records but also in academic and vocational training, employment, work habits, economic status, stability of family relations, and use of leisure time (Glueck and Glueck, 1968). Before age 17, 90.4% of the delinquents had become felons. Between 17 and 25 recidivism dropped to 59.6%; and between 25 and 31 the proportion of serious offenders fell to 28.9%. Glueck and Glueck further report that the "original nondelinquents largely continued to be law-abiding with the passage of time and their growth into adulthood." Unfortunately, the report traces neither the delinquents nor the nondelinquents in terms of the patterns identified in table 13.1.

The later phases of their work focused on developing predictive instruments for postadolescent and adult criminal behavior, and their work became highly controversial. Legitimate criticisms were leveled at their sampling techniques, the extensive reliance on Rorschach tests, and their causal analysis procedures. Nevertheless, their work stands as a landmark in providing longitudinal data on subsequent behaviors of delinquents and young adults. However, their interests were focused on prediction; and the reports of their investigations and data analyses, therefore, reflect a concern with improvement. By design, Glueck and Glueck's data do not provide information concerning individuals involved in criminal activity during middle or older age; Glueck and Glueck dealt primarily with adjudicated delinquents and incarcerated young adults. The decreases they report in criminal behavior to age 30 correspond with the observation from the 1976 *Uniform Crime Reports*. However, they did not address a question of great interest from the perspective of life course: Who are the perpetrators of the very large absolute number of criminal acts committed by individuals in our society in the middle and older age categories? Are there any parallels in the early life of the habitual offender to that of the middle-aged offender with no prior criminal experience? It is not appropriate to criticize Glueck and Glueck for not answering a question that is of interest to us but was not high on their priority list and therefore not a major factor in the design of their investigations.

In 1959 William McCord and Joan McCord (1959) reported the results of their evaluation of the Cambridge-Somerville Youth Study. Although the purpose of their study was to determine the efficiency of a treatment program, which during the years 1939-1945 provided regular counseling and interaction between adult project staff members and young boys, their report provides some data on the subsequent behavior of former juveniles. The original Cambridge-Somerville Youth Study was a social action program designed to prevent delinquency and "develop stable elements in the characters of children." In this program 650 boys, ranging in age from 8 to 13 with a median age of 10.5 years, were identified by schools, churches, social welfare agencies, and police departments as "predisposed to delinquency"; 325 pairs were formed by matching the boys on age, physical health, intelligence, emotional adjustment, home background, neighborhood, and delinquency prognosis. One boy from each pair was randomly chosen for the counseling and interaction treatment, and the other was assigned to a control group. The treatment consisted of an average of two meetings per month between the counselor and the boy, frequently including the family and teachers. The boys received counseling, tutoring, medical care, and trips to local museums or even summer camps. When the project ended in 1945, 253 of the original 325 pairs were still in the program.

The results of McCord and McCord's evaluation, which included ten-year follow-up data on the remaining 253 pairs, showed little difference in delinquent or criminal behavior between the treatment and control groups. About 40% of those in both groups had criminal records by 1955. The report presented a series of detailed analyses and produced assessments of causal factors for criminal behavior, including intelligence, socioeconomic status, home atmosphere, parental discipline, parental personality, and sibling order. In testing the possibility that treatment might have a delayed impact, McCord and McCord presented data on the age at which both treatment and control subjects were convicted of criminal offenses. Table 13.3 is a summary of these data; it reports the number of individuals convicted of four types of crime by four age categories.

Table 13.3. Summary of McCord and McCord's data on number of individuals convicted by age and type of offense (percents).

Offense	Under 13	13-18	19-22	Over 22
Property	91.4	80.9	44.8	40.7
Person	5.7	6.1	9.1	10.7
Sex	2.9	5.3	9.1	6.0
Drunkenness	0.0	7.7	37.0	42.9
Number	35	131	143	84

Source: Adapted from McCord and McCord, 1959, table 4, p. 21.

Although the age categories used by McCord and McCord do not correspond to those used in this chapter, their original groupings are retained in table 13.3. Ages in the "over 22" group could be as high as 30 years. Since the differences between treatment and controls are small and not relevant for this chapter, the data for both groups have been collapsed in table 13.3. The table reports the number of individuals convicted, and it is probable that some individuals appear more than once. Unfortunately, McCord and McCord's presentation of their data does not make this clear. However, they do report that these are all the convictions among 506 of the original 650 individuals in the program.[6] The data do not correspond to the ideal research design presented above. However, despite the problems of multiple counts, comparability, and attrition, the table shows several interesting patterns, which correspond to earlier observations.

Property offenses are by far the most prevalent; but they decrease from 91.4% under age 13 to 40.4% over the age of 22. Drunkenness increases from zero incidence at the youngest age to 42.9% for those over 22, and both person and sex crimes show low incidence and gradual increases over the periods covered in the study. These patterns are consistent with the observations made from the *Uniform Crime Reports* and from the other longitudinal studies. However, although McCord and McCord had the data available, their analyses and presentations do not make it possible to look for patterns of constancy or change in individual criminal career progressions.

Jackson Toby has completed a ten-year follow-up of a small group of 72 adolescents who were in residence at the Highfields Treatment Center in Hopewell, New Jersey, between 1955 and 1957.[7] With a great deal of effort, Toby was able to maintain contact with 65 of the men over a ten-year period. He conducted numerous interviews in a wide variety of contexts, including one dinner meeting with 16 men and their wives. He was able to trace the adult behavior of these individuals (Toby and Liebman, undated).

Toby reported that 37% of the white panel members and 69% of the blacks had been arrested at least once during the ten years after their release from Highfields. His analysis showed that the difference between black and white criminal adult adjustment is explained primarily by the white males' social integration with girl friends, fiancées, and wives who exerted strong pressures toward noncriminal adult behavior patterns. His data suggest that integration with close female friends and family members predicts successful adult adjustment and that continued involvement with male friends and peer-group gangs presages additional criminal behavior in adulthood.

This finding that mixed-sex social integration for whites may deter adult criminal behavior is based on a very small number of cases. But it suggests an important conceptual perspective. The whites in Toby's study who became integrated into families or developed close relations with girl friends or fianceés experienced social environments very different from those experienced by the men who continued their close affiliations exclusively with male peers. Presumably, the former environment provides fewer opportunities to experience situations defined as favorable to crime. On the other hand, the black males in Toby's sample less frequently developed relationships with the opposite sex and had much higher arrest rates as adults.

Toby's finding suggests that the social environment may be a major factor in accounting for both constancy and change in criminal behavior. This is not a new concept in the field of criminology or in social science research. The belief that adolescent or young adult criminals should be removed from the social milieus in which they first became involved in criminal behavior has been basic to European and American penal philosophies for at least two centuries. Yet a wide variety of studies have demonstrated that rates of recidivism remain intractably and frustratingly high. The causal factors of criminal career patterns are not yet understood, and Toby's findings may provide an important clue to uncovering the intricate causal mechanisms of criminal behavior, that is, constant and changing social interaction networks. Perhaps a noncriminal's transition from youth to adulthood is accompanied by a weakening of ties to the same-sex peer group and a strengthening of cross-sex ties. Toby's data suggests that this may occur more readily for white males than for black males.

Adolescence, Young Adulthood, and Middle Age

A major source of information on criminal behavior during adolescence, young adulthood, and middle age is Lee Robins's (1966) report of a 30-year follow-up of child guidance clinic patients in St. Louis, Missouri. Using personal interviews supplemented with data records available in local community agencies, she compared the 524 clinic patients with 100 nonpatient schoolchildren matched by age, sex, race, intelligence, and neighborhood. This study was designed to compare the natural histories and adult behaviors of children diagnosed as having sociopathic personalities with those of "normal children." At the time of referral to the clinic between 1924 and 1927, the children were 9-15 years of age, with a median of 13 years. Seventy-three percent of the patients were males, and 70% of the control group were males. Three-fourths of the patients were referred for "antisocial behavior," which included theft, incorrigibility, sexual offenses, runaway, truancy, aggression, and vandalism. The remaining 25% were referred for learning problems, temper tantrums, and other miscellaneous behavior problems. Robins was able to locate 91% of the clinic patients and 96% of the controls. The follow-up data covered a wide variety of aspects of adult life including marital history, parenthood, occupation, financial dependency, social participation, military records, health and medical data, use of alcohol and drugs, and arrest records.

Table 13.4 presents the arrest data for male and female clinic patients and controls. The patients are further broken down into those referred for antisocial behavior and others. The offenses reported by Robins are ordered according to the three categories—adolescence, young adulthood, and middle age—employed in table 13.1. Two-thirds of the boys and one-half of the girls who were referred to the clinic for antisocial behavior became adjudicated juvenile delinquents. Three-quarters of the boys and 40% of the girls referred for antisocial behavior were arrested as adults for criminal offenses. The most common adult offense for males was drunkenness; for females, the most common were drunkenness and prostitution. Adult arrests for every offense were more common among those referred for antisocial behavior than among other patients or control subjects. Arrests for crimes of violence occurred only among subjects referred to the clinic for antisocial behavior.

Almost 50% of the males referred for antisocial behavior had been imprisoned, whereas only 13% of the men referred for reasons other than antisocial behavior had served prison sentences and none of the control subjects had been incarcerated. Unfortunately, Robins did not break down the data on type of offense by specific ages during the thirty-year follow-up. However, she did present some arrest data with age categories.

Table 13.5 presents the arrest rate data for the subjects in Rob-

Table 13.4. Arrest data from Robins's study (percents).

	Males			Females		
Offense	Antisocial referral patients (N = 260)	Other patients (N = 90)	Controls (N = 69)	Antisocial referral patients (N = 83)	Other patients (N = 40)	Controls (N = 29)
Adolescence						
Larceny	23	6	1	7		
Burglary	16	2				
Auto theft	12	3				
Stolen property	2	2				
Young adulthood						
Robbery	14	1				
Vagrancy	12	3				
Prostitution				12		
Sex	4	1		1		
Rape	2					
Murder	1					
Middle age						
Drunkenness	38	13	13	19	7	
Family and children	7		3	3		
Forgery	7	1	1	1		
Embezzlement	5	2	1	2		

Source: Adapted from Robins, 1966, p. 47.

ins's study before and after age 30 for all offenses combined. The first row in the table indicates that 72% of the 260 male antisocial referral patients were arrested between the ages of 18 and 30. The second column shows that of the 90 male patients referred to the clinic in the "other" category, 36% were arrested between the ages of 18 and 30, a rate substantially lower than the antisocial referrals. And of the 69 males in the control group, 26% were arrested between the ages of 18 and 30. The corresponding arrest rates for the female antisocial referral patients, other patients, and controls are 30%, 8%, and 3% respectively. These rates provide the baseline comparisons for the rates in the second and third rows of the table, which are of particular interest from the perspective of constancy and change. These data reveal some information on the incidence of the patterns of criminal career outlined in figure 13.1.

Table 13.5. Arrest rates from Robins's study.

| | Males | | | | | | Females | | | | | |
| | Antisocial referral patients | | Other patients | | Controls | | Antisocial referral patients | | Other patients | | Controls | |
Arrest patterns	N	%	N	%	N	%	N	%	N	%	N	%
Arrested between age 18 and 30	260	72	90	36	69	26	83	30	40	8	29	3
Arrested after 30: arrested between age 18 and 30	183	59	32	53	18	44	25	48	36	7	1	100
not arrested between age 18 and 30	72	18	57	12	50	6	56	14	37	5	28	0

Source: Adapted from Robins, 1966, p. 47.

Both the second and third rows present data on rates of arrest after age 30, the period that I have called middle age. The second row represents those who have shown constancy in criminal behavior (arrested before and after age 30); for example, of the 183 male antisocial referrals who were arrested between the ages of 18 and 30, 59% were arrested again after age 30. The remaining 41% were not arrested after age 30, a change from criminal to noncriminal behavior.[8] Of the 32 male patients referred to the clinic for other reasons and who had been arrested between the ages of 18 and 30, 53% were arrested again after age 30, thus following a pattern of consistent criminal behavior, and 47% changed from criminal to noncriminal behavior. The number of female cases is very small and the percentages are unstable, but it seems clear that there is generally more constancy in criminal or noncriminal behavior than change from criminal to noncriminal behavior.

The third row of the table presents data on two additional patterns of criminal career progression. Of the 72 males referred to the clinic for antisocial behavior who were not arrested between the ages of 18 and 30, 18% were arrested after 30, a change from noncriminal to criminal behavior; thus 82% who were noncriminal before age 30 remained noncriminal after age 30.

The remaining data again show more constancy than change. However, there is sufficient change in all the data to preclude simple conclusions concerning criminal career progressions, and Robins's arrest data cannot be broken down further by type of offense, for there are not enough cases. Still, one may ask what accounts for both the constancy and change patterns identified in these data.

Two substantive patterns appear in the data. First, it appears that an early antisocial experience is difficult to shed. Of those referred to the clinic for antisocial behavior, 72% were arrested between 18 and 30. Well over half of these were arrested again after age 30, compared with only 26% of the controls. The high arrest rate for the controls may not be surprising given the matched character of the sample and the backgrounds of the subjects. Second, the data suggest that the effect of the early experience begins to diminish after age 30 and recent experiences become more significant. Those arrested between 18 and 30, in all three age groups, were substantially more likely to be arrested again after 30. Similarly, those not arrested between 18 and 30 were unlikely to be arrested after age 30. The relevant percentages here are 59, 53, and 44, compared with 18, 12, and 6. If early experience were the most powerful, there would not be such striking differences between these percentages.

In the Rand Study, which collected data on a very small group of 49 inmates in a California prison (Petersilia, Greenwood, and Lavin, 1977), information gathered in lengthy personal interviews was combined with data from official criminal records. The sample consisted of persistent, serious offenders, as judged from the "frequency, gravity, and length of their involvement with the criminal justice system" (p. v). Each had been convicted on at least one count of armed robbery and had served at least one prior prison term. Table 13.6 presents the offenses reported by the 49 inmates in interviews. In order of frequency, the crimes included drug sales, burglary, auto theft, property theft, forgery, robbery, aggravated assault, purse snatching, and rape. The offenses are grouped by adolescence, young adulthood, and middle age. Burglary and auto theft are most prevalent in adolescence, and robbery is most common in the adult period. These patterns correspond to findings in earlier studies. But the habitual offenders have the highest incidence of drug sales in the adult period, and the occurrence of theft of property valued over $50, forgery, and aggravated assault are fairly constant throughout the criminal careers. These patterns may be representative of all chronic offenders or simply the result of a very small and idiosyncratic sample. Table 13.6 also shows that the number of self-reported offenses declined substantially as the population aged.

There was no evidence that these criminals specialized in a particular type of crime. Although the incidence of criminal behaviors decreased with age, the probability of arrest, conviction, and incarcera-

Table 13.6. Self-reported offenses in the Rand study (percents; $N = 49$).

Offense	Juvenile period	Young adult period	Adult period	Entire career
Adolescent crimes				
Auto theft	19.7%	12.5%	2.4%	14.2%
Purse snatching	0.4			0.2
Theft over $50	9.5	9.3	9.7	9.5
Burglary	32.0	17.7	5.6	22.0
Young adult crimes				
Drug sales	27.7	39.2	40.9	34.4
Robbery	0.2	9.0	29.8	8.1
Aggravated assault	2.3	1.3	2.0	1.8
Rape	0.1			
Middle-age crimes				
Forgery	8.0	10.9	9.7	9.4
Number	4,551	4,477	1,477	10,505

Source: Adapted from Petersilia, Greenwood, and Lavin, 1977, p. 18.

tion per offense increased. The investigators also found that only 12% of the self-reported crimes were registered in official records. Offenses committed to obtain money for drugs and alcohol increased as the inmates aged. The investigators report that illegitimate income was, for the most part, quite low. They estimate an average annual income of several thousand dollars a year from crime. About half of the sample relied primarily on legitimate work as their primary source of income, but their employment was uneven and generally weak. About half of the offenders felt that they had maintained fairly strong family relationships throughout all phases.

The investigators distinguished two types of offenders in their sample. The first they labeled "intensive" criminals. These individuals had a conception of themselves as criminals. They planned their criminal activities in advance, derived more of their income from illegitimate sources, and were arrested for only about 5% of their crimes. The second category, the "intermittents," did not perceive themselves as criminals. Their offenses were not as well planned, and they were much more likely to be arrested and subsequently incarcerated. Approximately one-third of the sample were labeled intensives, and their crime rates were ten times greater than those of the intermittents.

Joan McCord (1978) reports new data in a thirty-year follow-up of the original 506 subjects in the Cambridge-Somerville Youth Study.

McCord has traced all the subjects and collected new follow-up data through questionnaires and agency records. As in the 1959 report, McCord focused on differences between the treatment and control groups in adult criminal behaviors. Like the 1959 report, the thirty-year follow-up showed very little difference in criminal behavior as well as in measures of health status, family patterns, and employment records. Indeed, the data suggest that the control group may have fared better as adults than the treatment group.

The new thirty-year follow-up data makes it possible to trace the 506 subjects from adolescence through middle age. Figure 13.3 shows the McCord data recast in criminal career progressions analogous to those presented in the hypothetical research design of figure 13.1. However, figures 13.1 and 13.3 are not identical. The McCord data do not distinguish between young adulthood and middle age, and therefore only two periods in the life span, adolescence and adulthood, can be examined. However, she does separate minor from serious crimes. The former includes crimes against "ordinances and order," and the latter includes burglary, larceny, auto theft, assault, rape, and homicide. The data for the treatment and control groups are combined.

The most common pattern among the Cambridge-Somerville subjects is a transition from nondelinquent status as an adolescent to minor crime as an adult. Over one-third of the subjects follow this pattern, which suggests change, albeit minor, from noncriminal to criminal behavior. The second most common pattern is pattern 6, with 27.9% of the subjects following this pattern. Pattern 6 corresponds to constancy of noninvolvement in criminal behavior. If one disregards the minor crimes, patterns 5 and 6 together account for almost two-thirds of the subjects. By comparison, all other patterns are quite low in incidence. The two patterns representing the greatest change are 3 and 4, with 5.7% and 8.1% of the subjects, suggesting that there may

Pattern	Adolescence	Young adulthood	N	%
1		Serious crime	50	9.9
2	Delinquent	Minor crime	60	11.8
3		Noncriminal	29	5.7
4		Serious crime	41	8.1
5	Nondelinquent	Minor crime	185	36.6
6		Noncriminal	141	27.9
		Total	506	100%

Figure 13.3. *Criminal career progressions from the Cambridge-Somerville Study. (Adapted from McCord, 1978, table 2.)*

be a slightly greater tendency to change from noncriminal to criminal behavior than vice versa.

Minor crimes aside, patterns 1 and 6 can be identified as representing constancy and patterns 3 and 4 as representing change. From this perspective constancy appears more prevalent than change among the Cambridge-Somerville subjects, but because of all the methodological problems with these data one should not draw such a conclusion. The data have been presented simply to demonstrate the potential power of this type of research design. The more fascinating analyses of these data would examine the relationships of psychological and sociological background with the incidence of constancy and change patterns.

Although the data are thin, one can discern certain clues from several of these studies and at least speculate on patterns of constancy and change in criminal behavior over the life span.

Almost all the studies report decreasing incidence of most types of property and personal crimes with age. In addition, the data from Wolfgang, Glueck and Glueck, McCord and McCord, and Robins suggest a shift from property crimes to crimes of violence during the transition from adolescence to adulthood. All these studies suggest certain patterns of constancy and change over the life span that require more systematic longitudinal research. There appear to be important differences by social class, educational level, and family characteristics. If one examines the theoretical conceptions of deviance and the programs and policies of the criminal justice system, it is clear that neither theory nor practice yet recognizes the complex, diverse patterns of criminal behavior over the life course. Indeed, they presume a rather fixed set of motivations, behaviors, and outcomes. However, with several minor exceptions these studies have focused on a deviant population. With the exception of the Glueck and Glueck sample of nondelinquents and the control groups in the Wolfgang, Robins, and McCord studies we still know very little about the transition from criminal and noncriminal careers in adolescence and young adulthood to adult criminality.

It is premature to point out the need for further longitudinal studies of deviant behavior over the life course and to propose a more general theoretical perspective involving social interaction and then at the same time to identify potential policy implications of such future research. Nevertheless, it seems clear that a life span perspective suggests a different view of certain policy questions. For example, there appears to be far more heterogeneity in types and patterns of deviant and criminal behavior than previous work has suggested. There is evidence that many juvenile offenders do not become career offenders. Appropriate criminal justice policies are required to sort career offenders from those who later adopt noncriminal behavior.

The small amount of available data suggests that a large proportion of juvenile delinquents and young adults mature out of their criminal behavior after age 30. It also seems that a small core of individuals either persist in these criminal patterns or are complemented by "new criminals." Should later research support these preliminary speculations and interpretations, programs of prevention, deterrence, and rehabilitation would need to recognize this diversity and tailor programs to individuals depending on their past behavior and future prognosis. For example, most efforts at deterrence assume that rational persons will weigh the costs and benefits of criminal activity, but there is some evidence that this assumption does not hold for the intermittent habitual offender, who rarely planned a crime. Perhaps a higher probability of apprehension might serve as a greater deterrent than conviction or long incarceration.

In the late 1970s there has been a trend throughout the United States toward uniformity in sentencing and incarceration policies. The changes are evident in federal, state, and local jurisdictions. The impetus for these changes is a growing disenchantment with the results of several decades of a therapeutic orientation in criminal justice systems. Attempts have been made to treat criminals as though they were ill and in need of individualized treatment. General dissatisfaction with intractable rates of recidivism and the alleged increase in crime rates have produced a new perspective in criminal justice systems, which focuses on uniform sentences based solely on the nature of convicted offenses. Unfortunately, the pendulum of professional and public opinions tends to swing to the extremes. The perspective of constancy and change that emerges from this chapter suggests that it would be unwise to adopt absolute uniformity in criminal justice policies. Existing longitudinal studies suggest a great deal of diversity in criminal behavior over the life course. The capacity to respond fairly and appropriately to individuals at different points in their lives should remain an important component of a criminal justice system. The life course perspective produces an eloquent plea to prevent a mindless adoption of uniformity in criminal justice systems without giving due consideration to life course patterns of criminal behavior.

With respect to the small group of persistent criminals, the question of long-range incapacitation must be considered. These and other policy questions can be explored only in a longitudinal successive cohort research program in which alternative arrangements for the criminal justice system can be developed and tested.

Notes

1. For a classic discussion of the problems of distinguishing between "publicly known criminality" and the volume of "real criminality," see Sellin and Wolfgang (1964).

2. These data were released by the FBI and reported in the *New York Times*, July 2, 1978.

3. Although the data analyses on the follow-up study are not completed, a preliminary report is now available (Wolfgang, 1977).

4. Glueck and Glueck have reported extensively on their research. Their publications include fourteen volumes and numerous articles. Major publications are listed in the references.

5. The findings in this study confirmed those of an earlier study by Glueck and Glueck which followed 500 male inmates in a Massachusetts reformatory (1930).

6. In 1941, sixty-five boys were dropped from the treatment group to ease the case load for the diminished counseling staff. Another seven boys had died. Their matches in the control were also eliminated. Thus McCord and McCord had follow-up data in 1955 on all available subjects.

7. For a report on the original Highfields experiment, see Lloyd W. McCorkle et al. (1958).

8. The arrest rates are undoubtedly contaminated by the many biases inherent in both the detection of criminal acts and processing of offenders; but this analysis points out that these types of data are rare in criminological research. It is crucial to pursue this type of question to untangle the questions of constancy and change in criminal behavior.

References

ABRAHAMSEN, DAVID. 1952. *Who are the guilty?* New York: Grove.

AKERS, RONALD L. 1973. *Deviant behavior: a social learning approach*. Belmont, Calif.: Wadsworth.

ALEXANDER, FRANZ, and STAUB, HUGO. 1956. *The criminal, the judge, and the public*. New York: Free Press.

BANDURA, ALBERT. 1973. *Aggression: a social learning analysis*. Englewood Cliffs, N.J.: Prentice-Hall.

BECKER, HOWARD S. 1964. *The other side: perspective on deviance*. New York: Free Press.

――― 1973. *Outsiders: studies in the sociology of deviance*, rev. ed. New York: Free Press.

CHAMBLISS, WILLIAM J. 1974. The state, the law, and the definition of behavior as criminal or delinquent. In Daniel Glaser, ed., *Handbook of criminology*. Chicago: Rand McNally.

CICOUREL, AARON V. 1968. *The social organization of juvenile justice*. New York: Wiley.

CLOWARD, RICHARD A., and OHLIN, LLOYD E. 1960. *Delinquency and opportunity: a theory of delinquent gangs*. New York: Free Press.

COHEN, ALBERT K. 1955. *Delinquent boys: the culture of the gang.* New York: Free Press.

COLLINS, JAMES J., JR. 1977. Offender careers and restraint: the probabilities and policy implications. Ph.D. dissertation, University of Pennsylvania.

CURTIS, LYNN A. 1975. *Violence, race, and culture.* Lexington, Mass.: D.C. Heath.

DOUGLAS, J. W. B., ROSS, J. M., HAMMOND, W. A., and MULLIGAN, D. G. 1966. Delinquency and social class. *British Journal of Criminology* 6: 924-302.

FEDERAL BUREAU OF INVESTIGATION. 1977. *Uniform Crime Reports.* Washington, D.C.: U.S. Government Printing Office.

FERGUSON, THOMAS. 1952. *The young delinquent in his social setting.* London: Oxford University Press.

FOX, JAMES ALAN. 1976. An economic analysis of crime data. Ph.D. dissertation, University of Pennsylvania.

GLUECK, SHELDON, and GLUECK, ELEANOR. 1930. *500 criminal careers.* New York: Knopf.

———— 1940. *Juvenile delinquents grow up.* New York: Commonwealth Fund.

———— 1943. *Criminal careers in retrospect.* New York: Commonwealth Fund.

———— 1957. *Unraveling juvenile delinquency.* New York: Commonwealth Fund.

———— 1968. *Delinquents and nondelinquents in perspective.* Cambridge, Mass.: Harvard University Press.

———— 1974. *Of delinquency and crime: a panorama of years of search and research.* Springfield, Ill.: Charles C. Thomas.

GOCDE, WILLIAM J. 1970. Violence among intimates. In Donald Mulvihill and Melvin Tumin, eds., *Violent crime: a task force report to the National Commission on the Causes and Prevention of Violence.* Washington, D.C.: U.S. Government Printing Office.

HALLOCK, SEYMOUR. 1967. *Psychiatry and the dilemmas of crime.* New York: Harper.

HAVIGHURST, ROBERT J., BOWMAN, PAUL HOOVER, LIDDLE, GORDON P., MATTHEWS, CHARLES V., and PEIRCE, JAMES V. 1962. *Growing up in River City.* New York: Wiley.

KITSUSE, JOHN I., and CICOUREL, AARON V. A note on the uses of official statistics. *Social Problems* 2: 131-139.

LANDAU, R., ET AL. 1972. The influence of psychotic parents on their children's development. *American Journal of Psychiatry* 124: 38-43.

LAW ENFORCEMENT ASSISTANCE ADMINISTRATION. 1976. *Criminal victimization surveys in eight American cities: a comparison of 1971/72 and 1974/75 findings.* Washington, D.C.: U.S. Government Printing Office.

———— 1980. *Expenditure and employment data for the criminal justice system, 1978 report.* Washington, D.C.: U.S. Government Printing Office.

LEMERT, EDWIN M. 1972. *Human deviance, social problems, and social control.* Englewood Cliffs, N.J.: Prentice-Hall.

———— 1973. Beyond need: the societal reactions to deviance. *Social Problems* 21: 457-468.

LOMBROSO, CESARE. 1876. *L'Uomo delinquente*. Translated with modifications by H. P. Norton, *Crime: its causes and remedies*. Boston: Little, Brown, 1911.

McCORD, JOAN. 1978. A thirty-year follow-up of treatment effects. *American Psychologist* 33: 284-289.

McCORD, WILLIAM, and McCORD, JOAN. 1959. *Origins of crime: a new evaluation of the Cambridge-Somerville Youth Study*. New York: Columbia University Press.

McCORKLE, LLOYD W., ELIAS, ALBERT, and BIXBY, F. LOVELL. 1958. *The Highfields story*. New York: Henry Holt.

MEDNICK, SARNOFF A., and CHRISTIANSEN, CARL OTTO. 1977. *Biosocial bases of criminal behavior*. New York: Gardner Press.

MERTON, ROBERT K. 1938. Social structure and anomie. *American Sociological Review* 3: 672-682.

MILLER, WALTER B. 1958. Lower class culture as a generating milieu of gang delinquency. *Journal of Social Issues* 14 (3): 5-19.

MULLIGAN, GLENN, DOUGLAS, J. W. B., HAMMOND, W. A., and TIZARD, J. 1963. Delinquency and the symptoms of maladjustment: the findings of a longitudinal study. *Proceedings of the Royal Society of Medicine* 56 (12): 1083-1986.

PETERSILIA, JOAN, GREENWOOD, PETER W., and LAVIN, MARVIN. 1977. *Criminal careers of habitual felons*. Santa Monica, Calif.: Rand Corporation R-2144-DOJ.

QUINNEY, RICHARD. 1970. *The social reality of crime*. Boston: Little, Brown.

RILEY, MATILDA WHITE, JOHNSON, MARILYN, and FONER, ANNE. 1972. *Aging and society*, vol. 3. New York: Russell Sage Foundation.

ROBINS, LEE N. 1966. *Deviant children grown up: a sociological and psychiatric study of sociopathic personality*. Baltimore, Md.: Williams and Wilkins.

RYDER, NORMAN B. 1965. The cohort as a concept in the study of social change. *American Sociological Review* 30: 843-861.

SELLIN, THORSTEN, and WOLFGANG, MARVIN E. 1964. *The measurement of delinquency*. New York: Wiley.

SHAH, SALEEM A., and ROTH, LOREN E. 1974. Biological and psychophysiological factors in criminology. In Daniel Glazer, ed., *Handbook of criminology*. Chicago: Rand McNally.

SHELDON, WILLIAM R. 1949. *Varieties of delinquent behavior*. New York: Harper.

SUTHERLAND, EDWIN H., and CRESSEY, DONALD R. 1970. *Criminology*, 8th ed. Philadelphia: Lippincott.

TOBY, JACKSON, and LIEBMAN, EDNA. The integration of adolescent delinquents into conventional society: the impact of girlfriends and wives as agents of further socialization. Rutgers University, undated.

TURK, AUSTIN T. 1969. *Criminality and the legal order*. Chicago: Rand McNally.

WALLERSTEIN, JAMES, and WYLIE, C. J. 1969. Our law-abiding lawbreakers. *Probation* 1969.

WEST, D. J. 1969. *Present conduct and future delinquency*. London: Heinemann.

WEST, D. J., and FARRINGTON, D. P. 1973. *Who becomes delinquent?* London: Heinemann.

———— 1977. *The delinquent way of life*. London: Heinemann.

WOLFGANG, MARVIN E. 1977. From man to boy—from delinquency to crime. Paper presented at the National Symposium on the Serious Juvenile Offender, Department of Corrections, State of Minnesota, Minneapolis, Minnesota. September.

WOLFGANG, MARVIN E., FIGLIO, ROBERT M., and SELLIN, THORSTEN. 1972. *Delinquency in a birth cohort*. Chicago: University of Chicago Press.

14 | Schooling and Occupational Careers: Constancy and Change in Worldly Success
David L. Featherman

WITH ITS HIGHLY URBANIZED, industrial economy, America has been called an achieving society (McClelland, 1961), the archetype of that ideal-typical class of modern society in which persons are achievement oriented, future directed, and materialistic (Inkeles and Smith, 1974). More recent social commentary has questioned the dominance of material values among contemporary Americans, particularly among the young. The "greening" of America (Reich, 1970) through self-exploration and self-expression is said to be replacing the older values—the residues of a new nation at the leading edge of a technoindustrial Western economy. If Americans were once inner directed by the intrinsic value of achievement and then other directed to get ahead within the secular world of material values (Reisman, 1950), today they might be said to be self-directed. In such a postmodern or postindustrial society, work and income may be less important than the conditions of work, and overtime pay may be less of an incentive than a long weekend (U.S. Department of Labor, 1974).

This chapter is not about societal or personal values per se but rather about the persistence of socioeconomic achievement over the life course as seen within the schools and the labor market. The relevance of values to this work is in its essential assumption that achievement is credibly indexed by worldly success—by work and graded performance rather than by some personal, self-relevant standards.[1] It is clear that this assumption is arbitrary, particularly given the plurality of values that seems to pervade modern American life. Yet empirical studies of personal satisfaction and happiness continue to reveal the substantial centrality of work to one's general sense of self-worth and well-being (Gurin, Veroff, and Feld, 1960; Campbell, Converse, and Rogers, 1976; Andrews and Withey, 1976). This is not to deny that other life domains are salient to perceived well-being, nor to argue that the material features of education and work dominate the nonmaterial. However, there persists a strong central orientation toward the socioeconomic value of work in most Western industrialized societies (Mayer, 1973; Hauser and Featherman, 1977, chap. 1). Most illustrative of this common orientation is that the relative preferability of specific occupations is similar across countries and among population groups within countries (see Treiman, 1977, for a review). In addition, the preferences for various lines of work seem to manifest a common view that work is instrumental to economic well-being and to socioeconomic status (see Goldthorpe and Hope, 1972, 1974; and Featherman, Jones, and Hauser, 1975, for the empirical development of this notion). Thus for the purposes of this chapter achievement refers narrowly to the persistence and change in socioeconomic status through work and through scholastic performances related to the attainment of education and of jobs.

It is appropriate to think of socioeconomic achievement as a lifelong process and thus as a special instance of social mobility. The seeds of such a process are sown within families of orientation, nurtured and developed within the schools, and harvested within the domestic and market economies in adulthood. Such a view has been termed the socioeconomic life cycle (Duncan, 1967) and is schematized in figure 14.1. Persistence of the level of achievement can be assessed in several ways within this framework. First, one can measure the degree of socioeconomic "inheritance" from one generation to the next. Are inequalities passed from parents to offspring, or is socioeconomic mobility prevalent? Second, one can take the staging or sequencing of events in the socioeconomic life cycle as given and ask how achievement within one stage—schooling—affects achievement at the next—jobs and employment. Third, one can look across the work history at the succession of jobs and employment-unemployment sequences to establish career achievements. This chapter pursues all three approaches in an effort to understand the typical trajectories of achievement from entry into school to retirement.

The sociological approach to human development differs from classical psychological approaches in several respects. It examines constancy and change in achievement behaviors and experiences over the life course, by no means typical of only sociological treatments (Baltes and Schaie, 1973a; Baltes, 1979); in addition, it focuses on intergenerational linkages. Childhood behaviors have been systematically studied in relation to adulthood behaviors of the same person

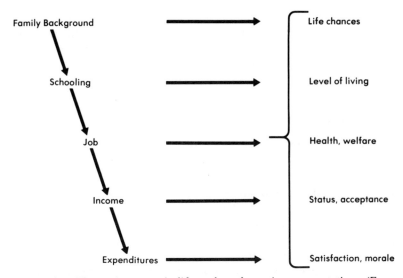

Figure 14.1. *The socioeconomic life cycle: schematic representation. (From Duncan, 1967, p. 87.)*

within conventional human development paradigms, but the corresponding behaviors or psychological characteristics of parents and offspring have less often been investigated in developmental psychology.

The legitimacy and importance of this intergenerational approach derive from a second emphasis of this chapter—its focus on social institutions as environments that affect achievement behaviors. Rather than look within microenvironments to detect ontogenetic features of development, the sociologist more typically compares behaviors across environments to observe changes that seem to vary with macroenvironments such as the social institutions that sequence and organize the life course (Clausen, 1972). In this chapter the central institutions are the home (family), the school, and the economy, the set of which suggests intergenerational features to continuity and change in achievement. The structural qualities of these environments, the linkages among them, and secular change in social institutions establish one set of limits—one context—for human development.

This chapter is concerned less with human development as manifested in intraindividual variability over time than in patterns of interindividual variability. Examining the latter patterns, while not necessarily following from the subject of achievement, is consistent with a sociological definition of worldly success in terms of relative performance within a set of peers (a birth cohort, a school grade).

These distinguishing emphases entail a concept of human development that encompasses more than maturational growth. An intergenerational and ontogenetic view of development requires a model of continuity and change that is more complex and flexible than the sequential, unidirectional, and irreversible model often used in ontogenetic child psychology (Baltes, 1979).

Scholastic Achievement

Individual potentials for worldly success are most often given their first substantial tests within the schools (Sorokin, 1927; Parsons, 1959). Schools play at least two major roles in modern society. First, they serve as the communal mechanism for social selection into practical and academic training. That is, education for life tends to be controlled by the community (society), not individual families. Neither curriculum nor student evaluation procedures are influenced primarily by individual families; rather they are subject to the combined jurisdictions of professional educators and community representatives. Thus the schools are social inventions that, at least in theory, educate the individual without regard to family or social background. Whether in fact the schools practice such universalism is open to debate (Bowles and Gintis, 1976; Blau and Duncan, 1967; Jencks et al., 1972).

A second role is the creation of education cohorts defined by age and scholastic ability. Federal legislation controlling the employment of children in enterprises of interstate commerce was enacted in the late thirties and tested in the courts during the early forties. After World War II provisions of the Fair Labor Standards Act of 1938 were broadened to include nearly all instances of child labor, except those in agriculture and those involving work during school vacations (Panel on Youth, 1974, pp. 35-38). Together with the relatively greater affluence of families during the postwar period, this legislation stimulated new universal school enrollment among children through at least a portion of adolescence (Ferriss, 1969, fig. 2.1; B. Duncan, 1968, table 12). Public regulation of school enrollment and attendance to a certain age (14 in most states) has assisted in this creation of educational cohorts from birth cohorts. Most children begin first grade at age 6 or 7, although at least 6% of the first graders are younger and another 9%-10% are older (B. Duncan, 1968, table 2). Thus each birth cohort enters the formal school system at approximately the same age, changing the locus of socialization from the nuclear family to the community (school).

Yet school entrance cohorts are not identical to birth cohorts; neither are graduation or school exit cohorts. In any year 10%-20% of a first-grade class does not belong to the modal birth cohort(s); similarly those graduating or leaving the schools in a given year are even less representative of one or two (single-year) birth cohorts, for the obvious reasons that individuals progress through the grades at variable speeds and leave school at different levels or grades.

Since the schools reorganize birth cohorts as substantially as they do, it is important to understand the basis for the winnowing and sifting—the selection for speed of progress and for length of school attendance. If the schools sort individuals from the same birth cohort into different graduation cohorts (obversely, first job, marriage, or next-stage-of-life cohorts) mainly on the basis of meritocratic principles, then interpretations of constancy and change in individual achievement become fundamentally different from those that one would draw if promotion were based on nonmeritocratic principles such as social class, race, or political ideology (Turner, 1960). If the social aggregates that leave the schools and enter adulthood as education cohorts are formed primarily by their scholastic ability and not by social background, then the schools facilitate social mobility rather than perpetuating socioeconomic inequalities from generation to generation.

Thus in interpreting the extent to which an individual's achievements vary through the years spent in schools and the linkages between academic performance and the jobs and earnings of later life, it is essential to keep in mind the school's social functions and the principles on which it is organized.

In this essay three indexes of scholastic achievement are used and investigated: intelligence and scholastic aptitude, grades, and years of formal school completed.

Intelligence

In the first decade of the twentieth century Binet and Simon developed the first instruments to diagnose "intelligence," the ability to do school work. Under commission by the minister of public instruction in Paris, they designed their Metrical Scale of Intelligence to predict which students were likely to fail and, by their early identification, to permit educators to place these students in special schools before they fell too far behind their age peers. Binet and Simon formulated their instrument to discriminate between "bright" and "dull" students, just as a classroom teacher in direct contact with the pupils might be able to diagnose intellective performance and capacity. Thus whatever intelligence tests measure, it is by design correlated with aptitude for scholastic achievement in conventional classroom situations. More modern tests such as the American version of the Stanford-Binet Intelligence Scale, created by Lewis Terman, predict other

measures of scholastic achievement with an average validity coefficient of 0.5 to 0.6, and in longitudinal studies they correlate with other
performance measures almost to the limits of their own reliability
(Jensen, 1969, p. 508).

Given the purpose for which intelligence tests were developed,
they are by definition culturally biased. That is, since they are constructed to diagnose which students will succeed in the schools, the
tests favor students who have mastered the language and conceptual
processes on which the teachers and curricula of the schools operate.
Schools have historically been elite or middle-class in origin; hence
students who are more able to learn and use the language and conceptual forms of those who design and staff the schools are both more
likely to succeed in their studies and to score higher on intelligence
tests.

Some psychologists, such as Raymond Cattell (1963), distinguish
between *fluid* and *crystallized* intelligence. The latter is a product of
education and experience, while the former is thought to be relatively
free of such cultural or environmental influences and to evince latent
capacities for conceptual learning and problem solving. While crystallized intelligence seems to correspond more closely to the substantive
content of schooling, fluid intelligence is only slightly less linked to the
curriculum in conventional schools. For example, were curricula
heavily devoted to affective content and style rather than to logicode-
ductive reasoning, such so-called culture-free tests as Raven's Progressive Matrices would have little predictive validity for scholastic
aptitude. One might legitimately conclude the culture-free tests of intelligence would be highly undesirable instruments for predicting
achievement in the schools as they have been organized in the United
States and Europe for decades.[2]

The most thorough and concise study of continuity and change in
intelligence—now understood as a form of scholastic performance as
well as aptitude for such performance—appears in Benjamin Bloom
(1964). Basing his analysis on five longitudinal studies that followed
children's intellective growth for periods ranging from five to twenty-
one years, Bloom concluded that no accurate predictions of ultimate
intelligence (by the end of schooling, or age 17) were possible prior to
the age of 3 or 4. In part, this inability reflected the lack of consolidation in children's cognitive development by that age, the validity of the
tests, and the tests' lower reliabilities. However, combining test results
from a series of administrations increased reliability after age 4 and
thus increased the predictive validity of the tests. Based on data
pooled across tests and corrected for measurement reliability, Bloom
estimated that the product-moment correlation between intelligence at

age 3 and age 17 was about 0.65; between age 5 and age 17, about 0.80; and at age 8 (and after) and age 17, 0.90 or higher. (The results for boys and girls were not distinguishable, but the data from the five longitudinal studies were not necessarily representative of a cross section of American children.)

From these data Bloom constructed a hypothetical model of intellectual growth, based on the assumption of an absolute scale of measurement (one with a fixed zero point and equal intervals)—an unlikely assumption. The model apparently accounted for the correlations from longitudinal studies and led Bloom to the following generalizations: "[In] terms of intelligence measured at age 17, at least 20 [percent] is developed by age 1, 50 [percent] by age 4, 80 [percent] by age 8, and 92 [percent] by age 13. Put in terms of intelligence measured at age 17, from conception to age 4 the individual develops 50% of his mature intelligence, from ages 4 to 8 he develops another 30 [percent] and from ages 8 to 17 the remaining 20 [percent]" (1964, p. 68). (For a critical evaluation of the legitimacy of such developmental interpretations from correlational evidence as adduced by Bloom, see chapter 9 in this volume.)

After the late teens, intelligence (as it is currently defined and tested; hence reference is to IQ hereafter) continues to change, albeit slightly and in apparent response to the presence or absence of stimulation from postsecondary education and careers (Bayley, 1966). Christopher Jencks and his colleagues (1972, pp. 60, 112) report a series of longitudinal studies of special populations tested in adolescence and at mid life (between ages 30 and 45) documenting positive correlations ranging between 0.7 and 0.9. Bloom's (1964, p. 81) review of longitudinal studies led him to conclude that intellective growth was possible at least through age 50, despite the substantial plateau in the growth curve after the early teen years. Even among the intellectually gifted, for whom the capacity of tests to capture positive changes is hampered by their ceiling effects and the severely truncated variance in measured abilities, small gains in IQ are not uncommon (Terman and Oden, 1959, pp. 61-63).

Interpreting the developmental course of IQ is far more problematic than documenting it, although the lack of national longitudinal data for panels of children who are broadly representative of their U.S. birth cohorts is not a secure base for this development, either. In any case high positive correlations between distributions of scores at two ages do not imply that the intelligence of an individual does not grow in the interval. Neither do they mean that persons who score high at an early age will learn more over a year or two than persons who score low. In fact, the correlations between initial scores and gains in test scores between two administrations are customarily zero until age 7—the age after which extensive changes become less apparent (Bloom, 1964, p. 62, and chart 4; Terman and Oden, 1959, p. 63). The pattern of longitudinal correlations and the drift of mean scores suggest that those who are diagnosed as "bright" in their initial years of formal schooling retain their advantage in knowledge and abilities and build from them to higher levels as they matriculate.

The most interesting but also a problematic feature of the developmental course of performance on IQ tests is the considerable stability of scores (denoting relative position) after the initial years of enrollment in the schools (Jencks et al., 1972, pp. 60-62). It is likely that both differing rates of psychological development before age 4 and the extent to which IQ tests prior to that age tap functions different from those tapped later make it difficult to predict from these earlier tests (Sontag, Baker, and Nelson, 1958; McCall, Appelbaum, and Hogarty, 1973). In addition, home environments may nurture abilities different from those evoked by classrooms and teachers (or the same sets of skills but with different emphases among their elements). Were such a lack of consistency between environments of the home and the school extensive, it would not support contentions that the schools systematically favor middle-class over lower-class children (Bowles and Gintis, 1976). The relative stability of intelligence after age 8 to 10 may reflect some genetic base, particularly if the schools tend to standardize the learning environments to which children are exposed. It may also result from commonalities in the environments across schools, grades, occupations, and careers that tend to sort individuals by correlated criteria into nearly identical ranks throughout much of life (Spaeth, 1976). Finally, the stability of IQ may be an artifact of the tests that give the concept of intelligence its concrete manifestation—tests designed by trial and error to identify capacities that enable matriculation to higher grades and complex curricula (and, given the educational prerequisites for occupations in industrial societies, to higher-status and higher-paying careers). Current research does not permit one to choose among these or other explanations for the basis of the developmental course of intelligence.[3]

Among the many instances of incomplete information are unreliable estimates of the heritability of intelligence—estimates that might help assess the degree to which observed variations in IQ manifest genetic differences among a specific population. (This is not to suggest that such estimates of heritability might index the limits of the environmental nurturance of intelligence; see Goldberger, 1977a, pp. 22, 26). Correlations of IQ between natural parents and their offspring are typically 0.5 (Jensen, 1969; Jencks et al., 1972, appendix A). Beyond providing a measure of intergenerational continuity in scholastic aptitude, these correlations tell little about the basis of continuity. But together with data from persons sharing reasonably calculable degrees of common kinship and of putatively common environments (twins reared together versus apart, fraternal versus identical twins), such correlations have enabled social scientists to estimate the proportion of total variance in IQ that represents genetic variability (heritability). Using correlations reported across a series of unrelated studies within nonstandard populations, Jencks and his colleagues (1972, appendix A) estimate heritability at 45%. Other estimates tend to be higher (see Goldberger, 1977b, for a review).

The disagreements about heritability are moot, however, since Leon Kamin (1974) and Arthur Goldberger (1976a, 1977a, b) have discredited the scientific status of these estimates. They cite sampling biases in the original kinship studies, errors of attribution in some secondary reports about the studies, errors in statistical estimation of biometric model fitting, and, in a few instances, apparent "manufacturing" of data and their misrepresentation. Virtually all work purporting to estimate the heritability of intelligence is flawed by one or more of these discrediting aspects. Yet even if the knowledge about heritability were more credible, it would not be very informative about the reasons for changes (or lack of them) in IQ and related academic achievements over the life cycle because heritability tells about the likely intergenerational consequences of selective breeding under constant (or average) environmental conditions. Knowledge about heritability of intelligence is even less useful in the design and evaluation of educational intervention strategies (Morton, 1974; Goldberger, 1977a; compare Jensen, 1969, and Scarr-Salapateck, 1971).

If heritability is by itself not a very informative sociological datum, the associations between social background and intelligence and between intelligence and other forms of academic and career achievements do constitute interesting sociological phenomena. (No attempt is made to decompose total or phenotypic variance in intelligence into genetic and environmental components.) For example, considerable research in the United States and abroad has been conducted to ascertain whether the schools promote and educate the most intellectually able, irrespective of family and social backgrounds (Douglas, 1964; Scottish Council for Research in Education, 1953; MacPherson, 1958; Fägerlind, 1975; Coleman et al., 1966; Sewell and Shah, 1967). In addressing this question of unequal educational opportunity, such researches inevitably inquire into the relationship between the social backgrounds of children and measures of intelligence.

Estimates of the predictability of scholastic aptitude (IQ) from

indexes of family socioeconomic background and other social characteristics range from 10% to 40% (Jencks et al., 1972). At the high end
of this range, Jerald Bachman (1970, p. 75) accounts for roughly one-
third of the variance in intelligence (Ammons Quick Test) among
tenth-grade boys in the United States by an additive combination of
family socioeconomic status, number of siblings, and race. Race itself
accounts for roughly 20% of the variance and over 9% of mental ability among boys of equal family sizes and socioeconomic statuses. At
the lower end of the range, data for Wisconsin high school seniors
(Sewell and Hauser, 1972; Sewell, Hauser, and Wolf, 1977) suggest
that as little as 9% of mental ability (Hennon-Nelson test) reflects the
social backgrounds of boys and girls (including socioeconomic status,
size of family, parental education, and maternal employment). Inge-
mar Fägerlind (1975) reports similarly low connections between social
background and intelligence among Swedish ten-year-olds, as do Karl
Alexander, Bruce Eckland, and Larry Griffith (1975) for a national
U.S. sample of high school sophomores. (See also Kohen, 1971; O. D.
Duncan, 1968.) Lack of strict comparability among these studies pre-
cludes a definite conclusion, but the weight of available evidence implies that the total effect of social background is probably nearer to
the lower end of the range cited by Jencks and his colleagues (1972).

Virtually all studies of the sociocultural bases of intelligence concur about the effects of specific background variables. Parental income, occupational statuses, and educations are positively related to
filial intelligence, while rearing in large families and broken families,
and being black are negatively related to IQ. Robert Hauser (1973)
concludes that the impact of "socioeconomic status" (a hypothetical
composite) on IQ among Wisconsin men is a linear combination of
essentially equally weighted elements of paternal and maternal educational levels, paternal occupational status (prestige score), and parental income. That conclusion apparently applies less well to Wisconsin
women, however. Girls' IQ scores are more substantially influenced
by maternal education than by other parental status or family characteristics, and parental income has no appreciable net effect of its own
(Sewell, Hauser, and Wolf, 1977, tables 2, 3). For neither boys nor
girls does having an employed mother or being reared in a broken or
rural family setting affect IQ (once the size of one's sibship and parental education and income levels are statistically controlled). For
both sexes, the net negative effect of an additional sibling on one's IQ
is about the same as the average positive effect of other background
characteristics (all measured as standardized variables).

Most social psychologists interpret such multivariate influences
of social background on IQ as proxies for the dynamic phenomena of

psychosocialization which differentiates the genetic and cultural environments of individuals and families. R. Dave (1963) and Richard Wolf (1964) have attempted to measure home environments directly, developing measures of "achievement press," "language models," "work habits emphasized," and the like. Joe Spaeth (1976) interprets such efforts to quantify environments and to relate them systematically to socioeconomic status and IQ as providing evidence for differential "cognitive complexity" across families and socioeconomic strata. A somewhat different interpretation is provided by Trevor Williams (1974, 1976a) from analyses conducted in Canada and Australia.

Williams suggests that not only do families provide environments of varying complexity (of things and people) but through the style and content of their *mutual* interaction (parents to children and vice versa), *families* alter the school-related behaviors (including IQ) of children. This social learning model for the variation of home environments within and between socioeconomic strata contains four empirical components: (1) active parental efforts to create complex environments of people and things, (2) predominance of one or the other parent in rearing (reinforcement), (3) physical rather than non-physical modes of reinforcement, and (4) parental expectations and encouragements for academic performance of children. In this work higher intelligence is associated (simultaneously) with higher parental IQs, more complex environments of things and people (role models and learning situations), fewer normative pressures for achievement, and relatively more physical forms of behavioral reinforcement. Environmental complexity of the home (as indexed by Williams) is apparently more important in shaping academic aptitude than parental IQ per se (and both are more strongly related to filial IQ than are the other behavioral components of the social learning model). However, brighter parents tend to construct more complex learning situations for their children, to involve the father more centrally in child rearing, to use nonphysical forms of reinforcement, and to more frequently encourage academic excellence. In general, children from high-IQ (also high socioeconomic status) families typically enjoy the double benefit of intelligent parents and the intellectually facilitating environments that they create. But Williams's work also suggests that the stereotypical childrearing pattern of middle-class families (nonphysical reinforcement and higher expectations for academics) may not be the only salutary environment. In addition, Williams finds that high-IQ children evoke a further enrichment of their own home environments; they prompt others to create more complex social and objective environments that further stimulate their cognitive development.

Thus children from high-IQ-families benefit from genes, environment, and from the feedback of filial intelligence to the enrichment of their own context. They are triply endowed.[4]

Since interindividual variability in IQ among adults is rather stable, research into sources of variability has been rare. What little there is corroborates this essential constancy (Duncan, Featherman, and Duncan, 1972, chap. 5; Fägerlind, 1975), although continuation of schooling beyond late adolescence and experimental manipulation of environmental complexity apparently foster further growth of mental ability (Griliches and Mason, 1973; Fägerlind, 1975; Baltes and Willis, 1979). The factors that account for variability in intelligence after age 20 are not necessarily the same as those associated with earlier differences in academic ability. For example, the socioeconomic backgrounds and family size characteristics of Swedish boys account for 11% of intelligence measured at age 10. Upon induction into the military about ten years later, the combination of early intelligence and amount and type of additional schooling explain 66% of the variance in adult IQ (Fägerlind, 1975, table 7.1). Despite the rather high ten-year correlation in IQ ($r = 0.745$), changes in relative performance on IQ tests did occur and apparently in response to factors other than those (or not highly correlated with them) associated with early intelligence and length of schooling.[5]

Achievement Tests and Grades

A second category of scholastic achievement is tapped by achievement tests and grades. In no sense can these measures be construed as culture-free, for they are designed to assess acquired knowledge. Thus such scholastic achievement is customarily indexed by tests of verbal ability, reading comprehension, and mathematical ability. Student performances on such standardized instruments are regarded as measures of the outputs of schools—the products of formal education (Coleman et al., 1966). Grades differ from standardized achievement tests in that (at least in principle) they are subject to the influences of teachers' wider knowledge about the student's ability. However, this general information might also include such educationally "irrelevant" items as the family's socioeconomic status, the student's sex and race, and other ascribed characteristics. Whether grades provide less valid measures of scholastic achievement than standardized tests because they reflect subjective (teacher) expectations for ability is problematic.

Estimates of the correlations between IQ, achievement tests, and grades suggest that the relationships between them are ones of degree rather than kind; none of them is culture-free in the strictest sense.

Bloom (1964, p. 102), in surveying several studies of the concurrent performances on IQ tests and performance on achievement batteries, sets the correlation at 0.85 among adolescents. Williams's (1976b) correlations for boys and girls in Toronto high schools approximate this estimate, although the relationship for boys is apparently lower in those data ($r = 0.72$). Grades and IQ correlate somewhat lower, at around 0.50 to 0.60 (Sewell, Hauser, and Wolf, 1977; Williams, 1976a; Kerckhoff and Campbell, 1977), while grades and standardized measures of achievement seem to be the least related. (Williams, 1976a, estimates the concurrent correlation at 0.4 to 0.5; similar correlations appear in Hauser, 1971, p. 87.)

Despite these differential patterns of interrelationship, both grades and standardized achievement test scores seem to follow a developmental pattern not unlike that estimated for intelligence. Bloom (1964, p. 103) observes that the majority of achievement tests are based on verbal facility; therefore the growth of scholastic achievement likely parallels the development of language and vocabulary. Basing his calculations on studies of vocabulary testing (Seashore and Eckerson, 1940; Smith, 1941; Bryan, 1953), Bloom projects a theoretic developmental curve for scholastic achievement. This hypothetical model indicates that 50% of the general test pattern at age 18 (grade 12) has unfolded by age 9 (grade 3) and that 75% has developed by age 13 (grade 7). If one includes early IQ testing among preschool children in the pool of data from which such developmental models are estimated (see Bloom's use of Ebert and Simmons, 1943), one can infer perhaps as much as one-third of grade 12 achievement from students' test performances as they enter first grade (Bloom, 1964, p. 104).

Hypothetical as such developmental models may be, they summarize rather accurately the observed patterns of interage correlations for reading comprehension, general achievement test scores, and teacher-assigned grades. That generalization becomes substantially less valid when the correlations are not corrected for estimated unreliability in tests and grading practices or for the absence of conventional standards for grading across schools (Bloom and Peters, 1961).[6] For example, the correlation between senior year high school grades and college freshman grades is roughly 0.50; after correction the estimate is 0.80. Interannual grades among collegians correlate in excess of 0.90, virtually at the theoretic maximum of their reliability (Bloom, 1964, p. 127).[7]

A correlation of 0.8 between scores does not imply that individuals do not gain in knowledge and ability. For example, the correlation of reading comprehension scores among persons tested in ninth and twelfth grades is 0.77 for boys and 0.84 for girls. Yet the mean scores increased by an amount roughly equal to 60% of a standard deviation (Shaycoft, 1967, tables 5-2 and 5-4). This is essentially similar to the change in a student's knowledge about biology and social studies, information perhaps more subject to modification by curriculum and teaching than is the aptitude for reading comprehension.[8] Nor do relatively high correlations necessarily mean that the gap in achievement between the most and the least able remains constant. James Coleman and his colleagues (1966, pp. 272-273) find that the average verbal abilities of blacks in grades 6, 9, and 12 lie a standard deviation below the means of white students in metropolitan schools of the Northeast. Owing to the greater variability in which scores at grade 12, however, the absolute difference (expressed in grade-level equivalent) between the racial scores was greater at the end of high school than at the beginning. (Recall that Coleman and his colleagues analyze cross-sectional data.) The high positive correlations suggest that the relative rank of a student (by scholastic aptitude) is well established by the end of primary schooling; that rank remains quite stable particularly when assessed by standardized achievement.

Efforts to explain differences in scholastic achievement by reference to school or institutional characteristics have generally been disappointing (Sewell and Armor, 1966; Coleman et al., 1966; Hauser, 1971; Hauser, Sewell, and Alwin, 1976; Spady, 1976). It is primarily student characteristics such as parental socioeconomic status, race, sex, and mental ability that account for performance on achievement tests and for grade-point averages; the effects of school variation in average teacher experience, expenditures per pupil, and the compositional features of student bodies are far less consequential. Jencks and his colleagues (1972, chap. 3) summarize quite succinctly their evaluation of the best research on this subject:

> Overall, the evidence shows that differences between high schools contribute almost nothing to the overall level of cognitive inequality. Differences between elementary schools may be somewhat more important, but evidence for this is still inconclusive. The average effect of attending the best rather than the worst fifth of all elementary schools is almost certainly no more than 10 points and probably no more than 5. The difference between, say, the top and bottom halves is even less.

> Under these circumstances the reader should not be surprised to learn that it is very difficult to identify specific characteristics of schools that influence student achievement.

If Bloom's developmental curve of academic aptitude is valid, it is not too surprising that variations in the organization and composition of schools have such modest effects on scholastic aptitudes (contrasted with factual information in academic subjects; see Shaycoft, 1967). Since academic abilities as measured by standard tests and teacher grading are apparently most malleable during the preschool and primary school years, the contextual effects of high schools on student achievements are less than one might expect to observe were research directed at younger children. (Nearly all the large-scale assessments of interschool variation in achievement as a function of institution-level variables, such as per pupil expenditures, have been conducted at the postprimary level; [Hauser, 1971] or in cross-sectional designs [Coleman et al., 1966].) The social composition of high schools and their curricula and value "climates" affect students' performances. For example, black students achieve higher test scores in schools with a majority (critical mass) of white middle-class peers; this contextual effect is accentuated among blacks from higher-status homes (see Spady, 1976, for a review; also, Jencks et al., 1972). White students seem to profit from instruction in schools having many teachers certified beyond the baccalaureate level, with accelerated curricula for superior students, advanced placement credit courses, and accelerated graduation policies, and with operative values emphasizing academic excellence (McDill, Rigsby, and Meyers, 1969). Students learn more in schools with longer days and instructional years (Wiley, 1976). Yet the fraction of the tested achievement of students that lies among high schools of one kind or another is less than one-third; and about one-third of such school effects reflects compositional features of the student bodies as indexed by their intelligence levels and families' socioeconomic statures (Hauser, 1971).

Exposure to a preschool educational program such as Head Start raises the achievement scores of participants, but the gains are short-lived. Nonparticipants, mainly from white, middle-class families, quickly catch up, and by the end of first grade virtually all the relative benefits of these programs on cognitive development have dissipated (see Jencks et al., 1972, pp. 85-86 for a review of research).

Thus the main source of differential scholastic achievement (as mirrored in achievement tests and grades) appears to lie outside the schools. To a degree it is found within the homes and social backgrounds of preadolescents. It also rests on individual differences in intelligence, although this relationship is axiomatic (given the development of IQ tests to predict success in school).

Students from middle and upper socioeconomic strata typically achieve higher scores on standardized scholastic tests and are assigned higher grades by their teachers (see Lavin, 1965, for a bibliographic overview). The overlap of academic performance among the strata is substantial, however, implying that social background per se is neither a decided asset nor a liability in that sense. Furthermore, grades and class ranks follow more closely from the tested intelligence and academic aptitudes of students than from socioeconomic backgrounds. Since measures of aptitude and intelligence tend to vary widely within each social stratum, the total impact of background on grades is slight, and the combined influences of social background and academic ability are unable to account for the differences in assigned grades.

For example, if one eliminates differences in student grades between Wisconsin high schools, one finds that girls tend to be ranked about one-half a standard deviation above males of comparable ability (IQ) and social background within a given school. This net difference between the sexes is about the same as the grade advantage of a 10-point increase in IQ. But when all variables are put into a standardized metric (in units of their standard errors), grades are about five times as influenced by mental ability as by the additive combination of paternal and maternal education, family income, and father's occupation; and the effects of such aspects of social background are about half of those of the gender of students. Less than half of the variance in cumulative grade point average (rank in senior year) reflects the background, intelligence, and sex of students within a given high school (Hauser, Sewell, Alwin, 1976, table 11.3). Marks in particular subject areas may be even less dependent on background, intelligence, and aptitude (Hauser, 1971, p. 89). For instance, grades in arithmetic and English reflect both the mental abilities of high school students and their scores on achievement tests in mathematics and reading. But these aptitudes and the socioeconomic origins of students together cannot account for as much as one-half of the variance in either set of grades within schools.

Whether similar results apply to elementary school performance is still unknown, since the requisite longitudinal data on large and representative populations are not available. For youth who matriculate into high school (virtually all of recent birth cohorts), differential academic performance is fixed neither by social background nor by intelligence.[9] Intelligence tests provide useful predictions about scholastic achievement, particularly as indexed by standardized achievement instruments. To the extent that parents' socioeconomic circumstances and education affect the tested levels of academic achievement of their offspring, they do so indirectly—primarily through IQ (Hauser, 1971). The socioeconomically advantaged score higher on IQ tests, yet students' social backgrounds provide only modest predictions of how well they will score. The correlation between social background and scholastic achievement is therefore modest.[10] Students often achieve academic competence in spite of how well they test for intelligence, and the grade at which they terminate formal education is not fully determined by the combination of social background, intelligence, and performance on scholastic tests.

Teacher-assigned grades correlate less strongly with high school students' social backgrounds than do IQ scores (Hauser, 1971; Sewell, Hauser, and Wolf, 1977; Williams, 1972; Wilson and Portes, 1975).[11] On that basis there is little evidence of class bias in teachers' "prophecies" (Rosenthal and Jacobsen, 1968; Sexton, 1961) about students' abilities. But there appears to be a slightly closer association between socioeconomic background and placement in a precollegiate (versus general or vocational) curriculum than between background and grades (Hauser, Sewell, and Alwin, 1976). For example, Wisconsin youths whose parents are both college graduates are more likely by nearly 10 percentage points to complete a college preparatory program of study than a youth from a household of high school-educated parents, irrespective of their own intelligence and other factors. In addition, girls are less likely by about 10 percentage points to complete such a curriculum than males of equal ability, even though the grade averages of females tend to surpass that of males in high schools. These findings imply that to some degree students are channeled on the basis of sex and socioeconomic class. But curriculum placement is more heavily influenced by IQ than by gender or social background (Hauser, Sewell, and Alwin, 1976; Williams, 1976b), and the greatest variance in curricular placement of high school students is not affected by any of these factors (Heyns, 1974). It is, of course, possible that bias in grading and curriculum placement occurs prior to high school (Rist, 1973; compare Williams, 1976b), leading to differential dropout and opportunities and challenges for scholarships.

Length of Formal Schooling

Social and psychological factors permit youth to protract their schooling beyond the compulsory minimum. Mental ability and scholastic performance on tests and in courses are among the important ones, but high IQ and grade point average (GPA) are not sufficient for the ultimate educational accomplishment—the completion of a college or postgraduate degree program. Intelligence scores of 9-year-olds predict the highest grade that they will complete ($r = 0.50$ with a standard error of 0.10; see McCall, 1977) nearly as well as do the scores of youths still in school at grade 12 ($r = 0.35$ for females and 0.48 for males; see Sewell, Hauser, and Wolf, 1977).[12] Clearly, there is a smaller association between tested scholastic ability and highest grade completed than between tested mental abilities at two or more stages beyond preadolescence, perhaps because the highest grade completed reflects so substantially the separate influences of a variety of factors that no one of them—even IQ—offers a highly accurate prediction of educational achievement.[13]

One way to gauge the continuity in educational achievement among Americans is to compare the average length of schooling in the parental generation with that in the filial generation. Such a measure of intergenerational educational mobility—obversely, the parent-filial correlation—is analogous to the kinship correlations of intelligence as an index of continuity and change in a type of scholastic achievement. A comparison of sons born throughout the first half of this century with their fathers reveals an unmistakable pattern of upward educational mobility. Sons have typically completed three to four more years of formal schooling than their fathers (Hauser and Featherman, 1976). This difference apparently peaked within families with sons born during the Great Depression (who thus completed their schooling around World War II); since then the educational gap between the generations of males has declined somewhat. The correlation between fathers' and sons' educations (as estimated from a cross-sectional sample of U.S. men of ages 20-64 in 1973) has remained rather constant, varying unsystematically between 0.42 and 0.46 across cohorts of men born five years apart since the turn of the century. This is a modest degree of persistence in the educational achievements of individuals between generations, but there is substantial mobility as well. Persons from less well-educated families surpass the level of schooling attained by their parents, enjoying the similar trend of a rising floor of the distribution of schooling in the United States (Featherman and Hauser, 1978, chap. 5).

The parent-filial education correlation is in the range of the estimate of the analogous IQ correlation, although the causal processes that yield such similarities need not be (indeed, probably are not) the same. The correlation of the levels of schooling completed by pairs of brothers (r about 0.5-0.7) is about the same or slightly higher than might be anticipated for the phenotypic similarities in intelligence (Duncan, Featherman, and Duncan, 1972; Jencks et al., 1972; Hauser and Featherman, 1976). The implication is thus that families provide the means for substantial educational homogeneity within a sibship. Precisely which mechanisms yield such high similarity are more conjectural than well established. For example, a linear combination of social background variables including paternal occupational standing and education, number of siblings, whether living in an intact or a broken family, whether reared on a farm or not, region of birth, ethnicity, and race accounts for only 55% of the brother's correlation (Hauser and Featherman, 1976). Were intelligence added to this combination, perhaps the proportion of the similarity that can be explained would rise, but it is unlikely that this combination of social background characteristics would exhaust the sources of commonality.

A related observation about the brother's correlation of educational achievements is that families and society often have conflicting goals. The father-son correlation implies that social forces within but mainly outside the family tend to reorganize the pattern of educational inequality between generations by stimulating educational mobility of children relative to their parents. This would occur if, for example, the schools typically took able children from families of high school-educated parents and educated them to the same level as children of parents who completed college. While evidence suggests that a good deal of such induction of mobility goes on, the witting and unwitting actions of families to promote the best interests of their children would tend to offset the mobility induced by institutions such as the schools. This offsetting might occur through socialization, genes, economics, and whatever else produces greater homogeneity of scholastic ability and achievement within a family and, obversely, proportionately greater educational inequality among families.

A more detailed look at the trend in this implicit contradiction between the actions of families and those of the larger community and society produces two conclusions about continuity and change in educational achievement (length of schooling). First, there are fewer differences among the educational achievements of persons born after World War II than among persons born earlier in the century. The trend toward educational equality across successive cohorts born in this century is particularly noticeable in the primary and secondary grades. For example, take three cohorts of men: the first, those born around World War I; the second, born during the early thirties in the depression; the third, born during World War II. The percentages of men completing eight or fewer years of schooling declined from 32% to 15% to 7% across these cohorts. Percentages completing 12 or fewer years fell from 80% to 66% to 59%, while percentages of those who completed college or less changed less markedly—90% to 95% (Featherman and Hauser, 1978, chap. 5). Thus the rising level of compulsory education has fostered a clear trend toward fewer differences (less inequality) in achieved education.

A second conclusion is that intergenerational mobility has increased, as indicated by the diminution of educational inequality both between and within socioeconomic strata and important social cate-

gories. Over the three birth cohorts just described, the racial difference in length of schooling lessened from just under two years to virtually no difference among men from statistically similar family backgrounds. Likewise the net impact of rearing on a farm or in a blue-
collar family has declined as well. For the World War I cohort a combination of paternal education and occupation, number of siblings,
farm rearing, intact or broken family, and race variables accounts for
about one-third of the variance in its schooling; for the younger,
World War II cohort, about one-quarter of the variance is explained
by these six aspects of social background (Featherman and Hauser,
1978, chap. 5). Therefore, the educational benefits of a middle-class
background are apparently less today than in prior decades, and high
school graduates are increasingly commonplace within the households
of every stratum and ethnic category (Hauser and Featherman, 1976;
Featherman and Hauser, 1978, chaps. 6, 8). However, the looser connection between one's social origins and educational achievements
seems confined to those who quit their schooling with the high school
diploma. Access to and matriculation through college are no more
equally available to recent cohorts of different backgrounds than to
their parents (Featherman and Hauser, 1978, chap. 5).

Even as the consequences of social background are increasingly
attenuated, at least with regard to precollege educations, a variety of
other influences on schooling act in concert with background but also
somewhat independently from it (Duncan, Featherman, and Duncan,
1972; Jencks et al., 1972). Much of the research on such factors has
been conducted among American high school students who have been
followed into early or middle adulthood. The most systematic of these
studies involves a panel of Wisconsin high school seniors studied by
William Sewell and colleagues since 1957 (see Sewell and Hauser,
1975, and Clarridge, Sheehy, and Hauser, 1977, for a project overview). The "Wisconsin model" for the processes by which educational, occupational, and economic statuses of adults are attained
(Sewell and Hauser, 1972, 1975) has been cross-validated in other
samples within the United States and in several other countries (Alexander, Eckland, and Griffin, 1975; Wilson and Portes, 1975; Hout
and Morgan, 1975; Alexander and Eckland, 1974; Kerckhoff, 1974;
Alwin, Otto, and Call, 1976; Yuchtman and Samuel, 1975; Gilbert,
1973; Garnier and Hout, 1974) with a high order of consistency when
replicate or similar variables are employed. Aside from expressing
length of schooling as a function of social background, the Wisconsin
model includes measures of mental ability and scholastic grades and
several kinds of social psychological factors hypothesized to mediate
the influences of background, scholastic ability, and performance.

These social psychological measures include the perceived encouragements of parents and teachers to undertake postsecondary education, peer plans to enroll in college, and both educational and occupational aspirations. The Wisconsin social psychological model explains nearly 55% of the variation in schooling completed beyond grade 12, adding about 40 percentage points to the explanation of such achievement by the aspects of social background when taken by themselves (Sewell and Hauser, 1972).[14]

Among individuals from nominally the same social backgrounds, intelligence and grades in high school account for 13% of postsecondary educational achievement. These two aspects of academic ability mediate a large fraction of effects of social background—between 23% and 40%, depending on the indicator of background (Sewell and Hauser, 1972). Yet neither the association of education and grades nor the association of education and intelligence arises because of their mutual dependence (in the Wisconsin model) on background,[15] illustrating the degree to which ultimate educational achievement rests on merit rather than privilege.

The social psychological variables in the Wisconsin model (peer plans, parent-teacher encouragements, and aspirations) also reflect background differences among high school seniors, mediating 60% of the effect of mother's education on son's postsecondary schooling, 70% of the effect of father's education, 55% of father's occupational status, and all the effect of family income. But among students from the same social stratum and ability group, these social psychological influences explain about 28% of the variation in length of schooling. That percentage emphasizes the educational importance of social influence processes during the high school years. It implies that of the entire 54% of the variance in schooling explained by the Wisconsin model, about half reflects the net effects of educational influence by teachers and parents, college plans of peers, and student's own goals and ambitions. Further, it suggests that what transpires between adolescents and their significant others within schools and homes during the secondary school years has broad implications for further scholastic achievement, in contrast to the much more modest consequences of the institutional characteristics of the high schools themselves (Hauser, Sewell, and Alwin, 1976).

Given that parents, peers, and teachers represent important sources of educational inequality and of levels of scholastic achievement in the postsecondary school years, it is useful to consider the bases on which their influence rests. Parents and student peers apparently are much more likely than teachers to take a student's social origins into account in expressing encouragement. Teachers, by contrast, are more likely to reflect primarily on a student's grades and academic ability. (Although teachers' grades seem responsive not only to ability but also to behavior, evaluations of behavioral conformity are not highly related to the student's social background; see Williams, 1976b). Thus teachers (at least in Wisconsin) respond in a more meritocratic fashion than parents and peers. However, teachers' influences have less bearing on the amount of postsecondary education completed than encouragement from parents and peers (Sewell and Hauser, 1972).

Toward Equality of Scholastic Achievement?

Across the three indicators of scholastic achievement there appears a considerable measure of variability of an individual's accomplishments. It seems fair to conclude (from incomplete data) that developmental patterns for intelligence and academic aptitudes follow a similar course, yielding more or less crystallized relative mental abilities and academic achievements among students by early adolescence, but actual performance in the classroom, as indexed by teacher grades, for example, is only modestly related to either intelligence or aptitudes. Further, successful matriculation into and through postsecondary education, while obviously connected to intellectual capacities and grades, is also influenced by noncognitive components of personality as well as the character of the interpersonal network inside and outside the school. Thus high intelligence begets good grades and both assist one in acquiring above-average education, but since the correlations among the three scholastic domains are substantially less than their theoretical maxima, it is obvious that some persons fail to achieve their educational potentials while others ultimately obtain degrees and certification in spite of more modest accomplishments in school or average mental ability.

One of the major bases of unequal scholastic achievement is socioeconomic background. The tested mental abilities, scholastic aptitudes, and grades of children from various social strata differ, but only a small fraction of the variation in these aspects of achievement reflects social class per se. While tests and teachers tend to respond to students mainly in terms of their abilities and the quality of their school work, parents and peers are more likely to introduce class and family resources into the decisions that students make about their schooling and careers.[16] Yet despite considerable meritocratic variance and apparently random (residual or unexplained) variation in length of schooling, perhaps as much as 50% of educational differences reflect family background (based on the comparison of male siblings' schooling; Hauser and Featherman, 1976). Even among high school graduates, social background continues to influence the amount of schooling that is completed (although the gross impact of background is less among such persons than for all persons of the same age whether or not they completed high school; see Featherman and Hauser, 1978, chap. 5). While most of the educational impact of social origins seems to be indirect—through such intermediate factors as scholastic ability, parent and peer influences—parental education and income continue to have a small direct bearing on the postsecondary achievements of young men and women (Sewell, Hauser, and Wolf, 1977). In gross terms, if families in all social strata were as able to send their children for additional schooling as was the highest-status quartile of Wisconsin families (circa 1960)—and allowing for differential mental ability—one might expect the number of persons matriculating in colleges and universities to have increased by over one-third and the number of college graduates to have risen by roughly 40% (Sewell, 1971). Thus while the institutional structure of American society provides for considerable educational mobility between generations—achievement without regard to socioeconomic background—the aggregate supply of persons whose scholastic achievements are misaligned with their potentials is numerically large. The apparent persistence of the social class effect on postsecondary education (albeit small as a proportion of total educational variance) even among more recent birth cohorts (Featherman and Hauser, 1978, chap. 5) gives little reason to suppose that this circumstance has changed markedly.[17]

Two other elements of social background that affect changes in scholastic achievement between generations as well as constancy of achievement throughout the course of schooling are race and gender. Girls in the United States typically earn higher grades than boys, but despite this achievement they have less usually been oriented toward college preparatory programs in high school (Hauser, Sewell, and Alwin, 1976; Williams, 1976b; Alexander and Eckland, 1974).[18] In the population at large women have generally completed as much or more schooling as males in the same birth cohort (Featherman and Hauser, 1976; Treiman and Terrell, 1975b), reflecting the greater likelihood that young men discontinue their schooling at the secondary school level. Among high school students, however, young women have been less likely to enroll in and complete postsecondary degree programs (Sewell and Shah, 1967; Sewell, 1971; Sewell, Hauser, and Wolf, 1977; Alexander and Eckland, 1974). Underlying these findings are historical patterns of sex role socialization that customarily orient men toward occupational careers and toward schooling as occupational preparation. Young men were often constrained to drop out of school and go to work or they chose to do so; yet if they remained in high school until their senior year, they typically undertook advanced training for white-collar jobs.

In light of declining educational differentials within and among most population subgroups, these historical sex differences in average length of schooling will probably disappear. If they do, women may actually complete more schooling than men, particularly if present reconsiderations of sex role socialization and stereotyping lead to more nearly equal educational opportunities. For example, the educational aspirations and attainments of young women have been more narrowly restricted by the socioeconomic and geographic circumstances of their backgrounds than have men's (Sewell and Shah, 1967). Also women's length of schooling has been less responsive to differences in their academic ability than to social background, even among college students (Alexander and Eckland, 1974); the reverse has occurred among males (Carter, 1972). Thus efforts to equalize educational opportunities and to remove gender stereotypes could raise the average educational achievement of women above the male mean, mainly in response to career-linked educational initiatives and to an enhancement of the benefits to young women's (relatively higher) academic abilities.

Ethnic heritage and race in particular are social attributes with significant educational consequences. Variation in average length of schooling among European ethnic groups, however, manifests mainly the levels of family resources (both economic and cultural) that create differential educational advantages for their offspring (Duncan and Duncan, 1968; Duncan and Featherman, 1972; Featherman, 1971). New immigrant groups, especially those from Mexico and Puerto Rico, appear to experience educational discrimination; their lower than average schooling reflects more than the disadvantage of their socioeconomic background (below-average parental education, family income; larger family sizes) per se (Featherman and Hauser, 1978, chap. 8). The same holds for black children, especially those reared in the South (Coleman et al., 1966; Featherman and Hauser, 1978, chaps. 6, 7), although the net educational disadvantage of being black appears to be less consequential than being a foreign-born Mexican or a Puerto Rican. For instance, black men of ages 21-64 who were born in the South and still living there in 1973 completed about 0.8 year less schooling than other men of similar family backgrounds. However, new arrivals to this country from Puerto Rico and Mexico completed almost 2.5 years less than men of similar socioeconomic origins (Featherman and Hauser, 1978, chap. 8).

The lesser net disadvantage for blacks than for other minorities represents recent improvements in the educational opportunities for that racial minority, especially in the South. In the early sixties the gap in schooling associated with race per se was as large as two years (Featherman and Hauser, 1978, chap. 8). Educational achievement (although perhaps not the quality of education within each grade) in the North now appears to be almost equal among blacks and whites from the same socioeconomic strata, and at least in that region black families are able to apply their socioeconomic resources toward the schooling of their children with nearly the same efficiency as white families (Hogan and Featherman, 1977; Featherman and Hauser, 1978, chap. 7). Whether the trend toward equal educational achievement implies that black and white children are being treated more similarly within the schools is unknown. Research has suggested that in the not too remote past black achievement in high school rested more heavily on behavioral conformity, ambition, and grades than did white achievement (Kerckhoff and Campbell, 1977; Porter, 1974). Whites have tended to profit from the educational resources of their families in ways that blacks have not (Portes and Wilson, 1976; Duncan, 1967).

It is beyond dispute that scholastic achievements are unequal among American children and young adults. Still one can conclude from the essential consistency across empirical investigations that such inequality of achievement exists more because social institutions are organized to recognize and reward merit than because of class interests or racial privilege. In that respect American society may not be unique (Hope, 1977). Trends across a series of indicators of scholastic achievement cannot be ascertained from current research, but a shift toward more equal educational achievement through length of school is clear from the experiences of recent adolescents. Therefore educational mobility between generations continues to provide new "talent" for the society.

Achievement in the World of Work

Linkages between formal schooling and occupations are forged in all industrial societies. Expansion and diversification of occupational pursuits have followed from technological innovation and in turn have created a demand for a more highly skilled, knowledgeable, and trainable labor force. Accompanying these shifts is a pattern of economic rationality, most visible in the microeconomics of supply and demand and of cost analysis within firms. Industrial fabrication, mainly in growing urban places, and geographic mobility of labor have become more common; and in the context of these economic and demographic changes the organizing principles of the social stratification order are altered (Treiman, 1970).

Qualifications of persons for work and economic pursuits were nurtured within the family in preindustrial society, especially those with extensive cottage industries. Economic status and occupations were often passed from generation to generation. With the relocation of industry into factories and urban places in the United States, families could no longer proffer sufficient training for the new jobs. They did not provide on-the-job experiences, as they once had for deployment in farming or cottage industry, nor were they likely to prepare offspring for the unconventional and problematic features of the emerging urban, industrial economy. Family background gradually became a less useful basis for screening potential employees, especially since this information was often not available for rural-to-urban migrants (compare Hareven, 1975). As the schooling of the population increased, especially after children participated less actively in the economy, educational certification became a major screening device for employment and occupational placement. Together with the fact that most children did not inherit the farms and businesses of their families, these restructurings of the economy and the shift of "human capital" development from the home to the school changed the basis of the social stratification system from ascription to achievement. That is, allocation of persons to positions in the socioeconomic system, namely on the basis of their access to occupations, occurred primarily through their schooling rather than through their social backgrounds; not surprisingly, education came to be defined as a common good.

Since World War II, the economies of most Western nations have shifted from the production of goods to the provision of services (Fuchs, 1968). In this crescive postindustrial society (Bell, 1973) employment in the industries supplying social services—education, government, medicine—has grown rapidly, and the labor force's white-collar jobs have burgeoned, especially among the professional and technical ranks. The importance of research and development to the evolving economies, and the ascendance of computer-based forecasting and decision making, have created new demands for personnel with advanced technical and scientific, theoretic training.

One is thus not surprised to find positive correlations between scholastic achievements and occupational and economic attainments in the world of work. Among several industrial nations schooling is central to socioeconomic achievements in work careers. In addition, while level of education is more important for socioeconomic achievement over the life cycle than social background or any other personal attribute, the correlations between education and occupational status or earnings in all nations (for which there are data) are far below unity. Thus continuity of worldly success in the transition from school to work (and from job to job) is partially prescribed by the social structure of (post) industrial society, although in reality it is of a modest magnitude.

To illustrate these general conclusions, one can cite correlations from selected national studies, particularly those between education and current occupational status for men in the prime working ages and between current occupation and that of their fathers' occupations during the sons' adolescence. In Great Britain these are 0.62 and 0.36, respectively (Treiman and Terrell, 1975a); in Australia, 0.52 and 0.29 (Featherman, Jones, and Hauser, 1975); in Denmark, 0.72 and 0.35; Finland, 0.76 and 0.38; Norway, 0.80 and 0.39; and Sweden, 0.78 and 0.44 (Pöntinen and Uusitalo, 1975); in Israel, 0.32 and 0.27 (Matras, Kraus, and Noam, 1976); in Poland, 0.47 and 0.11 (Pohoski, 1977; these data are for men and women combined); and in the United States, 0.56 and 0.34 (Featherman, Jones, and Hauser, 1975).

The relative importance of educational achievement for occupational accomplishments in the United States is illustrated in figure 14.2, based on two national samples of men in two decades. Figure 14.2 expresses the variability of the current occupations in terms of socioeconomic status scores;[19] it shows the percentage of this variation that can be assigned to various causes of occupational achievement. By comparing results from the two surveys, one senses both the major role played by education and the changes in the impact of schooling relative to that of other factors such as social background.

Three important changes are under way. First, the persistence of socioeconomic inequality between generations—as indicated by the percentage of occupational status variation that reflects the measures of social and economic background—is small and declining. The pure, or "net," effects of background on sons' achievement declined from 11% to 7% between 1962 and 1973. Second, the impact of education on differential occupational achievements remained about the same, but the mobility-facilitating role of schooling strengthened while its role as a vehicle of status persistence weakened. The latter role arises because socioeconomic background lends a differential advantage for educational achievement, with persons from higher-status families completing more. Insofar as education is an important precondition of occupational success and socioeconomic level, then the schools help perpetuate socioeconomic inequality from generation to generation. The significance of that function of education is indexed by what is called the "overlapping influence of social background and education" in figure 14.2, which implies that such a mechanism of status persistence through the schools accounted for about 14% of occupational achievement in 1962 and 1973. But a large and increasing frac-

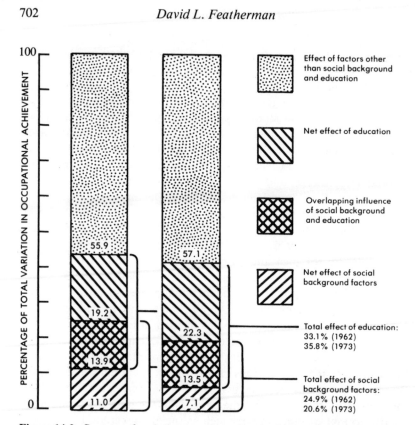

Figure 14.2. *Sources of variation in occupational achievement, men in the experienced civilian labor force aged 25-64 in March 1962 and 1973. Occupations scored in units of socioeconomic status, reflecting income and education of average incumbents (Duncan, 1961). Social background includes family head's occupational status and education, number of siblings, farm origin, broken family, and race. (From March 1962 and 1973 Current Population Surveys and Occupational Changes in a Generation Surveys [Blau and Duncan, 1967; Featherman and Hauser, 1975].)*

tion of educational differences among persons does not stem from variability in socioeconomic background. This major portion of educational variability also influences occupational achievements and might be regarded as the mobility-inducing role of schooling, since it does not reflect a person's background. In figure 14.2 that role is called the "net effect of education." The mobility-inducing effect of schooling is larger than its other role in transmitting inequalities between generations, and to the extent that shifts are apparent in figure 14.2, the mobility-inducing role is increasing relative to the other. To that extent there is little evidence that the capacity of education to provide resources for social mobility is dwindling.

The third shift in figure 14.2—in the postulated causes of occupational achievement—involves the increased importance of factors other than social background and schooling. Since these factors are not formally represented, it would be improper to infer their identity. The collection of such residual causes is largely unassociated with the specific features of family background and education shown in figure 14.2. Given the slight increase in the importance of unspecified, residual factors in accounting for differences in men's occupational statuses, one might conclude that socioeconomic achievement is no more rigidly determined by the home and the school than in the recent past. Occupational achievements today may be more independent of family resources and schools than in the past.

Can Occupational Achievement Be Inherited?

Generational similarities in intelligence prompt an interest in the role of genetic inheritance in achievements such as schooling and socioeconomic status. There is little reason to suppose that intergenerational continuity of careers and status is the consequence of genetic inheritance (Jencks et al., 1972), yet parent-filial correlations of occupational status are not trivial. It is important to assess the degree to which this positive association (r about 0.4) is due to the literal inheritance of jobs—the undertaking of farms, businesses, professional practices of parents—or to the pursuit of careers and occupations whose socioeconomic standing is similar to that of the parents.

Table 14.1 suggests that both processes of social inheritance occur in the United States, at least among men, although direct inheritance of specific jobs is less prevalent than generational continuity of employment in broad occupational groups. Table 14.1 shows the mobility of men from the occupations of their fathers (or other family heads) when the sons were about 16 years old to the occupations they held as adults in March 1962 or March 1973. The five broad categories of occupation in the table can be ranked from high to low, in the order given, according to the average incomes and educational levels of their incumbents. Two findings are obvious from the table. First, occupational positions tend to persist across generations in the United States, but there is also a great deal of occupational mobility. There has been a general movement out of farming, and elsewhere there is considerable movement up and down the social scale. About two-thirds of the sons of white-collar workers gain white-collar jobs, but so do 30%-40% of the sons of manual workers. At the same time 30% or more of the sons of white-collar workers take up manual or farm occupations. As one can see by comparing the occupational distributions of sons and their fathers in either 1962 or 1973, there is more upward than

Table 14.1. Mobility from father's (or other family head's) occupation to current occupation: U.S. men in the experienced civilian labor force aged 20 to 64 in 1962 and 1973.[a]

Father's occupation	Son's current occupation						Father's percent- age
	Upper white collar	Lower white collar	Upper manual	Lower manual	Farm	Total	
1962							
Upper white collar	53.8%	17.6%	12.5%	14.8%	1.3%	100.0%	16.5%
Lower white collar	45.6	20.0	14.4	18.3	1.7	100.0	7.6
Upper manual	28.1	13.4	27.8	29.5	1.2	100.0	19.0
Lower manual	20.3	12.3	21.6	43.8	2.0	100.0	27.5
Farm	15.6	7.0	19.2	36.1	22.2	100.0	29.4
Total	27.8	12.4	20.0	32.1	7.7	100.0	100.0
1973							
Upper white collar	52.0	16.0	13.8	17.1	1.1	100.0	18.2
Lower white collar	42.3	19.7	15.3	21.9	0.8	100.0	9.0
Upper manual	29.4	13.0	27.4	29.0	1.1	100.0	20.5
Lower manual	22.5	12.0	23.7	40.8	1.0	100.0	29.7
Farm	17.5	7.8	22.7	37.2	14.8	100.0	22.6
Total	29.9	12.7	21.7	31.5	4.1	100.0	100.0

Source: Data are from March 1962 and March 1973 Current Population Surveys and Occupational Changes in a Generation Surveys (Blau and Duncan, 1967; Featherman and Hauser, 1975).

a. Upper white collar: professional and kindred workers and managers, officials, and proprietors, except farm; lower white collar: sales, clerical and kindred workers; upper manual: craftsmen, foremen, and kindred workers; lower manual: operatives and kindred workers, service workers, and laborers, except farm; farm: farmers and farm managers, farm laborers, and foremen.

downward mobility across generations. In 1973, 49% were upwardly mobile and 19% were downwardly mobile, and in 1962 the corresponding figures were 49% and 17%. The second main finding in table 14.1 is that the results of the 1962 and 1973 surveys are much alike. There are essentially no differences between the mobility patterns of U.S. men in 1962 and in 1973. In a sense this similarity is to be expected, for occupational mobility is portrayed here as a lifelong process, and most of the cohorts of men in the labor force in 1962 were still working in 1973.

While mobility patterns have been stable in the total population, there have been marked changes in generational mobility within the black population. Table 14.2 shows the occupational mobility of adult black men in 1962 and in 1973. In 1962 there was little relationship between the occupational position of a black man and that of his father (or other family head). As among whites, there was a massive shift away from farm occupations. In other cases black men born at the bottom of the occupational hierarchy stayed at the bottom, and even those few born into white-collar families entered primarily lower manual occupations. Men in the majority population enjoyed a form of socially inherited advantage—the modest persistence of occupational standing across generations—but the black minority did not. Black sons typically could not enter lines of work similar to those pursued by their parents, unless the family head held a lower manual job

Table 14.2. Mobility from father's (or other family head's) occupation to current occupation: black U.S. men in the experienced civilian labor force aged 20 to 64 in 1962 and in 1973.[a]

Father's occupation	Son's current occupation						Father's percentage
	Upper white collar	Lower white collar	Upper manual	Lower manual	Farm	Total	
1962							
Upper white collar	10.4%	10.3%	19.7%	59.6%	0.0%	100.0%	4.5%
Lower white collar	14.4	13.5	0.0	72.1	0.0	100.0	1.9
Upper manual	8.5	9.7	10.4	67.9	3.6	100.0	9.0
Lower manual	7.6	8.0	10.8	71.4	2.3	100.0	37.2
Farm	3.2	3.3	7.0	66.7	19.8	100.0	47.4
Total	5.9	6.1	9.1	68.3	10.6	100.0	100.0
1973							
Upper white collar	33.2	21.8	10.1	34.8	0.0	100.0	5.0
Lower white collar	23.8	17.2	12.3	45.8	0.9	100.0	3.5
Upper manual	15.2	14.7	15.0	54.9	0.2	100.0	10.2
Lower manual	12.4	11.2	13.9	61.4	1.1	100.0	46.1
Farm	5.6	6.2	16.8	62.9	8.5	100.0	35.1
Total	11.8	10.6	14.8	59.4	3.6	100.0	100.0

a. See table 14.1 for description of occupational groups and source of data.

or was a farmer. A comparison of table 14.1 and 14.2 in 1962 suggests that black men used to be subjected to a perverse form of equality of opportunity in the world of work, a perversity that denied the advantages of birth into a white-collar family and constrained nearly 80% of black sons from higher-status origins to be downwardly mobile. At the base of this perverse form of opportunity was the limitation of the types of occupations open to blacks.

By 1973 the mobility table for black men was more like that of all men than it had been a decade earlier. Mobility to white-collar occupations was more prevalent among the sons of farmers and manual workers, and the tendency for sons of white-collar workers to enter white-collar work was intermediate between that of black men in 1962 and that of all men in 1962 or 1973. These changes in occupational mobility occurred mainly among the young black men who entered the labor force between 1962 and 1973.

These mobility trends can be described in more detail using a measure of status persistence. Each of the several hundred occupations identified by the U.S. Bureau of the Census was assigned a socio-economic status score (ranging from 0 to 96; Duncan, 1961), which is an average of the schooling and income of men in the occupation. Table 14.3 shows the number of units of status of a man's occupation associated with a one-unit change in the social standing of his father's occupation for black and white men at several ages in 1962 and in 1973. Among white men a unit of the status of father's occupation was associated with about 0.4 unit of current occupational status, regardless of age or the year of the survey. This level of status persistence across generations is far from complete, but it is also two-thirds as strong as the association of a man's occupational status with the length of his schooling. Among white men the association between the statuses of fathers and sons may have decreased slightly from 1962 to 1973, except at ages 55-64. The largest decreases occurred at younger ages, so in 1973 there was a direct relationship between age and the persistence of occupational status among white men.

Among blacks there was a marked increase in status persistence at every age. At ages 25-34 in 1973 the degree of status persistence was greater among black than among white men, and in 1973 there was an inverse relationship between age and status persistence among black men, which contrasts with the opposite pattern among white men. Thus it appears that black and white men are converging in the degree to which their social standing is associated with that of their fathers.

Father's occupational status is not the only background factor that affects a man's occupational standing. Table 14.4 shows the effects of several social background variables on the occupational status

Table 14.3. Average increase in the socioeconomic status of a man's occupation associated with a unit increase in the social status of his father's (or other family head's) occupation: U.S. men in the experienced civilian labor force by age and race, 1962 and 1973.[a]

Race and age	1962	1973
Black	0.175	0.383
24-34	0.180	0.429
35-44	0.252	0.326
45-54	0.103	0.303
55-64	0.168	0.244
White and other	0.461	0.410
25-34	0.450	0.373
35-44	0.469	0.419
45-54	0.467	0.434
55-64	0.445	0.458

a. Data are from March 1962 and March 1973 Current Population Surveys and Occupational Changes in a Generation Surveys (Blau and Duncan, 1967; Featherman and Hauser, 1975). Detailed 1960-basis census occupations are scaled in Duncan's (1961) socioeconomic index for occupations.

of white and black men in 1962 and in 1973. These effects are less than the associations in table 14.3 because they have been statistically freed of correlation with the other background variables. In the majority population (white and other) the effects of each social background variable were similar in 1962 and in 1973. A unit of father's occupational status was worth about a quarter of a unit of son's occupational status, and a year of father's schooling was worth 0.87 units of son's occupational status. Each additional sibling in the family of orientation reduced a man's occupational standing by an average of more than a unit, and growing up in a broken family handicapped a man by 2.5 to 3 units of occupational status. Finally, farm background (having a father who farmed) reduced a man's occupational status by 5 or 6 units.

Excepting farm origin, each of the social background variables had a much smaller effect on the occupational standing of black men than of white men in 1962. Neither a highly educated nor a high-status father was much of an advantage to a black man, and growing up in a large family or in a broken family did not handicap a black man as much as it did a white man. By 1973 each of the effects (except that of farm background) had increased substantially among black men, and here as in the mobility tables the data suggest growing similarity be-

Table 14.4. Effects of social background on occupational status: U.S. men aged 25 to 64 in the experienced civilian labor force by race, 1962 and 1973.[a]

Social background variable	1962		1973	
	Black	White and other	Black	White and other
Father's occupational status	0.067	0.286	0.200	0.249
Father's years of schooling	0.563	0.873	1.062	0.866
Number of siblings	−0.221	−1.097	−0.513	−1.266
Farm origin	−4.978	−5.949	−5.009	−4.789
Broken family	−0.576	−3.245	−1.946	−2.472

Source: Data are from March 1962 and March 1973 Current Population Surveys and Occupational Changes in a Generation Surveys (Blau and Duncan, 1967; Featherman and Hauser, 1975).

a. Entries are regression coefficients, controlling all variables listed.

tween the races. It is paradoxical that convergence in processes of achievement between the black and white populations may come about by the development of more inequality of opportunity within the black minority.

The total effect of social background (as indexed by the combined variables in table 14.4) accounts for less than 20% of the variation in current occupational status of majority men and about 14% among the black minority (in 1973). Therefore the tendency for occupational status to persist across generations is but a small part of the total process by which men enter socioeconomic strata.

Occupational Achievements of Women

Despite increasing participation of women in work outside the home (Sweet, 1975), the opportunities for occupational achievement for men and women remain unequal in at least two respects. First, institutionalized customs of child-rearing and household management persist, with the result that a disproportionate number of women from all socioeconomic strata are limited to roles outside the regular labor force (Hauser and Featherman, 1977, chaps. 4, 8). Access to the means of economic independence is unequal for the sexes, at least among married persons and especially so during the childbearing and childrearing phases of the family cycle (Sweet, 1973; Taeuber and

Sweet, 1976). One finds distinctive patterns of occupational attainment for the two genders, even among men and women reared within the same social background (occupational class of the head of the family of orientation; Tyree and Treas, 1974; Chase, 1975; Hauser and Featherman, 1977, chaps. 4, 8). Aside from the greater probability that a woman is less likely than her brother to be in the economically productive labor force, she is also less likely to hold an occupation that is functionally similar to her family head's occupation. That is, women in the labor force are less able than men to "inherit" the occupations of their fathers.[20] Obversely, women are more likely than men to be occupationally mobile (Chase, 1975), rendering their life courses less consistent with regard to socioeconomic status.

But when gauged by the relationship between a woman's father's (family head's) occupational status and her spouse's occupation, a woman's intergenerational opportunities for socioeconomic continuity (or change) are less differentiable from the opportunities of men (Tyree and Treas, 1974; Chase, 1975). Thus women's social mobility through marriage is more similar to men's mobility through occupational careers than is women's mobility through employment and occupations. Vicarious achievement (through spouse) remains a major mechanism for intergenerational continuity or change in status for women, supplementing or complementing the opportunities for achievement through independent economic pursuits outside marriage and the home economy.

One of the explanations for the unequal patterns of intergenerational continuity in status for the genders lies in the second major difference in overall occupational achievement. Women are less likely to find employment at the top of the socioeconomic hierarchy and less likely to be working in the menial jobs at its lower levels. Sexual segregation is an obdurate aspect of the American occupational structure (Wolf and Rosenfeld, 1978; Williams, 1977), but differences in the typical occupations of men and women do not fully account for the unequal pattern of intergenerational status persistence and mobility. Even if sexual segregation of occupations were to disappear, working women would still tend to be more mobile than men, who more typically gain employment in jobs whose status is similar to that of their parental family heads. The racial differentials in intergenerational status persistence and mobility are mainly a consequence of occupational segregation, whereas the sexual differentials are not (Hauser and Featherman, 1977, chap. 8). This suggests that occupational achievements of men and women, particularly married women, are subject to different sets of conditions and contingencies, despite apparent equality in the average socioeconomic levels of jobs held by both sexes (Featherman and Hauser, 1976; Treiman and Terrell, 1975b; McClendon, 1976). These factors may include sex role socialization, pauses in labor force participation related to marriage and family formation, and the impacts of spouse's career decisions, for example.

Aside from the social forces that shape distinctive courses of intergenerational mobility for men and women, there appear to be substantially different consequences of school achievement and early career occupations for later socioeconomic achievements (Sewell, Hauser, and Wolf, 1977). For instance, the net effect of years of school completed tends to be greater for women than for men of similar social origins; for persons of similar backgrounds and levels of schooling, the status of women's first jobs (after leaving school) is more consistently related to their occupational achievements at mid life than is men's. These tendencies are stronger among women with more frequent interruptions in their work histories (Wolf, 1975; Rosenfeld, 1976). Thus women encounter less socioeconomic change within their work careers. Women apparently must rely more heavily on formal credentials for access to jobs, while more continuous employment histories enable men to supplement their formal education with job-related experiences and training. The more frequent interruptions in women's working lives probably tend to limit employers' investments in the training of female employees and to encourage women to reenter occupations similar to those they formerly held (those that permit irregular work attachments without substantial loss in skill level or earning capacity; Mincer and Polachek, 1974). Given the more frequent reapplication for jobs, it is probable that educational credentials retain their importance across the working lives of women; men use credentials for initial career entry and then experience becomes more prominent (Sewell, Hauser, and Wolf, 1977).

The distinction between the adult life cycles of men and women appears to be the major basis for the lesser variation in female occupational achievements. Among men and women of equivalent social backgrounds, equivalent schooling, and equivalent first jobs, the net variations in the socioeconomic status of later occupations are nearly identical for male and female workers (Sewell, Hauser, and Wolf, 1977). By implication, the occupational achievements of women are contingent on their enactment of the simultaneous roles of spouse, parent, and worker in ways which men's achievements are not. Married women have fewer options in occupational careers than unmarried women and most men, and women's overall socioeconomic achievement may depend not only on their own scholastic and work achievements but also on the attitudes and achievements of their spouses.

Does Schooling Still Matter for Occupational Success?

Both the basis and significance of the connection between scholastic achievements and success in the world of work have been subjects of popular and scholarly inquiry for some time. Recent commentary has criticized society for relying too heavily on educational credentials for allocating persons into positions in the economy (Berg, 1970; Bowles and Gintis, 1976). At the same time, some have suggested that the economic value of schooling, particularly postsecondary education, has declined since the early seventies (Bird, 1975; Freeman, 1976), as shown by the relatively higher unemployment and underemployment for college graduates. These allegations are worthy of closer examination, but so too are the suggestions from empirical research that performance on the job is not closely connected to success in school or to academic aptitude (Thorndike and Hagen, 1959; Jencks et al., 1972).

The effect of schooling on occupational achievement (measured in arbitrary units of a "socioeconomic scale" of the standing of detailed occupations) has risen relative to the effect of social background (figure 14.2). Comparison of the occupational benefits of each unit increment in schooling for men in the labor force in 1973 and in 1962 leads to the conclusion that the absolute effect of schooling on socioeconomic achievement is large and increasing. Table 14.5 shows the influence of a year of schooling on occupational status among black and white (nonblack) men by age in 1962 and in 1973; in these results the association between schooling and occupation has been freed of the correlation that arises from their respective correlations with social background. Among white men, the occupational value of each additional year of schooling rose from 3.6 units in 1962 to 4.3 units (on the occupational status scale) in 1973. The occupational returns to schooling have historically been much lower for black men than for whites, but recently they have increased rapidly for blacks. A year of school was worth almost three times as much in occupational status to a white worker as to a black one in 1962, but its value was only about one and one-half times as much in 1973.

The gains in absolute effects of schooling on access to the more desirable jobs are evident at all ages in table 14.5, but especially among black men. Absolute increases over the decade were greater among black workers than among whites below age 55, giving rise to a sharp cross-sectional age gradient in occupational effects of schooling among blacks. Further, the effect of schooling on the status of a man's first civilian job (after schooling) was larger in each successive birth cohort (age category) regardless of race. One striking piece of evidence of recent increases in the occupational returns to schooling

Table 14.5. Average increase in the socioeconomic status of a man's occupation associated with an additional year of schooling: U.S. men in the experienced civilian labor force by age and race, 1962 and 1973.[a]

	1962 survey	*1973 survey*	
Race and age	*Current occupation*	*Current occupation*	*First occupation*
Black	1.272	2.666	2.248
25-34	1.830	3.827	3.046
35-44	1.153	3.487	3.008
45-54	1.271	2.406	1.862
55-64	1.418	1.506	1.600
White and other	3.597	4.258	4.517
25-34	4.435	4.897	5.257
35-44	3.978	4.430	4.816
45-54	3.494	4.183	4.445
55-64	2.998	3.601	3.445

Source: Data are from March 1962 and March 1973 Current Population Surveys and Occupational Changes in a Generation Surveys (Blau and Duncan, 1967; Featherman and Hauser, 1975).

a. Occupations are scaled in Duncan's (1961) socioeconomic index for occupations. Entries are coefficients in regression equations controlling father's occupational status and years of schooling, farm origin, intact family, and number of siblings.

among black workers is in the comparison of first and current occupations for men in the labor force in 1973. Among all but the oldest white men, the effect of schooling on the status of first job was larger than its effect on the status of the current occupation; in the same three cohorts of black men, the effect of schooling was greater at the later than at the earlier point in the life cycle.

A closer examination of the relation of scholastic achievement to occupational careers forces some reservations about these conclusions. The exception concerns white men in their late twenties and a comparison of the relative socioeconomic benefits of college and pre-college education. The occupational achievements and earnings of young white college graduates have become less distinguishable from those of white high school graduates. A parallel shrinkage in the socioeconomic premium for a college education since the early sixties is not apparent among black workers (Freeman, 1976; Featherman and Hauser, 1978, chap. 6). This racial difference in the occupational value of a college education has helped the black minority catch up with the occupational levels of whites at these ages.

Why the apparent erosion in the socioeconomic premium for college education only among young white workers? Some economists argue that the national budget for research and development declined in the early seventies, leading to cutbacks in aerospace, petrochemical, and other industries that typically employed college-trained workers. Coincident with this reduction, the substantially smaller birth cohorts of the post-baby boom period—then in the schools—lowered the demand for college-trained teachers. These shifts on the demand side of the economic equation were linked to effects on the supply side: the pool of college-trained workers was very large in the early seventies owing to the large proportions of high school graduates entering postsecondary education in the late 1960s (an all-time high, about 55% of a graduating class) and to the absolute size of the age groups, the adults who were the baby boom.[21] Because of shifts in both supply and demand, unemployment of the college-educated rose, underemployment was more prevalent, and the occupational and economic returns to college education fell in relation to those to precollege education. Since these shifts took place recently, their prevalence should have been most noticeable among the young workers who were just seeking first full-time jobs in the early seventies—persons in their mid to late twenties.

It remains to be seen whether the apparent downturn in the market for the college-trained has in fact occurred and, if so, what impact it will have on economic inequality and social mobility in the 1980s. Other events in the early seventies cloud the interpretation of the data from which the conclusions about the benefits of higher education have been drawn. The withdrawal of U.S. troops from Vietnam and the dismantling of the draft distinguish the experiences of young men who were in their twenties in the mid sixties from those who were the same age nearly a decade later. As a result, the compositions of the civilian labor forces of 20-year-olds were not equivalent in the periods during which change in the returns to education was apparently occurring.

A related and perhaps more significant event concerns the duration of the complete transition from youth (student) to adult (worker). In the early 1960s about 86% of the young men then in their early and mid twenties were in the labor force (at work or actively looking for a job) and 11% were enrolled in school. Of those who were working, 13% were also enrolled in postsecondary education. In the early seventies, with the Vietnam involvement winding down and the draft a less impending eventuality in the plans of young men, fewer were in the labor force (81%), more were enrolled in school (15%), and a greater fraction of those at work were also enrolled in school (18%). By implication, the Vietnam war and the draft probably speeded up the transition from school to work; World War II apparently had a similar effect (Winsborough, 1979; Hogan, 1978). Near the end of Vietnam involvement young men resumed a more protracted transition through schooling and into the labor force. Perhaps the rapidly rising costs of higher education influenced them to mix part-time education with employment. Perhaps the higher rates of unemployment in this period made school enrollment or reenrollment an attractive alternative—as a way to wait for the job market to brighten and as a means to improve one's current marketability through upgraded skills and specialization.

The upshot of these speculations about shifts in life-stage transitions is that larger fractions of men in their 20s during the early 1970s had not yet completed the full process of schooling, compared with men of the same ages in the 1960s. More of the former may have taken jobs that permitted them to complete their schooling while they worked. Thus until a larger proportion of these men complete the full transition into their posteducational careers, the calculations of economic and occupational returns to their schooling may be premature. (For another interpretation of this change as a temporary phenomenon, see Welch, 1979.)

Predicting Occupational Success

Given that additional formal education fosters access to occupations within successively higher socioeconomic strata, it is not surprising to observe correlations between measures of scholastic performance (grades) and ability (IQ and aptitude test scores) and occupational success. The important research question is whether achievements in the world of work vary for persons who have differing mental and academic abilities but the same level of education. That is, do educational aptitudes and abilities in adolescence affect the achievements of adults whose access to occupations through educational credentials was nominally the same? Alternatively, do the correlations arise solely through the access to jobs afforded by different lengths of schooling?

Jencks and his colleagues (1972, chap. 6) review a wide body of research on this question and conclude that the direct effects of grades, intelligence, and aptitude on occupational success are virtually zero among persons of equivalent schooling: "In general, if we compare two men whose [IQ] test scores differ by 15 points, their occupational statuses will typically differ by about 12.5 points. If they have the same amount of education and the same family background, their statuses will differ by only 2.5 points" (p. 186).

It is important to qualify these generalizations by differentiating between statistical and substantive effects. Recent studies that have followed birth or school cohorts into maturity report statistically significant net effects of grades and IQ on occupational status (Fägerlind, 1975; Sewell, Hauser, and Wolf, 1977). For instance, the Pearsonian correlations between adolescent IQ (measured at grade 11) and occupational status (in units of Duncan's socioeconomic index) at about age 35 are roughly 0.40 for men and 0.30 for women; those between high school grade point average (converted into rank) and occupational status are virtually the same (Sewell, Hauser, and Wolf, 1977, table 1). When the effects of social background on occupation are statistically controlled, the standardized net regression coefficients for the effects of grades and for mental ability are statistically significant for both sexes. Controlling for levels of schooling and first job as well as for measures of aspiration and the achievement influences of parents, peers, and teachers still leaves a statistically significant effect for grades and intelligence (although for men the net effect of grades is not statistically significant). Yet, substantively, the net social impact of mental ability and grades on mid-career occupations is small. For instance, two women who are reared in the same social backgrounds but were a full standard deviation different on mental ability and on high school grade point average would hold occupations roughly 7 points apart on the Duncan (1961) socioeconomic scale—one-third of a standard deviation of occupational status at age 35. But controlling for education, first job, social influences, and aspirations leaves a net occupational difference of just over 2 points, despite the statistical significance of these net differences. Thus the social impact of scholastic performance and ability is essentially indirect, through the completion of formal education and certification.[22]

Occupational Careers and Earnings

Few persons remain in the same occupation throughout their economically productive years. Even among those who do, many have changed employers or industry (construction, manufacturing, public administration, agriculture). If one tallies the incidence of job changes by the ages at which they occur, counting any change in duties or occupational title, employer, or industrial setting, one observes a decreasing tendency to change at older ages. That is, the correlation between age and mean duration of employment at a given job through the middle years of the working life is about 0.43 (Sørensen, 1975b).

This suggests that the early work histories of most persons are marked by job shifts but also that job-related investments, family responsibilities, and material and social ties to communities probably combine to limit employment changes in subsequent years. Not all lines of work are equally likely to show this age pattern of job shifts (Reynolds, 1951). For example, Spilerman (1977) reports that mail carriers, truck drivers, and construction carpenters show different tendencies to remain in the same jobs as a function of age. Truck drivers display the typical pattern of fewer changes at successively older ages, whereas carpenters tend to remain rather stable during the years of greatest physical endurance and strength and then to find other work in the preretirement years.

If there is a positive correlation between mean duration of jobs and age, there is also an inverted-U-shaped relation between age and socioeconomic achievement (Reynolds, 1951; Palmer, 1954; Sørensen, 1975b; Becker, 1964). Mean socioeconomic status of occupations plateaus and average annual earnings peak around age 40-45 for men. Again, different educational and industrial categories have somewhat distinctive patterns of age-occupational and age-income profiles (Becker, 1964; Stolzenberg, 1975; Spilerman, 1977).[23] Still, these two age-related patterns—the incidence of job shifts and the mean socioeconomic achievements of workers—show that a change in jobs is typically an improvement in absolute status. Obversely, they suggest that most job shifts are voluntary (Sørensen, 1975a, table 1) and that in market economies persons do not ordinarily change jobs voluntarily when socioeconomic improvements are not entailed.

There are contrasting explanations for the facts that most men enjoy few improvements (and some deterioration) in socioeconomic standing in their 50s and 60s and that job shifts become the exception rather than the rule. These explanations are more complementary than contradictory (Sørensen, 1975a, 1977). Human capital theories in economics (Becker, 1964) formalize achievement in terms of individuals' stocks of resources (abilities, knowledge, training, wealth) that can be exchanged in the labor market for jobs and income. Individuals invest in their own education, just as employers invest in the training of their workers, to enhance productivity and, thereby, socioeconomic benefits. Thus differences in socioeconomic status across the individual's working life follow from changes in human capital, through investment in and deterioration of aptitudes, knowledge, and physical abilities. Human capital theory also suggests that economic inequality within a society reflects inequalities in the supply of human capital; thus differential achievements across the work histories of individuals should ensue from equalizing education and overcoming the benefits and handicaps of social backgrounds. Within this conceptualization, the inverted-U-shaped pattern of achievement by age arises from a reduction in the marginal utility of investment (in additional training) after mid life, since the time horizon over which the costs of such investment could be amortized (by productivity and income) is decreasing. In addition, physical and mental skills deteriorate, on average reducing productivity and the efficiency of new learning (see Mincer, 1974, for the impacts on earnings). Employers open fewer jobs to older workers, and since fewer investments in the stock of capital are being made, job stability and socioeconomic stationarity are more common than among younger workers.

Rather than emphasizing the consequences of change in workers' characteristics, other analysts interpret the concave pattern of socioeconomic achievement over the life course as due to the effects of job changes within the economic structure of the labor market. Aage Sørensen (1974, 1975a, 1975b), for example, fits the concave empirical distribution with a model that assumes that workers' characteristics remain constant as they age. What changes is the economic value of each level of a given resource as persons move into different jobs. It is the jobs themselves that offer different rates of pay for a high school or college diploma, for example. (Jobs are differentiated by specific firms, industries, and occupations. Thus the pay for teaching varies by one's employer, by academic field, by occupational level, and by employment in a public versus a private educational industry.) Persons move (voluntarily) into better jobs (where rates of return on past investments are more favorable) more frequently at younger than at older ages because the supply of better jobs than the one currently held is smaller for mature workers. Sørensen finds that voluntary job changers experience more favorable returns on investments than do involuntary job changers at each age, although voluntary changes are more prevalent (at least through age 40, the upper bound of his sample). It appears that the consequence of job changing and its relative frequency by age induces the concave lifetime earnings trajectories; the earnings curves of stationary workers are substantially more horizontal than the curves of job changers (Spilerman, 1977, p. 568).

Others also stress the predominance of the labor market in shaping occupational careers and lifetime income flows. Some (Thurow and Lucas, 1972; Thurow, 1975; Sørensen, 1977) suggest that stocks of human capital may sort workers into queues (by preferability as an employee) for specific jobs but that not all jobs are open to all workers with equivalent credentials and experiences. The issue is not discrimination or preferability as such; rather it is the organization of the national economy into segments or subeconomies (Thurow, 1975; Bluestone, 1970; Braverman, 1974; Hodson, 1977), intrafirm or internal labor markets (Doeringer and Piore, 1971), and occupation-industry career lines (Spilerman, 1977; Stolzenberg, 1975) that channels individuals along achievement trajectories.

These theories collectively take exception to a simplified conceptualization of career achievement as issuing from the utilization of human resources in a free market, where neoclassical economics of supply and demand fashions the socioeconomic life histories of persons and the aggregate level of socioeconomic inequality in the society. They call attention to evidence that the American economy is organized into core, peripheral, and state segments, each having unique patterns of unemployment and underemployment, wage contours, degrees of unionization, and attendant prospects for the careers and lifetime socioeconomic achievements of its workers. In addition, some firms develop internal labor markets for vacant jobs, so that persons external to that market cannot enter the queue of eligibility. All this writing lends complexity to the summarizing of the conditions under which persons develop sustained employment histories and careers in the normative sense (Slocum, 1966) of an orderly sequence of work roles into successively more responsible and rewarding ones (see Spilerman, 1977, for instances of less orderly sequences).

At the risk of oversimplification, it is possible to generalize about the course of work histories, viewed narrowly in terms of the socioeconomic status implied by incumbency in specific occupations (Featherman, 1973; Kelly, 1973; Featherman and Hauser, 1978, chap. 5). These generalizations are illustrated in table 14.6, in which the current occupational statuses of birth cohorts in 1962 and 1973 (two points in their work histories) are related to each other and to first jobs, schooling, and social background.

All birth cohorts appear to share several features of a socioeconomic life cycle. For example, the differential potentials for occupational achievement that are provided by social background are more effective at career beginnings than at any other stage of the working life. Father's occupation and farm background continue to affect the current occupations of sons even beyond their first jobs, but the net regression coefficients for the effects of these background factors decline regularly with each successive occupation and as increasing proportions of the total effects of paternal status and farm rearing are expressed indirectly through intervening occupations. Father's education and rearing in a broken family have no appreciable bearing on occupations except through their association with schooling prior to first job. The number of siblings in the respondent's household affects the first job levels of men but subsequently plays no direct role in occupational achievement. There is one major exception to the declining direct effects of social background on career achievements, and that is the net handicap of being a black worker. In all cohorts the net effect fails to decline from first jobs to later ones. The continuing occupational handicap of race may actually have increased between first and later occupations held in 1962, as the race coefficients for all cohorts born prior to 1932 (and entering the labor market in the early to mid 1950s) increase.

Another feature common to the careers of all seven birth cohorts in table 14.6 is the tendency for socioeconomic achievements in first jobs to reflect the direct consequences of differential schooling more forcefully than later occupations. Coupled with this, the comparative benefit of college (relative to graded schooling) is largest at the beginning of the career. The total causal association between college education and occupational attainment (reduced-form coefficients not displayed here) drops regularly from about 8 points on the Duncan socioeconomic scale (for occupations; Duncan, 1961) per unit of increment in college at career beginnings to roughly 6 points of socioeconomic status (Duncan scale) for current occupations in 1973. While the occupational premium for college declines over the life cycle, the net value of graded schooling (its reduced-form coefficient) increases slightly after the first job and then remains constant at around 2 points on the Duncan scale per year of graded schooling. Consequently, the largest relative value of college arises at the first job.

Both graded schooling and college education become less influential on occupational achievement once the career is under way, as indicated by the declining direct effects of each form of schooling in the equations for 1962 and 1973 current occupations (which estimate these effects with levels of social origin and first job controlled). But the total association between college and socioeconomic achievement at successive points in the career is mediated through intervening occupations to a far greater degree than the association between graded schooling and achievement. For example, in the cohort born in 1917-1921, about 25% of the total effect of graded schooling and 45% of the effect of college are expressed indirectly as influences on current occupational status in 1962; the percentages increase to 54% and 75%, respectively, for occupational status in 1973. As the occupational career progresses, education has an increasing effect on the jobs and occupational statuses of men. College education, more than graded schooling, appears to serve its occupational purpose early, by launching men into their careers; it provides them with access to higher-status first jobs, which become stepping-stones to later achievements. Precollege education, on the other hand, appears to exercise a

Table 14.6. Metric regressions of 1962 and 1973 occupational statuses on socioeconomic background, schooling, and career beginnings, men in the experienced civilian labor force of March 1973 by birth cohort.[a]

Birth cohort (Age in March 1962) (Age in March 1973)	Independent variables					
	Father's occupation	Father's education	No. of siblings	Farm origin	Broken family	Race
1907-1911						
(51-55)	0.130	− 0.075	− 0.307	− 3.536	1.547	− 5.849
	(0.037)	(0.174)	(0.226)	(1.354)	(1.564)	(2.282)
	− 0.019	0.037	− 0.124	− 2.972	0.176	− 2.124
(61-65)	(0.032)	(0.149)	(0.194)	(1.166)	(1.343)	(1.966)
1912-1916						
(46-50)	0.117	0.082	− 0.058	− 2.284	0.460	− 5.108
	(0.028)	(0.141)	(0.178)	(1.121)	(1.260)	(1.873)
(56-60)	0.026	0.199	0.010	− 1.602	1.522	− 3.861
	(0.024)	(0.120)	(0.152)	(0.954)	(1.071)	(1.596)
1917-1921						
(41-45)	0.075	0.198	− 0.358	− 2.140	0.716	− 6.503
	(0.025)	(0.123)	(0.160)	(0.982)	(1.084)	(1.574)
(51-55)	0.035	− 0.041	− 0.126	− 0.898	0.203	− 2.454
	(0.022)	(0.110)	(0.144)	(0.881)	(0.972)	(1.417)
1922-1926						
(36-40)	0.089	0.109	− 0.203	− 0.276	− 0.024	− 6.066
	(0.022)	(0.111)	(0.146)	(0.911)	(0.981)	(1.342)
(46-50)	0.056	− 0.068	− 0.080	0.196	0.706	− 3.852
	(0.020)	(0.104)	(0.136)	(0.851)	(0.917)	(1.260)
1927-1931						
(31-35)	0.061	− 0.023	-- 0.043	− 2.892	− 0.097	− 4.893
	(0.021)	(0.111)	(0.143)	(0.928)	(0.968)	(1.314)
(41-45)	− 0.002	0.222	− 0.155	− 1.405	0.167	− 3.068
	(0.020)	(0.109)	(0.140)	(0.911)	(0.948)	(1.291)
1932-1936						
(26-30)	0.102	− 0.031	− 0.173	− 2.287	− 0.764	− 3.422
	(0.021)	(0.116)	(0.149)	(0.978)	(1.018)	(1.311)
(36-40)	0.011	0.038	− 0.019	− 2.425	0.990	− 3.955
	(0.022)	(0.118)	(0.151)	(0.993)	(1.032)	(1.331)
1937-1941						
(21-25)	0.051	− 0.228	− 0.336	− 2.699	− 0.986	− 3.461
	(0.023)	(0.133)	(0.174)	(1.148)	(1.115)	(1.448)
(31-35)	0.042	0.016	− 0.246	− 0.942	− 0.197	− 4.263
	(0.024)	(0.141)	(0.184)	(1.219)	(1.182)	(1.537)

Source: Featherman and Hauser (1978), table 5.21.

a. Approximate standard errors in parentheses. Net regression coefficients reflect the following metrics: all occupation variables are in units of Duncan's (1961) socioeconomic index, all education variables are single years of completed formal schooling, number of siblings is

	Independent variables						
Graded schooling	*College education*	*First job*	*1962 occupation*	*Constant*	*Error of estimate*	*R²*	
1.581	3.833	0.309		8.91	17.74	.474	
(0.258)	(0.497)	(0.036)					
0.611	2.031	0.104	0.590	6.97	15.23	.622	
(0.226)	(0.440)	(0.032)	(0.028)				
1.846	2.960	0.395		3.24	17.76	.488	
(0.214)	(0.417)	(0.028)					
0.848	1.688	0.101	0.589	2.00	15.10	.637	
(0.186)	(0.360)	(0.025)	(0.022)				
1.422	3.745	0.360		8.70	17.62	.491	
(0.197)	(0.367)	(0.025)					
0.869	1.718	0.077	0.606	4.10	15.80	.608	
(0.179)	(0.338)	(0.024)	(0.021)				
1.683	3.764	0.381		3.84	16.72	.551	
(0.189)	(0.298)	(0.022)					
1.274	1.918	0.094	0.557	1.02	15.62	.626	
(0.180)	(0.289)	(0.022)	(0.020)				
1.652	3.165	0.418		4.03	16.38	.557	
(0.187)	(0.283)	(0.021)					
1.128	2.002	0.129	0.499	3.39	16.04	.598	
(0.186)	(0.285)	(0.022)	(0.021)				
1.356	2.973	0.435		4.00	16.17	.583	
(0.200)	(0.303)	(0.022)					
1.209	2.833	0.142	0.443	4.52	16.39	.602	
(0.205)	(0.315)	(0.024)	(0.023)				
1.405	0.340	0.462		3.08	16.41	.434	
(0.260)	(0.321)	(0.023)					
1.509	3.881	0.241	0.253	3.77	17.40	.534	
(0.278)	(0.341)	(0.028)	(0.026)				

sum of brothers and sisters, broken family is binary indicator of rearing in something other than a mother-father arrangement, race is a binary indicator of black, and farm origin is a binary indicator of rearing in a farmer-headed family.

lesser but continuing influence directly on the career at several points. The effect of graded schooling seems to be to certify and train for basic competence, trainability, or preferability—traits that differentiate experienced workers and enable them to compete for occupations at each stage in the career. College also certifies, but it apparently does so by permitting early career access to higher-status, nonmanual occupations, and thereafter it has a much attenuated direct effect on attainments.

Given this interpretation of the roles of precollege and college education, it is not surprising that the advantage of college is greatest at career beginnings. For example, in the cohort born 1917-1921, its comparative value declined from 7.3 points on the Duncan scale upon entry into first jobs (not shown in table 14.6) to 2.3 points of difference in 1962 occupations (when this cohort was aged 40-44) to 0.8 point in 1973 (when the men were aged 51-55; see table 14.6). Neither is it surprising that these results are less applicable among the younger cohorts, since they are still in the early or middle stages of their work careers (compare data for the cohort born 1932-1936—age 36-40 in 1973—with data for the World War I cohort).

A final common aspect of the socioeconomic life cycle concerns the role of successive occupations in the attainments of men from similar social background and schooling. First, statuses of first jobs continue to influence later achievements, even forty to fifty years after career beginnings (the direct effect of first job is statistically significant for all cohorts in the equations of table 14.6 for current occupation in 1973). The absolute size of these continuing effects is small, amounting to less than 1 point on the Duncan scale (with a range of 100 points), after the occupational consequences of education and social background are controlled statistically. About half of the total effects of first jobs on current occupations in 1973 are expressed through intervening occupations (1962 occupation; reduced-form tabulations not shown). Among more mature workers, the impact of a 6- to 8-unit difference in first job status on level of 1973 occupation is nearly equivalent to a difference of one year of graded schooling. Second, intermediate occupations, such as those held in 1962, have more substantial consequences on careers than first full-time jobs. For most cohorts the structural coefficients in the 1973 equations are about five times larger for the effects of the 1962 occupations than for those of first jobs, and the net consequence is about half a point on the Duncan scale. Both observations lead to the transparent conclusion that socioeconomic careers have some modest continuity, with occupations separated by short intervals being more similar in their socioeconomic character than those separated by longer intervals.

The eleven-year interval between 1962 and 1973 highlights the last generalization about occupational careers, although this aspect of careers emerges from the collective experiences of the birth cohorts in table 14.6—taken as a single synthetic cohort—rather than as a common aspect of each. Since the direct effects of 1962 occupation on occupation in 1973 are larger for successively older cohorts, one can conclude that occupational changes and status dissimilarity are more common in the careers of younger men than in those of mature workers (see Sørensen, 1974; 1975b, for a more systematic analysis of this idea). This conclusion is made more credible by the pattern of R^2 and the errors of estimate by age within each of the birth cohorts in table 14.6. At each successive stage of the life cycle the combination of social background, schooling, and prior occupational attainments accounts for greater fractions of the variance in socioeconomic status, and the degree of variation in status among men with similar career experiences declines with age. For instance, in the cohort born 1922-1926, social background accounts for about 23% of the variance in first jobs and the combination of background and education accounts for about 56% of the variance. In 1962, when these men were aged 35-39, the combination of background, education, and first job accounts for 55% of the variance in the current socioeconomic status—about the same as at career beginnings. But by age 46-50, the extent of status inequality among men of similar career experiences (social background, education, and prior occupational statuses) declines from 16 to 15 points on the Duncan scale, and the amount of variation in current socioeconomic achievement explained by those experiences rises from 55% (in 1962) to 63% (in 1973).

Unfortunately, the surveys from which these data are drawn lack the measurements by which this crystallization of the socioeconomic life cycle might be explicated. There come to mind a variety of intrapersonal and institutional means by which occupational statuses tend to cohere with increasing age and experience in the labor force. Some of these potential explanations—such as tenure rights and accumulation of experience through on-the-job training—are perhaps more properly phrased in terms of job changes (or their lack) than in terms of status shifts over occupations (compare Kelley, 1973, and Featherman, 1973). Explanations that refer to the structure of labor markets and to occupational "families" or "situses" (Doeringer and Piore, 1971; Spilerman, 1977), are not properly represented by the equations estimated in table 14.6. In any event, the greater continuity of achievement in the later stages of occupational careers is a matter of degree. Despite increasing continuity of socioeconomic level achieved over successive stages of a man's occupational history, some one-half to two-thirds of a standard deviation of current occupational status lies within classes of men with similar social backgrounds, education, and prior occupational attainments. Perhaps measurements excluded from this analysis might reduce unexplained variation to a significant degree, but until career models of achievement that include these missing variables are estimated, the "reduced-forms" model embodied in table 14.6 suggests that achievement throughout the occupational career is far from determinate or fixed.

Sociohistorical Perspectives on Achievement in the Life Course

This chapter has focused on constancy and change in worldly success over the life cycle in a rather ahistorical fashion. However, there is nothing immutable or inevitable about the statistical connections between scholastic achievements and economic success through jobs and occupational careers or about the volume and direction of socioeconomic mobility between generations. Persons born in dynamic periods of history or those who experience unusual events such as economic depression or warfare during critical stages and transitions in the life cycle—such as the initial years of career building or the transition from school to work—often evidence distinctive achievement histories (Elder, 1974; Elder and Rockwell, 1977). Such histories are illustrated by intercohort variation in the correlations between schooling and earnings or between parental and filial socioeconomic statuses. More global shifts in economic demand and in technological efficiency strongly condition the opportunities for social mobility through schooling and jobs (Hauser et al., 1975; Pampel, Land, and Felson, 1977). Indeed, wars and the periodicity of prosperity and depression during this century have been mirrored in the sequencing and age scheduling of demographic events like schooling, labor force entry, marriage, and parenting in the socioeconomic life cycles of Americans (Winsborough, 1979; Hogan, 1978; Taeuber and Sweet, 1976; Elder, 1977). Thus the pattern to achievement over the life course, while quite properly viewed as a developmental phenomenon, is heavily conditioned by sociohistorical context and contemporary arrangements in the political economy.

This last point implies two further conclusions. First, generalizations about constancy and change in worldly success drawn from population averages are timebound and misleading. They are timebound in the sense of being limited to the present and past organizations of the economy and other institutions as manifested in the lives of the successive birth cohorts that compose the population at the time of measurement.[24] They are misleading because they are averages of unique cohort experiences (see Ryder, 1965, on the use of cohorts as a basis for studying the record of history and social change). By implication, this chapter should have been written with an eye toward cohort variation as well as to variation by race, class, gender, and the like.

A second conclusion is that achievements in school and in work histories are not under the sole control of the persons who experience them. To the contrary, the observable consequences of individuals' motivations, values, and aspirations on their differential achievements are quite slight in comparison with the effects of institutional, demographic, and historical sources of variation (see Spenner and Featherman, 1978, for a current review of the literature on this point). The influence of factors such as effort and goal orientation appears to be greater during the adolescent years than in adulthood—namely, prior to entry into work careers (Spenner and Featherman, 1978). By implication, achievement orientation or achievement motivation may not be a stable characteristic of the personality (Atkinson and Raynor, 1974; Atkinson, Lens, and O'Malley, 1976; compare Weiner, 1974) nor equally efficacious at all stages of the life cycle.

Finally, available research suggests that achievements over the life course are at most modestly predictable from those at earlier ages and in preceding stages of the life cycle (related event domains). Obviously, more precision in conceptualization and measurement of constancy and change in worldly success could alter this generalization. But present research implies that comparative achievement levels are far from constant over the life course—success does not necessarily beget success and the vicious (intergenerational) cycle of poverty may be broken almost as often as not (see Duncan and Morgan, 1976, for an instance of reliable economic research on this topic), although not necessarily with equal facility by all social groups. Such a condition recommends that more research be conducted on subjective evaluations of achievement over the life course, including an assessment of how objective statuses are perceived and compared with those of others, of self at a prior time, and of one's aspirations. Accommodations and stabilities in such subjective aspects of achievement over the life cycle, although excluded from this chapter, merit attention in their own right.

Notes

This manuscript was prepared with support from the Agricultural Experiment Station, University of Wisconsin-Madison, and the Foundation for Child Development, New York City. Revisions were completed while the writer was a Fellow at the Center for Advanced Study in the Behavioral Sciences, with financial support from the National Institute of Mental Health (32MH14581-03) and the Andrew W. Mellon Foundation. The editoral assistance of Mary Balistreri and Stephanie Haller is acknowledged. William H. Sewell and Paul B. Baltes kindly read and commented on an early draft.

1. "Achievement" herein refers to one's standing on a hierarchically ranked distribution. It assumes the existence of stratified rewards that have at least nominal utility for broad segments but not necessarily all of the American population. It does not by definition imply some psychological attribute, although it could be the behavioral consequence or correlate of such. Rather, the term refers to behavior subject to social evaluation such that performances are ranked into statuses. Thus the focus on persistence and change in worldly achievement attends to the maintenance of relative position (rank) across successive roles as student and worker.

2. It is beyond the purposes of this essay to discuss the conceptual integrity and measurement of intelligence per se. Intelligence has no ahistorical, asocial substance. Its content reflects the times and the nature of the contemporary social structure, just as intelligence refers to something different in a hunting and gathering society than it does in a postindustrial one. Viewed in this manner, no intelligence test can be culture-free except in the most relative sense of being based less directly on concrete knowledge and more on style of cognitive functioning and process. But both content and functioning (knowledge and style) are historically, socially, and culturally specific. If this interpretation is valid, then the public debate about the bias of intelligence tests is somewhat irrelevant, for the implied assumption that there could be fairer tests—on which all population groups have equal chances—is false. That assumption could be tenable only if there were such a thing as innate intelligence, or ahistorical, asocial intelligence, and if the schools were designed to reward a wider range of knowledge and capacities among students than they do now. For still another view of what intelligence tests measure, see John W. Atkinson, Willy Lens, and P. M. O'Malley (1976).

3. Joachim Wohlwill (chapter 9 in this volume) is highly critical of Bloom's use of stability coefficients (essentially test-retest correlations) as a basis for estimating the developmental course of an individual's cognitive capacities such as measured, both qualitatively and quantitatively, by repeated IQ tests. Wohlwill's argument and review of research are compelling on that point, but his frame of reference for "development" is somewhat different from the one adopted in this chapter. Here the relative standing of an individual in his birth cohort or in the general population is the issue. Constancy and change in that relative standing, interpreted as an instance of scholastic achievement, are the developmental issues at hand; tracing the (mean) level of intelligence of individuals or groups or monitoring the variability of intelligence in a population across an age dimension is not the central matter here. If one assents to the conceptual integrity of intelligence as measured by IQ tests, then indexes of association (linear or not) that preserve the ordinal relationships among persons are useful for the developmental purposes at hand, just as these same correlations might be employed to assay the predictability of occupational achievement from scholastic achievement (see Baltes and Schaie, 1973b, p. 374, for a compatible conceptualization of developmental phenomena and change).

4. Behavioral geneticists also have begun to measure qualitative aspects of environment, particularly those that might account for within-family commonalities and between-family differences in intelligence (Morton, 1974; Rao, Morton, and Yee, 1974; see critique by Goldberger, 1977b).

5. Given the loose statistical connection between schoolchildren's IQ scores and their social backgrounds and the less than fully deterministic relationship among these same factors, length of schooling, and later intelligence, there is little scientific basis to the claim that in practice the socially disadvantaged are not well served by the administration of intelligence tests. If the argument were true, then (for example) SES differences in educational achievement should be explained by SES variation in IQ scores and the relationship between IQ and scholastic performance. The evidence for these relationships is not favorable for the thesis of bias through testing. Neither does it support the educational revisionists' view that IQ tests are part of the elitists' design to control the schools in favor of elite children (Bowles and Gintis, 1976; compare Jencks et al., 1972, p. 81). The fundamental issue is the degree to which the lower than average scholastic achievements of the disadvantaged might deteriorate (particularly in relation to those from more favorable social backgrounds) without the benefit of standardized diagnostic tests to counteract any tendencies to evaluate scholastic abilities in a more subjective manner.

6. Again issues of sampling and population coverage are pertinent. Adjustments of data for unreliability of measurement assume that the population being adjusted is the same as the norming population, that from which the correction factor was estimated. But, in addition, models for the development of scholastic achievements and aptitudes, such as those developed by Bloom, are customarily based on samples of unknown representativeness and generality. Bloom himself laments the conspicuous absence of panel studies of elementary students, a hiatus that constrains him to utilize crude estimates of stability in achievement from intelligence test-achievement test correlations.

7. Williams (1972, 1976b) reports an uncorrected correlation of about 0.6 between grade point average for tenth and twelfth graders in Ontario; among Toronto students in grades 10 and 11 the correlation is about 0.7. Allen Kerckhoff and Richard Campbell (1977) compute a raw correlation of about 0.6 between junior high (grades 7 and 8) and senior high (average across years) grades among students in Fort Wayne. Marion Shaycoft (1967, table 5-4) estimates both corrected and raw correlations for information, achievement, and aptitude scores for ninth and twelfth graders in a Project Talent national longitudinal panel. While stability varies across tests, the median corrected value is roughly 0.8. Since only a few studies report data separately for the sexes, it is probably not safe to conclude that the observed higher intertemporal correlations for girls signal an established pattern of greater stability in academic aptitude and achievement.

8. Some educationists worry about the apparently small gains in learning from year to year, basing their evaluation on the mean difference in achievement scores at successive testings in relation to the variation among students at any one testing. Often the average gains are smaller than variation within a given grade level (Shaycoft, 1967, table 5-5).

9. This is not to say that there is no variation in achievement by economic stratum, race, or geographic region; see Coleman et al (1966).

10. Standardized achievement and intelligence tests discriminate between individuals, but it does not follow that these tests are heavily biased (giving capricious benefit) toward middle and upper socioeconomic strata. That could be so only if the within-stratum variance in intelligence and tested achievement were much more homogeneous than this evidence suggests. Hauser (1971), for example, reports correlations of under 0.2 between indicators of parental status and students' scores on math and reading achievement tests.

11. W. Sewell, R. M. Hauser, and W. Wolf (1977) report R^2 values (explained variance) of 0.35 for male and 0.42 for female Wisconsin high school students in regression equations linking teacher-assigned grades (normalized within the state sample of 10,000 cases and expressed as ranks) to IQ and social background. The latter included parental income, paternal occupational status, paternal and maternal educational levels, maternal employment during rearing, rural or urban residence, intact or broken family status, and number of siblings. The standardized regression coefficient for IQ was five to six times larger than any of the coefficients for social background; and, in the regression of IQ scores on the same social background factors, the R^2 values indicated that less than 10% of the IQ variance could be assigned to additive effects of these indexes of background. Thus most of the net effect of IQ on grades (rank) was not a reflection of the (small) effect of background on IQ. The IQ data refer to tests in eleventh grade, and the patterns of correlation may differ among younger students. In imagining these other data, however, one must recall the stability correlation of IQ tests taken in (say) sixth grade and later in high school.

12. See similar estimates for Sweden in Fägerlind (1975) and Kenneth Wilson and Alejandro Portes (1975) for the United States. Correlations between high school grade point average and ultimate grade of completed education are essentially the same.

13. Here is the other side of the ability-aptitude testing controversy. Since the tests are not highly accurate in discriminating between those who do and those who do not go on beyond grade 9 or grade 12, why use them—especially if they are biased with regard to race, class, or sex? The tests themselves appear not to discriminate capriciously among individuals. Their interpretation and use by educators are the real issues, but again that issue is not unambiguous. Are the predictions low because the tests themselves are unreliable instruments or because length of schooling is not solely a function of scholastic aptitudes and educability within the schools as presently structured? See Warren Willingham (1974) for a thoughtful analysis of predicting success at higher levels of education from tests of ability and performance at lower levels.

14. Inasmuch as the most sociologically interesting variation in educational achievement in contemporary America involves high school graduation and postsecondary schooling (given the trend in the lower tail of the distribution of schooling), the discussion of the alleged determinants of the length of schooling focuses on the post-high school years.

15. Less than 20% of the covariation reflects this common cause (Sewell and Hauser, 1972).

16. One can argue that since teachers tend to define the abilities to be tested and the curriculum to be learned, they, too, are agents of class ideology (Bowles and Gintis, 1976). To a degree that assertion is definitional, but if it were an essentially valid generalization about class bias in education, one would expect to see much higher correlations between social background and grade or amount of school (or postsecondary schooling) completed than international research has documented.

17. A number of international studies also find that schooling varies by socioeconomic background, even among persons of equal mental ability. Variation among countries in the size of the net "class" effect is hard to assess in current research, but it may not be as large as conventional wisdom might have it (Fägerlind, 1975; Treiman and Terrell, 1975a; Kerckhoff, 1974; Douglas, Ross, and Simpson, 1968; Maxwell, 1969; Boudon, 1973).

18. Differential performance by gender across subjects of curricula are reviewed by Shaycoft (1967).

19. Using each of several hundred detailed occupational titles identified by the U.S. Bureau of the Census, one can calculate "status" scores for specific occupations that reflect the average schooling and income of incumbents in each occupation; scores range arbitrarily from 0 to 96 (Duncan, 1961).

20. Paul Menchik (1977) examines differential bequests upon the death of parents as an illustration of the general case of social inheritance.

21. Fully 5.6 million fewer children of ages 6-14 were enrolled in school in 1970 than in 1960. During the same decade the number of adults aged 20-24 —the category containing persons with new college degrees—increased by 5 million among whites and by 6.5 million among blacks.

22. There is some evidence that intelligence may affect earnings more directly than it affects occupational achievement (Duncan, Featherman, and Duncan, 1972, chap. 5). In addition, there is some small change in abilities during young adulthood that reflects continuing education (Duncan, Featherman, and Duncan, 1972; Griliches and Mason, 1973; Fägerlind, 1975), but neither of these observations changes the generalizations advanced here and by Jencks et al. (1972).

23. The work histories of most women are different from those of men. Hence sex is another social category in which age-income and age-occupation profiles deviate from the modal varieties. This discussion is limited to male workers.

24. A related point is that one's data ought to be drawn from representative samples of real populations of interest, rather than those of convenience, as has been the pattern of much research.

References

ALEXANDER, K. L., and ECKLAND, B. K. 1974. Sex differences in the educational attainment process. *American Sociological Review* 30: 668-682.

ALEXANDER, K. L., ECKLAND, B. K., and GRIFFIN, L. J. 1975. The Wisconsin model of socioeconomic achievement: a replication. *American Journal of Sociology* 81: 324-342.

ALWIN, D., OTTO, K. B., and CALL, V. 1976. The schooling process in the development of aspirations: a replication. Boys Town Center for Youth Development, Omaha, Nebraska.

ANDREWS, F. M., and WITHEY, S. B. 1976. *Social indicators of well-being: Americans' perceptions of life quality*. New York: Plenum.

ATKINSON, J. W., LENS, W., and O'MALLEY, P. M. 1976. Motivation and ability: interactive psychological determinants of intellective performance, educational achievement, and each other. In W. H. Sewell, R. M. Hauser, and D. L. Featherman, eds., *Schooling and achievement in American society*. New York: Academic Press.

ATKINSON, J. W., and RAYNOR, J. O. 1974. *Motivation and achievement*. Washington, D.C.: Winston.

BACHMAN, J. G. 1970. *The impact of family background and intelligence on tenth-grade boys*. Youth in Transition, vol. 2. Ann Arbor, Mich.: University of Michigan, Institute of Social Research.

BALTES, P. B. 1979. Life-span developmental psychology: some converging observations on history and theory. In P. B. Baltes and O. G. Brim, Jr., eds., *Life-span development and behavior*, vol. 2. New York: Academic Press.

BALTES, P. B., and SCHAIE, K. W., eds. 1973a. *Life-span developmental psychology: personality and socialization*. New York: Academic Press.

—— 1973b. On life-span developmental research paradigms: retrospects and prospects. In P. Baltes and K. W. Schaie, eds., *Life-span developmental psychology: personality and socialization*. New York: Academic Press.

BALTES, P. B., and WILLIS, S. L. 1979. The critical importance of appropriate methodology in the study of aging: the sample case of psychometric intelligence. In F. Hoffmeister, ed., *The evaluation of old age related changes and disorders of age functions*. Heidelberg: Springer.

BAYLEY, N. 1966. Learning in adulthood: the role of intelligence. In H. J. Klausmeier and C. W. Harris, eds., *Analyses of concept learning*. New York: Academic Press.

BECKER, G. 1964. *Human capital*. New York: Columbia University Press.

BELL, D. 1973. *The coming of post-industrial society*. New York: Basic Books.

BERG, I. 1970. *Education and jobs: the great training robbery*. New York: Praeger.

BIRD, C. 1975. *The case against college*. New York: Bantam.

BLAU, P., and DUNCAN, O. D. 1967. *The American occupational structure*. New York: Wiley.

BLOOM, B. S. 1964. *Stability and change in human characteristics*. New York: Wiley.

BLOOM, B. S., and PETERS, F. 1961. *The use of academic prediction scales for counseling and selecting college entrants*. Glencoe, Ill.: Free Press.

BLUESTONE, B. 1970. The tripartite economy: labor markets and the working poor. *Poverty and Human Resources Abstracts* (supplement) 5(4): 15-35.

BOUDON, R. 1973. *Education, opportunity and social inequality*. New York: Wiley.

BOWLES, S., and GINTIS, H. 1976. *Schooling in capitalist America*. New York: Basic Books.

BRAVERMAN, H. 1974. *Labor and monopoly capital.* New York: Monthly Review Press.

BRYAN, F. E. 1953. How large are children's vocabularies? *Elementary School Journal* 54: 210-216.

CAMPBELL, A., CONVERSE, P. E., and ROGERS, W. L. 1976. *The quality of American life: perceptions, evaluations, and satisfactions.* New York: Russell Sage Foundation.

CARTER, N. D. 1972. The effects of sex and marital status on a social-psychological model of occupational status attainment. Master's thesis. Madison, Wis.: University of Wisconsin.

CATTELL, R. B. 1963. Theory of fluid and crystallized intelligence: a critical experiment. *Journal of Educational Psychology* 54: 1-22.

CHASE, I. 1975. A comparison of men's and women's intergenerational mobility in the United States. *American Sociological Review* 40: 483-505.

CLARRIDGE, B. K., SHEEHY, L. S., and HAUSER, T. S. 1977. Tracing members of a panel: a 17-year follow-up. In K. F. Schuessler, ed., *Sociological methodology 1978.* San Francisco: Jossey-Bass.

CLAUSEN, J. A. 1972. The life course of individuals. In M. W. Riley, M. Johnson, and A. Foner, eds., *Aging and society: a sociology of age stratification.* New York: Russell Sage Foundation.

COLEMAN, J., CAMPBELL, E. R., HOBSON, C. J., McPARTLAND, J., MOOD, A. M., WEINFELD, F. D., and YORK, R. L. 1966. *Equality of educational opportunity.* Washington, D.C.: U.S. Government Printing Office.

DAVE, R. H. 1963. The identification and measurement of environmental process variables that are related to educational achievement. Ph.D. dissertation. Chicago: University of Chicago.

DOERINGER, P., and PIORE, M. 1971. *Internal labor markets and manpower analysis.* Lexington, Mass.: D.C. Heath.

DOUGLAS, J. W. B. 1964. *The home and the school.* London: MacGibbon and Kee.

DOUGLAS, J. W. B., ROSS, M. J., and SIMPSON, H. R. 1968. *All our future.* London: Peter Davis. Mimeographed appendixes available from author, London School of Economics.

DUNCAN, B. 1968. Trends in output and distribution of schooling. In E. B. Sheldon and W. E. More, eds., *Indicators of social change.* New York: Russell Sage Foundation.

DUNCAN, B., and DUNCAN, O. D. 1968. Minorities and the process of stratification. *American Sociological Review* 33: 356-364.

DUNCAN, G. J., and MORGAN, J. N. 1976. *Five thousand American families: patterns of economic progress,* vol. 4: *Family composition change and other analyses of the first seven years of the panel study of income dynamics.* Survey Research Center, Institute for Social Research, University of Michigan.

DUNCAN, O. D. 1961. A socioeconomic index for all occupations. In A. J. Reiss, ed., *Occupations and social status.* New York: Free Press.

———— 1967. Discrimination against Negroes. *Annals of the American Academy of Political and Social Science* 371: 85-103.

———— 1968. Ability and achievement. *Eugenics Quarterly* 15: 1-11.

DUNCAN, O. D., and FEATHERMAN, D. L. 1972. Psychological and cultural factors in the process of occupational achievement. *Social Science Research* 1: 121-145.

DUNCAN, O. D., FEATHERMAN, D. L., and DUNCAN, B. 1972. *Socioeconomic background and achievement.* New York: Seminar Press.

EBERT, E., and SIMMONS, K. 1943. *The Brush Foundation study of child growth and development.* Monographs of the Society for Research on Child Development 8, no. 2. Washington, D.C.

ELDER, G. H., JR. 1974. *Children of the Great Depression.* Chicago: University of Chicago Press.

——1977. Family history and the life course. *Journal of Family History* 2: 279-304.

ELDER, G. H., JR., and ROCKWELL, R. C. 1977. Economic depression and postwar opportunity in men's lives: a study of life patterns and health. In R. G. Simmons, ed., *Research in community and mental health: an annual compilation of research.* Greenwich, Conn.: JAI Press.

FÄGERLIND, I. 1975. *Formal education and adult earnings.* Stockholm: Almquist and Wiksell.

FEATHERMAN, D. L. 1971. The socioeconomic achievement of white religio-ethnic subgroups: social and psychological explanations. *American Sociological Review* 36: 207-222.

—— 1973. Comments on models for the socioeconomic career. *American Sociological Review* 38: 785-790.

FEATHERMAN, D. L., and HAUSER, R. M. 1975. Design for a replicate study of social mobility in the United States. In K. Land and S. Spilerman, eds., *Social indicator models.* New York: Russell Sage Foundation.

—— 1976. Sexual inequalities and socioeconomic achievement in the U.S., 1962-1973. *American Sociological Review* 41: 462-483.

—— 1978. *Opportunity and change.* New York: Academic Press.

FEATHERMAN, D. L., JONES, F. L., and HAUSER, R. M. 1975. Assumption of social mobility research in the United States: the case of occupational status. *Social Science Research* 4: 329-360.

FERRISS, A. 1969. *Indicators of trends in American education.* New York: Russell Sage Foundation.

FREEMAN, R. B. 1976. *The over-educated American.* New York: Academic Press.

FUCHS, V. R. 1968. *The service economy.* New York: New York National Bureau of Economic Research (distributed by Columbia University Press).

GARNIER, M., and HOUT, M. 1974. Inequality of educational opportunity in France and the United States. Indiana University.

GILBERT, S. N. 1973. Educational and occupational aspirations of Ontario high school students: a multivariate analysis. Ph.D. dissertation, Carleton University.

GOLDBERGER, A. S. 1976a. Jensen on Burks. *Educational Psychologist* 12: 64-78.

—— 1976b. Mysteries of the meritocracy. In N. J. Block and G. Dworkin, eds., *The IQ controversy: critical readings.* New York: Pantheon.

—— 1977a. The genetic determination of income. Social Systems Research Institute Workshop Series No. 7707, University of Wisconsin-Madison.

—— 1977b. Models and methods in the IQ debate. Social Systems Research Institute Workshop Series No. 7710, University of Wisconsin-Madison.

GOLDTHORPE, J. H., and HOPE, K. 1972. Occupational grading and occupational prestige. In K. Hope, ed., *The analysis of social mobility: methods and approaches*. Oxford: Clarendon Press.

—— 1974. *The social grading of occupations: a new approach and scale.* Oxford: Clarendon Press.

GRILICHES, Z., and MASON, W. M. 1973. Education, income, and ability. In A. S. Goldberger and O. D. Duncan, eds., *Structural equation models in the social sciences*. New York: Seminar Press.

GURIN, G., VEROFF, J., and FELD, S. 1960. *Americans view their mental health*. Joint Commission on Mental Illness and Health Monograph Series No. 4. New York: Basic Books.

HAREVEN, T. K. 1975. Family time and industrial time: family and work in a planned corporation town, 1900-1924. *Journal of Urban History* 1(3):365-385.

HAUSER, R. M. 1971. *Socioeconomic background and educational performance*. Rose Monograph Series, Washington, D.C.: American Sociological Association.

—— 1973. Disaggregating a social-psychological model of educational attainment. In A. S. Goldberger and O. D. Duncan, eds., *Structural equation models in the social sciences*. New York: Seminar Press.

HAUSER, R. M., DICKINSON, P. J., TRAVIS, H. P., and KOFFELL, J. N. 1975. Temporal change in occupational mobility: evidence for men in the United States. *American Sociological Review* 40: 279-297.

HAUSER, R. M., and FEATHERMAN, D. L. 1976. Equality of schooling: trends and prospects. *Sociology of Education* 49: 99-120.

—— 1977. *The process of stratification: trends and analyses*. New York: Academic Press.

HAUSER, R. M., SEWELL, W. H., and ALWIN, D. F. 1976. High school effects on achievement. In W. H. Sewell, R. M. Hauser, and D. L. Featherman, eds., *Schooling and achievement in American society*. New York: Academic Press.

HEYNS, B. 1974. Social selection and stratification within schools. *American Journal of Sociology* 76: 1434-51.

HODSON, R. 1977. Labor force participation and earnings in the core, peripheral, and state sectors of production. Master's thesis, University of Wisconsin-Madison.

HOGAN, D. 1978. The variable order of events in the life course. *American Sociological Review* 43: 573-586.

HOGAN, D., and FEATHERMAN, D. L. 1977. Racial stratification and socioeconomic change in the American North and South. *American Journal of Sociology*: 100-126.

HOPE, K. 1977. As others see us: a study of merit, advantage, and deprivation in Scotland. Oxford University, Nuffield College.

HOUT, M., and MORGAN, W. R. 1975. Race and sex variations in the causes of the expected attainments of high school seniors. *American Journal of Sociology* 81: 364-394.

INKELES, A., and SMITH, D. H. 1974. *Becoming modern: individual change in six developing countries.* Cambridge, Mass.: Harvard University Press.

JENCKS, C., SMITH, M., ACLAND, H., BANE, M. J., COHEN, D., GINTIS, H., HEYNS, B., and MICHELSON, S. 1972. *Inequality.* New York: Basic Books.

JENSEN, A. R. 1969. How much can we boost IQ and scholastic achievement? *Harvard Educational Review* 39: 1-123.

KAMIN, L. 1974. *The science and politics of IQ.* New York: Halstead Press.

KELLY, J. 1973. Causal chain models for socioeconomic career. *American Sociological Review* 38: 481-493.

KERCKHOFF, A. C. 1974. Ambition and attainment. Rose Monograph Series. Washington, D.C.: American Sociological Association.

KERCKHOFF, A. C., and CAMPBELL, R. T. 1977. Black-white differences in the educational attainment process. *Sociology of Education* 50: 15-27.

KOHEN, A. I. 1971. Determinants of early labor market success among young men: ability, quantity, quality of schooling. Paper presented at the meeting of the American Educational Research Association, New York.

LAVIN, D. E. 1965. *The prediction of academic performance.* New York: Russell Sage Foundation.

MACPHERSON, J. S. 1958. *Eleven-year-olds grow up.* Publications of the Scottish Council for Research in Education, 42. London: University of London Press.

MATRAS, J., KRAUS, V., and NOAM, G. 1976. Factors in status attainment in Israel. Hebrew University.

MAXWELL, J. 1969. *Sixteen years on: a follow-up of the 1947 Scottish survey.* London: University of London Press.

MAYER, K. 1973. Dimensions of mobility space: some subjective aspects of career mobility. In W. Muller and K. Mayer, eds., *Social stratification and career mobility.* The Hague: Mouton.

MCCALL, R. B. 1977. Childhood IQ's as predictors of adult educational and occupational status. *Science* 197: 482-483.

MCCALL, R. B., APPELBAUM, M. I., and HOGARTY, P. S. 1973. *Developmental changes in mental performance.* Monographs of the Society for Research in Child Development 38 (3, whole no. 150). Washington, D.C.

MCCLELLAND, D. C. 1961. *The achieving society.* Princeton, N.J.: Van Nostrand.

MCCLENDON, M. J. 1976. The occupational status attainment processes of males and females. *American Sociological Review* 41: 52-64.

MCDILL, E. L., RIGSBY, L. C., and MEYERS, E. D. 1969. Institutional effects on the academic behavior of high school students. *Sociology of Education* 40: 181-199.

MENCHIK, P. L. 1977. Primogeniture, equal sharing, and the U.S. distribution of wealth. Institute for Research on Poverty, University of Wisconsin-Madison.

MINCER, J. 1974. *Schooling, experience, and earnings.* New York: National Bureau of Economic Research.

MINCER, J., and POLACHECK, S. 1974. Family investments in human capital. *Journal of Political Economy* 82: s76-s108.

MORTON, N. E. 1974. Analysis of family resemblance. I: Introduction. *American Journal of Human Genetics* 26: 318-330.

PALMER, G. 1954. *Labor mobility in six cities*. New York: Social Science Research Council.

PAMPEL, F., LAND, K., and FELSON, M. 1977. A social indicator model of changes in the occupational structure of the United States: 1947-1974. *American Sociological Review* 42: 951-964.

PANEL ON YOUTH OF THE PRESIDENT'S SCIENCE ADVISORY COMMITTEE 1974. *Youth: transition to adulthood*. Chicago: University of Chicago Press.

PARSONS, T. 1959. The school class of a social system: some of its functions in American society. *Harvard Educational Review* 29: 297-318.

POHOSKI, M. 1977. Presentation to ISA Research Committee on Stratification and Mobility. Dublin, April.

PÖNTINEN, S., and UUSITALO, H. 1975. Socioeconomic background and income. *Acta Sociologica* 18, no. 4.

PORTER, J. N. 1974. Race, socialization and mobility in educational and early occupational attainment. *American Sociological Review*, 39: 303-316.

PORTES, A., and WILSON, K. 1976. Black-white differences in educational attainment. *American Sociological Review* 41: 414-431.

RAO, D. C., MORTON, N. E., and YEE, S. 1974. Analysis of family resemblance. II: A linear model for familial correlation. *American Journal of Human Genetics* 26: 331-359.

REICH, C. 1970. *The greening of America*. New York: Random House.

REISMAN, D., with GLAZER, N., and DENNEY, R. 1950. *The lonely crowd*. New Haven, Conn.: Yale University Press.

REYNOLDS, L. G. 1951. *The structure of labor markets*. New York: Harper.

RIST, R. C. 1973. *The urban school: a factory for failure*. Cambridge, Mass.: MIT Press.

ROSENFELD, R. A. 1976. Women's employment patterns and occupational achievements. Ph.D. dissertation, University of Wisconsin-Madison.

ROSENTHAL, R., and JACOBSEN, L. 1968. *Pygmalion in the classroom*. New York: Holt, Rinehart and Winston.

RYDER, N. B. 1965. The cohort as a concept in the study of social change. *American Sociological Review* 30: 843-861.

SCARR-SALAPATECK, S. 1971. Race, social class, and IQ. *Science* 174: 1285-95.

SCOTTISH COUNCIL FOR RESEARCH IN EDUCATION. 1953. *Social implications of the 1947 Scottish Mental Survey*, 35. London: University of London Press.

SEASHORE, H. G., and ECKERSON, L. D. 1940. Measurement of individual differences in general English vocabularies. *Journal of Educational Psychology* 31: 14-38.

SEWELL, W. H. 1971. Inequality of opportunity for higher education. *American Sociological Review* 36: 793-809.

SEWELL, W. H., and ARMOR, M. J. 1966. Neighborhood context and college plans. *American Sociological Review* 31: 159-168.

SEWELL, W. H., and HAUSER, R. M. 1972. Causes and consequences of higher education: models of the status attainment process. *American Journal of*

Agricultural Economics 54: 851-861.

———— 1975. *Education, occupation, and earnings: achievement in early career*. New York: Academic Press.

SEWELL, W. H., HAUSER, R. M., and WOLF, W. 1977. Sex, schooling, and occupational careers. Center for Demography and Ecology Working Paper No. 77-31. University of Wisconsin-Madison.

SEWELL, W. H., and SHAH, V. P. 1967. Socioeconomic status, intelligence, and the attainment of higher education. *Sociology of Education* 40: 1-23.

SEXTON, P. C. 1961. *Education and income*. New York: Viking Press.

SHAYCOFT, M. F. 1967. *The high school years: growth in cognitive skills*. Pittsburgh, Pa.: American Institutes for Research and University of Pittsburgh, Project Talent.

SLOCUM, W. 1966. *Occupational careers*. Chicago: Aldine.

SMITH, M. K. 1941. Measurements of the size of general English vocabulary through the elementary grades and high school. *Genetic Psychological Monographs* 24, no. 2: 313-345.

SONTAG, L., BAKER, C., and NELSON, V. 1958. *Mental growth and personality: a longitudinal study*. Monographs of the Society for Research in Child Development 23, no. 2: 1-143.

SØRENSEN, A. B. 1974. A model for occupational careers. *American Journal of Sociology* 80: 44-57.

———— 1975a. Growth in occupational achievement: social mobility or investment in human capital. In K. Land and S. Spilerman, eds., *Social indicator models*. New York: Russell Sage Foundation.

———— 1975b. The structure of intragenerational mobility. *American Sociological Review* 40: 456-471.

———— 1977. The structure of inequality and the process of attainment. *American Sociological Review* 42: 965-978.

SOROKIN, P. 1927. *Social mobility*. New York: Harper and Brothers.

SPADY, W. G. 1976. The impact of school resources on students. In W. H. Sewell, R. M. Hauser, and D. L. Featherman, eds., *Schooling and achievement in American society*. New York: Academic Press.

SPAETH, J. L. 1976. Cognitive complexity: a dimension underlying the socioeconomic achievement process. In W. H. Sewell, R. M. Hauser, and D. L. Featherman, eds., *Schooling and achievement in American society*. New York: Academic Press.

SPENNER, K., and FEATHERMAN, D. 1978. Achievement ambitions. In the *Annual Review of Sociology*, vol. 4. Palo Alto, Calif.: Annual Reviews.

SPILERMAN, S. 1977. Careers, labor market structure, and socioeconomic achievement. *American Journal of Sociology* 83: 551-593.

STOLZENBERG, R. M. 1975. Occupations, labor markets and the process of wage attainment. *American Sociological Review* 40: 645-665.

SWEET, J. 1973. *Women in the labor force*. New York: Seminar Press.

———— 1975. Recent trends in the employment of American women. Center for Demography and Ecology Working Paper No. 75-14. University of Wisconsin-Madison.

TAEUBER, K. E., and SWEET, J. A. 1976. Family and work: the social life cycle of women. In J. M. Kreps, ed., *Women and the American economy: a look to the 1980s*. New York: Columbia University Press.

TERMAN, L. M., and ODEN, M. H. 1959. *The gifted group at midlife*. Palo Alto, Calif.: Stanford University Press.

THORNDIKE, R. L., and HAGEN, E. 1959. *Ten thousand careers*. New York: Wiley.

THUROW, L. C. 1975. *Generating inequality*. New York: Basic Books.

THUROW, L. C., and LUCAS, R. 1972. *The American distribution of income*. Washington, D.C.: U.S. Government Printing Office.

TREIMAN, D. J. 1970. Industrialization and social stratification. In E. O. Laumann, ed., *Social stratification research and theory for the 1970s*. New York: Bobbs-Merrill.

―――― 1977. *Occupational prestige in comparative perspective*. New York: Academic Press.

TREIMAN, D. J., and TERRELL, K. 1975a. The process of status attainment in the United States and Great Britain. *American Journal of Sociology* 81: 563-583.

―――― 1975b. Sex and the process of status attainment: a comparison of working women and men. *American Sociological Review* 40: 174-200.

TURNER, R. H. 1960. Sponsored and contest mobility and the school system. *American Sociological Review* 25: 855-867.

TYREE, A., and TREAS, J. 1974. The occupational and marital mobility of women. *American Sociological Review* 39: 293-302.

U.S. DEPARTMENT OF LABOR. 1974. *Job satisfaction: is there a trend?* Manpower Research Monograph No. 30. Washington, D.C.

WEINER, B. 1974. *Achievement motivation and attribution theory*. Morristown, N.J.: General Learning Press.

WELCH, F. 1979. Effects of cohort size on earnings: the babyboom babies' financial bust. Department of Economics, University of California, Los Angeles.

WILEY, D. E. 1976. Another hour, another day: quantity of schooling, a potent path for policy. In W. H. Sewell, R. M. Hauser, and D. L. Featherman, eds., *Schooling and achievement in American society*. New York: Academic Press.

WILLIAMS, G. 1977. The changing U.S. labor force and occupational differentiation by sex: a longitudinal analysis. Paper presented at the 1977 meeting of the Population Association of America, St. Louis, Missouri.

WILLIAMS, T. 1972. Educational aspirations: longitudinal evidence on their development in Canadian youth. *Sociology of Education* 45: 107-133.

―――― 1974. Competence dimensions of family environments. Presented at the annual meeting of the American Educational Research Association, Chicago, Illinois.

―――― 1976a. Abilities and environments. In W. H. Sewell, R. M. Hauser, and D. L. Featherman, eds., *Schooling and achievement in American society*. New York: Academic Press.

―――― 1976b. Teacher prophecies and the inheritance of inequality. *Sociology of Education* 49: 223-236.

WILLINGHAM, W. W. 1974. Predicting success in graduate education. *Science* 183: 273-278.

WILSON, K. L., and PORTES, A. 1975. The educational attainment process: results from a national sample. *American Journal of Sociology* 81: 343-363.

WINSBOROUGH, H. H. 1979. Changes in the transition to adulthood. In M. W. Riley, ed., *Aging from birth to death*. Boulder, Colo.: Westview Press.

WOLF, R. M. 1964. The identification and measurement of environmental process variables related to intelligence. Ph.D. dissertation, University of Chicago.

WOLF, W. C. 1975. Occupational attainment of married women: do career contingencies matter? Ph.D. dissertation, Johns Hopkins University.

WOLF, W. C., and ROSENFELD, R. A. 1978. Sex structure of occupations and job mobility. *Social Forces*, March.

YUCHTMAN, E., and SAMUEL, Y. 1975. Determinants of career plans: institutional versus interpersonal effects. *American Sociological Review* 40: 521-531.

Index

739